THE ECONOMICS OF JOHN STUART MILL
VOLUME II POLITICAL ECONOMY

STUDIES IN CLASSICAL POLITICAL ECONOMY/III

SAMUEL HOLLANDER

The economics of John Stuart Mill

Volume II
Political Economy

BASIL BLACKWELL

Basil Blackwell Ltd.
108 Cowley Road, Oxford OX4 1JF, UK

British Library Cataloguing in Publication Data

Hollander, Samuel
   The economics of John Stuart Mill. – (Studies
in classical political economy)
   1. Mill, John Stuart – Economics   2. Economics
 – Great Britain – History – 19th century
   I. Title   II. Series
   330.15'3   HB103.M7

   ISBN 0-631-14045-X (Set)

X7600 74 878

Phototypeset by Dobbie Typesetting Service, Plymouth, Devon
Printed in Great Britain by T.J.Press Ltd, Padstow

CONTENTS

7
MONEY AND BANKING:
THEORY AND POLICY 483
I The law of markets:
general issues 483
II The law of markets:
early formulations 487
III The *Principles*: the
cyclical context 513
IV The quantity theory 520
V Money and the rate of
interest 531
VI Bank finance and the
cycle: implications for
monetary policy 544
VII On the control of
central banking 583
VIII Concluding note 598

8
ON UTILITY AND LIBERTY 602
I Introduction: the
Schumpeterian version of
Benthamism 602
II The Benthamite position:
a summary statement 607
III The greatest happiness
principle: the reaction from
Bentham 617

IV The greatest happiness
principle post-1840: the
return to Bentham 638
V The return to Bentham
continued: on 'utilitarianism'
and the status of justice 645
VI The greatest happiness
principle: some comparisons
and problems 656
VII Liberty, utility and
social control 661
VIII The labour problem and
private property: some
preliminary implications 669
IX On compensation 672
X Utility versus natural
rights: applications to
labour and property 673

9
ECONOMIC POLICY: THE
ROLE OF GOVERNMENT 677
I Introduction 677
II The case for 'free trade' 685
III Government provision:
negative considerations 689
IV The case from liberty:
consumer choice 693
V Market failure 696

VI Elementary education 700
VII 'Superior' education 718
VIII Professional training 720
IX Mill and education: an overview 724
X Foreign trade policy 729
XI Government and economic development 738
XII Population control, poor relief and full employment policy 741
XIII On local and central administration 747
XIV The labour market: regulation of hours and unions 749
XV Colonization 753
XVI Monopoly and the state 758
XVII Patent protection 762
XVIII Summary: progress and the state 763

10
ECONOMIC POLICY: SOCIAL ORGANIZATION 770
I Introduction 770
II Aspects of the indictment of capitalism 776
III The Communist solution 786
IV The St Simonian and Fourierist solutions 800
V Profit-sharing 808
VI Co-operation: prospects and advantages 810
VII The collectivist option rejected 819
VIII On Socialism: summary 820

11
ECONOMIC POLICY: THE REFORM PROGRAMME 825
I Introduction 825
II Equality of opportunity and property rights 827
III Land reform: distributive aspects 833
IV Land reform: efficiency aspects 839
V Land reform: Ireland 847
VI On endowment and property rights 855
VII Income distribution and public finance 858
VIII On inheritance 876
IX Limitations on bequests and distribution: diminishing utility 880
X The desirability of economic development and the stationary state 881
XI The condition of the people: the poverty trap and the solution 888
XII The condition of the people: trade unionism 897
XIII Mill and 'bourgeois' bias 907

CONCLUSION: SOME CENTRAL THEMES 913
I Mill, Ricardianism and the historical school 913
II Mill and neo-classicism 928
III Mill and marginal utility 934
IV Mill and mathematical economics 936
V Mill and Malthusianism 945
VI The charge of 'scientism' 955
VII The empirical dimension: on the 'reality' of axioms and model improvement 958

Appendix: Attitudes towards
birth control   968
Appendix: The Hubbard
Issue   971
Appendix: On the Socialist
Conference   977

BIBLIOGRAPHY   979
INDEX   1006

SEVEN

Money and banking: theory and policy

I THE LAW OF MARKETS: GENERAL ISSUES

We shall refer to the version of Say's law of markets according to which the money value of goods supplied is *identically* equal to that of goods demanded as Say's identity, a view which precludes attempts to add to money balances out of sales proceeds. An alternative version of Say's law has it that the equality of the aggregate value of goods demanded and supplied reflects solely an *equilibrium* state of affairs. On this version disequilibrium might entail excess supplies of goods in the aggregate (at going prices), having a counterpart in an excess demand for money to hold. On the first version it is implied that money as such has no utility to recipients who accordingly attempt to disburse it on goods as soon as acquired, with the consequence that, assuming a positive money stock, the level of prices must rise to infinity. This *reductio ad absurdum* underscores that the entire conception has relevance only to a purely barter system. By contrast, the alternative view is consistent with a monetary system. In its full-fledged version an excess supply of goods will depress prices thereby raising the real value of the monetary stock, holders thereof becoming increasingly satisfied and accordingly reducing attempts to add thereto from sales proceeds, in which manner the disequilibrium comes to be corrected. The latter version is a mirror image of the quantity theory of money in at least one of its formulations – that according to which a doubling in the stock of money acts on prices not mechanically but by way of increased outlays on goods, a consequence of the initial exogenous increase in (the real value of) money balances which generates an excess demand for goods at the initial set of prices. Only in equilibrium, when the price level has been doubled, will the excess be corrected. Conversely, in the event of a halving of the money stock, an excess supply of commodities will be created which will be corrected by a general fall in prices raising the real value of the lower stock until holders are satisfied.[1]

Where did J. S. Mill stand on these issues? As is well known, in his famous essay composed in 1830 on 'The Influence of Consumption on Production' – described by Sir John Hicks as 'to modern taste, the deepest of Mill's writings on the subject' and 'one of the finest productions of Classical Economics' (1973, 58) – Mill formally allowed for excess demand for money to hold.[2] The historiographic, analytical and policy implications of his allowance will be our concern in what follows.

Conspicuous in the secondary literature is an opinion that the essay is unique in Mill's voluminous writings on the monetary issues at stake, the argument kept in the shade in the *Principles*. Thus according to Lord Robbins, this 'view of the operations of the speculative motive which affords what is in effect a theory of the trade cycle . . . can be detected between the lines in the treatment of speculation in the *Principles*, but it is nowhere so overtly developed' (1967, *CW*, IV, x; cf. Robbins, 1976, 66–8).[3] Sir John Hicks has addressed himself to the apparent mystery: 'There can be no doubt', he writes of the essay, 'that Mill did have a short-period theory' involving a non-neutral monetary perspective; 'but it is a remarkable thing' that in 1848 'we find no reference at all to the argument of the essay. In the *Principles* (see especially the chapter on "Excess of Supply") Mill appears, on all this side, to be just a hard-boiled "classic". The argument of the essay is not withdrawn, but it is just not there' (1967, 163). Hicks does not discern an actual change in position between 1830 and 1848; rather the supposed silence of 1848 reflects, he believes, a concern on Mill's part 'that if too much weight were given to short-period [monetary] effects, it would play into the hands of the crude inflationists. The long-period, it would be said, is just a succession of short-periods. Why not keep the stimulus going, when the first dose is exhausted, by another dose? . . . [We] can best explain Mill's position by supposing that he always held to what

---

1 For technical details see Baumol and Becker (1960 [1952]), Balassa (1959), Lange (1942), Schumpeter (1954, 615f).
2 Cf. Baumol and Becker (1952): 'In reading it one is led to wonder why so much of the subsequent literature (this paper included) had to be written at all' (1960, 765).
3 Cf. Robbins (1968), 64: 'Mill himself, in writing his *Principles*, was obviously careful to avoid the dogmatism which his article had been intended to dissolve; and, reading between the lines, one can detect the fundamental outlook which it expressed. But he made no special point of it, as might have been expected; and what is said has little of the cutting edge of the original article.'

he had said in the essay, but did not want to emphasize it, for he held that
it was *dangerous*' (162–3).[4]

In his important monograph on the history of monetary theory B. A. Corry
goes yet further. The essay is said to be 'remarkable for its discussion of
the effects of changes in the demand for money, but the puzzle is its timing,
for both before and after it, Mill produced unquestioning support for the
unqualified Classical position' (Corry, 1962, 101). This perspective leads
Corry to seek to understand how it was that Mill's monetary economics
'changed from the radicalism of the early Essay to the conservatism of the
Principles' (101), a work reiterating (so runs the contention) those notions
of an impossibility of general over-production and monetary disequilibrium,
characterizing Mill's pre-1830 position and showing 'no trace at all' of the
qualifications in the essay regarding the possibilities of changes in the desire
to hold cash: 'The complete "neutrality" of money is argued without
qualification' (106). The resolution of the "puzzle" of a unique statement
distinguished from what came before and what came after is expressed
hesitantly:

There appears to be no really satisfactory explanation of this changing attitude
towards the possibility of monetary disturbance. It is possible to use Mill's extreme
youth to account for the earliest [pre-1829] articles; speculation – which was beyond
the control of any authority – was a common view of the Classical school, and Mill,
at this stage, can hardly be regarded as more than a very able *rapporteur*. *Of the
Influence of Consumption Upon Production* clearly shows a more independent frame of
mind; the present writer is inclined to suspect the influence of Torrens here although
there is no direct evidence available. The prolonged depression of the post-war years
must have made the simple equilibrium analysis of James Mill's *Elements* appear
more than somewhat unrealistic. Then presumably with the relatively increased
prosperity of the thirties and early forties – although interspersed with periodic
financial crises – the qualifications so necessary to the statement of all economic
principles were gradually dropped from the younger Mill's analysis.

This general evaluation should be contrasted with an alternative
interpretation offered by Pedro Schwartz in his *New Political Economy of John
Stuart Mill*. Here it is urged that Mill departed from Ricardian orthodoxy
in monetary matters as early as 1826 (in his paper on 'Paper Currency

---

4 See Hicks (1983), 62–3 for an abandonment of this perspective in favour of one much
closer to our own in the present chapter: 'I do not now believe that Mill thought that
in the two works he says anything substantially different. He always thought that there
were two sides to the argument. In the essay they appear together; but in the *Principles*
they are too widely separated.' Hicks alludes here to the discussions of 'disequilibrium'
in III, Chs. xii and xiv – albeit rather underemphasized in the latter compared with the
former; and the equilibrium analysis of I, Chs. iv and v.

and Commercial Distress') under the influence of Thomas Tooke, adopting 'new doctrines of monetary theory and policy that were to last him until the end of his life':

Here his departure from the Ricardian doctrine was not due to philosophical or political considerations, and it was not in the same direction as in other areas of his thought. Indeed, whereas in the questions of trade unions, socialism or *laissez faire* Mill, in a greater or less degree, breathed new life into the old political economy, in the question of money and employment he changed his analytical stance and moved a step backwards in respect of his orthodox position (1972, 33).

It is Mill's abandonment of the Ricardian (bullionist) position to which Schwartz alludes here. But this, he insists, did not amount to a diversion towards 'a more "Keynesian" position' – rather to the contrary, Mill in 1826 argued for 'a more passive attitude to monetary phenomena than that held by Ricardo and his disciples, let alone the Attwoods and other Birmingham reflationists, the true "Keynesians" in this plot' (35). On this view the puzzle posed for so many by the essay of 1830 falls away for it too, on Schwartz's reading, must not be read through anachronistic lenses:

Our Keynesian times could not refrain from hailing this article as an important contribution to economic thought and wondering why Mill did not follow it up with more radical departures from the 'classical' position. However, we should beware of taking it out of context. To say that the existence of money allows psychological factors to affect the economic situation, is not the same as to say that the cycle may be controlled by deliberate variations of the money supply (and still less by variations in public expenditure) . . . Mill was not moving nearer to Malthus, Sismondi and Attwood when he wrote this essay. Quite the contrary; he was moving still further away from them than the strict Ricardians . . . (39).

From this perspective, Schwartz concludes, the relative unconcern with the issues of 1830 in the *Principles* merely indicates 'how peripheral monetary questions were to his New Political Economy' (41).

Schwartz's insistence that we avoid anachronistic readings is fully justified, for a neglect of that seemingly obvious requirement has led to serious misrepresentations of Mill's position in the *Principles* as well as the early papers. Moreover, that the paper of 1826 contains much of substance that was to appear in the essay of 1830 is also true; the latter is by no means a unique production. But here we part company. For, as J. A. Schumpeter has always recognized (1954, 621f.), far from proceeding to treat the allowance for excess money demand as a skeleton in the family cupboard Mill continued to give it pride of place in 1848 and thereafter. Indeed, the cyclical phenomena are much elaborated in a linkage made between them and the secular trend of the return on capital, a relationship only touched on lightly in some of the early papers and not at all in the essay of 1830. Moreover, notwithstanding Mill's horror of monetary unorthodoxy of the Birmingham variety, he yet championed flexibility and intelligent judgement on the part of the central bank rather than the automaticity required by the currency school whose rules, designed to reduce central banking to the issue of gold certificates, were embodied in Peel's Act of 1844. To categorize his position as one of extreme *laissez-faire* is going much too far. There is also the matter of Mill's new allowances in the *Principles* for government expenditure in countries 'at a hand's breadth' of a stationary state, although this position admittedly cannot be interpreted in 'Keynesian' terms.

We proceed by analysis of Mill's formulations of the law of markets in essays prior to the *Principles* and in the *Principles* itself (Sections II and III). In Sections IV and V we consider technical issues relating to the quantity theory and the interest rate. Thereafter we turn to bank finance with particular reference to cyclical fluctuations and banking policy (Section VI). The control of central banking is considered separately in Section VII.

II   THE LAW OF MARKETS: EARLY FORMULATIONS

In this section we trace the evolution of Mill's monetary perspective, with special reference to the law of markets, prior to the *Principles* in various articles: 'War Expenditure' (1824); 'The Quarterly Review on Political Economy' (1825); 'Paper Currency and Commercial Distress' (1826); 'Of the Influence of Consumption on Production', first composed in 1830 and published in 1836; 'The Currency Juggle' (1833); and 'The Currency Question' (1844).[5] Before proceeding to these formal articles, however, it will be helpful to have in mind the methodological perspective and the substance of Mill's first ever published review, a two part review of Tooke's *Thoughts and Details on the High and Low Prices of the Last Thirty Years* (1823), for a variety of general issues arise to be further elaborated in the formal papers.

The polemical tone directed at Western, Attwood and their followers, is pure James Mill. The possible effects on prices of bank restriction (and the return to gold of 1819) had been 'settled long ago by general reasoning to the satisfaction of every thinking man' – namely that restriction *per se* could raise prices by a percentage not exceeding the difference between the market and mint price of gold (*The Globe and Traveller*, 4 March 1823). The fact that 'many commodities' varied in price to a far greater degree had, therefore, to be accounted for by other causes than currency variation. Tooke's merit was partly to adduce

5   For a brief review of this literature see Robbins (1967), xiiif.

general reasoning, which alone sufficed to prove the absurdity of attributing to depreciation any greater effect [than the difference in value between paper and gold]; but as there are many, who, not being capable of comprehending general reasoning, are inclined to regard it with distrust, Mr. Tooke fortified his position by a statement of facts, proving conclusively that during the last 30 years enhancement of prices was seldom, if ever, coincident with increase in the issues of Bank paper, but was sometimes coincident with a diminution. To attribute, therefore, any considerable part of the enhancement to depreciation, is inconsistent not only with principle, but with facts – not only with general, but with specific experience (*The Morning Chronicle*, 9 Aug. 1823, 3).

It was, of course, variations in the price of corn that most interested Tooke and these, as Mill reported favourably, were largely explicable by 'variations of the seasons, and the variations in the amount of private paper and credit, arising from speculation and over-trading', which (Mill adds) 'Tooke also analyses, and refers to their real sources' (4 March 1823).[6]

The nature of the credit variation and its source in 'speculation and overtrading' are not elaborated upon in the review and this is unfortunate considering the high profile of the topic in the later articles and the *Principles*. As for seasonal variations Mill reports at some length on the effects of expectation in complicating the standard supply–demand mechanism. That 'demand and supply, as affecting prices' are 'prospective' as well as 'actual' accounted for the fact that 'the lowest prices sometimes coincide with the smallest stock for sale, and the highest prices with the largest stock' (9 Aug. 1823). More generally, the inelasticity of demand for corn is referred to as the basic cause for sharp variation in total farm revenue, the increase in the first two decades generating false signals of permanent prosperity and encouraging long-term investment 'thereby increasing the quantity of produce, and aggravating their distress when low prices returned'.[7] It is interesting that the upward trend 1793–1812 is in no way related to diminishing agricultural returns; indeed that phenomenon is not even mentioned.[8]

Tooke's position was designed also to counter those who attributed the

---

6 Mill was impressed by Tooke's case that changes in credit were not peculiar to an inconvertible paper. For a general account of Tooke's position see Gregory (1828), 31f, Laidler (1972), Arnon (1984). Ricardo saw eye to eye with Tooke concerning price movements following resumption, drawing on Tooke's evidence before the Select Committee on the Agriculture of the United Kingdom (1821); cf. Hollander (1979), 496–7n.

7 Malthus (1823 [1963]) also emphasized that high demand elasticity for agricultural produce constituted a source of instability, and commended Tooke for his analysis.

8 A short while later, however, Mill alluded to the effect of the Corn Laws on the profit rate.

price movements to war expenditure and its cessation. Here we arrive at the central issue taken up the following year in the review of Blake:

Independently of taxation[9] war could have raised prices only by creating demand, or by obstructing supply.

Those who affirm that war increased demand, think that the whole of the extra government expenditure creates a new source of demand; that not only the prices of naval and military stores are raised, but that the additional consumption of fleets and armies must raise the price of food; that the demand for soldiers and sailors must raise wages; also the increased demand for manufactures to supply fleets and armies must farther raise wages, and thus increase the consumption by the labouring classes, &c.

This would be true if the extra government expenditure consisted of new funds; but these reasoners forget that what is consumed by government comes out of the pockets of the people, and would by them have been expended in the purchase of labour and commodities. In this way, therefore, war cannot raise prices. It can only raise those commodities which are the objects of sudden demand, such as naval and military stores, and these only until the supply has accommodated itself to the demand (9 Aug. 1823).

* * *

Mill's earliest contribution to economic theory (apart from his letters to the press) – the review of William Blake in 1824 – is conspicuous for its denial of post-war 'universal distress' described by Blake in his 'Observations on the Effects produced by the Expenditure of Government during the Restriction of Cash Payments' (1823) as a general depression involving 'landed proprietors without rents; farmers and manufacturers without a market, the monied capitalists ready to lend, and the merchant not wanting to borrow; a redundant capital, yet a redundant population; and the industrious poor compelled to apply, like mendicants, at the parish workhouses' (cited *CW*, IV, 3). The post-war difficulties were limited to the agricultural sector, insisted Mill, in a sarcastic denunciation of the 'landed interest'. 'We are very sceptical as to that universal distress, of which, at one time we heard so much'. It is clear enough that, eighteen years old and firmly under his father's thumb, Mill was shackled by 'general principles', which precluded as contradictory 'a redundant capital, yet a redundant population' (3).[10] The paper concludes with a tirade against

9 On Ricardian grounds taxation is in fact rejected as a cause of high general prices. The income tax does not affect prices at all; and indirect taxes play on relative prices only.

10 Blake had originally subscribed to Bullionist orthodoxy, but subsequently changed his mind and in 1823 accounted for war and post-war price movements in terms of changes

appeal to 'practical men', in this case in support of the supposed 'difficulty
of finding employment' for new capital since the end of the war:

A reasoner must be hard pressed, when he is driven to quote practical men in aid
of his conclusions. There cannot be a worse authority, in any branch of political
science, than that of merely practical men. They are always the most obstinate
and presumptious of all theorists. Their theories, which they call practice, and affirm
to be the legitimate results of experience, are built upon a superficial view of the
small number of facts which come within the narrow circle of their immediate
observation; and are usually in direct contradiction to those principles which are
deduced from a general and enlarged experience. Such men are the most unsafe
of all guides, even in matters of fact. More bigotted to their own theories than the
most visionary speculator, because they believe them to have warrent of past
experience; they have their eyes open to such facts alone as square with those
theories. They are constantly confounding facts with inferences, and when they
see a little, supply the remainder from their own imagination (19).[11]

The 'general principles' to which Mill appealed include pre-eminently
that 'saving' entails a form of spending (productive spending), and what
was later to be labelled the treasury view. On these grounds Mill rejected
Blake's position that the high range of prices during the war and the high
level of activity were due to 'a supposed extra demand . . . produced by
the [loan financed] war expenditure of government', and the low prices
and output of the post-war period to the cessation of such spending. As
to the *saving is spending* theorem:

Two fallacies are involved in this reasoning: first, that of supposing that expenditure,
as contradistinguished from saving, can by any possibility constitute an additional
source of demand: and secondly, that of conceiving that capital which being
borrowed by government becomes a source of demand in its hands, would not have
been equally a source of demand in the hands of those from whom it is taken.
A mass of capital which is lent to government, and an equal mass which remains
in the hands of the capitalist, are both consumed, and both, possibly, within the
same space of time. The difference is, that the first, when consumed, leaves nothing
behind it, the other, leaves in its place another capital not only equal, but greater:
for, having been productively consumed, it has been re-produced with a profit.
Both, while the consumption is going on, are equally sources of demand: but no

in government expenditure. In his review Mill used Tooke's *High and Low Prices* to argue
that changes in the price level were due mainly to seasonal and to a small degree to
currency fluctuations, but not at all to war expenditure and the transition to peace (except
in so far as war tended to obstruct imports).

11 Oddly enough, Mill himself engaged to the kind of appeal to facts he here condemned,
when it came to exchange rate movements (7f).

sooner is the one consumed, than the demand which it afforded ceases to exist: the other continues to afford a demand, which instead of diminishing, continually increases, as often as the capital is re-produced with a profit (13–14).

All this is prologue to the treasury view. Since it is untrue that 'a fund' of capital becomes a source of demand only if 'spent' rather than 'saved', it follows that government borrowing merely *transfers* expenditure from 'perennial' (investment) to 'transitory' (consumption) uses. In stark contrast stood Blake's view 'that the capital borrowed by government is not removed from a productive employment, but would have lain dormant in the hands either of the lender or of some one else, in the shape of goods for which no market could be found'.[12]

It is important to recognize Blake's apparent acceptance of the proposition – which Mill here ascribes to his father – that 'commodities are a measure of [a nation's] purchasing power', (16) and rejection only of the further presumption that an expanded purchasing power will necessarily be expended to absorb increased output at profitable prices. There was, Blake objected, no assurance that such expenditures would be made since it could not be taken for granted 'that new tastes, new wants, and a new population, increase simultaneously with the new capital' (cited, 15). Accordingly, excess supplies of commodities in general might be generated:

neither the corn grower, nor the cloth maker, could know that there would be an excess, till the excess occurred. Each depended upon a market, and was mistaken.

12 Apart from his complaint in his 1824 review that Blake had gone overboard by ascribing *all* the price movements of the preceding three decades to war demand by government and its cessation – including that part that could legitimately be accounted for in terms of the currency (and seasonal fluctuations in the case of agricultural products specifically) – Mill objected also to Blake's presumption that the adverse exchanges and excess of the market over the mint price of the war period was due mainly to large government expenditures abroad (5). Mill admitted that 'sudden' increases in government requirements to make foreign purchases could well have raised the premium on foreign bills and the price of bullion – that even an anticipation of such requirements could have had that effect – but insisted that any such disturbance 'remedies itself', and rapidly, by compensatory commodity flows (7f). (As we shall see, in 1848 Mill was readier to allow that exchange rate correction might be sluggish; below, p. 546.)

   Mill objected to Blake's assertion that Ricardo had positively denied that the exchanges depended on the 'balance of debts and credit', by observing that the balance was itself dependent upon the comparative values of currencies; and that if gold movement occurred between countries following some disturbance, this could only be due to a variation in the comparative values or else gold would not be an advantageous remittance (10–11). By taking this line Mill rather fudged his concession that the exchanges could be adversely affected by disturbances totally unrelated to internal price-level variation. And there can be no doubt that his primary objective was indeed to emphasize that 'the high price of gold, and the depression of the exchanges' afforded 'conclusive evidence of a depreciation . . .' (12).

If every thing could be foreseen, mankind would not miscalculate, and there would be no overstocking of the market. But they do miscalculate, and the market is overstocked. When savings are devoted to re-production, each manufacturer employs the additional capital in fabricating that class of commodities which he has been in the habit of making. But if there was already more than sufficient, the addition must still further increase the excess. How is it possible for this process to continue without a fall in prices, and a lower rate of profit to the capitalist? (cited 15–16).

Mill's reply runs along standard Ricardian lines: Blake was in error regarding the implied notion of a *limit* to human desires and, more important (because Mill chose to fight it out on this issue) regarding his implied opinion that even in the event of such limit producers will continue to expand output: 'It would be absurd to suppose, that men would forego the satisfaction of present desires in order to have the means of gratifying wants which they do not feel. New tastes and new wants may, or may not, spring up with new capital; but it is certain, that if a man continues to produce, he has either acquired new tastes and wants, or some of his old ones still remain unsatisfied' (16–17).

Blake was indeed skating on thin ice. He was obliged to introduce mistaken expectations into his argument which would perhaps be acceptable had he limited himself to the very short run. But, on the contrary, his case was designed for secular purposes implying the *necessity* of excess commodity supply in consequence of capital accumulation, the act of saving entailing a surrender of the right to consume.[13] Mill is on firm ground in objecting that 'if it be correct, it proves that there can be no addition to capital, without producing a glut. All accumulation is from saving. If it be true, that he who saves shows his disinclination to consume, it follows, that an increase of produce can never find a market, since no one else has the means of increasing his consumption, and he who accumulates, has not the will. Every increase of wealth would, on this supposition, be an increase of poverty' (17).

Blake had spoiled his case. But while Blake applied a short-run argument unconvincingly to the secular case Mill reversed the procedure. For he too leaped to a *non sequitur*. Having argued convincingly against the notion of a secular constraint to activity generated by over-production, he applies the conclusion to deny the possibility of a glut of commodities in general, however generated, without recognizing (although Blake too was negligent here) the possibility of excess supplies due, let us say, to what he was later

---

13 That it was indeed designed for secular purposes is particularly conspicuous in Blake's representation of the orthodox view of profit-rate determination as involving the inverse wage–profit relationship, the wage rate itself dependent on the quality of marginal land – evidently a long-run perspective (cited Mill, 15).

conspicuously to allow, a net increase in the demand for money to hold reflected in attempts to add to money balances from sales proceeds:

We, therefore, conclude that the funds, which were appropriated by government and spent during the war, were not lying dormant before that period for want of a market. The only remaining supposition then, since they were not a new creation, is, that they must have been withdrawn from a productive employment; an employment in which they were expended in the purchase of goods, and of labour, just as completely as they afterwards were; and constituted fully as sufficient a source of demand.
Mr. Blake's attempt, therefore, to prove that government expenditure created an extra demand for commodities and labour, a demand which would not otherwise have existed, entirely falls to the ground; and with it, the whole of the theory which ascribes to that expenditure the high prices which prevailed during the war (18).

It would be misleading to leave the impression that the exchange proceeded entirely in the rarified atmosphere of pure theory. The debate sometimes came down to earth, Blake questioning the orthodox view on grounds of lack of empirical evidence which pointed to absolute contraction in *civilian* industries during the war, and Mill countering with evidence, derived from Thomas Tooke, (*High and Low Prices*, 2nd ed., 1824) showing that there were scarcely any civilian industries with a larger activity during the war than after 1815, and that while general output had increased during the war the upward trend had set in before 1792 and indeed proceeded with greater rapidity after 1815 (19–20). (The rapid rate of capital accumulation throughout the war would, Mill believed, have permitted an 'enormous increase' in the community's capital stock but for the extractions due to the government expenditure (14–15).)
Mill's polemic against 'practical men' thus did not extend to Tooke who was one of those 'who join[ed] to their personal experience a knowledge of principle' (19). But one cannot escape the impression that his central case against the general possibility of aggregative excess supply was made on theoretical grounds. He himself said as much: 'No general reasoning could have added to the conviction which every one must feel, who has perused Mr. Tooke's detail of facts, that Mr. Blake's theory is totally erroneous. What cannot, however, be proved by any detail of facts, but which it is of the highest importance to prove, is, that a state of war cannot, under any circumstances, generate an extra demand. This proposition can be proved only by general reasoning' (21). Quite clearly, this denial of the very conception of general excess capacity (in which circumstance government expenditure might act as a stimulus) was a conclusion Mill stood by with or without Tooke.

In taking this stance Mill went far beyond Ricardo. For Ricardo distinctly allowed for the facts of excess capacity and unemployment in the manufacturing sector after 1815 (the 'stagnation of trade' and 'present distressed situation of the labouring classes') and sought to account for them – albeit in terms of severe frictions which hindered the transfer of resources from declining to prosperous industries attempting to expand, rather than general excess commodity supply or excess demand for money to hold (Hollander, 1979, 516f).[14] Mill, still under the baneful influence of his father, allowed himself to be totally blinded to the facts, refusing to concede the existence of 'distress' and 'stagnation' beyond the agricultural sector.[15]

* * *

In the following year the same unsatisfactory perspective reappears in a general defence of McCulloch – including his notion that excess of one good must necessarily be matched by deficiency of another since there could be no general excess – against Malthus's strictures. Where, Malthus had inquired, was the market 'which would absorb a large capital, was in the most prosperous and flourishing state, and inviting additional stock by high prices and high profits' – for 'no one ever heard, as a matter of fact, from competent authority, that for some years together since the peace there was a marked deficiency of produce in any one considerable department of industry'? (cited, *CW*, IV, 41–2). Once again the elder Mill's methodology governs the son's reaction – his allusion here to 'the *naïveté* with which [Malthus] thus proposes to rebut demonstration by testimony'. As in 1824 the theoretical point elaborated upon alludes solely to the proposition that secular expansion comes up against no deficiency of demand flowing from the fact of expansion in itself. Once again this sound argument is illegitimately applied to rule out excess commodity supply deriving from no matter which source.

* * *

14 But Ricardo also came out the worse in his debate with Blake (Hollander, 1979, 522–3).
15 The tone is unmistakably James Mill's. The younger Mill concedes that the landlords had suffered, but was not sympathetic since their distress was no more than 'is implied in the necessity of contracting the expenses to which they had become habituated in the days of that good fortune, which was altogether unlooked-for and unearned, and of which, had they studied general principles, instead of scoffing at them, they would have forseen the speedy termination'. Other classes were prosperous, and 'although we are aware that, in the estimation of a great majority of members of parliament, the "landed interest" is the nation, and agricultural distress is national ruin, it is not so in ours; and we are very sceptical as to that universal distress, of which, at one time, we heard so much' (3–4).

We come next to a watershed in Mill's development, as important in some respects as the better known essay of 1830 which it presaged, namely the contribution of 1826. For here at last (appropriately, for we have reached the year of the nervous breakdown) intrude the facts of 'commercial distress' and 'revulsion' characterizing the early months of that year in the wake of an extended period during 1824–5 of 'rash speculation':

Very rarely, at any former period, have mercantile miscalculations been carried to so great a length. A vast majority of these enterprises failed; but not until, for the purpose of carrying them on, many persons had come under engagements, which nothing but the success of the speculation could enable them to fulfil. The speculations proving unsuccessful, these persons became insolvent; and their ruin drew after it that of many others, who had not speculated, but who were dependent, for the means of fulfilling their engagements, upon the fulfilment of engagements towards themselves by persons who had (73).[16]

Speculation as such, as described here, merely involves mercantile transactions 'attended with more than ordinary risk'; whereas by *rash* speculation is intended transactions 'in which the risk is great, and the prospect of gain not a sufficient equivalent'. Subsequently, reference is made to 'gambling' (78). The process is graphically described. The focus is upon over-trading in established lines of business (rather than fraudulent share issues in new projects ('bubbles') or the inflation of share prices unwarranted by 'rational calculation').[17] The initiation of the over-trading process is qualitatively similar to that reaction to anticipated excess demand – a short-fall due to anticipated contraction of supply or increase in demand – which characterizes *stabilizing* price adjustments. Assuming 'moderate' expectations of excess demand in the case of a given commodity, dealer purchases will stimulate an increase in price which 'probably' would suffice to produce 'the required addition to the supply, and . . . in the meantime, the necessary limitation of consumption' (75). The effects of such speculation are wholly

16 Schwartz (1972), 35, sees Mill's *volte face* as a reflection of changing circumstances forcing upon him the need 'to face the realities of earlier capitalism'.
    Apart from two early 'calamitous periods' (1784 and 1793) Mill isolates four commercial revulsions each preceded by speculation: 1810–11, 1814–15, 1819 and 1826 (IV, 74; 1815–16, 75). Mill refers readers to 'Part I of Mr. Tooke's able and important work on High and Low Prices' for 'fuller information concerning the events of these remarkable periods'.
17 Mill had no sympathy for losers in the latter category, those who bought shares 'at a price which they knew that *no rational calculation* would warrant, in the hope of finding dupes, or knaves of their own stamp, to purchase them again at a further advance (74, emphasis added).
    Mill did not have in mind by his rash speculation those '*bonâ fide* projects' which might turn out to be advantageous, albeit in the long run.

beneficial. Problems arise only where conditions are ripe for *self-justifying* price increases. Such destabilizing speculation is likely when a variety of major commodities are subject to significant anticipated excess demand to which dealers react, the initial price increases attracting the attention of those outside the professional trading community, those 'who look no further than to the immediate turn of the market, to purchase in expectation of a still further advance. These speculative purchases produce the very effect, in anticipation of which they were made', the price increases now extending 'far beyond what the prospect of deficiency, or of increase demand, will justify' (75).

The effect on commodity supply is also vividly described. Individuals who place massive orders with foreign and domestic manufacturers to take advantage of their estimate of the level of future prices, neglect to consider that others are doing the same. In the aggregate the addition supplies necessary to satisfy the initial short-fall – presumably the quantities that would suffice in a 'quiescent' state where only *professionals* are engaged – are 'enormously over-estimated' (76). Thus while those who sell early at inflated prices will make net gains, once attempts to realize gains become general prices will tend downwards, and cumulatively so with panic sales, in fact falling below their original levels in consequence of the extensive excess supplies, at those levels, which have been generated.

The picture now is one of 'enormous over-production and over-trading . . . the market is glutted, the holders suffer immense losses, many of them become insolvent, and their ruin draws along with it the ruin of many among the many others, who have given them credit . . .'.[18] It is noteworthy that amongst the holders are manufacturers, stocks remaining unsold in their warehouses, or saleable only at a loss.

There is a marked break in this paper with the smug, indeed the irresponsible, outlook of 1824 and 1825. There are further indications in 1826 of the later position. First, the role of credit in the speculative period and its aftermath. Although little emphasis is placed upon it in the account of the speculative price and output increases, Mill evidently had in mind that the process was fueled, at least partly, by credit. Reference is made to 'the failure of a few great commercial houses' – the implication being that they had supplied finance for the upswing[19] – '[which] occasions the ruin of many of their numerous creditors' thereby generating 'a general

18 Tooke was first in the field in his account of the manner in which the panic of 1825–6 followed necessarily upon the preceding speculation. Mill cites at length Tooke's *Considerations on the State of the Currency* (1826) regarding the speculation and over-trading of 1824 and 1825. Cf. also Robert Torrens, *An Essay on the External Corn Trade*, 3rd ed. 1826, 317–32. For an excellent discussion of this literature see Tucker, 1960, 186f.

19 Subsequently (97f) it is clarified that credit expansion is not the initiating factor (by way of reduced interest) in the speculation.

alarm . . . and an entire stop . . . for the time to all dealings upon credit: many persons are thus deprived of their usual accommodation, and are unable to continue their business' (76). That the 'over-production' and 'glutted markets' extend throughout the system is thus partly explained by a general failure of credit.

Equally important as a foretaste of what was to follow is Mill's elaboration upon the net demand for loanable funds (more accurately, money to hold) which characterizes the crisis and the implications thereof for the interest rate considering the legal maxima imposed by the usury laws of the day:

One of the chief peculiarities of a period of commercial distress is, that every body wishes to borrow, while nobody is willing to lend. From a fall of prices, or the failure of some one who is indebted to him, a merchant is disappointed of a sum which he expected to receive, and which was his only immediate means of meeting an engagement falling due the same day. Failure to pay a bill when it becomes due, is an act of insolvency; and a merchant will raise money at any sacrifice to avoid it. When many persons are placed simultaneously in this situation, it may be supposed for what an extraordinary amount, beyond the usual quantity of loans, a demand is produced. But the same cause which produces this desire to borrow, produces at the same time a disinclination to lend: not only by reason of the little confidence which at such a period is likely to be felt in the solvency of the borrower; but because the fall in the public securities, and in the prices of goods, occasioned by the same attempts to raise money immediately, enables him who has funds at his command, to invest them at a profit greatly exceeding the legal rate of interest. Who would lend to a merchant at five per cent, at the risk of losing all by his insolvency, when by buying into the three per cents at 75, he can obtain immediately four per cent upon his money; and by selling out a year afterwards, when they have risen to 83, realize a profit of about ten per cent more, independently of the dividends accruing in the intermediate period, amounting in all to a gain of fourteen per cent in one year? The same persons might perhaps be willing, if they were permitted, for the sake of the immediate gain, to discount at short dates, at the rate of seven or eight per cent. Thus, by not being permitted to borrow money for a few weeks, at two or three per cent above the legal rate, many merchants have no doubt been ruined; while a far greater number have possessed themselves of the means of continuing their payments by the most enormous sacrifices in other ways (108–9).

Finally, the reader is struck by Mill's allusions to the implications for speculation of a low rate of profit, a connection that clearly presages the more general discussion in the *Principles* of the consequences of a secularly falling return on capital for cyclical phenomena: '[T]he Corn Laws . . . by lowering the rate of ordinary mercantile profit, really produce that tendency to hazardous speculations which is so erroneously, though so commonly, imputed to the system of our currency' (109–10; cf. 103).[20]

* * *

At this point we turn to the celebrated essay 'On the Influence of Consumption on Production'.

The general context of this paper is economic growth, Mill commencing his argument by reference to the importance attached to the stimulation of consumption from this perspective prior to the achievement by political economy of its 'comparatively scientific character'. The true view, 'triumphantly established' in place of the 'palpable absurdities', amounted to the savings-is-spending theorem – formulated now as implacably as in 1824, perhaps more so: 'The person who saves his income is no less a consumer than he who spends it: he consumes it in a different way; it supplies food and clothing to be consumed, tools, and materials to be used, by productive labourers' (262–3).[21] Consequently, governmental attempts to encourage consumption merely divert funds from 'reproductive' (investment) uses, an application of the treasury view. The conclusion seems unambiguous – that 'there will never . . . be a greater quantity produced, of commodities in general, than there are consumers for':

What a country wants to make it richer, is never consumption, but production. Where there is the latter, we may be sure that there is no want of the former. To produce, implies that the producer desires to consume; why else should he give himself useless labour? He may not wish to consume what he himself produces, but his motive for producing and selling is the desire to buy. Therefore, if the producers generally produce and sell more and more, they certainly also buy more and more. Each may not want more of what he himself produces, but each wants more of what some other produces; and, by producing what the other wants, hopes to obtain what the other produces. There will never, therefore, be a greater quantity produced, of commodities in general, than there are consumers for. But there may be, and always are, abundance of persons who have the inclination to become consumers of some commodity, but are unable to satisfy their wish, because they have not the means of producing either that, or anything to give in exchange for it. The legislator, therefore, needs not give himself any concern about consumption. There will always be consumption for everything which can be produced, until

20 Cf. Torrens, *An Essay on the External Corn Trade*, 4th ed. 1829, 318.
21 On Mill's historical overview see the highly critical remarks by Hutchison, 1953, 349: 'So much for the youthful J. S. Mill's account of the history of "the new economics", and how it had finally superseded (or "exploded") a doctrine held by a great line of writers all through the seventeenth and eighteenth centuries.'

the wants of all who possess the means of producing are completely satisfied, and then production will not increase any farther. The legislator has to look solely to two points: that no obstacle shall exist to prevent those who have the means of producing, from employing those means as they find most for their interest; and that those who have not at present the means of producing, to the extent of their desire to consume, shall have every facility afforded to their acquiring the means, that, becoming producers, they may be enabled to consume (263-4).

But now, unlike the reply to Blake or the defence of McCulloch, though in line with the paper of 1826, Mill admitted to 'some strong appearance of evidence' which had misled those who maintained the 'palpable absurdities' regarding consumption. He proceeds to 'inquire into the nature of the appearances, which gave rise to the belief that a great demand, a brisk circulation, a rapid consumption (three equivalent expressions), are a cause of national prosperity', in order 'that no scattered particles of important truth are buried and lost in the ruins of exploded error'. While Mill is conscious of the fallacy of composition, he none the less is troubled in the present case by a theorem that apparently holds good at the aggregate level – the impossibility of 'general gluts' – but not for the individual producer whose fortunes obviously 'in a great measure depend upon the number of his customers, and . . . every additional purchase does really add to his profits' (266). The conclusion reached – and there is a stop-go flavour to the argumentation suggesting a mental struggle – is that the fallacy of composition is not here relevant, for even at the aggregate level expanded consumption may act as a stimulus.

The argument turns upon the fact that advanced economies are never operating at full capacity in the literal sense, since inventories and money funds must be available at various stages of production to satisfy expected sales in the one case and make necessary purchases in the other. This is a purely 'technological' matter. If the turnover period were somehow reduced – the emphasis in this part of the argument is on inventory levels – 'capital' hitherto idle might be actively utilized in the expansion of physical plant, materials and wage goods. It is essential to distinguish this argument from a separate (and better known) allowance, applicable to a short-run excess demand for money to hold of a speculative nature, which emerges subsequently in the paper. We shall trace out Mill's argument on both matters in what follows.

Narrow and broad definitions of 'capital' are distinguished at the outset, the latter including sales proceeds accumulated but not yet disbursed in the hiring of labour and the purchase of equipment and materials, and inventories not yet sold:

The capital, whether of an individual or of a nation, consists, we apprehend, of all matters possessing exchangeable value, which the individual or the nation has in his or in its possession for the purpose of reproduction, and not for the purpose of the owner's unproductive enjoyment. All unsold goods, therefore, constitute a part of the national capital, and of the capital of the producer or dealer to whom they belong. It is true that tools, materials, and the articles on which the labourer is supported, are the only articles which are directly subservient to production: and if I have a capital consisting of money, or of goods in a warehouse, I can only employ them as means of production in so far as they are capable of being exchanged for the articles which conduce directly to that end. But the food, machinery, &c., which will ultimately be purchased with the goods in my warehouse, may at this moment not be in the country, may not be even in existence. If, after having sold the goods, I hire labourers with the money, and set them to work, I am surely employing capital, though the corn, which in the form of bread those labourers may buy with the money, may be now in warehouse at Dantzic, or perhaps not yet above ground.

Whatever, therefore, is destined to be employed reproductively, either in its existing shape, or indirectly by a previous (or even subsequent) exchange, is capital. Suppose that I have laid out all the money I possess in wages and tools, and that the article I produce is just completed: in the interval which elapses before I can sell the article, realize the proceeds, and lay them out again in wages and tools, will it be said that I have no capital? Certainly not: I have the same capital as before, perhaps a greater, but it is locked up, as the expression is, and not disposable (266–7).

The matter of the turnover rate, which in large part governs the quantity of 'idle' capital, is next taken up:

If every commodity on an average remained unsold for a length of time equal to that required for its production, it is obvious that, at any one time, no more than half the productive capital of the country would be really performing the functions of capital. The two halves would relieve one another, like the semichori in a Greek tragedy; or rather the half which was in employment would be a fluctuating portion, composed of varying parts; but the result would be, that each producer would be able to produce every year only half as large a supply of commodities, as he could produce if he were sure of selling them the moment the production was completed.

Mill emphasizes further that the 'perpetual non-employment of a large portion of capital, is the price we pay for the division of labour. The purchase is worth what it costs; but the price is considerable' (268). The point here is that specialized producers and dealers 'have not found the means of fulfilling the condition which the division of labour renders indispensable to the full employment of capital, – viz., that of exchanging their products with each other. If those persons could find one another out, they could mutually relieve each other from this disadvantage' (269). An increase in the turnover rate[22] would permit the use of capital, otherwise locked up in inventory, in a real expansion of capacity, and one that is sustainable in the long run:

The reasoning cited in the earlier part of this paper [262f], to show the uselessness of a mere purchase or customer, for enriching a nation or an individual, applies only to the case of dealers who have already as much business as their capital admits of, and as rapid a sale for their commodities as is possible. To such dealers an additional purchaser is really of no use; for, if they are sure of selling all their commodities the moment those commodities are on sale, it is of no consequence whether they sell them to one person or to another. But it is questionable whether there be any dealers in whose case this hypothesis is exactly verified; and to the great majority it is not applicable at all. An additional customer, to most dealers, is equivalent to an increase of their productive capital. He enables them to convert a portion of their capital which was lying idle (and which could never have become productive in their hands until a customer was found) into wages and instruments of production; and if we suppose that the commodity, unless bought by him, would not have found a purhaser for a year after, then all which a capital of that value can enable men to produce during a year, is clear gain – gain to the dealer, or producer, and to the labourers whom he will employ, and thus (if no one sustains any corresponding loss) gain to the nation. The aggregate produce of the country for the succeeding year is, therefore, increased; not by the mere exchange, but by calling into activity a portion of the national capital, which, had it not been for the exchange, would have remained for some time longer unemployed (268-9).

A basic implication of Mill's analysis thus far is that the sustainable growth rate of the system can be increased by 'technological' advances which, reducing the uncertainty and ignorance characterizing even normal exchange relations, permit lower minimum inventory holdings. At this juncture, however, Mill introduced a warning. The flexibility provided by inventories in a world of imperfect knowledge is essential to the smooth working of the system, and excess capacity of this nature can never safely be totally

---

22 Mill illustrates thus the concern of producers with the turnover rate: 'Of the importance of the fact which has just been noticed there are three signal proofs. One is, the large sum often given for the goodwill of a particular business. Another is, the large rent which is paid for shops in certain situations, near a great thoroughfare for example, which have no advantage except that the occupier may expect a larger body of customers, and be enabled to turn over his capital more quickly. Another is, that in many trades, there are some dealers who sell articles of an equal quality at a lower price than other dealers. Of course, this is not a voluntary sacrifice of profits: they expect by the consequent overflow of customers to turn over their capital more quickly, and to be gainers by keeping the whole of their capital in more constant employment, though on any given operation their gains are less' (268).

dispensed with.[23] Indeed, only in speculative times – times of 'general delusion' – is the turnover period radically reduced with dire consequences:

From the considerations which we have now adduced, it is obvious what is meant by such phrases as a *brisk demand*, and a rapid circulation. There is a brisk demand and a rapid circulation, when goods, generally speaking, are sold as fast as they can be produced. There is slackness, on the contrary, and stagnation, when goods, which have been produced, remain for a long time unsold. In the former case, the capital which has been locked up in production is disengaged as soon as the production is completed; and can be immediately employed in further production. In the latter case, a large portion of the productive capital of the country is lying in temporary inactivity.

From what has been already said, it is obvious that periods of 'brisk demand' are also the periods of greatest production: the national capital is never called into full employment but at those periods. This, however, is no reason for desiring such times; it is not desirable that the whole capital of the country should be in full employment. For, the calculations of producers and traders being of necessity imperfect, there are always some commodities which are more or less in excess, as there are always some which are in deficiency. If, therefore, the whole truth were known, there would always be some classes of producers contracting, not extending, their operations. If *all* are endeavouring to extend them, it is a certain proof that some general delusion is afloat. But when the delusion vanishes and the truth is disclosed, those whose commodities are relatively in excess must diminish their production or be ruined: and if during the high prices they have built mills and erected machinery, they will be likely to repent at leisure (274–5).

Conspicuous here is the danger that real capacity increases undertaken during periods of 'general delusion' will prove to be excessive relaive to 'normal' requirements. Unfortunately little is said of the initiating cause of such delusions apart from a statement that they are most commonly generated by 'some general, or very extensive, rise of prices (whether caused by speculation or by the currency), which persuades all dealers that they are growing rich'. The implications of the statement for the real effects attributable to expansion of the money supply will be taken up presently.

23 Cf. Hayek (1978), 207: Mill called for 'full employment at high wages' but not the maximum level of employment achievable in the short run. The objective required a 'properly functioning market which, by the free play of prices and wages, secures in each sector a correspondence of supply and demand'. Also Hicks (1973), 58–9: 'There is implied, in that essay, something which is very near to our concept of Full Performance. Mill is perfectly aware, and indeed insists, that a condition in which the national economy is less than Fully Performing is perfectly possible, and must indeed be expected to occur from time to time. He is aware that lapses from Full Performance are associated with accumulations of stocks; but that the carrying of normal stocks is no sign of a lapse.'

At this point our concern is with speculative reactions apart from currency disturbance. In so far as such reactions are to exogenous events – the appearance of excess demand in some major markets – we are carried no further than the position of 1826. But the warning against unjustified increases in turnover rates reflecting speculative purchases (allowing increased output and even real capital construction but of an unsustainable order) was prologue to a discussion of regular or cyclical variation in speculative mood:

In the present state of the commercial world, mercantile transactions being carried on upon an immense scale, but the remote causes of fluctuations in prices being very little understood, so that unreasonable hopes and unreasonable fears alternatively rule with tyrannical sway over the minds of a majority of the mercantile public; general eagerness to buy and general reluctance to buy, succeed one another in a manner more or less marked, at brief intervals. Except during short periods of transition, there is almost always either great briskness of business or great stagnation; either the principal producers of almost all the leading articles of industry have as many orders as they can possibly execute, or the dealers in almost all commodities have their warehouses full of unsold goods (275).

These cyclical swings in speculative mood are, unfortunately, taken for granted and not further analysed.[24] Yet they play a fundamental role in precluding 'unemployment equilibrium' of a Keynesian order as we shall now see.

The theoretical analysis proceeds on a plane above that of the 1826 paper in drawing the famous contrast between a barter and a money system allowing formally and with eminent clarity for excess supply of goods in general with a counterpart in an excess demand for money to hold:

There can never, it is said, be a want of buyers for all commodities; because whoever offers a commodity for sale, desires to obtain a commodity in exchange for it, and is therefore a buyer by the mere fact of his being a seller. The sellers and the buyers, for all commodities taken together, must, by the metaphysical necessity of the case, be an exact equipoise to each other; and if there be more sellers than buyers of one thing, there must be more buyers than sellers for another.
This argument is evidently founded on the supposition of a state of barter; and, on that supposition, it is perfectly incontestable. When two persons perform an act of barter, each of them is at once a seller and a buyer. He cannot sell without

24 Corry (1962), 103, makes the point that an increase in the demand for money was not itself seen to be the initiating cause of falling output and prices but 'the factor which changed the re-alignment of prices after a period of excessive speculation into prolonged deflation'.

buying. Unless he chooses to buy some other person's commodity, he does not sell his own.

If, however, we suppose that money is used, these propositions cease to be exactly true. It must be admitted that no person desires money for its own sake, (unless some very rare cases of misers be an exception,) and that he who sells his commodity, receiving money in exchange, does so with the intention of buying with that same money some other commodity. Interchange by means of money is therefore, as has been often observed, ultimately nothing but barter. But there is this difference – that in the case of barter, the selling and the buying are simultaneously confounded in one operation; you sell what you have, and buy what you want, by one indivisible act, and you cannot do the one without doing the other. Now the effect of the employment of money, and even the utility of it, is, that it enables this one act of interchange to be divided into two separate acts or operations; one of which may be performed now, and the other a year hence, or whenever it shall be most convenient. Although he who sells, really sells only to buy, he needs not buy at the same moment when he sells; and he does not therefore necessarily add to the *immediate* demand for one commodity when he adds to the supply of another. The buying and selling being now separated, it may very well occur, that there may be, at some given time, a very general inclination to sell with as little delay as possible, accompanied with an equally general inclination to defer all purchases as long as possible. This is always actually the case, in those periods which are described as periods of general excess . . .

In order to render the argument for the impossibility of an excess of all commodities applicable to the case in which a circulating medium is employed, money must itself be considered as a commodity. It must, undoubtedly, be admitted that there cannot be an excess of all other commodities, and an excess of money at the same time (276–7).

It is worthwhile repeating that this argument stands apart from the allowance for unused 'capital' in the form of inventories as a necessary feature even at quiescent or normal stages of the cycle.

Professor Patinkin maintains of Mill's essay that while it provides a picture of temporary stagnation 'generated, if for some reason, people "liked better to possess money than any other commodity" . . . [it] does not explain why the stagnation is only temporary, and certainly does not say – or even imply – that the positive real-balance effect of a declining price level, plays any role in the recovery' (1956, 476n).[25] That there is no suggestion of a

25 On this matter Patinkin takes issue with Becker and Baumol (1960), 360–1, 374. Patinkin (1956) himself, 255–6, emphasizes the role of the real-balance effect as the *logical* key to the classical equilibration process without ascribing it to the classicists themselves. His charge that they neglected the equilibrization process not only in the secular case, but 'what is worse, they transferred this neglect of detail to the short-run cyclical problem as well. And for this analytical lacuna they were rightly criticized by Malthus and Sismondi, in their times, and by Keynes, in ours'.

real-balance effect in Mill's account is true enough, but there are in fact strong hints of a mechanism at work upon which Mill relied to assure recovery.

Consider the insistence that real losses are suffered by firms in so far as sales at low prices during periods of crisis yield a revenue the purchasing power of which will fall upon a recovery of prices:

> For whom there is a general anxiety to sell, and a general disinclination to buy, commodities of all kinds remain for a long time unsold, and those which find an immediate market, do so at a very low price. If it be said that when all commodities fall in price, the fall is of no consequence, since mere money price is not material while the relative value of all commodities remains the same, we answer that this would be true if the low prices were to last for ever. But as it is certain that prices will rise again sooner or later, the person who is obliged by necessity to sell his commodity at a low money price is really a sufferer, the money he receives sinking shortly to its ordinary value. Every person, therefore, delays selling if he can, keeping his capital unproductive in the mean time, and sustaining the consequent loss of interest. There is stagnation to those who are not obliged to sell, and distress to those who are (276-7).

Mill here suggests, it will be noted, that the expectation of recovery encourages firms to delay sales wherever possible. Evidently then, at some stage during the crisis, the state of expectations has reversed itself for the original feature under analysis had been the general attempt to add to money balances from sales proceeds – the 'general anxiety to sell'. The juxtaposition of this transition in mood with the emphasis upon the temporary nature of the crisis suggests that recovery is presumed to set in with expanded purchases in response to expected price increases:

> It is true that this state can be only temporary, and must even be succeeded by a reaction of corresponding violence, since those who have sold without buying will certainly buy at last, and there will then be more buyers than sellers. But although the general over-supply is of necessity only temporary, this is no more than may be said of every partial over-supply. An overstocked state of the market is always temporary, and is generally followed by a more than common briskness of demand (277).[26]

26 Cf. the account by Hicks (1983), 64: 'Slumps are times of low prices, relatively to some norm; if the norm is firm, that means that the low prices themselves hold out a prospect of recovery, which sooner or later, must become actual. So there is an underlying stability, provided that the norm remains.' Hicks clarifies that the nature of the norm must be appreciated in terms of the maintenance of the gold standard. All this is true; but the argument leaves out of account the key role for bank intervention to aid recovery – to prevent prices from collapsing in depression. This matter we take up later (p. 544).

This, apparently, is as far as Mill went in explaining the presumption against a Keynes-like 'unemployment equilibrium'.

A word regarding the historiographical implications of the formulation. In the first place, Mill took great pains to insist that recognition of excess demand for money to hold in no way conceded anything to the 'general glut' or 'over-production' theorists:

But those who have, at periods such as we have described, affirmed that there was an excess of all commodities, never pretended that money was one of these commodities; they held that there was not an excess, but a deficiency of the circulating medium. *What they called a general superabundance, was not a superabundance of commodities relatively to commodities, but a superabundance of all commodities relatively to money.* What it amounted to was, that persons in general, at that particular time, from a general expectation of being called upon to meet sudden demands, liked better to possess money than any other commodity. Money, consequently, was in request, and all other commodities were in comparative disrepute. In extreme cases, money is collected in masses, and hoarded; in the milder cases, people merely defer parting with their money, or coming under any new engagements to part with it. But the result is, that all commodities fall in price, or become unsaleable. When this happens to one single commodity, there is said to be a superabundance of that commodity; and if that be a proper expression, there would seem to be in the nature of the case no particular impropriety in saying that there is a superabundance of all or most commodities, when all or most of them are in this same predicament.

It is, however, of the utmost importance to observe that excess of all commodities, in the only sense in which it is possible, means only a temporary fall in their value relatively to money. To suppose that the markets for all commodities could, in any other sense than this, be overstocked, involves the absurdity that commodities may fall in value relatively to themselves; or that, of two commodities, each can fall relatively to the other, A becoming equivalent to B − x, and B to A − x, at the same time. And it is, perhaps, a sufficient reason for not using phrases of this description, that they suggest the idea of excessive production. A want of market for one article may arise from excessive production of that article; but when commodities in general become unsaleable, it is from a very different cause; *there cannot be excessive production of commodities in general* (277–8, italics added).

The essentials of the doctrine are preserved when it is allowed that *there cannot be permanent excess of production, or of accumulation*; though it be at the same time admitted, that as there may be a temporary excess of any one article considered separately, so may there of commodities generally, not in consequence of over-production, but of a want of commercial confidence (279, italics added).

Indeed, the paper closes on the same orthodox theme – there are no constraints to growth emanating from demand deficiency. Once again the contrary view is lambasted as absurd:

The argument against the possibility of general over-production is quite conclusive, so far as it applies to the doctrine that a country may accumulate capital too fast; that produce in general may, by increasing faster than the demand for it, reduce all producers to distress. This proposition, strange to say, was almost a received doctrine as lately as thirty years ago; and the merit of those who have exploded it is much greater than might be inferred from the extreme obviousness of its absurdity when it is stated in its native simplicity. It is true that if all the wants of all the inhabitants of a country were fully satisfied, no further capital could find useful employment; but, in that case, none would be accumulated. So long as there remain any persons not possessed, we do not say of subsistence, but of the most refined luxuries, and who would work to possess them, there is employment for capital; and if the commodities which these persons want are not produced and placed at their disposal, it can only be because capital does not exist, disposable for the purpose of employing, if not any other labourers, those very labourers themselves, in producing the articles for their own consumption. Nothing can be more chimerical than the fear that the accumulation of capital should produce poverty and not wealth, or that it will ever take place too fast for its own end. Nothing is more true than that it is produce which constitutes the market for produce, and that every increase of production, if distributed without miscalculation among all kinds of produce in the proportion which private interest would dictate, creates, or rather constitutes, its own demand (278).

Secondly, sharply contrasting with the denial of the facts of post-war depression which characterized the polemic against Blake, is Mill's claim that no orthodox economist who subscribed to the law of markets would deny the possibility of an excess demand for money to hold: 'no one, after sufficient explanation, will contest the possibility of general excess, in this sense of the word. The state of things which we have just described, and which is of no uncommon occurrence, amounts to it' (276). Similarly, after reiterating the orthodox insistence upon the proposition that 'it is produce which constitutes the market for produce', so that expanded output – if appropriately allocated – 'creates, or rather constitutes, its own demand', Mill insists that his own account of excess money demand added nothing to what was known by 'the authors of the doctrine', who at most were sometimes 'inadvertent' in formulation and left the (unfortunate) impression that their doctrine contradicted 'well-known facts' (278–9):

This is the truth which the deniers of general over-production have seized and enforced; nor is it pretended that anything has been added to it, or subtracted from it, in the present disquisition. But it is thought that those who receive the doctrine accompanied with the explanations which we have given, will understand, more clearly than before, what is, and what is not, implied in it; and will see that, when properly understood, it in no way contradicts those obvious facts which are universally known and admitted to be not only of possible, but of actual and even frequent occurrence. The doctrine in question only appears a paradox, because it has usually been so expressed as apparently to contradict these well-known facts; which, however, were equally well known to the authors of the doctrine, who, therefore, can only have adopted from inadvertence any form of expression which could to a candid person appear inconsistent with it.

There is considerable justification for these assertions since J. B. Say generally (and Ricardo on significant occasions) did not insist upon the extreme version of the law of markets – Say's identity (see Hollander, 1979, 79f, 512f). But they are none the less unbecoming since Mill himself, though only while under the direct influence of his father, had subscribed to that version and this had governed his perspective on monetary matters before 1826 to the extent of blinding him to the very 'facts' which now forced themselves upon his attention and with which he at last felt able to deal. Here then is a case where, considering Mill's personal history, the intrusion of 'anomalous' facts brought about the abandonment of a faulty theoretical construct.[27]

* * *

27 Corry (1962), 106, suspects the influence of Torrens while admitting that 'there is no direct evidence available'. Notwithstanding Torrens's recognition of the possibility of changes in the relative valuation of money and goods (see Robbins, 1958, 176f on the *Essay on the Production of Wealth* 1821), Lord Robbins has urged that it is Mill himself who deserves the main credit for breaking the contemporary *impasse*: 'while conceding nothing to the general argument against saving and accumulation [he] broke through the sterile logic of Say's Law and showed how, from time to time, a holding back of expenditure might produce the appearance of a general glut' (1968, 61). Similarly: 'I think it must be agreed that this is a very remarkable article. It does not, it is true, deal with the possibility that, because of some hold-up in the capital market, attempted savings may run to waste for considerable periods. But at least it provides, what earlier statements of the orthodox classical position had conspicuously failed to provide, a possible explanation of the *appearance* of over production, without surrendering the general position that the effects of accumulation are beneficial. It would not have satisfied Malthus. But at least it put a plausible gloss on Smith and Ricardo' (64).
The view that Mill's analysis 'would not have satisfied Malthus' relates to a belief that Malthus stood firmly by the 'no hoarding' theorem so that, while recognizing that the 'orthodox' theory failed to account for depression, he himself provided no satisfactory alternative which allowed for fluctuations in the demand for money (Robbins, 1968, 60–1). This seems too harsh an evaluation, since Malthus went far in the appreciation of the post-war depression, allowing in his account for leakages from the expenditure stream (cf. Hollander, 1979, 528f).

As noted above Mill pointed to 'the currency' as one possible cause of 'general delusion'. This allowance led him to comment that while 'an increase of production really takes place during the progress of depreciation' this is so 'as long as the existence of depreciation is not suspected; and it is this which gives to the fallacies of the currency school, principally represented by Mr. [Thomas] Attwood, all the little plausibility they possess' (275). When the 'delusion' dissipates these extended projects are proved, as we know, unsustainable.[28] This fundamentally important theoretical observation was elaborated upon in the 'Currency Juggle' of 1833 to which we turn next.[29]

Mill addressed himself in this paper to the case made by Thomas Attwood before the Commons Committee on the Bank Charter (1832), supporting expanded issues of (an inconvertible) paper money to reduce the real pressure of debts and taxes and thus (by stimulating demand) to act on employment and capital usage: 'A large portion of the national capital, especially that part which consists of buildings and machinery, is now, he affirms, lying idle, in default of a market for its productions; those various productions being, as he admits, the natural market for one another, but being unable to exchange for each other, for want of a more plentiful medium of exchange . . .' (IV, 190).[30]

The initial response to the argument is simply that a small nominal quantity of currency at low general prices is as effective as a motive to produce as a larger one at higher general prices. But it emerges that Mill

This is not, of course, to deprecate the quality of Mill's formulation. Hutchison (1953), 346f, on the other hand is highly critical of Mill's treatment in certain respects: 'a profound and confusing ambivalence runs through the essay as a whole which is quite certainly very unfair to the eighteenth-century thinkers condemned in such sweeping terms and whose entire approach is dismissed from any consideration as a "palpable absurdity". What one wishes that Mill (and his followers for several decades subsequently) had done, is to have elucidated more carefully the distinction between those "periods of general excess," the possibility of which "no one denies," and the periods of "general over-production" when "produce in general increases faster than the demand for it," which it is such a monstrous error even to conceive of, and the proof of the impossibility of which had apparently constituted such an amazing intellectual revolution'. But this is unfair. Mill does convincingly justify the key distinction between production as such, which is not the culprit, and breaks in the expenditure stream under certain conditions where the problem lies.

28 This position bears a close resemblance to that of Hayek. Cf. Machlup (1976), 22: 'The inevitability of the crisis attending the adjustment of the economy after its overextension, a crisis resulting in excess capacity of durable capital equipment and in unemployment of labor, is probably the most characteristic . . . thesis in Hayek's theory of the trade cycle.'
29 Mill commented in the *Autobiography* on the importance of this paper (*CW*, I, 191).
30 More generally in his evidence before the Committee, Attwood gave as his ideal an inconvertible currency regulated to the end of creating 'full employment' (cf. Fetter, 1965, 145).

accepted the real stimulus provided by the process of inflation in certain circumstances, denying however that such output and employment gains are sustainable – the position of the essay on the 'Influence of Consumption'.

Attwood's conclusions (in so far as they implied the possibility of permanent real gains) are attributed to erroneous method – the appeal to 'practical experience' or an inductive logic, namely that because in 1825 general full-employment had been achieved at a high level of prices it was desirable to return to that situation on the presumption that the former had been caused by the latter (190). Mill (after some initial hesitancy) accepts that full capacity was achieved in 1825, and in fact that capacity was expanded, but attributing these facts to a 'state of insane delusion, in its very nature temporary' – the excessive pressure on capacity usage and unjustifiable additions to capacity during the upswing constituting 'partly the cause of their lying idle now' (191). As in 1830, therefore, Mill warns of the requirement, if steady growth is to be achieved, for short-term flexibility:

From the impossibility of exactly adjusting the operations of the producer to the wants of the consumer, it always happens that some articles are more or less in deficiency, and others in excess. The healthy working of the machinery, therefore, requires that in some channels capital should be in full, while in others it should be in slack, employment. But in 1825, it was imagined that *all* articles, compared with the demand for them, were in a state of deficiency. The extension of paper credit, called forth by the speculations in a few leading articles had produced a rise of prices, which *not* being supposed to be connected with a depreciation of the currency, each man considered to arise from an increase in the effectual demand for his particular article, and so fancied there was a ready and permanent market for any quantity of that article which he could produce. Mr. Attwood's error is that of supposing a depreciation of the currency *really* increases the demand for all articles, and consequently their production, because under some circumstances, it may create a *false opinion* of an increase of demand, which false opinion leads, as the reality would do, to an increase of production, followed, however, by a fatal revulsion as soon as the delusion ceases.

On this account, however, it was the speculative response to circumstances affecting a 'few leading articles' that 'called forth' bank-note expansion; the expansion was not the initiating feature. (This relationship was to be made more explicit in a revision of 1859 which attributes the phenomena of 1825 to 'an unusual extension of the spirit of speculation, accompanied rather than caused by a great increase of paper credit'.)[31] But the central

31 Cf. a similar formulation in the paper of 1826, IV, 91. In the paper of 1830 Mill wrote of *either* speculation *or* the currency as initiators (275; above, p. 503).

implication of Mill's perspective is that depreciation not accompanied by speculative delusion – inflation as such – has no 'real' effects whatsoever. The discussion of the collapse late in 1825 is also revealing. The ultimate cause is seen to lie not, as Attwood maintained, in the contraction of the currency; that was an effect of the crisis itself. The ultimate cause rather was the collapse of the speculative 'delusion'. This response to Attwood has been termed 'paradoxical', considering the essay of 1830 coined at roughly the same time, and viewed as a 'superficial' and 'facetious' attack on the Birmingham School' (Corry, 101, 105). We shall take up these charges presently.

* * *

In his final monetary paper before the *Principles* – the 'Currency Question' (1844) – Mill again describes the features of commercial crisis, concentrating however on price movements and paying little attention here to variations in the real dimensions of the economy:

A commercial crisis is the recoil of prices, after they have been raised by speculation higher than is warranted by the state of the demand and of the supply. Speculation is almost always set in motion by something which affords apparent grounds for expecting either an extra demand or a deficient supply. But the anticipation may, in the first place, be erroneous; in the second, however rational it may be, the speculation (especially where the prospect of gain is considerable) is very likely to be overdone, each speculator conducting his operations as if he alone knew the circumstances on which the hope of profit is grounded. The rise consequent upon the speculative purchases attracts new speculators, insomuch that, paradoxical as it may appear, the largest purchases are often made at the highest price. But at last it is discovered that the rise has gone beyond the permanent cause for it, and purchases cease, or the holders think it is time to realise their gains. Then the recoil comes; and the price falls to a lower point than that from which it had risen, because the high price has both checked the demand, and, by stimulating production or importation, called forth a larger supply. Besides, many of those who during the high price have contracted engagements, which they trusted to a further rise for giving them the means of fulfilling, are unable to hold on until the crisis is past, but must sell at any sacrifice.

When this series of effects is confined to some one article of commerce, individuals may be ruined, but the mercantile world generally is not disturbed. When, however, as in 1825 and at several other periods in the present century, the opening of new markets, or some expected deficiency of supply extending to various important articles, has set speculation at work in several great departments at once, the spirit is apt to become general, and other commodities rise in price without any reasonable cause whatever. In such cases, the ultimate revulsion is most extensive and calamitous.

As long as the seasons vary, as markets fluctuate, and men miscalculate, or the passion of gain (as in gamblers) over-rides their calculations, so long will these alterations of ebb and flow, these 'cycles,' as Colonel Torrens calls them, 'of excitement and depression,' continue. They are worse in America than in England, because American commerce is conducted in a more gambling spirit; they are worse at Liverpool than in London, for the same reason. But whatever aggravates the natural fluctuations of the markets, or creates fluctuations when they would not otherwise exist, increases both the frequency and the destructiveness of such convulsions. This the corn laws do; and it is one of their principal evils (*CW*, II, 348–9).

The reference to the corn laws as culprit doubtless refers to the fundamental proposition, alluded to in 1826, that by 'lowering the rate of ordinary profit' the corn laws 'really produce that tendency to hazardous speculations which is so erroneously, though so commonly, imputed to the system of our currency' (above, pp. 497–8 citing 110), thereby implying a secular or endogenous force at work aggravating cyclical instability.

The passage continues, as in several of the earlier papers but now more forcefully, to absolve the currency as such from blame for contributing to the frequency and severity of commercial crises. Those supporting the forthcoming Bank Act to regulate convertible note issues (Torrens, Norman, McCulloch, Loyd and Sir Robert Peel – theorists and practitioners constituting the Currency School) claimed for the new system 'that this artificial cause of fluctuation will be cut off'. For Mill (as he already casually implied in 1826) it was because speculative purchases are fuelled by expansion of *credit in general*, that 'periods of general confidence, when large prospects of gain seem to be opening themselves, and when there is a disposition among dealers to employ not only all their money but all or much of their credit in enlarging their operations, are attended with so great a rise of general prices' – an outcome that would result 'if no such thing as a transferable acknowledgement of debt [in the form of notes] had ever been known in the country' (354). A major qualification to this rejection of the currency position is given in a note,[32] but this we shall take up in our discussion of the *Principles*.

* * *

What emerges from this review of the essays prior to the *Principles* is an allowance for crisis periods characterized by excess commodity supply, and excess capacity above and beyond the normal margin of quiescent periods.

---

32 Mill allows (352n) that the use of small-denomination notes – prohibited since 1823 – and available for wage payments would alter the picture.

These crises are represented in some of the statements to be part of a cyclical process involving swings in expectations of an endogenous order, swings which explain why 'unemployment equilibria' are not a feature of the argument. In two of the papers (those of 1826 and 1844) we find a linkage between the downward secular trend of the profit rate and the state of expectations. Notwithstanding, the law of markets stands sentinel as firmly as ever, if by that term is meant the impossibility of over-production as such. For secular expansion of output can never be checked by lack of purchasing power. Our next task is to discern how these issues are treated in the *Principles* itself.

Also to be investigated are the fortunes of the pregnant suggestions in the early papers regarding the role played by credit-in-general and paper credit in particular in the generation of cycles.

III THE *PRINCIPLES*: THE CYCLICAL CONTEXT

We proceed having in mind the common view that the early allowances, especially in the essay of 1830, regarding the possibility of excess commodity supply are significantly played down in the *Principles* (above, pp. 484–5). In what follows it will become quite clear that this view has no basis whatsoever in fact (see also the account in Sowell, 1972, 48f).

Brief reference is made to demand for money as a 'reserve for future contingencies' in the course of a preliminary analysis of the determinants of the price level, where it is argued that hoarded money stocks do not act on prices (*CW*, III, 508; cf. 515, 539). But it is in the analysis of commercial crises as well as the chapter formally devoted to 'Excess of Supply' where we find full-fledged statements of the arguments in the early essays.

The chapter 'Of the Influence of Credit on Prices' (III, Ch. xii) traces out the process whereby expectations of future price increases held on rational grounds by professional traders dealing in specific commodities in excess demand (or expected excess demand) extend to speculative purchases beyond the levels justified by the extent of excess demand and, indeed, to commodities in general (540f). The upward price movement is fired by an extension of credit, without which – with 'money', narrowly defined, alone – there would be limited potential; in fact, an enormous rise could be envisaged 'even if there were no increase of money, and no paper credit, but a mere extension of purchases on book credits' (541). The perception of the nature of the upward trend brings the movement to an end and a collapse sets in with the unloading of stocks, prices falling to levels below those ruling at the outset, in consequence of a cessation of credit even for reputable firms. The excess demand for money to hold and excess commodity supply characterizing the crises are portrayed as clearly as in 1830:

There is said to be a commercial crisis, when a great number of merchants and traders at once, either have, or apprehend that they shall have, a difficulty in meeting their engagements. The most usual cause of this general embarrassment, is the recoil of prices after they have been raised by a spirit of speculation, intense in degree, and extending to many commodities. Some accident which excites expectations of rising prices, such as the opening of a new foreign market, or simultaneous indications of a short supply of several great articles of commerce, sets speculation at work in several leading departments at once. The prices rise, and the holders realize, or appear to have the power of realizing, great gains. In certain states of the public mind, such examples of rapid increase of fortune call forth numerous imitators, and speculation not only goes much beyond what is justified by the original grounds for expecting rise of price, but extends itself to articles in which there never was any such ground: these, however, rise like the rest as soon as speculation sets in. At periods of this kind, a great extension of credit takes place. Not only do all whom the contagion reaches, employ their credit much more freely than usual; but they really have more credit, because they seem to be making unusual gains, and because a generally reckless and adventurous feeling prevails, which disposes people to give as well as take credit more largely than at other times, and give it to persons not entitled to it. In this manner, in the celebrated speculative year 1825, and at various other periods during the present century, the prices of many of the principal articles of commerce rose greatly, without any fall in others, so that general prices might, without incorrectness, be said to have risen. When, after such a rise, the reaction comes, and prices begin to fall, though at first perhaps only through the desire of the holders to realize, speculative purchases cease: but were this all, prices would only fall to the level from which they rose, or to that which is justified by the state of the consumption and of the supply. They fall, however, much lower; for as, when prices were rising, and everybody apparently making a fortune, it was easy to obtain almost any amount of credit, so now, when everybody seems to be losing, and many fail entirely, it is with difficulty that firms of known solidity can obtain even the credit to which they are accustomed, and which it is the greatest inconvenience to them to be without; because all dealers have engagements to fulfil, and nobody feeling sure that the portion of his means which he has entrusted to others will be available in time, no one likes to part with ready money, or to postpone his claim to it. To these rational considerations there is superadded, in extreme cases, a panic as unreasoning as the previous overconfidence; money is borrowed for short periods at almost any rate of interest, and sales of goods for immediate payment are made at almost any sacrifice. Thus general prices, during a commercial revulsion, fall as much below the usual level, as during the previous period of speculation they have risen above it: the fall, as well as the rise, originating not in anything affecting money, but in the state of credit; an unusually extended employment of credit during the earlier period, followed by a great diminution, never amounting however to an entire cessation of it, in the later (541–3).

It will be noted that during the upswing from a state of quiescence, expanded credit plays a necessary but not an initiating role – the initiation involves 'some accident' stimulating expectations of generalized excess demand. A rather more positive role seems to be accorded credit during the downturn. But still the downturn itself is not attributed to credit contraction; and the reduced availability of credit itself while aggravating the downswing can perhaps be understood as a reflection of the altered mood, which would be fully in line with the formulation of 1844.[33] (A later statement in the *Principles*, however (574, below, p. 519), adds rather to the ambiguity surrounding this point.)

The expectational pattern implied in the foregoing extract merits further attention. As for the upper turning point all Mill has to say is that 'the reaction comes, and prices begin to fall, though at first perhaps only through the desire of the holders to realize . . .' It is possible to see here a recoil of prices which turns on 'the rather vague notion that speculators decide that prices have reached a peak and so cease their purchases', a notion suggesting a shift in attitude towards inventory investment because speculators have an idea of a normal price level, and if the deviation extends too far, expectations of a price fall set in (Link, 1959, 157–8).[34] As Link further points out 'the transition from the period of revulsion to the quiescent state does not receive any attention' and occurs 'somewhat mysteriously' (167, 177). This he claims to be the 'most striking' feature of the account – that in some 'obscure' way 'revulsion is rapidly replaced by the quiescent state' (179; also 160). But this problem can be overcome if we assume that Mill stood by his position in the essay of 1830, where there can be no question of an upturn from the trough based upon expectations of a price-level norm (above, p. 505).[35]

The stimulating effects on output and employment of an increase in inconvertible paper presupposed by Thomas Attwood are alluded to critically, and it is appropriate to have Mill's objections in mind at this

33 The account in the *Principles* relates to situations such as 1825 where credit contraction followed 'an irrational extension of it' (543). To this extent *all* movements of credit reflect indirectly if not directly swings in expectational mood. (The year 1847, on the other hand, involved a crisis of a different order wherein an unusual set of circumstances forced interest high depriving some firms, which were short of funds, of renewed credit, and whose failure spread general distrust.)

34 Link plays down the role of gold drains as inessential to the end of upward speculation, and on the basis of the present text justifiably so.

35 See (III, 509) for an allusion to this mechanism: 'Persons may indeed refuse to sell, and withdraw their goods from the market, if they cannot get for them what they consider a sufficient price. But this is only when they think that the price will rise, and that they shall get more money by waiting. If they thought the low price likely to be permanent, they would take what they could get. It is always a *sine qua non* with a dealer to dispose of his goods.'

point (III, Ch. xiii).[36] Attwood's general argument was suspect (563–4). An increase of *all* prices could evidently have no stimulatory effect, so that the case must presume expectations by each producer that his own output will sell at a higher *relative* price when it reaches the market, an expectation inevitably disappointed. That people never discover the increase in their sales revenues to be purely nominal Mill refused to believe. For Attwood to seek support in the periods of high prices experienced periodically would not do for these were not 'times of prosperity', but 'simply (as all periods of high prices, under a convertible currency, must be) times of speculation'; and at such times speculators 'did not think they were growing rich because the high prices would last, but because they would not last, and because whoever contrived to realize while they did last, would find himself after the recoil, in possession of a greater number of pounds sterling, without their having become of less value'.

This latter assertion is fair enough in so far as it applies to the peak of the cycle, since the first to unload doubtless do so with the prospect of falling or at least unchanged prices in mind. But Mill in his essays had always conceded a temporary stimulus to output, even additions to capacity, during the upturn, and that stimulus certainly implied upward price expectations (fueled by credit) which were ultimately to be disappointed. It is unlikely that Mill had abandoned the allowance for real temporary effects.[37] We can appreciate the decision to bypass the full case to the extent that his concern in the critique of Attwood was primarily to deny the possibility of a *secular* inflationary stimulus to output, capital and employment.

In the celebrated chapter 'Of Excess of Supply' (III, Ch. xiv) Mill turns his attention to those such as Malthus, Chalmers and Sismondi who, generalizing from the admissible case of one product asserted that expansion of products in the aggregate is necessarily accompanied by a deficiency of purchasing power thereby precluding sales at unchanged prices and profits (571; cf. 66–8).[38] In line with the earlier papers this position is rejected as far as concerns *the ability to purchase* on the grounds that

each person's means of paying for the productions of other people consists of those which he himself possesses. All sellers are inevitably and *ex vi termini* buyers. Could

---

36 Mill also addressed himself briefly to David Hume's analysis of the real effects of monetary expansion.

37 For allusions to real output effect during speculative periods see Book III, Ch. xxvi, 664.

38 Sowell (1972; 1974) takes issue with those who believe that the great controversy turned upon the question of secular stagnation (e.g. Blaug, 1958a, 93). Both the general glut and the orthodox economists, he insists, accepted that there were no permanent or secular growth constraints, and the debate turned entirely upon the possibility of short-run excess supply. But the fact is that Mill does reason as if secular stagnation were a problem for Malthus *et al.*

we suddenly double the productive powers of the country, we should double the supply of all commodities in every market; but we should, by the same stroke, double the purchasing power . . . A general over supply, or excess of all commodities above the demand, so far as demand consists in means of payment, is . . . an impossibility (571–2).[39]

It is, as usual, conceded that allowance must be made for a distribution of the supposedly doubled aggregate capacity between commodities which inappropriately meets the pattern of demand pertaining to a doubled expenditure, a distribution assured by the allocative process. As for *the will to purchase* (a second sense of the notion of a deficiency of demand) Mill insists that the decision to produce itself indicates a will to purchase. He concedes, again as is usual with him, the abstract possibility that the community might be satiated with products and choose to enjoy higher incomes in the form of leisure – in which case there would be no increase in output of which to dispose (574). The act of accumulation itself is not problematic even if capitalists save and invest 'out of habit' in the presence of scarce labour supplies, since purchasing power is thereby transferred to the working classes, and 'until the working classes have also reached the point of satiety – there will be no want of demand for the produce of capital, however rapidly it may accumulate: since, if there is nothing else for it to do, it can always find employment in producing the necessaries or luxuries of the labouring class' (573–4).

The argument is supplemented by a more formal case – that it is self-contradictory to maintain that all commodities 'should fall in value' (Mill evidently intended *relative* value) 'and that all producers should, in consequence, be insufficiently remunerated'. But 'if values remain the same, what becomes of price is immaterial, since the remuneration of producers does not depend on how much money, but on how much of consumable articles, they obtain for their goods. Besides, money is a commodity; and

---

39 This passage is cited by Keynes (1936) to imply the doctrine that 'the whole of the costs of production must necessarily be spent in the aggregate, directly or indirectly, on purchasing the product' (1973 [1936], 18). This old saw is reiterated to the present day; cf. Robinson (1980), 81.

Patinkin (1956, 472f) justifiably protests that the passage deals with power to purchase and merely expresses the social accounting identity that national income equals national product. But although Patinkin strongly defends Mill against the charge by Lange (1942) as well as Keynes that he maintained the law of markets as an identity, he is none the less critical (as he is critical of the entire classical school), of a failure, beyond casual hints, to specify how precisely – in the secular context – the market mechanism validates the law. For Patinkin an expansion of aggregate supply, reflecting higher capacity and population or technical change, generates a deflationary gap which sets in motion a corrective adjustment process stimulating aggregate demand, i.e. a real balance effect at, it must be assumed, the secular level (252f; cf. 351, 475).

if all commodities are supposed to be doubled in quantity, we must suppose money to be doubled too, and then prices would no more fall than values would' (572). Now this issue of the secular adequacy of the money supply had been earlier addressed by Mill, though only in the editions of 1849, 1852 and 1857 (562–3n.), in a critique of John Gray's case against convertibility (*Lectures on the Nature and Use of Money*, 1848). That 'commodities are the real market for commodities' and 'Production is essentially the cause and measure of demand' Gray had accepted in the case of barter only, but regarded as fallacious under a metallic monetary system 'because if the aggregate of goods is increased faster than the aggregate of money, prices must fall, and all producers must be losers; now neither gold nor silver, nor any other valuable thing "can by any possibility be increased *ad libitum*, as fast as all other valuable things put together:" a limit, therefore, is arbitrarily set to the amount of production which can take place . . .' To this argument Mill objected that a general fall in prices would in fact stimulate an expansion of gold supply; although a reduction in general of prices would in any event be merely nominal and have no serious deflationary consequences.[40]

To return to the 'over-production error'. Its source was seen to lie in a misconceived appeal to experience – a reference, in the first place, to certain 'mercantile facts' – accountable, Mill insisted, in terms of his own conception of commercial crisis. This statement supplements that already given in the earlier chapter on credit, and contains all the key elements of the earlier essays with their allowance for excess commodity supply:

At such times there is really, an excess of all commodities above the money demand: in other words, there is an under-supply of money. From the sudden annihilation

---

40 The increased weight of fixed nominal obligations is said in the note to be a minor consideration from the point of view of the 'productive classes'; they 'would suffer almost solely in the
increased onerousness of their contribution to the taxes which pay the interest on the National
Debt'. There would be something cavalier about this response – after all, Attwood's case for
inflation had turned in part on the reduction of this kind of burden – were it not for the fact
that Mill expected an automatic expansion of the money supply under a convertible regime.
   It is not clear why Mill chose to delete this discussion of Gray in the fifth edition.
Possibly it was because the pamphlet was no longer in the public eye.
   See also the correspondence of 1852: 'I do not see how Mr. Tooke's doctrine, that
prices depend on the aggregate of money incomes, at all helps to prove that increase
of capital by savers lowers general prices. Whether £100 is employed in business or in
personal expenditure it equally becomes part of somebody's money income. Increase
of production will not, I conceive, lower prices unless the production of money is an
exception to the general increase. If it is so prices will fall, no doubt, but even then the
fall of prices or what is the same thing, the increased value of money does not lower
profits or incumber the markets with unsold goods: it only increases the burthen of all
fixed money engagements' (3 July 1852, XIV, 93–4).

of a great mass of credit, every one dislikes to part with ready money, and many are anxious to procure it at any sacrifice. Almost everybody therefore is a seller, and there are scarcely any buyers; so that there may really be, though only while the crisis lasts, an extreme depression of general prices, from what may be indiscriminately called a glut of commodities or a dearth of money. But it is a great error to suppose, with Sismondi, that a commercial crisis is the effect of a general excess of production. It is simply the consequence of an excess of speculative purchases. It is not a gradual advent of low prices, but a sudden recoil from prices extravagantly high: its immediate cause is a contraction of credit, and the remedy is, not a diminution of supply, but the restoration of confidence. It is also evident that this temporary derangement of markets is an evil only because it is temporary. The fall being solely of money prices, if prices did not rise again no dealer would lose, since the smaller price would be worth as much to him as the larger price was before (574).[41]

It will be remarked that Mill in this passage – and it is a feature of all the earlier accounts – is presuming that the Sismondi view alludes to secular trends, the growth process forcing down prices in consequence of inadequate purchasing power. As Mill viewed the matter, the facts of the case, as far as concerned commercial crises, pointed only to temporary price and profit movements, the problem of profitability residing precisely in their non-permanent character. This objection is important from a methodological viewpoint, for appeal is made to facts which are convincingly shown to accord better with an alternative theoretical model.

Reference is also made to an error of interpretation on the part of the overproduction writers involving that 'fall of profits and interest which naturally takes place with the progress of population and production', which, for Mill, reflects 'the increased cost of maintaining labour, result[ing] from an increase of population and of the demand for food, outstripping the advance of agricultural improvement', and is totally unrelated to a 'want of market for commodities' (575; cf. 739–40). For 'the true interpretation of the modern or present state of industrial economy is, that there is hardly any amount of business that may not be done, if people will be content to do it on small profits', while the alternative approach was 'essentially self-contradictory' and 'chimerical'. His tone here brings to mind that of his juvenile pronouncements. It is relevant that at precisely this juncture Mill directs his readers not only to J. B. Say, but to the 'conclusive exposition' in the *Elements* of James Mill and to his *Commerce Defended*, where

41 In this passage Mill asserts that 'the immediate cause' of the price decline is 'a contraction of credit'. As we have seen he had earlier put the direct blame on a reversal of the expectational mood. But the notion that the remedy for depression is the 'restoration of confidence' again points the finger at expectations.

the correct doctrine was set forth 'with great force and clearness' (576). It is these statements which, perhaps, are responsible for the common belief that Mill reappears in 1848 in the guise of a 'hard-boiled classic'. This, however, is positively not the case. His objections were solely to the 'over-production' theorists who purported to account for a 'permanent decline in the circumstances of producers, for want of markets' (575), using their case in support of 'unproductive consumption', and a check to accumulation (571). The allowances for short-run excess commodity supply are made in 1848 with all the force of the earlier essays.

Mill, in fact, carries the matter further, for while in the earlier essays attention was paid to excess commodity supply in periods of 'revulsion', little note was taken of its counterpart in the labour market. Indeed, on one conspicuous occasion Mill had asserted that one person's gain is another's loss during crisis periods suggesting no net reduction in wages and employment (below, p. 549).

This hiatus has been remarked upon in the literature, but it clearly is not true of the *Principles* where Mill is explicit regarding both excess capacity and unemployment as well as undesired inventory accumulations: 'Establishments are shut up, or kept working without any profit, hands are discharged . . .' (741).

This allowance for excess labour supply is also to be found in the context of the celebrated first proposition on capital – that 'industry is limited by capital' (II, 338–9; cf. 57, 65). Mill evidently presumed that the basic doctrine regarding aggregate employment is to be supplemented by a function allowing for the state of aggregate demand for final goods. Moreover, far from playing down the qualifications required for the law of markets to apply – allowance for (disequilibrium) periods of excess supply – Mill defined more closely than ever he had done in his essays the linkage between the secular tendency of the profit rate to decline and the cyclical phenomena in question, and paid particular attention to actual leakages of savings of a secular order, particularly capital outflows abroad (see above, p. 467).

IV   THE QUANTITY THEORY

As with Ricardo the selection of the precious metals as a medium of exchange or circulating medium was seen to turn on their relatively stable 'value' – in the sense of general purchasing power – a consequence of relative constancy in supply: 'Of all commodities, they are among the least influenced by any of the causes which produce fluctuations of value . . . But on the whole, no commodities are so little exposed to causes of variation. They fluctuate less than almost any other things in their cost of production. And from their durability, the total quantity in existence is at all times so great in proportion to the annual supply, that the effect on value even of a change in the cost of production is not sudden: a very long time being required to diminish materially the quantity in existence, and even to increase it very greatly not being a rapid process (*CW*, III, 504; cf. 558). Like that of all other commodities the value of money is determined 'temporarily by demand and supply, permanently and on the average by cost of production' (507; cf. 517) – an unfortunate formulation since it has been read to imply that changes in cost of production for Mill act on value independently of supply variation, while in fact 'even in the case of a metallic currency, the immediate agency in determining its value is its quantity' (556).

The value of money in the short run and long run – its 'temporary' and its 'permanent' value – is dealt with in two successive chapters (III, Chs. viii and ix). It is most appropriate to deal with the latter issue in the context of value and distribution (see above, p. 295) and limit the discussion here to 'temporary' value.[42]

In the simplest model – a model excluding credit – the determination of the level of prices in the short run turns in part on the supply of money understood as 'the quantity of it which people are wanting to lay out; that is, all the money they have in their possession, except what they are hoarding, or at least keeping by them as a reserve for future contingencies. The supply of money, in short, is all the money in *circulation* at the time' (509; cf. 515). Emerging thus tangentially in the specification of the index of money supply appropriate for price determination is recognition of a demand for money to hold for other than transactions purposes. This formulation is supplemented, however, by a subsequent elaboration of both the speculative and precautionary components of the demand for money of particular importance for its insistence upon a short-run context:

Money acts upon prices in no other way than by being tendered in exchange for commodities. The demand which influences the prices of commodities consists of the money offered for them. But the money offered, is not the same thing with the money possessed. It is sometimes less, sometimes very much more. In the long run indeed, the money which people lay out will be neither more nor less than the money which they have to lay out: but this is far from being the case at any given time. Sometimes they keep money by them for fear of an emergency, or in expectation of a more advantageous opportunity for expending it. In that case the money is said not to be in circulation: in plainer language, it is not offered, nor about to be offered, for commodities. Money not in circulation has no effect on prices (539).

---

42 Mill's basic money in the quantity theory context is metallic currency, but the same analysis could be applied to fiat notes (see, e.g., 556).

The leading proposition of this passage unfortunately lends itself to misinterpretation. Taken literally it implies that an exogenous increase in the non-transactions component would not exert downward pressure on the level of prices. As we shall see, however, the general tenor of Mill's argument suggests that this could not have been his intention. Rather his point is that an increase in the money supply coinciding with (or in response to) an increase in the non-transactions component will not generate an increase in the price level. We shall allude frequently to this point.

Formally, the demand for money – in so far as it is pertinent to the analysis of the price level – is simply defined as 'all the goods offered for sale' (509).[43] This formulation has been read to imply the proposition that 'the amount of the individual's *excess demand* for money – at a given set of relative prices, real income and real balances – is necessarily equal to the aggregate money value of the amounts of his *excess supplies* of commodities – corresponding to this same set of prices, income, and balances' (Patinkin, 1956, 25).[44] It is doubtful whether this interpretation is an accurate attribution in each detail, but the general proposition seems to reflect Mill's intentions.[45] It is certainly the case (as we shall see) that it is by generating an excess demand for commodities that an injection of money acts on prices; and there is no reason to preclude the converse relationship.

Let us look now more closely at the analysis of the impact of an exogenous increase in the money supply on prices in general. Mill took great care to specify the experiment. It is an essential part of the argument, we have observed, that 'money acts on prices in no other way than by being tendered in exchange for commodities' (539). Accordingly, changes in relative prices might occur, depending upon how precisely the increase impinges on the system: 'it is of course possible that the influx of money might take place through the medium of some new class of consumers, or in such a manner

---

43 In this context (510) Mill uses the term 'reciprocal demand', more familiar in the foreign trade context. Mill emphasizes that it is goods *of all sorts* on the one side, and money on the other.

44 Excess money demand is a *flow* concept on a par in dimension with commodity supply; whereas demand for money as such is a *stock* demand; it is therefore not true that an individual's demand for money equals the aggregate money value of his commodity supplies.

45 That Mill distinguished the stock and flow concepts is clear from the proposition that the 'money offered [for goods] is not the same thing with the money possessed'; it is easy enough to apply this notion of *excess* to the case of money demand.

     Mill also distinguished the stock of commodities from the market supply: Individuals 'may indeed refuse to sell, and withdraw their goods from the market, if they cannot get for them what they consider a sufficient price' (509). This complexity is, however, played down; it occurs 'only when they think that the price will rise, and that they shall get more by waiting. If they thought the low price likely to be permanent, they would take what they could get. It is always a *sine qua non* with a dealer to dispose of his goods'.

as to alter the proportions of different classes of consumers to one another, so that a greater share of the national income than before would thenceforth be expended in some articles, and a smaller in others; exactly as if a change had taken place in the tastes and wants of the community' (510). Such disturbances would, however, be temporary, lasting 'until production had accommodated itself to this change in the comparative demand for different things . . .'[46] To rule out such disturbances to the structure of prices and focus upon the 'effect of an increase in money, considered by itself' and 'apart from accessory circumstances' Mill proposed as the experimental change that each individual be supposed to wake up to find an extra pound added to each pound already in his possession,[47] following which – always supposing 'the wants and inclinations of the community collectively in respect of consumption remaining exactly the same' – 'there would be an increased money demand, and consequently an increased money value, or price, for things of all sorts' (511).

General prices will change in proportion to the change in money supply, at least after the passage of sufficient time for the increase 'to permeate all the channels of circulation' (511). Here lay a fundamental distinction between non-monetary commodities and money (albeit itself a commodity) – the 'peculiar property' of money that its value 'other things being the same, varies inversely as its quantity' (512). For money is desired not for itself but 'as the means of universal purchase, the demand [consisting] of everything which people have to sell; and the only limit to what they are willing to give, is the limit set by their having nothing more to offer. The whole of the goods being in any case exchanged for the whole of the money which comes into the market to be laid out, they will sell for less or more of it, exactly according as less or more is brought.'[48]

Allowance is, of course, made for velocity or the 'rapidity of circulation' of money. This Mill rephrased as 'the efficiency of money' to avoid any suggestion of 'the number of purchases made by each piece of money in a given time' which is an irrelevant consideration, and focus rather on 'the average number of purchases made by each piece [in a given time] in order to effect a given pecuniary amount of transactions [in that same time]' (513–14).[49] With this in mind the value of money can be said to vary in

46 Mill is implicitly presuming constant-cost industries.
47 Hume's experiment of adding a guinea to each individual's money stock would weight disproportionately the impact on workers' outlays.
48 Mill insists that the result holds good even if, for whatever reason, the price structure should be permanently affected by the injection, for 'it is a necessary consequence of the fact, that a fourth more money would have been given for the same quantity of goods. *General* prices, therefore, would in any case be a fourth higher' (511). But see the criticisms of this proposition in Balassa (1959), 266n6, Patinkin (1956), 30–1.
49 In his *Treatise on Money*, Keynes distinguishes the national money stock relative to national

direct proportion with the volume of transactions and inversely with the quantity of money weighted by the velocity index.[50]

All this is of the first importance from an analytical perspective. Mill's emphasis upon the increase in the level of prices reflecting a prior impact of the increased money supply upon the demand for commodities, supplemented by his observation that the injection of money affects relative prices according to how and where it impinges reflects a clear recognition that 'the causal relation between money and prices is not at all a mechanical one' (Patinkin, 1956, 98). Moreover, the argument is logically consistent with a process involving the real-balance effect. Yet here we must exercise caution, for Mill does not formally spell the process out in precisely those terms; and to absolve Mill entirely of the charge directed against later writers such as Marshall and Pigou of confusing the demand curve for money and the 'market-equilibrium' curve (as does Balassa, 1959, 265–6) would be going too far.[51] The argument leading up to the notion of a proportionate

income from the money stock relative to volume of transactions, and attributes the first to Mill (1930, II, 23–4). In the present context, however, it is apparently the latter to which Mill refers. It is not clear whether this is what he had in mind in the essay of 1844 (IV, 352). See below (pp. 559–60).

50 Mill notes that a correction on the commodity side is also required to the extent that the same goods are bought repeatedly 'in speculative times' (512).

51 On these matters see Patinkin, Chs. II, III. Patinkin here points out that a real balance effect impinges on money itself as well as for commodities; part of any increase in the money supply will be used to add to money balances, involving a shift in the 'demand curve' for money. (This is a special case where a shift of supply cannot be assumed to leave demand unaffected.) The so-called unitary-elastic demand for money is then a locus of market equilibria, not a genuine curve of demand, *ceteris paribus* with money supply held constant. The following figure (42) summarizes the issue:

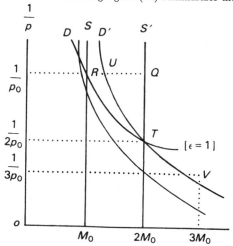

Nominal amount of money demanded and supplied

relation between prices and money supply seems indeed, as Patinkin suggests, to deal with market-equilibrium positions; but the rationale offered to explain why prices are precisely doubled following a doubling of the money supply, entailing allusions (by way of contrast) to the demand elasticities of regular commodities, strongly suggests that at least at some places in his exposition Mill had in mind a 'genuine' demand curve for money of unitary elasticity.[52]

The foregoing qualification scarcely detracts from the high quality of Mill's general account. This account has been taken to task for a deficiency usually reserved for later neo-classicists, namely a failure – despite the obvious desire to integrate monetary and value theory – to include in his chapter on 'The Value of Money as Dependent on Demand and Supply' a counterpart to the stability discussion of his earlier chapter on 'Demand and Supply in their Relation to Value' (Patinkin, 1956, 376, 438f).[53] But this reservation implies high praise, for it is Mill's own achievement that awakens the expectation.

Mill's objective throughout his exposition was, however, to bury not to praise simple-minded applications of the quantity theory. These are disturbances to the key variables which do not generate the 'expected' results. Thus an increase in the money stock will not generate an increase in prices in the event that it does not raise the amount offered for sale against commodities: 'money hoarded does not act on prices. Money kept on reserve by individuals to meet contingencies which do not occur, does not act on prices. The money in the coffers of the Bank, or retained in a reserve by private bankers, does not act on prices until drawn out, nor even then unless drawn out to be expended in commodities' (*CW*, III, 515; cf. 508, 539).[54] Needless to say, this phenomenon can be treated formally as a reduction in velocity and imposes no conceptual difficulty from the perspective of

Following a doubling of the money supply, from S to S', the demand for money to hold shifts from D to D'. At the original level of prices (p_0) RU of the net increase is absorbed by the increase in demand, with UQ representing an excess money supply, with its counterpart in an excess demand for commodities generating upward pressure on prices. The market-equilibrium locus joining positions such as R and T has unitary elasticity.

52 Thus Mill's account (512) seems to suggest that only if the entire net increase in the money supply (RQ in the preceding note) is expended in commodities will the price level rise proportionately.

53 Mill's account of stability conditions in the context of the interest rate must, however, be kept in mind (below, p. 533).

54 But, as noted above, Patinkin demonstrates that the proportionate change in prices occurs notwithstanding some shift in the demand for 'hoards' and 'reserves'. In Mill's discussion the increase in money demand is an exogenous increase, independent of, rather than induced by, the supposed expansion of money supply, i.e. there is apparently no real balance effect playing on the demand for money.

the framework given above. But it is more helpful to focus on what is directly involved, namely an increase in the supply for money which would generate an increase in the level of commodity prices were it not for the supposed increase in the demand for money to hold.[55] In this same context we encounter a fundamentally important observation to which we shall revert in our discussion of Mill's monetary policy, namely that 'an increase of the circulating medium, conformable in extent and duration to the temporary stress of business does not raise prices, but merely prevents their fall' (516) – an obvious allusion to the virtually unlimited demand for 'ready money' during business depression.[56]

* * *

55 Diagrammatically:

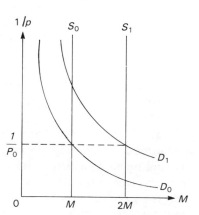

We draw Mill's demand curves with unitary elasticity having in mind the 'error' discussed above. Another example: An increase in transactions entailing an excess demand for money will involve no price reductions, if the money supply is expanded (515–16). If not, either resort is made to money substitutes, or velocity expands, or indeed prices will decline. (On this case see Patinkin, 117.)

56 This case can be represented thus:

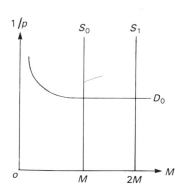

More important than the foregoing complications – all of which are amenable
to treatment within Mill's basic (if extended) model – is his insistence that
the entire analysis pertains in an economy without credit:

The proposition which we have laid down respecting the dependence of general
prices upon the quantity of money in circulation, must be understood as applying
only to a state of things in which money, that is, gold and silver, is the exclusive
instrument of exchange, and actually passes from hand to hand at every purchase,
credit in any of its shapes, being unknown. When credit comes into play as a means
of purchasing, distinct from money in hand, we shall hereafter find that the
connexion between prices and the amount of the circulating medium is much less
direct and intimate, and that such connexion as does exist, no longer admits of
so simple a mode of expression (514).[57]

There were qualifications to the proposition that the value of the circulating
medium varies inversely with its quantity, qualifications (Mill added in
1857) 'which, under a complex system of credit like that existing in England,
render the proposition a totally incorrect expression of the fact' (516).[58]

Two chapters of the *Principles* are devoted to credit (III, Chs. xi, xii),
the first of which constitutes a descriptive account of various 'substitutes
for money', including bank notes, bills of exchange – on which topic Henry
Thornton is cited *verbatim* at length (531f.), promissory notes (*inter alia* those
issued by government) and 'deposits and cheques' (536);[59] book or trade
credit is not mentioned, although this must be an oversight for it figures
extensively in the formal discussion of the impact of credit on prices. By
means of the various credit instruments 'the immense business of a country
like Great Britain is transacted with an amount of the precious metals
surprisingly small . . .' (537).

> A fresh set of issues is raised by the proposition that an increase in the money supply,
> should it act in the first instance on security prices and thus the interest rate, might
> generate an equivalent outflow of the metals and for this reason have no impact on
> commodity prices: 'This is a case highly deserving of attention: and it is a fact now
> beginning to be recognised, that the passage of the precious metals from country to country
> is determined much more than was formerly supposed, by the state of the loan market
> in different countries, and much less by the state of prices' (515). But see Patinkin's
> conclusion (115, 162) that price movements are in fact generated.

57 Mill should have added that the analysis applies to the case of *fiat* money also.
58 Modified in 1862 to an 'extremely incorrect expression of the fact'.
59 'A fourth mode of making credit answer the purposes of money, by which, when carried
far enough, money may be very completely superseded, consists in making payments
by cheques.' This practice, Mill adds, was 'spreading to a continually larger portion
of the public'. Bankers are said to know what reserve to keep on hand and lend out
the 'far greater part'. There is no hint, however, that the banking system 'creates money',
although Mill describes the clearing-house process. Banks are accorded only a 'cloakroom'
function, as it was later to be called.

'Credit' creation is distinguished from 'capital' creation and represented as a means of transferring saved funds from owners to users (527–8).[60] But to the extent that in the absence of a credit mechanism such funds would have lain idle for want of skill, knowledge or time on the part of capitalists to engage personally in business operations, savings (while not increased by credit operations) are called into a 'more complete state of productive activity' (529).[61] The implications of credit for interest-rate determination are not here taken up, for Mill's primary concern is with credit as 'purchasing power' in which capacity it acts upon general prices: 'In a state of commerce in which much credit is habitually given, general prices at any moment depend much more upon the state of credit than upon the quantity of money. For credit, though it is not productive power, is purchasing power; and a person who, having credit, avails himself of it in the purchase of goods, creates just as much demand for the goods, and tends quite as much to raise their price, as if he made an equal amount of purchases with ready money' (530).[62]

That general prices depend upon the state of credit more than the supply of money, narrowly defined, *'at any moment'* is a crucial qualification that must never be lost sight of, since the *'permanent'* value (purchasing power) of money – the 'natural and average prices of commodities' – was not the issue and not at all a disputed matter. 'Natural' value was 'determined by the cost of producing or of obtaining the precious metals' (538).[63] It was the level of 'immediate and temporary' prices that concerned Mill and on that matter there was no 'general assent'.

---

60 Cf. Ricardo's position, *Works*, IV, 436–7: '[Credit] does not create capital, it determines only by whom that capital should be employed.'

61 A further allowance is added in 1865 (528n). The change is probably due to Cairnes (cf. 1060). If notes are loaned to producers who use them as 'capital', then though the national stock of commodities is unchanged a greater share is transferred to productive ends and real expansion results.

62 The emphasis on pressure on prices emanating from current expenditure is consistent with that approach later termed the 'Income Theory of Prices'. This is even clearer in the paper of 1844, taken up again below (p. 558).

63 Cf. *ibid.*, 'the fluctuations in the value of the currency, are determined, not by its quantity, whether it consist of gold or paper, but by the expansion and contraction of credit' (544). This distinction is all nicely summarized in correspondence regarding the consistency of Mill's essay on trade and the *Principles*: '[T]he speculations in that Essay do not relate to the effects of *fluctuations* but only of *permanent changes* in the amount of bullion in the country & *those* I imagine even Tooke would allow to have an effect on prices, governed as these changes must be by changes in the *costs* (not indeed of producing bullion at the mines – but) of purchasing & importing it into the country' (1 Oct. 1847, XVII, 2006).

See also letter to Cliffe Leslie of 1863 for a complex case involving the general principle: 'With respect to the question whether *credit* in any of its shapes is to be counted on either side in addition to the metals, is not the real state of the case, that the increase of gold

Here Mill gives his own position. As we know in this context he insisted that an injection of (metallic) currency absorbed into 'hoards' leaves prices unchanged. This proposition is prologue to an elaboration of the reverse relationship – that (always in the 'short run') expenditures playing on prices may be financed far *beyond* the means provided by the available money stock, as for example, purchases by banker's cheque even though there is no cover in the reserves, or purchase with money to which the individual has but a claim, or with the mere promise to pay in the future, namely 'simple book credit'. In brief, '[t]he amount of purchasing power which a person can exercise is composed of all the money in his possession or due to him, and of all his credit. For exercising the whole of this power he finds a sufficient motive only under peculiar circumstances; but he always possesses it; and the portion of which he at any time does exercise, is the measure of the effect which he produces on price' (540). The specific instruments of credit – whether bank notes, bills of exchange, promissory notes, cheques, or book credit – is not the essential matter. It is credit *per se* – when drawn on – that acts on prices, 'in whatever shape given, and whether it gives rise to any transferable instruments capable of passing into circulation, or not' (538–9). The impact on prices will occur even in the absence of any 'written instruments called substitutes for currency' (540).

* * *

A main purpose of the analysis is to reduce the odium attached to notes: 'From the time of the resumption of cash payments by the Act of 1819, and especially since the commercial crisis of 1825, the favourite explanation of every rise or fall of prices has been "the currency"; and like most popular theories, the doctrine has been applied with little regard to the conditions necessary for making it correct' (514). On an analogy with simple velocity Mill conceded a differential impact on prices of alternative forms of credit, concluding that 'credit transferable from hand to hand' is 'more potent, than credit which only performs one purchase' so that prices are likely to rise higher if (speculative) purchases are made with notes rather than bills

would not produce any increase of credit until prices have first risen? As soon as they had risen from the action of the gold alone, larger sums would be required for all purchases, & as the ordinary object of credit is to make purchases, the nominal amount of credit called into operation would (all other things remaining the same) increase exactly in the ratio in which prices had risen. So that the difference in the credit employed before & after would not be a cause but an effect of the different state of prices before & after, & might be struck out of the account on both sides, so far as the consequences of the increase of gold are concerned – only taking care to remember that every fluctuation of credit from *other* causes would act as a disturbing cause and vitiate the comparison' (14 Nov. 1863, XV, 898–9).

or book credits (546). For all that, he adhered to the Tooke–Fullarton position that the inflationary process characterizing the speculative phase of the cycle is financed almost entirely by trade credit, generating, only at a second stage, pressure for increased bank accommodation.

Whether bank notes are or are not to be counted as 'money' Mill dismissed as a problem only for those still 'adhering to the doctrine of the infancy of society and of political economy, that the quantity of money compared with that of commodities, determines general prices', and who seek to prove that only bank notes (and no other form of credit) constitute 'money' and act on prices; whereas in fact 'money and credit are . . . exactly on a par, in their effect on prices; and whether we choose to class bank notes with the one or the other, is in this respect entirely immaterial' (552–3).[64]

This approach seems to invite the expansion of the definition of 'money supply' to incorporate the full variety of credit forms, at least for purposes of analysis of the price level. Yet Mill did not wish to follow this line, and we must try to appreciate why this might be so. As we have seen, a distinction was drawn between 'written instruments' acting as substitutes for currency – some instrument that can pass 'from hand to hand' – and trade or book credit. Conceivably then it is because the former could be defined quantitatively that they might be included within the money supply. Trade credit, its availability or the amount actually drawn upon, could not. And it is a characteristic that immediately raises problems for monetary policy, for if the 'money supply' in the broad sense cannot be quantitatively defined its variations cannot be regulated – unless some proxy for it can be devised.

That the note issue was the basis of a 'superstructure of credit' – and might serve as proxy – a further view attributed to the currency school, Mill also denied. Credit made available by dealers to a customer turned not on the volume of notes or coins in circulation but 'on their opinion of his solvency: if any consideration of a more general character enters into their calculation, it is only in a time of pressure on the loan market, when they are not certain of being themselves able to obtain the credit on which they have been accustomed to rely; and even then, what they look to is the general state of the loan market, and not (preconceived theory apart) the amount of bank notes'. As for the *use* of credit, that also turned on the 'expectation of gain' the fulfilment of which 'depends upon prices, but not especially upon the amount of bank notes' (554–5).[65]

---

64 Thus 'money left with a banker, and not drawn against, or drawn against for other purposes than buying commodities, has no effect on prices, any more than credit which is not used'. Conversely, credit which is used to purchase commodities, affects prices in the same manner as money.

65 Speculative periods involve 'circumstances calculated to lead to an unusually extended use of credit' (546); or a desire 'to employ . . . credit in a more than usual degree, as a power of purchasing' (663). Clearly then the collapse of credit characterizing the

The implied moral of all this is that direct control of trade credit – it is primarily *use* of credit that matters – is ruled out as a means of regulating prices. To regulate notes alone would certainly not suffice. These implications we take up in Section VI.

V MONEY AND THE RATE OF INTEREST

In his account of classical monetary theory Don Patinkin reserves the highest praise for Mill's analysis of the impact of a monetary increase upon the market rate of interest, having in mind above all its allowance for an explicit interrelation between the commodity and bond (loanable fund) markets: 'Mill's exposition is decidedly more precise and systematic than Marshall's. More generally, it is difficult to understand why, in its analysis of a monetary increase, the Cambridge school as a whole failed to make use of the specific interrelationship between price and interest movements that Mill and his predecessors had consistently employed' (1956, 259). In particular, Keynes's celebrated charge against the classics was completely misplaced:

[I]t has been usual to suppose that an increase in the quantity of money has a tendency to reduce the rate of interest, at any rate in the first instance and in the short period. Yet no reason has been given why a change in the quantity of money should affect either the investment demand-schedule or the readiness to save out of a given income. Thus the classical school had quite a different theory of the rate of interest in Volume I dealing with the theory of value from what they had in Volume II dealing with the theory of money. They have seemed undisturbed by the conflict and have made no attempt, so far as I know, to build a bridge between the two theories (Keynes, 1973 [1936], 182–3).

In what follows we shall demonstrate the broad validity of Patinkin's objections to Keynes's view.

A brief word first regarding Mill's position in 1826. Here he rejected an argument of the critics of paper money that its injection, by reducing the interest rate encourages 'hazardous speculations' on the part of small capitalists (*CW*, IV, 97f).[66] The basic principle is at stake – whether an increase in paper money can affect the interest rate. And surprisingly, considering the tone of his formal argument, Mill's answer is a positive one.

---

downturn of the cycle reflects the collapse of confidence rather than the reverse, a matter Mill sometimes left opaque.

66 Mill rejected that interpretation which saw the 'hazardous speculation' of 1824–6 as a response to a low interest rate available on regular ventures by small capitalists, itself due to sudden and large increases in country bank notes issued by way of discount and other advances. On this view Bank of England notes were said to have followed, generating further reductions in the rate of interest (97–8).

There were those 'practical men' who confused 'money' in the sense of currency or circulating medium with 'money' in the sense of loanable funds concluding that interest is a function of the money supply in the former sense. A 'more intelligent class of reasoners' recognized that the interest rate is the price of loanable funds, but erroneously argued that since paper currency is injected by way of the loan market the interest rate is inevitably reduced in consequence. Now Mill conceded that this latter argument was 'less absurd in principle' but objected to an error of 'fact', namely the neglect of a preceding increase in the demand for loanable funds – in the case at hand increased applications to the country banks for credit.[67] The expansion of Bank of England issues was, however, 'spontaneous' and designed to 'carry off superfluous specie'; and such issues would, Mill conceded, have forced down the interest rate – at least 'for a short time' – had they been injected by way of the discount market (100). But in actuality the loans had been made to government – a new borrower – and merely prevented an increase in the interest rate that otherwise would have occurred; indeed, the accommodation was partly at the expense of bank discounts to private individuals (101–2).

Mill's concern throughout this account was with 'permanent' variations in the rate of interest, and the (potential) effect of an injection of paper money was evidently categorized as a temporary matter, the implicit presumption being that such injections (even where exogenous) are once and for all and amenable to treatment in comparative-statics terms. The actual fall in the interest rate of 1823 was seen to be part of a secular decline and Mill, rather ungraciously and tentatively, offered an explanation in terms of the path of the profit rate making full use of the fundamental Ricardian theorem on distribution:

We protest against the supposition, that we are under any sort of obligation, because we negative an alleged cause, to assign the real one. We will, however, make the attempt; premising that we do not pretend to do more than conjecture; nor are we by any means certain that in a case of this sort, any more than a conjecture can be made.

The rate of interest, like the prices of commodities, though it is subject to casual variations, has nevertheless a point to which it converges; and this point is regulated by the rate of profit upon mercantile capital. The rate of interest on the average of a considerable number of years, always bears some proportion to the rate of profit . . . [The] great increase of our population, combined with the Corn Laws, which have only come into operation since 1815, has raised the price of the necessaries of life greatly above the average of the years preceding the war. This has raised nominal wages, and by increasing that part of the cost of production

---

67 These applications reflected farm price movements after 1822 (87).

of all commodities which consists of the subsistence of the labourer, has lowered the general profits of stock (102–3).[68]

In the *Principles* the interest rate is treated in the chapter formally devoted to the subject (III, Ch. xxiii) as the price of loanable funds in a splendid account of the process whereby quantities demanded and supplied come to be equalized (647f).[69] The interest rate is said to be more volatile than other prices but as in the standard theory of price 'there must be . . . some rate which (in the language of Adam Smith and Ricardo) may be called the natural rate; some rate about which the market rate oscillates, and to which it always tends to return. This rate partly depends on the amount of accumulation going on in the hands of persons who cannot themselves attend to the employment of their savings, and partly on the comparative taste existing in the community for the active pursuits of industry, or for the leisure, ease, and independence of an annuitant' (648).[70] Close attention is given the matter of stability of equilibrium. In the event of an excess supply, the interest rate will be 'forced down to the point which would either tempt borrowers to take a greater amount of loans than they had a reasonable expectation of being able to employ in their business, or would so discourage a portion of the lenders, as to make them forbear to accumulate, or endeavour to increase their income by engaging in business on their own account, and incurring the risks, if not the labours, of industrial employment' (648). In the reverse case, the interest rate tends upwards. When the excess of profits over interest narrows 'many borrowers may no longer be willing to increase their responsibilities and involve their credit for so small a remuneration: or some who would otherwise have engaged in business, may prefer leisure, and become lenders instead of borrowers: or others, under the inducement of high interest and easy investment for their capital, may retire from business earlier, and with smaller fortunes, than they otherwise would have done' (649).

In a fuller account of the constituents of the demand for loanable funds there is included (in addition to business borrowing for production and trade) borrowing by government and by 'unproductive' consumers;[71] while, on the side of supply, the 'general loan fund' includes – in addition to 'the funds

---

68 Mill in fact denied that there had occurred much of a change in the interest rate after December 1823. The sudden rise in public security prices in early 1824 was clearly unrelated to the profit rate, and seen to reflect Stock Exchange speculation (104).

69 Pure interest is the payment for abstinence by the capitalist. Mill deals with interest on good security to avoid questions of risk remuneration (see also 400–2).

70 Interest is thus formally represented as a function of supply and demand for loanable funds, not of savings and investment as Keynes maintained of the classical school.

71 On the impact of government borrowing see 'On Profits and Interest' (written in 1830), IV, 304.

belonging to those who, either from necessity or preference live upon the interest of their property' (657), – 'the disposable capital deposited in banks; that represented by bank notes; the capital of the bankers themselves, and that which their credit in any way in which they use it, enables them to dispose of' (649–50).[72] It is the equality of demand and supply, each interpreted in this global sense, that determines 'the permanent' or 'average rate of interest; which must always be such as to adjust these two amounts to one another'. But, despite these extensions, the emphasis throughout is on the demand and supply of loanable funds as a reflection of investment and savings decisions respectively. Thus, despite the amplification, bankers are still accorded a cloakroom function of lending out of the 'general loan fund' (650) – national savings; and in concluding the argument Mill summarizes with the statement that the rate of interest 'depends essentially and permanently on the comparative amount of real capital offered and demanded in the way of loan' (657) – the demand by government and unproductive consumers dropping out of the picture.[73]

To identify savings with the supply of loanable funds (the demand for bonds), and investment with the demand for loanable funds (the supply of bonds) logically implies a barter economy wherein the excess demand for cash balances is identically equal to zero and the price level therefore indeterminate – Say's identity.[74] Yet we have shown that Mill's versions of the law of markets allowed for an excess demand for money to hold, a position reinforced in the formal analysis of the quantity theory. It is most unlikely that he was aware of the technical objection to any identification of savings with lending, and investment with borrowing. In any event, as we shall see, there are situations where Mill allowed explicitly for borrowing to the end of adding to cash balances; while his full treatment of the interest rate is not impeded by the general propensity to draw too close a relation

72 Professional money lenders (bankers) earn profits on their activity. Bankers lend their own 'capital' and also capital borrowed from the community ('their credit') for which they pay either no interest or less than they receive on their loans. (On bank profits see also IV, 305.) The reference to the bankers' own capital and their credit was added in 1865. There seems to be double counting in Mill's full enumeration; Cairnes was much troubled by this part of Mill's discussion (cf. 1059f), moreover, nothing is said of book credit that figures so conspicuously elsewhere in the monetary analysis.

73 This is achieved by the unjustified assumption that even when borrowed for unproductive consumption or by government, 'the amount borrowed is taken from a previous accumulation, which would otherwise have been spent to carry on productive industry; it is, therefore, so much subtracted from what may correctly be called the amount of loanable capital' (654).

74 Cf. Patinkin (1956), 187, 257. For example, excess commodity demand implies $I > S$; if I is identified with borrowing, and S with lending, this entails an excess of borrowing over lending – excess commodity demand is covered by an excess supply of *bonds*, rather than by a change in money balances. The implication is a zero excess demand for cash balances.

between savings and the supply of loans and investment and the demand for loans.

We have outlined elsewhere Mill's account of the *secular* trend in the interest rate – the decline reflecting the 'gradual process of accumulation' and the downward trend of profits (651; see p. 462). As for fluctuations about the trend (our present concern) much weight is placed on the demand side of the market in that '[t]he demand for loans varies much more largely than the supply, and embraces longer cycles of years in its aberrations' (652). Here Mill has in mind the effects of government borrowing to finance wars, and of the sudden opening of new investment opportunities such as the railways (653). As far as concerns the supply side, fluctuations are said to be 'almost exclusively' the consequence of changes in bank lending; for the portion of 'capital', in the sense of the general loan fund, in the hands of bankers 'being lent for short periods only, is continually in the market seeking an investment' (650). Here Mill reverts to speculative cycles and the variation in loans during the course of the cycle – a high willingness and, accordingly, a low interest rate characterizing the early stages of speculation, and a low willingness and high interest rate characterizing the 'revulsion'.[75] These, however, are disturbances which are corrected by the reversal of the initial shift, reflecting the supposed temporary nature of the disturbance. More interesting for us is the treatment of a 'permanent' change, specifically a permanent injection of money into the system, in order to see the extent of the parallel between the theories of interest and value – Mill's transfer to interest analysis of the concept of a 'natural rate'

---

75   In speculative times, bankers are 'inclined to extend their business by stretching their credit' (650). This expression refers back to the idea that money lenders are engaged in lending out the savings of others: 'they lend more than usual (just as other classes of dealers and producers employ more than usual) of capital which does not belong to them'. Conversely, in the revulsion 'interest always rises inordinately, because, while there is a most pressing need on the part of many persons to borrow, there is a general disinclination to lend' (651). A 'panic' 'occurs when a succession of unexpected failures has created in the mercantile, and sometimes also in the non-mercantile public, a general distrust in each other's solvency; disposing every one not only to refuse fresh credit, except on very onerous terms, but to call in, if possible, all credit which he has already given'.

   Thus when banks lend their notes Mill writes as if they are just extending credit to X, of what they have received from Y. Conversely, in a panic people call in deposits to the end of keeping cash on hand: 'Deposits are withdrawn from banks; notes are returned on the issuers in exchange for specie; bankers raise their rate of discount, and withhold their customary advance; merchants refuse to renew mercantile bills.' Mill adds an historical gloss: 'At such times the most calamitous consequences were formally experienced from the attempt by the law to prevent more than a certain limited rate of interest from being given or taken.' For the law forced people to sell securities and goods for ready cash; or pay a huge interest rate to cover the risk of illegal lending.

and the oscillation of the market rate about it, namely the 'tendency' of the market rate to reflect the natural rate.

The essence of Patinkin's version of Mill in this regard – attributed also to Thornton and Ricardo and subsequently to Fisher – is that the monetary increase, assumed to enter the system by way of expanded loans, pushes the market rate of interest down below the natural rate; and the increased profitability of investment under these conditions – comparison made between expected profitability and cost of finance – by generating increased investment outlays and (assuming full employment) thus raising prices, then acts back on the bond market increasing the demand for loanable funds to cover the higher cost of the capital projects (Patinkin, 162, 257f). In the final analysis there is necessarily a 'symmetrical effect' on the demand and supply for loans (260).[76] How accurate is this account?

Throughout his analysis Mill formally played down the monetary aspects of interest-rate determination, while at the same time fully conceding an impact of an injection of money on the interest rate. Thus he cautioned in 1865: 'I have, thus far, considered loans, and the rate of interest, as a matter which concerns capital in general, in direct opposition to the popular notion, according to which it only concerns money' (*CW*, III, 653).[77] None the less, loanable capital 'is all of it in the form of money';[78] and although when borrowed for productive purposes it is used to acquire purchasing power over commodities, it remained true that the interest rate will be affected by various causes 'which act, directly at least, only through money' (655).

This allowance applies to the immediate impact of a change in the money supply (and also, as Mill goes on to clarify, to the effects of an ongoing process of monetary increase). And since in full equilibrium the interest rate reverts to the original (unaltered) natural rate; the effect would go unnoticed in a comparative statics analysis of equilibrium states:

The rate of interest bears no necessary relation to the quantity or value of the money in circulation. The permanent amount of the circulating medium, whether great

76 'Or, alternatively, approaching the problem from the viewpoint of the commodity market, classical economists argued that the monetary increase does not change any of the real characteristics of the economy; that, in particular, it does not change the marginal productivity of capital; and that, therefore, it does not change the natural rate of interest. More specifically, the monetary increase causes an equiproportionate increase in the money cost of any investment project and in the money value of its anticipated returns; hence it leaves the rate of profit – and hence the long-run equilibrium rate of interest – unchanged.'

77 Cf. 657: there can be an 'action on loans which does not happen to be accompanied by any action on the currency'.

78 Mill regretted the common parlance of referring to interest as 'the value of money'; for loans were loans of 'capital' and money was a mere 'instrument of transfer' (508).

or small, affects only prices; not the rate of interest. A depreciation of the currency, when it has become an accomplished fact, affects the rate of interest in no manner whatever. It diminishes indeed the power of money to buy commodities, but not the power of money to buy money. If a hundred pounds will buy a perpetual annuity of four pounds a year, a depreciation which makes the hundred pounds worth only half as much as before, has precisely the same effect on the four pounds, and cannot therefore alter the relation between the two. The greater or smaller number of counters which must be used to express a given amount of real wealth, makes no difference in the position or interests of lenders or borrowers, and therefore makes no difference in the demand and supply of loans. There is the same amount of real capital lent and borrowed; and if the capital in the hands of lenders is represented by a greater number of pounds sterling, the same greater number of pounds sterling will, in consequence of the rise of prices, be now required for the purposes to which the borrowers intend to apply them.
But though the greater or less quantity of money makes in itself no difference in the rate of interest, a change from a less quantity to a greater, or a greater to a less, may and does make a difference in it (655–6).

That the interest rate falls below the (given) natural rate in consequence of the injection follows from the presumption that the initial impact occurs by way of an increase in the supply of loanable funds both in the case of note issues and gold inflows:

In England, and in most other commercial countries, the paper currency in common use, being a currency provided by bankers, is all issued in the way of loans, except the part employed in the purchase of gold and silver. The same operation, therefore, which adds to the currency also adds to the loans: the whole increase of currency in the first instance swells the loan market. Considered as an addition to loans it tends to lower interest, more than in its character of depreciation it tends to raise it; for the former effect depends on the ratio which the new money bears to the money lent, while the latter depends on its ratio to all the money in circulation. An increase, therefore, of currency issued by banks, tends, while the process continues, to bring down or to keep down the rate of interest. A similar effect is produced by the increase of money arising from the gold discoveries; almost the whole of which, as already noticed, is, when brought to Europe, added to the deposits in banks, and consequently to the amount of loans; and when drawn out and invested in securities, liberates an equivalent amount of other loanable capital. The newly-arrived gold can only get itself invested, in any given state of business, by lowering the rate of interest; and as long as the influx continues, it cannot fail to keep interest lower than, all other circumstances being supposed the same, would otherwise have been the case (656–7).[79]

79 Cf. 651–2 on money expansion following a gold inflow. Conversely, a drain of gold

Since the market rate of interest for Mill is determined in the loanable funds market, and its initial fall following the monetary increase is due to a shift in the supply curve in that market, the only possible justification for the presumption that the market rate returns to its original level must be that there occurs a compensatory increase in the demand for loanable funds reflecting the higher money cost of the original investment projects. And this Mill spells out explicitly, as we have seen: 'There is the same amount of real capital lent and borrowed; and if the capital in the hands of lenders is represented by a greater number of pounds sterling, the same greater number of pounds sterling will, in consequence of the rise of price, be now required for the purposes to which the borrowers intend to apply them.'

The role of higher money prices in raising the demand for loanable funds to finance investment projects also emerges explicitly in the analysis of a different experiment – a case where money is injected in the form of inconvertible notes to pay for government purchases rather than by way of the loanable funds market. In this event an 'increase of currency really affects the rate of interest, but in the contrary way to that which is generally supposed; by raising not by lowering it' (656). This is precisely because of the impact on the demand for loanable funds of an increase in the money cost of investment goods.

Mill's account here seems to be flawed; for he insists that the (upward) effect on the interest rate occurs only while the depreciation is 'in process of taking place', whereas it is not at all clear why this is so, since there occurs in this case no initial increase in the supply of loanable funds to be compensated. None the less, if (following Mill) this analysis is transposed to the main case – and there is no doubt that currency injection by way of increased loans is the main case – we again arrive at Patinkin's reading. Indeed, Mill himself, as we have seen, refers to the process of adjustment as entailing an impact on prices pushing interest up although outweighed by the direct effect in the bond market involving downward pressure until the full effect on prices works its way through. There can therefore be no question of the intimate linkage drawn between the commodity and bond markets, a linkage fully to be expected considering Mill's adherence to the

---

is taken from deposits and starves the loanable fund market: 'As the introduction of additional gold and silver, which goes into the loan market, tends to keep down the rate of interest, so any considerable abstraction of them from the country invariably raises it; even when occurring in the course of trade, as in paying for the extra importations caused by a bad harvest, or for the high-priced cotton which, under the influence of the American civil war, was imported from so many parts of the world. The money required for these payments is taken in the first instance from the deposits in the hands of bankers, and to that extent starves the fund that supplies the loan market' (657).

equality version of the law of markets and his sophisticated analysis of the quantity theory.[80]

As noted earlier, it is characteristic of Mill that he attempts to formulate his allowances for an impact of money upon the interest rate within a 'real capital' framework. This is true even when the disturbance involves an increase in borrowing solely for purposes of adding to cash balances, as in periods of 'crisis'. Here the interest rate rises, unless banks increase their issues by way of the loan market:

[The borrower's] need is specifically for money, not for commodities or capital. It is the demand arising from this cause, which produces almost the great and sudden variations in the rate of interest . . . But although, in this case, it is not capital, or purchasing power, that the borrower needs, but money as money, it is not only money that is transferred to him. The money carries its purchasing power, with it wherever it goes; and money thrown into the loan market really does, through its purchasing power, turn over an increased portion of the capital of the country into the direction of loans. Though money alone was wanted, capital passes; and it may still be said with truth that it is by an addition to loanable capital that the rise of the rate is met and corrected (654–5).

But this is to insist on a matter of terminology. It does not detract from the fact that money is represented as important as far as the interest rate is concerned.

The foregoing discussion follows the sixth edition of 1865. The formulation owed much to J. E. Cairnes, for the treatment in earlier editions had been extremely brief (653–4n). There was a formal proposition that: 'An increase of the currency has in itself no effect, and is incapable of having any effect, on the rate of interest'[81] – to which Cairnes strongly objected (1061) – illustrated by the case involving an inconvertible currency issued by government in payment of its purchases. In the new equilibrium, upon which Mill focusses, the interest rate is unchanged; nothing is said of the period

80 A problem of consistency, however, arises if we note Mill's insistence in the essay of 1844, on Tooke's grounds, that a lower interest need not stimulate higher expenditures (below, p. 559).
81 Cf. letter to Herford, 26 Oct. 1854: 'I quite agree . . . that many fallacies are engendered by the vague & ambiguous use of the word Capital even among political economists. I do not think however that anyone entitled to the name of a political economist ever confounds capital with money, or with the right to receive money . . . The phrases which you cite as examples appear to me to arise from a confusion of another sort, viz. the employment of both these words, money & capital to express loanable capital, or capital seeking investment, a misuse of terms extremely frequent, & leading to the notion that the causes which influence the loan market & the rate of interest have something to do with the quantity of currency, than which in my opinion no notion can be more erroneous' (CW, XIV, 241–2).

immediately after the injection. On the other hand, it is conceded (as in 1844 and the earlier papers) that an increase in the money supply issued by way of the loan market does act on the interest rate since 'the same operation . . . which adds to the currency, also adds to the loans, or to the capital seeking investment on loan; properly, indeed, the currency is only increased in order that the loans may be increased. Now, though as currency these issues have no effect on interest, as loans they have'.[82] (It is not made clear whether this effect is a 'temporary' one, thereby leaving open the nature of the full corrective process.)

There can thus be no question of a certain unwillingness until 1862 to emphasize the impact of changes in the money supply on the interest rate, an unwillingness which generated the criticisms of Cairnes; who in fact mistakenly seems to have understood Mill as actually denying any impact of money on the interest rate:

I venture to maintain . . . that 'an increase' of the currency *is* capable of affecting the rate of interest . . .
An increase of the currency (understanding by currency for the present simply circulating medium in any form which practically possesses purchasing & paying power) must take effect in one or other of two ways: – either through the medium of a loan, or through that of purchase: the persons into whose hands the new currency first comes either *lend* it, or *spend* it. Now in either case I contend that the augmentation will tend to affect the rate of interest. I observe you draw a distinction . . . between issues 'as currency' and issues 'as loans'. But this distinction seems to me exactly to beg the question in dispute. You say the issues are 'loans' – no doubt – but loans of what? – of capital? This I deny . . . I say they are 'loans of currency' just as truly as money handed over the counter in exchange for a commodity is payment in currency. Well if I am right in this it certainly follows that an increase of currency is capable of affecting the rate of interest . . . (1061).

[T]he view for which I seek to obtain a hearing . . . regards the rate of interest as essentially a '*monetary*' phenomenon; whereas it has hitherto been represented as expressing a relation of '*capital*' as distinguished from money (1064).

What, however, was Cairnes's substantive contribution to Mill's thought? From him Mill took the case of an injection of money by way of purchases generating an *increase* in the interest rate (above, p. 538) leading him to conclude that while the rate of interest depends 'essentially and permanently

---

82 Cf. 1844: 'Fluctuations of price do not, we believe, depend upon bank issues; but the operations of banks, as of other money-lenders, of course act upon the loan market, or as it is improperly called, the money market; in other words, upon the rate of interest, and what is almost synonymous, the prices of securities' (IV, 357).

on the comparative amount of real capital offered and demanded in the way of loan' it is 'subject to temporary disturbances of various sorts, from an increase and diminution of the circulating medium; which derangements are somewhat intricate, and sometimes in direct opposition to first appearances' (657). More generally, Cairnes evidently obliged Mill to spell out the process of adjustment whereby the market rate tends to the natural rate. Yet Cairnes could not overcome Mill's insistence upon phrasing the matter such as to focus attention upon 'capital' rather than 'currency' (1061). As Mill himself put it in correspondence, after thanking Cairnes warmly for various notes on the fifth edition (1862): 'I have rewritten the fourth section of the chapter on the Rate of Interest and have much enlarged it; completing my exposition of the causes on which the rate of interest depends, by adopting nearly all you have said on the subject that involves doctrine. In what merely involves the mode of stating the theory, I still prefer my own: but I see that the whole truth of the subject may be expressed in either way, and may usefully be so in both' (20 Dec. 1864, *CW*, XV, 983).[83]

Mill also adopted Cairnes's position regarding an impact of gold discoveries on the rate of interest (Mill, III, 657; Cairnes, *ibid.*, 1062f). He claimed, however, that he had already decided to make the allowance independently: 'even before I heard from you, [I had] inserted a passage pointing out how the new gold, as long as it continues to flow in, must tend to keep down the rate of interest' (12 Dec. 1864, XV, 976).

As for the main case – here we revert to Patinkin's general interpretation – it is unlikely whether Mill's full account of 1865 involves more than a spelling out of what was already well understood. After all, Ricardo in 1810 had said nearly all there was to say, recognizing that at the higher level of prices ruling in the new equilibrium situation a lower interest rate is not required to stimulate increased borrowing, taking account of the impact of prices on the demand for loanable funds to counterbalance the initial increase in supply (1951, III, 91).

There are further elaborations in the sixth edition that call for brief comment. First, the role of expectations. Already in the original formulation of the chapter on the rate of interest Mill recognized that it will not be the case that an increase in paper currency issued by government to pay its expenses raises the level of prices in proportion leaving the interest rate unchanged, if 'it is known and reckoned upon that the depreciation will only be temporary; for people might certainly be willing to lend the

---

83 Mill publicly thanked Cairnes for his help. Cf. preface to the edition of 1865: 'The chapter in which the greatest addition has been made is that on the Rate of Interest; and for most of the new matter there introduced, I am indebted to the suggestions and criticism of my friend Professor Cairnes, one of the most scientific of living political economists' (II, Ch. xciv).

depreciated currency on cheaper terms if they expected to be repaid in money of full value' (*CW*, III, 653–4n). In the edition of 1865, which allows (following Cairnes) for upward pressure on the interest rate, Mill notes that 'the expectation of further depreciation adds to this effect; because lenders who expect that their interest will be paid and the principal perhaps redeemed, in a less valuable currency than they lent, of course require a rate of interest sufficient to cover this contingent loss' (656).

Secondly, there is an allowance for forced savings and its impact on the interest rate.[84] This notion is first formulated by Mill in the essay 'On Profits and Interest' (written 1830, first published 1844) where it is related specifically to injections of inconvertible paper currency: 'If the paper is inconvertible, and instead of displacing specie depreciates the currency, the banker by issuing it levies a tax on every person who has money in his hands or due to him', and might entail the conversion of revenue – what would have otherwise been spent – into capital:

and thus, strange as it may appear, the depreciation of the currency, when effected in this way, operates to a certain extent as a forced accumulation. This, indeed, is no palliation of its inequity. Though A might have spent his property unproductively, B ought not to be permitted to rob him of it because B will expend it on productive labour.

In any supposable case, however, the issue of paper money by bankers increases the proportion of the whole capital of the country which is destined to be lent. The rate of interest must therefore fall, until some of the lenders give over lending, or until the increase of borrowers absorbs the whole (IV, 307).

Mill prefaces the remark by commenting that the phenomenon constituted one of the 'anomalies in the rate of interest, which have not, so far as we are aware, been hitherto brought within the pale of exact science' (305). A similar analysis is introduced into the 1865 edition of the *Principles*, where explicit allowance is made for the resultant 'real increase of capital', and by implication therefore for an effect on the interest rate. The effect on 'capital' however, is said to be temporary; it 'ceases, and a counter-process takes place, when the additional credit is stopped, and the notes called in' (III, 528n). The analysis of 1830, by contrast, seems to allow for a permanent effect, although possibly only because the disturbance envisaged concerns an inconvertible paper.

Thirdly, the edition of 1865 also allows for a 'more or less permanent' impact exerted by gold discoveries:

---

84 The extensive literature on the subject of forced saving, including early formulations by Bentham and Malthus, is discussed by Hayek (1939).

The rate of interest is, at times, affected more or less permanently by circumstances, though not of frequent, yet of occasional occurrence, which tend to alter the proportion between the class of interest-receiving and that of profit-receiving capitalists . . . One is, the gold discoveries. The masses of the precious metals which are constantly arriving from the gold countries, are, it may safely be said, wholly added to the funds that supply the loan market. So great an additional capital, not divided between the two classes of capitalists, but aggregated bodily to the capital of the interest-receiving class, disturbs the pre-existing ratio between the two, and tends to depress interest relatively to profit (651–2).

It is possibly this passage that Mill had in mind as already written independently of, though in accordance with, Cairnes's notes (above, pp. 540–1). It is not absolutely clear whether Mill intends to say that the interest rate is 'permanently' affected, i.e. even after the gold inflow ceases, or whether he is presuming 'permanency' in the sense of a supposedly continuous inflow (this latter reading would be more consistent with the passage at 657).

* * *

The analysis of interest in the sixth edition of the *Principles* is as rich as Patinkin has claimed. Yet any reader of the earlier editions might have come away with a feeling of disappointment. And Mill, even in the final versions and despite the elaborations, seems to do his best to leave *an impression* of the irrelevance of money in interest-rate determination by emphasizing, as always, the 'capital' rather than the monetary property of loanable funds. Doubtless his approach reflects a burning hostility towards mercantilist residues. That nothing but an impression was involved we have attempted to demonstrate here.

It will be helpful to review the broad conclusions of this section by reference to the well-known article dealing with Cairnes and Mill on the rate of interest by L. C. Hunter (1959). Hunter points out (65–6, 69–70, 84) that Mill's early paper on 'Profits and Interest' of 1830 (1844) contains suggestions of dissatisfaction with the 'Ricardian' emphasis on the interest rate as a reflection of the rate of return on physical capital; the former might vary independently of the latter as Mill suggests at the close of his paper alluding to an increase in inconvertible currency through the banking system which affects the interest rate even in long-run equilibrium (cf. *CW*, IV, 307–8). In the first five editions of the *Principles* Mill is said to revert back to the 'real' dimension. But even in the sixth edition – with Cairnes's notes at hand – 'although Mill was prepared to admit a certain amount of truth in the monetary approach, he continued to stress as more important the capital–interest relationship' (83). Thus 'while at the early stage Mill was prepared to admit that monetary or banking policies could have a determining influence on the long-run equilibrium level of business activity, and hence on output and employment, he now in the sixth edition allows only that institutional changes, and not monetary policies are capable of influencing the long run, during which the consequences of the added injection of loans will have time to work themselves out' (84). In Hunter's view, he thus refused to accept Cairnes's position.

This evaluation is not in all respects convincing. The allowance of 1830 for a 'long-run' effect on interest of a monetary injection is limited to the forced saving case; and it is not clear that the analysis of 1865 would be any different in the event of an injection of inconvertible paper. Secondly, Hunter tends to minimize Mill's allowances in 1865 for the impact of gold discoveries merely because they take effect through 'real' or institutional forces (but see his position, 82). Most important, he fails to show that Cairnes actually emphasized a long-term impact on interest emanating from the monetary side (84). On the contrary, the texts utilized play up Cairnes's adherence to Mill's view of the ultimate role of capital productivity and insistence only on *temporary* variations of the interest rate of a monetary nature (77). (The notion (74–5) that note issues displace gold which is exported for commodities affecting real activity is indeed accepted by Cairnes, but goes back of course to Adam Smith and was quite standard.)

The primary difference between Mill and Cairnes, as I read it, thus turns on the strategic question whether or not to *emphasize* the short-run impact of money on the interest rate. There was agreement on the substance. That this is so is further suggested by a supplementary consideration – that Cairnes showed no displeasure in print with Mill's final performance, a fact that Hunter, quite rightly from his perspective, regards as 'curious' and 'hard to reconcile' with his reading of the evidence (86). That Cairnes did not take the many opportunities he had to express his own 'novel' position might be explained, Hunter suggests, either by a change of opinion – a 'highly improbable' solution since 'he was adamant in his emphasis on the money-interest as opposed to the capital–interest relationship' – or 'by a belief that Mill had fairly presented the essential arguments of the notes'. It is precisely the latter which seems to be the actual case, although Hunter is forced by his reading of the evidence to see this too as 'unlikely'.

VI BANK FINANCE AND THE CYCLE:
IMPLICATIONS FOR MONETARY POLICY

In this section we consider further Mill's position regarding the responsibility of bank-note issues for cyclical instability, with particular attention to policy implications. Our major concern is with the early papers of 1826 and 1833;

that of 1844 on Peel's Act; and the *Principles*, III, Ch. xxiv on 'The Regulation of a Paper Currency'.

There are three propositions regarding the note issue[85] which drew Mill's critical attention in 1826: That even in 'quiescent' periods, a paper currency (although convertible) is yet liable to 'over-issue'; that 'over-issue' is an invariable feature of speculative periods, heightening the speculation itself, while the subsequent revulsion is aggravated since paper is then withdrawn from circulation;[86] and that sudden increases of the note issue when occurring by way of loans (as in Britain) generate a decline in the interest rate thereby reducing the incomes of small capitalists and encouraging 'hazardous speculation' on their part (*CW*, IV, 81).[87]

Mill's definition of over-issue was simply the '*lowering of the value* of the currency' or '*raising general prices*' (81). Now it was inconceivable that the currency could be thus depreciated with coins still in circulation since an increase in notes simply displaces coin (82). (On the standard argument of Smith and Ricardo paper was desirable on efficiency grounds.)[88] Only 'when an issue of paper *ceases* to displace a corresponding quantity of gold . . . is the currency depreciated; then, and not till then, is there an over-issue. But this, by universal admission, cannot happen while the Bank continues to pay in specie on demand.'[89]

That some lag is entailed between the injection of additional paper and the displacement of an equivalent value in gold – during which interval there

85 Formally, the discussion turned on the government's decision to prohibit issues of small notes; but Mill generalized to notes as such.

86 Specifically the extra paper initially 'called into existence' by the speculation.

87 The second and third propositions were said, by those Mill opposed, to have characterized the 1824–6 period.

88 'Since the paper, which costs nothing, performs all the functions of currency as well, the large notes indeed much better, than gold; while every sovereign exported causes the importation of a sovereign's worth of productive capital, or consumable produce; the country gains, by the substitution, the whole value of the gold. There is a gain to the currency in cheapness.' These real effects constitute a celebrated classical theme much emphasized by Adam Smith (1937, 278, 480).

89 The full logic of this 'Ricardian' argument is very nicely explained in the *Principles* (*CW*, III, 557–8), although doubtless Mill had it in mind in 1826. An injection of paper by the government in payment of its purchases and salaries into a metallic-currency system generates upward pressure on general prices. An ounce of coined gold will fall in value below that of manufactured gold (by more than the cost of manufacture), but coins will then be melted and general prices again decline. Thus an ongoing increase in paper entails no *net* increase in the money supply until coin has been totally displaced. The increase in plate implies a fall in its relative price so that even though – assuming a once-and-for-all injection of paper – the quantity of paper in circulation is equal to an amount of coin previously circulating, the remaining coin will be such as to assure that the value of the currency as a whole equals, in the first instance, the *reduced* value of the metallic material. But this is still a disequilibrium situation; for the relatively low value of the metals stimulates a cut-back in supply from the mines and/or a reduced supply by wear

is a net increase of currency and a depreciation in its value – is conceded; the depreciation, of course, is essential for the corrective process. But the sequence of events set in motion by the initial injection is said to be very rapid (83–4). Mill does not elaborate on the time involved before a price response to the increase in notes; but once prices rise it is a matter of days before commodities flow in and bills are drawn on London, such that the exchange rate rises in Paris and falls in London generating a gold outflow. Indeed, merely the *expectation* of such an exchange rate movement sets the gold outflow in motion:

The slightest excess above the expense of transit, is a sufficient motive to those who speculate on the exchanges; a class of men proverbially keen-sighted, and who are contented with very small gains, on account of the rapidity and certainty of the return. The exportation would in fact begin even *before* the exchange yielded such a premium as would be necessary to render the speculation a profitable one. There are transactions in anticipation of profit, as well as transactions for immediate profit, in this line of business as in others (85).

Apart from the presumption of a very rapid response of prices to an increase in money supply, the weakness of the argument lies in its comparative statics character; for nothing therein precludes 'permanent' effects on the price level even under convertibility of an on-going injection of notes.[90]

So much for quiescent periods. We come now to Mill's position regarding speculative periods such as 1824–5. In such circumstances the foregoing argument was inappropriate. That speculation always generates currency expansion is accepted without debate (86, 89); but it is no longer a self-corrective increase in so far as speculative moods, and correspondingly

and usage and then the metals and the currency revert to their 'natural' value. (All this assumes internal mines. In cases involving international metal flows, the process of losing coin rendered superfluous by paper will be yet speedier.)

Whether or not paper is convertible is immaterial until coin has been totally superseded. As before, an injection of paper forces prices upwards, including those of metallic articles, so that it becomes profitable to convert coin into bullion. But in the case of a *convertible* paper, coin can be acquired from the issuers in exchange for notes; notes therefore return to the issuers and there is no way their *net* quantity can be (permanently) expanded such that their value falls below that of the metal the paper represents. (Again, in an open system the corrective process, in the convertible case, will be still speedier.) But assume *inconvertible* paper, and there is no such limit to its issue and to the fall in the purchasing power of the currency. (On Ricardo's position regarding the possibility of over-issue in the inconvertible case and in the absence of coins in circulation, see Hollander, 1979, 437f.)

90 Mill concedes that in the period after 1822 (even prior to the onset of speculation) an exchange rate decline had not accompanied expansion of the money supply, but points to 'disturbing causes' at work which precluded the expected outcome, including the impact of the Corn Laws (87f).

increases in currency infect trading partners abroad. In that case there can exist an increase in domestic currency 'much above what would have been sufficient to drive out the excess, if the currencies of other countries had not been simultaneously increased; and although gold was at that very time flowing out at a most rapid rate, prices continued for many months at the same elevated range' (90).[91]

Yet the significance of this allowance for a depreciated paper currency under convertibility is minimized as far as any blame attaches to the note issue as such. Currency on Mill's account of 1826 includes coin and notes (issued by the Bank of England and the country bankers), but as Mill was to insist ever after the 'functions of currency, and the need for currency' were 'superseded to a very great extent, by mere *credit*'; and as Thornton had shown the 'circulating medium' included all three categories (90–1). Even in quiescent periods the abolition of bankers' notes would create a void rapidly filled by bills of exchange (93); whereas in periods of speculation, trade credit – what Mill refers to as 'book credit' – would expand to meet any needs for accommodation left by a contraction of bank notes: 'He who has credit enough to obtain a loan from a banker, has credit enough to obtain goods from a dealer. Whenever there is a disposition to give credit too easily, which there always is in periods of great speculation, we may be quite certain that this disposition is stronger among the other classes of the community, than among the bankers' (96).

Thus under the going monetary institutions even major fluctuations in the value of the currency could occur in the absence of bankers' notes, so that paper issues could not be said to be the 'cause' of the depreciation characterizing speculative periods (90). More generally, the speculative process had the property of 'creating the medium in which it is itself carried on' (90). In essence, variations in the money supply – defined to include all circulating media – were passive reactions, and symptoms of, inflation rather than its cause, further reducing the onus upon bankers' paper. In these propositions regarding the relation between the money supply and prices lies the key to Mill's position:

It is well known that every increase of speculation is accompanied by an extended issue and circulation of mercantile paper, and with an extended use of credit.

91 Hawtrey (1928) amongst others was later greatly to emphasize this complexity: 'The problem of unemployment, as we knew it before the war, is the problem of the trade cycle. I have already pointed out how active trade promotes borrowing by traders, and the borrowing tends to make trade more active. With a gold standard the limit upon borrowing is ultimately felt in a shortage of the bank's cash reserves. But in a world system this shortage only comes about gradually. It is possible for a credit expansion to go on gathering impetus for several years before the effect upon the demand for cash is such as to require the banks to take action to check it' (78).

A period of speculation is invariably marked by great confidence. While prices are rising, every one seems to be growing rich, and on the strength of his supposed riches, every one finds his neighbour ready to give him credit. The speculator wishing, as the term implies, to extend his transactions, avails himself of this facility of obtaining credit, to the full extent which his speculations require. For most purposes, it is evidently more convenient to obtain a banker's note, for the purpose of making purchases, than to make purchases with a bill. Notwithstanding, however, the superior convenience of notes, a large increase is constantly made, in periods of speculation, to the quantity of mercantile paper performing the functions of currency. And the same, or a still greater increase, takes place in the amount of transactions which are settled without the intervention either of bills or of money; by mere transfers in a banker's or a merchant's books. These additions to the currency have the same effect in lowering its value, which a similar increase in the issues of the country banks would have (91).

It is thus in the nature of a credit company that a generalization of price increases occurs from specific commodities (subject to expected excess demand) to commodities in general. From this perspective, responsibility for the 'exaggerated recoil' of prices which inevitably follows (92) can be laid at the door of credit. In all this Mill followed Tooke (1826).

There was then no particular advantage to a metallic over a paper currency (and, by implication no reason to regulate a currency so that it operates as if it were wholly metallic) in so far as concerns the speculative period – commercial paper and credit are overriding forces. But a positive case is made out for bank notes in periods of 'revulsion' or 'crisis'. For then credit fails, and there arises a net demand for money narrowly defined. Here is an early allowance for hoarding and its deflationary consequences and to the role of bank notes in minimizing its consequences:

During a commercial crisis, credit almost entirely ceases. None but the very best bills, and of the shortest dates, will pass current in the market; and for all other payments, ready-money must be provided. Those who have it, are unwilling to let it out of their hands; knowing that nobody who has demand upon them, will receive payment in any other medium. They therefore postpone all ready-money purchases. Thus, at the very moment when money and nothing else will be received in purchases, scarcely any money is offered; its purchasing power consequently is prodigiously increased, prices fall ruinously low, and insolvencies are multiplied a hundred-fold beyond what the mere destruction of the paper of the original insolvents could have produced. Now then, if a supply of paper, of undoubted security, can be poured into the market, sufficient to compensate the undue contraction of the currency, all this unnecessary evil is obviated. But if not, it must wait the tardy process of importing bullion from abroad: which, after all, may perhaps be hoarded as fast as it comes in (97).[92]

The 'tardiness' of the corrective process in the absence of injections of notes is not clarified here, but doubtless reflects a presumption that similar price movements are occurring abroad (the counterpart to the case made out in the discussion of the speculative period).

The deflationary characteristics of the revulsion described above refer only to reductions in the level of prices. There is reference also to the effect on the interest rate: 'Commercial distress, by producing a great immediate demand for ready-money, always lowers greatly the price of, in other words, increases the interest on, all securities which are immediately convertible' (103; see also 108–9, discussed above, p. 497). There is perhaps still discernible a hesitancy to allow for contemporaneous excess of capital and labour. For Mill asserts that in times of crisis one person's gain is another's loss – the evil from the perspective of national wealth amounting only to the loss of interest on the capital 'lying unemployed during the stagnation' (77); and that 'national happiness' (rather than national wealth) is reduced. Mill, it might be said, failed to draw out the full implications of his own discussion. Yet it is improbable that he neglected the real (output and employment) dimension. Allusion is made to expansion of manufacturing employment during speculative periods (96) and the observations regarding revulsion conclude in terms suggesting that unemployment was in mind: 'If the distress of last winter was what it was, notwithstanding the issue of several additional millions of Bank of England notes; what might it not have been if the enormous contraction, natural at such a crisis, had been suffered to continue?' (97).

Mill's concern with the necessity for alleviation of crises and 'distress' is actually reflected in the initial formulation of his objections to contemporary monetary policy based as it was upon the view that the currency system was responsible for over-trading and subsequent revulsion, necessitating restrictions of notes to those exceeding £5 in value (78). Hasty legislation was regrettable unless absolutely essential. But in this case the rules were not introduced in 'mitigation of immediate suffering; which might have been some excuse for precipitation. It was never contended that the proposed measures had any tendency to alleviate the existing distress. It was even admitted, that the small-note measure was calculated to aggravate the distress by discrediting an important part of the circulation; by which

---

92 Cf. A. F. Burns (1968), II, 229: 'During much of the nineteenth century, interest was focused on commercial crises – that is, the sharp rise of money rates, scramble for liquidity, drop of prices, and spread of bankruptcies that frequently marked the culmination of a boom.'

means the currency was further contracted, and additional force given to that recoil of prices, which was the immediate cause of the distress' (78).

That positive intervention on the part of the monetary authorities was required – to provide 'a supply of paper, of undoubted security' to satisfy the excess demand for money to hold in depression – is clear beyond doubt. And this demonstration must be borne in mind, for in the same paper the government is said to be preoccupied with a 'vain attempt to remove the causes of mercantile revulsions' (105), and the problem of 'commercial distress' to be unamenable to legislation (77). This was so since the root of the problem lay in the 'universal propensity of mankind to over-estimate the chances in their own favour', so that 'while this propensity subsists, every event which stimulates hopes, will give rise to extensive miscalculation; and every miscalculation upon a sufficiently extensive scale, will terminate in the ruin of multitudes'. The long-term solution lay with education for the rising generation entering merchant houses – including an appreciation of the 'circumstances which regulate the prices of commodities' – in the hope that improved mental habits would give 'sober calculation a solid ground to rest upon . . . [in] place of gambling; that traders may one day require sufficient prudence to abstain from risking their own property in *rash* speculations, and sufficient probity to abstain from risking in *any* speculations the property of others' (78).

It is easy to be misled by this apparently resigned outlook. The fact is that Mill was objecting specifically to those controls over the note issue under discussion as a means to mitigate or even entirely eradicate crises. There were steps, however, that could be taken to reduce the impact of 'revulsions' when they occurred and as we have seen they include monetary intervention. It is, therefore, only on a surface view that Mill was less 'interventionist' than Tooke who, taking a position in 1826 closer to the 'Currency School' than he was later to do (see below, p. 600), favoured the replacement of low denomination notes by coin, or their backing by a larger specie reserve. As Laidler argues this was 'as much to protect the poor from the consequences of commercial crises, as because he expected such a measure to mitigate the causes of such crises' (1972, 171n). Mill was very much concerned with the latter objective.

* * *

At first sight the attack upon Thomas Attwood in 1833 may appear anomalous, considering the desirable function ascribed to the Bank of England by Mill himself of increasing the note issue during times of 'revulsion', a recommendation made forcefully as early as 1826 and, we shall see, reiterated equally forcefully in 1848.

Mill's critique opens with a statement that Attwood's evidence before the House of Commons Committee on the Bank Charter was sufficiently dangerous for it to be necessary to respond, although by so doing he adopted 'the garb and attitude of a Conservative' and made public a clash between radical reformers (183). What was at stake was a 'gigantic plan of confiscation [of private property] . . . - a depreciation of the currency' (184). 'That men who are not knaves in their private dealings', Mill proceeds, 'should understand what the word depreciation means, and yet support it, speaks but ill for the existing state of morality on such subjects.' The paper closes with a reference to the Attwood plan as 'an execrable crime' - 'a national iniquity' in 1859 - discrediting the cause of Radical reform; a matter of 'brute force over right, and a perpetually impending spoliation of everything which one person has and another desires' (192).[93] For the first time in history, Mill contends, it was a *deliberate object* to depreciate the currency by increasing the issues of inconvertible paper money - rather than an unthought of consequence - thereby taking 'from all who have currency in their possession, or who are unlikely to receive any fixed sum, an indefinite aliquot part of their property or income; making a present of the amount to the issuers of the currency, and to the persons by whom the fixed sums are payable' (184-5).[94] And this objective - 'the contemplated fraud upon creditors' - was disguised by a fallacious claim that the purpose of the exercise was to avoid an injustice to debtors since more than half the national debt and a mass of private debts had been contracted when the currency was depreciated, so that a policy of depreciation was now called for to assure that creditors are not paid more than they lent (186).[95]

93 Mill's objection to violent revolution comes to the fore in this context. The Birmingham views would have been particularly dangerous if combined with revolutionary political forces: 'The real misfortune would be, if they should wave their currency juggle, and coalesce with the clear-sighted and more numerous tribe of political swindlers, who attack public and private debts directly avowedly' (192).

94 Mill alludes here to cases of paper issues 'without restraint of convertibility, or any limitation of the amount', but where there was no express purpose to depreciate the currency. The notion that an increase in currency will (*ceteris paribus*) reduce its value was known to Locke and Hume, but 'the practicals had never heard of it; or if they had, disdained it as visionary theory', believing that if paper money rested on good security representing real wealth - the so-called 'real bills' doctrine - it could never be depreciated by an increase in notes.

95 The claim was false because the fundholders and other creditors were not, by and large, the same people who unduly benefited from the return to gold and deflation. To claim damages from one set because another set were overpaid was unjust, not reparation (186-7). Secondly, '[t]he restoration of the ancient standard, and the payment, in the restored currency, of the interest of a debt contracted in a depreciated one, was no injustice, but the simple performance of a plighted contract' (187). For lenders knew that the original restriction was temporary and that the standard would be restored at the original par; indeed instead of returning to gold six months after peace, as sanctioned by Parliament, the return to gold was delayed for years so that fundholders were actually

It was, moreover, a fraud achieved in a manner which gave 'a set of bankers the power of taxing the community to an unlimited amount at their sole pleasure, by pouring forth paper which could only get into circulation by lowering the value of all the paper already issued' (189). Mill predicted the end of pecuniary transactions, for '[n]o one in his senses would take money in exchange for anything, except he were sure of being able to lay it out before the next day' (189).[96]

That Attwood attributed secular output effects to currency depreciation was recognized by Mill (186). But he objected that any real output effects turn upon a delusion on the part of producers that an increase in the price for their respective commodities is a relative increase; once it is recognized that general inflation is under way the increase of production ceases and is followed 'by a fatal revulsion' (191). Already in 1830 (and with an eye on Attwood) Mill had cautioned that any real effects of inflation turned upon faulty expectations – 'speculative delusion'; and as Sir John Hicks has put it with special reference to Mill 'the Classical Economists were quite right in refusing to look that way', for all that could be found along that route was a depreciated currency without (permanent) countervailing advantage (1967, 163).[97]

paid interest in 'depreciated paper' although the nation was bound by contract to pay it in cash. In brief, '[w]e covenanted to pay in a metallic standard; we therefore are bound to do it. To deliberate on such a question is as if a private person were to deliberate whether he should pick a pocket' (189).

96 Mill represented William Cobbett (Thomas Attwood's adversary), who favoured cancellation of part or all the existing debt, as *knavish* but not *foolish* except in thinking that such an act would be a national benefit (185–6). Cobbett was clever enough to realize how *absurd* it is 'for sake of operating upon existing contracts, to render all future ones impracticable except on the footing of gambling transactions, by making it impossible for any one to devine whether a shilling he undertakes to pay will be worth a penny or a pound at the time of payment'. On Cobbett's scheme future creditors would at least 'have the benefit of knowing what they bargained for . . .' (186).

In the paper of 1844 which concerned the proposed Bank Act, an aspect of Attwood's position is referred to that plays no part in 1833, namely the recommendation 'periodically to degrade the standard (or to authorize an increase of inconvertible paper exactly equivalent) in proportion as the progress of industry creates an increase of production and a multiplication of pecuniary transactions' (345). Although this proposal might seem to be less irresponsible than one to inflate the currency as a stimulus to increased output – the emphasis of the 'Currency Juggle' – Mill's hostility is no less strong.

97 'Inflation does give a stimulus, but the stimulus is greatest when the inflation starts – when it starts from a condition that has been non-inflationary. If the inflation continues, people get adjusted to it. But when people are adjusted to it, when they *expect* rising prices, the mere occurrence of what they had expected is no longer stimulating . . .' Cf. also Friedman (1968), 11: 'there is always a temporary trade-off between inflation and unemployment; there is no permanent trade-off. The temporary trade-off comes not from inflation per se, but from unanticipated inflation, which generally means, from a rising rate of inflation'. This is *precisely* Mill's position in his rejection of Attwood.

The cyclical problem also arises conspicuously. The revulsion of 1825 was not 'caused', as Attwood maintained, by a contraction of the currency: 'the only cause of the real ruin, was the imaginary prosperity' (*CW*, I, 191). On this view currency contraction was the consequence: 'So many merchants and bankers having failed in their speculations, so many, therefore, being unable to meet their engagements, their paper became worthless, and discredited all other paper.' Now at this point Mill declared that while 'an issue of inconvertible paper might have enabled these debtors to cheat their creditors . . . it would not have opened a market for one more loaf of bread, or one more yard of cloth; because what makes a demand for commodities is commodities, not bits of paper'. It is precisely this formulation that for some creates a problem of interpretation since Mill had himself in 1826 recommended expanded note issues in depression and was to do so again in his later publications.

However, the problem is rather apparent than real. In the first place, Mill's recommendation involved, it will be recalled, Bank of England notes of 'undoubted security' (convertible notes). To reject out of hand expansion of inconvertible paper (even in depression) is not to be generalized to all paper issues, the distinction lying presumably in the danger attached to the inconvertible case alone that one injection would be followed by another threatening secular inflation.

Secondly, Mill had specifically warned in 1830 against any short-run 'full-employment' policy which precluded that degree of flexibility called for by a program of steady growth (above, pp. 501-2). It was quite consistent then for him to insist in 1833 that any positive real effects flowing from a deliberate policy of inflation – the achievement of permanent 'full' capacity usage – would be undesirable.

Moreover, to deny that the 'cause' of depression is a monetary one is not necessarily to deny that, once generated, monetary measures might be required to relieve the pressure. Mill had already recorded his position very clearly in 1826:

A discussion of some interest took place in parliament, upon a proposition for authorizing the issue of several millions of exchequer bills to relieve the immediate distress. Ministers refused their assent to this proposition but, in lieu of it prevailed upon the Bank to make advances to the extent of three millions upon the security of goods.

The propriety of this course appears unquestionable: yet, strange to say scarcely any part of their conduct excited so much reproach. The practical men not only gave them no thanks for what they did, but would not cease urging them to do what they had refused to do: and ministers were bitterly inveighed against, for unfeelingly suffering such a depth of distress to continue unassuaged, merely because they would not deviate from a general principle, which was not applicable to such extreme cases. Of those from whom this lachrymation proceeded, there was not one who seemed capable of seeing that an advance by the Bank afforded all the relief which an issue of Exchequer bills *could* afford; probably much more than it *would*.

Two evils were expected to be remedied by this measure: first, the depression of prices, owing to the contracting of the currency by the immense destruction of mercantile and country paper; and, secondly, the difficulty, or rather the utter impossibility, of obtaining loans, except at extravagant interest. Both these evils were materially mitigated by the advances of the Bank (IV, 120).

This theme was to be repeatedly reiterated in later formulations.

Here arises a significant distinction. For Attwood, as Mill read him, an increase in currency acts upon output by way of the stimulus given to prices, the presumption being that the increased loans generate increased expenditure on commodities. This Mill did not allow; for him the role of the Bank is to satisfy excess demand for money to hold, literally understood, not to generate outlays on goods and services. This is well clarified in the *Principles* where he argued that the response by the Bank of England to an excess demand for money would check forced sales of commodities – the increase in notes filling a gap created by an 'undue contraction' of private credit – but would not positively increase the demand for commodities. This qualified perspective is quite consistent with the statement of 1833 according to which 'an inconvertible paper' (Mill might have said any paper) would not open 'a market for one more loaf of bread, or one more yard of cloth . . . because what makes a demand for commodities is commodities, not bits of paper'.

It may, however, be conceded that in some respects Mill was too polemical in the heat of debate. Thus he implies that a contraction of the currency not only was not responsible for the 'revulsion' of 1825, but could not have been responsible, whereas even Ricardo (not to speak of Thornton) had strenuously warned against sudden contractions of the currency.[98] Conversely, currency inflation, even in the absence of 'speculative delusion' might have real effects in the event of cost rigidities which (unlike Attwood) Mill did not consider.[99]

* * *

98 e.g. Thornton (1802), 117–18. Ricardo, for his part allowed that even devaluation might be legitimate to avoid severe deflation; cf. *Works*, IX, 73–4; V, 208.

99 On Attwood's position see Viner (1937), 198–200. Hawtrey in his celebrated *Trade and Credit* (1928), gives Attwood a fair reading concerning his 'inflationism' (65f). It is clarified that in his earliest presentation – an open letter of 1817 to Vansittart, Chancellor of the Exchequer – Attwood focussed on the damage to activity of falling prices, a short-run concern, based on the (reasonable) proposition that at such times an excess demand for

The paper on the 'Currency Question' (1844) constitutes a panegyric for the gold standard as a guarantee against over-issue. Here we have reference to those who see 'no harm in emancipating a paper currency from the constraint of convertibility, and from every definite principle of limitation, provided only that it is grounded on the security of actual property; forgetful that even the *assignats* were issued on no less a security than the principal portion of the soil of France, and that a paper so guaranteed is no more protected from depreciation, if issued in excess, than the land itself would be if offered for sale in unusual quantity' (344). But the case for an inconvertible currency was not at issue – and Attwood is mentioned only in passing – since all the major parties to the contemporary debate regarding the currency 'admit, that the proper standard of currency is the precious metals, at an unaltered mint valuation; that a pound (precisely as stated by Sir Robert Peel) should mean, a fixed quantity of gold of a given fineness; and that no one who has contracted to pay that given quantity, should be allowed on any pretext to discharge his debt by paying a smaller quantity, or making over paper equivalent to a smaller quantity'. The limitations of gold as a standard – its admittedly variable cost of production (and thus, it is implied, its purchasing power) – is conceded; but gold approached closer to the ideal than any other commodity. In any event, 'were [it] far more subject to fluctuation than it is, it would be less so than the policy of a government, – especially one which takes for its principle of guidance "the wants of trade," which in this case simply means the convenience of debtors' (345). Mill thus maintained a strong line on the necessity for a standard,

money to hold is encouraged. Expansion of the currency was required to reverse the movement. But while he was unconcerned with depreciation of the currency in terms of gold, he was concerned to guard against secular inflation, and proposed (also in 1817) a managed currency on the basis of a rule of thumb (stable money wages) that he believed was more effective than tying the currency to gold. Hawtrey's main point is that Attwood 'did not wish to push the circulation of bank notes beyond what was necessary to keep the population of the country employed . . . Far from being an inflationist at this stage, Attwood wanted a measure of value more stable than gold. He was more royalist than the king' (69–70). It was only later that his argument – especially in the hands of his followers – was 'debauched by the exigencies of political controversy' into pure inflationism amounting in part to the case for *higher*, not stable, prices whereby the real burden of fixed charges on industry and agriculture might be reduced (notwithstanding the implications for fixed income recipients).

There is a further dimension to 'inflationism' to which Hawtrey refers (79) – opposition to credit restriction during the cyclical upswing for fear of bringing about a price decline and lapse into depression. 'Sound currency', by contrast, requires steps to avoid or moderate the rise as well as the fall in prices. Mill falls into the 'sound currency' school because he championed constraints on credit in general including note issues on the upswing, while his proposals also included expansions of the note issue in depression to prevent excessive deflation. This of course in addition to his objections both on positive and normative grounds to reductions in the purchasing power of nominally fixed incomes.

taking the Ricardian position in general, but going beyond Ricardo in refusing to countenance a devaluation of the pound in terms of gold 'on any pretext' since Ricardo in his day had justified such a measure in circumstances where a return to gold at par would entail severe deflation of output and employment.

The position of the currency school – of Torrens, Norman, McCulloch, Loyd and Peel – is represented as involving a *novel* idea that an increase even of a convertible note issue will be destabilizing since 'the check of convertibility' – although it assures against '*permanent* depreciation' – 'acts too slowly, and admits of great mischief from excess of issues before it begins to operate' (345).[100] It is to increased issues of paper that, according to this school, could be attributed many of the features of the commercial cycle; for the price level increase (prior to any metal outflow) and subsequent decrease

is already a mischief; it deranges mercantile calculations, creates unexpected gains to some at the expense of others, and adds to the gambling character in a certain degree inherent in all the great operations of commerce. But the evil seldom ends here. All advance of prices tends to encourage speculation; especially when the same cause which creates the advance (being increased issues made by bankers, in the form of increased advances to their customers) occasions, as its very first effect, a reduction of the rate of interest. The conjunction of rising markets and a low rate of interest leads to speculative purchases, by which the rise itself is heightened and prolonged. The rise, however, not being grounded on any permanent cause of increased price (such as a deficiency of supply); in proportion to its continuance, the fall, when the tide turns, is from a greater height, and also to a lower depth. Those who during the rise of prices obtained credit upon the apparently increasing value of the goods which they held, are only enabled to fulfil their engagements by parting with the goods at almost any sacrifice, and prices sink for a time as much below their accustomed rate as they had previously been raised above it (346).

The proposed bank legislation would 'place the issuers under a legal impossibility of ever increasing their issues (beyond a certain moderate minimum), except in exchange for bullion'.[101] Coupled with this would

100 For excellent accounts of the banking and currency school controversy see Robbins (1958), Ch. 4; (*CW*, IV, xviif).
101 The currency principle is nicely summarized thus: 'To avert these evils, in the opinion of Colonel Torrens and Mr. Loyd, and we may now add of Sir Robert Peel, something more than convertibility is necessary. Their remedy is to place the issuers under a legal impossibility of ever increasing their issues (beyond a certain moderate minimum), except in exchange for bullion, which, if refused to them, would probably be sent to the mint and coined. By this contrivance the paper currency is prevented from being arbitrarily increased. It can only, under such a system, be extended, when, if the augmentation

be a rule which prevents the Bank from actively contracting its issues (as for example by sale of bank securities) in an effort to check an outflow of bullion during periods of falling prices, a practice which 'raises the rate of interest and increases the difficulty of obtaining loans, . . . thus heightening all the evils of a commercial revulsion' (346–7).[102] The currency should not be diminished 'otherwise than by not re-issuing notes which are presented for payment: 'By the plan proposed, that of compelling the issuers to keep their securities at a fixed amount, and to let the currency contract or expand only by the exchange of gold for notes and of notes for gold, the paper will, according to this theory, be preserved exactly the same in quantity as the metallic money which would otherwise circulate in its place; this identity of quantity being, it is supposed, indispensable to secure identity of value.' And in such a program would be found the solution to cyclical instability:

Under the system thus established, we are confidently told that the calamity of almost periodical recurrence, commonly known by the name of a 'commercial crisis,' will be greatly diminished both in frequency and in severity. Some permit themselves to use language which at least seems to import that these convulsions will be rendered impossible. Colonel Torrens looks upon the measure as one which 'will effectually prevent the recurrence of those commercial revulsions, those cycles of excitement and depression, which as Mr. Loyd has so felicitously explained, result from the alternate expansion and contraction of an ill-regulated circulation' [*Inquiry*, iv]. He admits, indeed, that undue speculation, and the consequent reaction, might prevail to a great extent even under a metallic currency. But he attributes to the measure now proposed, an efficacy in counteracting those evils, sufficient to constitute that measure 'the most important and the most salutary, as regards the reform of our monetary system, which has been brought under the consideration of parliament since the act of 1819 for the resumption of cash payments.'[103]

were not made, an equivalent increase would probably take place in the portion of the currency which consists of coin.'

102 'Under the present system, the Bank, when it finds its treasure leaving it, does not remain passive, and allow the exchange of notes for specie to go on until, the needful contraction having been effected, the drain stops of itself. It becomes alarmed, and endeavours by calling in its issues to stop the efflux of bullion in an earlier stage. It diminishes its loans to merchants, depriving them in a period of falling prices of the accustomed accommodation, which is then more than usually necessary. Or it throws some of its securities upon the market, and by absorbing a portion of the capital which is seeking investment, deprives the merchants of an equivalent amount of pecuniary advances. By either process, it raises the rate of interest and increases the difficulty of obtaining loans, at a period which is already one of pressure, thus heightening all the evils of a commercial revulsion.' Mill cites Tooke's account (350–1) of the process by which securities are purchased with Bank of England notes.

103 The citation is from Torrens (1844). Torrens' refutation was of Tooke, (1844).

All of this Mill denied outright partly on empirical grounds of a kind that he normally claimed it desirable to avoid.[104] More important are matters of principle, Mill following Tooke in his objections to Torrens and summarizing thus:

That the proposed changes in the mode of regulating the currency will be attended with none of the advantages predicted; that, so far as intended to guard against the danger of over-issue, they are precautions against a chimerical evil; that the real evil of commercial vicissitudes, of 'cycles of excitement and depression,' [See Torrens, *Inquiry*, iv; cf. Tooke, *Inquiry*, 55] is not touched by them, nor by any regulations which can be adopted for bank notes or other mere instruments of credit; and that in what Mr. Tooke justly calls (next to solvency and convertibility) 'the main difference between one banking system and another,' namely, 'the greater or less liability to abrupt changes in the rate of interest and in the state of commercial credit,' [Tooke, *Inquiry*, 106] the present arrangements, under the condition of a larger bank reserve, have a decided advantage over the new system (360–1).

In this summary passage, regulation (either of the convertible note issue or of credit in general) is ruled out, beyond the requirement for a larger reserve. Did Mill then retract the earlier allowance for a degree of flexibility on the part of the Bank of England?

We must first establish whether or not Mill in 1844 allowed an impact on prices exerted by the note issue – and did not view them merely as the passive response to an increase in demand for bank finance – for only in that case would Bank intervention be meaningful, even in principle. Despite appearances, when the paper of 1844 is examined in detail, one discerns important allowances for a positive impact on prices by the note issue.

In a convenient summary Mill defines Tooke's rejection of the imputations made against bank issues as responsible for cyclical price movements:

The imputations are – First: That the banks, by arbitrary extension of their issues, raise prices; and thus create fluctuation, and speculation, and ultimate revulsions, where such would not otherwise exist.
Secondly: That when speculations have commenced from causes unconnected with the banks, they, by extending their issues, concurrently with the rise of prices, prevent the rise from being checked in an early stage. And when the rise of prices, by its operation on the exports and imports, has caused an efflux of gold, they hasten to stop it by a contraction of the currency equal to or beyond the previous expansion;

---

104 For example, commercial revulsions were said to be as severe in France where metal was the common medium of payment, as in England and the US. If fluctuations characterized a purely metal system they would not be prevented by making 'paper conform exactly to the variations of a metallic currency . . .' (348).

which contraction being effected by a forced operation upon the loan market, aggravates the difficulties of persons already distressed.

Mr. Tooke disputes both these assertions.

He denies that an extension of issues can be arbitrarily made by the banks; or that, if made, it has any necessary tendency to raise prices.

He denies that, when prices are rising, the extension of issues, which frequently takes place simultaneously, retards the action of the causes which tend to check the rise; or that by preventing such increase of issues, improvident speculation would be earlier arrested, and the consequent calamities confined within a narrower range [Tooke, *Inquiry*, pp. 56ff.] (349–50).

Now Mill comes to the defence of Tooke in his debate with Torrens but in so doing effectively concedes the cases where an increase in the currency *does* act upon prices.

There is first Mill's insistence that increased note issues do not *necessarily* raise the net money supply. Citing Tooke's *History of Prices*, Mill (350–1) observes that when the Bank buys securities in the market with its notes the interest rate indeed falls, but the seller might invest the funds abroad (as he would be encouraged to do by the fall in interest itself) rather than add to purchases domestically. In fact, since the capital transmission occurs by exchanging notes for gold there is no (permanent) net addition to the money supply. As a second instance, the issue by country banks of notes to farmers (to allow them to hold stocks) may be counterbalanced by merchants who, finding no grain on the market, place their notes on deposit or repay outstanding loans. Again there occurs no net expansion of notes. Mill alludes to 'innumerable witnesses' to this effect, thus appealing to experience; but this experience, he asserts, is 'perfectly consistent with the theory of the subject'.

Secondly, Mill argues that even when a net increase in notes does occur this need not entail an increase in general 'purchasing power'. To do so, it is necessary for the issues to impinge upon the production–income–expenditure process:

The purchasing power which determines prices is of two kinds, – *ultimate* purchasing power, which determines permanent prices; and the portion of that power which is an actual exercise at a given time; this determines the fluctuations of prices. The ultimate purchasing power of the community is, in the words of Mr. Tooke, 'the quantity of money constituting the revenues of the different orders of the state, under the head of rents, profits, salaries, and wages' [Tooke, *Inquiry*, 71] We think he should rather have said their 'gross incomes,' to include that portion of their receipts which is employed in replacing material, and in renewing machinery and buildings as they wear out. The whole of these incomes is destined to be, and is, expended in purchases, either for personal consumption or for reproduction. The aggregate of money incomes, compared with the whole annual produce of the country, determines general prices, as between the dealer and the consumer. If you add to the currency in a way which increases the aggregate of incomes, you raise prices; but this condition can be satisfied by nothing short of a permanent increase of the quantity of money in the country; either from an influx of the metals, caused by a diminution in the cost at which they can be produced and imported, or from increased issue of an inconvertible paper currency. We say inconvertible, because it is admitted that of that alone could any increase have the character of permanence (352).[105]

All of this reinforces what we already know of Mill's approach to general quantity theory reasoning, namely his refusal to adopt an 'automatist' approach in considering the impact of a change in money supply on the price level (cf. above, p. 520f).[106]

That any impact on expenditures could result from the reduction in the rate of interest in consequence of expanded note issues is very forcibly rejected (357–8n) with citations from Tooke's *Inquiry*:

[T]o suppose that persons entitled to credit are likely to be induced – *stimulated* is the favourite term – by the mere circumstance of a low rate of interest, to enter into speculations in commodities (using the term speculation in its obnoxious sense), argues a want of knowledge of the motives which lead to such speculations. These are seldom, if ever, entered into with borrowed capital, except with a view to so great an advance of price, and to be realized within so moderate a space of time, as to render the rate of interest or discount a matter of comparatively trifling consideration [81–2].

But why should this purchasing power be directed to the purchase of commodities, if there was nothing in the state of supply relatively to the rate of consumption, to afford the prospect of gain on the necessary eventual resale? The error is in supposing the *disposition* or *will* to be co-extensive with the power. The limit to the motive for the exercise of the power is in the prospect of resale with a profit [79].

---

105 Cf. the remarks by Gregory (1928), 21–2 on Tooke's perspective: '[I]n his search for an explanation of the causes of general price movements, which would . . . reject the rigid connection between the quantity of money and the state of the price level postulated by the Currency School, he evolved a theory which, in its general tendency, is singularly close to those Income Theories of Prices which in recent years have been adumbrated by Wieser, Hawtrey, Aftalion and others'.

106 As Gregory (1928), 22, observes 'there is ultimately no antithesis between the Quantity Theory – in that modern interpretation of it which takes account of variations in individual desire to hold money – and Income Theories of Money'.

Now it is clearly 'permanent prices' rather than their fluctuations that Mill has in mind when he maintains that (under convertibility) 'nothing short of a permanent increase' of the money supply reflecting an influx of gold can be effective in raising prices (352). Yet there are two concessions which, though relating to non-permanent increases in the note issue are said to 'add to the aggregate of incomes' and evidently do entail (temporary) price increases:

To be scientifically accurate, it must be admitted that if the increased issues were made in advances to employers of labour (for instance, in a loan to a manufacturer, who expends them in the direct payment of wages to his workpeople), there would be, to that extent, as long as the expenditure was going on, an increase of the aggregate money income of the community, and hence a corresponding rise of prices. But this supposition is not applicable to our present currency, of which the smallest notes are of too high a denomination to be employed, in any extent worth considering, for the payment of wages.

We may add, with Mr. Tooke [*Inquiry*, 68f.], that the issues of a *Government* paper, even when not permanent, will raise prices; because Governments usually issue their paper in purchasing for consumption. If issued to pay off a portion of the national debt, we believe they would have no such effect.[107]

Mill concludes weakly that 'an extension of issues, may not' – not *cannot* – 'increase the aggregate money incomes of the community, nor raise general prices between dealer and consumer, upon which prices all dealers depend for their ultimate returns, and on the anticipation of which they necessarily ground all their transactions with one another'. Evidently then the category of (net) note issues which he maintains does not act on prices is one that fails to generate increased outlays on commodities. We have one example in the discussion elsewhere (above, pp. 748–9) of notes injected in times of depression which merely satisfy liquidity preference. Doubtless such notes may be represented as an increase in 'wealth' rather than 'income'. And that Mill indeed had this kind of situation in mind is suggested by the form taken of his rejection of the contention that a (net) increase in note issues must raise money demand for commodities 'at the particular moment' – i.e. even if not permanently – 'because the person who obtains the bank notes does so for the purpose of using them, and may be supposed to bring them immediately into the market and make purchases to their full extent' (352–3). This argument Mill turns down on grounds of its neglect of velocity,[108]

107 See also p. 527 above for a further example of a note issue that generates no price increase – the case involving capital export.

108 Because of his supposed neglect of changes in velocity Torrens is accused of having 'built an elaborate superstructure upon a foundation of sand' (353n).

the implication being that increased notes may find their way into hoards or at any event may be accompanied by a fall in the average rapidity of circulation – a case most likely in depression.

What of the positive effects as prices of increases in the note issue which occur *during* periods of speculation? These surely cannot be dealt with in the foregoing manner. In fact Mill retreats, as it were, to a second line of defence: Increases in purchasing power due to net increases in note issue would have occurred even in the absence of such issues. Here we have a repetition in more developed form of the basic argument of 1826, namely that even were there no such thing as bankers' notes such expansions (acting on prices) would occur under speculative circumstances since increases in notes involve one way amongst numerous others of drawing upon available credit:

The purchasing power of an individual at any moment is not measured by the money actually in his pocket, whether we mean by money the metals, or include bank notes. It consists, first, of the money in his possession; secondly, of the money at his banker's, and all other money due to him and payable on demand; thirdly, of whatever credit he happens to possess. To the full measure of this three-fold amount he has the power of purchase. How much he will employ of this power, depends upon his necessities, or, in the present case, upon his expectations of profit. Whatever portion of it he does employ, constitutes his demand for commodities, and determines the extent to which he will act upon price.

Now, of these three elements of money demand, the first alone is grounded upon a corresponding amount of money actually *in esse*. The second, or the deposit at his banker's, is in part grounded upon actual money, namely, to the extent of about one-third, that being the proportion which prudent bankers profess to keep in their coffers to meet the drafts of their depositors. The third element of money demand, namely credit, has no basis of actually existing money at all. It is an additional money demand, created over and above that which is constituted by all the money in actual circulation. But it is exactly as operative upon prices as the money itself, provided the possessor chooses to make use of the purchasing power which it confers. This explains why periods of general confidence, when large prospects of gain seem to be opening themselves, and when there is a disposition among dealers to employ not only all their money but all or much of their credit in enlarging their operations, are attended with so great a rise of general prices. The effect is sometimes ascribed to the bills of exchange and other transferable paper which these transactions generate, and which are said to perform the functions of currency. Those who use this language mistake the effect for the cause. Bills of exchange are mere evidences of credit. The credit itself is the operating cause. It is manifest that when buyers are willing to employ their credit as well as their money in making purchases, their demand for commodities becomes so much greater, and prices must rise. They would rise if no such thing as a transferable acknowledgement of debt had ever been known in the country.

We may observe, parenthetically, that these considerations remove the puzzle which has been made of whether deposits, and cheques, and bills of exchange, are to be considered as money. With those who think that money alone confers power of purchase, these questions are very pertinent. When they ask whether deposits, or whether anything else, is money, they mean, does it operate on money prices? If it does, they think it a necessary consequence that it should be called money. But when once it is clearly seen that credit, so far as employed in the purchase of commodities, operates upon prices in exactly the same degree as money, the question what forms of credit should be called money, becomes extremely unimportant. It would probably be best that no form whatever should be so called.

If the views now stated be sound, it seems not easy to understand how an increased creation of the written evidences of credit called bank notes, can, of itself, create an additional demand, or occasion a rise of price. Admitting bank notes to be money (which is, in truth, a mere question of language), what does the person do who issues them, but take so much from the third element of purchasing power, namely credit, and add it to the first element, money in hand – making no addition whatever to the total amount? More properly, he merely converts so much credit from an unwritten into a written, and from a cumbrous into a convenient, form. Bank notes are to credit precisely what coin is to bullion; the same thing, merely rendered portable and minutely divisible. We cannot perceive that they add anything, either to the aggregate of purchasing power, or to the portion of that power in actual exercise. The person to whom the notes are advanced is proved by that very fact to have credit, and his requiring the advance proves that to that extent he intends to use his credit in making purchases. Is it supposed that having credit, and intending to buy goods by means of it, he will be disabled from doing so because a banker is prohibited from one particular mode of giving him credit? (353–5).

Again, as in 1826, the onus upon bankers' notes is further reduced, by the observation, following Tooke, that the increased issues which do occur are a passive response to price increases not their cause, such increases – rather than other forms of credit – reflecting the particular institutional arrangements at play but not in any way essential to the process:

That bank notes, as such, have any peculiar power on prices, we see no reason whatever to believe: and we hold with Mr. Tooke, that when they are increased, their increase is a consequence of a rise of prices, not a cause. It is a known fact that the country issues almost invariably increase when the prices of agricultural produce are rising. The reason is, that the buyers, having larger payments to make, apply for more notes to make them with, it being the custom in the provision and cattle markets not to buy on credit, but to pay immediately in bank notes. A rise of other prices does not necessarily lead to increased issues; because, in almost all other transactions between dealers, bank notes are already superseded by cheques, or book credits; and these would soon be introduced into the markets for agricultural produce, if the obtaining bank notes were rendered difficult. Even the small quantity of bank notes which are employed at the clearing house or elsewhere, to effect the ultimate liquidation of these cheques and credits by the payment of balances, might, as Mr. Tooke remarks, have their place supplied by exchequer bills (as in Scotland), or by drafts on the Bank of England.

Whether the credit which necessarily exists in a commercial country assumes the form of bank notes or no, is, in short, a mere matter of convenience. In whatever form or vesture the credit is given, its influence on price is the same. He who has credit, and desires to employ it in purchases, will find the means of doing so without bank notes, and will act upon prices accordingly; while if he does not think the time favourable for making purchases, even having the notes in his possession will not induce him to do it; he will either keep them by him until they are wanted, or they will go into deposit.

It appears, then, that any increase of issues which is likely to take place under the present system of convertibility, is in itself quite inoperative to raise prices, and cannot, therefore, be an exciting cause of commercial revulsions; but that a spirit of speculation, or an undue extension of credit, does raise prices, and raises them equally whether bank notes are generated by it or not; and that by preventing the increase of bank notes during such periods, nothing would be done to check the rise, since it is not bank notes which, as it is sometimes expressed, *sustain* prices, but the state of credit generally. No mode of regulating bank notes would either arrest the rise, or moderate the subsequent revulsion, which is always proportional (355–6).[109]

In all of this it is 'undue extension of credit' in speculative periods that is said to be responsible for the generalized upward price movement, which seems to imply that credit as such *is*, at least under certain conditions, an active force with respect to prices. If this is so we discern an important deviation from 1826 regarding credit in general. But it is doubtful whether Mill had abandoned the weight placed upon speculative mood as the 'ultimate' determinant – credit in general being regarded as a passive reaction – for that seems to be the position of the *Principles*.

There are, however, concessions regarding the impact of note issues – important concessions – that appear in the shadows in the present context. Even notes can under certain circumstances have a net impact on prices:

It must be conceded, and Mr. Tooke does fully concede, that if bankers urged, by competition or caught by the contageous confidence of speculative times, make advances to persons who otherwise have *not* credit and cannot give good security, in that case the foregoing arguments do not apply. To that extent they do create

---

109 Cf. also 358–9n., where Mill draws on Tooke regarding the possibility of an immense purchasing power engaged in speculation without notes or even bills of exchange.

a new purchasing power, a new demand, and, as its consequence, a rise of price (355).[110]

This vital concession Mill seems to wish to play down. For regarding the impact of notes on prices even under convertibility he proceeds to insist that it is not by notes 'as such' that such impact occurs. There may be imprudent advances by bankers of all kinds; indeed, '[a]ll extensions of credit, legitimate or illegitimate, tends, in proportion as it is made use of, to a rise of price. And all contraction of credit produces an equivalent collapse'.

* * *

We turn next to the *Principles* for an amplification of the impact of the note issue. A brief word first regarding Mill's reactions in 1848 to inconvertibility.

The value (purchasing power) of an inconvertible currency is represented as always, to be wholly arbitrary (III, Ch. xiii, 556f). A proposal to regulate the currency, by reference to the 'fictitious rule' of a purely nominal exchange rate between paper currency and coin is rejected, since governments would be easily induced to tamper with it (559). The notion of backing paper by property is also rejected (562–3n). The inevitable 'variations' in the value of the circulating medium 'disturb existing contracts, and expectations, and the liability to such changes renders every pecuniary engagement of long date entirely precarious' (558). Worse still, the degradation in value was not an accidental matter but a deliberate consequence of the fact that each issue was a source of profit to the issuing authority – especially so when the authority's own debts were computed in terms of the currency – an allusion to government promissory notes.[111]

We have referred elsewhere to the rejection in the present context of the Hume–Attwood ascription of a real stimulus to inflation, on the grounds

---

110 Cf. also Mill's gloss on the observation 'that any increase of issues which is likely to take place under the present system of convertibility, is in itself quite inoperative to raise prices': 'We say *likely* to take place – not any increase which *can* take place; because there have been instances, both with joint-stock banks and private bankers, of imprudent advances, on insufficient security, resembling, on a smaller scale, the gigantic mismanagement of the American banks. These must have tended, as we have already admitted, to raise prices: and though it was not peculiarly in their character of issuers that the banks thus misconducted themselves, their issues, no doubt, enabled them to do so on a larger scale' (356n).

111 The replacement of metal by paper was a national advantage: The issuers gained since until their notes returned to them they derived use from them as from real capital (and the cost of maintaining the currency is reduced). But if no gold or silver is superceded, so that the increase in notes represents a net increase in currency, the gains of the issuers is at the expense of note holders (565).

that any such stimulus presumes a 'continuous delusion' (pp. 515–16). There remains to recall the fact that Mill does make brief allowance for the 'forced saving' phenomenon which, for his part, is outweighed by considerations of 'integrity and good faith' (565).[112]

As in his earlier papers, Mill rejected the post-war arguments favouring inflation on grounds of justice. Quite apart from the fact that there would be no practical way of rectifying any injustices, of the kind often supposed, to specific individuals generated by 'returning to cash payments without lowering the standard', Mill went further in insisting that resumption at par had not constituted an injustice: 'Parliament had no alternative; it was absolutely bound to adhere to the acknowledged standard' (567). For even were it the case that all outstanding debts had been contracted in a depreciated pound (in terms of purchasing power) Parliament had pledged to return to gold at par within six months of the cessation of hostilities, so that when the government borrowed it did so on the implicit condition of a promise to repay on these conditions. Were it possible to correct injustices to specific individuals, it would be found that fundholders were the injured parties because of the delayed return to gold (568).

The entire issue of inconvertibility is briefly disposed of. It is the convertible case that takes centre stage. In the chapter 'On the Regulation of a Convertible Currency' (III, Ch. xxiv) Mill repeated the Tooke–Fullarton position regarding the 'passivity' of the note issue under convertibility. With the evidence of the country bankers before various Parliamentary Committees in mind 'it is argued by Mr. Tooke and Mr. Fullarton, that bank issues, since they cannot be increased in amount unless there is an increased demand, cannot possibly raise prices; cannot encourage speculation, nor occasion a commercial crisis; and that the attempt to guard against that evil by an artificial management of the issue of notes, is of no effect for the intended purpose, and likely to produce other consequences extremely calamatous' (662).[113]

---

112 Cf. to forced savings in general: 'There is no way in which a general and permanent rise of prices . . . can benefit anybody except at the expense of somebody else. The substitution of paper for metallic currency is a national gain: any further increase of paper beyond this limit is but a form of robbery' (565).

Mill concedes that producers who are accommodated by loans gain, though their gain is part of that reaped by the issuer and is at the expense of all holders of currency. Those under a fixed nominal obligation also gain, and a real stimulus arises in so far as the 'productive classes' are net borrowers from the 'unproductive'. Here Mill concedes Attwood's 'positive' argument – the stimulus resulting from reducing the tax burden falling on producers, required to pay off the national debt (cf. 566).

A bitter denunciation of any such program as Attwood's will also be found in a letter of 24 Sept. 1868, XVI, 1443f. The issue arose from a contemporary US controversy.

113 Regarding the testimony of the country bankers, Mill wrote: 'I am convinced that they cannot increase their issue of notes in any other circumstances than those which are

Here the distinction between the 'quiescent' and 'speculative' states is critical. During the quiescent period there is, runs the argument, no special demand for loans, and any (exogenous) increase in notes cannot remain in circulation to finance increased demand for commodities: 'In this case, therefore, there can be no addition at the discretion of the bankers, to the general circulating medium: any increase of their issues either comes back to them, or remains idle in the hands of the public, and no rise takes place in prices' (663).[114]

Considering the fact that the quiescent period is one of net investment, Mill's insistence upon the constancy of the note issue is surprising. And we have established that the capital accumulation proceeding during quiescence is central to the link envisaged between trend and cycle. But while Mill here neglects the growth component of the quiescent period, clearly his main concern is to refute the notion of an independent ability on the part of the banks to expand monetary demand; a response to an increased demand for bank finance reflecting 'the gradual process of accumulation' can, so one might suppose, be formally classified as passive. We shall return shortly to this problem.

Attention is also given to the finance of those increased operations by speculators which characterize the 'expectant' state, 'when an impression prevails, whether well founded or groundless, that the supply of one or more great articles of commerce is likely to fall short of the ordinary consumption', and when traders are 'disposed to make a more than ordinary use of their credit' (663).[115]

Here it is helpful to refer back to the earlier chapter on the 'Influence of Credit on Prices' (III, Ch. xii) where a differential impact exerted by various forms of credit is allowed, notes constituting the most potent and

there stated. I believe, also, that the theory, grounded by Mr. Fullarton upon this fact, contains a large portion of truth, and is far nearer to being the expression of the whole truth than any form whatever of the currency theory' (662).

Cf. 661: The Tooke–Fullarton view 'denies to bank notes, so long as their convertibility is maintained, any power whatever of raising prices, and to banks any power of increasing their circulation, except as a consequence of, and in proportion to, an increase of the business to be done'. Mill charged opponents of this position with tampering with the data. He cites Tooke's evidence of 1832 before the Commons Committee on the Bank Charter to the effect that price level increases *preceded* changes in bank note circulation.

114 The recipient either keeps them at hand or deposits them or repays past loans but there occurs no increase in commodity demand under the supposed conditions. A note is added in 1862: even if notes are expanded by way of reduced interest – Mill refers to an 'artificial' increase in demand – the borrower makes his deal and the recipient places his notes in deposit, having no use for them.

115 Similarly, a sudden large increase in foreign demand for home goods, or the expectation of it will generate an increase in the price of exportables and stimulate 'speculations, sometimes of a reasonable, and (as long as large proportion of men in business prefer excitement to safety) frequently of an irrational or immoderate character' (663).

book credit the least.[116] Now, as we know, Mill always formally insisted on the passivity of credit expansion in the sense that the extent of the available total of credit actually drawn upon depends upon the demand for accommodation. In the present context too the point is made that 'all this purchasing power . . . is operative upon prices, only according to the proportion of which it is used' (546). But the allowance for a differential impact depending upon the form of credit selected undermines the notion of the passivity of credit extension – a notion, we have seen, that was poorly founded in the earlier essays. Mill's concern, however, was to minimize the onus upon notes for cyclical price increases, on the grounds that while in speculative periods prices were indeed likely to rise higher if purchases were financed with notes, Tooke had shown that such purchases were 'in the majority of cases . . . made almost exclusively on book credit', an increase in the demand for bank accommodation only occurring when the speculative tide was already turning:

'Applications to the Bank for extended discount', says the highest authority on such subjects [Tooke, *History of Prices*, 1848, Vol iv, 125–6], (and the same must be true of applications to other banks) 'occur rarely if ever in the origin or progress of extensive speculations in commodities. These are entered into, for the most part if not entirely, in the first instance, on credit, for the length of term usual in the several trades; thus entailing on the parties no immediate necessity for borrowing so much as may be wanted for the purpose beyond their own available capital. . . . It is . . . when by the vicissitudes of events, or of the seasons, or other adventitious circumstances, the forthcoming supplies are found to exceed the computed rate of consumption, and a fall of prices ensues, that an increased demand for capital takes place; the market rate of interest then rises, and increased applications are made to the Bank of England for discount.' So that the multiplication of bank notes and other transferable paper does not, for the most part, accompany and facilitate the speculation; but comes into play chiefly when the tide is turning, and difficulties begin to be felt (547).

[T]hough the great instrument of speculative purchases is book credits, it cannot be contested that in speculative periods an increase does take place in the quantity both of bills of exchange and of bank notes. This increase, indeed, so far as bank notes are concerned, hardly ever takes place in the earliest stage of the speculations: advances from bankers (as Mr. Tooke observes) not being applied for in order

---

116 'Credit, in short, has exactly the same purchasing power with money; and as money tells upon prices not simply in proportion to its amount, but to its amount multiplied by the number of times it changes hands, so also does credit; and credit transferable from hand to hand is in that proportion more potent, than credit which only performs one purchase' (546).

to purchase, but in order to hold on without selling when the usual term of credit has expired, and the high price which was calculated on has not arrived . . . [The] tea speculators mentioned by Mr. Tooke could not have carried their speculations beyond the three months which are the usual term of credit in their trade, unless they had been able to obtain advances from bankers, which, if the expectation of a rise of price had still continued, they probably would have done (549).

Moreover, the practical import of the concession that since 'credit in the form of bank notes is a more potent instrument for raising prices than book credits, an unrestrained power of resorting to this instrument may contribute to prolong and heighten the speculative rise of prices, and hence to aggravate the subsequent recoil' (549) is almost immediately withdrawn, on the grounds that even relative to forms of credit other than book credit (such as bills) the (belated) expansion of the note issue was quantitatively small;[117] while – here Fullarton is cited – cheques on bankers (and transfers in a banker's books) are 'parallel in every respect to bank notes, giving equal facilities to an extension of credit, and capable of acting on prices quite as powerfully' (551). These were considerations which 'abate very much from the importance of any effect which can be produced in allaying the vicissitudes of commerce, by so superficial a contrivance as the one so much relied on of late, the restriction of the issue of bank notes by an artificial rule' (552).

In the chapter on the regulation of a convertible currency, however, one discerns a rather greater allowance for a positive impact on prices emanating from the note issue. That bankers very often unduly administer to the increased demand for credit characterizing the 'expectant state', and that such periods are attended 'during some part of their progress, by a considerable increase of bank notes' (664), is allowed, although such expansions are still regarded with Tooke and Fullarton, as the consequence not the cause of rising prices – the cause being largely simple book credit and cheques to a lesser extent. But Mill's adherence to the Tooke–Fullarton position was now subject to a qualification: 'I regard it as proved, both scientifically and historically, that during the ascending period of speculation, *and as long as it is confined to transactions between dealers*, the issues of bank notes

117 The data drawn on indicated that in speculative periods the change of bank notes amounted to some 5% – a fraction of the total of all bills in existence at any time, let alone of all forms of credit. Moreover, 'even this, as we have seen, hardly ever comes into play until that advanced period of the speculation at which the tide shows signs of turning, and the dealers generally are rather thinking of the means of fulfilling their existing engagements, than meditating an extension of them: while the quantity of bills in existence is largely increased from the very commencement of the speculations' (549–50).

are seldom materially increased, nor contribute anything to the speculative rise of prices' (italics added). This qualification is much emphasized. The notion of passivity 'can no longer be affirmed when speculation has proceeded so far as to reach the producers. Speculative orders given by merchants to manufacturers induce them to extend their operations, and to become applicants to bankers for increased advances, which if made in notes, are not paid away to persons who return them into deposit, but are partially expended in paying wages, and pass into the various channels of retail trade, where they become directly effective in producing a further rise of prices'.

Thus although the initial note issues are the response to a preceding demand for increased advances, once they filter through into the labour market they take on an active life of their own in generating a kind of multiplier effect. This qualification already appears in a note to the essay of 1844, as we have seen (IV, 352n). In his later evidence on the Bank Act Mill reiterated the same point:

You stated that you objected to an issue of 1 l. notes, because it was more liable to over-issue. What do you mean by over-issue? In order to explain that, it is necessary to go into some particulars. I think that as long as the Bank confines its advances to merchants and general dealers, to what is called the mercantile public, people who deal in goods but who do not pay wages, its issues never originate a rise of prices, because a dealer only uses notes for the purpose of fulfilling previous engagements. Dealers never make purchases in the first instance with Bank notes; the dealers to whom Bank notes are paid usually either send them into deposit, or pay them to persons who send them into deposit. But the operation is different when advances are made to manufacturers or others who pay wages. When that is the case, the notes do or may get into the hands of labourers and others who expend them for consumption, and in that case the notes do constitute in themselves a demand for commodities, and may for some time tend to promote a rise of prices; and when they do so, and there is not any other cause for that rise of prices than the issue of notes, that constitutes over-issue, that is to say, an issue that will be followed by a revulsion. *In that case the Bank would have been the moving power to raise the prices?* The notes would have been the moving power to raise the prices: but that I do not think is ever the case now (V, 512).

Doubtless the prohibition of notes of small denomination was behind Mill's confidence that expansions of note issues do not play on prices. Yet the allowance in principle makes it difficult to appreciate the formal assertion that the note issue is totally passive during the *quiescent* period in so far as net capital accumulation, which presumably affects the labour market, is underway.

To return to the *Principles* (III, Ch. xxiv). There is a second qualification to the presumption of passivity of the note issue. This refers to the final stages of the speculative period when advances are requested by those unsuccessful speculators who, after the tide shows signs of turning, struggle to avoid selling in a falling market. An expanded note issue (while formally a passive response) in this case 'tends to prolong the duration of the speculations' enabling 'the speculative prices to be kept up for some time after they would otherwise have collapsed' (665). For the extension of credit via note issues 'long after the recoil from over-speculation has commenced', prevented the increase in the interest rate which would otherwise have taken place in consequence of the demand for disposable capital and which would have obliged speculative holders 'to submit earlier to that loss of resale, which could not have been prevented from coming on them at last' (668).[118]

In contrast to III, Ch. xii, serious consequences are now said to flow from the artificial maintenance of prices (and depression of the interest rate), namely an aggravated drain of the precious metals, 'a leading feature of this stage in the progress of a commercial crisis' (665), necessitating a more stringent contraction of notes than would otherwise be required, thereby worsening the subsequent deflation. For since the prolongation of the drain 'endanger[ed] the power of the banks to fulfil their engagement of paying their notes on demand, they are compelled to contract their credit more suddenly and severely than would have been necessary if they had been prevented from propping up speculation by increased advances, after the time when the recoil had become inevitable'. This applied to the Bank of England itself, which was compelled to contract its discounts sharply to avoid the danger of suspended payments. The resultant increases in the interest rate, inflicted 'much greater loss and distress on individuals and destroy[ed] a much greater amount of ordinary credit of the country, than any real necessity required' (670).

It was Mill's repeatedly stated view that the rising prices of the speculative period were inconceivable without the support of a variety of credit forms including book credits granted by manufacturers and importers to their clients. And, in fact, his opposition to expanded note issues after the 'recoil' from over-speculation had set in, was not to an increase in currency as such but to inappropriate extensions of credit (which happened to take the form of notes): 'Prices, having risen without any increase of bank notes, could well have fallen without a diminution of them; but having risen in

---

118 Mill here denies that to restrict the note issue is irrelevant because the bank will allow deposits to be drawn out (667–8). The events of 1847 are said to show that while similar problems occur if the bank acts through its deposits alone – expanding its discounts and advances when it should be cutting them, rendering the ultimate contraction 'more severe and sudden than necessary' (670) – the situation is worsened when expanded lending occurs via note issue as well as via deposits.

consequence of an extension of credit, they could not fall without a contraction of it' (669) – a contraction prevented by the supposed note issue.[119] But this is a formal matter. The concessions themselves regarding the 'active' impact of notes on prices stood firm. The implications for policy are taken up next.

* * *

In the first chapters of the subset dealing with money, Mill describes its function in facilitating exchange much as Adam Smith had done: 'There cannot . . . be intrinsically a more insignificant thing, in the economy of society, than money; except as a contrivance for sparing time and labour. It is a machine for doing quickly and commodiously, what would be done, though less quickly and commodiously, without it' (506).[120] To this Mill adds the observation that 'like many other kinds of machinery, it only exerts a distinct and independent influence of its own when it gets out of order'. This latter observation has been read to imply a rather restricted view of the potentialities for monetary policy.[121]

Similarly, Mill's championship of the gold standard has given the impression of a limited potential for an active monetary policy. This perspective has been very nicely put by Sir John Hicks:

[Mill] makes it clear that it is confidence in the maintenance of a Gold Standard (in his days a full Gold Standard with gold coins in circulation) which is the basis of the required belief that in the long run prices cannot depart very far from normal. He is therefore opposed to the regulation of the Quantity of Money, however defined; the objective of monetary policy should be the maintenance of convertibility. That will not prevent fluctuations, nor could control of Quantity prevent fluctuations; for booms can start with an expansion of trade credit, without the banks themselves being, at that stage, much involved. As the boom develops, it requires to be fortified by more secure forms of credit, so the pressure is carried back from the circumference to the centre of the banking system. It is essential,

119 The period preceding the collapse of prices involves a gold drain in consequence of a rising level of prices itself generated by speculative extensions of credit whether or not notes are involved. In principle, the outflow generates its own correctives by reducing prices and raising interest. But this dual consequence is prevented 'so long as the unduly expanded credit is upheld by the continued advances of bankers' (669).
120 Cf. also, 7: 'Money, as money, satisfies no want; its worth to any one, consists in its being a convenient shape in which to receive his incomings of all sorts, which incomings he afterwards, at the times which suit him best, converts into the forms in which they can be useful to him.' And 633: 'In international, as in ordinary domestic interchanges, money is to commerce only what oil is to machinery, or railways to locomotion – a contrivance to diminish friction.'
121 Friedman (1969), 105, 107. See also Samuelson (1968), 3.

at that point, that the centre should hold firm; it must protect itself, but only in order to be able to spread security around it. Booms are thus more dangerous than slumps; for a slump will cure itself, while in a boom there is a threat to the convertibility, on which the underlying stability is based. But once it is recognized that there is this threat, wise policy can ward it off (1983, 64; cf. 1967, 164–6).

We shall now see, however, that the scope for a discretionary policy allowed by Mill in the *Principles* was rather wider than may appear at first sight.

As in the paper of 1844 Mill appreciated that a primary concern of policy makers must be the mitigation of the severity of the 'painful series' of 'commercial crises', a phenomenon peculiar to the nineteenth-century British economy, and that in part to this end the Bank Charter Act itself was introduced (III, 660).[122] His opposition to the legislation reflects, as he now phrased the matter, a rejection of the 'popular view' of the 'currency theory' which discerned in an arbitrary issue of notes the 'cause' of the initial price increases generating a 'spirit of speculation in commodities', with its reaction in a 'commercial crisis'.[123] To focus on the currency as the prime agent diverted attention from the real 'circumstances . . . influencing the expectation of supply' (661). Yet the qualification alluded to above (p. 571) which allows an active force to the note issue after the upper turning point is of the first importance, for it implied a concession to the champions of the Act of 1844. Mill indeed frankly recognized that the legislation helped avoid the 'retardation of the recoil, and the ultimate aggravation of its severity' (665). Similarly, 'I am compelled to think that the being restricted from increasing their issues, is a real impediment to

122 For a convenient listing of its provisions see Mill's account (665–6): 'The issue of promissory notes for circulation was to be confined to one body. In the form adopted by Parliament, all existing issuers were permitted to retain this privilege, but none were to be hereafter admitted to it, even in the place of those who might discontinue their issues: and, for all except the Bank of England, a maximum of issues was prescribed, on a scale intentionally low. To the Bank of England no maximum was fixed for the aggregate amount of its notes, but only for the portion issued on securities, or in other words, on loan. These were never to exceed a certain limit, fixed in the first instance at fourteen millions. All issues beyond that amount must be in exchange for bullion; of which the Bank is bound to purchase, at a trifle below the Mint valuation, any quantity which is offered to it, giving its notes in exchange. In regard, therefore, to any issue of notes beyond the limit of fourteen millions, the Bank is purely passive, having no function but the compulsory one of giving its notes for gold at 3*l*. 17*s*. 9*d*., and gold for its notes at 3*l*. 17*s*. 10½*d*., whenever and by whomsoever it is called upon to do so.'

123 Here we find a nice instance of Mill's objections to the practical men. For the 'popular view' involved a 'remarkable instance to what lengths a favourite theory will hurry, not the closet students whose competency in such questions is often treated with so much contempt, but men of the world and of business, who pique themselves on the practical knowledge which they have at least had ample opportunities of acquiring'.

their making those advances which arrest the tide at its turn, and make it rush like a torrent afterwards' (670).[124] (On his concessions to 'the more moderate' or 'more sober' members of the currency school, Overstone, Norman and Torrens, see also 664, 667.) In 1857 Mill reiterated that from his perspective the 'mitigation of commercial revulsions is the real, and only serious, purpose of the Act of 1844' (665n). He denied the case made out by some currency school proponents that the maintenance of convertibility itself required the legislation, for (citing Lord Overstone) 'the Bank can always, by a sufficiently violent action on credit, save itself at the expense of the mercantile public' and would do so under any system.[125] The advantage of the Act of 1844 lay precisely in the fact that it 'mitigates the violence of that process, . . . a sufficient claim to prefer in its behalf'.

Notwithstanding these concessions the balance of the case still rested with Tooke and Fullarton. What was required was a degree of flexibility on the part of the banking system deliberately precluded by the legislation of 1844. For the 'panegyrists of the system . . . boast[ed], that on the first appearance of a drain for exportation – whatever may be its cause, and whether, under a metallic currency, it would involve a contraction of credit or not – the Bank is at once obliged to curtail its advances. And this, be it remembered, when there has been no speculative rise of prices which it is indispensable to correct, no unusual extension of credit requiring contraction; but the demand for gold is solely occasioned by foreign payments on account of government, or large corn importations consequent on a bad harvest' (678). This position, Mill maintained, presumed too hastily that in the case of a purely metallic currency a gold drain necessarily entails a contraction of the internal circulation. A gold drain resulting from extraneous factors such as extraordinary foreign expenditures by government, private capital exports, and the need for unusual imports because of poor home harvests (and not from an increase in the price level generated by an undue expansion of currency or credit) would in all probability not be drawn from circulation, but 'from the hoards, which under a metallic currency always exist to a very large amount; in uncivilized countries, in the hands of all who can afford it; in civilized countries chiefly in the form of bankers' reserves. Mr. Tooke, in his 'Inquiry into the Currency Principle', bears testimony to this fact; but it is to Mr. Fullarton that the public is indebted for the clearest and most satisfactory elucidation of it' (673). Even a system designed

124 On Mill's position see also his evidence before the Select Committee on the Bank Acts of 1857 (CW, V, 502, 505–6, 519, 529–30).
125 On the other hand, if convertibility was threatened by irresponsible management before 1844, it was no different after 1844; there remained a danger of suspension by the banking department. Indeed it was yet more likely given the separation of departments.

to assure that the paper currency fluctuated in exact conformity to the variations of a metallic currency required no contraction of the currency (or credit) in such cases. What, however, would be required was an adequate gold reserve to cover the drain:

In a country in which credit is carried to so great an extent as in England, one great reserve, in a single establishment, the Bank of England, supplies the place, as far as the precious metals are concerned, of the multitudinous reserves of other countries. The theoretical principle, therefore, of the currency doctrine would require, that all those drains of the metal, which, if the currency were purely metallic, would be taken from the hoards, should be allowed to operate freely upon the reserve in the coffers of the Bank of England, without any attempt to stop it either by a diminution of the currency or by a contraction of credit. Nor to this would there be any well-grounded objection, unless the drain were so great as to threaten the exhaustion of the reserve, and a consequent stoppage of payments; a danger against which it is possible to take adequate precautions, because in the cases which we are considering, the drain is for foreign payments of definite amount, and stops of itself as soon as these are effected (677).[126]

In fact, 'in all systems . . . the habitual reserve of the Bank should exceed the utmost amount to which experience warrants the belief that such a drain may extend; which extreme limit Mr. Fullarton affirms to be seven millions, but Mr. Tooke recommends an average reserve of ten, and in his last publication, of twelve millions. Under these circumstances, the habitual reserve, which would never be employed in discounts, but kept to be paid out exclusively in exchange for cheques or bank notes, would be sufficient for a crisis of this description; which therefore would pass off without having

---

126 Cf. paper of 1844 (IV, 356–7): 'There is, however, one way in which the present administration of the currency does heighten the evils of a commercial revulsion. The rise of prices in periods of exaggerated confidence checks exportation and greatly increases importation. A balance has to be paid in gold, and this is demanded from the Bank. To stop the drain, it hastily contracts its issues, that is, it sells securities and diminishes its loans, thus aggravating, in a period of difficulty, the already existing pressure upon the loan market; and this, it is urged, will be prevented by the ministerial measure, since the bank will not be permitted to contract its issues, except by not re-issuing the notes which have been returned to it for payment. But, as Mr. Tooke remarks, to attain this object it is only necessary that the bank should habitually hold so large a reserve of bullion as will admit of allowing any probable drain to proceed until it has reached its limits. Whatever amount of reserve is needed for this purpose will be equally necessary on the plan of Sir Robert Peel, since the bullion, against which all notes beyond the fixed amount of securities are to be issued, must be sufficient to meet the greatest drain which can ever be supposed to occur. We shall see presently that, in reality, the amount of reserve which would suffice on Mr. Tooke's plan will not be sufficient on Sir Robert Peel's.' See also the evidence of 1857, V, 502f.

its difficulties increased by a contraction either of credit or of the circulation' (677–8).

Mill saw in the separation of the departments according to the 1844 legislation a measure dictating far larger reserves than would otherwise be required, and necessitating unnecessary upward pressure on the rate of discount.[127] Accordingly, 'notwithstanding the beneficial operation of the Act of 1844 in the first stages of one kind of commercial crisis (that produced by over-speculation), it on the whole materially aggravates the severity of commercial revulsions. And not only are contractions of credit made more severe by the Act, they are also made greatly more frequent' (682).[128]

The deflationary consequences implied by the theoretical error regarding the operation of a purely metallic system had been spelled out by Fullarton; and in the first three editions of the *Principles* Mill added a note alluding to the fulfilment of his dire prediction during the events of 1847:

Are not the events of 1847 a fulfilment of this prediction? The crisis of that year was preceded by no inflation of credit, no speculative rise of prices. The only speculations (the corn market expected) were those in railway shares, which had no tendency to derange the imports and exports of commodities, or to send any gold out of the country, except the small amounts paid in instalments by shareholders in this country to foreign railways. The drain of gold, great as it was, originated solely in the bad harvest of 1846 and the potato failure of that and the following year, and in the increased price of raw cotton in America. There was nothing in these circumstances which could require either a fall of general prices or a contraction of credit. An unusual demand for credit existed at the time, in consequence of the pressure of railway calls, and this necessitated a rise of the rate of interest. If the bullion in the Bank of England was sufficient to bear the drain without exhaustion, where was the necessity for adding to the distress and difficulty of the time, by requiring all who wanted gold for exportation, either to draw it from the deposits, that is, to subtract it from the already insufficient loanable capital of the country, or to become themselves competitors for a portion of that inadequate fund, thus still further raising the rate of interest? The only necessity was created by the Act of 1844, which would not suffer the Bank to meet this extra demand of credit by lending its notes, not even the notes returned to it in exchange for gold. The crisis of 1847 was of that sort which the provisions of the Act had not the smallest tendency

---

127 On this matter cf. 679–81; also the paper of 1844, IV, 359–60; the evidence of 1857, V, 503–4, 507–8, 518, 524–5, 528–9; and the evidence of 1867, V, 607.

128 'To make the Act innocuous, therefore, it would be necessary that the Bank, in addition to the whole of the gold in the Issue Department, should retain as great a reserve in gold or notes in the Banking Department alone, as would suffice under the old system for the security both of the issues and of the deposits.'

to avert; and when the crisis came, the mercantile difficulties were probably doubled by its existence (678–9n).[129]

Flexibility was required also during periods of crisis. That notes should conform to the metallic standard as far as concerned its 'permanent' value was not in question; Mill and the banking school denied only that they should conform to *fluctuations* in the value of the metallic currency and, therefore, be required to vary in quantity in conformity with all the variations that would have occurred if metal alone circulated. For 'the fluctuations in the value of the currency are determined, not by its quantity, whether it consist of gold or of paper, but by the expansions and contractions of credit'; and a paper currency fluctuating in quantity according to the 1844 rules, in fact generated 'more violent revulsions of credit than one which is not held to this rigid conformity' and, therefore, *destabilized* the value of the currency (667).[130]

In taking this position Mill had in mind pre-eminently the desirability for an active role on the part of the Bank of England *during depression*, a role sufficiently important to outweigh even the disadvantages of too free a hand at the peak of the cycle (and notwithstanding the allowances made for the 'ultimate aggravation' of the 'recoil' itself by such freedom):

In the first place, a large extension of credit by bankers, though most hurtful when, credit being already in an inflated state, it can only serve to retard and aggravate

129 Cf. evidence of 1857, V, 522: '*Have not almost all the great drains in this country, the drain in 1847, the drain in 1849, the drain in 1839, and the drain in 1836 all been, if not entirely, in a great measure caused by over-speculation previously occurring?* That can hardly be said, I think, in the case of the drain of 1847, because the over-speculation which there had been at that time was principally in railway shares, which had very little tendency to produce a drain.'
    The 1863–4 crisis in France was also said to involve a 'drain' for reasons of a non-speculative order – including the high prices of cotton imports, and an immense demand for foreign capital (cf. evidence of 1867, V, 601). A high interest rate as a feature of the crisis is alluded to in that context (603, 607).

130 Cf. V, 544: 'It does not follow, because we ought to make the permanent value of the paper currency conform to the value of a metallic currency, that therefore we ought to have the same fluctuations which occur in the value of a metallic currency. The fluctuations to which the value of a convertible currency is subject, depend not upon anything that affects either the metals or the bank notes, but upon general extensions or contractions of credit. The currency which is the least liable to violent contractions of credit, will be the currency with the fewest fluctuations. Therefore, if a convertible paper currency, issued by bankers and not restricted by Act of Parliament, is likely to lead to fewer variations in credit than a metallic currency, it appears to me better than a metallic currency, and better than a paper currency which is obliged to conform to a metallic currency.' See also evidence of 1857, V, 543: 'in a system of credit like what we have in this country, you may have a very much more steady currency than a purely metallic currency would be'.

the collapse, is most salutary when the collapse has come, and when credit instead of being in excess is in distressing deficiency, and increased advances by bankers, instead of being an addition to the ordinary amount of floating credit, serve to replace a mass of other credit which has been suddenly destroyed. Antecedently to 1844, if the Bank of England occasionally aggravated the severity of a commercial revulsion by rendering the collapse of credit more tardy and hence more violent than necessary, it in return rendered invaluable services during the revulsion itself, by coming forward with advances to support solvent firms, at a time when all other paper and almost all mercantile credit had become comparatively valueless. This service was eminently conspicuous in the crisis of 1825–6, the severest probably ever experienced; during which the Bank increased what is called its circulation by many millions, in advances to those mercantile firms of whose ultimate solvency it felt no doubt; advances which if it had been obliged to withhold, the severity of the crisis would have been still greater than it was. If the Bank, it is justly remarked by Mr. Fullarton, complies with such applications, 'it must comply with them by an issue of notes, for notes constitute the only instrumentality through which the Bank is in the practice of lending its credit' (670–1).[131]

Mill realized, of course, that the principles of 1844 allowed an expansion of notes when gold inflows occur, as they do when the general level of prices declines, but regarded such flows as occurring too late to prevent distress (672). It will be recalled (above, p. 546) that already in 1826 Mill had doubted the rapidity of the corrective process involving gold outflows, when speculative moods are of an international order. It seems then that the same principle was now being extended to the depression stage.[132]

Here it is essential to note Mill's insistence (always following Fullarton) that the expanded note issues in depression were still, in a crucial sense, 'passive'. This was so since they did not result in increased expenditures on commodities:

But those notes are not intended to circulate, nor do they circulate. There is no more demand for circulation than there was before. On the contrary, the rapid decline of prices which the case in supposition presumes, would necessarily contract the demand for circulation. The notes would either be returned to the Bank of England, as fast as they were issued, in the shape of deposits, or would be locked

131 Mill observes that the circumstances of 1847 'might have produced a destruction of credit equal to that of 1825, had not circumstances which may almost be called accidental, given to a very simple measure of the government' – the suspension of the Bank Charter Act – 'a fortunate power of allaying panic, to which, when considered in itself, it had no sort of claim' (544). The government had again been forced to suspend the provisions of the Act in 1857 and 1865 (660, 672).
132 But in that case Mill seems to have altered his position compared with various pre-1848 formulations.

up in the drawers of the private London bankers, or distributed by them to their correspondents in the country, or intercepted by other capitalists, who, during the fervour of the previous excitement, had contracted liabilities which they might be imperfectly prepared on the sudden to encounter. In such emergencies, every man connected with business, who has been trading on other means than his own, is placed on the defensive, and his whole object is to make himself as strong as possible, an object which cannot be more effectually answered than by keeping by him as large a reserve as possible in paper which the law has made a legal tender. The notes themselves never find their way into the produce market; and if they at all contribute to retard' (or, as I should rather say, to moderate) 'the fall of prices, it is not by promoting in the slightest degree the effective demand for commodities, not by enabling consumers to buy more largely for consumption, and so giving briskness to commerce, but by a process exactly the reverse, by enabling the holders of commodities to hold on, by obstructing traffic and repressing consumption' (671–2).[133]

The same point recurs in the evidence of 1857: 'in the case of an internal panic . . . there is no knowing how far the panic may reach; the longer it goes on the longer it is likely to go on, because panic creates panic. Any amount of issue of notes which the Bank could possibly make at such a time could not under any circumstances do any harm, because all that people would want them for would be to keep by them; they would never go into circulation' (V, 529). In the *absence* of intervention there must occur, in consequence of the high rate of discount, general deflation of prices upon forced commodity sales:

Does a high rate of discount necessarily accompany a low price of public securities or of commodities, generally speaking? Not necessarily a low price of commodities. It is possible that the prices of commodities might not vary; but in most cases the prices of

133 Cf. 516. Also regarding the nature of demand for money in crisis periods: 'His need is specifically for money, not for commodities or capital. It is the demand arising from this cause, which produces almost all the great and sudden variations of the rate of interest. Such a demand forms one of the earliest features of a commercial crisis. At such a period, many persons in business who have contracted engagements, have been prevented by a change of circumstances from obtaining in time the means on which they calculated for fulfilling them. These means they must obtain at any sacrifice, or submit to bankruptcy; and what they must have is money. Other capital, however much of it they may possess, cannot answer the purpose unless money can first be obtained for it; while, on the contrary, without any increase of the capital of the country, a mere increase of circulating instruments of credit (be they of as little worth for any other purpose as the box of one pound notes discovered in the vaults of the Bank of England during the panic of 1825) will effectually serve their turn if only they are allowed to make use of it. An increased issue of notes, in the form of loans, is all that is required to satisfy the demand, and put an end to the accompanying panic' (654–5).

commodities are ultimately affected. When the low price of securities is owing to commercial difficulties, if those commercial difficulties continue, and there is great difficulty in raising money by discount or otherwise for temporary exigencies, the natural effect is to lower the prices of commodities, because the holders of goods, being unable to get money in any other way, are obliged to sell at a forced reduction of price (526).[134]

Mill's denial that a correction of excess commodity supply can be achieved by monetary means therefore applies in the limited sense that there is no positive increase in purchases. But expansion of notes is seen to have the effect of checking forced sales and to this extent does alleviate the excess. Any 'passivity' of the note issue in this context turns out to be rather a formal matter.

* * *

As we know Mill conceded that the 1844 Act had the desirable consequence of enforcing some restraint on the Bank in reducing its note issues at or near the turning point of a 'speculative rise in prices' thereby allowing prices to decline and the gold drain (typical of such periods) to ease. His insistence that the Bank avoid such constraint where gold outflows originate in non-monetary circumstances implies the allowance of a degree of discretion to the Bank authority in distinguishing different categories of drain. Clearly in Mill's estimate the legitimate degree of restraint dictated by the Act would in practice be applied even without legislation. (On this issue see below, p. 587f.)

The constraint required of the Bank at the upper turning point, where speculation is involved, would avoid delaying the downturn, thus 'mitigating its intensity' (III, 669). But the Bank also had a positive responsibility to alleviate the crisis when it occurred though it was the (inevitable) outcome of a preceding speculation. What was appropriate at one period of the cycle was totally inappropriate at another – the different reactions required to the same end of dampening the fluctuations. Again, discretion is of the essence. Mill indeed found Adam Smith at fault for neglecting the emergency borrowing requirements of generally 'prosperous mercantile firms' during periods of 'commercial difficulty' by his famous assertion that only 'prodigals

---

134 Mill's observation in his evidence of 1867 that credit rationing was even more harsh than interest rate increases should also be borne in mind: 'le refus de la Banque d'escompter et la limitation des bordereaux seraient infiniment plus graves pour le commerce, en temps de crise, que la hausse la plus extrême de l'intérêt. Dans celle-ci, il ne s'agit que de payer très-cher pendant quelques semaines le secours dont on a besoin; mais l'impossibilité d'obtenir un secours suffisant pourrait entraîner la faillite' (V, 610).

and projectors' ever want to borrow at a rate of interest above the standard market rate (925).

There is little here to suggest that hesitancy to countenance an anti-cyclical monetary policy which, it is sometimes said, characterizes Mill's position. To reject monetary unorthodoxy of the Attwood variety as an invitation to secular disaster – involving as it does an inconvertible currency – in no way implied a denial that cyclical instability could be assuaged by monetary means while yet retaining convertibility (itself to be defended by the maintenance of adequate reserves).[135]

It had been Henry Thornton's position that a credit system required central bank management which could not be reduced to a matter of mechanical rules. And, as Sir John Hicks has recognized, Mill was on 'the same side as Thornton; he believes in monetary management' (1967, 166). Hicks, however, sees a lesser concern on Mill's part with the prevention of slumps. To attribute this to a lack of social conscience would, he argues, be unconvincing; it reflected rather the view that checking the boom – avoiding over-expansion of credit – the disorganization caused by the crisis would be prevented and also the slump that emerges from such disorganization. Now this is true. But it is not the whole truth. For it neglects Mill's very positive insistence upon credit expansion by the Bank of England during periods of depression to help satisfy the increased liquidity preference of those periods.

There is another matter that requires reiteration. It has been asserted that 'Mill could hardly have neglected the problems of unemployment during the cycle so easily but for the fact that the revulsion is quickly followed by a state of affairs characterized by full employment. Apparently the economic system tended to spring back rapidly to full employment, rapidly enough as a rule to make the problem of cyclical unemployment unimportant' (Link, 1959, 177).[136] But Mill did not neglect the unemployment and excess capacity of the revulsion period;[137] the 'painful' character of the contemporary 'commercial crisis' (Mill, 660) obviously

---

135 Cf. Schwartz's (1972) reference to Mill on 'the advantage of a convertible paper currency over a purely metallic currency in a crisis, when a timely issue could prevent many unjustified bankruptcies' (37); and Mill's rejection of the 'recommendation of any cure for social evils based on the manipulation of the monetary system' (41).

136 Cf. *ibid.*, 168: 'The elimination or mitigation of the commercial cycle was not a leading problem for Mill'; *ibid.*, 69: 'Commercial revulsion . . . was clearly undesirable. But here the problem appeared relatively unimportant because such periods were probably short, merging quickly into the quiescent state. Thus, whatever, the drawbacks of revulsion, they were not a serious social problem'; and *ibid.*, 179: 'Mill's conception of the cycle is probably a leading reason for his neglect of depression as a social problem . . . the belief that depression was very brief and that the normal state of affairs was a state of full employment was certainly most important.'

137 e.g., above pp. 392–3, 520, 549.

referred to more than price movements. And while there were forces at work generating the ultimate recovery of expenditures and thus the correction of the excess demand for money (above, p. 505) it is also the case that Mill did not wish to rely upon them alone, and accordingly ascribed a positive role to the monetary authorities.[138]

* * *

What is the source of the view attributing to Mill a denial of an active monetary policy? There are a number of possible explanations in addition to the erroneous deductions drawn from Mill's hostility towards inflationary proposals of the Attwood variety.

The formal insistence upon the passivity of the note issue is partly responsible: 'The existence of money . . . in Mill's view enabled hoarding to take place and a certain deferment in the sale of commodities; but since money supply was conceived as a passive variable, there was nothing to guarantee that an active monetary policy would restore the sway of Say's law' (Schwartz, 1972, 39). But we have seen that while an injection of credit in depression is said (following Fullarton) not to generate increased outlays on commodities, it does have the effect of checking forced sales of commodities. This is a highly qualified form of 'passivity'. We have seen too a variety of other concessions on Mill's part regarding an active role of note issues in generating price movements near the upper turning point.

It is also certainly true that Mill did not countenance counter-cyclical variation in public expenditure; as we have seen in Chapter 6, various proposals for increased public expenditure were made with an eye to secular trends. Yet any prevention of the downward trend of the profit rate, as might be achieved by increased unproductive outlays, would act indirectly to check speculation and dampen fluctuations. (And there was no modification of position, compared with 1826, despite the assertion then that the ultimate 'cause' of the commercial crisis – speculation rather than monetary expansion – was one 'which legislation cannot reach', namely the 'universal propensity of mankind to over-estimate the chances in their own favour'; above, p. 550).[139] But in any event, rejection of government

138 From our discussion it will be clear that Mill had in mind largely open-market operations. For a discussion of contemporary debate regarding Bank Rate as such see Cramp (1962).

139 Mill in the *Principles* did not envisage the total eradication of cyclical movements by monetary means. The underlying problem was a psychological one – albeit amenable to influence – and to this view he continued to adhere. Conversely, even in 1826, Mill had recognized that institutional reform might assuage the problem. Abolition of the Corn Laws, for example, would reduce one of the 'causes' of speculation by checking the fall in profits (above, p. 497).

spending of a cyclical variety must not be mistaken for a rejection of monetary intervention.[140]

Mill's paper of 1844 must also surely have misled readers. For its conclusion is phrased in a manner so forceful, as to suggest the preclusion of any socially desirable function for the bank managers. It can only be surmised that the strong formulation reflects the purpose of the moment which was specifically to reject the currency school rules regarding the note issue. To this must be added the striking fact that while the Bank of England was to remain a private company, Mill did not address himself in any concerted fashion to the precautions required to assure the authority carried out its social obligation. To this issue we turn next.

VII ON THE CONTROL OF CENTRAL BANKING

It is allowed in the *Principles* that while notes were quantitatively of lesser importance than other forms of credit yet an exclusive privilege of issue would be the source of great profit, which 'should be obtained for the nation at large' (*CW*, III, 683).[141] Were a gold-certificate system of notes to be instituted the bank of issue might indeed be the national bank: 'if the management of a bank-note currency ought to be so completely mechanical, so entirely a thing of fixed rule, as it is made by the Act of 1844, there seems no reason why this mechanism should be worked for the profit of any private issuer rather than for the public treasury'. But this was not so if discretionary policy was allowed:

If, however, a plan be preferred which leaves the variations in the amount of issues in any degree whatever to the discretion of the issuers, it is not desirable that to the ever-growing attributions of the Government, so delicate a function should be superadded; and that the attention of the heads of the state should be diverted from larger objects, by their being besieged with the applications, and made a mark for all the attacks, which are never spared to those deemed to be responsible for any acts, however minute, connected with the regulation of the currency. It would be

---

140 This writer has found but one favourable reference by Mill to public works. It occurs tangentially during the discussion in the first two editions of the *Principles* of Government expenditures in Ireland: 'The millions lavished during the famine in the almost nominal execution of useless works, without any result but that of keeping the people alive, would, if employed in a great operation on the waste lands, have been quite as effectual for relieving immediate distress, and would have laid the foundation broad and deep for something really deserving the name of social improvement' (III, 1000). These remarks, however, evidently refer to a special case. Mill's objections to public works but allowance for monetary intervention in depression are very nicely put in the paper of 1826 (IV, 120, cited above, pp. 553–4).

141 Ricardo, of course, proposed his 'National Bank' for the purpose of capturing the profits of note issue for the public (*Works*, IV, 271f).

better that treasury notes, exchangeable for gold on demand, should be issued to a fixed amount, not exceeding the minimum of a bank-note currency; the remainder of the notes which may be required being left to be supplied either by one or by a number of private banking establishments. Or an establishment like the Bank of England might supply the whole country, on condition of lending fifteen or twenty millions of its notes to the government without interest; which would give the same pecuniary advantage to the state as if it issued that number of its own notes.

As we know Mill emphasized the need for discretion on the part of the note-issuing authority, involving restraint on note issues in the case of gold drains reflecting inflationary or speculative price increases but not in response to other drains; and to increased issues (independently of gold inflows) to satisfy the excess demand for liquidity in periods of revulsion. Mill's unwillingness to countenance a government bank of issue clearly then does not reflect the 'unimportance of money'. It was rather his wish to protect the institution of government from the odium that inevitably attaches to the exercise of so 'delicate a function' as discretionary note issue entailing contact with individual borrowers.

It is essential to appreciate what regulations, if any, were to be imposed on a private company to assure that it fulfilled its discretionary functions. Mill's evidence given in 1857 before the Parliamentary Committee on the Act of 1844 is particularly pertinent to this matter.

The opposition to a government bank of issue is reiterated, as well the desirability of tapping the profits of the private authority for the public:

As far as the management and control of the circulation itself is concerned, you think that would be as well left in private hands? Yes. I would add, that if it were thought that there should be only one bank of issue, I do not think that bank of issue should be the Government itself. I think the currency should not be provided by the Government, but by such an establishment as the Bank of England, the public making a bargain with it for so much of the profit as they thought they could reasonably require (V, 510–11).

Here too the social obligation of the Bank of England – its counter-cyclical role – is repeatedly emphasized with particular reference to the need to maintain reserves exceeding on average those required by ordinary business calculation, for 'an establishment like the Bank is not like other bankers', and has a responsibility 'to prevent or to mitigate a commercial crisis' (507).[142] In the interest of stability it was desirable to insulate the internal

142 Cf. Pigou (1936) regarding the correction of 'disharmonies' of various orders: 'The interest of the community as a whole . . . requires the banks to restrict credit more in good times and to expand it more in bad times than bank shareholders, looking to their private profit, desire' (123). It is not clear whether Pigou was aware of Mill's early formulations of this proposition.

note circulation from changes in the external position at least in some circumstances, while the legislation of 1844 had actually exacerbated cyclical fluctuations by obliging the bank to contract credit in response to any and every gold drain no matter what the cause. More specifically:

The occasions on which the operation of the Act seems to me to be decidedly mischievous, are those cases of drain which do not arise from previous over speculation; such as those arising from a great import of corn, or a greatly increased price of raw materials of manufacture, such as cotton, or great foreign remittances by the government, or exportations of capital (508–9).

There is a distinction to be drawn between two kinds of drains. One may be called an unlimited, another a limited drain. A drain occasioned by a revulsion from a state of over-speculation is in its nature unlimited; unless there be something done to stop it, it will go on. If the high state of prices, occasioned by an inflated state of credit, continues, the drain will continue; and it can only be stopped when the high prices have ceased by a diminution of the currency, or a diminution of loans. But the case is different with all other drains; for instance, a drain occasioned by payments for the import of corn, or by foreign payments by Government, or the exportation of capital for foreign investment. That drain stops of itself as soon as the purpose is effected which caused it; and, therefore, it seems to me that the reserve should always be such as may be equal to the probable demand on account of a drain of this sort; and that in the case of such a drain, bullion may be allowed to run out from the reserve, without any violent action on credit to stop it. For that reason it seems to me necessary now, when drains to a large amount are liable to arise from causes of that sort, that the Bank should keep habitually a much larger reserve than it used to keep, in order to meet a drain (513–14).

In evidence given before the French banking committee of 1867 the distinction between the two kinds of drain is reiterated, with a forcefully expressed insistence on the obligation to contract note issues where the external drain is generated by excessive speculation (602–4, 607).

Also objectionable was the encouragement given to speculation by increased lending at low interest at a time when the reserves were growing but in consequence of circumstances likely to be reversed:

Previously to 1844 the Bank never lowered their rate of discount below 4 per cent., but you are aware that the Bank when they had large amounts of money at their disposal made use of it, and were consequently obliged to employ it at the current rates of interest? Yes, they have I know been charged with having almost caused some commercial crises, by the use they have made of their large funds at certain periods of speculation and of consequent revulsion: I mean by the use which they made of extraordinary public deposits which they had for a time.

You think that at a time when the Bank of England has large deposits in its hands, and when the current rate of interest is from any causes below 4 per cent., it is not expedient for the Bank to enter into competition in the money market, or to employ that money at all? I would not lay down any general rule, but I think they are bound not to do it without great consideration of the circumstances; that is to say, not without considering whether there is likely to be a demand on their reserve; in fact, whether their superfluity of reserve is likely to last.

You think that in those particular times they ought to depart from such principles of actions as would guide any ordinary banking establishment? I think so, because a private banker may fairly think that his operations cannot produce any great effect upon the general circumstances of the money market, and that, therefore, it is enough if he considers himself (537–8).

And thirdly, the responsibility to expand note issue independently of any expansion of the reserves during depression was thwarted by the legislation of 1844:

[I]f in the first stage of this process the Act operates usefully, it operates exceedingly injuriously in the latter stage; that is to say, when the revulsion has actually come, and when, instead of there being an inflated state of credit, there has been an extraordinary destruction of credit, and there is nothing like the usual amount of credit that there is at other times. At such a time the Bank can hardly lend too much; it can hardly make advances to too great an extent, as long as it is to solvent firms, because its advances only supply the place of the ordinary and wholesome amount of credit, which is then in deficiency. But the Bank, under the operation of the Act, can only make those advances at such a time from their deposits. Now it is very true that the deposits are likely to be large at those times, because at those times people leave their money in deposit; they leave it within call, to be able to have it at any moment when they want it, and therefore the Bank deposits are larger than usual. But still this resource is not sufficient, as was proved in 1847, when the Bank Directors, after doing the very utmost which they could do from their deposits to relieve the distressed state of trade by advances to solvent firms, were obliged to go to the Government to ask for a suspension of the Act, and the Government were obliged to grant it (506).

I am supposing the case of a drain in consequence of over speculation; in that case I understood you to say that the advantage of the system of unrestricted issue which you advocated, would be this; that when a panic did come after periods of over speculation, the Bank then would be able to use its whole reserve, consisting of the bullion that is now in its banking department, and so much of the bullion as is now in the issue department, as it would keep under such circumstances; and that it would therefore have a larger fund to draw upon to sustain credit than it has now? I would state it even more strongly; because in the case you are supposing, which is not a case where there is any doubt about the convertibility of the Bank note, the Bank might issue notes to any extent they were asked for, as they did after 1825.

You admit that there might be a very great extension of its issues under those circumstances? I think there ought to be in those circumstances, because there is such a destruction of ordinary credit, that it is necessary that some credit should come in to take the place of what is destroyed, in order to prevent great calamities.

Such extension of issues would increase the total amount of circulation much beyond what it would be, if it were a purely metallic currency? Very much beyond. That is a great advantage, because one of the great inconveniences of a metallic currency is, that it is impossible for it to come to the assistance of a drain in those emergencies. *You do not agree with Mr. Tooke in thinking that a mixed circulation of convertible paper must fluctuate always as a metallic currency?* I am not aware that Mr. Tooke thinks that it must fluctuate in quantity as a metallic currency would; I think it is a great advantage of our currency, as it would be without the Act, that it does not fluctuate exactly as a metallic currency would (544–5).

Having in mind these very clearly formulated statements of central bank responsibility for stabilizing cyclical fluctuations by discretionary discounting independently of external gold movements we turn to the manner of assuring its achievement. First, we note Mill's rejection of formal regulation – apart from convertibility itself – even concerning the magnitude of the reserves:

In the first place, what is your opinion as to the policy of imposing by law any restriction upon the Directors of the Bank of England with respect to the issue of notes? My opinion is that there should not be any restriction by law, except that of convertibility, which appears to me to be sufficient for all the purposes for which restriction is intended. *Are you aware of the nature of the limit which Mr. Tooke has proposed in his book with respect to the bullion reserve of the Bank?* Mr. Tooke, I believe, proposes what cannot possibly be imposed by law, namely, a limit which should consist in the Bank's retaining a much larger average reserve than it has hitherto done, an average reserve of 12,000,000 *l*. Public opinion might enforce a restriction of that sort, but it is incapable in its terms of being enforced by law (501).

At most there would be *a sort of understanding that the capital of the Bank should vary from 10,000,000 l. to 12,000,000 l. on the average*' (513). And in the context of a recommendation to restrain discounts in speculative periods even when a gold inflow might suggest the desirability of expanding issues we see Mill's wish to avoid the imposition of 'any general rules':

Would it not be rather difficult for the Bank Directors to foresee what may happen two or three months hence? Do you think that the Bank, having a large amount of money which had been paid in from taxation, ought to be prevented from circulating it among the public because the rate of interest was not 4 per cent? Do you think that that would be a wise, a wholesome action on the part of the Bank Directors? I should think that it would be necessary that they should consider a great many circumstances in order to decide that. I do not think any general rule can be laid down.

But without laying down a general rule, do you not think there are many cases which would justify the Bank in lending out money at the current rate of interest? I think they are bound to consider well the disadvantage which would be occasioned, at a time when there was a low rate of interest, by lending a very large sum of money in addition to what had been lent before, which would tend to encourage speculation, and whether that would be a greater evil than leaving a portion of their deposits for a time in their coffers (538).[143]

Mill's position turns in part upon a belief that the rules of 1844 had themselves had a destabilizing effect by instituting the separation of the banking and issue departments thereby precluding mutual relief and diminishing the efficacy of any given volume of reserves (e.g. 503, 504, 507–8, 518, 528–9).

Quite apart from this particular defect of the law, however, and allowing for the recognition that the Act of 1844 had the desirable feature of curbing credit expansion in late phases of the speculative period, there was still no need for formal rules since the appropriate policy could be achieved in their absence: 'I do not think that this mode of operation is so much required now as it perhaps was at one time, because the commercial public generally, and the Bank Directors, understand much better than they did the nature of a commercial crisis, and the extreme mischief which they do both to themselves and to the public by upholding over speculation, and I do not think that they at all need the provisions of the Act in order to induce them in that case to conduct themselves as the Act would make them' (506). Thus legislation was not required to achieve monetary constraint, where appropriate, assuming a competent and socially conscious directorship – an assumption justified by growing experience, and public awareness of 'the necessity of checking speculation':

I understand you to say that you would recommend the Committee to return to the provisions of the law as it was before 1844, only with some understanding as to the amount of the reserve that the Bank should keep? That would be my idea. Although, as I have already stated, I think in the commencement of a revulsion from a state of over speculation the Act at times has operated beneficially, yet I am of opinion that with the experience that we now have, and the principles on which the Bank of England is likely to continue to act, even if the Act were repealed the Directors would probably do spontaneously, in that particular case, what the Act now compels them to do; that is, they would not reissue notes sent back to them in exchange for bullion (514).

143 But see Mill's qualifications (602, 513) below (p. 585).

Therefore the Act of 1844 has really no merit, inasmuch as this one beneficial action which you ascribe to it, might and ought to follow from the intelligence and discretion of the Directors? At the same time I must say, that I am not aware that the Directors have ever been in intelligence of commercial affairs behind the commercial public generally. I think they have always had quite as enlightened views as the bulk of the public had. They have not always had the best views. They had not in the time of the Bank restriction; but then neither had the public. They had improved views quite as soon as the public. When Sir Robert Peel found that the Bank of England had not been observing the requisite caution in checking speculation in its commencement, he might very naturally think that it would be beneficial to compel them to do so. But whether compulsion was required or not at that time, I think that the effect has now been produced. The feeling of the public is now even of an exaggerated kind on the subject of the necessity of checking speculation. The alarm is sounded very early, sometimes earlier than is necessary; and I do not think it is to be apprehended that, under the present constitution, the Bank of England is ever likely to be less alive than the commercial world in general are to that object, so as to require the restraint of the Act.

Therefore you would not recommend the continuance of this Act of 1844 in order to accomplish that beneficial action, which you say it may have produced in certain cases, but which you believe would be effected without the Act by the spontaneous action of the Bank Direction, with the improved intelligence and the experience that they now possess? Decidedly. I think that the degree of enlightenment of the Bank Directors has been constantly progressive; that they have advanced with the public, and are likely still to do so. I think they are now kept back more by the false theory upon which this Act rests, than by anything else; and that they would act in a more judicious way than the Act prescribes, if they had larger discretion entrusted to them (530–31).[144]

It is worth noting Mill's belief that the legislation of 1844 had itself been responsible for encouraging a less than responsible attitude on the part of the Bank directors, the experience of 1847 acting as a corrective, albeit partial only because of the unnecessary complications introduced by the separation of the departments:

Is it your opinion that the measures of the Bank, during the last two years with respect to high rate of discount and the duration of bills, have been more restrictive than was judicious? I think the Bank has acted on the principle which was laid down for them by great

---

144 Mill was, in fact, optimistic regarding the need to maintain adequate reserves: 'I think the tendency of the opinion of competent persons of late years has been in favour of the necessity of keeping a much larger reserve than was formerly thought necessary; and the circumstances of trade have really required a larger amount of reserve, because the great increase in the magnitude of transactions, and particularly the unexampled drains of bullion which have occurred, have rendered it necessary to keep a larger reserve in order to meet those drains' (503).

authorities at the time when the Act of 1844 was passed, viz., that in the management of their banking department they had nothing whatever to consider but their interest as a bank. I think they have taken that view of their position. They have thought, therefore, that they were not under the necessity of keeping a much larger reserve than ordinary banking principles required. I think they at first began, after the Act of 1844, to act entirely upon that principle; they took the word of Sir Robert Peel, the author of the Act, anything they did as mere bankers, in the management of their deposits, was no concern of the public, but only their own concern. I think that in 1847 that error was, to a great degree, corrected. I think that since that time the Bank have been quite aware, and the public have been aware, that that view of the theory of the Act of 1844 is not sustainable; and that an establishment like the Bank is not like other bankers, who are at liberty to think that their single transactions cannot affect the commercial world generally, and that they have only their own position to consider. The transactions of the Bank necessarily affect the whole transactions of the country, and it is incumbent upon them to do all that a bank can do to prevent or to mitigate a commercial crisis. This being the position of the Bank, and the Bank being much more aware of it since 1847 than they were before, they have not acted so entirely as before on the principle that they had nothing to consider but their own safety. Still, however, as bankers, they have not kept in the banking department the whole reserve necessary to meet a drain, and being obliged, as bankers, to consider the solvency of their banking department, they have been obliged to vary their rates of discount more violently and more frequently than they did before; which, I think, is owing to the Act (507).

And more generally the philosophy behind the Act had exerted an unfortunate influence:

At certain times the Bank of England raises its rate of interest in order to maintain its reserve of notes; and in that case you think the operation of the Act of 1844 has tended to increase the rate of interest charged at certain times? Yes.

Do you think it has had the effect of lowering the rate of interest at other times? It has had that effect in point of fact, but I am not sure that it is fair to charge it upon the Act, because it is rather the effect of the doctrines put forth by the supporters of the Act than of the Act itself. When the Act was introduced, the language usually held by its supporters was, that the Bank in the management of its deposits was no more bound to consider the public interest than any other bank, and that it was to regulate its conduct with a view solely to its own safety; and so far as the Bank have acted upon that opinion, they have no doubt been led by it, not only to contract their discounts when they otherwise might not have been obliged to do so, but also to extend them at periods when probably otherwise they would not have done so; because seeing that they were at liberty, like other bankers, to lend their money to any extent that they thought prudent for their own interest, at the market rate, that they have lent money at less than 4 per cent., and upon some occasions at as little as 2 per cent. But that is not a necessary effect of the Act. The Act does not oblige them to do that, and the Bank may, if they please, abandon the doctrine that they are at liberty to act in the same way as other bankers; and seeing that such a body as the Bank must, in the management of its ordinary banking business, produce so great an effect upon the public interest, they may come to the conclusion that they are bound to consider that, and therefore ought not to lend below 4 per cent. or some such rate.

Then so far as the lowering the rate of interest is concerned, that has been the effect of the course taken by the Bank Directors, rather than any effect produced by the Act itself? I think it is more the effect of the mistaken grounds upon which the Act was first defended, and which have been partly abandoned by its defenders, than any effect of the Act itself (520).[145]

From this perspective, the repeal or modification of the legislation of 1844 would itself be an encouragement to responsible bank policy as Mill saw it.

Mill's two-fold presumption of an ability on the part of the Bank to distinguish between different categories of drain, and a willingness to react differentially even in the absence of legislative rules is reiterated frequently, for the examiners pressed him over and again on precisely these features of his position:

That seems to involve a sort of foreknowledge on the part of the Bank as to how long a drain is to continue; but, with knowing that, surely they must exercise some power of controlling it? Of course they have that power; and they may in any case be obliged at last to contract their discounts; but if they have a large reserve, and if, from the circumstances of the times, and from the knowledge which they have, and which the public have, of the causes producing the drain, they think that the drain that is existing is of the one kind, and not of the other, they will act accordingly. If they find that the drain exceeds their provision for it, notwithstanding their having kept so large a reserve, then they must take measures to replenish their reserve; but the effect of this would only be, that they would be then obliged to bring on the public in a smaller degree, and at a later period, inconveniences which, under the present system, they must bring on at once, and much more frequently, and in a much greater degree (514).

Do you think that the Bank can, with sufficient certainty, distinguish between the separate causes of drain, so as to be able to pursue a different course according to the cause which, in their

---

145 Cf. also the French evidence of 1867: 'Il est impossible de prévenir les variations du taux de l'intérêt, et par conséquent de l'escompte. Elles dépendent de l'offre et de la demande des capitaux disponibles. Il n'y a aucun moyen de les mitiger, mais on peut les aggraver, et c'est l'effet des règles restrictives comme celle de la loi anglaise de 1844' (610).

opinion, produces the drain? The causes are matters of public notoriety. Everybody knows whether there has been a bad harvest, or whether the price of cotton has risen in America to a great extent, and generally whether a considerable export of capital is taking place. Then, on the other side of the question, all persons who pay attention to commercial transactions know well when there has been an inflation of credit, and, great speculation going on in goods; therefore, I think, the Bank have very sufficient means of distinguishing between the causes of a drain. The only case in which there can be any difficulty is, when there are causes of both sorts operating; in which case it may be difficult to determine exactly how much of the effect is due to each; but still, even in such a case as that, a course of action founded upon the judgment that experienced men can form upon the subject, seems to me much better than deciding by a mechanical rule that is only applicable to the extreme of one case, and pernicious in every other (519).

I understood you to say, that after the experience we have had of the discretion of the Bank of England, you think it might be thoroughly trusted not to re-issue notes in cases when they might be called for to strengthen the banking department? Not to re-issue notes in cases in which the return of those notes upon their hands was the effect of previous over-speculation (522).

Rejection of full-fledged state control of central banking thus by no means implied a denial of a responsibility for counter-cyclical intervention on the part of the bank directors. The justification for an absence of formal control turned on a presumably 'capable' and 'experienced' management. As Mill summarized the matter in evidence of 1867: 'Une banque dirigée par des hommes capables, dès que sa réserve commence à s'en aller, trouvera dans sa connaissance des antécédents commerciaux le moyen de reconnaître les causes particulières qui ont produit l'écoulement; elle saura si le numéraire tend à sortir en quantité indéfinie ou seulement en quantité définie. Si l'on a laissé à cette banque sa pleine liberté d'action, c'est seulement dans le premier cas qu'elle se hâtera de protéger sa réserve, qu'elle aura eu soin de tenir normalement à un montant suffisant pour faire face, sans aucune mesure spéciale, à tout écoulement probable à limite définie' (604). What Mill's precise position would have been had his optimism (both regarding the expertise of private management in its discretionary obligations and its willingness to sacrifice its own interest for the public good) been proved unjustified it is impossible to say; but there is little reason to doubt that he would have modified his case in favour of private management. After all, Mill was open-minded on the issue of state intervention and if he had a particular bias against a state-run central bank it was partly to protect the reputation of the government by avoiding its day-to-day contact with borrowers (above, p. 584). Doubtless were private managers demonstrably inadequate to the discretionary task, civil servants might prove equally so;

on the other hand if the problem was an unwillingness to sacrifice private interest for the public good, a state bank of issue might prove necessary.[146]

Yet we are still faced by an apparent difficulty. We recall the sharp distinction by Tooke and his supporters between note issues, which they played down as an active destabilizing force, and credit extensions by way of variations in deposits:

[I]n considering the effect produced by the proceedings of banks in encouraging the excesses of speculation, an immense effect is usually attributed to their issues of notes, but until of late hardly any attention was paid to the management of their deposits; though nothing is more certain than that their imprudent extensions of credit take place more frequently by means of their deposits than of their issues. 'There is no doubt,' says Mr. Tooke [*Inquiry into the Currency Principle*, Ch. xiv, 88, 91], 'that banks, whether private or joint stock, may, if imprudently conducted, minister to an undue extension of credit for the purpose of speculations, whether in commodities, or in overtrading in exports or imports, or in building or mining operations, and that they have so ministered not unfrequently, and in some cases to an extent ruinous to themselves, and without ultimate benefit to the parties to whose views their resources were made subservient' (III, 657–8).

Now the Bank of England itself was taken to task:

In the discussions, too, which have been for so many years carried on respecting the operations of the Bank of England, and the effects produced by those operations on the state of credit, though for nearly half a century there never has been a commercial crisis which the Bank has not been strenuously accused either of producing or of aggravating, it has been almost universally assumed that the influence of its acts was felt only through the amount of its notes in circulation, and that if it could be prevented from exercising any discretion as to that one feature in its position, it would no longer have any power liable to abuse. This at least is an error which, after the experience of the year 1847, we may hope has been committed for the last time. During that year the hands of the bank were absolutely tied, in its character of a bank of issue; but through its operations as a bank of deposit it exercised as great an influence, or apparent influence, on the rate of interest and the state of credit, as at any former period; it was exposed to as vehement accusations of abusing that influence; and a crisis occurred, such as few that preceded it had equalled, and none perhaps surpassed, in intensity.

---

146 Cf. Henry Thornton's (1802) view that English bank directors were more responsible than their Continental counterparts since they were not government employees (105f, 109–10; but see 316, 348).

It is difficult to appreciate Mill's seeming confidence in the potential for responsible behaviour by private management considering this evaluation of its credit policies.

The experience of 1847 might have been seen as a lesson sharp enough to be remembered and acted upon. But there is also the fact that Mill had not yet reached a final conclusion on the matter of banking control. This becomes clear in his evidence of 1857 on the Bank Charter Act:

Would there be any advantage to a rule, which required the Bank to keep more than was necessary at certain times, because it had kept less than was desirable at other times? It is desirable, I think, that the Bank should keep a larger reserve than the average at some times as well as a smaller at others, in order to prevent the Bank, at times when there is a tendency to over-speculation, from encouraging that tendency by making loans at a lower rate of interest than the average rate. I am not prepared to say that I would impose on the Bank any compulsory rule in respect to the amount of the reserves. It might probably be better done by fixing a rate of interest below which they should not be permitted to lend. I am not giving an opinion in favour of any restriction, but if any were necessary, I think that would be the best restriction to impose (V, 502).

Here Mill indicates a preference for a minimum bank rate over a rule relating directly to the reserves,[147] but does not commit himself to the need for control of either kind. Subsequently he frankly states that he had not made up his mind on appropriate bank rate regulation:

Is it your opinion that the Bank should in any manner be limited to a minimum rate of discount according to the practice that existed before the passing of the Act of 1844? I think that since the Act of 1844, the Bank have lowered their rate of interest very unnecessarily and undesirably, at times when they might have foreseen that the low rate of interest would not last, that the then replenished state of their reserve which induced them to lower the rate of discount was only temporary, and that there would soon be a demand on their reserve again. I think the Bank has several times made that mistake. Whether it would be desirable to cut them off from ever lowering their rate of discount below a certain rate, is a question upon which I have not made up my mind (513).

You are not able to say whether or not they should be fettered in the discretion which an ordinary banker exercises of doing as he pleases with his own money and taking any rate of interest that he thinks fit? I think that the Bank, as being a great public body, exercising public

---

147 Cf. evidence of 1867: '*L'émission des billets doit-elle être limitée? Convient-il de proportionner l'émission à l'encaisse ou au capital?* Toute limitation de l'émission des billets, autre que la limite naturelle imposée par la convertibilité, me semble déplacée. Ce n'est pas l'émission qu'il faut proportionner à l'encaisse, mais bien l'encaisse à l'émission' (608).

functions, cannot in all respects be properly guided only by its banking interest. Whether it should be subject to restriction by law in this particular I do not know; but I think that it cannot rightly be governed by its pecuniary interest, in circumstances in which a private banker might reasonably be so; that the Directors ought not always, when the market rate of interest is temporarily low, to conform their rate to it, but rather to allow their reserve to accumulate at those times, in order not to minister to a spirit of speculation, which a low rate of interest does.[148]

There is also the matter of notes of small denomination. Whereas in 1826 Mill defended small notes on grounds of economy (IV, 104–5), by 1844 he stressed their disadvantage in allowing to paper a positive capacity to act on consumer expenditure and prices. This argument is reiterated in the *Principles*; and in 1857 a further disadvantage is cited:

Do you think that there would be any advantage in the issue of any denomination of notes under 5l., in England? I think it is much better that there should be no notes below 5l., because this retains a quantity of gold in the country which may be used to replenish the banking reserve in case of necessity, without waiting for the slower process of its importation. Besides, 1l. notes are liable to be used in the payment of wages, and a currency which is used in payment of wages is much more liable to produce evils from over issue, than any currency which is only issued to the mercantile public (V, 509–10).[149]

Mill played down the matter of the number of institutions of note issue: 'I do not think it is of very much consquence whether there is one bank of issue or many in the country. It seems to me quite a minor question; but inasmuch as there have always been many, and I believe the local feeling

---

148 It is noteworthy also that in 1867 the case against regulation of the discount rate (in this case a maximum with an eye to the regulation of bank profits) is said to be questionable but only on grounds of injustice – the injustice of treating some borrowers more favourably than others, and more favourably than the labouring class as a whole: '*Est-il possible d'imposer à une banque privilégiée un taux fixe d'escompte ou même un maximum?* Imposer à une banque privilégiée soit un taux fixe, soit un maximum du taux de l'escompte, pourrait être licite en droit, mais ne saurait, à mon avis, être utile a l'intérêt générale. Si l'état du marché des capitaux, en dehors de la Banque, determinait un taux d'intérêt au-dessus de ce maximum, alors, en défendant à la Banque de profiter de cette hausse, on ne ferait que créer un privilège en faveur de ceux dont on aurait fait escompter le papier à un taux exceptionnellement favorable. En supposant même, ce qui est difficile à concevoir, qu'on pût ménager un moyen de partager également ce bénéfice entre tous les commerçants, on ne voit pourtant pas pourquoi l'Etat s'occuperait de donner le capital aux commerçants au-dessous de sa valeur, plutôt que de donner le pain au-dessous de sa valeur aux classes laborieuses' (V, 610).

149 Cf. evidence of 1867: 'Les coupures ne devraient pas être assez petites pour passer communément entre les mains de personnes qui, par défaut d'éducation et d'expérience, seraient facilement portées aux paniques' (610–11).

is always in favour of having many, it probably is desirable that there should be' (509). The standard objection that plurality of institutions implied excessive note issue he rejected: 'we have seen that the power which bankers have of augmenting their issues, and the degree of mischief which they can produce by it, are quite trifling compared with the current over-estimate. As remarked by Mr. Fullarton, the extraordinary increase of banking competition occasioned by the establishment of the joint-stock banks, a competition often of the most reckless kind, has proved utterly powerless to enlarge the aggregate mass of the bank-note circulation; that aggregate circulation having, on the contrary, actually decreased' (III, 684). In 1865 he added that in 'the absence of any special case for an exception to freedom of industry, the general rule ought to prevail'.[150]

The basic principle that increased issues beyonds the needs of trade are not to be feared is applied to the matter of the country banks in the evidence of 1857: 'As far as excess of issues is concerned, I think there is no reason for any restriction' (V, 509), clarifying however the limitations of that proposition:

You said that you were in favour of allowing country banks, as well as the Bank of England, to issue notes without any other restriction than convertibility, or, at all events, that you saw no need of restriction from the fear of over-issues; will you state what you mean by 'over-issues,' because you have already told us that you admit that it is possible that issues of paper may be in excess of that which a metallic circulation would supply? By over-issues, I mean such as create undue speculation, or maintain it when it ought to be checked. In any other sense I do not conceive that there can be over-issues so long as convertibility is maintained.

Then your opinion is a theoretical opinion; it is not deduced from the fact that there have been no such issues? It is my interpretation of the facts that have taken place.

Do you remember the case of the American banks in 1835, when the issues rose from about 100,000,000l. to about 150,000,000l. in the course of one year? Yes, but I have always understood that there was not practical convertibility at that time.

They were legally convertible, were they not? The fact was, that either through the influence of the banks, or for some other reason, they were not convertible. In the next place, I admit that in a period of violent speculation, that speculation may be ministered to by banks; not that they do so in the commencement, at least not by means of their notes, but they may prevent speculation from being early checked by the necessity of re-selling goods that had been speculated upon (546–7).[151]

150 Country banks were championed as a convenience to customers (V, 534). Some required note issuing rights to survive: 'In some districts it is probable that a bank could not maintain itself by its deposits only, unless it had a profit on its issues also; and so far the inconvenience referred to in the question would certainly be produced, if there were only one bank of issue.'

151 Cf. 512 on 'over-issue'.

The full implications of the latter allowance for the general proposition Mill did not, unfortunately, spell out; and in 1867 he reiterated that a multiple system would operate exactly as a unitary one, any single bank finding it impossible by offering favourable terms to increase its issues at the expense of others:

Je crois qu'après quelques tâtonnements, et peut-être quelques excès temporaires dans l'usage d'une liberté nouvellement acquise, la circulation des billets se trouverait partagée entre un certain nombre d'établissements solides et prudents, qui se conduiraient collectivement à peu près comme la banque unique se conduit, et qu'on n'éprouverait ni les bienfaits ni les inconvénients auxquels on s'attend. Les banques ne manqueraient pas d'établir, selon l'usage de celles de l'Ecosse, un échange hebdomadaire, sinon journalier, de leurs billets respectifs. Il en arriverait qu'une banque qui chercherait à accaparer la circulation en donnant de plus grandes facilités de crédit que les autres, ne pourrait augmenter ses émissions que momentanément: elle verrait rentrer ses billets, présentés par les autres banques, en quantité supérieure aux billets de ces banques qu'elle-même aurait en caisse, et il lui faudrait liquider le surplus en numéraire. L'extension du crédit, que les uns appellent de leurs voeux et que les autres repoussent, n'aurait donc lieu que lorsqu'elle serait provoquée ou favorisée par des causes générales, agissant sur toutes les banques à la fois, et tendant à determiner une baisse générale de l'intérêt. Mais, toutes les fois que ces causes existent, elles exercent, comme on le voit toujours, une influence exactement pareille sur une banque unique. En fait, la hausse et la baisse de l'escompte auraient toujours lieu à peu près simultanément chez toutes les banques, et, selon toute probabilité, par un accord, au moins tacite, entre elles. Il n'y aurait donc, à mon avis, que très-peu de différence pratique entre les deux systèmes, une fois que les esprits et les habitudes s'y seraient accommodés (606–7).[152]

For all that some control was required. Thus the Bank of England alone would be required to pay in gold; the reserves of other banks would be Bank of England notes: 'The object of this is that there may be one body, responsible for maintaining a reserve of the precious metals sufficient to meet any drain that can reasonably be expected to take place. By disseminating this responsibility among a number of banks, it is prevented from operating efficaciously upon any: or if it be still enforced against one, the reserves of the metals retained by all the others are capital kept idle is pure waste, which may be dispensed with by allowing them at their option to pay in Bank of England notes' (III, 684). Secondly, there were restrictions to assure against bank insolvency. In the early editions of the *Principles* Mill

---

152 In the paper of 1844 Mill had observed that even the Bank Charter Act could be applied to a case of multiple issues (IV, 347).

maintained that guarantees against bank failures involved 'vexatious meddling', but in 1857 he modified this position pointing to instances of fraudulent joint-stock institutions. In his evidence of 1857 he reserved final judgement, pointing out that (despite instances of 'gross mismanagement and consequent insolvency of banks') 'as long as there are no notes in England below 5*l.*, the probability is that the holders of 5*l.* notes can as well take care of themselves as the depositors, who have generally been the greatest sufferers by those mismanagements' (V, 509). But in the French evidence a decade later he allowed for some insurance against insolvency:

Sur la nécessité absolue de la convertibilité constante et immédiate des billets, il n'y a plus de différence d'opinion parmi les hommes compétents. Elle me paraît la seule condition indispensable. Avec cette convertibilité suffisamment garantie, il n'y a pas de mauvais système de banques d'émission. La convertibilité serait évidemment illusoire si des billets pouvaient être émis par tout le monde. Même dans le système de la pluralité, il faudrait imposer la condition d'un capital considérable et de la publicité la plus complète. On pourrait en outre, et peut-être on devrait, éxiger un dépôt de rentes sur l'Etat, égal à la somme de tous les billets émis et destiné à leur servir de garantie spéciale (605).

VIII CONCLUDING NOTE

There is a paradoxical flavour to the story of Mill on money and banking. He counted himself amongst the strongest defenders of the gold standard, at no time wavering in this position. In this, of course, he was like other banking school adherents totally at one with the currency school – a unanimity of opinion on policy that has been termed 'one of the most remarkable facets of nineteenth century British economic doctrine' (Laidler, 1972, 169). Moreover, his dismissal of the currency school's concern with excess note issue under convertibility applied only to periods of 'quiescence', for he emphasized an 'active' impact of note issues at late speculative stages of the cycle, considering the internationalization of speculative moods and the consequential weakening of the significance of reflux. There was much then about which Mill agreed with the currency school. Indeed, notwithstanding his extremely high regard for Tooke,[153] he was in some respects closer to Loyd (Lord Overstone), for while Overstone took the

153 Cf. 20 March, 1858, *CW*, XV, 551: 'Few persons have rendered greater services to Political Economy & its applications than Mr. Tooke, & the value of what he has done is likely to be rated more & more highly as the subject is better understood & as the ephemeral controversies of the present time die away.' Also 21 Sept. 1840, XIII, 444: 'I have been much pressed to write on the Report (or rather Minutes of Evidence) of the Committee on Currency & Banks – especially by Mr. Tooke with whom I agree on the subject more than with anybody else who has written on it . . .'

position that ' "fluctuations in the amount of the currency are seldom, if ever, the original and exciting cause of fluctuations in prices and the state of trade" [he] always maintained, what Tooke gradually tended to lose sight of, that "the management of the currency . . . may and often does exert a considerable influence in restraining or augmenting the violence of commercial oscillations" ' (cited in Gregory, 1928, 20n).[154] On the other hand, notes could not, Mill insisted, be treated as gold certificates as the formulators of the Act of 1844 would have it; judgement was called for since, where gold drains were underway but unrelated to speculative price increases, limitations of issue must be avoided to prevent generating unnecessary deflationary pressure. It is this call for a discretionary insulation of the internal circulation from changes in the external position that appears so self-contradictory from the perspective of a champion of convertibility – and convertibility without allowance for periodic devaluation. To this must be added the further insistence upon expanded issues during depression to satisfy the demand for liquidity and prevent forced sales – a very nice example of an 'active' monetary policy.

Mill may be said to have drawn widely from a variety of sources, as is usual for him, which allowed for a somewhat greater degree of intervention than that of Tooke. The precise extent and nature of Mill's independence, of course, depends in large part on the interpretation one makes of Tooke, and this is no easy matter. Laidler in his first-rate account recognizes Tooke's allowances for discretionary bank policy, particularly the insistence on adequate reserves to allow the Bank to finance temporary external drains and avoid domestic deflation; having in mind that the major sources of external drain are of a purely commercial nature (such as poor harvests) and, even when of a monetary nature, are unrelated to preceding note expansion – involving rather increase in bank deposit business and in private credit as part of a speculative upswing (Laidler, 1972, 170–1, 179). Laidler shows further that while, for Tooke, control of notes was inadequate – indeed the supply of notes was beyond the *direct* control of the banking system hinging as it did on the demand by the public for notes to hold in place of other money forms – he was none the less 'willing to admit that the volume of bank advances could affect the level of economic activity, and hence the volume of notes in circulation' (173; cf. 181, 183). Similarly, Tooke's lack of a theory connecting bank advances with bank liabilities – his failure (in line with most of his contemporaries except Joplin and Pennington) to

154 Cf. Gregory (1928), 81: Tooke had long insisted that changes in the level of prices *cause* changes in the amount of circulation rather than the reverse but had originally allowed that the increased issues sustain the rise in prices. And this he came to deny in 1840. (On the dating of Tooke's position in this and other respects see the criticisms of Gregory by Arnon 1984. Arnon insists on a transitional period beginning in 1838 and culminating finally in the *Inquiry* of 1844.)

appreciate the idea of multiple credit creation – did not preclude him, as some commentators have believed, 'from having a monetary theory of the determination of the level of economic activity' (177n; also 174–6, 183, 184n). In particular, a short-run impact of the banking system on the price level and the level of aggregate demand was allowed, acting via lending activities independently of note issue (180–1, 183, 184n). All this is to be found in Tooke's works of 1844 and thereafter, and (as we have seen) much of it was acceptable to Mill. But it also emerges from our study that in Mill's case a somewhat more positive effect on activity and prices was attributed to the note issue *per se* at least in non-quiescent situations (and most situations were such) and this even after the appearance of Tooke's major work of 1844.[155] We fully concur with Professor Fetter that while Mill opposed the 1844 Act he diverged from Fullarton and Tooke on the 'passivity' of the note issue (1965, 190, 226–7). It may be added, however, that nowhere did Mill emphasize a difference with Tooke, but rather pointed to Tooke's own concessions (e.g. above, pp. 564–5).

A further index of Mill's effective independence is provided by his attitude to state control of banking compared with that of Tooke. In his early period Tooke had followed Ricardo in rejecting free trade – an exception to the general rule of *laissez-faire*. By 1844 he had come to withdraw the exception on the grounds that 'convertibility into gold, together with unlimited competition as to issue, does give sufficient security against an excessive issue of paper currency' (cited in Arnon, 1984, 323). According to Arnon's account Tooke came to argue 'that free trade in banking is not dangerous to the production of wealth, its influence on prices is negligible, and so there is no reason not to leave this business outside the "province of police"

155 Arnon (1984) refers to Tooke's abandonment of his earlier orthodox reasoning, including the quantity theory and the need to assure by regulation that a mixed currency of coin and notes acts as a purely metallic currency, and his adoption (by 1844) of the banking school views that notes do not play on prices (in fact the Bank cannot increase notes in circulation – the Law of Reflux) and that the quantity theory must be rejected in favour of an income theory of prices whereby prices govern the volume of medium in circulation (312–13, 315–16). But we have seen that from a very early stage Mill had questioned any simple minded version of the quantity theory – injections of money had to impinge on the income–expenditure stream (above, p. 561); on Gregory's reading (unlike Arnon's) Tooke, also, adhered to an income theory of prices both early and late in his career (Gregory, 1928, 22, 82). Equally important, allowance must be made for Mill's early case for bank intervention acting on notes when account is taken of speculative or cyclical forces (above, pp. 548–9). These views were carried over to Mill's paper of 1844 and the *Principles* (above, pp. 564, 569f, 573f). There does not seem to be a break in Mill's intellectual development.

As for Tooke's allowance for regulation of the note issue in 1826, the weight of emphasis is as much on the protection of holders of small-denomination paper as upon the belief that control would mitigate crises; in 1826 Mill was very much preoccupied with the latter issue (above, p. 550).

outside the hands of the greedy state'. Now it will be recalled that while for Mill the bank was to remain a private company, this did not reflect the 'unimportance' of notes, but hinged upon the presumption that the bank managers would adopt a socially responsible attitude in its policy, including counter-cyclical monetary intervention. Moreover, while Mill (unlike the proponents of the Act of 1844) did not countenance a single bank of issue he did allow for some degree of government control of the system as a whole. The apparent difference with Tooke is, however, reduced when we extend our attention beyond notes, for Tooke and Fullarton were very conscious of over-banking considering all forms of bank credit: 'in their controversial zeal to show that there was no basis for restriction of note issues [they] came very close to building up a case that the abuses of deposit banking called for regulation' (Fetter, 1965, 191).

The apparently paradoxical tone to which we have alluded reflects Mill's standard quest for balance – in the present case his appreciation of the exquisitely difficult task of mitigating cyclical pressures, but yet avoiding secular depreciation of the currency. It is most unfortunate that Mill's strong statements regarding a 'passive' note issue – statements that can perhaps be appreciated in terms of a taste for polemic which he never outgrew (apart from the neglect, characteristic of Tooke as well, of the role of Bank of England liabilities as a reserve base for other components of the circulating medium) – have clouded his true position. He gave the impression that money was unimportant, and thereby backed himself into a corner. Thus, for example, one of our foremost Mill scholars has been led to conclude that 'the only measure of monetary policy that really wins his approval is the suspension of Peel's law during the 1847 crisis'; and to treat his monetary contribution with a dismissive comment that 'the generation of British students who were to learn their monetary theory from the *Principles* might have found better teachers in other economists among Mill's contemporaries' (Schwartz, 1972, 41).

It remains to remark that the 'paradox' discernible in Mill's formulations is present also in those of Ricardo. With Ricardo too we find not only a recommendation for bank accommodation to satisfy the demand for liquidity in periods of 'want of confidence' but also – and here Ricardo surpasses Mill – a recommendation for devaluation of the currency if that is necessary to avoid severe deflation (above, p. 31).

EIGHT

On utility and liberty

A system of political economy may be defined as a comprehensive set of economic policies based upon some normative, unifying principle such as Socialism or Liberalism (Schumpeter, 1954, 38). Mill, of course, is traditionally considered a 'liberal', but this is a mere label; fully to appreciate his policy recommendations we must examine closely the normative, unifying principle or principles at play, particularly so considering his celebrated utilitarian odyssey and his much discussed attitude towards Socialism.

The present chapter is designed to provide an appropriate context for a closer examination of Mill's conceptions of the role of government in economic life, socio-economic organization and income distribution. These matters can only be appreciated in terms of the 'greatest happiness' principle, allowing a conspicuous place for individual liberty in that principle (combined, of course, with recourse to a body of economic analysis, for there may be desirable ends which cannot be achieved, perhaps because they are self-contradictory, a characteristic revealed by economic theory).[1] The fact that Mill finally formalized his position on ethics and social philosophy rather late in the day should not be taken to imply that his conclusions were inapplicable at an early stage. His vaccilations regarding utility, we shall show, do not so much reflect changes of substance – for the 'greater good' necessarily entails value judgements which were, by and large, unchanged over time – but rather an altered perspective on the nature of the original Benthamite doctrine, ultimately allowing for the formal incorporation of liberty *within* the doctrine. (Had Mill not reacted so strongly against his upbringing he presumably would have reached the solution earlier,

---

1 Robbins (1952), provides an essential introduction and background to our topic. See particularly the sections (176f) 'The Theory of policy and the Principle of Utility', 'Individualism as an End'.

since, as will become clear, it is consistent with Bentham's original position.)

Rawls (1971, vii–viii) has very fairly recognized that 'the great utilitarians, Hume and Adam Smith, Bentham and Mill, were social theorists and economists of the first rank; and the moral doctrine they worked out was framed to meet the needs of their wider interests and to fit into a comprehensive scheme'. A close investigation of Mill's position on economic policy will, therefore, it is hoped, also contribute indirectly to a deeper appreciation of what the moral doctrine amounted to, although that will not be our major preoccupation.

I INTRODUCTION: THE SCHUMPETERIAN VERSION OF BENTHAMISM

A vast range of perspectives exists regarding the nature of Benthamite utilitarianism itself – even if we limit ourselves to historians of economics – a particularly pertinent matter considering the vicissitudes in Mill's own approach.[2] A word first regarding the hostile account given by Schumpeter (1954), which turns (it transpires) on an unjustifiably severe version of the doctrine close to J. S. Mill's own interpretation during the period 1832–40. This 'boisterous and vulgar' doctrine, as Schumpeter labels it ominously early in his book (66) is conceived in the following terms: 'The pleasures and pains of each individual are assumed to be measurable quantities capable of being (algebraically) added into a quantity called the individual's happiness . . . These individual "happinesses" are again summed up into a social total, *all of them being weighted equally:* "everyone to count for one, nobody to count for more than one." Finally, that social total is substituted for, or identified with, the common good or welfare of society, which is thus resolved into individual sensations of pleasure or pain, the only ultimate realities. This yields the normative principle of Utilitarianism, namely the Greatest Happiness of the Greatest Number, which is chiefly associated, in recognition of ardent advocacy, careful elaboration, and extensive application, with the name of Bentham' (131).[3] Schumpeter recognized ancient antecedents to the general doctrine, but distinguished the scholastics, who applied it to 'the sphere of stable, barn, shop, and market' thereby confining it 'to purely utilitarian activity where it is (nearly – not even there wholly) adequate', from the eighteenth-century utilitarians who 'reduced the whole world of human values to the same schema, ruling out, as contrary

---

2   For detailed accounts of these vicissitudes see Viner (1958), 306–31, Robson, (1964), 245–68, Priestley (1969), viif.

3   Schumpeter (1954), 130–1, finds the term 'Greatest Good of the Greatest Number' first used by Hutcheson (1725); and the general doctrine in (*inter alia*) Helvetius (1758), Beccaria (1764), Priestly (1768) and Paley (1785). David Hume is also included in the group of eighteenth-century advocates. On the origins see also Stephen (1900), I, 235f, Robbins (1952), 49–55.

to reason, all that really matters to man. Thus they are indeed entitled to the credit of having created something that was new in literature . . . namely, the shallowest of all conceivable philosophies of life that stands indeed in a position of irreconcilable antagonism to the rest of them' (133). Utilitarianism, 'fitted to perfection the streak of materialistic (antimetaphysical) rationalism, that may be associated with liberalism and the business mind' (408). Similarly, 'this unitary social science of utilitarianism was individualist, empiricist, and "rationalist," the last term meaning here simply that the system, both in its analytic and in its normative aspects, strictly excluded everything that would not pass the test of utilitarian or hedonist rationality' (428). Such a system was 'incapable of taking account of the facts of political life and of the way in which states, governments, parties, and bureaucracies actually work', although 'its preconceptions did little harm in fields such as that of economics where its "logic of stable and barn" may be considered as a tolerable expression of actual tendencies' (428–9).[4] Schumpeter himself recognized his own 'strong personal aversion to utilitarianism' (1153), and his account indeed tells us much of his personal value judgements, including his antipathy towards the 'liberalism' of the British classical school. (It may well be to this bias that his celebrated but perverse account of Adam Smith can be attributed.)

Schumpeter treated J. S. Mill somewhat apart from Bentham and James Mill, although grudgingly, conceding that Mill 'rose above his early Benthamism' although 'he never shook off its shackles entirely: though his essays *On Liberty* and *Considerations on Representative Government* are no doubt redeemed, in part, by wider horizons and deeper insight, they are still "philosophical radicalism"'. It will thus remain forever a matter of the historian's personal equation whether J. S. Mill's theory spells abandonment or improvement of that of his father' (430).[5] The distinction emerges also during the

---

4 James Mill's *Essay on Government* is described as 'unrelieved nonsense' based on 'the freely voting rational citizen, conscious of his (long-run) interests, and the representative who acts in obedience to them, the government that expresses these volitions – is this not the perfect example of a nursery tale?' The premises of Mill's political theory were mere *postula* reflecting a 'completely imaginary agent, the rational voter'. By contrast are James Mill's economics, the premises of which, albeit involving abstraction from reality as theory requires, none the less are 'induced from realistic observation of the profit-seeking and calculating business man' (429, 430n).

5 Cf. 411: '[Mill] grew to realize that the scheme of utilitarian rationality is quite inadequate beyond a limited range of problems. But he was not the man to make anything of it . . .'. The strongest statement will be found in a comment on Mill's critique of Benthamite philosophy in *A System of Logic* (1843) and positive response to Coleridge and his group in 'Bentham' (1838) and 'Coleridge' (1840): 'Mill goes a long way toward accepting their criticism of eighteenth-century rationalism – and the "interest philosophy of the Bentham school" – and shows himself quite open to their romanticist conception of history: in fact, I do not think that the man who wrote these articles – and the passages on James Mill's theory of government in the *Logic* [VI, Ch.8,3] – can properly be called a utilitarian at all' (528n).

course of a contention to the effect that amongst prominent, nineteenth-century classical economists only Bentham, James Mill and *with qualification* J. S. Mill can be counted as 'prominent and militant utilitarians . . . It was natural for Bentham and the Mills to see themselves in the role of philosophical patrons of economics and to assume responsibility for an alliance between economics and utilitarianism, that was acquiesced in by many later economists, such as Jevons and Edgeworth; but it was neither necessary nor useful' (408). Similarly, 'J. S. Mill cannot be called a utilitarian without qualification. In some respects he outgrew the creed; in others he refined it. But he never renounced it explicitly . . .' All this raises a number of general issues for us.

The above account of utilitarianism turning on the all-pervasiveness of the hedonistic, rational, self-interest axiom, turns out to be precisely the interpretation by J. S. Mill at the time of his reaction against his upbringing (discussed above in Chapter 2 on methodology). Even at that time he, like Schumpeter, justified the self-interest axiom within the sphere of the (anonymous) market place, and on Schumpeter's grounds, too, namely that all theory requires *abstraction* but is yet valid provided that actual tendencies are incorporated rather than totally arbitrary or unrealistic postulates drawn from a hat. This after all is the essence of the essay on definition in economics prepared in the early 1830s and rewritten in 1833 at the height of his revolt. This position was not to change. What was modified, we shall see, is his negative interpretation of Benthamism in the broad – its extra-economic extensions. It will be one of our tasks to attempt to discern the nature of Mill's increasingly warm evaluation of 'Benthamite' utilitarianism as time passed. What emerges is his realization that his earlier critical stance had misrepresented Bentham. Thus his mature position can be interpreted as a *return to Bentham*.

In this context we shall raise the relationship between the utilitarian expediential criterion and *justice*. We shall demonstrate Mill's representation of justice as a matter of expediency but one accorded the very highest (qualitatively speaking) weighting. This was the resolution which fully justified his return to the fold. (As for justice itself, the emphasis throughout is upon the protection of 'individual liberty' in a very broad sense of that term extending (*inter alia*) to equality of opportunity, and 'high' living standards.) Mill's resolution turns out to be fully in line with Bentham's early formulations.

Now the possibility that J. S. Mill may have come to recognize that he had misrepresented Bentham is ruled out entirely by Schumpeter's version of Benthamism.[6] Yet the evidence points precisely towards that

6 Also by that of Priestley (1969) who regards Mill's concessions to Bentham as mere lip service for strategic purposes. The issue is of great current interest for the view which we dispute cf. Taylor 1984, 54: 'Mill wanted to introduce qualitative discrimination of better and worse courses of conduct or ways of leading lives. Mill wished to introduce such discrimination into the utilitarian theory of Bentham which had been irreducibly hostile to them'.

conclusion. The next section sets out Bentham's position in *An Introduction to the Principles of Morals and Legislation* (1789) and *A Table of the Springs of Human Action* (1815).[7]

A second general issue raised by Schumpeter's account will concern us in this chapter. On general methodological principle (and this runs through the *History of Economic Analysis*) Schumpeter denied any 'necessary link between ideology and economic "analysis" '. This principle emerges, very clearly, in his account of utilitarianism.[8] But what of utilitarianism and *economic policy*? Schumpeter himself leaves the matter open: 'As regards the "classic" recommendations, there are no doubt many that are wholly neutral with respect to any philosophy of life: one need not be a utilitarian in order to recommend peasant proprietorship for Ireland, or in order to recommend or condemn return to the gold standard after the Napoleonic Wars. But there are others – unconditional free trade, for example – that did imply views of general policy and attitudes to life that do seem, to say the least, to link up with utilitarianism better than with any other philosophy of life' (1954, 409).[9] In fact, Schumpeter goes so far as to suggest, in a context relating to nineteenth-century critics of mercantilist trade restrictions, that 'their opinions about policy were represented as "scientific inferences" from premises that had been laid down in a scientific spirit. Especially the English utilitarians, such as John Stuart Mill, looked upon their recommendations concerning policy as an engineer would look upon his recommendation about the construction of an engine. Their present was invariably "this enlightened age." Hence *practical* and *theoretical* "error" was for them equally definite and indeed the same thing. This standpoint, which partly accounts for their pontifical attitude, is of course wholly untenable . . .'(336–7).

---

7 For the significance of these works in J. S. Mill's accounts see Robson (1964), 262–3.

8 Cf. citation above (p. 605) from Schumpeter (1954), 408. Also 409: '[A]s regards that part of economic analysis which works with rational schemata, utilitarian philosophy, though superfluous, does no harm. And this fact, as critics would have recognized if they had been competent economists, salvages the bulk of the work in economic analysis done by the utilitarians'; and 528n, regarding J. S. Mill's criticisms of 'the interest philosophy' of the Bentham School in the late 1830s and early 1840s, but his appreciation of the nature of technical economics which assured that he did not abandon it on account of his philosophical doubts: 'To critics who did not understand it equally well, this looked like hesitation and endless shifting of viewpoint. Actually, however, his views were, *in this respect*, perfectly consistent and, in addition, far ahead of his time.' (see also 134, 430n).

Cf. Robbins (1970a), 57: 'I fully agree with Schumpeter that the logical coherence of [the classical economists'] analytical propositions does not stand or fall with this [utilitarian] background'.

9 The example drawn from free trade – setting aside the question of its historical validity – is highly illustrative of Schumpeter's own philosophy; as is his commendation of Carlyle who he believed saw much more clearly than Bentham 'what a nation is and really wants and what are the real determinants of its fate' (411).

What precisely, however, one is immediately led to ask, were the implications (if any at all) of the vicissitudes in Mill's perception and evaluation of the utility principle for his approach to economic policy? This question emerges also when full allowance is made – an allowance which Schumpeter fails to make – for the *conventional* nature of the greater happiness principle as a rough index for legislative purposes (or for the guidance of moral leaders indirectly concerned with legislation). For we must resolve the issue of the constituents of the 'general good'. This indeed was precisely J. S. Mill's overriding problem, a particularly acute problem for one who came to be so conscious of the (potential) variability of custom and attitudes. While 'the greatest good of the greatest number', as ultimate policy end, is ever present as a governing consideration in policy analysis in Mill's *Principles of Political Economy*, what to include in the maximand? As one instance of the problem – apparently minor but in fact most revealing of a matter of principle – restriction of food exports during a scarcity is said to be 'sound policy' but only given the prevailing state of international morality (*CW*, III, 917, discussed below, pp. 736–7). One deduces that, in practice, 'the greatest amount of good' provides the key for evaluation of policy at the *national* level – a constraint determined by the state of opinion. The pervasiveness of this perspective for policy requires that close consideration be given to Mill's own interpretation of the doctrine of utilitarianism with an eye to changes over time therein.

We shall show in this chapter that once his naive youthful utilitarianism and his initial reaction therefrom had been set aside, Mill's further vaccilations reflect an attempt to arrive at an appropriate interpretation – 'appropriate' given his value judgements – of the precise scope of the 'general good'. For the principle of utility itself provided no detailed blueprint of 'ends', so that *subjective* judgements were always required to fill the gap. Utilitarianism for Mill was positively not a scheme of 'ultimate values'. It might well transpire on this view, Mill realized, that the specific policy recommendations of utilitarianism are no different from those emerging within, let us say, a natural rights framework – that 'secondary' principles are of greater practical import than 'primary' principles. There is *a fortiori* no necessary reason why Mill's vaccilations regarding utilitarianism should have influenced his perspective on socio-economic policy. It is certainly not the case, it will emerge, that Mill regarded any policy position as definitive in an 'engineering' sense.

II THE BENTHAMITE POSITION: A SUMMARY STATEMENT

The first point to observe is Bentham's insistence that standard appeals to such concepts as 'justice' or 'virtue' turn out to mean anything and nothing: 'Take away *pleasures* and *pains*, not only *happiness*, but *justice*, and *duty*, and *obligation*, and *virtue* – all of which have been so elaborately held up to view as independent of them – are so many empty sounds' (1815, 3). And that this is so is brilliantly demonstrated in the major work of 1789 where he concluded that 'there is no such thing as any sort of motive which is a bad one in itself: nor, consequently, any such thing as a sort of motive, which in itself is exclusively a good one'; and even as regards consequences 'it appears too that these are sometimes bad, at other times either indifferent or good . . .'. '[W]e see the emptiness of all those rhapsodies of common-place morality, which consist in taking of such names as lust, cruelty, and avarice, and branding them with marks of reprobation: applied to the *thing*, they are false; applied to the *name*, they are true indeed, but nugatory. Would you do a real service to mankind, show them the cases in which sexual desire *merits* the name of lust; displeasure, that of cruelty; and pecuniary interest, that of avarice' (1789, 114–15).[10]

True morality in short has its source in *utility*:

On this basis must also be erected, and to this standard must be referred, – whatsoever clear explanations are capable of being suggested, by the other more anomalous appellatives above spoken of; such as *emotion, affection, passion, disposition, inclination, propensity, quality* (viz. *moral quality*), *vice, virtue, moral good, moral evil*. Destitute of reference to the ideas of *pain* and *pleasure*, whatever ideas are annexed to the words *virtue* and *vice* amount to nothing more than that of groundless *approbation* or *disapprobation*. All language in which these appellations are employed is no better than empty declamation. A *virtuous disposition* is the disposition to give birth to *good* – understanding always *pathological* good, – or to prevent, or abstain from giving birth to, *evil*, understanding always *pathological* evil, – in so far as the production of the effect requires *exertion* in the way of *self-denial* : i.e. sacrifice of supposed lesser good to supposed greater good. In so far as the greater good, to which the less is sacrificed, is considered as being the good of *others*, the virtue belongs to the head of *probity* or *beneficence* : in so far as it is considered as being the good of *self*, to that of *self-regarding prudence* (1815, 14).[11]

10 Breaking 'lust' down into components Bentham (1815) isolates, as one constituent element, sexual desire, and this – when the *consequences* are not regarded as undesirable – is not called lust but designated by some other term (*ibid.*). Similarly, 'self interest', in the strict sense of selfishness, is also not *per se* a 'bad' motive, for if weeded out 'the thread of life is cut, and the whole perishes' (24).
   On *malice* see Bentham (1789), 94. Bentham here spells out, by way of illustration of a general theme, that to this corresponds 'a kind of pleasure that is his motive: the pleasure he takes at the thought of the pain which he sees, or expects to see, his adversary undergo'. Here is a further instance of Bentham's insistence on comprehensive analysis. Since such pleasure is present, malice cannot be designated 'bad' in *all* its aspects.

11 'For *pathological* might here have been put the more ordinary adjunct *physical*, were it not that, in that case, those pleasures and pains, the seat of which is not in the *body*, but only in the *mind*, might be regarded as excluded' (3).

That is the primary message and we see particularly well in this context the fruitfulness for clear thought of the Benthamite method of breaking down for close analysis any complex notion.

Now the great error of Schumpeter is to confuse Benthamite utilitarianism with some form of selfishness. Probably the error arises from a failure to note that the *formal Table of the Springs of Human Action* is limited to a narrow range of considerations – only those which act on the will 'in the way of immediate contact', that is 'pleasures and pains [which] are, every one of them, *simple* and *elementary*' (1815, 1, 5),[12] coupled with a careless reading of the declaration that '[a] man is said *to have an interest in any subject* in so far as that *subject* is considered more or less likely to be to him a source of pleasure or exemption [from pain] . . .' (*ibid.*, 5). But any such misconception should dissipate when one considers the further analysis of compound motives and the nature of 'interest'.[13]

Consider, for example, the complex pleasures of sexual love, love of justice and love of liberty. The former is compounded of sexual desire, the desire of goodwill (goodwill on the part of the beloved with an eye to what it might yield!), but also goodwill *per se*, that is sympathy 'in contemplation of the qualities, intellectual or moral, ascribed to that same person'. The second includes justice for oneself (self-preservation), sympathy (justice for another party) but also '*sympathy* for *the community* at large, in respect of the interest, which it has in the maintenance of *justice* : i.e. as being liable, in an indefinite extent, to become a sufferer by *injustice*'. While the third comprises *inter alia* 'self preservation', sympathy for some other individual, but also that sympathy 'which has for its object *the community* at large, considered as liable to be made to suffer from the misrule' (10–11). It is clear beyond doubt that *disinterested* motives are fully recognized and that these fall within the 'utility' rule.

Let us now look more closely at the notion of 'interest'. That concept, Bentham insisted, entails merely efficient selection of means to some end 'whether that interest be of the *self-regarding* class, or of the *extra-regarding* ; viz. of the *social* or of the *dissocial class*' (14). But all human acts are 'interested' (in *that* sense) even if quite 'disinterested': 'In regard to *interest*, in the most extended, – which is the original and only strictly proper sense, – of the word *disinterested*, no human act ever has been or ever can be *disinterested*. For there exists not ever any voluntary action, which is not the result of the operation of some *motive* or *motives* : nor any motive, which has not for its accompaniment a corresponding *interest*, real or imagined' (15). To insist upon interested behaviour is *not* to deny benevolence or 'the absence of all interest of the *self-regarding* class' (even though pleasure is derived from it). And if that is so, 'the most *disinterested* of men, is not less under the

---

12 On this see Stephen (1900), I, 250f, Viner (1958), 323–4.
13 For recent balanced accounts of Bentham see Steintrager (1977) and Long (1977).

dominion of *interest* than the most *interested*. The only cause of his being styled *disinterested* is – its not having been observed that the sort of *motive* (suppose it *sympathy* for an individual or a class of individuals) has as truly a corresponding *interest* belonging to it, as any other species of motive has' (15).[14]

A further word is in order regarding the ethical dimension of Bentham's preoccupations in *Morals and Legislation* for the light thrown on the self-interest issue. Personal ethics comprises a moral duty to oneself ('the art of directing a man's actions in this respect, may be termed the art of discharging one's duty to one's self: and the quality which a man manifests by the discharge of this branch of duty . . . is that of *prudence*'); and a moral duty towards others, partly negative (probity) to avoid reducing their happiness and partly positive (beneficence) to increase their happiness. Bentham himself raises the question: '[w]hat motives (independent of such as legislation and religion may chance to furnish) can one man have to consult the happiness of another? by what motives, or, which comes to the same thing, by what obligations, can he be bound to obey the dictates of *probity* and *beneficence*?' And in his reply the social motives are allowed for:

In answer to this, it cannot but be admitted, that the only interests which a man at all times and upon all occasions is sure to find *adequate* motives for consulting, are his own. Notwithstanding this, there are no occasions in which a man has not some motives for consulting the happiness of other men. In the first place, he has, on all occasions, the purely social motive of sympathy or benevolence: in the next place, he has, on most occasions, the semi-social motives of love of amity and love of reputation. The motive of sympathy will act upon him with more or less effect, according to the *bias* of his sensibility: the two other motives, according to a variety of circumstances, principally according to the strength of his intellectual powers, the firmness and steadiness of his mind, the quantum of his moral sensibility, and the characters of the people he has to deal with (1789, 284–5).

'Disinterested' behaviour is, we have seen, clearly meritorious on Bentham's account: Although disinterested acts are 'the product of *interest*, as any other action ever is or can be, whatsoever *merit* may happen to belong

14 Cf. Viner (1958), 312–13, who insists that pleasure and pain, the individual's 'sovereign masters' for Bentham – and a standard eighteenth-century position – are not identifiable with self-interest, but with 'whatever men are interested in'. The term *pleasure* was an inclusive one allowing 'not only the pleasures of the senses but also those of the heart and the mind'. Moreover, 'pleasures of self . . . could become associated with the pleasures of others. Man, by living in society, by education, and by acts of parliament, could be made good'. Viner concedes a frequent overemphasis in Bentham's exposition on the selfish sentiments but finds James Mill the more guilty party, for he systematically argued that even 'affectionate sentiments' reflect (consciously) the individual's *own* pleasures.

to any action, to which, in the loose and ordinary way of speaking, the epithet *disinterested* would be applied, is not in any the slightest degree lessened' (1815, 16). But on what grounds is merit – the morality of an action – based? Specifically are there external points of reference? This question will prove to be of profound importance when we come to Mill. The answer Bentham gives is that *utility* itself – the 'general good' – is the sole reference point:

as there are some motives, the force of which, they being either of the *self-regarding*, or of the *dissocial* class, is more liable than the force of those of the remaining class, viz. the *social* class, to operate in the breast of each particular individual, to the prejudice of the general good – of the interest of mankind at large; so, on the other hand, there are others, – and more particularly among those which belong to the *social* class, – which, in a particular degree, are capable of being employed, and with success, in checking the operative forces of the above *comparatively* dangerous motives, and restraining it from applying itself with effect to the production of acts of the tendency just mentioned (22).

The foregoing perspective had long before suggested to Bentham classification of motives in a hierarchy, an 'order of pre-eminence among motives' (1789, 116), in which 'good-will' stands highest in the light of its relation to social good. The ranking turns on 'the tendency which they appear to have to unite, or disunite' an agent's interests and those of other members of the community:

On this plan they may be distinguished into *social, dissocial,* and *self-regarding.* In the social class may be reckoned, 1. Good-will. 2. Love of reputation. 3. Desire of Amity. 4. Religion. In the dissocial may be placed, 5. Displeasure. In the self-regarding class, 6. Physical desire. 7. Pecuniary interest. 8. Love of power. 9. Self-preservation . . . Of all these sorts of motives, good-will is that of which the dictates, taken in a general view, are surest of coinciding with those of the principle of utility. For the dictates of utility are neither more nor less than the dictates of the most extensive and enlightened (that is *well-advised*) benevolence. The dictates of the other motives may be conformable to those of utility, or repugnant, as it may happen (116–17).

'Good-will' then stands highest 'because of the social tendency [is] much more constant and unequivocal' than in any other of the social motives (116). Similarly: while 'there is no sort of motive by which a man may not be prompted to engage in acts that are of a mischievous nature; that is, which may not come to act in the capacity of seducing motive', yet 'there are some motives which are remarkably less likely to operate in this way than others', 'the least likely of all [being] that of benevolence or good-will' (135).[15]

The ultimate task of government falls easily into place. It is precisely to encourage *socially* desirable behaviour:

The effects of the peculiar power of the magistrate are seen more particularly in the influence it exerts over the quantum and bias of men's moral, religious, sympathetic, and anti-pathetic sensibilities. Under a well-constituted, or even under a well-administered though ill-constituted government, men's moral sensibility is commonly stronger, and their moral biases more conformable to the dictates of utility: their religious sensibility frequently weaker, but their religious biases less unconformable to the dictates of utility: their sympathetic affections more enlarged, directed to the magistrate more than to small parties or to individuals, and more to the whole community than to either: their antipathetic sensibilities less violent, as being more obsequious to the influence of well-directed moral bias, and less apt to be excited by that of ill-directed religious ones: their antipathetic biases more conformable to well-directed moral ones, more apt (in proportion) to be grounded on enlarged and sympathetic than on narrow and self-regarding affections, and accordingly upon the whole, more conformable to the dictates of utility (68).

More briefly '[t]he business of government is to promote the happiness of the society, by punishing and rewarding' (74); or in the familiar language, 'the only *right* and justifiable end of Government [is] the greatest happiness of the greatest number. . .' (14n). And from this same perspective the concept of *justice* is approached – a central matter, it transpires, for J. S. Mill:

[J]ustice, in the only sense in which it has a meaning, is an imaginary personage, feigned for the convenience of discourse, whose dictates are the dictates of utility, applied to certain particular cases. Justice, then, is nothing more than an imaginary instrument, employed to foreward on certain occasions, and by certain means, the purposes of benevolence. The dictates of justice are nothing more than a part of the dictates of benevolence, which, on certain occasions, are applied to certain subjects; to wit, to certain actions (120n).

Justice can only be understood in terms of utility but it reflects 'the dictates of benevolence', and is high in the hierarchy.

To appreciate Bentham's full intentions his frequent charges against 'interest-begotten prejudice' and 'sinister interest' (e.g. 1815, 7, 9, 27) must

---

15 Bentham admits that an act may be benevolent to some group A and yet have hostile effects for another group B. But this is because 'his good-will is imperfect and confined: not taking into contemplation the interests of all the persons whose interests are at stake . . .'

be considered. The following strongly-worded charges added to *Morals and Legislation* in 1822 captures nicely the spirit of his position in historical context:

Not long after the publication of the Fragment on Government, anno 1776, in which, in the character of an all-comprehensive and all-commanding principle, the principle of *utility* was brought to view, one person by whom observation to the above effect was made was *Alexander Wedderburn*, at that time Attorney or Solicitor General, afterwards successively Chief Justice of the Common Pleas, and Chancellor of England, under the successive titles of Lord Loughborough and Earl of Rosslyn . . . The *principle of utility* was an appellative, at that time employed – by me, as it had been by others, to designate that which, in a more perspicuous and instructive manner, may, as above, be designated by the name of the *greatest happiness principle.* 'The principle (said Wedderburn) is a dangerous one.' Saying so, he said that which, to a certain extent, is strictly true: a principle, which lays down, as the only *right* and justifiable end of Government, the greatest happiness of the greatest number – how can it be denied to be a dangerous one? dangerous it unquestionably is, to every government which has for its *actual* end or object, the greatest happiness of a certain *one*, with or without the addition of some comparatively small number of others, whom it is matter of pleasure or accommodation to him to admit, each of them, to a share in the concern, on the footing of so many junior partners. *Dangerous* it therefore really was, to the interest – the sinister interest – of all those functionaries, himself included, whose interest it was, to maximize delay, vexation, and expense, in judicial and other modes of procedure, for the sake of the profit, extractable out of the expense (1789, 14–15n).

In his account Jacob Viner has rightly insisted upon the need to differentiate Bentham's own utilitarianism from that of James Mill, a distinction that emerges conspicuously in the analysis of the ideal constitution: 'Setting out from the proposition that the sole proper purpose of government is to promote the greatest happiness of mankind, James Mill proceeded by purely *a priori* analysis, without any reference to history or contemporary facts, from the premise that legislators served *only* their "sinister interests" . . . to the conclusion that good government was therefore obtainable only by making it, through popular suffrage and frequent elections, the self-interest of the elected to serve the interests of the electors.' The exercise proved an embarrassment for Bentham (not only J. S. Mill) who 'always conceded that men, even legislators, could not only be influenced by the praise and blame of other men, but could even display some measure of pure benevolence' (Viner, 1958, 310). As I have shown elsewhere this was precisely Ricardo's objection to James Mill, and in the same general context (Hollander, 1979, 593f).

While the contrast between ethics and legislation should not be drawn too sharply, Bentham's major preoccupations were legal and legislative.

After his outline of the valuation scheme which has attracted so much amusement (the intensity, duration, probability, propinquity, purity, fecundity and extent which comprise 'the value of a pleasure'), he observed that, in so far as the application of this valuation to reward, punishment or compensation is ignored, 'the business of *law* and *government* is carried on blindfold' (1815, 3); and the work of 1789 was originally intended to serve 'as an introduction to a plan of a penal code . . .' (1789, 1, 4).[16] But it must also be noted for accurate perspective that Bentham positively did not intend to suggest *precision* in the calculation whether in private ethics or legislation: 'It is not to be expected that this process should be strictly pursued previously to every moral judgement, or to every legislative or judicial operation. It may, however, be always kept in view: and as near as the process actually pursued on these occasions approaches to it, so near will such process approach to the character of an exact one' (1789, 40).

A sympathetic commentator has accurately diluted the essence of the

---

16 Bentham (1789) was conscious that much was lacking as a theory of morals: 'As an introduction to the principles of *morals*, in addition to the analysis it contains of the extensive ideas signified by the terms *pleasure, pain, motive,* and *disposition,* it ought to have given a similar analysis of the not less extensive, though much less determinate, ideas annexed to the terms *emotion, passion, appetite, virtue, vice,* and some others, including the names of the particular *virtues* and *vices*' (3). He also recognized an excess of emphasis on penal as distinct from civil laws.

As for the ethical sphere, it was the ethics of moral leaders (who were to attempt to influence legislators) rather than the ordinary man that mainly concerned Bentham. Viner (1958) warns rightly against interpreting Benthamism 'as a system of private ethics, didactic as well as descriptive'. Private morals however, do enter the story, for the élite must operate upon them in the interests of the 'greatest happiness' principle: 'Men normally are interested to some extent in the happiness of others than themselves, and in exceptional cases are capable of "universal benevolence," or a dominating concern with the happiness of mankind at large, but generally, if they are left to themselves, there will be serious discrepancy between the actual behavior of individuals and the behavior which would conduce to "the greatest happiness of the greatest number." It is the function of legislation to coerce or bribe individuals to make their behavior coincide with that required by the greatest-happiness principle, and of education and moral leaders to mould men's desires so that they spontaneously associate the happiness of others with their own happiness' (311–12).

However, Bentham (1789), it must never be overlooked, was careful to delimit the legislative role: 'There is no case in which a private man ought not to direct his own conduct to the production of his own happiness, and of that of his fellow-creatures: but there are cases in which the legislator ought not (in a direct way at least, and by means of punishment applied immediately to particular *individual* acts) to attempt to direct the conduct of the several other members of the community. Every act which promises to be beneficial upon the whole to the community (himself included) each individual ought to perform of himself: but it is not every such act that the legislator ought to compel him to perform. Every act which promises to be pernicious upon the whole to the community (himself included) each individual ought to abstain from of himself: but it is not every such act that the legislator ought to compel him to abstain from' (285).

Benthamite doctrine (attributed to the entire school of classical economists from Hume to Cairnes and Sidgwick) as 'the habit of judging actions and policies by their consequences rather than by reference to some intuitive norm', a characteristic standing in sharp contrast to that of the continental metaphysicians. 'The question, what is to be done if we reject considerations of utility', and put our reliance in innate feelings of right and wrong 'is typical of the attitude of the main tradition of English political economy' (Robbins, 1970a, 56–7). And aside from some extreme passages Bentham, within that tradition, used the greatest happiness principle as a 'working rule by which to judge generally applicable laws and procedures. Bentham knew perfectly well the logical limits of his procedure' (81). He did not take too seriously utility quantification itself; the postulates relating to interpersonal comparisons and summation were purely *conventional*:

Tis in vain to talk of adding quantities which after the addition will continue distinct as they were before, one man's happiness will never be another man's happiness: a gain to one man is no gain to another: you might as well pretend to add twenty apples to twenty pears, which after you had done that could not be forty of any one thing but twenty of each just as there was before . . . This addibility of the happiness of different subjects, however, when considered rigorously, it may appear fictitious, is a postulation without the allowance of which all political reasoning is at a stand: nor is it more fictitious than that of the equality of chances to reality, on which the whole branch of the Mathematics which is called the doctrine of chances is established (cited in Halévy, 1928, 495; cf. Robbins, 1952, 180; 1981, 5).[17]

The same applies to Bentham's postulate 'everyone to count for one, nobody to count for more than one'. For by this postulate every individual is considered equally capable of the same degree of happiness in the same circumstances, while he explicitly recognized the *varying* sensibilities of different individuals to pleasure and pain (cf. 1789, Ch, vi).

To suggest then, as Schumpeter does by his dismissive remarks regarding Bentham's 'equalitarianism' in contexts entailing 'the whole world of human values' or the 'interest philosophy' (1954, 131f discussed above), that the 'calculus' was intended to reflect in some sense *reality* is thoroughly misleading.[18]

The postulate can be upheld, and without inconsistency, by one who simultaneously stresses differences in sensibility, character and motivation from individual to individual. (It is doubtful whether, even at the height of his reaction against Benthamite utilitarianism in the early 1830s

17 Cf. Viner (1958), 314: 'The "calculus" as [Bentham] actually used it was merely a mental comparison of the comparative weights of the pros and cons' where a balance between individual happiness is called for. See also Stephen (1900), I, 271.

18 But see the preliminary and incomplete discussion in Schumpeter (1954), 1071n, 7, which draws back somewhat.

J. S. Mill objected to the Benthamite postulates in so far as they were designed for purposes of rough 'Welfare' calculation.)

The principle of utility itself was, Bentham himself emphasized, not susceptible of direct proof: '[T]hat which is used to prove every thing else, cannot itself be proved: a chain of proofs must have their commencement somewhere. To give such a proof is as impossible as it is needless' (1789, 13). The general rule was a postulate. But there were, Bentham maintained, many who combatted the principle while actually using it, their arguments proving 'not that the principle is *wrong*, but that, according to the applications he supposes to be made of it, it is *misapplied*'. 'Is it possible for a man to move the earth?' Bentham asked. 'Yes; but he must first find out another earth to stand upon' (14–15). The point here is that, ultimately, even his opponents, who insist on some absolute sense of 'right', are forced to have reference to a criterion akin to utility. The use of the principle even by opponents was to be much emphasized by Mill as we shall see.

We must raise also in this context the vexed question of the precise constituents of the greater good. The general rule is *axiomatic* but this does not preclude differences between adherents and changes over time in their conception of the axiom. Consider, for example, 'the greatest number'. Who or what to include? The matter is taken up by Bentham in the context of slavery and cruelty to animals: Why, he asks, have the interests of animals been generally neglected?

The day has been, I grieve to say in many places it is not yet past, in which the greater part of the species, under the denomination of slaves, have been treated by the law exactly upon the same footing, as, in England for example, the inferior races of animals are still. The day *may* come, when the rest of the animal creation may acquire those rights which never could have been withholden from them but by the hand of tyranny. The French have already discovered that the blackness of the skin is no reason why a human being should be abandoned without redress to the caprice of a tormentor. It may come one day to be recognized, that the number of the legs, the villosity of the skin, or the termination of the *os sacrum*, are reasons equally insufficient for abandoning a sensitive being to the same fate. What else is it that should trace the insuperable line? Is it the faculty of reason, or, perhaps, the faculty of discourse? But a fullgrown horse or dog, is beyond comparison a more rational, as well as a more conversible animal, than an infant of a day, or a week, or even a month, old. But suppose the case were otherwise, what would it avail? the question is not, Can they *reason*? nor, Can they *talk*? but, Can they *suffer*? (1789, 283n).

That the 'axiom' reflects a value judgment is brought out with crystal clarity in this passage.[19] We shall find this to have become one of J. S. Mill's major concerns.

III THE GREATEST HAPPINESS PRINCIPLE:
THE REACTION FROM BENTHAM

Let us now trace out J. S. Mill's position on the 'greatest happiness' principle and his reading of Benthamite utilitarianism. We shall evaluate its accuracy at a later stage. The retrospective account of the early years – the years before his breakdown – given in the *Autobiography* is a convenient point of departure:

My previous education had been, in a certain sense, already a course of Benthamism. The Benthamite standard of 'the greatest happiness' was that which I had always been taught to apply; I was even familiar with an abstract discussion of it, forming an episode in an unpublished dialogue on Government, written by my father on the Platonic model. Yet in the first pages of Bentham it burst upon me with all the force of novelty. What thus impressed me was the chapter in which Bentham passed judgement on the common modes of reasoning in morals and legislation, deduced from phrases like 'law of nature,' 'right reason,' 'the moral sense,' 'moral rectitude,' and the like, and characterized them as dogmatism in disguise imposing its sentiments upon others under cover of sounding expressions which convey no reason for the sentiment, but set up the sentiment as its own reason . . . The feeling rushed upon me, that all previous moralists were superseded, that here indeed was the commencement of a new era in thought. This impression was strengthened by the manner in which Bentham put into scientific form the application of the happiness principle to the morality of actions by analyzing the various classes and orders of their consequences (*CW*, I, 67).[20]

As for the legislative and institutional implications (as distinct from those for personal morality) the effect was similarly devastating:

But what struck me at that time most of all, was the Classification of Offences; . . . and when I found scientific classification applied to the large and great complex subject of Punishable Acts, under the guidance of the ethical principle of Pleasurable and Painful Consequences followed out in the method of detail introduced into these subjects by Bentham, I felt taken up to an eminence from which I could survey a vast mental domain . . . [at] every page he seemed to open a clearer and broader conception of what human opinions and institutions ought to be, how they might be made what they ought to be, and how far removed from it they now are. When

---

19 Bentham (1851) recognized the possibility that sympathy might extend from 'at one end *unity*' to 'the other, the number of the whole of the human race, – or rather of the whole sensitive race, all species included, – present and future' (25).

20 The references are to *Morals and Legislation*.

I laid down the last volume of the *Traité* I had become a different being. The 'principle of utility,' understood as Bentham understood it, and applied in the manner in which he applied it through these three volumes, fell exactly into its place as the keystone which held together the detached and fragmentary component parts of my knowledge and beliefs. It gave unity to my conception of things. I now had opinions; a creed, a doctrine, a philosophy . . . (67, 69).[21]

Early in 1833, however, Mill was writing to Carlyle of 'the dogmatic disputatiousness of my former narrow and mechanical state' (18 May 1833, *CW*, XII, 153). His transformation he described shortly afterwards as a progressive one:

This change has been progressive, and had barely *begun* to take place when you were in London two years ago. I was then, and had been for some years, in an intermediate state – a state of *reaction* from logical-utilitarian narrowness of the very narrowest kind, out of which after much unhappiness and inward struggling I had emerged, and had taken temporary refuge in its extreme opposite. My first state had been one of intense philosophic intolerance; not arising from the scornfulness of the heart but from the onesidedness of the understanding: seeing nothing myself but the distorted image, thrown back from many most oblique and twisted reflectors, of *one* side only of the truth. I felt towards all who saw any other side, not indeed a feeling of disdain, for that never was in my character but the very utmost excess of intellectual *vilipending*. At that time I was thought to *outrer* the doctrines of utilitarianism, even by those who now consider me a lost sheep who has strayed from the flock and been laid hold of by the wolves. That was not wonderful; because even in the narrowest of my then associates, they being older men, their ratiocinative and nicely concatenated dreams were at some point or other, & in some degree or other, corrected and limited by their experience of actual realities, while I, a school-boy fresh from the logic-school, had never conversed with a reality; never seen one; knew not what manner of thing it was; had only spun, first other people's & then my own deductions from assumed premises. Now when I had got out of this state, and saw that my premises were mere generalizations of one of the innumerable aspects of Reality, & that far from being the most important one; and when I had tried to go *all* round every object which I surveyed, and to place myself at all points of view, so to have the best chance of seeing all sides; I think it is scarcely surprising that for a time I became catholic and tolerant in an extreme degree, & thought one-sidedness almost the one great evil in human affairs, seeing it was the evil which had been the bane of my own teachers, & was also that of those who were warring against my teachers (12 January 1834, XII, 204–5).

His excessive catholicism was, however, soon corrected: 'I also am

---

21 Mill in this passage refers to P. E. L. Dumont's (1802) *redaction* of Bentham.

conscious', he remarked to Carlyle in October 1833, 'that I write with a greater appearance of *sureness* and strong belief than I did for a year or two before, in that period of *recovery* after the petrification of a narrow philosophy, in which one feels *quite sure* of scarcely anything respecting Truth, except that she is many sided' (5 October 1833, XII, 181).

The transformation in perspective is apparent in Mill's obituary article for Bentham of 1832 in the *Examiner*. Formally speaking, it is not, by and large, an unfavourable piece. Bentham is represented as having demolished a body of law which lacked 'a comprehensive consideration of ends and means', and was constructed 'in utter defiance of logic' by appeal to 'vague cloudy generalities arbitrarily assumed *à priori*, and called laws of nature, or principles of natural law' (*CW*, X, 495). Yet more important, Bentham had proceeded to lay the foundation of a new legal structure. Similarly, in the field of morals: 'Mr. Bentham's real merit, in respect to the foundation of morals, consists in his having cleared it more thoroughly than any of his predecessors, from the rubbish of pretended natural law, natural justice, and the like, by which men were wont to consecrate as a rule of morality, whatever they felt inclined to approve of without knowing why.' At the same time, Mill insisted, Bentham was by no means the *founder* of either the science of morals or legislation by dint of his adoption of 'the principle of general utility', for that doctrine, 'as the foundation of virtue', derived from Hume although Bentham applied it 'more consistently and in greater detail, than his predecessors'. And Bentham's characteristic *one-sidedness* is criticized: 'There is something very striking, occasionally, in the minute elaborateness with which he works out, into its smallest details, one half-view of a question, contrasted with his entire neglect of the remaining half-view, though equally indispensable to a correct judgement of the whole' (497–8).[22]

Early in 1833, it will be recalled, Mill referred to 'the dogmatic disputatiousness of my former narrow and mechanical state'. And in this year he published his 'Remarks on Bentham's Philosophy', the anonymity of which he took pains to assure.[23] Bentham's fundamental

22 Mill complained that Bentham failed to study and take into account the views of others and for that reason did not correct this weakness. For further references to the narrowness of the school of utilitarians, cf. letters to Sterling, 20–22 Oct. 1831, *CW*, XII, 81, and to Carlyle, 22 Oct. 1832, *ibid.*, 128. There is a reference to James Mill's narrowness in a letter to Carlyle, 2 Aug. 1833, *ibid.*, 170: '[Grote] is a Utilitarian; in one sense I am so too, but *he* is so in rather a narrow sense . . . He is a man of good, but not first-rate intellect: hard and mechanical; not at all quick; with less *subtlety* than any able and instructed man I ever knew: with much logical and but little aesthetic culture; *narrow* therefore; even narrower than most other Utilitarians of reading and education: more a disciple of my father than of any one else: industrious, brave, *not* very active or spirited . . .'

23 See letters to Carlyle, 11–12 April 1833, *ibid.*, 152, and to Nichol, 14 Oct. 1834, *ibid.*, 236.

principle of utility is laid out in descriptive and prescriptive terms:

> The first principles of Mr. Bentham's philosophy are these; – that happiness, meaning by that term pleasure and exemption from pain, is the only thing desirable in itself; that all other things are desirable solely as means to that end: that the production, therefore, of the greatest possible happiness, is the only fit purpose of all human thought and action, and consequently of all morality & government; and moreover, that pleasure and pain are the sole agencies by which the conduct of mankind is in fact governed, whatever circumstances the individual may be placed in, and whether he is aware of it or not (*CW*, X, 5).[24]

But Mill was now not satisfied. In Bentham's account, those who made reference to the 'law of nature', 'right reason', 'natural rights', a 'moral sense' were supposedly engaged in dogmatic and unjustified assertions regarding the feelings of particular persons. This charge Mill rejected as a misrepresentation flowing from a characteristic failure to do justice to the literature. The philosophers opposed by Bentham[25] contended rather (on the basis of 'an inductive and analytical examination of the human mind') that while 'the pursuit of happiness is natural to us', so also is 'the reverence for, and the inclination to square our actions by, certain general laws of morality'; that the moral sentiments – 'as much part of the original contribution of man's nature as the desire of happiness and fear of suffering' – constituted universally rooted human instincts (and, as such, not further explicable) and not the unjustified personal feelings of particular individuals as Bentham thought (6). Mill did not formally state his actual agreement with the philosophers even when more fairly represented. But a comparison with the obiturary statement suggests at the least that he was now less inclined to dismiss their position out of hand; and taking the 1833 paper as a whole, it does appear that he gave his support to the notion of universal moral sentiments independent from, and with the same status as, the principle of utility – in contrast with his earlier view (described in the *Autobiography*) where morality involves nothing but an 'analysis of consequences'.[26]

To some extent Mill objected merely to a failure on Bentham's part to apply suitably the 'general happiness' rule in the *ethical* context, a complaint

---

24 'Remarks on Bentham's Philosophy', Appendix B in E. L. Bulwer, *England and the English* (1833).

25 Mill cites Reid, Stewart and the German metaphysicians.

26 Even in 1832 we find, in correspondence, a notion of a *permanent* source of morality which is suggestive: 'The *spirit* of all morality, right self-culture' – unlike the details of conduct which 'must be, like all other maxims of prudence, *variable*' – is based on principles 'which cannot change, since man's nature changes not, though surrounding circumstances do . . .' (24 May 1832, *CW*, XII, 101). This observation may be compared with an earlier one whereby even 'the mind of man' is temporally variable (7 Nov. 1829, *ibid.*, 43).

which is in itself consistent with continued adherence to the general Benthamite rule itself: '[T]he mode in which [Bentham] understood and applied the principle of Utility, appears to me far more conducive to the attainment of true and valuable results in [the art of legislation] than in [that of morals] . . .'; for Mill (who identified the latter aspect of Bentham's position with Paley's 'doctrine of expedience') found much wanting:

Now, the great fault I have to find with Mr. Bentham as a moral philosopher, and the source of the chief part of the temporary mischief which in that character, along with a vastly greater amount of permanent good, he must be allowed to have produced is this: that he has practically, to a very great extent, confounded the principle of Utility with the principle of specific consequences, and has habitually made up his estimate of the approbation or blame due to a particular kind of action, from a calculation solely of the consequences to which that very action, if practised generally, would itself lead (*CW*, X, 7-8).

On this view an act which is neutral with respect to the happiness of the agent or of others affected is justified even in the face of general disapproval, which disapproval Bentham saw merely as prejudice and superstition. On Mill's view, by contrast, while the act or the habit in itself may not be pernicious it may reflect a '*character* essentially pernicious, or at least essentially deficient in some quality currently conducive to the "greatest happiness" ' (8).

However, much more was involved than a failure to evaluate correctly the full consequences of an act in estimating the 'greatest happiness' – albeit a serious failure with practical consequences (9). Mill's objections extended from the discourse of prescription to that of description. For he did 'not rank Mr. Bentham very high' as an 'analyst of human nature', since he had 'done little in this department, beyond introducing . . . a very deceptive phraseology, and furnishing a catalogue of the "springs of action," from which some of the most important are left out' (12). Thus by Bentham's first principle that 'the actions of sentient beings are wholly determined by pleasure and pain' or more specifically, 'by our *interests*, by the *preponderant* interest, by the *balance* of motives', Bentham allowed solely for 'pains and pleasures in *prospect*, pains and pleasures to which we look forward as the *consequences* of our acts'. This, Mill insisted, was not universally so, for conduct is also frequently based on the pain and pleasure preceding the contemplated act.[27] To call this 'interest' was not helpful since 'interest' implied an 'end' to which the proposed conduct is a 'means', while at stake was often 'a feeling (call it an association if you think fit) which has no ulterior end, the act or forbearance becoming an end in itself' – an 'impulse' not subject to

---

27 e.g. one recoils from an act because of the 'pain' felt in its very contemplation.

calculation in any strict sense of that term and which defined 'virtuous' behaviour (12–13).

More generally, Mill strongly objected to Bentham's formal enumeration of motives: ' [M] otives are innumerable; there is nothing whatever which may not become an object of desire or dislike by association'. And worse still, Bentham's list actually omitted some powerful operative motives – though, as mentioned above, not strictly speaking calculable 'interests' – pre-eminently 'conscience, or the feeling of duty: one would never imagine from reading him that any human being ever did an act merely because it is right, or abstained from it merely because it is wrong' (13).[28]

Mill allowed that Bentham's notion whereby actions are always governed by 'interests' did not necessarily impute 'universal selfishness to mankind', although Bentham himself believed in the predominance of the selfish principle in human nature', since he counted sympathy (benevolence) as an interest (14). But the formulation adopted by Bentham gave a damaging impression with the most regrettable consequences for those 'with any rational hope of good for the human species':

There are, there have been, many human beings, in whom the motives of patriotism or of benevolence have been permanent steady principles of action, superior to any ordinary, and in not a few instances, to any possible, temptations of personal interest. There are, and have been, multitudes, in whom the motive of conscience or moral obligation has been thus paramount. There is nothing in the constitution of human nature to forbid its being so in all mankind. Until it is so, the race will never enjoy one-tenth part of the happiness which our nature is susceptible of. I regard any considerable increase of human happiness, through mere changes in outward circumstances, unaccompanied by changes in the state of the desires, as hopeless; not to mention that while the desires are circumscribed in self, there can be no adequate motive for exertions tending to modify to good ends even those external circumstances. No man's individual share of any public good which he can hope to realize by his efforts, is an equivalent for the sacrifice of his ease, and of the personal objects which he might attain by another course of conduct. The balance can be turned in favour of virtuous exertion, only by the interest of *feeling* or by that of *conscience* – those ''social interests,'' the necessary subordination of which to ''self-regarding'' is so lightly assumed.
But the power of any one to realize in himself the state of mind, with out which his own enjoyment of life can be but poor and scanty, and on which all our hopes of happiness or moral perfection to the species must rest, depends entirely upon his having faith in the actual existence of such feelings and dispositions in others,

---

28 The motive of 'dury' is identified with the moral sentiments or moral obligation or the moral sense. (Mill observed that Harley, unlike Bentham, had made due allowance for this sense.)

and in their possibility for himself. It is for those in whom the feelings of virtue are weak, that ethical writing is chiefly needful, and its proper office is to strengthen those feelings. But to be qualified for this task, it is necessary, first to have, and next to show, in every sentence and in every line, a firm unwavering confidence in man's capability of virtue. It is by a sort of sympathetic contagion, or inspiration, that a noble mind assimilates other minds to itself; and no one was ever inspired by one whose own inspiration was not sufficient to give him faith in the possibility of making others feel what *he* feels (15–16).

Let us return to Mill's criticism of Bentham on grounds of neglecting the 'general bearing of an action on the entire moral being of the agent' (8). This limitation, Mill maintained, applied with particular force in the domain of ethics. As for legislation he was less concerned provided, however, that institutional arrangements are presumed given. Indeed he had the warmest praise (as in 1832) for Bentham's services to the 'philosophy of legislation':

he was the first who attempted regularly to deduce all the secondary and intermediate principles of law, by direct and systematic inference from the one great axiom or principle of general utility. . . .
This then was the first, and perhaps the grandest achievement of Mr. Bentham; the entire discrediting of all technical systems; and the example which he set of treating law as no peculiar mystery, but a simple piece of practical business, wherein means were to be adapted to ends, as in any of the other arts of life. To have accomplished this . . . is to have equalled the glory of the greatest scientific benefactors of the human race (10). [29]

But for the analysis of these 'greater social questions' themselves Bentham's perspective had little to offer:

Those of the bearings of an action, upon which Mr. Bentham bestowed almost exclusive attention, were also those with which almost alone legislation is conversant. . . A theory . . . which considers little in an action besides that action's *own* consequences, will generally be sufficient to serve the purposes of a philosophy of legislation. Such a philosophy will be most apt to fail in the consideration of the greater social questions – the theory of organic institutions and general forms of polity; for those (unlike the details of legislation) to be duly estimated, must be viewed as the great instruments of forming the national character; of carrying forward the members of the community towards perfection, or preserving them

---

29 Mill went further: Bentham 'was the first who conceived with anything approaching to precision, the idea of a Code, or complete body of law; and the distinctive characters of its essential parts, – the Civil Law, the Penal Law, and the law of Procedure' (10 – 11).

from degeneracy . . . And this signal omission is one of the greatest of the deficiencies by which his speculations on the theory of government, though full of valuable ideas, are rendered, in my judgement, altogether inconclusive in their general results (9).

The potential implications of such a perspective for the subsequent *Principles of Political Economy*, given its objective as defined in the subtitle to that work are clear.

When we turn to the theory of government as such we find further strictures all deriving from a common source, the endemic narrowness of perspective implied by Bentham's presumptions regarding the universality of human motive and environment which led him to recommend a single form of government for all circumstances:

Mr. Bentham's speculations on politics in the narrow sense, that is, on the theory of government, are distinguished by his usual characteristic, that of beginning at the beginning. He places before himself man in society without a government, and, considering what sort of government it would be advisable to construct, finds that the most expedient would be a representative democracy. Whatever may be the value of this conclusion, the mode in which it is arrived at appears to me to be fallacious; for it assumes that mankind are alike in all times and all places, that they have the same wants and are exposed to the same evils, and that if the same institutions do not suit them, it is only because in the more backward stages of improvement they have not wisdom to see what institutions are most for their good. How to invest certain servants of the people with the power necessary for the protection of person and property, with the greatest possible facility to the people of changing the depositaries of that power, when they think it is abused; such is the only problem in social organization which Mr. Bentham has proposed to himself. Yet this is but a part of the real problem. It never seems to have occurred to him to regard political institutions in a higher light, as the principal means of the social education of a people. Had he done so, he would have seen that the same institutions will no more suit two nations in different stages of civilization, than the same lessons will suit children of different ages. As the degree of civilization already attained varies, so does the kind of social influence necessary for carrying the community forward to the next stage of its progress. For a tribe of North American Indians, improvement means, taming down their proud and solitary self-dependence; for a body of emancipated negroes, it means accustoming them to be self-dependent, instead of being merely obedient to orders: for our semi-barbarous ancestors it would have meant, softening them; for a race of enervated Asiatics it would mean hardening them. How can the same social organization be fitted for producing so many contrary effects? (16)

Bentham's perspective on political obligation – that it derived from a reasoned perception of the necessity of legal protection and a common interest in obedience to the law (a presumption utilized in the recommendation for representative government) – was equally fallacious. For it neglected the force of habit: '[Bentham] was not, I am persuaded, aware, how very much of the really wonderful acquiescence of mankind in any government which they find established, is the effect of mere habit and imagination, and therefore, depends upon the preservation of something like continuity of existence in the institutions, and identity in their outward forms; cannot transfer itself easily to new institutions, even though in themselves preferable; and is greatly shaken when there occurs anything like a break in the line of historical duration – anything which can be termed the end of the old constitution and the beginning of a new one' (17). A powerful conservative dimension to the problem of institutional change is apparently introduced by Mill: 'The very fact that a certain set of political institutions already exist, have long existed, and have become associated with all the historical recollections of a people, is in itself, as far as it goes, a property which adapts them to a people, and gives them a great advantage over any new institutions in obtaining that ready and willing resignation to what has once been decided by lawful authority, which alone renders possible those innumerable compromises between adverse interests and expectations, without which no government could be carried on for a year, and with difficulty even for a week.'[30] Yet we must always remember that Mill was attempting to trace a middle road. For he also wrote of constitutional writers prior to Bentham who carried the matter of custom 'to the height of a superstition; they never considered what was best adapted to their own times, but only what had existed in former times, even in times that had long gone by ', in an 'absurd sacrifice of present ends to antiquated means'.

There will be found also in Bulwer's *England and the English* (1833) a passage by Mill[31] summarizing his new position but in terms which substantially reinforce the objection to the greater happiness principle. Thus he refers to his Appendix to Bulwer as a statement of 'the principal tenets of Bentham, with an exposition of what I conceive to be his errors; pointing out at once

30 See also letter to Carlyle, 9 March 1833, *CW*, XII, 145 on the reformed Parliament, which he described as 'so ridiculously like what I expected' implicitly mocking his father's grandiose expectations from constitutional change. '[Some] of our Utilitarian Radicals are downcast enough', he proceeded, 'having deemed that the nation had in it more wisdom and virtue than they now see it has, and that the vicious state of the representation kept this wisdom & virtue out of parliament. At least this good will come out of their disappointment, that they will no longer rely upon the infallibility of Constitution-mongering: they admit that we have as good a House of Commons as *any* mode of election would have given us, in the present state of cultivation of our people . . . For myself, I have well-nigh ceased to feel interested in politics. The time is not yet come for renovation, and the work of destruction goes on of itself without the aid of hands.'

31 See editorial comments *CW*, X, 499.

the benefits he has conferred, and also the mischief he has affected . . . I have there, regarding him as a legislator and a moralist, ventured to estimate him much more highly in the former capacity than the latter; endeavouring to combat the infallibility of his application of the principle of Utility, and to show the dangerous and debasing theories, which may be, and are deduced from it.' But more than that: even in legislation 'his greatest happiness principle is not so clear and undeniable as it is usually conceded to be. "The greatest happiness of the greatest number" is to be our invariable guide! Is it so? – the greatest happiness of the greatest number of men living, I suppose, not of men to come; for if of all posterity, what legislator can be our guide? Who can prejudge the future? Of men living, then? – well – how often would *their* greatest happiness consist in concession to their greatest errors' (*CW*, X, 501–2).

This latter objection (which does not appear so clearly in the Bulwer Appendix) is profoundly disturbing for it raises the question: how is the 'greatest good' to be defined? In medieval times the rule 'demanded a bonfire of old women'. The greatest happiness principle was, Mill concluded, 'an excellent general rule, but it is not an undeniable axiom'.

Mill's 'Corporation and Church Property' published in the same year points further still from Bentham. Here a sharp distinction is made between 'expediency' and 'morality', the former a relative matter depending on circumstances, the latter (incorporating 'justice' or 'right') absolute and universal:

It is a twofold problem; a question of expediency, and a question of morality: the former complex and depending upon temporary circumstances; the latter simple and unchangeable. We are to examine, not merely in what way a certain portion of property may be most usefully employed; that is a subsequent consideration: but, whether it can be touched at all without spoliation; whether the diversion of the estates of foundations from the present hands, and from the present purposes, would be disposing of what is justly our own, or robbing somebody else of what is his; violating property, endangering all rights, and infringing the first principles of the social union . . . And, if this were so, it would already be an act of immorality even to discuss the other question. It is not a fit occupation for an honest man, to cast up the probable profits of an act of plunder. If a resumption [i.e. redirection] of endowments belongs to a class of acts which, by universal agreement, ought to be abstained from, whatever may be their consequences; there is no more to be said (*CW*, IV, 195–6).

Mill's divergence from (his interpretation of) Bentham and from his own earlier position which entailed 'the ethical principle of Pleasurable and Painful Consequences' is apparent.[32] There is now said to be appeal to

---

32 In a striking letter to Carlyle of 12 Jan. 1834 *CW*, XII, 207–8) Mill formally classified himself as a 'utilitarian', but in a very special sense, placing much weight upon each

an absolute standard apart from utility (and this, moreover, even in a context relating to legislation).[33]

* * *

A word next regarding Mill's famous analysis of Sedgwick's *Discourse* (1835), a most difficult item to evaluate. In correspondence Mill described it as a representation of 'the "utilitarian theory of morals" . . . for the first time in its true colours. At all events, I have incidentally represented my own mode of looking at ethical questions; having never yet seen in print any statement of principles on the subject to which I could subscribe' (26 Nov. 1834, XII, 238). But we must proceed cautiously, for we know from the *Autobiography* that Mill suppressed certain passages which his father read as an 'attack on Bentham and on him' (I, 209); and he warned in the Preface to *Dissertations and Discussions* that the review 'might give an impression of more complete adhesion to the philosophy of Locke, Bentham, and the eighteenth century, than is really the case, and of an inadequate sense of its deficiencies . . .' (1859, V).

In the course of his paper Mill describes the conflict between those who regard our ideas of right and wrong as 'ultimate and inexplicable' facts perceived by a peculiar faculty of human nature (*CW*, X, 51), [34] and the utilitarians who account for such ideas (as all other complex ideas and corresponding feelings) in terms of our intellect and senses and, more

individual's conception of his greater good and the means to achieve it best: 'Another of our differences is, that I am still, & am likely to remain, a utilitarian; though not one of "the people called utilitarians"; indeed, having scarcely one of my secondary premises in common with them; nor a utilitarian at all, unless in quite another sense from what perhaps any one except myself understands by the word . . . I have never, at least since I had any convictions of my own, belonged to the benevolentiary, soup-kitchen school. Though I hold the good of the species (or rather of its several units) to be the *ultimate* end (which is the alpha & omega of my utilitarianism) I believe with the fullest Belief that this end can in no other way be forwarded but by the means you speak of, namely be each taking for his exclusive aim the development of what is best in *himself*. I qualify or explain this doctrine no otherwise than as you yourself do, since you hold that every human creature has an appointed task to perform which task he is to know & find out for himself; this can only be by discovering in what manner such faculties as he possesses or can acquire may produce most good in the world . . .' It is most unlikely, however, that this constitutes the entirety of the picture, for the principles of legislation are not here allowed for.

33 Cf. also 219 where an independent source of moral obligation is implied: '[A]ny deviation from it [a reference to a man's declared will], not called for by high considerations of social good, even when not a violation of property, runs counter to a feeling so nearly allied to those on which the respect for property is founded, that there is scarcely a possibility of infringing the one without shaking the security of the other'.

34 And 'the pleasures and pains, the desires and aversions, consequent upon this perception' also as 'ultimate facts in our nature'.

precisely, for whom 'the particular property in actions, which constitutes them moral or immoral . . . is the influence of those actions, and of the dispositions from which they emanate, upon human happiness'.[35] In this context Mill repeats the fundamentally important observation made in the Bulwer text of the previous year but now applies it to both parties: 'Whether the ethical creed of a follower of utility will lead him to moral or immoral consequences, depends on what he thinks useful; – just as, with a partizan of the opposite doctrine – that of innate conscience – it depends on what he thinks his conscience enjoins' (52). Whichever of the two doctrines was the 'true' one – and Mill only observes (unfortunately without elaboration) that 'those who maintain that human happiness is the end and test of morality are bound to prove that the principle is true' – it would remain to establish 'such secondary and intermediate maxims, as may be guides . . . into the application of the principle . . .' The first principle by itself, in either case, is in terms of practice *empty*; and further specification of what both the 'greatest happiness' and the 'moral sense' enjoins was always required to fill the gap.[36] This perspective was to be rehearsed time and again.

In the paper at hand Mill played down the problem of defining and evaluating the consequences of actions as far as concerned 'the outward interests of oneself and of other people'; just behaviour in this local sense was 'in general sufficiently pointed out by a few plain rules, and by the laws of one's country' (56). This (in effect) was a reply to Sedgwick's objection that 'if utility be the standard, different persons may have different opinions on morality' (67). There was less uncertainty than Sedgwick believed in approaching the question: '[W]hat is justice? – . . . what are those claims of others which we are bound to respect? and *what is* the conduct required by "regard to the common good?"' (64). For individuals were not isolated: 'Every one directs himself in morality, as in all his conduct, not by his own unaided foresight, but by the accumulated wisdom of all

35 Mill refers also to the utilitarian contention 'that the morality of actions is perceived by the same faculties by which we perceive any other of the qualities of actions, namely, our intellects and our senses. They hold the capacity of perceiving moral distinctions to be no more a distinct faculty than the capacity of trying causes, or of making a speech to a jury' (61). This applies also to, e.g., ambition, honour, envy – all are feelings created by 'association' rather than distinct or peculiar in themselves. Mill himself did not accept this position as is made clear later in the paper. There was, he maintained, a 'moral sense' (below, p. 629).

36 Mill took a totally fair position. Thus Sedgwick objected that if utility were the 'end' it would be made to justify the means, to which Mill replied: 'just as far as in any other system, and no further. In every system of morality, the end, when good, justifies all means which do not conflict with some more important good . . . According to the principle of utility, the end justifies all means necessary to its attainment, except those which are more mischievous than the end is useful . . .' (72).

former ages, embodied in traditional aphorisms' (65–6).[37] Thus while Mill denied the pretense 'that nature tells what is right' and challenged Sedgwick to show what rules of conduct were yielded by 'the moral sense' (67, 64) – and thus seems to have moved away from the allowance for an absolute and universal standard of justice made in 'Corporation and Church Property' – he himself recognized that the utilitarian, in arriving at moral evaluations, must also make appeal to some external source – apparently customary standards.

The customary state of opinion which Mill had in mind, he knew, however, to be an imperfect source for moral rules. He had said as much in the previous year, and again repeats the warning here: '[T]he progress of experience, and the growth of the human intellect, succeed but too slowly in correcting and improving traditional opinions' (66). But there did exist at any time, a more objective or 'correct' standard which was recognizable with the aid of 'cultivated reason':

According to the theory of utility . . . the question, what is our duty, is as open to discussion as any other question. Moral doctrines are no more to be received without evidence, nor to be sifted less carefully, than any other doctrines. An appeal lies, as on all other subjects, from a received opinion, however generally entertained, to the decisions of cultivated reason. The weakness of human intellect, and all the other infirmities of our nature [interest, passion], are considered to interfere as much with the rectitude of our judgements on morality, as on any other of our concerns; and changes as great are anticipated in our opinions on that subject, as on every other, both from the progress of intelligence, from more authentic and enlarged experience, and from alterations in the condition of the human race, requiring altered rules of conduct (74).

That there were problems he did not deny, but they were no greater than those faced by the opponents of utility: '[W]here there is uncertainty, men's passions will bias their judgment. Granted; this is one of the evils of our condition, and must be borne with. We do not diminish it by pretending that nature tells us what is right . . .' (67).

Whether or not the standard of reference was a changing one – and Mill seems here to believe (unlike Sedgwick) that it was – there was no escape from the basic conclusion that the greatest happiness principle did not *in itself* yield rules of just behaviour. This conclusion is reinforced when consideration is made of the consequences of actions for character[38] – an

37 Mill devoted an entire paper to 'aphorisms' (*CW*, I, 419–29).
38 Mill's concern specifically was with the effects of action 'upon [an individual's] susceptibilities of pleasures or pain, upon the general direction of his thoughts, feelings, and imagination, or upon some particular association' (56). Although Paley was guilty of overemphasizing the objective consequences of actions, this was not inherent in the

issue raised against Bentham in the 'Remarks on Bentham's Philosophy' of the previous year; for there was 'as much difference in the moral judgments of different persons, as there is in their views of human nature, and of the formation of character'. Accordingly, 'clear and comprehensive views of education and human culture must therefore precede, and form the basis of, a philosophy of morals . . .' (56). Here we have it again: Even a utilitarian perspective must turn upon some conception or other of 'morality' *drawn from an external source* which defined 'right' or 'true human feeling'.

Some of the broader consequences of actions were, however, not a matter of concern for the average citizen, a point used by Mill in partial rebuttal of Sedgwick: 'Mr. Sedgwick's argument resembles one we often hear, that the principle of utility must be false, because it supposes morality to be founded on the good of society, an idea too complex for the majority of mankind, who look only to the particular persons concerned. Why, none but those who mingle in public transactions, or whose example is likely to have extensive influence, have any occasion to look beyond the particular persons concerned. Morality, for all other people, consists in doing good and refraining from harm, to themselves and to those who immediately surround them' (59). The major problems of defining the nature and scope of just behaviour from a utilitarian perspective were problems for the legislator and the educator.[39]

Here Mill elaborates somewhat more clearly his own conception of the source of moral feelings – the status of their natural and artificial components, as it were. He did not maintain (as did Mandeville) that such feelings 'are factitious and artificial associations, inculcated by parents and teachers purposely to further certain social ends, and no more congenial to our natural feelings than the contrary associations'. It is from our 'natural constitution' that we derive our affections of love and aversion to human beings, and here in 'the unselfish part of our nature [in 'sympathy'] lies *a foundation*, even independently of inculcation from without, for the generation of moral feelings'. But 'because it is not inconsistent with the constitution of our nature that moral feelings should grow up independently of teaching' it did not follow 'that they generally do so, or that teaching is not the source

doctrine of utility itself which extended to 'our internal sources of happiness or unhappiness' (69). It was, in short, untrue 'that utility estimates actions by this sort of consequences ['worldly' standards of wealth, power, social position]; it estimates them by all their consequences'.

39 In earlier correspondence (letter to Carlyle, 12 Jan. 1834, cited above note 32) it will be recalled, Mill had observed that it was each one's individual definition of the greatest good and choice of means that constituted together the general good. That formulation, however, neglected entirely the question of legislation so there is no necessary conflict with the present context.

of almost all the moral feeling which exists in the world . . .' (60).[40] Sympathy in brief, is a 'natural' sentiment upon which, with the indispensable aid of education, is founded moral feelings – the evaluation of just behaviour. In this manner Mill attempted to trace a path between the more extreme versions of the two doctrines he was describing.

Mill later referred to this paper as a 'vindication of the fundamental principles of Bentham's philosophy'.[41] Seen from Sedgwick's viewpoint this might be so. But the fact that Mill deleted sections formally critical of Bentham must not be forgotten. We do not have the full picture.

* * *

The essay of 1838 for the *London and Westminster Review* devoted specifically to 'Bentham' is rather more critical, although still attempting to steer a middle course.[42] Mill praises Bentham for his great innovation in morals

40 Thus a very young child has affections of sympathy (e.g. towards its mother) and may refrain from some indulgence in consequence. But this is not a matter of morality. Morality enters the picture with an act of imagination – of the pain caused to any other. Now this act of imagination is *taught* though the pains of others may be 'naturally painful to us'.

An observation in Mill's paper 'On the Definition of Political Economy' (1836) is relevant here: 'Those laws of human nature which relate to the feelings called forth in a human being by other [individual (1844)] human or intelligent beings, as such, namely the *affections*, the *conscience*, or feelings of duty, and the love of *approbation*; and to the conduct of man, so far as it depends upon, or has relation to, these parts of his nature – form the subject of another portion of pure mental philosophy, namely, that portion of it on which *morals*, or *ethics* are founded. For morality itself is not a science, but an art; not truths but rules. The truths on which the rules are founded are drawn (as is the case in all arts) from a variety of sciences; but the principal of them, and those which are most nearly peculiar to this particular art, belong to a branch of the science of mind' (*CW*, IV, 319–20).

Here morality, it appears, is not itself represented as an absolute concept but rather as 'rules' based on appropriate laws of human nature (including, presumably, a moral sense). This would be consistent with the position in 'Sedgwick', and diverges from the strong position taken in 'Corporation and Church Property' (1833). (But this paper though first published in 1836, was written five years earlier and rewritten in 1833 (cf. *ibid.*, 309) so there is something of a problem of consistency.)

41 *Autobiography*, *CW*, I, 227 (below p. 639). Robson (1964), 259 refers to the item as 'a defence of utilitarianism which does not deal with Bentham . . .'

42 Cf. Viner (1958), 322: 'In these articles Mill was clearly endeavoring to salvage, or at least shrinking from abandoning a utilitarian system of ethics while rejecting such features of Bentham's system as he could no longer tolerate. There was high praise, therefore, for Bentham as well as high blame. His main criticism of Bentham related to his treatment of private morals and of psychology, and especially the stress Bentham put on the role played in human behaviour by calculation of gain or loss. He objected

and politics – his application thereto of scientific method, 'a value beyond all price, even though we should reject the whole, as we unquestionably must a large part, of the opinions themselves' (*CW*, X, 83). Most satisfactory was Bentham's belief that 'error lies in generalities' leading to his rejection of phrases (appeals, e.g., to the 'moral sense', 'rule of right', the 'fitness of things', the 'law of nature', 'natural justice') as attempts to impose opinion without reference to a genuine standard of appeal.[43] But to this latter charge itself Mill gave a mixed response:

Few, we believe, are now of opinion that these phrases and similar ones have nothing more in them than Bentham saw. But it will be as little pretended, now-a-days, . . . that the phrases can pass as reasons, till after their meaning has been completely analysed, and translated into more precise language: until the standard they appeal to is ascertained, and the *sense* in which, and the *limits* within which, they are admissible as arguments, accurately marked out (86).

It is a fine line that Mill attempts to tread.[44]

Very harsh charges are made in this paper against the narrowness of Bentham's conception of human nature – a narrowness reflecting, Mill maintained, the use of introspection as almost the sole source for the behavioural axioms. Envisaging behaviour as a susceptibility to pleasures and pains governed partly by self-interest and the selfish passions and partly by sympathies and antipathies toward others – led him to neglect entirely the pursuit of 'spiritual perfection' as an end in itself, namely, 'the desire

> also that Bentham, by shifting from a technical (or broad) meaning of terms – and especially of the term ''interest'' – to a popular (or narrow) meaning, often slid into an account of human behaviour which pictured it as inherently selfish.'

43 Mill (86) makes much of Bentham's 'method of detail': 'It is the introduction into the philosophy of human conduct, of this method of detail – of this practice of never reasoning about wholes until they have been resolved into their parts, nor about abstractions until they have been translated into realities – that constitutes the originality of Bentham in philosophy, and makes him the great reformer of the moral and political branch of it.' As for the 'generalities of his philosophy' he had little to offer that was novel. The doctrine that general utility is the foundation of morality he derived from Helvetius and other eighteenth century (and earlier) writers (86–7). Any doctrine, not just this, could be approached in terms of the method of detail. Bentham himself was unaware of these characteristics of his work (90). (Bentham's failure to do justice to the literature had been already commented on in 1833; see above, note 22).

44 The passage was reformulated in the second edition (1867), although remaining critical of Bentham: 'Few will contend that this is a perfectly fair representation of the *animus* of those who employ the various phrases so amusingly animadverted to; but that the phrases contain no argument, save what is grounded on the very feelings they are adduced to justify, is a truth which Bentham had the eminent merit of first pointing out.'

of perfection, or the feeling of an approving or of an accusing conscience' (95 – 6);[45] an almost total neglect of other ends;[46] and even a constrained version of sympathy (97).[47] Apart from this constrained sympathy 'There remained, as a motive by which mankind are influenced, and by which they may be guided to their good, only personal interest. Accordingly, Bentham's idea of the world is that of a collection of persons pursuing each his separate interest of pleasure, and the prevention of whom from jostling one another more than is unavoidable, may be attempted by hopes and fears derived from three sources – the law, religion, and public opinion', that is from *sanction*, whether legal, religious and popular. The charges, it may be noted, are specifically directed against Bentham rather than his followers:

he has not been followed in this grand oversight by any of the able men who, from the extent of their intellectual obligations to him, have been regarded as his disciples. They may have followed him in his doctrine of utility, and in his rejection of a moral sense as the test of right and wrong: but while repudiating it as such, they have, with Hartley, acknowledged it as a fact in human nature; they have endeavoured to account for it, to assign its laws; nor are they justly chargeable either with undervaluing this part of our nature, or with any disposition to throw it into the background of their speculations. If any part of the influence of this cardinal error has extended itself to them, it is circuitously, and through the effect on their minds of other parts of Bentham's doctrines (97).

This is an ambiguous formulation, for where precisely Mill himself stood on the spectrum is not made absolutely clear. The existence of a moral sense is definitely asserted (as in 1835) but whether Mill included himself amongst those who accepted the moral sense *as the test of right and wrong* is less certain. That he regarded himself as one of the 'followers' of Bentham – using the term as here defined – is suggested by a subsequent comment in the paper that Bentham was on the right track in his emphasis on '*the consequences of actions* in considering their morality, his failure being a 'lack of adequate

---

45 The reference is to the capacity 'of desiring, for its own sake, the conformity of his own character to his standard of excellence, without hope of good or fear of evil from other source than his own inward consciousness'. (It is not denied that Bentham allowed for 'conscience'. But he identified it with philanthropy with an eye on the affection of God or man – to opinion.)

46 Mill refers to Bentham's almost total neglect of the sense of honour (acting independently of other people's opinion); and of the love of beauty, order, power (though not in the sense of power over others) and of action.

47 Thus sympathy is not extended to the love of loving. Benthamite 'sympathy' was inadequate, Mill maintained, as a security for virtuous action. For personal affection could be turned to the disadvantage of third parties, while general philanthropy (when divorced from a feeling of duty) is weak.

knowledge regarding character formation and thus the consequences of actions for the agent's own frame of mind' (111 – 12). On the other hand, he also greatly played down the doctrine. The first principle of utilitarianism (or any other doctrine) had always to be supplemented by secondary principles and by itself did not carry one far:

All we intend to say at present is, that we are much nearer to agreeing with Bentham in his principle, than in the degree of importance which he attached to it. We think utility, or happiness, much too complex and indefinite an end to be sought except through the medium of various secondary ends, concerning which there may be, and often is, agreement among persons who differ in their ultimate standard; and about which there does in fact prevail a much greater unanimity among thinking persons, than might be supposed from their diametrical divergence on the great questions of moral metaphysics . . . Those who adopt utility as a standard can seldom apply it truly except through the secondary principles; those who reject it, generally do no more than erect those secondary principles into first principles. We consider, therefore, the utilitarian controversy as a question of arrangement and logical subordination rather than practice, important principally in a purely scientific point of view, for the sake of the systematic unity and coherence of ethical philosophy. Whatever be our own opinion on the subject, it is from no such source that we look for the great improvements which we believe are destined to take place in ethical doctrine (110–11).

This passage is profoundly significant. It relegates the entire utility principle to the sidelines – except as providing an organizational discipline for accurate thought – and reiterates that adherents are obliged to seek further principles in supplement, which may be none other than the first principles of their opponents: utilitarianism cannot dispense with external standards of reference.

It should, however, be remarked that the statement was somewhat toned down for a later edition, by alterations of the first sentence to read:

At present we shall only say, that while, under proper explanations, we entirely agree with Bentham in his principle, we do not hold with him that all right thinking on the details of morals depends on its express exertion . . . It is when five or more of the secondary principles conflict, that a direct appeal to some first principle becomes necessary; and then commences the practical importance of the utilitarian controversy; which is, in other respects, a question of arrangement . . .

But the greater significance here accorded to the first principle applies only in special cases. And Mill did not alter a passage designed apparently to separate himself from Bentham, namely 'that to the principle of utility we owe all that Bentham did; that it was necessary to him to find a first principle that he could receive as self-evident, and to which he could attach all his other doctrines as logical consequences: that to him systematic unity was an indispensable condition of his confidence in his own intellect'.

It is relevant that Mill left unstated his own conception of 'the end to which morality should be referred'. What he here insisted upon was rational discourse: '[T]hat it be referred to an *end* of some sort, and not left in the dominion of vague feeling or inexplicable internal conviction, that it be made a matter of reason and calculation, and not merely of sentiment, is essential to the very idea of moral philosophy; is, in fact, what renders argument or discussion on moral questions possible. That the morality of actions depends on the consequences which they tend to produce, is the doctrine of rational persons of all schools; that the good or evil of those consequences is measured solely by pleasure or pain, is all of the doctrine of the school of utility which is peculiar to it' (111). This passage too remained unaltered in later editions.

Bentham's narrowness of perspective, Mill complained further, was disastrous as far as concerned personal ethics, for overlooking 'the existence of about half of the whole number of mental feelings which human beings are capable of, including all those of which the direct objects are states of their own mind' he could give no guidance at all:

Morality consists of two parts. One of these is self-education; the training, by the human being himself of his affections and will. That department is a blank in Bentham's system. The other and coequal part, the regulation of his outward actions, must be altogether halting and imperfect without the first; for how can we judge in what manner many an action will affect even the worldly interests of ourselves or others, unless we take in, as part of the question, its influence on the regulation of our, or their, affections and desires? (98)[48]

The foregoing criticism of Bentham brings to mind that to similar effect in his 'Remarks on Bentham's Philosophy' five years earlier, and in his discussion of Sedgwick's *Discourse* in 1835, although Mill now goes further in charging that the faulty appreciation of human nature actually impeded an evaluation of the morality of personal conduct even in the narrow sense of 'worldly interests'. Equally serious were the consequences for an adequate appreciation of the material interests of society as a whole – of the evaluation of the laws and institutions appropriate for economic development in various

---

48 At most Bentham's rules prescribed for the individual 'worldly prudence, and outward probity and beneficence'.

temporal and geographical settings. For 'a philosophy of laws and institutions, not founded on a philosophy of national character, is an absurdity'. At best Bentham could 'indicate the means by which, in any given state of the national mind, the material interests of society can be protected; saving the question . . . whether the use of those means would have, on the national character any injurious influence' (99). Mill's summary of his estimate speaks for itself:

We have arrived, then, at a sort of estimate of what a philosophy like Bentham's can do. It can teach the means of organizing and regulating the merely *business* part of the social arrangements. Whatever can be understood or whatever done without reference to moral influences, his philosophy is equal to; where those influences require to be taken into account, it is at fault. He committed the mistake of supposing that the business part of human affairs was the whole of them; all at least that the legislator and the moralist had to do with . . . (99–100).[49]

The moralist and legislator, Mill insisted, had to do with moral influences in evaluating the 'greatest happiness'.

Mill complained similarly of the weight placed by Bentham upon the forseeable consequences of an action, which gave his moral philosophy a 'cold, mechanical, and ungenial air'; Bentham wrote as if that 'ought to be the sole master of all our actions, and even of all our sentiments; as if either to admire or like, or despise or dislike a person for any action which neither does good nor harm . . . were an injustice and a prejudice . . . He thought it an insolent piece of dogmatism in one person to praise or condemn another in a matter of taste: as if men's likings and dislikings, on things in themselves indifferent, were not full of the most important inferences as to every point of their character; as if a person's tastes did not show him to be wise or a fool, cultivated or ignorant, gentle or rough, sensitive or callous, generous or sordid, benevolent or selfish, conscientious or depraved' (112–13).[50]

There remains Mill's reactions in 1838 to Bentham on legislation and government for which issues what has just been said is highly relevant. By and large the critical stance of 1833 is reiterated. While Bentham's 'greatest triumph' was his scientific contribution to law (its codification and systematic arrangement), and while his 'On the Influence of Time and Place in Matters of Legislation' recognized the varying needs of different nations with respect to law, his contribution to constitutional (in contrast to civil and penal)

49 Cf. also 96, 113, on the obligation to take into account character.
50 Cf. 'To say either that man should, or that he should not, take pleasure in one thing, displeasure in another, appeared to him as much an act of despotism in the moralist as in the political ruler' (96).

legislation suffered from the 'limitations . . . which were set to all his speculations by the imperfections of his theory of human nature. For, taking . . . next to no account of national character and the causes which form and maintain it, he was precluded from considering except to a very limited extent, the laws of a country as an instrument of national culture' (100, 105).

Thus Bentham's approach to government – his case for majority rule – was much weakened. Abuses of government authority were to be controlled by requiring responsibility to persons whose 'interest' accorded with the end of good government (defined as the interest of the whole community), which control would be assured by responsibility to the numerical majority (106). 'But is this fundamental doctrine of Bentham's political philosophy an universal truth?' Mill objected. 'Is it, at all times and places, good for mankind to be under the absolute authority of the majority of themselves? . . . Is it, we say, the proper condition of man, in all ages and nations, to be under the despotism of Public Opinion?' (107). Mill's particular concern was cultural dictatorship and the threat 'to the further improvement of man's intellectual and moral nature' – a clear index of the existence of 'secondary principles' to which appeal must be made even by formal adherents to utilitarianism. 'The power of the majority is salutary', Mill allowed, 'so far as it is used defensively, not offensively – as its exertion is tempered by respect for the personality of the individual, and deference to superiority of cultivated intelligence' (108-9).[51] A mere parroting of the 'greatest happiness' rule, Mill believed, could entail gross injustice – a point, we have seen, already insisted upon in 1833.

The informal correspondence provides a remarkable summary of Mill's position at the time he penned his major paper on Bentham. I have in mind a statement to Bulwer regarding the opportunity provided by the death of James Mill to reform the *Westminster Review*, which summarizes, in effect, the essence of the paper as far as it pertains to government:

As good may be drawn out of evil – the event which has deprived the world of the man of greatest philosophical genius it possessed & the review (if such little interest may be spoken of by the side of great ones) of its most powerful writer, & the only one to whose opinions the editors were obliged to defer – that same event has made it far easier to do that, in the hope of which alone I allowed myself to become connected with the review – namely to soften the harder & sterner features of its

51 Bentham, Mill conceded, was admirable in promoting 'one of the ideal qualities of a perfect government – identity of interest between the trustees and the community for whom they hold the power in trust', and in showing how this requirement had been sacrificed in modern Europe to the 'sinister interest of rulers'. But Bentham was one-sided in his emphasis on public opinion. The majority might be the least unjust of all possible alternatives but institutions were required as corrective, to assure an 'opposition to the will of the majority'.

radicalism and utilitarianism, both which in the form in which they originally appeared in the Westminster, were part of the inheritance of the 18th century. The Review ought to represent not radicalism but neoradicalism, a radicalism which is not democracy, not a bigotted adherence to any forms of government or to one kind of institutions, & which is only to be called radicalism inasmuch as it does not palter nor compromise with evils but cuts at their roots – & a utilitarianism which takes into account the whole of human nature not the ratiocinative faculty only – the utilitarianism which never makes any peculiar figure as such, nor would ever constitute its followers a sect or school – which fraternizes with all who hold the same *axiomata media* (as Bacon has it) whether their first principle is the same or not – & which holds in the highest reverence all which the vulgar notion of utilitarians represents them to despise – which holds Feeling at least as valuable as Thought, & Poetry not only on a par with, but the necessary condition of, any true & comprehensive Philosophy (23 Nov. 1836, XII, 312).

His differences with the vulgar utilitarians had been 'growing wider and wider' since 1829:

[W]hat is the meaning of *your* insisting upon identifying me with Grote or Roebuck or the rest? Do you in your conscience think that my opinions are at all like theirs? Have you forgotten, what I am sure you once knew, that my opinion of their philosophy is & has for years been *more* unfavourable by far than your own? & that my radicalism is of a school of the most remote from theirs, at all points, which exists? They knew this as long ago as 1829, since which time the variance has been growing wider & wider (to Fonblanque, 30 Jan. 1838, XIII, 370).[52]

IV THE GREATEST HAPPINESS PRINCIPLE POST-1840:
THE RETURN TO BENTHAM

There is some difficulty in getting a grip on Mill's centre of gravity. *The Autobiography* dates a third period of 'mental progress' – the Harriet Taylor period – from approximately 1840: 'In this third period (as it may be termed) of my mental progress, which now went hand in hand with hers, my opinions gained equally in breadth and depth. I understood more things, and those which I had understood before, I now understood more thoroughly. I had now completely turned back from what there had been in excess in my reaction against Benthamism' (*CW*, I, 237). This retrospective view implies a change in position after 1840. But it is not clear that the interpretation was consistently maintained. For a somewhat different formulation given in the preface to the *Dissertations and Discussions*, 1859 implies less a substantive change of perspective over time than a deliberate alteration in the weighting

52 Cf. letter to Comte, 8 Nov. 1841: His 'sortie définitive de la section benthamiste de l'école révolutionnaire' was hastened by reading Comte's treatise on *Politique Positive* (*ibid.*, 489).

of the argument at various stages to meet particular audiences. Thus any impression that the paper on Sedgwick's *Discourse* (1835) had taken too uncritical a view of 'Bentham and the eighteenth century' Mill hoped would be rectified by the essay on 'Bentham' (1838) and that on 'Coleridge' (1840) with its sympathetic treatment of Coleridge's ethical and political views. These papers, however, were not the last word: 'These, again, if they stood alone, would give just as much too strong an impression of the writer's sympathy with the reaction of the nineteenth century against the eighteenth: but this exaggeration will be corrected by the more recent defence of the "greatest happiness" ethics against Dr. Whewell [1852]' (*CW*, X, 494). Indeed this latter interpretation may be supported from a further passage in the *Autobiography* itself which maintains continued adherence to the substance of the 1838 paper on Bentham – including its demonstration of the 'errors and deficiencies of his philosophy' – despite questions regarding the strategic wisdom of its publication:

[W]hile doing full justice to the merits of Bentham, I pointed out what I thought the errors and deficiencies of his philosophy. The substance of this criticism I still think perfectly just; but I have sometimes doubted whether it was right to publish it at that time. I have often felt that Bentham's philosophy, as an instrument of progress, has been to some extent discredited before it had done its work, and that to lend a hand towards lowering its reputation was doing more harm than service to improvement (I, 225, 227).

It is in this context too that Mill represented the (1835) review of Sedgwick's *Discourse* – and not only the later review of 'Whewell on Moral Philosophy' (1852) – as a 'vindication of the fundamental principles of Bentham's philosophy',[53] a position we have seen already to be an exaggeration (above, p. 63). In all of this Mill seems to be attempting to play down any notion of a substantive alteration in position over time on his part.[54]

Mill is not very convincing. The materials of 1833 appeal to some absolute standard apart from utility (above pp. 620, 627). This is implied in 1835 (p. 628) – 'General happiness' reappears as the ultimate standard in 1838 but is all but relegated to the sidelines, with the weight of emphasis placed on secondary principles, which (in practice) might transpire to be the first principles of other ethical doctrines. Mill treads a fine line in attempting to avoid a *formal* appeal to some absolute external standard of reference

53 'Now however when a counter-reaction appears to be setting in towards what is good in Benthamism, I can look with more satisfaction on this criticism of its defects, especially as I have myself balanced it by vindications of the fundamental principles of Bentham's philosophy . . .' (*CW*, I, 227).
54 Cf. also the statement in the *Autobiography*, I, 175, to the 'truths' of his 'early opinions' from which 'in no essential part' he 'at any time wavered'.

which would have placed him in the same camp as the natural or providential moralists.

When we turn to the materials of the 1850s and 1860s a sharp change in tone, and (more important) of substance, is discernible regarding these matters. First, however, a word on the *System of Logic* (1843, *CW*, VIII, 889f) which contains the famous charge that Bentham's political science was 'unscientific' envisaged as it was to be of *universal* applicability based upon, at best, locally relevant axioms – that self-interest is the predominant motive of rulers (as of everyone else) and that the sole method of assuring a coincidence of their self-interest and the interest of the governed is by acting upon it. All of this recalls the items of 1833 (above, p. 624) and it apparently constituted a 'permanent' objection to Benthamite procedure since the work was reissued in eight editions during Mill's own lifetime (ed. 8, 1872). This criticism, therefore, was not considered by Mill to detract from his *defence* of Bentham in 1851–2, a fact which raises some potential problems of consistency, considering his 'rereading' of Bentham on the ubiquity of the purely self-regarding motive, a matter taken up in the present section.

Consider first a statement of 1851 regarding the argument for private property in terms of 'natural right'. Here Mill denies any genuine meaning to that expression except as a reflection of 'fitness', i.e. of consequences in terms of the effect on 'human happiness':

We apprehend that what is called natural right, would be more properly described as a first appearance of right; it is a perception of fitness, grounded on some of the more obvious circumstances of the case, and requires, quite as much as any other first impression, to be corrected or controlled by the considerate judgement. So partial and imperfect are these supposed natural impressions of justice, that almost every disputed moral or social question affords them on both sides. Mr. Newman appeals to a natural feeling of the right of a person to what he has made; socialists appeal to a natural feeling of the right of every one who is born, to be born to as advantageous a lot as every other human being. The question is a very complex one, into which the not offending these supposed instincts about rights, may be allowed to enter as one consideration, but not a principal one, of the many involved. The ultimate standard is the tendency of things to promote or impede human happiness ('Newman's *Political Economy*'; V, 443).[55]

The correspondence of the spring 1849 yields the same notion: 'I am convinced that competent judges who have sufficient experience will not agree . . . that they have a natural idea of right or duty. I am satisfied that all such ideas in children are the result of inculcation and that were it not for inculcation they would not exist at all except probably in a few

55 'Newman's Political Economy', *Westminster Review*, Oct. 1851. This argument is almost identical to that made eighteen years later (see below, pp. 673–5).

persons of pre-eminent genius and feeling' (XIV, 25).[56] Here but for the
closing qualification it would seem that the earlier doubts regarding the
role played by natural constitution in the evaluation of right and wrong
had been totally set aside. (Yet the ambiguous qualification is potentially
revealing; Mill apparently allows that superior characters, if not normal
mortals, are able somehow to tap a source of inspiration.) The paper on
Whewell of 1852 carries us a little further.

The favourable tone there adopted towards Bentham can, at least
partly, be accounted for by the context – Mill's profound opposition to
what he understood as Whewell's defensive attitude towards the social
and institutional *status quo* (an attitude attributed generally to the ancient
British Universities) and which was the unfortunate outcome of an
appeal to 'self-evident' or 'necessary' truths in the sciences in general
as far as concerned morals in particular (*CW*, X, 168–9).[57] Whewell's
Elements of Morality, Mill complained, 'could be nothing better than
a classification and systematizing of the opinions which he found prevailing
among those who had been educated according to the approval methods
of his own country; or, let us rather say, an apparatus for converting those
prevailing opinions, on matters of morality, into reasons for themselves';
while the *Lectures on the History of Moral Philosophy in England* constituted a
critique of writers 'who derive their ethical conclusions, not from internal
intuition, but from an external standard . . . the only methods of
philosophising from which any improvement in ethical opinions can be
looked for . . .'[58]

However, more than a reaction against apologetics is involved. There
seems to be a genuine return to Bentham – the orignial version as outlined

56 Cf. 22 Nov. 1850, *ibid.*, 53: 'How can morality be anything but the chaos it now is,
    when the ideas of right & wrong, just & unjust, must be wrenched into accordance either
    with the notions of a tribe of barbarians in a corner of Syria three thousand years ago,
    or with what is called the order of Providence . . .'
57 'Whewell on Moral Philosophy', *Westminster Review*, Oct. 1852. The earlier part of the
    paper constitutes an attack on the Universities.
58 Here Mill digresses to point out that the eighteenth-century adherents to utility, or the
    'tendency to happiness, as the principle or test of morality', had themselves been engaged
    in a defence of contemporary orthodoxy, against criticism by Shaftesbury (and even
    Hume) – who had argued from the standpoint of 'instinctive feelings of virtue, and the
    theory of moral taste or sense'. With changed circumstances and the efforts of the French
    Philosophers, Godwin and Bentham, the same moral philosophy founded on utility led
    to conclusions 'very unacceptable to the orthodox'; and the unacceptibility of the
    conclusions ultimately led to a reaction against the principle *per se*: 'Utility was now
    abjured as a deadly heresy, and the doctrine of *à priori* or self-evident morality, an end
    in itself, independent of all consequences, became the orthodox theory' (170). Eighteenth-
    century utilitarianism culminated with Paley who proclaimed 'not only expediency as
    the end, but (a very different doctrine) simple self-interest as the motive, of virtue, and
    deducing from these premises all the orthodox conclusions . . . .'.

above (Section II). One has the impression that Mill, as it were, has reread the original documents freed of self-imposed blinkers.

Although the 'greatest happiness' principle itself may not generate a *specific* program – the position of 1835 or 1838 – yet Bentham (unlike Paley) had in fact *used it appropriately* as a foundation for 'secondary or middle principles, capable of serving as premises for a body of ethical doctrine not derived from existing opinions, but fitted to be their test'; and his service was outstanding:

Without such middle principles, an universal principle, either in science or morals, serves for little but a thesaurus of commonplaces for the discussion of questions, instead of a means of deciding them. . . [Bentham] was the first who, keeping clear of the direct and indirect influences of all doctrines inconsistent with it, deduced a set of subordinate generalities from utility alone, and by these consistently tested all particular questions. This great service, previously to which a scientific doctrine of ethics on the foundation of utility was impossible, has been performed by Bentham (though with a view of the exigencies of legislation more than to those of morals) in a manner, as far as it goes, eminently meritorious, and so as to indicate clearly the way to complete the scheme(173).

Whewell's *Lectures*, Mill had further maintained, entirely misrepresented the ethics of utility: 'We are as much for conscience, duty, rectitude, as Dr. Whewell. The terms, and all the feelings connected with them, are as much a part of the ethics of utility as of that of intuition. The point in dispute is, what acts are the proper objects of those feelings; whether we ought to take the feelings as we find them, as accident or design [God] has made them, or whether the tendency of actions to promote happiness affords a test to which the feelings of morality should conform' (172). In response to Whewell's insistence that 'we must do what is right, at whatever cost of pain and loss', Mill complained: 'As if this was not everybody's opinion: as if it was not the very meaning of the word right. The matter in debate is, what *is* right, not whether what is right ought to be done'; similarly, everybody agreed that 'reason has a rightful authority over desire and affection' but 'what *is* reason? and by what rule is it to guide and govern the desires and affections?' (172). Here Mill warmly applauded Bentham's demonstration of what was, in fact, implied by placing the test of right and wrong in supposedly universal feelings: '[W]hen called on to say anything in justification of their approbation or disapprobation [they] produce phrases which mean nothing but the fact of the approbation of disapprobation itself . . . All experience shows that those feelings are eminently artificial, and the product of culture'. Indeed, 'the contest between the morality which appeals to an external standard' – the utility standard – 'and that which grounds itself on internal conviction, is the contest of progressive morality against stationary – of reason and argument against the deification of mere opinion and habit' (178–9). 'It may . . . be pertinently remarked', Mill added, 'that the moral ideas which this approval [of fellows] presupposes, are no other than those of utility and hurtfulness . . . [i.e.] in proportion as mankind are aware of the tendencies of actions to produce happiness or misery, they will like and commend the first, abhor and reprobate the second' (184). 'Utility, as a standard', Mill concluded, 'is capable of being carried out singly and consistently; a moralist can deduce from it his whole system of ethics, without calling to his assistance any foreign principle' (194).

This perspective stands in sharp contrast with that of the 1830s. Mill's paper of 1838 on Bentham is at one with Schumpeter bearing the message that the Benthamite principle is really valid only for the 'business' part of life. And that paper had relegated the principle of utility to the sidelines. Now, however, morality is explicitly said to *have its source in utility* (as Bentham indeed had insisted), and much weight is placed on the relationship.

Furthermore, notwithstanding the reiterated charge of narrowness on Bentham's part,[59] Mill came to his defence against Whewell's strictures by insisting – quite accurately as our account of Bentham has shown – that by the 'greatest happiness' principle Bentham intended 'the greatest happiness of mankind, and of all sensitive beings' – *not the self-interest* of the agent; and, on the other hand, that Bentham did not intend, as the basis of morality, an appeal to 'public opinion' or the 'approbation of neighbours' (183). The opinion of one's fellows was not for Bentham the constituent of virtue, but acted as a motive towards virtuous behaviour – to assure that the self-interest of the agent coincides with the 'greatest happiness' principle (184). The approval or disapproval of others – popular sanction – would keep 'the conduct of each in the line which promotes the general happiness' (185). It is this latter upon which Bentham had insisted as 'true morality', and the so-called moral sentiments were ideally to be 'trained to act in this direction only'. Mill complained strongly of Whewell's confusion of the 'Happiness theory of Morals with the theory of Motives sometimes called the Selfish System' (184n).[60] We need but contrast this with Mill's own

59 The account of 1852 was not, one must add, totally laudatory. It was Bentham's *method* that Mill found eminently acceptable, not necessarily all the applications: '[N]ot that his practical conclusions [in morals: 1859] were often wrong . . . but . . . there were large deficiencies and hiatuses in his scheme of human nature and life, and a consequent want of breadth and comprehension in his secondary principles, which led him often to deduce just conclusions from premises so narrow as to provoke many minds to a rejection of what was nevertheless truth. It is by his *method* chiefly that Bentham, as we think, justly earned a position in moral science analogous to that of Bacon in physical. It is because he was the first to enter into the right mode of working ethical problems, though he worked many of them, as Bacon did physical, on insufficient data' (173–4).

60 See Petrella (1977), esp. 224–5 for a critical view of the consistency of the relationship between 'egoistic' and 'universal' hedonism adopted by Bentham and Mill. The problem is perhaps less severe than Petrella suggests in so far as legislative interference with the individual will often be ruled out even in cases involving conflict with community welfare. Satisfaction of universal hedonism in all respects is the ideal not necessarily the norm.

earlier charge that Bentham viewed the world as 'a collection of persons pursuing each his separate interest or pleasure' reliance placed on legal, religious and popular sanction to assure against 'jostling one another more than is unavoidable' (above, p. 633).

What can be said of the character of the secondary principles required by ethical utilitarianism? How is 'the greatest happiness' to be defined? Mill lauded Bentham's own observation that the day might come when animals are included within the maximand – that if some practice caused more pain to animals than gave pleasure to man it would be immoral and perhaps the subject of legislation (185f). There is implied here a notion of progress in ethical standards as distinct from the hidebound standards embodied in the appeal to supposedly universal judgements which might in fact reflect 'grovelling superstitions' (195).

This same issue arises in the context of legislation, specifically Whewell's charge that Bentham in his *Influence of Time and Place* . . . had neglected the historical element by championing a general plan with allowance only for modification of detail according to local circumstances including national opinion and feeling. Mill pointed out, in a complete abandonment of the reservations of the 1830s, that Bentham had admitted fully the need to allow for local opinion, but 'did not look upon these opinions and feelings as affecting, in any great degree, what was desirable to be done, but only what could be done' (196). More specifically:

The fact that, in any of these matters, [property, contract, family, government] a people prefer some particular mode of legislation, on historical grounds – that is, because they have been long used to it, – is no proof of any original adaptation in it to their nature or circumstances, and goes a very little way in recommendation of it as for their benefit now. But it may be a very important element in determining what the legislator can do, and still more, the manner in which he should do it; and in both these respects Bentham allowed it full weight. What he is at issue with Dr. Whewell upon, is in deeming it right for the legislator to keep before his mind an ideal of what he would do if the people for whom he made laws were entirely devoid of prejudice or accidental presupposition: while Dr. Whewell, . . . enjoins legislation not in simple recognition of existing popular feelings, but in obedience to them.

Thus while the 'national view' might countenance slavery, and there may be need to make legal provision for it, it was essential for the legislator 'to regard the equality of human beings as the foundation of . . . legislation', and 'the "historical element" as a matter of temporary expediency . . . while yielding to the necessity, to endeavour, by all the means in his power, to educate the nation into better things'. 'No one, more than Bentham', Mill claimed, 'recognises that most important, but most neglected, function of the legislator, the office of an instructor, both moral and intellectual' (197). In brief, 'the moral sentiments should be guided by the happiness of mankind' and 'the moral sentiments, so guided, should be cultivated and fostered'.

There remains to point out in this context a reiteration of the principle of 1835, that 'clear and comprehensive views of education and human nature must . . . precede, and form the basis of, a philosophy of morals . . .' (above, p. 630). But now it will be noted the ultimate appeal is said unambiguously to be the 'greatest happiness': 'An adherent of "dependent morality" [utility]', Mill wrote in 1852, 'would say that, instead of deriving right from rights, we must have a rule of right before it can be decided what ought to be rights; and that, both in law and in morals, the rights which ought to exist are those which for the greatest happiness it is expedient should exist' (189).

Mill closed his paper by asserting that Whewell's 'attempts . . . to construct a moral philosophy without [the philosophy of utility], have been . . . failures' (201). Here he had in mind an earlier observation that, despite all, Whewell (and other opponents) had been drawn into the utility camp in practice, with special reference to the end of creating and continuing the social bond:

Moral rules are . . . spoken of as means to an end. We now hear of the peace and comfort of society; of making man's life tolerable; of the satisfaction and gratification of human beings; of preventing a disturbed and painful state of society. This is utility – this is pleasure and pain. When real reasons are wanted, the repudiated happiness principle is always the resource . . . [Moral] rules are necessary, because mankind would have had no security for any of the things which they value, for anything which gives them pleasure or shields them from pain, unless they could rely on one another for doing, and in particular for abstaining from, certain acts . . . Though Dr. Whewell will not recognise [formally] the promotion of happiness as the ultimate principle, he deduces his secondary principles from it, and supports his propositions by utilitarian reasons as far as they will go (192–3; cf. 189).

Benevolence, justice, truth, purity (Mill maintained) *could all be derived from utility* – with which view, he now insisted, the opponents of Bentham were effectively in agreement albeit unawares. This theme – stated by Bentham himself it will be recalled – reappears in the 1861 pamphlet on utilitarianism to which we turn next.

V THE RETURN TO BENTHAM CONTINUED:
ON 'UTILITARIANISM' AND THE STATUS OF JUSTICE[61]

In his major dissertation on *Utilitarianism* (1861) Mill defined the creed as one 'which accepts as the foundation of morals, Utility, or the Greatest

61 This work should be read together with the essay 'Nature', *CW*, X, 373f., composed

Happiness Principle' whereby 'actions are right in proportion as they tend to promote happiness, wrong as they tend to produce the reverse of happiness', meaning by happiness 'pleasure, and the absence of pain; by unhappiness, pain, and the privation of pleasure' – the position that 'pleasure and freedom from pain, are the only things desirable as ends; and that all desirable things (which are as numerous in the utilitarian as in any other scheme) are desirable either for the pleasure inherent in themselves, or as means to the promotion of pleasure and the prevention of pain' (*CW*, X, 210). This view is represented as standing in opposition to that which conceives right and wrong 'as something absolute – generically distinct from every variety of the Expedient . . .' (240). This was standard Benthamism as too was the principle that 'all action is for the sake of some end, and rules of action, it seems natural to suppose, must take their whole character and colour from the end to which they are subservient. When we engage in a pursuit, a clear and precise conception of what we are pursuing would seem to be the first thing we need, instead of the last we are to look forward to' (206).[62] But in this work, in answer to a variety of criticisms over the years, Mill spelled out in some detail what ethical utilitarianism included in the ideas of pain and pleasure and what was left an open question, and expounded more fully than in the earlier statements the precise nature of the first principle of utility itself. In all of this Mill's 'return to Bentham' is again conspicous.

Mill conceded at the outset that the utility theory is not subject to 'proof' in the ordinary sense since 'questions of ultimate ends are not amenable to direct proof. Whatever can be proved to be good, must be so by being shown to be a means to something admitted to be good without proof'. Thus 'medical art is "good" if it improves health – but who is to say health is good; music is good if it generates pleasure, but who is to say pleasure is good?' (207–8). (Here Mill abandoned his own demand for proof in the paper of 1835 (above, p. 628) and accepted Bentham's position, although he did attempt to define a sense in which the intellect 'can be pursuaded either to give or withhold its assent to the doctrine' carrying the matter beyond Bentham in an attempt to strengthen the latter's argument.[63]) The

---

between 1850 and 1858 and published posthumously in *Three Essays on Religion*. This essay constitutes a clear demonstration of the absurd implications flowing from appeal to nature: 'Conformity to nature, has no connection whatever with right and wrong' (400); 'the duty of man is to co-operate with the beneficient powers [in nature], not by imitating [them] but by perpetually striving to amend the course of nature – and bringing that part of it over which we can exercise control, more nearly into conformity with a high standard of justice and goodness' (402).

62 Unlike the sciences where first principles are not initially required; first principles are there, in practice, the last.

63 For a sympathetic analysis of Mill's argument see Wilson (1982, 1983), also Dryer (1969), and West (1982).

prerequisite for some end in morals and legislation – practical arts – 'All action is for the sake of some end, and rules of action . . . must take their whole character and colour from the end to which they are subservient' (206) – was in any event accepted even by Kant despite his precept regarding moral obligation ('So act, that the rule on which thou actest would admit of being adopted as a law by all rational beings'), for when dealing with practical deductions from the rule 'he fails, almost grotesquely, to show that there would be any contradiction, any logical (not to say physical) impossibility, in the adoption by all rational beings of the most outrageously immoral rules of conduct. All he shows is that the *consequences* of their universal adoption would be such as no one would choose to incur' (207). In brief, 'as men's sentiments, both of favour and of aversion, are greatly influenced by what they suppose to be the effects of things upon their happiness, the principle of utility, or as Bentham latterly called it, the greatest happiness principle, has had a large share in forming the moral doctrines even of those who most scornfully reject its authority' (207) – a point made in the earlier criticism of Whewell.

* * *

For our purposes the key chapter is that dealing with the distinguishing character of justice in both the ethical and legislative contexts – the 'modes of conduct' and the 'arrangements of human affairs' designated as *just* – and the legitimization of these specifications. Mill proceeds (Ch. v, 'Justice and Utility') by first surveying popular or widely-held opinion regarding justice:

In the first place, it is mostly considered unjust to deprive anyone of his personal liberty, his property, or any other things which belongs to him by law . . . it is just to respect, unjust to violate, the *legal rights* of any one . . . [A] second case of injustice consists in taking or withholding from any person that to which he has a *moral right*. Thirdly, it is universally considered just that each person should obtain that (whether good or evil) which he *deserves*; and unjust that he should obtain a good, or be made to undergo an evil, which he does not deserve . . . Fourthly, it is confessedly unjust to *break faith* with any one: to violate an engagement, either express or implied, or disappoint expectations raised by our own conduct, at least if we have raised those expectations knowingly and voluntarily . . . Fifthly, it is, by universal admission, inconsistent with justice to be *partial* ; to show favour or preference to one person over another, in matters to which favour and preference do not properly apply . . . Nearly allied to the idea of impartiality, is that of *equality* (241–3).

But the common feature in this catalogue of constituents – the essence of the popular idea of justice – is summarized as a right residing in an individual:

In our survey of the various popular acceptations of justice, the term appeared generally to involve the idea of a personal right – a claim on the part of one or more individuals . . . Whether the injustice consists in depriving a person of a possession, or in breaking faith with him, or in treating him worse than he deserves, or worse than other people who have no greater claims, in each case the supposition implies two things – a wrong done, and some assignable person who is wronged . . . It seems to me that this feature in the case – a right in some person, correlative to the moral obligation – constitutes the specific difference between justice, and generosity or beneficence. Justice implies something which it is not only right to do, and wrong not to do [a question of morality-in-general], but which some individual person can claim from us as is his moral right (247).

The source of the individual's claim to protection reflects a moral right but one based on 'general utility'. That is the key to Mill's argument:

To have a right . . . is, I conceive, to have something which society ought to defend [one] in the possession of. If [an] objector goes on to ask why it ought, I can give him no other reason than general utility . . . The interest involved is that of security, to every one's feelings the most vital of all interests . . . security no human being can possibly do without; on it we depend for all our immunity from evil, and for the whole value of all and every good, beyond the passing moment; . . . Now this most indispensable of all necessaries, after physical nutriment, cannot be had, unless the machinery for providing it be kept unintermittedly in active play (250–1).

Mill insisted further that the end of security is so profoundly significant that it gives a peculiar stamp to conceptions of justice: 'Our notion . . . of the claim we have on our fellow-creatures to join in making safe for us the very groundwork of our existence, gathers feelings round it so much more intense than those concerned in any of the more common cases of utility, that the difference in degree . . . becomes a real difference in kind' (251). Mill denied 'the existence of imaginary standards of justice not grounded in utility' but yet regarded justice grounded in utility as 'the most sacred and binding part of all morality':

Is, then, the difference between the Just and the Expedient a merely imaginary distinction? Have mankind been under a delusion in thinking that justice is a more sacred thing than policy, and that the latter ought only to be listened to after the former has been satisfied? By no means. The exposition we have given of the nature and origin of the sentiment, recognises a real distinction; and no one of those who profess the most sublime contempt for the consequences of actions as an element in their morality, attaches more importance to the distinction than I do. While I dispute the pretensions of any theory which sets up an imaginary standard of justice not grounded on utility, I account the justice which is grounded on utility to be the chief part, and incomparably the most sacred and binding part, of all morality. Justice is a name for certain classes of moral rules, which concern the essentials of human well-being more nearly, and are therefore of more absolute obligation, than any other rules for the guidance of life; and the notion which we have found to be of the essence of the idea of justice, that of a right residing in an individual, implies and testifies to this more binding obligation.

The moral rules which forbid mankind to hurt one another (in which we must never forget to include wrongful interference with each other's freedom) are more vital to human well-being than any maxims, however important, which only point out the best mode of managing some department of human affairs. . . . [T]he moralities which protect every individual from being harmed by others, either directly or by being hindered in his freedom of pursuing his own good, are at once those which he himself has most at heart, and those which he has the strongest interest in publishing and enforcing by word and deed. . . Now it is these moralities, primarily, which compose the obligations of justice. The most marked cases of injustice . . . are acts of wrongful aggression, or wrongful exercise of power over some one; the next are those which consist in wrongfully withholding from him something which is his due; in both cases, inflicting on him a positive hurt, either in the form of direct suffering, or of the privation of some good which he had reasonable ground, either of a physical or of a social kind, for counting upon (255–6).

In this manner Mill attempted to extricate the utility doctrine from the charge that it denied to justice a 'more sacred' quality than 'mere' expedience or policy. His perspective removed 'the only real difficulty of the utilitarian theory of morals':

It appears from what has been said, that justice is a name for certain moral requirements, which, regarded collectively, stand higher in the scale of social utility, and are therefore of more paramount obligation, than any others; though particular cases may occur in which some other social duty is so important, as to overrule any one of the general maxims of justice . . . It has always been evident that all cases of justice are also cases of expediency: the difference is in the peculiar sentiment which attaches to the former, as contradistinguished from the latter [ordinary cases]. If this characteristic sentiment has been sufficiently accounted for; if there is no necessity to assume for it any peculiarity of origin; if it is simply the natural feeling of resentment, moralized by being made co-extensive with the demands of social good; and if this feeling not only does but ought to exist in all the classes of cases to which the idea of justice corresponds; that idea no longer presents itself as a stumbling-block to the utilitarian ethics. Justice remains the appropriate name for certain social utilities which are vastly more important, and therefore more absolute and imperative, than any others are as a class (thought not more so than others may be in particular cases); and which, therefore, ought to be, as well as naturally are, guarded by a sentiment not only different in degree, but also in kind, distinguished from the milder feeling which attaches to the mere idea of promoting human pleasure or convenience, at once by the more definite nature of its commands, and by the sterner character of its sanctions (259).

This 'solution' to 'the only real difficulty of the utilitarian theory of morals' is quite in line with Bentham's own approach, which we have seen allowed for a hierarchical ladder of moralities (above, p. 611).

Let us look more closely at the 'exalted rank' accorded equality and impartiality among the precepts of justice by both popular and advanced opinion. This weighting is explained partly as a reflection or corollary of the principle of desert – itself one of the precepts of justice: society 'should treat all equally well . . . who have deserved equally well of [it], that is who have deserved equally well absolutely. This is the highest abstract standard of social and distributive justice; towards which all institutions, and the efforts of all virtuous citizens, should be made in the utmost possible degree to converge' (257). But much more was involved than 'a mere logical corollary from secondary or derivative doctrines'. The moral duty in question (of equality and impartiality) was implicit in 'the very meaning of Utility, or the Greatest-Happiness Principle': 'That principle is a mere form of words without rational signification, unless one person's happiness, supposed equal in degree (with the proper allowance made for kind), is counted for exactly as much as another's. Those conditions being supplied, Bentham's dictum, "everybody to count for one, nobody for more than one" [*Plan of Parliamentary Reform*, 817] might be written under the principle of utility as an explanatory commentary'. That 'equal amounts of happiness are equally desirable, whether felt by the same or by different persons' is not represented as a presupposition but rather as the very essence of the principle of utility. (If anything is an 'anterior principle', Mill suggested (258n), it would be 'that the rules of arithmetic are applicable to the valuation of happiness, as of all other measurable qualities'.)

The notion of qualitative differences between utilities, with special reference to the supreme social utility of security (on a par, it will be recalled, with that of subsistence), was formally introduced in reply to critics of utilitarian ethics. Mill applauded the 'exalted rank' which the maxims of equality and impartiality were accorded in both 'popular' and 'enlightened' estimation (257). But his allowance was quite general – pleasures had a non-quantitative as well as a quantitative dimension: 'It is quite compatible with the principle of utility to recognise the fact, that some *kinds* of pleasure are more desirable and more valuable than others' (211) – an illustration of a formal failure to consider the relevance of the incremental dimension.[64] In elucidating this

64 Cf. Viner (1958), 326–7.

proposition Mill attempts to render commensurable the 'qualitative' with the 'quantitative' – as he must do given the so-called 'anterior principle' that the rules of arithmetic are applicable to the 'valuation of happiness, as of all other measurable qualities' – and in so doing comes very close to adopting an *élitist* criterion of judgement: '[T] he test of quality, and the rule of measuring it against quantity, being the preference felt by those who, in their opportunities of experience, to which must be added their habits of self-consciousness and self-observation, are best furnished with the means of comparison' (214).[65] It is conceded that people may deteriorate in their 'capacity for nobler feelings' and alter their choices in favour of lower pleasures, but in that case it is not 'because they deliberately prefer them', but because, (for example) they have fallen under a bad influence; for 'it may be questioned whether any one who has remained equally susceptible to both classes of pleasures, ever knowingly and calmly preferred the lower . . .' The evaluation of competent judges was the sole means for arriving at evaluations of the qualitative rankings of 'the pleasures derived from the higher faculties' over those derived from 'animal nature' (213). At all events, Mill insisted that in practice the utility criterion of morality – and accordingly of legislation too – was not an empty one: 'It is truly a whimsical supposition that if mankind were agreed in considering utility to be the test of morality, they would remain without any agreement as to what *is* useful, and would take no measures for having their notions taught to the young, and enforced by law and opinion . . . mankind must by this time have acquired positive beliefs as to the effects of some actions on their happiness . . .' (224).

In all this Mill was, so to speak, on the defensive. The utility standard, he observed in this context, was the *general* happiness so that even were it doubted that a 'noble character' is always a happier character for its nobleness, it indubitably made others happier. Utilitarianism, accordingly, 'could only attain its end by the general cultivation of nobleness of character . . .' (213–14). Even this was carefully qualified in the light of misunderstandings regarding what was entailed by right conduct:

---

65 Cf. 211–12 where Mill refers in a clumsy passage to two conditions which determine the relative status of different pleasures. Of two pleasures, if there is one preferred by all, or almost all, who have experience of both ('irrespective of any feeling of moral obligation') then that is the more desirable pleasure. If one is so much preferred to the other by those 'competently acquainted with both' that, even though 'attended with a greater amount of discontent', it is selected (over any amount of the other 'their nature is capable of') then it is superior in quality (outweighing quantity which is significant in comparison). 'It is an unquestionable fact', Mill proceeds to assert, 'that those who are equally acquainted with, and equally capable of appreciating and enjoying both, do give a most marked preference to the manner of existence which employs their higher faculties'; and would refuse to surrender them even for satisfaction of all the desires of a lower order despite various liabilities attached. This choice does not entail 'a sacrifice of happiness'; on the contrary.

The utilitarian morality does recognise in human beings the power of sacrificing their own greatest good for the good of others. It only refuses to admit that the sacrifice is itself a good. A sacrifice which does not increase, or tend to increase, the sum total of happiness, it considers as wasted. The only self-renunciation which it applauds, is devotion to the happiness, or to some of the means of happiness, of others . . .

I must again repeat, what the assailants of utilitarianism seldom have the justice to acknowledge, that the happiness which forms the utilitarian standard of what is right in conduct, is not the agent's own happiness, but that of all concerned. As between his own happiness and that of others, utilitarianism requires him to be as strictly impartial as a disinterested and benevolent spectator (218).

Mill's self-righteous tone regarding 'the assailants' of the principle is a little unbecoming considering that he himself had adopted their misinterpretation in earlier years.

This perspective was prologue to an important statement regarding appropriate social and institutional arrangements to encourage right action – ideally the entire preclusion of actions promoting a self-happiness opposed to the general good, more practically the encouragement of impulses to promote the general good as one of the motives to action (218).[66] This matter we take up later. Here we note only how careful Mill was to point out that the utilitarian standard was not beyond reach of ordinary mortals as some critics, from the other end of the spectrum, had contended:

The objectors to utilitarianism cannot always be charged with representing it in a discreditable light. On the contrary, those among them who entertain anything like a just idea of its disinterested character, sometimes find fault with its standard as being too high for humanity. They say it is exacting too much to require that people shall always act from the inducement of promoting the general interests of society . . . [But] no system of ethics requires that the sole motive of all we do shall be a feeling of duty; on the contrary, ninety-nine hundredths of all our actions are done from other motives and rightly so done, if the rule of duty does not condemn them . . . The great majority of good actions are intended, not for the benefit of the world, but for that of individuals, of which the good of the world is made up; and the thoughts of the most virtuous man need not on these occasions travel beyond the particular persons concerned, except so far as is necessary to assure himself that in benefiting them he is not violating the rights – that is, the legitimate and authorized expectations – of any one else (219–20).

Here Mill rehearsed an old theme appearing in the 1835 review of Sedgwick, namely that only public benefactors, including (doubtless) legislators, need concern themselves with public utility as such. In other cases, 'private utility,

66 See also the note regarding prospects for the future (216).

the interest or happiness of some few persons, is all [an individual] has to attend to. But in any event prospects for future mental improvement were good: 'Genuine private affections, and a sincere interest in the public good, are possible, though in unequal degrees, to every rightly brought up human being' (216). A more striking case of begging the question than that implied in the foregoing assertion is difficult to conceive!

Mill struggled none the less with the relationship of justice to the moral sentiments; – was the *feeling* which accompanied the notion of justice 'a special dispensation of nature' or did it develop from the notion itself 'in considerations of general expediency?' (248). This is a fundamental matter, when we recall how troubled he had been in 1838.

A letter of November 1859 (XV, 649–50) sets the stage for Mill's clarification. Some individuals, Mill there argued, lack 'a feeling of approving & condemning conscience' – they cannot have any intuitive notion of right and wrong. But some do possess such feeling 'independently of any expected consequences to themselves'; 'to them the word *ought* means, that if they act othewise, they shall be punished by this internal, & perfectly disinterested feeling'. What of the source of this feeling? James Mill's position is considered whereby the pains of conscience derive by association from a 'dread of disapprobation', a process which produces 'a general & intense feeling of recoil from wrongdoing' but in which 'no conscious influence of other people's disapprobation may be perceptible'. This, however, Mill maintained was not the usual case:

I do not hold this to be the normal form of moral feeling. I conceive that feeling to be a natural outgrowth from the social nature of man: a state of society is so eminently natural to human beings that anything which is an obviously indispensable condition of social life, easily comes to act upon their minds almost like a physical necessity. Now it is an indispensable condition of all society, except between master & slave, that each pay regard to the other's happiness. On this basis, combined with a human creature's capacity of *fellow-feeling*, the feelings of morality properly so called seem to me to be grounded, & their main constituent to be the idea of punishment. I feel conscious that if I violate certain laws, other people must necessarily or naturally desire that I sh[d] be punished for the violation. I also feel that I sh[d] desire them to be punished if they violated the same laws towards me. From these feelings & from my sociality of nature I place myself in their situation, & sympathize in their desire that I sh[d] be punished; & (even apart from benevolence) the painfulness of not being in union with them makes me shrink from pursuing a line of conduct which would make my ends, wishes, & purposes habitually conflict with theirs.

The approach in *Utilitarianism* follows this line. The sentiment accompanying justice does not itself 'arise from anything which would commonly, or correctly, be termed an idea of expediency; but though the sentiment does not, whatever is moral in it does' (X, 248).[67] This view is again restated in later correspondence with W. T. Thornton: 'I never contended that the *feeling* of justice originates in a consideration of general utility, though I think it is that consideration which gives it its binding, & properly moral, character . . .' (17 April 1863, XV, 853-4).[68] At all events, he added, 'the feeling of justice (except where, being divided against itself, it can be appealed on *both* sides) never need come into conflict with the dictates of utility'.

Since justice is not a standard recognized by simple introspection it must inevitably vary with the variety of opinion regarding what precisely, in any situation, is required to assure the general good – specifically the 'security' of society. There might, Mill concedes, be wide differences in opinion about justice as about all questions touching upon 'what is useful in society', although this did not justify recourse to so-called 'immutable, ineffaceable, and unmistakable dictates of Justice, which carry their evidence in themselves, and are independent of the fluctuations of opinion' (X, 251). On the contrary, a great variety of contradictory views regarding, for example, the justification of punishment, or (closer to home for us) income distribution and taxation could be made out on grounds of 'justice' *tout court*, whereas 'social utility alone can decide the preference' (254–5). Indeed, 'from these confusions there is no other mode of extrication than the utilitarian'.

Mill's insistence upon the subjective nature of justice comes to the fore with particular force during various elaborations regarding equality:

But in this, still more than in any other case, the notion of justice varies in different

---

67 More specifically, 'the two essential ingredients in the sentiment of justice are, the desire to punish a person who has done harm, and the knowledge or belief that there is some definite individual or individuals to whom harm has been done' (248). These two 'natural sentiments' are related (1) to the impulse to self-defence, and (2) to the feeling of sympathy: '[T]he sentiment of justice appears to me to be, the animal desire to repel or retaliate a hurt or damage to oneself, or to those with whom one sympathizes, widened so as to include all persons, by the human capacity of enlarged sympathy, and the human conception of intelligent self-interest. From the latter elements, the feeling derives its morality; from the former, its peculiar impressiveness, and energy of self-assertion' (250). Alternatively put, morality is that feeling of resentment divorced from self or 'standing up for the interest of society' (249).

For a similar position, see Bentham, (1815), 29: 'The sort of motives, to the influence of which a man would in general be best pleased that his breast should be regarded as most sensible, – this, for the present purpose, may serve for the explanation of what is meant by *good* motives: the reverse may serve for *bad* motives.'

68 In this letter Mill considers a case where a community is required to surrender a citizen to the enemy or face extermination: '[I]n such a case as this I think there can be no doubt that the morality of utility requires that the people should fight to the last rather than comply with the demand'. His case turns both on making tyrants pay a price, thereby dissuading them, and on the special tie between the community and its individual members.

persons, and always conforms in its variations to their notion of utility. Each person maintains that equality is the dictate of justice, except where he thinks that expediency requires inequality . . . Those who think that utility requires distinctions of rank, do not consider it unjust that riches and social privileges should be unequally dispensed; but those who think this inequality inexpedient, think it unjust also . . . Even among those who hold levelling doctrines, there are as many questions of justice as there are differences of opinion about expediency. Some Communists consider it unjust that the produce of the labour of the community should be shared on any other principle than that of exact equality; others think it just that those should receive most whose needs are greatest; while others hold that those who work harder, or who produce more, or whose services are more valuable to the community, may justly claim a larger quota in the division of the produce (243-4).

Similarly, he emphasized the subjectivity involved in defining exceptions to any general rule – including that of equality and impartiality: 'The equal claim of everybody to happiness in the estimation of the moralist and the legislator, involves an equal claim to all the means of happiness, except insofar as the inevitable conditions of human life, and the general interest, in which that of every individual is included, sets limits to the maxim; and those limits ought to be strictly construed.' Thus a principle of justice based upon a fundamental matter of expediency, may none the less be set aside for another principle that has precedence in special cases:

As every other maxim of justice, so this, is by no means applied or held applicable universally; on the contrary . . . it bends to every person's ideas of social expediency. But in whatever case it is deemed applicable at all, it is held to be the dictate of justice. All persons are deemed to have a *right* to equality of treatment, except when some recognised social expediency requires the reverse. And hence all social inequalities which have ceased to be considered expedient, assume the character not of simple inexpediency, but of injustice . . . The entire history of social improvement has been a series of transitions, by which one custom or institution after another, from being a supposed primary necessity of social existence, has passed into the rank of a universally stigmatized injustice and tyranny (258-9).

A most interesting application of these principles emerges in a letter to Mazzini regarding contemporary British constitutional opinion. Here Mill's own subjective evaluation – 'justice', for him, ideally includes both 'liberty' and 'equality' – is represented as clashing with the general view:

The English, of all ranks and classes, are at bottom, in all their feelings, aristocrats. They have some conception of liberty, & set some value on it, but the very idea of equality is strange & offensive to them. They do not dislike to have many people above them as long as they have some below them. And therefore they have never sympathized & in their present state of mind never will sympathize with any really democratic or republican party in other countries. They keep what sympathy they have for those whom they look upon as imitators of English institutions – Continental Whigs who desire to introduce constitutional forms & some securities against personal oppression – leaving in other respects the old order of things with all its inequalities & social injustices and any people who are not willing to content themselves with this, are thought unfit for liberty (15 April 1858, *CW*, XV, 553).

VI THE GREATEST HAPPINESS PRINCIPLE:
SOME COMPARISONS AND PROBLEMS

There can be no doubt of a negative stance in the papers of the 1830s, compared with those of the 1850s and 1860s, not only towards Bentham but towards the utility principle itself; Bentham and utility were more or less identified. In his early papers of 1833 Mill flirted with the notion of moral sentiments existing universally, which govern feelings of right and wrong without ulterior end; he was troubled by Bentham's focus upon specific consequences and corresponding neglect of the effect of actions on the character of the agent; and he was much concerned by the open-endedness of the notion of the 'general good' – the subjectivity of the ends – having in mind the danger that opinion might justify the most abominable standards. By the late 1830s the 'general happiness' was formally re-established in primary position although Mill remained very troubled by the problems of specifying the maximand in practical detail and the source of moral feelings. These doubts were to be more or less assuaged by the early 1850s.

Mill himself, it will be recalled, preferred to interpret these vicissitudes as altered weightings of emphasis with an eye to the state of contemporary debate. There is some truth to this. But Mill's growing ease with the doctrine of utility seems also to flow from a new-found ability to answer the criticisms, his own doubts, by allowing a broader interpretation of that doctrine. This re-evaluation went hand in hand with an increased willingness to 'reinterpret' Bentham himself in more catholic terms. And the reinterpretation is certainly called for. Bentham had never championed the narrow utilitarianism originally attributed to him by Mill, and repeated to this day, as in Schumpeter's account. Thus whereas in the 1830s Mill had found the utility doctrine inadequate as a source of morality (either, as in 1833, recourse was made to independent principles or, as in 1838, the status of the 'general good' is left ambiguous), by 1852 Mill was satisfied with the pre-eminent role of utility as the source of morality – which had always been Bentham's position. The further step of allowance within the utility framework for a 'sacred' quality accorded justice was actually taken by Bentham in his early formulations (see above, p. 612) although it is not clear whether Mill owed them a specific debt or whether he arrived at his position independently.[69]

In the same spirit, the open-endedness of the greater happiness principle was no longer considered a disadvantage; thus its ideal extension to animals is attributed favourably to Bentham. Mill in fact grew confident that intellectual progress would assure an adequate degree of unanimity regarding what in fact at any time is useful and to be counted among the constituents of the 'general good' – or at the least (as in 1852) that *advanced minds* could discern accurately, and (as in 1861) 'every rightly brought up human being' to some degree, in what consisted the general good. That even Kant and Whewell were in practice forced to have recourse to the utilitarian rule is asserted both in 1852 and 1861; and it is allowed in 1852 that Bentham had recognized that 'the moral sentiments should be guided by the happiness of mankind' – a far cry from the earlier charge against him of severe myopia or one-sidedness – for nothing precluded the incorporation within the 'general good' of such imponderables as 'nobleness of character'.

Robson questions whether there were changes of substance in Mill's position towards Bentham over time. The 'apparent changes of opinion' he suggests were 'the combined result of polemical considerations and personal history' (1964, 261; cf. also 1968, 271). Now in our account there is a discernible break and discernible return to the fold. Nevertheless, it must be conceded that the later solutions to Mill's original problems are present in muted form in the earlier statements of the 1830s. There is some truth to Mill's own position that once the breakaway from his youthful position had been made it was a matter only of finding precisely the right balance with an eye to the state of opinion – always bending the stick appropriately. Thus it was allowed even in 1833 that the notion of utility can, in principle, be extended to cover the effect of actions on character, and that the supposed Benthamite limitations – the narrowness at least of Bentham's formal conception of 'interest' – posed a lesser problem where fundamental changes in socio-economic organization and institutions with their implications for the formation of character were not at stake. The prospects for the sublimation of narrow self-interest with the advance of society are stated in similar language both in 1861 and 1833; there is little to distinguish the intermediate and later Mills on this fundamental issue. The later recourse to the morality of expediency in the analysis of justice – the end of social security in the broadest sense – is presaged by the discussion in 1833 of the immorality of

69 But cf. Priestley (1969). Priestley argues that Mill never rejected the utility principle as such, but attacked Bentham in the 1830s (xi, xxv, xxiv) and came to his defence in the 1850s for purely tactical reasons (xxxv–xxxviii, xlvi). Although Priestley does not concern himself formally with the accuracy or justice of Mill's interpretation of Bentham (xiv), it is strongly implied that the 'Bentham' Mill came to defend was *not* the real Bentham.

spoliation, its 'infringing the first principles of the social union . . .'; while
in 1835 the 'natural constitution' is looked to as providing a foundation
for moral feelings which none the less develop by way of teaching and
experience – an approach not too far removed from the formulation of 1861
where, in some measure, the 'moral sense' is allowed for. And from the
mid-1830s, as in 1861, it had been observed that personal morality in many
cases did not require formal reference to the *general* good.

The more positive tone towards utilitarianism of the later years can also be
in part accounted for in terms of intellectual context. Most striking are the
strong allusions in 1852 to the apologetic implications flowing from
Whewell's doctrine of a priori or self-evident morality. (Mill, however, was
supremely honest in pointing out that in different historical circumstances, as
in the late eighteenth century, it was the utility doctrine that had been misused.)

Yet for all that the contrast between a Mill hostile to Bentham in the
1830s and a Mill well disposed towards him by the 1850s does stand out.
The evidence on balance points to a change both in tone of argument and
in substance – particularly regarding the status of the utility principle as
source of morality (directly attributed to Bentham) and the *qualitative*
differentiation of justice and its constituents (consistently with Bentham's
own formulations).

That Mill came to recognize his error regarding Bentham is implicit in
Viner's celebrated account. Mill, Viner suggested regarding the articles
of 1833, reserved for Bentham blows which 'could more justly have been
directed against James Mill. The harshness and vehemence of the attack
on Bentham was no doubt a subconscious manifestation of the urge he was
under to free himself from what he had come to feel was an intellectual
straitjacket, but it had been his father rather than Bentham who had placed
it on him' (1958, 321).[70] Mill's awareness of his misunderstanding
becomes clear when we compare his criticisms in the 1830s regarding private
morals and psychology – the emphasis supposedly placed on calculations of
gain and loss and a tendency to picture behaviour as inherently selfish,
which he blamed on Bentham's character – and the paper of 1852 wherein
'conceding very little error in the Benthamite doctrine, Mill rejected
vehemently Whewell's objections to utilitarian ethics in general and to
Bentham in particular, even when they were very similar indeed to his own
criticism of Bentham in 1838' (322, 325).[71]

70 See also Robbins (1952), 144–5: 'The nature of [Mill's] mental crisis and the means
    whereby he nursed himself back to spiritual health all involved a break with family
    influences which he associated with early utilitarianism; far more than was intellectually
    justifiable, he tended to identify Benthamism and the classical system with his father,
    James Mill . . .' (also 156n).
71 Viner, 323, illustrates from Mill's charges (1838) that the *Table of the Springs of Action*
    treats 'conscience', 'principle', 'moral rectitude', 'moral duty' as 'love of reputation'

This is in line with our own interpretation. Viner further, however, suggests that in *Utilitarianism* Mill in some respects went far beyond Bentham:

In form, these [essays] still represented an adherence to the doctrine, but so modified by the admission without obvious absorption of foreign elements that they have been the despair of its friends and the delight of its critics ever since. Acts were to be morally appraised solely in terms of their consequences for happiness – a strictly Benthamite proposition. *All* consequences, however, were to be taken into account, including the effects on the character of the agent – an early doctrine of Mill's which he derived from Coleridge and which he regarded as contrary to Bentham's views, mistakenly, I think. Happiness was conceived broadly enough to cover every type of wish or aspiration man could experience. Mill – unwisely, I think – went a step further than Bentham ever ventured by offering a 'proof' that happiness was the proper criterion of virtue: namely, that competent judges accepted it as such, a type of proof which eighteenth-century critics of the 'moral sense' school of ethics had exposed to ridicule for its circularity. Mill now attempted also to incorporate into utility a novel element for it and one which many moral philosophers hold to be incompatible with it, namely, the recognition of non-homogeneity of pleasures and consequently the existence of qualitative differences of a hierarchical nature, as well as quantitative difference between pleasures (325).

The matter of proof is an attempt to strengthen Bentham's position, as is also recognition of qualitative differences of a hierarchical nature. We have argued, however, that far from being a 'novel element' the latter is to be found in Bentham's own work.

* * *

The foregoing account raises some problems of regarding Mill's consistency which will be only briefly outlined.

It has frequently been pointed out that the alleged obligation to seek the greatest happiness of the greatest number rather than of one self, or some group, itself rests upon a kind of moral judgement – a value judgement – such as those which Bentham condemned (Robbins, 1952, 179–80; 1970a, 80; 1970c, 423; 1971a, 148–9). Bentham himself, we have seen, admitted readily the impossibility of *proving* the principle – 'that which is used to prove everything else, cannot itself be proved' (above, p. 616) – envisaging it as axiomatic which assuredly implies value judgement, for argument is closed if proof is ruled out. We have also Bentham's explicit recognition

rather than something distinct from philanthropy, affection, or self-interest in this or the next world, and neglects entirely 'self-respect'. Both charges were unfair, as Viner shows with reference to the *Table* itself.

(p. 615) that the additivity of happiness is a 'fictitious postulatum'. Now the conventional nature of Bentham's axioms may indeed reflect the object of assuring 'that in making recommendations for action, *all* the effects of all the different sets of people liable to be affected are given due consideration. It is as a working rule rather than an ultimate moral norm that the greatest happiness principle finds its justification' (Robbins, 1970a, 81). But that an ultimate moral norm is implied cannot be gainsaid. Bentham early on suggested not only the inclusion within the maximand of all human kind regardless of colour, but of *all sentient beings*, animals included, with appropriate 'discounting', so to speak – a value judgement with profound normative significance if ever there was one.

The utility principle itself one concludes is not self-contained; it requires supplement from outside sources which defines the utilitarian's value judgement. Value judgement is entailed both in formulation of the rule and in spelling out the constituency presumed to be at stake. In fact, unless the constituency is spelled out the rule is an empty one. This was clear to Mill who, in 1833, pointed out that while the greatest happiness principle is an 'excellent general rule, it is not an undeniable axiom'; the rule might demand, as in medieval times, 'a bonfire of old women' (above, p. 626). Similarly, it will be recalled, he asked rhetorically: "The greatest happiness of the greatest number" is to be our invariable guide! Is it so? – the greatest happiness of the greatest number of men living, I suppose, not of men to come; for if of all posterity, what legislator can be our guide? who can prejudge the future? of men living, then? – well – how often would *their* greatest happiness consist in concession to their greatest errors' (above, p. 626). It is strikingly expressed in 1835 in the declaration that from a utility perspective 'clear and comprehensive views of education and human culture must precede, and form the basis of a philosophy of morals' and these may differ from person to person (above, p. 630).

Yet there seems to be some hesitancy – some considerable hesitancy – on Mill's part to accept the value-laden nature of the principle despite his own striking statements. For in 1835 he demanded proof that human happiness is the end and test of morality (above, p. 628); and in 1838 he wrote critically of Bentham seeking a first principle that to *him* was self-evident and from which all else flowed as logical consequences (above, pp. 634–5). What, however, of his later years, the years of his return to Bentham?

Again his hesitancy is apparent. In 1849 he rejected the evaluation of right and wrong in terms of some 'natural idea', yet allowed for some such appeal by 'a few persons of pre-eminent genius and feeling' (above, pp. 640–1). In 1852 he interpreted the utilitarian principle as implying the equality of all human beings and referred favourably to Bentham's hopes for a time when cruelty to animals would be ruled out on utility grounds yet asserted also that 'a moralist can deduce from [utility as a standard] his whole system of ethics, without calling to his assistance any foreign principle' (above, p. 643) – as if the requirement for 'foreign principles' reflecting the 'value judgments' implicit in the specification of the maximand were not the very essence of the matter!

The problem is complicated further in the work of 1861 where Mill again maintains the position that utility is the source of justice. Mill is quite clear that 'questions of ultimate ends are not amenable to direct proof' (above, p. 646): 'Whatever can be proved to be good, must be so by being shown to be a means to something admitted to be good without proof – . . . who is to say pleasure is good?' That value judgement is entailed seems clear enough. Yet he attempted a proof of sorts as we have seen. And once again one must ask: Whose pleasures, and how to weight pleasures of the constituents selected for inclusion in the maximand? Now Mill recognizes that what precisely is meant by justice (which he reduces to 'equality') varies with one's perspective of the general good – about 'what is useful in society' (above, p. 654) – evidently then a matter of personal preference. But in that case it should be clear that supplementary sources are required to flesh out the utility rule – sources that may not be the same for all adherents. To declare that instead of deriving 'rights from rights' one must have 'a rule of right before it can be decided what ought to be right' – a rule provided by the 'greatest happiness' principle – is to argue in a circle. And that 'absolutist' criteria of the very kind condemned, standards of justice 'generically distinct from every variety of the Expedient' (X, 240), do creep in is suggested by the references to qualitative differentials between pleasures amenable to specification by persons of 'nobler feelings' (above, p. 651), and by the assertion that the utility principle is 'without rational significance, unless one person's happiness . . . is counted exactly as much as another's (above, p. 650). These difficulties reappear in the statement in *On Liberty*, our next topic.

VII LIBERTY, UTILITY AND SOCIAL CONTROL

'If it were felt' Mill declared in the famous third chapter of *On Liberty*, 'that the free development of individuality is one of the leading essentials of well-being; that it is not only a co-ordinate element with all that is designated by the terms civilisation, instruction, education, culture, but is itself a necessary part and condition of all those things, there would be no danger that liberty should be undervalued, and the adjustment of the boundaries between it and social control would present no extraordinary difficulty . . . (*CW*, XVIII, 261). This allusion to the limits of social control is restated in a summary of the main outcome of the work – 'the two maxims which together form the entire doctrine of [the] essay', a reference to the celebrated *self-* and *other-regarding* distinction:

The maxims are, first, that the individual is not accountable to society for his actions, in so far as these concern the interests of no person but himself. Advice, instruction, persuasion, and avoidance by other people if thought necessary by them for their own good, are the only measures by which society can justifiably express its dislike or disapprobation of his conduct. Secondly, that for such actions as are prejudicial to the interests of others, the individual is accountable, and may be subjected either to social or to legal punishment, if society is of opinion that the one or the other is requisite for its protection (292).[72]

In the body of the third chapter Mill elaborates upon individuality as 'One of the Elements of Well-Being'. Specifically, it is one of the key constituents of the general good with special reference to the development of human character along appropriate lines: 'It is desirable . . . that in things which do not primarily concern others, individuality should assert itself. Where, not the person's own character, but the traditions or customs of other people are the rule of conduct, there is wanting one of the principal ingredients of human happiness, and quite the chief ingredient of individual and social progress' (261). That freedom in the sense of respect for individuality is actually a matter of 'justice' is also made quite explicit: '[W]hatever crushes individuality is despotism, by whatever name it may be called, and whether it professes to be enforcing the will of God or the injunctions of men' (266). And to crush individuality is to crush spiritual development: '[I]t is only the cultivation of individuality which produces, or can produce well-developed human beings . . .' (267). The non-uniformity of individual utility functions is brought out here with eminent clarity (confirming, incidentally, the purely conventional nature of the axiom whereby each is to count for one for legislative purposes) while the general utility principle, defined with reference to (Mill's conception of) the character of human kind, dictated a case for genuine freedom of choice to encourage appropriate training of that character:

[D]ifferent persons . . . require different conditions for their spiritual development . . . Such are the differences among human beings in their sources of pleasure, their susceptibilities of pain, and the operation on them of different physical and moral agencies, that unless there is a corresponding diversity in their modes of life, they neither obtain their fair share of happiness, nor grow up to the mental, moral, and aesthetic stature of which their nature is capable (270).

[T]o conform to custom, merely *as* custom, does not educate or develope in him

72 Cf: '[T]he sole end for which mankind are warranted, individually or collectively, in interfering with the liberty of action of any of their number, is self-protection . . . the only purpose for which power can be rightfully exercised over any member of a civilized community, against his will, is to prevent harm to others. His own good, either physical or moral, is not a sufficient warrant' (223).

any of the qualities which are the distinctive endowment of a human being. The human faculties of perception, judgment, discriminative feeling, mental activity, and even moral preference, are exercised only in making a choice. He who does anything because it is the custom, makes no choice. He gains no practice either in discerning or in desiring what is best. The mental and moral, like the muscular powers, are improved only by being used. The faculties are called into no exercise by doing a thing merely because others do it, no more than by believing a thing only because others believe it. If the grounds of an opinion are not conclusive to the person's own reason, his reason cannot be strengthened, but is likely to be weakened, by his adopting it: and if the inducements to an act are not such as are consentaneous to his own feelings and character (where affection, or the rights of others, are not concerned) it is so much towards rendering his feelings and character inert and torpid, instead of active and energetic (262).

Tribute is paid to F.H. Von Humboldt according to whom 'the end of man, or that which is prescribed by the eternal or immutable dictates of reason, and not suggested by vague and transient desires, is the highest and most harmonious development of his powers to a complete and consistent whole', to which end two requisites were required: 'freedom and variety of situation' (261).

The formulation in *On Liberty* constitutes an elaboration of the argument in *Utilitarianism* by spelling out in greater detail the nature of the maximand – 'the general good' *as perceived by Mill*. For clearly not only 'security' (above, p. 648) is involved, but human character formation itself, and ultimately social progress. The importation of external criteria in the definition of what constitutes well-being is thus clear, as is also the nature of 'liberty' as means to the end thus defined.[73]

The establishment of 'individuality' as means to an end with special reference to Mill's own conception of character formation (and ultimately social progress in general) created apparent dilemmas. Mill, for example, complained of 'the philanthropic spirit abroad' towards the 'moral and prudential improvement of our fellow-creatures', a movement which Mill warned, encouraged standardization (271); but he himself championed moral 'improvement', and regarded education as a form of social control designed to train people in youth 'to know and benefit by the ascertained results of human experience' (262) and render them 'capable of rational conduct in life' (282). There is scope here for a moulding of personality. But Mill seems to have been satisfied that education programs might be devised to encourage in the adult the use and interpretation of such experience 'in his own way' (262) without actually dictating choice and opinion; and this is not patently unreasonable.[74]

73 See the account in Robson (1968), Ch. 7.
74 On this problem, see West, 1965.

It is, however, somewhat paradoxical that Mill was prepared to see his view of genuine individuality imposed on those who chose to be governed in their patterns of consumption by opinion as his recommendations regarding taxation make clear. (See the discussion below, p. 880, of conspicuous consumption.) But dilemmas for the liberal of this order (which reflect the justification of forcing individuals to be free) are inevitable, and they are the exception not the rule in Mill's case. That he was aware of the problem is certain; what could at any time be achieved depended on the state of opinion and, ideally, desirable reforms were to be precluded if premature.

There are difficulties with the analysis that require brief comments. It is implied in some of Mill's formulations that liberty, a basic human need, constitutes an end in itself as well as a means to other ends, appropriate character development. Some commentators have discerned here a severe dilemma. It has been observed, for example, that if Mill 'is a utilitarian committed to one supreme principle as yielding all reasons for or against any action, how can Mill at the same time endorse a principle – his principle of liberty – according to which the fact that an act promotes utility is no reason at all in its favor if the act happens to be one that violates the liberty principle?' (Gray, 1981, 95).[75]

This problem should not, however, be overstated. *For the utility principle constitutes the final appeal.* Thus the mere fact that an act violates the liberty

---

75 Gray himself comes to Mill's defence taking into account Mill's conception of human nature. Gray's article contains an extensive review of an enormous literature on the topic. Cf. also Grampp (1965), II, 136: 'As a utilitarian [Mill] believed in freedom as a means and not as something that was always worthwhile in itself. He believed men should be free because only by being so could they reach their goals. But if one supposes they may reach their goals without being free, does that mean freedom has no value? One cannot be sure. At other times, he wrote that freedom was an end in itself, and then he was not a utilitarian.' See too the evaluation in Robbins (1952), 186: '[I]t is difficult to read Mill on social philosophy without feeling that insensibly he had reached a position which, in fact, involved a plurality of ultimate criteria'.

  Robson (1968) concedes only a 'tension' in Mill between two justifications of individual liberty: that it is conducive to utility, and that it is a basic human need (186), but plays down the problem: 'While Mill's devotion to the utilitarian end in *On Liberty* is clear, and only a recognition of the over-riding importance of general happiness can allow one to see the proper dimensions of liberty, it must be admitted that Mill attaches more importance to liberty than utility demands' (128n); but Mill's basic position was that 'freedom is not an end in itself' rather it provides a fuller experience from which truth may be induced and belief made conformable to fact' (215).

  Rawls (1971) may be read as an attempt to escape Mill's supposed dilemma by formally placing justice, appeal made to intuition, at the summit. See, however, the balanced analysis by Gordon (1980), who bases a positive case on the presumptions 'that freedom is intrinsically good', and 'that freedom is a primary social good, which may indeed be instrumental to the attainment of other goods, but must also be treated as an end in itself' (28).

principle by affecting adversely second parties need not rule it out. This is strikingly revealed in Mill's insistence that while aspects of competition (e.g. the entry of firms into a profitable industry) may entail damage by A of B's interests, the 'social good' none the less requires that such consequences be overlooked: '[I]t is, by common admission, better for the general interest of mankind, that persons should pursue their objects undeterred by this sort of consequences. In other words, society admits no right, either legal or moral, in the disappointed competitors, to immunity from this kind of suffering; and feels called on to interfere, only when means of success have been employed which it is contrary to the general interest to permit – namely fraud, or treachery, and force' (XVIII, 292-3). Conversely, liberty is represented as '*one* of the elements of well-being', and '*one* of the principal ingredients of human happiness' implying that it is an end amongst others. And in that case the need for some external principle of valuation is required to weigh these ends, and this can only be provided by the 'general good'. The distinction between self- and other-regarding acts reflects indeed the importance of liberty in the hierarchy – Mill's attempt to assure that liberty will not be too readily constrained in the interests of other *desiderata*.[76] But the so-called 'inviolability' of self-regarding acts is not an absolute, and must bow to circumstances.[77] One notes, for example, that Mill did not preclude reasoned persuasion in the matter of 'self-regarding' defects: 'Considerations to aid [a person's] judgment, exhortations to strengthen his will, may be offered to him, even obtruded on him, by others', although the individual alone 'is the final judge. All errors which he is likely to commit against advice and warning, are far outweighed by the evil of allowing others to constrain him to what they deem his good' (277). There were also 'moral vices' which merited even stronger disapprobation (279), although again provided we have to do

76 Allett (1981), 185, cites the strictures against Mill by J. A. Hobson (1901): 'If [an individual] . . . is living as a member of a society, since he is an organic being in an organic society, no action of his can be considered purely self regarding or wholly void of social import . . . "individual rights" can have . . . no absolute validity; for society, and not the individual, must clearly claim, in the social interest, to determine what actions fall within this "self-regarding" class.' Allett's defence of Mill seems convincing: Mill intended the 'self-regarding' category for which he claimed 'inviolability' to include acts not affecting *adversely* the interests of others (not acts that do not affect them at all). The class is by no means an empty one.

77 Cf. Robson (1968), 184-5: 'A proper understanding of *On Liberty*, and in particular of the rule concerning intervention in individual affairs is impossible without reference to the principle of utility, and is extremely difficult without reference to the rest of Mill's social thought. The rule or principle, it must be remembered, is a practical one, and therefore to be interpreted according to an actual situation. Mill is providing a guide to action and, as always for him, such guides should be tested by the ultimate principle, when subordinate utilities conflict.'

only with 'the merely contingent, or, as it may be called, constructive injury which a person causes to society, by conduct which neither violates any specific duty to the public, nor occasions perceptible hurt to any assignable individual except himself; the inconvenience is one which society can afford to bear, for the sake of the greater good of human freedom' (282).[78] It is quite clear that the individual's 'inviolability' in self-regarding acts is, in practice, a matter of the general good.[79]

Quite logically then allowance had to be made for exceptions to the rule – cases where the general good dictates the actual repression of individuality. There is the question of the prevention of suicide attempts. And, more generally, the case of 'backward' societies in contrast to the British case. There was no absolute rule:

[The] danger which threatens human nature is not [in contemporary Britain] the excess, but the deficiency, of personal impulses and preferences. Things are vastly changed, since the passions of those who were strong by station or by personal endowment were in a state of habitual rebellion against laws and ordinances, and required to be rigorously chained up to enable the persons within their reach to enjoy any particle of security. In our times, from the highest class of society down to the lowest, every one lives as under the eye of a hostile and dreaded censorship. Not only in what concerns others, but in what concerns only themselves, the individual or the family do not ask themselves – what do I prefer? or, what would suit my character and disposition? or, what would allow the best and highest in me to have fair play, and enable it to grow and thrive? They ask themselves, what is suitable to my position? What is normally done by persons of my station and pecuniary circumstances? or (worse still) what is usually done by persons of a station and circumstances superior to mine? I do not mean that they choose what is customary in preference to what suits their own inclination. It does not occur to them to have any inclination, except for what is customary. Thus the mind itself is bowed to the yoke: even in what people do for pleasure, conformity is the first thing thought of; they like in crowds; they exercise choice only among things commonly done; peculiarity of taste, eccentricity of

78 Mill warned further regarding control of 'self-regarding conduct' that public opinion means 'some people's opinion of what is good or bad for other people' and, this is 'quite as likely to be wrong as right' (283). In this context we find a formulation which might imply that justice (liberty) is an end in itself on a par with utility; but it is yet more probable that by 'policy' Mill merely intended elements conducive to the general good *apart from* justice (liberty) without intending to exclude the latter from the general good: '[L]et not society pretend that it needs . . . the power to issue commands and enforce obedience in the personal concerns of individuals, in which, on all principles of justice and policy, the decision ought to rest with those who are to abide the consequences' (282).

79 For this reason we find Himmelfarb's charge of inconsistency to be exaggerated: 'The primary goods in *Utilitarianism* were morality and a sense of unity; the primary goods in *On Liberty* were liberty and individuality' (1974, 107). For a further criticism of this charge, see Levy, 1980, 9.

conduct, are shunned equally with crimes: until by dint of not following their own nature, they have no nature to follow: their human capacities are withered and starved: they become incapable of any strong wishes or native pleasures, and are generally without either opinions or feelings of home growth, or properly their own (264–5).[80]

The perspective championed by Mill should be appreciated as part of a reform program directed against the repression of individuality by the force of opinion merely for the sake of conformity. But Mill was very careful indeed to insist on the *social* benefits deriving from such a program; his case was the very reverse of a license for anti-social behaviour. Even the degree of social control which could be justified, reflecting the restriction that 'the liberty of the individual must be thus far limited; he must not make himself a nuisance to other people' (260), encouraged an enrichment of true individuality:

In proportion to the development of his individuality, each person becomes more valuable to himself, and is therefore capable of being more valuable to others. There is a great fulness of life about his own existence, and when there is more life in the units there is more in the mass which is composed of them. As much compression as is necessary to prevent the stronger specimens of human nature from encroaching on the rights of others, cannot be dispensed with; but for this there is ample compensation even in the point of view of human development. The means of development which the individual loses by being prevented from gratifying his inclinations to the injury of others, are chiefly obtained at the expense of the development of other people. And even to himself there is a full equivalent in the better development of the social part of his nature, rendered possible by the restraint put upon the selfish part. To be held to rigid rules of justice for the sake of others, develops the feelings and capacities which have the good of others for their object (266).

Mill denied, therefore, that the 'individualism' he championed was in any way 'anti-social'. This is much insisted upon: 'It would be a great misunderstanding of this doctrine to suppose that it is one of selfish indifference, which pretends that human beings have no business with each other's conduct of life, and that they should not concern themselves about the well-doing or well-being of one another, unless their own interest is involved. Instead of any diminution, there is need of a great increase of

80 Mill conceded that 'to a certain extent it is admitted that our understanding should be our own: but there is not the same willingness to admit that our desires and impulses should be our own likewise; or that to possess impulses of our own, and of any strength, is anything but a peril and a snare' (263). On the role of 'opinion' in a contemporary context in *On Liberty*, see Hamburger (1976), Burnell (1983).

disinterested exertion to promote the good of others' (277). Let us recall here a similar and striking passage from *Utilitarianism*:

I must again repeat, what the assailants of utilitarianism seldom have the justice to acknowledge, that the happiness which forms the utilitarian standard of what is right in conduct, is not the agent's own happiness, but that of all concerned. As between his own happiness and that of others, utilitarianism requires him to be as strictly impartial as a disinterested and benevolent spectator . . . As the means of making the nearest approach to [the] ideal, utility would enjoin, first, that laws and social arrangments should place the happiness, or (as speaking practically it may be called) the interest, of every individual, as nearly as possible in harmony with the interest of the whole; and secondly, that education and opinion, which have so vast a power over human character, should so use that power as to establish in the mind of every individual an indissoluble association between his own happiness and the good of the whole; especially between his own happiness and the practice of such modes of conduct, negative and positive, as regard for the universal happiness prescribes: so that not only he may be unable to conceive the possibility of happiness to himself, consistently with conduct opposed to the general good, but also that a direct impulse to promote the general good may be in every individual one of the habitual motives of action, and the sentiments connected therewith may fill a large and prominent place in every human being's sentient existence (*CW*, X, 218).

This perspective we have seen, is consistent with the original formulations of Bentham, who had insisted on the same ideal.[81]

81 Robson (1968) insists on a rather sharper distinction between Mill and Bentham in the light of the Coleridge influence: 'Just because he brings them together, however, one would expect to find a difference between his position and Bentham's. It occurs in consideration of the pre-eminence of individual or institutional reform. Both work for social utility, but Mill argues that social ends cannot be understood, much less achieved, except by individuals. Here is the central import of *On Liberty*. As Sterling said, Mill believed "that individual reform must be the groundwork of social progress." The individual must not be shut up within a controlled and restrictive system of social morality; he must be free to choose his own destiny in the light of his moral views – consideration always being given to the happiness and equal development of others. In a restrictive system, society cannot advance, for moral attitudes and practices remain stagnant. The rulers may, of course, change their decrees, but unless the rules are felt by individuals as a living internal force, as duty or conscience, no real improvement can result. A necessity for social advance and freedom of thought is, therefore, such freedom of action as makes freedom of thought more than a phrase . . .' (126–7).
   Cf. also 143: 'Again one is led to Mill's most important modification of utilitarianism, his concentration on the individual. Perhaps the greatest charm which utility held for Bentham was that it permitted of calculation. Acts could be objectively classified according to their beneficial or harmful consequences, and a needy and easy way to the best of all commonwealths could be thus described. Mill alters the whole scheme by insisting that individual development is the only and difficult way . . .'; 129, regarding a peculiarly complex and vital element in the 'moral good' ascribed to Mill; and 185; 'Mill is not

VIII THE LABOUR PROBLEM AND PRIVATE PROPERTY:
SOME PRELIMINARY IMPLICATIONS

A supposedly widespread opinion regarding 'individual independence'
governs Mill's perspective on the measures required by the dictates of *justice*
'to improve either the bodily or mental condition of the labouring classes':

[L]et it here be remembered that we have to do with a class, a large portion of which
reads, discusses, and forms opinions on public interests. Let it be remembered also,
that we live in a political age; in which the desire of political rights, or the abuse of
political privileges by the possessors of them, are the foremost ideas in the minds of
most reading men – an age, too, the whole spirit of which instigates every one to
demand fair play for helping himself, rather than to seek or expect help from others.
In such an age, and in the treatment of minds so predisposed, justice is the one
needful thing rather than kindness ('Claims of Labour', 1845; *CW*, IV, 383).[82]

Satisfactory living standards for the masses could be achieved by paternalistic
measures, but at the cost of 'the spirit of equality and love of individual independence' characterizing contemporary British opinion – including that of the
masses (374–5).[83] Justice, in the sense of 'fair play for helping himself',
required rather the removal of 'every restriction, every artificial hindrance,
which legal and fiscal systems oppose to the attempts of the labouring

preaching anarchy, but a rational approach to individual rights. Private actions are not
amoral to him, as they often seem to be for Bentham. A utilitarian justification for
individual liberty is not simple for Mill, for he includes the full development of each
and every human being in the ethical end. Morality is dynamic for him, not static as
it is for Bentham, and the elements of happiness are seen in terms of the possessors of
happiness, individual citizens.' It is conceded, at the same time, that there is at least
a 'superficial consistency' between Mill and Bentham who reach the 'same apparent
result by working from different ends' (127–8).
   On the degree of common ground between Bentham and Mill regarding the appropriate
provinces of liberty and authority see Long (1977), 108, 115f and Lyons, 1972, 211n.
The picture is a mixed one (Long, 1977, 9, 116–17).
82 'It is not enough that they should no longer be objects of pity. The conditions of a positively
happy and dignified existence are what he demands for them, as well as for every other
portion of the human race' cf: 'Thornton on Labour and its Claim,' (1869; V, 650n).
Adam Smith (1937) had also expressed the *desideratum* in terms of justice: '[I]t is but
equity . . . that they who feed, cloath and lodge the whole body of the people, should
have such a share of the produce of their own labour as to be themselves tolerably well
fed, cloathed and lodged' (78–9).
83 The case against slavery is formulated in the *Principles* in these terms: '[T]here are .
. . things which are or have been subjects of property, in which no proprietory rights
ought to exist at all. But as the civilized world has in general made up its mind on most
of these, there is no necessity for dwelling on them in this place. At the head of them,
is property in human beings. It is almost superfluous to observe, that this institution
can have no place in any society even pretending to be founded on justice, or on fellowship
between human creatures' (II, 232–3).

class to forward their own improvement'. And along these lines Mill provides what proves to be a characteristic perspective on government intervention – that it should be designed wherever possible to *stimulate* ultimate independence:

Of schemes destined specially to give them employment, or add to their comforts, it may be said, once for all, that there is a simple test by which to judge them. Is the assistance of such a kind, and given in such a manner, as to render them ultimately independent of the continuance of similar assistance? If not, the best that can be said of the plans is, that they are harmless. To make them useful, it is an indispensable condition that there be a reasonable prospect of their being at some future time self-supporting. Even upon the best supposition, it appears to us that too much importance is attached to them. Given education and just laws, the poorer class would be as competent as any other class to take care of their own personal habits and requirements (386–7).

A body of just law would thus avoid discrimination (and certainly discrimination against the majority class) and encourage the development of individual potential and initiative.[84] *In contemporary circumstances the utility criterion implied that of justice understood as respect for individual independence.*

This sets the stage for the *Principles*. The conditions of human happiness were assured by a variety of material and spiritual means with an eye always to the going state of opinion. At the most mundane level, and having in mind one of the central concerns of the age, 'the condition of the people' was of fundamental importance. But only if the principle of individuality is respected would high standards (or equality) be at all meaningful (an evaluation, we shall later find, determining Mill's attitude towards Socialism):

After the means of subsistence are assured, the next in strength of the personal wants of human beings is liberty; and (unlike the physical wants, which as civilization

84 Desirable steps towards the end of increased independence include *inter alia* the framing of laws of partnership to encourage the accumulation of small savings; and the removal of stamp levies on the purchase of small plots of land and legal fees on transfers. Defects in these domains constituted the source of deeply felt grievances on the part of 'the most intelligent and right-thinking of the [working] class – those who are most fitted to acquire, and best qualified to exercise, a beneficial influence over the rest' (386). Particularly important was the abolition of measures which positively involved class discrimination: the corn laws (equivalent to a tax on bread) Mill represented as the source of a 'rankling sense of gross injustice, which renders any approximation of feeling between the classes impossible while even a remembrance of it lasts . . .'; the game laws as a lamentable 'want of just feeling,' and 'source of crime and bitterness in a class which it is now so much the fashion to patronize'; and the loss by the poor of rights of way and commons as a transfer to the rich (384–5). Mill pointed to the contradictions of corn laws side by side with alms-giving; the game laws yet games of cricket between rich and poor; and no rights of way on private land yet parks for workers.

advances become more moderate and more amenable to control) it increases instead of diminishing in intensity, as the intelligence and the moral faculties are more developed. The perfection both of social arrangements and of practical morality would be, to secure to all persons complete independence and freedom of action, subject to no restriction but that of not doing injury to others: and the education which taught or the social institutions which required them to exchange the control of their own actions for any amount of comfort or affluence, or to renounce liberty for the sake of equality, would deprive them of one of the most elevated characteristics of human nature (II, 208–9).

The end of high wages and low hours we shall find is further qualified. It is championed by Mill subject to the condition that satisfactory living conditions are not fraudulently obtained. The good society in the broadest sense (including character formation) stands ever sentinel.

A mutual reinforcement of ends and means emerges in the present context and is pertinent for a full appreciation of Mill's conception of the 'greatest good' principle. Individual fulfilment and initiative, an end in itself, acts to encourage high real earnings:

[The] efficiency of industry may be expected to be great, in proportion as the fruits of industry are insured to the person exerting it: and . . . all social institutions are conducive to useful exertion, according as they provide that the reward of every one for his labour shall be proportioned as much as possible to the benefit which it produces. All laws or usages which favour one class or sort of persons to the disadvantage of others; which chain up the efforts of any part of the community in pursuit of their own good, or stand between those efforts and their natural fruits – are . . .violations of the fundamental principles of economic policy; tending to make the aggregate productive powers of the community productive in a less degree than they would otherwise be (II, 114–15; cf. III, 880f, esp. 884–5).

Like the case for high earnings, that for private property was a complex one. Mill rationalized it both in terms of expediency – as a means to an end, specifically as a motive to increased wealth; but also as an end in itself (given the contemporary state of morals and opinion): 'I do not, indeed, quite agree . . . that, from the utilitarian point of view, the right of private property is founded *solely* on the motives it affords to the increase of public wealth; because independently of those motives, the feeling of security of possession and enjoyment which could not (in the state of advancement mankind have yet reached) be had without private ownership, is of the very greatest importance as an element of human happiness . . .' (26 June 1870, XVII, 1739–40).

It will be noted immediately how marked is the subjective and provisional nature of the maximand. The greatest happiness allows for the pleasure derived from possession of property in the given state of opinion. This accords with the presumption of the doctrine whereby each individual is presumed to be the best judge of his own interest. But that judgement is not irrevocable; it is subject to influence. And to influence opinion in favour of Mill's own vision of the greatest good is a conspicuous characteristic of the *Principles*. Perhaps not surprisingly there are instances when his perception of 'right' opinion carried him rather far, so that a degree of paternalism regarding what the judgement should be is not always avoided.[85]

IX ON COMPENSATION

The subjective nature of the 'greatest happiness' principle may be equally well illustrated in terms of the compensation issue. The principle might be understood to justify measures which are advantageous to the majority even when at the cost of some individuals or groups. But this was positively not Mill's reading. Throughout his work a (qualified) right to compensation is recognized which formally runs in terms of 'justice'.

Compensation is thus justified even for slave owners upon abolition, despite the iniquity of the institution, for 'when the state has expressly legalized it, and human beings, for generations, have been bought, sold, and inherited under sanction of law, it is another wrong, in abolishing the property, not to make full compensation' (*CW*, II, 233). Compensation could 'probably not with justice be refused' upon the abolition of state monopolies. But a condition is here interposed of general relevance:

There are other cases in which this would be more doubtful. The question would turn upon what, in the peculiar circumstances, was sufficient to constitute prescription [ancient privilege]; and whether the legal recognition which the abuse had obtained, was sufficient to constitute it an institution, or amounted only to an occasional license. It would be absurd to claim compensation for losses caused by changes in a tariff, a thing confessedly variable from year to year; or for monopolies like those granted to individuals by the Tudors, favours of a despotic authority, which the power that gave was competent at any time to recall.[86]

85 His disapproval of conspicuous consumption to be discussed presently provides a case in point. A second illustration we shall find in his presumption regarding the desirability of economic development and the role of government in achieving that end.

86 Cf. 'I might illustrate my meaning by saying that it is my opinion . . . that it was an exceedingly improper act of Hen. 8th to give away the lands of the monasteries to individuals, whose successors now possess those lands, but I conceive it would be now unjust to take those lands, or any portion of them, from the present possessors' ('The Income and Property Tax', 1852; V, 484).

Mill's support for the adoption of machinery whenever justified on efficiency grounds, despite recognition of the inevitability that some group will suffer from technological change – even the possibility that the current generation of workers as a whole might be disadvantaged – must also be understood subject to the obligation upon governments 'of alleviating, and if possible preventing, the evils of which this source of ultimate benefit is or may be productive to an existing generation':

If the sinking or fixing of capital in machinery or useful works were ever to proceed at such a pace as to impair materially the funds for the maintenance of labour, it would be incumbent on legislators to take measures for moderating its rapidity: and since improvements which do not diminish employment on the whole, almost always throw some particular class of labourers out of it, there cannot be a more legitimate object of the legislator's care than the interests of those who are thus sacrificed to the gains of their fellow-citizens and of posterity (98–9).

X UTILITY VERSUS NATURAL RIGHTS: APPLICATIONS TO LABOUR AND PROPERTY

W. T. Thornton's demonstration in 1867 that the wage rate was not irresistibly determined by some 'supposed natural law' but rather involved (within limits) a matter of choice, gave added urgency to the question (as Mill phrased it) 'whether there are any *rights* of labour on the one hand, or of capital on the other, which would be yielded if the opposite party pushed its pretensions to the extreme limit of economic possibility'. Mill's reply (1869; *CW*, V, 646–7) provides a splendid summary of his general position.

Thornton had adopted the view that neither side had any 'rights', and that provided employers did not resort to force or fraud any terms offered by them were 'just', for labour had no claim to employment, and certainly none to employment at a particular wage, since it could not be shown that the institution of private property deprived anybody of anything that would have existed in its absence (647–8). On the contrary, property was the condition for wealth: '[Society] is not bound in equity, whatever it may be in charity, to find food for the hungry because they are in need, nor to find occupation for the unemployed because they are out of work. By withholding aid, it is not guilty of the smallest injustice . . . [The] poor, as such, have no unliquidated claim against the rich' (649).

With this Mill took issue. As in his major formal works here too he made the point that moralists who appealed to some standard of justice other than the general good mistook a corollary of the principle of general utility for a first principle, being misled by the fact that the corollary 'had taken a deep root in the popular mind, and gathered round itself a considerable amount of human feeling' (651; cf. 'Newman's Political Economy',

1851; V, 443). It was only because of its profound consequences that a particular standard became thus impregnated in the imagination.

Mill noted Thornton's allowances of the general happiness as the criterion of social *virtue* but complained that he had failed to extend it to *justice*. In fact the general interest provided the standard for both, the difference turning on the seriousness of the consequences at stake: 'There are many acts, and a still greater number of forbearances, the perpetual practice of which by all is so necessary to general well-being, that people must be held to it compulsorily, either by law, or by social pressure'; in other cases 'it is, on the whole, for the general interest that they should be left free; being merely encouraged, by praise and honour, to the performance of such beneficial actions as are not sufficiently stimulated by benefits flowing from them to the agent himself' (650–1).

Since a supposedly intuitive rule of justice was not in fact a first principle at all, it could always be faced by a rival with equal authority. Thornton himself had counterposed his own perspective on social justice against that of Rousseau and Proudhon 'according to which all private appropriation of the instruments of production was a wrong from the beginning, and an injury to the rest of mankind', both approaches claiming to be evident by intuition. But the axioms on which each was based were 'all of them good', so that the choice between them could only be decided 'by the thoroughly practical consideration of consequences . . . by the general interest of society and mankind, mental and bodily, intellectual, emotional, and physical taken together'. This same point was made in correspondence with Thornton regarding his volume: 'I find in it what I always find where a standard is assumed of so called justice distinct from general utility & supposed to be paramount whenever the two conflict, viz. that some other standard might just as well have been assumed. Not only do I not admit any standard of right which does not derive its sole authority from utility, but I remark that in such cases an adversary could always find some other maxim of justice equal in authority but leading to opposite conclusions' (19 Oct. 1867, XVI, 1318).

In the case at hand the Rousseau approach 'satisfied [the] highest conceptions of justice and moral right', and had 'the "note" of intuitive truth as completely as the principles from which [Thornton's] own system is a deduction'. The moderate version of that approach whereby a labourer's pay should correspond to 'his wants and his merits' ('that each should have what he deserves, and that, in the dispensation of good things, those whose wants are more urgent should have the preference') had even stronger appeal than Thornton's for 'we [were] guided to it by the immediate and spontaneous perceptions of the moral sense' (V, 651–2).[87]

---

87 While Mill is accepting the methodological position of his opponent for argument's sake

* * *

That a priori theories of justice could not be relied upon, was also suggested by the fact that characteristically their most important conclusions could be shown inapplicable while the axiom remained intact. Thus Thornton's claim that property in land deprived no one of anything quantitatively consequential – what would have been available in an unappropriated system – might be accepted, but was irrelevant in circumstances where people were fit to manage their affairs co-operatively for the general benefit (652–3). Similarly, Mill pointed to a claim based on 'intuitive morality' by Thornton that since the rights of capital reflect the rights of past labour, capital had the right to impose any contract of present labour short of fraud or force. This too Mill countered by asking, 'how many of the great commercial fortunes have been, at least partly, built up by practices which in a better state of society would have been impossible – jobbing contracts, profligate loans, or other abuses of Government expenditure, improper use of public positions, monopolies, and other bad laws, or perhaps only be the manifold advantages which imperfect social institutions gave to those who are already rich, over their poorer fellow-citizens, in the general struggle of life?' This quite apart from force or fraud strictly defined. Moral intuition, once allowed, thus pointed away from Thornton's case for the free use of property. On the other hand, there was a case *in general utility* why bad title to property should be recognized after the lapse of time – the fact that 'reversal of the wrong would cause greater insecurity, and greater social disturbance than its condonation' (654). Mill, in practice, was well disposed to Thornton's case for the free disposal of property: '[O]n utilitarian grounds, there probably would be little difference between Mr. Thornton's conclusions and my own. I should stand up for the free disposal of property as strongly, and most likely with only the same limitations, as he would'.

Intuitive morality – again accepting it for argument's sake – might be said (against Thornton) to support the claims by the majority for the taxation of the rich alone or the guarantee of employment at a specific wage or the denial of legal protection to property above a certain amount, since 'the existing social arrangements, and law itself, exist in virtue not only of the forbearance but of the active support of the labouring classes'. On Thornton's own principles, this kind of argument stood up well. But there were strong utilitarian arguments against it, namely that 'the conditions imposed would be injurious, instead of beneficial, to the public weal' (654–5). Mill thus insisted on 'the prosaic consideration of consequences'. Labour had no *right* to anything other than what could be justified in terms of

it is difficult to avoid the impression that he himself actually recognizes, at the least, a 'moral sense' (see above, p. 653 on this issue).

'the permanent interest of the human race' (an extraordinary widening of the greater-good maximand if taken literally).

* * *

The foregoing chapter provides essential background for an appreciation of Mill's approach towards the role of government in economic life, economic organization in the broadest sense of that term, and income distribution. These matters are taken up in the following three chapters.

NINE

Economic policy:
the role of government

I INTRODUCTION

The general rule formalized in *On Liberty* which dictates the legitimate scope of social control (Chapter 8, Section VII) appears, we shall see, in the *Principles of Political Economy* with special reference to the role of government in economic affairs.[1] The role of government, within the same frame of reference, is also well stated in the defence of Bentham against Whewell's strictures in 1852, and again in the paper on centralization a decade later:

Government is entitled to assume that it will take better care than individuals of the public interest, but not better care of their own interest. It is one thing for the legislator to dictate to individuals what they shall do for their own advantage, and another to protect the interest of other persons who may be injuriously affected by their acts. Dr. Whewell's own instances suffice: 'What is the meaning of restraints imposed for the sake of public health, cleanliness, and comfort? Why are not individuals left to do what they like with reference to such matters? Plainly because carelessness, ignorance, indolence, would prevent their doing what is most for their own interest.' Say rather, would lead them to do what is contrary to the interests of other people. The proper object of sanitary laws is not to compel people to take care of their own health, but to prevent them from endangering that of others. To prescribe by law, what they should do for their own health alone, would by most people be justly regarded as something very like tyranny (*CW*, X, 197–8).

A legislature, as well as an executive, may take upon itself to prescribe how individuals shall carry on their own business for their own profit. It may bind the

---

1 See Robbins (1952), 'Individualism as a Means' (186–94) for the general background to our topic.

operations of manufacture to an unchangeable routine, by all the *minutieux* regulations of Colbert. But when, instead of protecting individuals against themselves, it only protects them against others, from whom it would be either difficult or impossible for them to protect themselves, it is within its province. This is the principle which legitimates laws against false weights and measures, and the adoption of a common standard of them for the whole country; which justifies the legal regulation of emigrant ships, and of the professional qualification of masters of merchant vessels; which requires that employers and parents shall not, by conspiring together, selfishly overwork children for their private gain, or work them at all, at times or in modes inconsistent with their proper education; which forbids that individuals should be allowed to build, and let out for dwelling in, places such as human beings cannot inhabit with decency or safety to their health. For though it may be alleged that, in this last case, acceptance of the conditions is voluntary, it is so only as regards the head of the family, who, being oftenest absent, suffers least from the evil; and it is not voluntary at all when better residences are not to be had; while, if bad ones are prohibited, the spontaneous provision of good ones follows as a matter of course (XIX, 602).

George Stigler has complained that Mill's position regarding state intervention in economic life was ambiguous:

He does not tell us how to determine whether a given public policy frees or inhibits individuals. Suppose I contemplate a program of public housing. If I bribe or force people into such housing, of course I have reduced their area of choice and responsibility. But I have also, I presumably hope, given a generation of children a chance to grow up in quarters that are not grossly unsanitary and inadequate for physical and moral health. Mill does not tell us whether this policy fosters or inhibits individualism – although I strongly suspect that he would have favoured public housing, as he did free public education and limitations of hours of work for young people. If an economist is to be a moral philosopher, however . . . he should develop his philosophy to a level where its implications for policy become a matter of logic rather than a vehicle for expressing personal taste (1975, 44; also 1982, 124–5).

Let us consider this charge. To allow us to focus on the main complaint we shall accept that 'spontaneous provision' of good housing follows the introduction of minimum housing standards (as Mill expected), or that Mill would have recommended public housing to remedy the situation if the private profit motive proved inadequate as is certain (see below, Section V). The essential point to note is Mill's insistence that the Stigler case falls *outside* the self-regarding category so that the argument against control based on the 'inviolability' *of the agent* is inapplicable. The householder's decision to choose sub-standard accommodation has nefarious consequences for *others* who have a claim on the state's protection which is to be granted on grounds of general utility – a criterion including the protection of the 'individuality' (liberty) of second parties incapable of acting on their own behalf. That value judgement is involved is certainly true. But, as Lionel Robbins has repeatedly insisted (e.g. Robbins, 1981, 9) this flows from the very nature of economic policy, to appeal for 'logic' or 'objective rules' in these matters is to ask for the moon. Neither is it desirable:

Except for playful intellectual exercise, or as a first stage of a first approximation in a sustained logical argument, universal principles seem to me to have no useful role in argument, and particular cases or restricted classes of cases to comprise almost everything that is worth arguing about – or dying for. And information, wisdom, judgment, measurement-of-a-kind of things not scientifically measurable, compassion for the weaker segments of mankind, always – or nearly always – need to be permitted to corrupt the logical rigor of abstract argument if the final result is to be reasonably applicable to particular cases, and if in a democratic society it is to find wide and lasting acceptance. Good abstract argument is an essential tool for the organization of knowledge and for bringing values to bear on public issues. But the rhetoric of abstract argument has no built-in devices to guard against neglect or oversight of relevant major values, and abstract argument is a tool for processing information, not a substitute for it (Viner, 1960, 62).

This, we shall find, was Mill's perspective.[2] Mill did, none the less, provide helpful *guidelines* – but not ever-ready rules – in addition to the distinction between self- and other-regarding acts, to reduce to a minimum the impact upon the individual agent even in cases falling within the latter category. Particularly important here is the distinction between 'authoritative' and 'unauthoritative' intervention, the former involving direction and enforcement, and the latter advice and information and even government agency in competition with private agency 'not trusting the object' to individual initiative alone, but not precluding it (*CW*, III, 937).[3] And not only should intervention, even where fully justified, leave the agent a maximum of choice, it should be 'self-destructive' wherever possible. Compensation for losses incurred in consequence of intervention is a further consideration to take into account. And it must always be recognized that Mill's full position can only be appreciated within a frame of reference which recognizes his programme for reform of social attitudes designed precisely

2 Robson (1968), 202: '[F]or Mill with his insistence on historical, geographical and institutional relativity, and with his demand for specific verification, no concrete, final, and comprehensive principle can be found to settle once and for all time the correct area of government actions'.
3 Examples include the Church Establishment, government schools and colleges, national banks and state factories, the post office, a state Engineering Corps, public hospitals, poor relief and scientific research – all of which not excluding private provision.

to reduce to a minimum troublesome divergences between interests including those between parents and children.

* * *

Jacob Viner has pertinently observed regarding Mill's perspective on the role of government, that 'except for the difference in tone and feeling, the fuller expression of lofty ideals and impracticable aspirations, it was substantially similar in method of analysis and nature of conclusions to Bentham's treatment. Like Bentham, and like all the major classical economists except perhaps Senior – who was not a Benthamite – J. S. Mill gave only a very qualified adherence to laissez-faire. It was for him only a rule of expediency, always subordinate to the principle of utility and never a dogma. The dogmatic exponents of laissez-faire of the time were the Manchester School . . . ' (1958, 330–1). Much the same could be said of Adam Smith (cf. Crouch, 1967). That the *laissez-faire* doctrine was, for Mill, a rule of expediency is certain and repeatedly he insisted that the legitimate functions of government could not be reduced to a simple formula more specific than that implied by reference to the 'general good'.

The protection of property narrowly defined did not suffice: 'It seems to me a very narrow view of the purposes of government to suppose that it is only of use to the possessors of accumulated capital. It protects, or at least it is bound to protect, every body's life, person and dignity from injury and insult; and even as regards pecuniary matters, those who spend all they get have as much objection to it being taken from them by malefactors as those who save' (28 Dec. 1867, *CW*, XVI, 338). In evidence given before the Select Committee on The Income and Property Tax in 1852 he was somewhat more satisfied with the benefit principle of tax obligation which utilized a broader notion of protection derived from the state, but still insisted upon an open-ended approach based upon expediency in terms of 'community benefit':

Did I understand you to say that the claim of the State to support by means of taxation was not in return for the protection afforded by the State to the different classes? It is in return for good government, which includes that and much beyond it.

What do you include beyond the protection of person and property which the State gives to parties? In answering that question it would be necessary to enter into a large consideration of what the Government can do for the benefit of those subject to it, and that is a very wide question, on which people may differ.

Will you state what, in your opinion, that includes? I should say that it includes the improvement and benefit of the community in all ways in which those objects can be promoted by legislation.

Will you state any instances so as to make clear what you mean? For example, the establishment of schools and universities; that cannot be called the protection of person or property; it is not in all cases a thing which I think the Government should do; but in many cases it is. It seems to me a matter of judicious discrimination in each case, what the Government can do for the benefit of the community. Whatever it can do usefully, which will be different in different circumstances, it ought to do (V, 495).

As for schemes relating to the well-being of labour, Mill's response was in similar terms: 'The more effectual performance by Government of any of its acknowledged duties; the more zealous prosecution of any scheme tending to the general advantage, is beneficial to the labouring classes' (*The Claims of Labour*, 1845; IV, 386). Mill was not disposed towards intervention specifically directed at one class, a matter to be amplified presently.

The same argument from expediency with reference to 'physical and moral good' determined the case for the protective functions of government on which theme Mill brings the discussion of the topic in the *Principles of Political Economy* to a close:

I have not thought it necessary here to insist on that part of the functions of government which all admit to be indispensable, the function of prohibiting and punishing such conduct on the part of individuals in the exercise of their freedom, as is clearly injurious to other persons, whether the case be one of force, fraud, or negligence. Even in the best state which society has yet reached, it is lamentable to think how great a proportion of all the efforts and talents in the world are employed in merely neutralizing one another. It is the proper end of government to reduce this wretched waste to the smallest possible amount, by taking such measures as shall cause the energies now spent by mankind in injuring one another, or in protecting themselves against injury, to be turned to the legitimate employment of the human faculties, that of compelling the powers of nature to be more and more subservient to physical and moral good (III, 971).

In Mill's view, however, even the 'admitted' or 'necessary' or 'indispensable' functions of government – functions 'universally acknowledged' to be essential in the sense that the expediency thereof amounts to evident necessity – 'embraced a much wider field than can easily be included within the ring-fence of any restrictive definition' (799). It was 'hardly possible to find any ground of justification common to them all, except the comprehensive one of general expediency; nor to limit the interference of government by any universal rule, save the simple and vague one, that it should never be admitted but when the case of expediency is strong' (803–4).

Mill proceeded to demonstrate how wide in practice is the coverage of governmental functions even where collective responsibility is limited to what is universally recognized as expedient – certainly far wider than could be accurately encompassed within the 'doctrine of non-interference' which formally constrains intervention to protection against force and fraud relating to person and property (799–800). The very definition of private property in natural resources is raised in this context – the rights allowed individuals to 'any portion of this common inheritance' – for 'no function of government is less optional than the regulation of these things, or more completely involved in the idea of civilized society'; and far more is entailed than the protection of a person's rights to what he has acquired by his own efforts or by voluntary consent (801). Laws of inheritance extending beyond giving effect to an individual's stated will (to cover, for example, intestate property) are similarly said to be widely justified on grounds of 'public interest, or perhaps only that of the particular persons concerned' (801); while the regulation of contracts extending beyond making operative a person's 'own expressed desire' to the validity of the contract itself, or the establishment of civil tribunals to arbitrate disputes and measures to assure against disputes, or rules of guardianship, are universally justified by appeal to 'the general interest of the State' or 'the public good' (802–3).

The series of illustrations ends with a passage which turns out to have far wider significance than its formal purpose of demonstrating the broad undisputed range of intervention:

There is a multitude of cases in which governments, with general approbation, assume powers and execute functions for which no reason can be assigned except the simple one, that they conduce to general convenience. We may take as an example, the function (which is a monopoly, too) of coining money. This is assumed for no more recondite purpose than that of saving to individuals the trouble, delay, and expense of weighing and assaying. No one, however, even of those most jealous of state interference, has objected to this as an improper exercise of the powers of government. Prescribing a set of standard weights and measures is another instance. Paving, lighting, and cleansing the streets and thoroughfares, is another; whether done by the general government, or as is more usual, and generally more advisable, by a municipal authority. Making or improving harbours, building lighthouses, making surveys in order to have accurate maps and charts, raising dykes to keep the sea out, and embankments to keep rivers in, are cases in point (803).

All of this is said to avoid 'disputed ground'. Yet several of these instances recur in the subsequent discussion of 'optimal' functions to illustrate cases of indiscriminate benefit. It is difficult to avoid the impression that Mill was engaged, so to speak, in a 'softening up' process designed to disarm extremist opponents of intervention by demonstrating the actual extent of the allowances which they themselves made and to introduce a wide range of his own allowances. A striking example of the apparent strategy is Mill's inclusion of contracts involving working conditions – certainly a much disputed issue – when illustrating supposedly uncontroversial intervention relating to the decision whether particular contracts satisfy 'the public good' (802).

When, in the chapter 'Of the Grounds and Limits of the *Laissez-Faire* or Non-Interference Principle', the discussion is formally extended to the 'optional' category or intervention – to disputed territory – the difficulties in the way of formulating a simple rule of thumb other than 'expediency' are, of course compounded. In his introduction to that discussion Mill promises to outline – consistently with 'a correct view of the laws which regulate human affairs – 'the nature of the considerations on which the question of government interference is most likely to turn', and 'the mode of estimating the comparative magnitude of the expediences involved' (804). But while, as we have already noted at the outset, he suggested general principles relating to the advantages and disadvantages of intervention he also conceded readily that the problem did not 'admit of any universal solution' (937). This is the substance of an important remark made in correspondence during preparation of the *Principles* to the effect that there are no '*axiomata media*' relating to the role of government 'which do not vary with time, place, & circumstance', so that little more could be achieved 'in a scientific treatment of the question than to point out a certain number of *pro's* and a certain number of *con's* of a more or less general application, & with some attempt at an estimation of the comparative importance of each, leaving the balance to be struck in each particular case as it arises' (13 April 1847, XIII, 712).

It would be a serious error, however, to leave the impression that Mill refused to take a position. The present issue provides a splendid illustration of the need always to have in mind the context of Mill's pronouncements. For, depending upon the audience addressed, so he weighed the case appropriately, often taking a more extreme position than his mature reflections justified and thereby suggesting far less consistency than actually exists. His stated objective at the outset of Book V ('On the Influence of Government') was, in fact, to achieve a degree of balance between 'impatient [Continental] reformers' who 'thinking it easier and shorter to get possession of the government than of the intellects and dispositions of the public are under a constant temptation to stretch the province of government beyond due bounds'; and the English 'spirit of resistance *in limine* to the interference of government' – the 'disposition to restrict its sphere of action within the narrowest bounds' (III, 799). This latter perspective (said to be 'decidedly' apparent in 1848 and 1849, but 'hitherto' apparent in 1852 – an important variation) Mill interpreted as a reaction to earlier 'interference for purposes other than the public good, or under an erroneous conception of what that good requires', and to 'rash proposals . . . by sincere lovers of improvement, for attempting, by compulsory regulation, the attainment of objects which can only be effectually or only usefully compassed by opinion and discussion . . . '

The outcome of the detailed analysis in the *Principles* of the role of government was, in fact, a general *presumption* 'in favour of restricting to the narrowest compass the intervention of a public authority in the business of the community'. The arguments suggested that 'the burthen of making out a strong case' rested 'on those who recommend government interference. *Laissez-faire*, in short, should be the general practice: every departure from it, unless required by some great good, is a certain evil' (944–5). Similarly: 'Believing with M. Comte that there are no absolute truths in the political art, nor indeed in any art whatever, we agree with him that the *laissez faire* doctrine, stated without large qualifications, is both unpractical and unscientific; but it does not follow that those who assert it are not, nineteen times out of twenty, practically nearer the truth than those who deny it' ('Auguste Comte and Positivism', 1865, X, 303). Moreover, Mill stated his preferences clearly regarding the form of intervention, when required, in line with the positions adopted in *Utilitarianism* and *On Liberty*. Non-authoritative intervention of the advisory or informative category, Mill complained, was a course 'seldom resorted to by government, and of which such important use might be made'; while the authoritative form of government had 'a much more limited sphere of legitimate action than the other' (III, 937–8). A closely related point is his hostility towards centralization; central government was to have a very carefully prescribed role. Mill's interventionism, like that of Adam Smith (see Crouch, 1967, 214; also Robbins 1958, 192–4) was far from that of the archetypal modern welfare state.

Professor Stigler has adopted a hypercritical attitude to Mill regarding both the issue of state intervention in economic life (the subject matter of this chapter), and socialism (that of the next):

John Stuart Mill was . . . ambivalent on the comparative merits of private enterprise and various forms of socialism. The ambivalence was attributable to three sources: his remarkable propensity to understand and state fairly almost any view; the influence of Harriet, the *femme fatale* of the history of economics; and the astonishing and absurd deficiencies which he assigned to private enterprise. He asserted that perhaps nine-tenths of the labour-force had compensation which at best was loosely related to exertion and achievement – indeed so loosely that he expressed indignation that the "produce of labour should be apportioned as we now see it, almost in an inverse ratio to the labour". He felt able to assert that a competitive market could not achieve a shortening of hours of work, even if all the labourers wished it. It has been said that only a highly educated man can be highly mistaken. Mill is no refutation (1982, 14–15).

It emerges from our study (both in this chapter and the next) that this is far from a fair evaluation. Mill had the most profound respect for the force of competition. Even where a role for government within capitalism was envisaged and when his ideal social system was under investigation the strengthening of competition was seen to hold the key. The two examples given by Professor Stigler are seriously misleading.

II THE CASE FOR 'FREE TRADE'

Mill's perspective on 'free trade' is neatly summarized in *On Liberty*. Since trade is, by its nature, 'a social act' – falling beyond that range of actions which solely concern the interests of the individual as such – the free-trade doctrine 'rests on grounds different from, though equally solid with, the principle of individual liberty asserted in this Essay'; similarly, 'the principle of individual liberty is not involved in the doctrine of Free Trade' (*CW*, XVIII, 292–3). These strong statements refer to the producer; from the perspective of the consumer matters are different as we shall see later. But even from the former perspective it is allowed (in a reference to public controls relating to product adulteration, work safety and sanitation) that 'considerations of liberty' are in fact involved 'in so far as leaving people to themselves is always better, *caeteris paribus*, than controlling them'; for trade restraints as such were 'an evil' precisely because they are constraints. The essence of Mill's position is that, where second parties are concerned, government has a presumptive *right* to intervene – although it may not find it expedient to use that right and when obliged to do so must limit its interference to a minimum; while the individual cannot protest on grounds of his *inviolable* individuality, because the restraints 'affect only that part of conduct which society is competent to restrain'. Intervention can be condemned only in so far as it fails to produce the results intended.

From this perspective Mill in general favoured 'free trade': 'It is now recognized, though not till after a long struggle, that both the cheapness and the good quality of commodities are most effectually provided for by leaving the producers and sellers perfectly free, under the sole check of equal freedom to the buyers for supplying themselves elsewhere' (292). Similarly, the presumption 'from political economy' is against government direction of activity on the grounds that there is no one so fit to conduct any business, or to determine how or by whom it shall be conducted, as those who are personally interested in it. This principle condemns the interferences, once so common, of the legislature, or the offices of government, with the ordinary processes of industry' (305).

The perspective of *On Liberty* is that of the *Principles* (III, 923f). There were, of course, 'large departments of human life from which [government] must be unreservedly and imperiously excluded'; irrespective of one's philosophy of the social union and appropriate political institutions 'there is a circle around every individual human being, which no government, . . . ought to be permitted to overstep' – a limit defining 'that part which concerns only the life, whether inward or outward, of the individual, and does not affect the interests of others, or affects them only through the moral influence of example'. But even where second parties are involved, authoritative intervention required 'a much stronger necessity to justify it in any case' – a significant consideration in the light of the problem raised by Stigler (above, p. 678). Indeed, it could be justified by 'scarcely any degree of utility, short of absolute necessity . . . ' and this because control is 'irksome' and impedes 'the development of some portion of the bodily or mental faculties'. And Mill's allowance for authoritative intervention in cases of 'absolute necessity' is, further qualified. Such intervention could be justified only if 'it can also be made to recommend itself to the general conscience; unless persons of ordinary good intentions either believe already, or can be induced to believe, that the thing prohibited is a thing which they ought not to wish to do' (937–8). Government, in short, may have a formal right to intervene where second parties are involved but this was not a free licence to do so. There must be a sound case from utility.

As for intervention in productive activity Mill was doubtful: '[I]n all the more advanced communities, the great majority of things are worse done by the intervention of government, than the individuals most interested in the matter would do them, or cause them to be done, if left to themselves' (941). Generally,

the business of life is better performed when those who have an immediate interest in it are left to take their own course, uncontrolled either by the mandate of the law or by the meddling of any public functionary. The persons, or some of the persons, who do the work, are likely to be better judges than the government, of the means of attaining the particular end at which they aim. Were we to suppose, what is not very probable, that the government has possessed itself of the best knowledge which had been acquired up to a given time by the persons most skilled in the occupation; even then, the individual agents have so much stronger and more direct an interest in the result, that the means are far more likely to be improved and perfected if left to their uncontrolled choice (946–7).

A variety of specific market controls are also considered to which we now turn.

'Desirable' ends

Control of food prices is one category of contracts which Mill takes up. While low average food prices are 'undeniably' desirable – the end could not be achieved by way of price control. The analysis runs in terms of the natural-price theory and therefore deviations between demand and supply (cost) prices: Thus a rate of return on capital below the average rate, due to price control, would lead to a failure of output. This outcome could be avoided by the grant of subsidies to agriculture (in the absence of state penalties). But these subsidies entail a grant from taxpayers to those who pay no tax – 'one of the forms of a practice essentially bad, that of converting the working class into unworking classes by making them a present of subsistence' (926).

Emergency shortages, by contrast, justified a degree of intervention. Here Mill applied market-price theory, with emphasis upon the rationing function of price and the notion of short-run equilibrium – that ' . . . the price of a thing cannot be raised by deficiency of supply, beyond what is sufficient to make a corresponding reduction of the consumption' (927). To assure generalized relief the richer classes must cut their consumption; government should intervene to this effect, and also (it seems) simultaneously extend cash grants to the poor. Not to check consumption by the wealthy and yet to grant cash relief to the poor (as some proposed) would further force prices up till 'the poorest competitors have no longer the means of competing, and the privation of food is thrown exclusively upon the indigent, the other classes being only affected pecuniarily', an outcome benefiting corn dealers alone. The role of government was otherwise limited for it could not normally fulfil the function of speculative trading more effectively than the competitive market:

All that governments can do in these emergencies, is to counsel a general moderation in consumption, and to interdict such kinds of it as are not of primary importance. Direct measures at the cost of the state, to procure food from a distance, are expedient when from peculiar reasons the thing is not likely to be done by private speculation. In any other case they are a great error. Private speculators will not, in such cases, venture to compete with the government; and though a government can do more than any one merchant, it cannot do nearly so much as all merchants (927; cf. 942, below p. 689, regarding individual agency in general).

A second case relates to control of the interest rate. Accepting for the sake of argument the 'public-policy' argument for an interest-rate maximum – that 'the general good' requires low interest – Mill proceeds to demonstrate that the result achieved by the imposition of maxima is the precise reverse of the objective: 'The [usury] laws which were intended to lower the price paid . . . for pecuniary accommodation, end . . . in greatly increasing it' (923).

The case sometimes made for control especially in favour of the borrower was totally misplaced since '[a] person of sane mind, and of the age at which persons are legally competent to conduct their own concerns, must be presumed to be a sufficient guardian of his pecuniary interest' (924). But the detailed argument hinged upon the 'fair' price automatically assured within a competitive environment, for the borrower with urgent needs who lacks adequate security is not subject to the dictate of a single lender; the latter may insist on a premium but 'competition will limit the extra demand to a fair equivalent' for the risk of insolvency. Here Mill takes Adam Smith to task for his view that only 'prodigals and projectors' ever want to borrow at a rate above the standard market rate. Smith had failed to allow for temporary borrowing emergencies encountered by otherwise 'prosperous mercantile firms' during periods of 'commercial difficulty' (925). The usury laws had in fact aggravated commercial crises, for state controls were always bypassed at yet greater cost to the borrower. Smith's 'prodigals' could only be saved from themselves by (unjustifiable) restraints on their property; while his approach to 'projectors' placed obstacles in the way of genuine innovation since '[m]any of the greatest improvements [an allusion to Robert Stephenson] were at first looked shyly on by capitalists, . . .' (926).[4]

'Undesirable' ends

While Mill in his general formulations frequently left undefined in any precise sense the end of government activity, satisfying himself with broad statements regarding 'the improvement and benefit of the community', he was certainly prepared to *exclude* certain ends, taking the position that 'whether right or wrong in itself, the interference must work for ill, if government, not understanding the subject which it meddles with, meddles to bring about a result which would be mischievous' (913). Thus in a review of 'erroneous theories' in Book V, Chapter X – said to be 'entirely discredited among all those who have not lagged behind the general progress of opinion' – the doctrine that domestic purchases are a national benefit and foreign importations a national loss (which implied that the consumer's interest conflicted with the public interest) was a proposition Mill totally rejected. And here an important aspect of his own conception of ends comes to the fore. Protection is condemned as entailing resource wastage and thus welfare loss, for importation never occurs 'except when it is, economically speaking, a national good, by causing the same amount of commodities to be obtained, at a smaller cost of labour and capital to the country' (914).[5] Mill alluded also to 'the specious plea of employing our own

---

4 Mill refers to the reform of the usury laws, but 'irrationally'. In the edition of 1857 their complete reform is recognized.

5 In the case of protection of manufactures the resultant price differential indemnifies the additional labour and capital unnecessarily used up. In that of agricultural goods, resource wastage is involved on marginal units only (the 'last instalment'), the extra price indemnifying not only that wastage but also constituting a tax on consumers paid to landlords.

countrymen and our national industry, instead of feeding and supporting the industry of foreigners' (915), the error lying in a failure to recognize that the choice is not between domestic and foreign employment but rather between different categories of the former, free international trade rendering the national resources more effective and, therefore, desirable. (cf. the case for efficiency, 114–15).[6]

III GOVERNMENT PROVISION: NEGATIVE CONSIDERATIONS

Active intervention by government in the form of provision of services which individuals are free to select or reject in favour of privately provided alternatives (a form of non-authoritative intervention) in no way entailed 'infringement of liberty' (*CW*, III, 938–9). Quite apart from the fact that a range of activities is involved entailing second parties, there was no restriction of choice. But while there could be no objection on grounds of liberty, other objections existed which Mill examined in the *Principles* and in *On Liberty*.

A common objection to any extension of the range of governmental activity, that it necessarily compromised the efficiencies deriving from specialization, was rejected, account taken of the potentialities for the devolution of administration on local authority (940–1). But the major economic objection remained. Any peculiar advantage governments might possess of superior access to information and acquisition to talented personnel was not 'an equivalent for the one great disadvantage of an inferior interest in the result' (942). This position is supported by allusion to the purported fact that in 'the common operations of industry or commerce' government agency was rarely able to meet the competition of private agency, at least in those cases where the latter possessed 'the requisite degree of industrial enterprise' and commanded 'the necessary assemblage of means'. (These qualifications are of prime significance, for they exclude underdeveloped economies from this range of considerations.)[7]

The further case is made that government activity in any field necessarily excludes individuals from engaging in the task although they are precisely those 'capable of doing it better or on cheaper terms than any other persons' and who would be thus engaged in a system of individual agency (942).[8] This is so, Mill maintained, even if the government's own hiring criteria turn on appropriate ability. But this is an argument which seems to be more relevant to a government monopoly – a prime case of 'authoritative'

6 See Section X for further discussion of Foreign Trade Policy.
7 See Section XI below.
8 Mill adds further that even if government had better intelligence and knowledge than a single individual, it must be inferior to *all* individuals together who would otherwise engage in the activity.

intervention rather than government provision in competition with private agency. That this is so is confirmed by the conclusion drawn from the argument which relates to the general advantages flowing from 'competition': 'So far as this is the case, . . . government, by excluding or even by superseding individual agency, either substitutes a less qualified instrumentality for one better qualified, or at any rate substitutes its own mode of accomplishing the work, for all the variety of modes which would be tried by a number of equally qualified persons aiming at the same end; a competition by many degrees more propitious to the progress of improvement, than any uniformity of system' (942).

Professor Stigler (1975, 196; also 1982, 124–5n.) asserts that the relative incompetence of state action did 'not play a major part in shaping [Mill's] attitude' which turned largely on the defence of individual liberty. But, however important was this latter consideration (and here a distinction should be made between the perspectives of producer and consumer), it is scarcely legitimate thus to play down the argument from efficiency. Moreover, a range of undesirable sociological consequences flowing from extended governmental activity must be taken into account. To these we now turn.

The strongest objection in the *Principles* to the extension of government agency relates to education in the very broadest sense of the term: 'Even if government could comprehend, within itself, in each department, all the most eminent intellectual capacity and active talent of the nation, it would not be the less desirable that the conduct of a large portion of the affairs of society should be left in the hands of persons immediately interested in them' (*CW*, III, 942–3). Mill alludes to the matter of 'practical education' – the inculcation of the habit of adapting means to ends which characterizes 'mental improvement': 'A people among whom there is no habit of spontaneous action for a collective interest – who look habitually to their government to command or prompt them in all matters of joint concern – who expect to have everything done for them, except what can be made an affair of mere habit and routine – have their faculties only half developed; their education is defective in one of its most important branches' (943). The argument is extended in an appeal for the 'diffusion of intelligence, activity and public spirit among the governed', an appeal supported by reference to the experienced difficulty of maintaining these characteristics in modern societies where the 'advance of civilization and security' removes the challenges facing individuals in more primitive states. Once again Mill warned of the dangers of democracy which provides 'an equal chance to everybody of tyrannizing' – in the case, that is, of a 'democratic constitution, not supported by democratic institutions in detail, but confined to the central government' (944). Centralized decision making seems to be at stake since the appeal for the encouragement of 'as many as possible of their joint concerns by voluntary co-operation' is much less relevant to cases of government intervention of a non-authoritative type which allows for private as well as government provision.

The extension of governmental functions, Mill clarified further, entailed an undesirable increase in the power of government – direct authority and the 'indirect form of influence', which constituted a danger even in a democratic society since the 'public collectively is abundantly ready to impose, not only its generally narrow views of its interests, but its abstract opinions, and even its tastes, as laws binding upon individuals', with potentially damaging consequences for the course of social progress. For progress required free reign for individual initiative in the broadest sense of that term; and 'there never was more necessity for surrounding individual independence of thought, speech, and conduct, with the most powerful defences, in order to maintain that originality of mind and individuality of character, which are the only source of any real progress, and of most of the qualities which make the human race much superior to any herd of animals' (939–40). The force of this observation, again, would seem to be much diluted in cases of government participation in the provision of services as distinct from authoritative intervention entailing government monopoly.

In *On Liberty* too Mill seems to slip unawares between the two cases. The formal context is one where 'the reasons against interference do not turn on the principle of liberty' (XVIII, 305) which would seem to exclude government monopoly.[9] Mill is not well disposed, even where government could excel, on the grounds that activity by individuals (or by individuals in voluntary combination) provided 'a means to their own mental education – a mode of strengthening their active faculties, exercising their judgment, and giving them a familiar knowledge of the subjects with which they are thus left to deal', encouraging thereby a breaking out of 'the narrow circle of personal and family selfishness, and accustoming them to the comprehension of joint interests, the management of joint concerns – habituating them to act from public or semi-public motives, and guide their conduct by aims which unite instead of isolating them from one another'. The consequences of such training for citizenship and political freedom were legion. And in addition, there were the advantages discussed earlier in *On Liberty* (217f.) flowing from the 'varied experiments, and endless diversity of experiment' which characterized individual activity and voluntary associations (306). 'What the State can usefully do', Mill concluded, 'is

9 '[The] question is not about restraining the actions of individuals, but about helping them: it is asked whether the government should do, or cause to be done, something for their benefit, instead of leaving it to be done by themselves, individually, or in voluntary combination.' This formulation does not imply the total preclusion of private enterprise.

to make itself a central depository, and active circulator and diffuser, of the experience resulting from many trials. Its business is to enable each experimentalist to benefit by the experiments of others; instead of tolerating no experiments but its own'. Clearly Mill has slipped into a condemnation of state monopoly.

The 'great evil of adding unnecessarily to [its] power' is represented in this context as 'the most cogent reason' – in addition to the questions of efficiency and mental education – 'for restricting the interference of government'. But again while the formal context is non-authoritative intervention, implicitly allowing for private alternatives, the substance of the argument relates to government monopolies:

The third and most cogent reason for restricting the interference of government is the great evil of adding unnecessarily to its power. Every function super-added to those already exercised by the government, causes its influence over hopes and fears to be more widely diffused, and converts, more and more, the active and ambitious part of the public into hangers-on of the government, or of some party which aims at becoming the government. If the roads, the railways, the banks, the insurance offices, the great joint-stock companies, the universities, and the public charities, were all of them branches of the government; if, in addition, the municipal corporations and local boards, with all that now devolves on them, became departments of the central administration; if the employees of all these different enterprises were appointed and paid by the government, and looked to the government for every rise in life; not all the freedom of the press and popular constitution of the legislature would make this or any other country free otherwise than in name. And the evil would be greater the more efficiently and scientifically the administrative machinery was constructed – the more skilful the arrangements for obtaining the best qualified hands and heads with which to work it . . . If every part of the business of society which required organized concert, or large and comprehensive views, were in the hands of the government, and if government offices were universally filled by the ablest men, all the enlarged culture and practised intelligence in the country, except the purely speculative, would be concentrated in a numerous bureaucracy, to whom alone the rest of the community would look for all things: the multitude for direction and dictation in all they had to do; the able and aspiring for personal advancement. To be admitted into the ranks of this bureaucracy, and when admitted, to rise therein, would be the sole objects of ambition. Under this régime, not only is the outside public ill-qualified, for want of practical experience, to criticize or check the mode of operation of the bureaucracy, but even if the accidents of despotic or the natural working of popular institutions occasionally raise to the summit a ruler or rulers of reforming inclinations, no reform can be effected which is contrary to the interest of the bureaucracy (306–7).

That Mill also recognized various positive advantages of bureaucracy must not be overlooked. He laid down a rule of thumb by which a balance could be achieved in practice: 'the greatest dissemination of power consistent with efficiency; but the greatest possible centralization of information, and diffusion of it from the centre' (309). For he conceded that 'a central organ of information and instruction for all the localities, would be equally valuable in all departments of administration. A government cannot have too much of the kind of activity which does not impede, but aids and stimulates, individual exertion and development' (310). The danger lay elsewhere:

The mischief begins when, instead of calling forth the activity and powers of individuals and bodies, it substitutes its own activity for theirs; when, instead of informing, advising, and, upon occasion, denouncing, it makes them work in fetters, or bids them stand aside and does their work instead of them. The worth of a State, in the long run, is the worth of the individuals composing it; and a State which postpones the interests of *their* mental expansion and elevation, to a little more of administrative skill, or of that semblance of it which practice gives, in the details of business; a State which dwarfs its men, in order that they may be more docile instruments in its hands even for beneficial purposes – will find that with small men no great thing can really be accomplished; and that the perfection of machinery to which it has sacrificed everything, will in the end avail it nothing, for want of the vital power which, in order that the machine might work more smoothly, it has preferred to banish.

In the *Principles* and *On Liberty* Mill, we have seen, reverts repeatedly to the case of government monopolies in listing the dangers of state provision from a sociological perspective – dangers which include a threat to individuality and thus progress. This practice suggests a horror of collective decision making – a matter of profound significance for the general issue of economic organization to be taken up later. It is apparent too that, in Mill's view, even in the (unlikely) event that government control could be justified on efficiency grounds it would be unacceptable. The sociological arguments seem to be less pertinent in cases of government provision alongside private provision but Mill had little doubt of the balance of advantage in terms of efficiency even in that case.

IV   THE CASE FROM LIBERTY: CONSUMER CHOICE

Mill's case for 'free trade' was not based on the 'liberty' of the producer but on efficiency and various socio-political advantages. On the other hand, and to this we now turn, the issue of liberty from the consumer's perspective is quite central: 'there are . . . questions of liberty; such as the Maine Law . . . ; the prohibition of the importation of opium into China; the restriction of the sale of poisons; all cases, in short, where the object of the interference is to make it impossible or difficult to obtain a particular commodity. These interferences are objectionable, not as infringements on the liberty of the producer or seller, but on that of the buyer' (*CW*, XVIII, 293). The general argument evidently applies to the broad issue of trade.[10] But a number of tricky cases – crime, prostitution, drunkenness and (by implication) suicide – are also taken up for discussion.

That governmental precautions against crime were in order was not at issue; '[the] right inherent in society, to ward off crimes against itself by antecedent precautions, suggests the obvious limitations to the maxim, that purely self-regarding misconduct cannot properly be meddled with in the way of prevention or punishment' (294). It was the avoidance of *illegitimate* infringement of personal liberty that was the problem. Thus, for example, to require that purchasers of drugs and poisons first obtain a medical certificate was not advisable (on grounds of liberty) since this measure would make it 'sometimes impossible, always expensive, to obtain the article for legitimate uses' (294). A preferable solution was to take the simple precaution of registering sales of poisons to dissuade buyers from any criminal usage (295).

Gambling and prostitution had to be tolerated on grounds of liberty – albeit 'blameable' – to the extent that the 'evil' touched the individual alone (296). As for drunkenness, only an individual who has already proven himself a danger to society when drunk might legitimately be controlled (295). Moreover, no one should be prevented from encouraging activities which were themselves permissible. But what if the instigator 'derives a personal benefit from his advice . . . to promote what society and the State consider to be an evil'? Mill does not reach a conclusive answer one way or the other, but certainly hesitated to recommend the outlawing of such enterprises considering 'the moral anomaly of punishing the accessary, when the principal is (and must be) allowed to go free; of fining or imprisoning the procurer, but not the fornicator, the gambling-house keeper, but not the gambler' (297). Yet some degree of social control was justified – control, be it noted, impinging on sellers:

Almost every article which is bought and sold may be used in excess, and the sellers have a pecuniary interest in encouraging that excess; but no argument can be

10 Cf. Robbins, 1981, 8: ' . . . if I were today to respond to Roy Harrod's challenge how to judge the repeal of the Corn Laws, I should not attempt to justify it in terms of the gain of utility at the expense of the producers. I should not know how to do this without comparisons which, to put it mildly, would be highly conjectural. I should base my vindication on the general utility of the extension of markets and the resulting enlargement of liberty of choice.' This seems by and large to have been Mill's position. See also Ten (1980) on the emphasis placed by Mill upon freedom of choice.

founded on this, in favour, for instance, of the Maine Law; because the class of dealers in strong drinks, though interested in their abuse, are indispensably required for the sake of their legitimate use. The interest, however, of these dealers in promoting intemperance is a real evil, and justifies the State in imposing restrictions and requiring guarantees which, but for that justification, would be infringements of legitimate liberty.

But what form should control take? To increase the costs of acquisition, is ruled out on grounds of liberty. Thus Mill rejected limitation of the number of sales outlets. The principle is an important one – the rejection of paternalism:

This is not the principle on which the labouring classes are professedly governed in any free country; and no person who sets due value on freedom will give his adhesion to their being so governed, unless after all efforts have been exhausted to educate them for freedom and govern them as freemen, and it has been definitely proved that they can only be governed as children . . . It is only because the institutions of this country are a mass of inconsistencies, that things find admittance into our practice which belong to the system of despotic, or what is called paternal, government, while the general freedom of our institutions precludes the exercise of the amount of control necessary to render the restraint of any real efficacy as a moral education (299).

Control by price is also rejected. For '[e]very increase of cost is a prohibition, to those whose means do not come up to the augmented price; and to those who do, it is a penalty laid on them for gratifying a particular taste. Their choice of pleasures, and their mode of expending their income, after satisfying their legal and moral obligations to the State and to individuals, are their own concerns, and must rest on their own judgment' (298). This conclusion is qualified when it comes specifically to revenue-raising impositions – inevitable in any event: 'It is . . . the duty of the State to consider, in the imposition of taxes, which commodities the consumer can best spare: and *à fortiori*, to select in preference those of which it deems the use, beyond a very moderate quantity, to be positively injurious. Taxation, therefore, of stimulants, up to the point which produces the largest amount of revenue (supposing that the State needs all the revenues which it yields) is not only admissable, but to be approved of.' But in the general case it is difficult to say what precisely Mill had in mind when he allowed for a degree of restriction on the sale of intoxicants. For it would seem that any form of control must inevitably raise the cost to consumers, monetary or otherwise.

The compulsory labelling of drugs was justified since 'the buyer cannot wish not to know that the thing he possesses has poisonous qualities' (294).

Similarly, since 'liberty consists in doing what one desires, and [one] does not desire to fall into the river' it would be legitimate to prevent a person from crossing a dangerous bridge. But Mill is clear that a person – a rational adult – who has been duly warned and yet chooses to cross the bridge should not be prevented, since 'no one but the person himself can judge of the sufficiency of the motive which may prompt him to incur the risk'. This, however, seems to apply only where there is merely a danger of accident. Where there is certainty (or more likely certainty of death) the conclusion may be otherwise although Mill is not clear in this context. The latter case would amount to a bid for suicide, and while Mill does not take up the issue, it is clear by deduction from an observation regarding one who sells himself into slavery that prevention of suicide would be justified:

The reason for not interfering, unless for the sake of others, with a person's voluntary acts, is consideration for his liberty. His voluntary choice is evidence that what he chooses is desirable, or at the least endurable, to him, and his good is on the whole best provided for by allowing him to take his own means of pursuing it. But by selling himself for a slave, he abdicates his liberty; he forgoes any future use of it beyond that single act . . . The principle of freedom cannot require that he should be free not to be free. It is not freedom to be allowed to alienate his freedom (299–300).

V MARKET FAILURE

Let us return to the central theme, the general presumption in favour of free enterprise when the problem is viewed from the perspective of the producer (and, a matter to be elaborated presently, assuming competition). The case for the market, Mill proceeded to argue, when considered from the perspective of the consumer, raised the issue of consumer ignorance:

[I]f the workman is generally the best selector of means, can it be affirmed with the same universality, that the consumer, or person served, is the most competent judge of the end? Is the buyer always qualified to judge of the commodity? If not, the presumption in favour of the competition of the market does not apply to the case; and if the commodity be one, in the quality of which society has much at stake, the balance of advantages may be in favour of some mode and degree of intervention, by the authorized representatives of the collective interest of the state (*CW*, III, 947).[11]

11 There is a much earlier statement, in 'Coleridge' (1840), X, 156, with this implication: 'All who are on a level with their age now readily admit that government ought not to *interdict* men from publishing their opinions, pursuing their employments, or buying and selling their goods, in whatever place or manner they deem the most advantageous. Beyond suppressing force and fraud, governments can seldom, without doing more harm

The consumer could indeed be presumed to be generally, though not universally, the best judge of objects 'destined to supply some physical want, or gratify some taste or inclination, respecting which wants or inclinations there is no appeal from the person who feels them'; and, similarly, regarding the demand for 'the means and appliances of some occupation'. The various conditions required to justify 'free trade' are nicely summarized in a later statement:

There are many things which free-trade does passably. There are none which it does absolutely well; for competition is as rife in the career of fraudulent pretence as in that of real excellence. Free-trade is not upheld, by any one who knows human life, from any very lofty estimate of its worth, but because the evils of exclusive privilege are still greater, and what is worse, more incorrigible. But the capacity of free-trade to produce even the humblest article of a sufficient degree of goodness, depends on three conditions: First, the consumer must have the means of paying for it; secondly, he must care sufficiently for it; thirdly, he must be a sufficient judge of it ('Endowments', 1869, V, 622).

human affairs are seldom improving in all directions at once, and it is doubtful if much of the improvement that is now going on is taking the direction of trade morality. Even in commerce properly so called – the legitimate province of self-interest – where it is enough if the ruling motive is limited by simple honesty, things do not look at present as if there were an increasing tendency towards high-minded honour, conscientious abhorrence of dishonest arts, and contempt of quackery. Even there the vastness of the field, the greatness of the stakes now played for, and the increasing difficulty to the public in judging rightly of transactions or of character, are making the principle of competition bring forth a kind of effects, the cure of which have to be sought somewhere else than in the corrective influence of competition itself (625).

If problems of market failure of this order existed in trade generally they were compounded in the case of *education*. Educational services indeed constituted the classic instance of 'things of which the utility does not consist in ministering to inclinations, nor in serving the daily uses of life, and the want of which is least felt where the need is greatest' (III, 947). As early

than good, attempt to chain up the free agency of individuals. But does it follow from this that government cannot exercise a free agency of its own? – that it cannot beneficially employ its powers, its means of information, and its pecuniary resources (so far surpassing those of any other association, or of any individual), in promoting the public welfare by a thousand means which individuals would never think of, would have no sufficient motives to attempt, or no sufficient power to accomplish? . . . [For example,] a State ought to be considered as a great benefit society, or mutual insurance company, for helping . . . that large proportion of its members who cannot help themselves.'

as 1833 (as he explained in the *Autobiography*) he had 'urged strenuously the importance of having a provision for education, not dependent on the mere demand of the market, that is, on the knowledge and discernment of average parents, but calculated to establish and keep up a higher standard of instruction than is likely to be spontaneously demanded by the buyers of the article. All these opinions have been confirmed and strengthened by the whole course of my subsequent reflections' (I, 191; regarding 'Corporation and Church Property', IV, 194). Similar allowances for intervention had to be made 'where there is no person in the situation of a consumer, and where the interest and judgement to be relied on are those of the agent himself' – a class of cases covering *irresponsible persons* (III, 950–1).

That individuals are the best judges of their own interest also presumed that their judgement is based on 'actual, and especially on present, personal experience'. It lacked validity when their judgement was arrived at and decided upon irrevocably, even before any experience. A case was thus made for control of '*engagements in perpetuity*' (953–4).

* * *

The general rule in favour of the individual's judgement of his own interest was also inapplicable where acts undertaken on behalf of others are involved – *charitable acts* in particular. For the question arose, from the perspective of recipients, 'whether it is better that they should receive help exclusively from individuals, and therefore uncertainly and casually, or by systematic arrangements, on which society acts through its organ the state (960).

Within this same category Mill formally placed his justification of the regulation of *colonization* and other acts by individuals which 'though intended solely for their own benefit, involve consequences extending indefinitely beyond them, to interests of the nation or of posterity, for which society in its collective capacity is alone able, and alone bound, to provide' (963).

Colonization and poor relief illustrate cases where the nature and degree of privately provided services fall short of the social optimum. An extension of the argument is made to all cases 'in which important public services are to be performed, while yet there is no individual specially interested in performing them, nor would any adequate remuneration naturally or spontaneously attend their performance' (968) – cases where the social exceeds the private return. More generally, 'anything which is desirable should be done for . . . the present interests of those members of the community who require external aid, but which is not of a nature to remunerate individuals or associations for undertaking it, is in itself a suitable thing to be undertaken by government' (970). Mill does qualify this extraordinarily broad statement by observing that governments should, before engaging in an activity, first consider the likelihood of its being undertaken more effectively by 'the voluntary principle'.[12] But the allowance opens the flood-gates by leaving undefined what end is socially 'desirable' and to what extent it should be met.

In this same context Mill provided the classic statement of indiscriminate benefit – the public good phenomenon – envisioning it apparently as a primary (though presumably not a necessary) feature of divergence between social and private return. This emerges in an illustration drawn from geographical exploration: 'The information sought may be of great public value, yet no individual would derive any benefit from it which would repay the expense of fitting out the expedition; and there is no mode of intercepting the benefit on its way to those who profit by it, in order to levy a toll for the remuneration of its authors' (968).[13] Government construction and maintenance of lighthouses provided a further example 'for since it is impossible that the ships at sea which are benefited by a lighthouse, should be made to pay a toll on the occasion of its use, no one would build lighthouses from motives of personal interest, unless indemnified and rewarded from a compulsory levy made by the state'. A case is made out on the same grounds for the subsidization of scientific research: 'If the government had no power to grant indemnity for expense, and remuneration for time and labour thus employed, such researches could only be undertaken by the very few persons who, with an independent fortune, unite technical knowledge, labourious habits, and either great public spirit, or an ardent desire of scientific celebrity.' 'Speculative knowledge' (pure theory) is similarly represented as 'a service rendered to a community collectively, not individually, and one consequently for which it is, *primâ facie*, reasonable that the community collectively should pay.'[14]

* * *

A further general category of market failure originates with the 'free rider' phenomenon – 'the case in which it would be highly for the advantage of everybody, if everybody were to act in a certain manner, but in which it is not the interest of any *individual* to adopt the rule for the guidance of his own

12 Mill is here taking for granted that regular individual initiative does not suffice. His allusion to the 'voluntary principle' refers to other forms of private initiative (e.g. philanthropic societies in the case of charity).

13 Mill again insists that account be taken of private associations in support of exploration, but observes that in general 'such enterprises have been conducted at the expense of government, which is thus enabled to entrust them to the persons in its judgment best qualified for the task'.

14 Mill (968–9) distinguishes 'savants' (theorists) who have poor earning opportunities in other endeavours, from other scientists.

conduct, unless he has some security that others will do so too. There are a thousand such cases; and when they arise, who is to afford the security that is wanted, except the legislature?' ('Employment of Children in Manufactories', *The Examiner*, 29 Jan. 1832, 67). The argument extends to the regulation of factory hours but also emerges elsewhere, as in the context of population control and colonization.

VI ELEMENTARY EDUCATION

In what follows we take up for closer examination the role of government in education, one of the most significant of Mill's 'exceptions' to the general case for 'free trade'. Our discussion involves the interconnected issues of the quality of contemporary educational services, the objectives to be met and the problem of finance and organization. (The special case of higher education will also be considered.) Despite the role accorded the state, what emerges is Mill's insistence upon competition in the provision of educational services on grounds both of general utility and of liberty (bearing in mind that liberty itself had desirable social implications). Here we find Mill's own reply to the charge of 'ambiguity' laid against him (above, p. 678). The problem of education entailed 'other-regarding' interests – 'Is it true that [children's] interest is completely identical with that of their parents? Certainly not . . . ' ('Rationale of Representation', 1835; *CW*, XVIII, 27n.) – so that intervention was not to be precluded on grounds of liberty, and yet restraints on parental choice had to be reduced to a minimum; in short, while the parent could not appeal to the *inviolability* of his own interest (the same applies, in principle to the case of sub-standard housing), the state had none the less to respect that interest as far as was practicable – subject, that is, to assuring the objectives sought by society.

It is worthwhile elaborating upon Mill's justifications for intervention in the present case before turning to the more detailed analysis of the objectives to be achieved, and the precise means to achieve them.

(1) Defects of the contemporary system

That the contemporary system of elementary education had failed dismally Mill had no doubt. In his celebrated article on the 'Claims of Labour' (1845) he noted (regarding poverty) that 'we have scarcely seen more than the small beginnings of what might be effected for the country even by mere schooling' (IV, 376).[15] Throughout all editions of the *Principles* he observed of elementary education that 'even in quantity it is, and is likely to remain, altogether insufficient, while in quality, though with some slight tendency

---

15 Blaug (1975), 579n, suggests that in this essay (unlike the *Principles*) Mill's emphasis is almost entirely on formal or schoolroom education. This is evidently not so as is clear tangentially from his reference to 'mere schooling', as well as from the very text to which Blaug refers us (IV, 378).

to improvement, it is never good except by some rare accident, and generally so bad as to be little more than nominal' (III, 949–50).[16] In the tract on 'Parliamentary Reform' (1859) the same complaint reappears: 'Society is at present as backward in providing education, as in recognising its claims; and the general standard of instruction in England is so low, that if anything more than the merest elements were required, the number of voters would be even smaller than at present' (XIX, 327). Two years later, in 'On Representative Government', he wrote of the 'disgracefully low existing state of education in the country' (530) and, in *Utilitarianism*, of the 'present wretched education, and wretched social arrangements, [which] are the only real hindrance to [a happy life] being attainable by almost all' (X, 215). In two articles devoted to endowments (written thirty-six years apart) the same point emerges: In the first ('Corporation and Church Property', 1833; IV, 214–15) he surmised that some 95 per cent of unendowed schools were 'an organized system of charlatanerie for imposing upon the ignorance of parents'; the 'desire to gain as much money with as little labour as is consistent with saving appearances' was not 'peculiar to the endowed teachers'. And in the second ('Endowments', 1869; V, 624–5), regarding (middle-class) secondary schools, he observed that 'the disclosures of the Schools Enquiry Commission have been as damning to the character of the private, as to that of the endowed, schools'.

Education, as we know, provided for Mill the classic example of market failure. For 'the uncultivated cannot be competent judges of cultivation' so that 'the demand of the market is by no means a test' (III, 947).[17] At least under contemporary conditions – an important proviso – the socially optimal demand would not be satisfied on 'the voluntary system', for 'the end not being desired the means will not be provided at all'; or 'the persons requiring improvement having an imperfect or altogether erroneous conception of what they want, the supply called forth by the demand of the market will be anything but what is really required'. On this matter he had taken issue with Adam Smith in 1833; Are parents, he asked, 'as solicitous, and as well qualified, to judge rightly of the merits of places of education as the theory of Adam Smith supposes?' (IV, 215).

The problem of deficient quality and quantity was particularly potent in the case of elementary education from the perspective both of the

16 Blaug (1975), 583–4, asserts that Mill writes as if state subsidies to elementary education were non-existent and concludes that the argument was not over state assistance as such, but rather over the religious character of state-aided schools. This is not totally convincing. It implies that the case for state aid required no championship, whereas the voluntary movement was scarcely dead; and state aid was minimal. But, as we shall see, Mill was indeed much concerned by the type of schooling received in church schools.

17 This position is represented by Blaug (*ibid.*, 582, 592) as a new and distinctive contribution to the contemporary debate.

individual and society: 'There are certain primary elements and means of knowledge, which it is in the highest degree desirable that human beings born into the community should acquire during childhood. If their parents, or those on whom they depend, have the power of obtaining for them this instruction, and fail to do it, they commit a double breach of duty, towards the children themselves, and toward the community generally, who are all liable to suffer seriously from the consequences of ignorance and want of education in their fellow-citizens' (III, 948). From this perspective – a protective function due the individual child and, moreover, one from which society as a whole also benefits – it followed that government could legitimately 'impose on parents the legal obligation of giving elementary instruction to children'. Similarly: 'A thorough system of instruction for the whole country we must have; & I do not see anything short of a legal obligation which will overcome the indifference, the greed, or the really urgent pecuniary interest of the parents' (8 Jan. 1868, XVI, 1348). But not unexpectedly, it is in *On Liberty* (1859) itself that the case for intervention is most conspicuously formulated:

I have already observed [299] that, owing to the absence of any recognised general principles, liberty is often granted where it should be withheld, as well as withheld where it should be granted; and one of the cases in which, in the modern European world, the sentiment of liberty is the strongest, is a case where, in my view, it is altogether misplaced. A person should be free to do as he likes in his own concerns; but he ought not to be free to do as he likes in acting for another, under the pretext that the affairs of the other are his own affairs . . . It is in the case of children, that misapplied notions of liberty are a real obstacle to the fulfilment by the State of its duties . . . Consider, for example, the case of education. Is it not almost a self-evident axiom, that the State should require and compel the education, up to a certain standard, of every human being who is born its citizen? . . . But while this is unanimously declared to be the father's duty, scarcely anybody, in this country, will bear to hear of obliging him to perform it. Instead of his being required to make any exertion or sacrifice for securing education to the child, it is left to his choice to accept it or not when it is provided gratis! It still remains unrecognised, that to bring a child into existence without a fair prospect of being able, not only to provide food for its body, but instruction and training for its mind, is a moral crime, both against the unfortunate offspring and against society; and that if the parent does not fulfil this obligation, the State ought to see it fulfilled, at the charge, as far as possible of the parent (X, 301–2).

It is important to be clear that what concerned Mill was not predominantly the absence of facilities to assure literacy. By 1859 he could say that 'reading, writing, and the simple rules of arithmetic, can now be acquired, it may be fairly said, by any person who desires them' (XIX, 327). But 'reading, writing and arithmetic are but a low standard of educational qualification'. This position apparently was maintained at least as early as 1845 as we shall now see; and that much more was involved than parental irresponsibility and poverty, will become apparent.

The abysmal state of affairs, as he saw it, Mill attributed in part to apologetic class bias. Education, he wrote in 1833, 'consists chiefly of the mere inculcation of traditional opinions' (I, 364). In the article of 1845, writing of the dissenting and established church schools, he complained that the responsibility for the parlous standards lay not with a lack of funding (indeed adequate finance had been available for some thirty years) but a 'lack of sincere desire to attain the end' of creating well-educated citizens:

[I]f we may judge from the zeal manifested, and the sums raised, both by the Church and the Dissenters, . . . , there is no deficiency of pecuniary means for the support of schools, even without the aid which the State certainly will not refuse. Unfortunately, there is something wanting which pecuniary means will not supply. There is a lack of sincere desire to attain the end . . . There may be a wish that children should learn to read the Bible, and, in the Church Schools, to repeat the Catechism. In most cases, there is little desire that they should be taught more; in many, a decided objection to it. Schoolmasters, like other public officers, are seldom inclined to do more than is exacted from them; but we believe that teaching the poor is almost the only public duty in which the payers are more a check than a stimulant to the zeal of their own agents (IV, 376–7).

His complaint was *not* that working-class children were being kept illiterate but that the supporters and managers of Church schools were positively eager not to 'over-educate' working-class children, and evaded their responsibilities by teaching the Bible in such fashion that their pupils were 'taught to understand nothing else'. Mill leaves little doubt as to the motive: '[A]ny education which aims at making human beings other than machines, in the long run makes them claim to have the control of their own actions . . . Whatever invigorates the faculties, in however small a measure, creates an increased desire for their more unimpeded exercise: and a popular education is a failure, if it educates the people for any state but that which it will certainly induce them to desire, and most probably to demand' ('Representative Government', 1861; XIX, 403).

The consequences for the character of the 'lowest class of the working people' of this deliberate neglect are laid out in a burning indictment:

all that is morally objectionable in the lowest class of the working people is nourished, if not engendered, by the low state of their understandings. Their infantine credulity to what they hear, when it is from their own class; their incapacity to observe what is before their eyes; their inability to comprehend or believe purposes in others which they have not been taught to expect, and are not conscious of in themselves – are the known characteristics of persons of low intellectual faculties in all classes. But what would not be equally credible without experience, is an amount of deficiency in the power of reasoning and calculation, which makes them insensible to their own direct personal interests. Few have considered how any one who could instil into these people the commonest worldly wisdom – who could render them capable of even selfish prudential calculations – would improve their conduct in every relation of life, and clear the soil for the growth of right feelings and worthy propensities ('Claims of Labour', IV, 377).

(2) Objectives of reform

Much was expected from educational reform involving the state: ' . . . there is reason to hope that great improvements both in the quality and quantity of school education will be effected by the exertions either of government or of individuals, and that the progress of the mass of the people in mental cultivation, and in the virtues which are dependent on it, will take place more rapidly, and with fewer intermittences and aberrations, than if left to itself' Principles, III, 764).[18] But what precisely constituted a desirable formal educational programme for the masses? A combination of book-learning (by recourse to cheap libraries as well as in schools) and practice provided the key:

It is by action that the faculties are called forth, more than by words – more at least than by words unaccompanied by action. We want schools in which the children of the poor should learn to use not only their hands, but their minds, for the guidance of their hands, in which they should be trained to the actual adaptation of means to ends; should become familiar with the accomplishment of the same object by various processes, and be made to apprehend with their intellects in what consists the difference between the right way of performing industrial operations and the wrong ('Claims of Labour', IV, 378).

This passage has profound implications, for it shows that Mill took seriously the purely economic implications of a good elementary education.[19] But it was not solely, or even predominantly, his objective to assure a more effective labour force; the objective was 'not to improve them as workmen merely, but as human beings', such as the products of the Scottish Parochial Schools – 'a reflecting, and observing, and therefore

18 Cf. letter to Carlyle, 5 Sept. 1833, XII, 176: 'I have just received a copy of some Evidence taken by the Poor Law Commissioners on the subject of Education, affording some striking instances of the good effect produced upon the very rabble of London by even such imperfect schooling as they now sometimes receive.'

19 Cf. 'Representative Government', 1861, XIX, 532, for a further index of Mill's belief that a good general education helps the acquisition of skills.

naturally a self-governing, a moral and a successful human being – because he has been a reading and a discussing one'. The object of education was, in short, to train the mind for 'the adaptation of means to ends' with hopefully beneficial consequences within both the narrow industrial sphere and the broad sphere of general citizenship.

This same perspective reappears throughout Mill's career. To illustrate from an early (unsigned) article of 1832:

Modern education is all *cram* – Latin cram, mathematical cram, literary cram, political cram, theological cram, moral cram. The world already knows everything, and has only to tell it to its children, who, on their part, have only to hear, and lay it to rote (not to *heart*). Any purpose, and any idea of training the mind itself, has gone out of the world. Nor can I yet perceive many symptoms of amendment . . .

Where, then, is the remedy? It is in the knowledge and clear comprehension of the evil. It is in the distinct recognition, that the end of education is not to *teach*, but to fit the mind for learning from its own consciousness and observation; that we have occasion for this power under ever-varying circumstances, for which no routine rule of thumb can possibly make provision. As the memory is trained by remembering, so is the reasoning power by reasoning; the imaginative by imagining; the analytic by analysing; the inventive by finding out. Let the education of the mind consist in calling out and exercising these faculties: never trouble yourself about giving knowledge – train the *mind* – keep it supplied with materials, and knowledge will come of itself . . . (I, 337–8).

The general objective is stated in clear terms in the *Principles*, and again extends far beyond inculcation of the three R's:

[I]t is to be hoped that opinion on the subject is advancing, and that an education of mere words would not now be deemed sufficient, slow as our progress is towards providing anything better even for the classes to whom society professes to give the very best education it can devise. Without entering into disputable points, it may be asserted without scruple, that the aim of all intellectual training for the mass of the people, should be to cultivate common sense; to qualify them for forming a sound practical judgment of the circumstances by which they are surrounded. Whatever, in the intellectual department, can be superadded to this, is chiefly ornamental; while this is the indispensable groundwork on which education must rest. Let this object be acknowledged and kept in view as the thing to be first aimed at, and there will be little difficulty in deciding what to teach, or in what manner to teach it (II, 375).

Or consider the same theme as it appears in 'Representative Government' (1861) with special reference to the function of popular institutions as a means of political instruction': 'It is but a poor education that associates ignorance with ignorance, and leaves them, if they care for knowledge, to grope their way to it without help, and to do without it if they do not. What is wanted is, the means of making ignorance aware of itself, and able to profit by knowledge; accustoming minds which know only routine, to act upon, and feel the value of, principles: teaching them to compare different modes of action, and learn, by the use of their reason, to distinguish the best' (XIX, 545).

As for the precise curriculum, reference may be made to a letter of 1852 where Mill's position is elaborated. Little was hoped for from science:

What the poor as well as the rich require is not to be indoctrinated, is not to be taught other people's opinions, but to be induced and enabled to think for themselves. It is not physical science that will do this, even if they could learn it much more thoroughly than they are able to do. After reading, writing, and arithmetic (the last a most important discipline in habits of accuracy and precision, in which they are extremely deficient), the desirable thing for them seems to be the most miscellaneous information, and the most varied exercise of their faculties. They cannot read too much. Quantity is of more importance than quality, especially all reading which relates to human life and the ways of mankind; geography, voyages and travels, manners and customs, and romances, which must tend to awaken their imagination and give them some of the meaning of self-devotion and heroism, in short, to unbrutalise them. By such reading they would become, to a certain extent, cultivated beings, which they would not become by following out, even to the greatest length, physical science. As for education in the best sense of the term, I fear they have a long time to wait for it (7 Jan. 1852, XIV, 80).[20]

(3) The role of the state

Let us look more closely at the precise role accorded the state. Immediately after his famous statement that the consumer is not a competent judge of education, Mill adds the following proposal which apparently involves the actual *government provision* of educational services:

Now any well-intentioned and tolerably civilized government may think, without presumption, that it does or ought to possess a degree of cultivation above the average of the community which it rules, and that it should therefore be capable of offering better education and better instruction to the people, than the greater

20 In 1871 Mill expressed concern with the narrowness of perspective of working-class politicians and looked to historical knowledge for a solution: 'Il est très vrai que le défaut d'instruction générale, et surtout de connaissances historiques, condamne la plupart des ouvriers qui sont des hommes politiques à une certain étroitesse de vues, même lorsque leurs idées sont foncièrement bonnes. Il n'y aura de remède à cela que graduelle-ment, par le progrès de l'enseignement populaire' (21 May 1871, XVII, 1820–1).

number of them would spontaneously demand. Education, therefore, is one of those things which it is admissable in principle that a government should provide for the people. The case is one in which the reasons of the non-interference principle do not necessarily or universally extend (III, 947–8).

A government advisory capacity, Mill added, would be insufficient: 'a thing of which the public are bad judges, may require to be shown to them and pressed on their attention for a long time, and to prove its advantages by long experience, before they learn to appreciate it, yet they may learn at last; which they might never have done, if the thing had not been thus obtruded upon them in act, but only recommended in theory' (948n.; cf. IV, 217–18).[21]

The key choice, in practice, was one between 'government provision and voluntary charity: between interference by government, and interference by associations of individuals, subscribing their own money for the purpose, like the two great School Societies'. And while it was 'not desirable that anything should be done by funds derived from compulsory taxation, which is already sufficiently well done by individual liberality', the quality and the quantity of education provided by charity schools were inadequate, so that it was 'the duty of the government to supply the defect, *by providing elementary schools* accessible to all the children of the poor, either freely, or for a payment too inconsiderable to be sensibly felt' (929–50; italics added). This was a matter of fairness: compulsion of parents to assure that their children received elementary schooling required that 'such instruction shall be always accessible to them either gratuitously, or at a trifling expense'. The bulk of the cost would be paid, as in Scotland, from the local rates so 'that the inhabitants of the locality might have a stronger interest in watching over the management, and checking negligence and abuse'.

Mill, it appears, supported a means test. The discussion in the *Principles* refers specifically to 'the children of the poor'.[22] In 1869 he referred to a 'rather strong opinion in favour of making parents pay something for their children's education when they are able, though there are considerable difficulties in authenticating their inability' (24 Oct. 1869, XVII, 1658);

21 The case was made against C. B. Dunoyer, *De la liberté du travail* (1845), who had recommended government advice but no more.
22 There is much in common between Mill's position and that of Senior in the Hand-Loom Weavers Report (1841): 'It is . . . obvious that, if the state be found to require the parent to educate his child, it is bound to see that he has the means of doing so. The voluntary system, therefore, the system which leaves to the ignorance, or negligence, or debauchery or averice of the parents of one age to decide how far the population of the succeeding age shall, or shall not, be instructed, has been repudiated; and we trust that, in a matter of this importance . . . a system which has been repudiated in principle, will not be permitted to continue in practice' (*Parliamentary Papers*, 1841, Vol. X, 121–1). This statement is consistent with a means test.

and it is unlikely that such authentication refers to the 'trifling' or 'insensible' charge recommended. Similarly he claimed widespread support for the principle he championed in the following terms: 'That those who are too poor to pay for elementary instruction, should have it paid for by others for them, has after a battle of above half a century, taken its place in opinion among admitted national necessities' ('Endowments', V, 622),[23] and a little later he states clearly that '[the] State does not owe gratuitous education to those who can pay for it' (627).

Let us return to the main recommendation itself. Mill rejected the objection (an application of the population principle) that free or almost free education would bring about a depression of the money wage, 'the springs of exertion and self-restraint' being relaxed, as would follow the reduction of any other expenditure item entering into 'necessary wages'. His proposal was not the substitution of public for private provision where the observation might apply. For education was typically not included 'among those necessary expenses which their wages might provide for, therefore the general rate of wages is not high enough to bear those expenses,and they must be borne from some other source'; more precisely, 'elementary education cannot be paid for, at its full cost, from the common wages of unskilled labour', and (he adds) 'would not if it could' (III, 949).[24]

A related objection that educational subsidies are inevitably self-perpetuating, also did not apply:

[T]his is not one of the cases in which the tender of help perpetuates the state of things which renders help necessary. Instruction, when it is really such, does not enervate, but strengthens as well as enlarges the active faculties: in whatever manner acquired, its effect on the mind is favourable to the spirit of independence: and when, unless had gratuitously, it would not be had at all, help in this form has the oppposite tendency to that which in so many other cases makes it objectionable; it is help towards doing without help.

Here we have a classic instance of a case for government intervention justified on grounds that it will ultimately *encourage* individual initiative, an aspect of his position to which Mill repeatedly reverted.

* * *

23 Mill adds that to accept the principle that *inability to pay* justifies subsidization is to concede that the *ignorance* and *selfishness* of parents should also be overcome.
24 But contrast III, 389 where Mill discusses the consequences of subsidized training for 'scholarly or bookish occupations generally' (such as the clergy, schoolteaching); incomes in these professions were lowered by such subsidies. The wages of skilled labour are represented as including a return covering 'the expense, trouble, and loss of time required in qualifying for the employment' (828).

The proposal in the first three editions of the *Principles* involved state *provision of elementary schools*. In the fourth (of 1857) the formulation is altered: The government's duty was 'to supply the defect *by giving pecuniary support to elementary schools*', to render them accessible at almost zero cost to (poor) parents (italics added). Secondly, the reference to financing from local rates is deleted.

The significance of the changes requires attention. The opening sentences of the section imply government provision of services, and these are unaltered. Moreover, in subsequent discussions we find throughout all editions references to an obligation on government 'in many cases [to] establish schools and colleges'.[25] Indeed, Mill goes out of his way (in unchanged passages) to insist upon the safeguards required if a government-supplied education is to be introduced:

One thing must be strenuously insisted on; that the government must claim no monopoly for its education; either in the lower or the higher branches; must exert neither authority nor influence to induce the people to resort to its teachers in preference to others, and must confer no peculiar advantages to those who have been instructed by them. Though the government teachers will probably be superior to the average of private instructors, they will not embody all the knowledge and sagacity to be found in all instructors taken together, and it is desirable to leave open as many roads as possible to the desired end.

It is not endurable that a government should, either *de jure* or *de facto*, have a complete control over the education of the people. To possess such a control, and actually exert it, is to be despotic . . . Though a government, therefore, may, and in many cases ought to, establish schools and colleges, it must neither compel nor bribe any person to come to them; nor ought the power of individuals to set up rival establishments, to depend in any degree upon its authorization. It would be justified in requiring from all the people that they shall possess instruction in certain things, but not in prescribing to them how or from whom they shall obtain it (950).

The validity of a common charge of paternalism against Mill in the sphere of education is vastly reduced by the foregoing perspective which, in fact, amounts to a frequently encountered matter of principle – that an element of competition between alternative means must be assured to guarantee the highest possible standards whether it be in education, science or industrial enterprise. In the present case, Mill's insistence on freedom for the establishment of private schools must be taken most seriously, since it was part of his doctrine that with progress the case for intervention would be

---

25 See also 8 Jan. 1868, XVI, 1347–8 which expresses continued support of finance from the local rate.

continuously weakened as citizens learned better to appreciate the service.[26]

It is apparent that despite the altered formulation of 1857, Mill continued to accord government the duty to establish and maintain its own schools to supplement the private sector *where necessary*. Yet is is essential to recognize the allowance in the formulation that state aid might also be accorded private schools. That this is indeed so, is yet more strongly confirmed by correspondence of 1868. Here it is recognized too that, under certain circumstances, the actual provision of schools by government might be made unnecessary by state aid to the private sector:

I entertain the strongest objections to any plan which would give a practical monopoly to schools under government control. But I have never conceived compulsory education in that sense. What I understand by it is that all parents should be required to have their children taught certain things, being left to select the teachers, but the sufficiency of the teaching being ensured by government inspection of schools & by a real & searching examination of pupils. The actual provision of schools by a local rate would not necessarily be required if any schools already existed in the locality which were sufficient for the purpose or which could be made so by aid from the local funds & by inspection (CVI, 1347–8).

And once again *On Liberty* provides a clear statement of Mill's ideal preferences:

If the government would make up its mind to *require* for every child a good education, it might save itself the trouble of *providing* one. It might leave to parents to obtain the education where and how they pleased, and content itself with helping to pay the school fees of the poorer classes of children, and defraying the entire school expenses of those who have no one else to pay for them. The objections which are urged with reason against State education do not apply to the enforcement of education by the State, but to the State's taking upon itself to direct that education; which is a totally different thing (XVIII, 302).

As always, it was the nefarious consequences of state monopoly for 'the individuality of character, and diversity in opinion and modes of conduct' that had to be avoided, while 'if the country contains a sufficient number of persons qualified to provide education under government auspices, the same persons would be able and willing to give an equally good education on the voluntary principle, under the assurance of remuneration afforded

---

26 Mill in fact expressed delight that at 'no time in our history' had 'mental progress ... depended so little on governments, and so much on the general disposition of the people . . . ' (II, 379).

by a law rendering education compulsory, combined with State aid to those unable to defray the expenses' (393).[27]

It seems from several of Mill's formulations that the state or local authority was not to subsidize parents *directly*, while allowing them free choice, as under the modern voucher proposal; pecuniary support would be given to the schools not the parents. But there seems nothing in the voucher proposal which conflicts with Mill's principles, and the proposition whereby the state 'might leave to parents to obtain the education where and how they pleased, and content itself with helping to pay the school fees . . . '[28] is certainly consistent with vouchers. There is, however, one qualification – although this applies generally. Mill regularly expressed opposition to sectarian education: 'I have been fighting all my life for the principle of Schools & Colleges for all, not for Churchmen or any other class of religionists . . .' (20 March 1858, XV, 552); and he referred to the 'principle of universal, and compulsory unsectarian education' (24 Oct. 1869, XVII, 1658). It is unlikely whether he would have recommended state support for church schools whether or not within a system of vouchers.[29]

A further safeguard against excessive state influence was alluded to as early as 1833 in the context of Roebuck's Commons speeches favouring a system of national education (XII, 171, 233). As Mill pointed out to a correspondent: 'Vous verrez qu'il donne à l'élection populaire le choix des instituteurs primaires. Vous mettrez peut-être cela sur le compte du radicalisme; mais radicalisme ou non, je crois que, dans notre pays, où la centralisation n'est nullement dans les moeurs, c'est là le seul moyen de faire accepter par la nation l'éducation forcée' (30 Nov. 1833, 198–9). It appears that Mill, at least at this stage, favoured the popular selection of teaching staff even in state-supported schools as a counter to any trend towards centralization.

Mill's position was a well-balanced one, and he was always open to persuasion. He was impressed by the evidence presented by Chadwick in 1861 of the advantages of large over small school districts as a means of hiring and retaining teachers 'of a high average of excellence' (1 March 1861, XV, 720). Consideration should also be given to the following comment to Chadwick regarding his resolutions on the Education Bill of 1870, which questions the efficacy of local management boards and refers to 'anti-centralisation prejudices':

The Resolutions go into details on which they might conflict with the line already taken up by the working classes at their public meetings, especially in the limitation

27 Cf. Robbins (1976), 121–2 on the significance of this passage in the present context.
28 Cf. Blaug (1975), 585n: 'It requires only one addition, the substitution of education vouchers for subsidized fees, to be pure Milton Friedman.'
29 Mill certainly considered 'improper' state support for institutions devoted to a particular group, such as the clergy of a sect ('Corporation and Church Property', 1833, IV, 281).

applied to the compulsory principle, and possibly in the constitution you propose for the school committees. The point which it is really of importance to impress on the working classes is the necessity of a skilled central initiative instead of leaving the initiation of measures to local boards: and on this I do not think the working classes likely to be unwilling listeners. It does not seem to me that they have anti-centralisation prejudices: it is the lower middle class, who are accustomed to get local management into their hands, that are unwilling to share power with a central authority . . . (24 May 1870, XVII, 1724).

The latter reference to a degree of joint central–local responsibility must, however, be kept in mind. We shall see that Mill opposed an observed trend towards centralisation in the context of policy towards endowment to which general topic we now turn.

(4) Education and endowments
Our perspective on Mill's position regarding the provision of educational services is much broadened when the matter of endowment is introduced. Here Mill diverged from Adam Smith.

The case for permitting and encouraging endowment in the field of education was forcefully argued by Mill as early as 1833. The disposition of the founder of educational endowments was to be protected for a certain number of years partly on grounds of the principle favouring variety of means and protection of minorities:

A perfect government would, no doubt, be always under the guidance of the wisest members of the community. But no government can unite all the wisdom which is in the members of the community taken together; much less can a mere majority in a legislative body. A nation ought not to place its entire stake upon the wisdom of one man, or one body of men, and to deprive all other intellect and virtue of a fair field of usefulness, whenever they cannot be made to square exactly with the intellect and virtue of that man or body. It is the wisdom of a community, as well as of an individual, to beware of being one-sided: the more chances it gives itself, the greater the probability that some will succeed. A government, when properly constituted, should be allowed the greatest possible facilities for what itself deems good; but the smallest for preventing the good which may chance to come from elsewhere . . .

We deem it important that individuals should have it in their power to enable good schooling, good writing, good preaching, or any other course of good instruction, to be carried on for a certain number of years at a pecuniary loss. By that time, if the people are intelligent, and the government wisely constituted, the institution will probably be capable of supporting itself, or the government will be willing to adopt all that is good in it, for the improvement of the institutions which are under the public care. For, that the people can see what is for their good, when it has long been shown them, is commonly true; that they can forsee it – seldom ('Corporation and Church Property', IV, 217–18).

'All improvements', Mill warned, 'either in opinion or practice, must be a minority at first'; and the danger to minorities was particularly great in democracies.[30]

Mill's concern with variety of means led him to warn in 1869 that public opinion – which happily had accepted the principle 'that the jurisdiction of the State over Endowments extends, if need be, to an entire alteration of their purposes' – was tending 'far beyond providing for the due application to public uses of funds given for the public benefit', and suggesting 'the apologies made in the over-centralised governments of the Continent' – as distinct from the United States – 'for not permitting any one to form the smallest act connected with public interests without the leave of the Government' ('Endowments', V, 615–16). There was danger in making 'education and beneficence an absolute monopoly in the hands of, at the best, a parliamentary majority' (617). For 'what the improvement of mankind and of all their works most imperatively demands is variety, not uniformity. What is called tampering by private persons with great public interests, as if it meant obstructing the Government in what it thinks fit to do for public uses with the funds at its disposal, means trying to do with money of their own something that shall promote the same objects better . . . It is healthy rivalry'. And once again, as in 1833, Mill insisted upon the need to protect minorities 'whose portion in the public interest deserves the attention of majorities equally with their own' (618); and warned of 'the intolerance of the majority respecting other people's disposal of their property after death' (620).[31]

30 Mill's concern is reflected in his critical (unsigned) comment on his father in the same year: 'Mr. Mill has given to the world, as yet, on the subject of morals, and on that of education, little besides generalities: not "barren generalities", but of the most fruitful kind; yet of which the fruit is still to come. When he shall carry his speculations into the details of these subjects, it is impossible that an intellect like his should not throw a great increase of light upon them: the danger is that the illumination will be partial and narrow; that he will conclude too readily that, whatever is suitable food for one sort of character, or suitable medicine for bringing it back, when it falls from its proper excellence, may be prescribed for *all*, and that what is *not* needful or useful to one of the types of human nature, is worthless altogether. There is yet another danger, that he will fail, not only in conceiving sufficient variety of excellence, but sufficiently *high* excellence; that the type to which he would reduce all natures, is by no means the most perfect type; that he conceives the ideal perfection of a human being, under *some* only of its aspects, not under all; or at least that he would frame his practical rules as if he so conceived it' ('A Few Observations on Mr. Mill', Appendix C to E. L. Bulwer, *England and the English*, 1833, I, 591–2).

31 Indeed Mill frequently maintained that the dangers of intolerance grew with progress (621).

Mill qualified his position somewhat. In the first place, 'a very small minority is able to support a private school suitable to its requirements' so that educational endowments were not the *sine qua non* for their survival. And conversely, there was even some danger that minorities might be at a disadvantage when the period of inviolability terminated and the endowment came under state control should they then 'fall into the power of the majority'. However: 'if endowed institutions, originally of a national character, or which have become so by the expiration of the term of inviolability, are open to all alike; and open in the true sense, that is, with full liberty to refuse one part of the teaching while accepting another part; minorities would enjoy all the benefits that the endowments could give, while retaining the full power of providing, at their own cost, any education which they may consider preferable' (621–2).

Mill had high hopes that a reform of the long-standing charity-school endowments would make it possible to minimize the need for direct government provision of services. In 1834 he wrote thus to a French correspondent regarding educational finance: 'En fait de fonds, les anciennes dotations suffisent, dès que le gouvernement les reprend d'entre les mains de mandataires infidèles, qui les gaspillent sans pitié. Je ne parle pas des Universités, mais des nombreuses Charity schools, et surtout des fondations, où les écoles devraient être et ne sont pas' (4 Sept. 1834, XII, 233). Mill in fact, placed greater faith in the right use of endowments than in direct government provision. For while government is 'probably a better judge of good education than an average man – even an average founder', none the less 'the full benefit of the superior wisdom of the government would be obtained, in the case of old foundations, by that discretionary power of modifying the dispositions of the founder, which ought to be exerted by the government as often as the purposes of the foundation require' ('Corporation and Church Property', 1833, IV, 215–16). There was also the likelihood that the public would be less receptive to recourse to taxation 'for every purpose of moral and intellectual improvement for which funds may be required', but would accept that educational endowments be thus used.

The themes reappear throughout as, for example, in the correspondence of 1868: 'a mere consolidation of the already existing school endowments, now mostly jobbed or, at best, very inefficiently applied, would probably enable good instruction to be provided in all localities in which it is not already afforded by private exertions. Of course there must be a Government department to control the employment of these funds, but it does not follow that the teachers need be appointed or directly controlled by any public office . . . ' (8 Jan. 1868, XVI, 134–8).

* * *

Robert Lowe's *Middle Class Education: Endowment or Free Trade* (1868) was the stimulus for the foregoing defence. The paper of 1869 involves matters of general principle extending beyond secondary schooling and therefore requires further elaboration here:

The question of educational endowments resolves itself into this: Is education one of those marketable commodities which the interest of rival dealers can be depended on for providing, in the quantity and of the quality required? Is education a public want which is sufficiently met by the ordinary promptings of the principle of trade? I should be the last to speak with sentimental disparagements of trade or its achievements, or to imagine that the motives which govern it can safely be dispensed with in any great department of the service of mankind. But the question is not quite fairly stated in the disjunctive programme, "Endowment or Free-Trade." Endowment *and* Free-Trade is the thing contended for. That there should be free competition in education; that law, or the State, when it prescribes anything on the subject, should fix what knowledge should be required, but not from whom it shall be procured, is essential to civil and political freedom. But will this indispensable free-trade in education provide what is wanted, better without than with the help, example, and stimulus of education aided by endowments? (V, 622).

Since market provision could not be relied upon (above, p. 697) a choice had to be made between direct public provision and endowments. Mill was un-ambiguous in his answer: 'Independently of the pecuniary question, schools and universities governed by the State are liable to a multitude of objections which those that are merely watched, and, in case of need, controlled by it are wholly free from; especially that most fatal one of tending to all alike; to form the same unvarying habits of mind and turn of character' (623).

Various objections are set aside. As for the curriculum, the variety of alternative endowed institutions and the influence of the state, *within its proper limits*, 'would ensure adequate provision for including in the course of education . . . whatever has any just claim to form a part of it' (624). Most important, the efficiency of schoolteachers could be assured if 'the fees of pupils would always be a part' – and they 'generally should always be the greatest part' – 'of his remuneration'. This was a matter of central import, for Lowe's main objection to educational endowments had been (in Mill's paraphrase) that 'injustice is done to private schools, and their improvement impeded, by subsidising their competitors – bribing parents by the pecuniary advantages of endowments, and enabling the endowed schools to undersell the unendowed' (626). Mill's reply turned partly on the notion of a positive slope to the supply curve – the presumption of a level of demand for educational services high enough to allow for higher cost provision. But more important, education would not be free even in endowed institutions for those who could afford to pay:

It may be true that, under the present abuses of endowments, parents are sometimes bribed to accept a bad education gratis; but the reformers of those institutions do not propose that their funds should be employed in giving gratuitous instruction to the children of the well-off classes, or in enabling those who can pay for a good education to obtain it at less than its value. Such, certainly, are not the intentions of the Schools Enquiry Commissioners, who propose a far other application of the funds of endowments than that of artificially cheapening education to those who are able, and whose duty it is, to pay its full price (626–7).

As far as possible the market principle was thus to be retained even within the framework of endowment.[32] Unfortunately the Commission of 1868, Mill observed, had been 'as damning to the character of the private, as to that of the endowed schools . . . ' (625);[33] and there were far greater obstacles in the way of reform of the former: 'The real principle of efficiency in teaching, payment by results, is easily applied to public teaching, but wholly inapplicable to private school speculations, even were they subject to a general system of public examinations; unless by special agreement between schoolmasters and parents, which also is a thing we have no chance of seeing until the fashion can be set' (624). Mill was sceptical since parents were easily fooled:

[Is] there any one so blind to the realities of life as to imagine that the emoluments of a private schoolmaster have in general any substantial connection with the merit and efficiency of his teaching? In the first place, he has a direct pecuniary interest in neglecting all studies not cared for by the general public, or by the section of it from whom he hopes for patronage. In those which they do care for, a little trouble goes much further in aiming at a mere appearance of proficiency, than at the reality . . .It is difficult to see, in the operation of the trading principle, any tendency to make these things better. When the customer's ignorance is great, the trading motive acts much more powerfully in the direction of vying with one another in the arts of quackery and self-advertisement than in merit (624–5).[34]

32 Even in the case of the great public schools and the universities where fees were paid to the collective body, payment of staff could still be made according to the number of students taught and the quality of instruction (624).
33 Mill pointed out (627) that the Commission had not formally dealt with elementary education in their investigation of endowments. But he believed that endowments 'evidently ought to be applied in aid of that general plan for making elementary instruction universal, which statesmen and the public almost unanimously agree that it has become a duty to provide'.
34 There were other alternatives however: 'Those parents who desire for their children something better than what the private schools afford, and do not find that something better in the endowed schools as at present conducted, sometimes combined to form the subscription schools commonly called proprietory.'

The disadvantage of the private system – the 'vices of a mere trading education' – could not, without assistance, be overcome even during the course of the 'general progress of human affairs'. There was some hope that an increasing number of parents 'are probably acquiring somewhat better notions of what education is, and a somewhat greater value for it', but this was a slow process and 'where each has to act individually, as in sending his children to school, and the power of the more advanced is only that of their opinion and their example, the general mass may long remain sadly behind' (625–6). But that Mill desired an improvement in the private sector is certain; and the solution was at hand:

Schools on the trading principle will not be improved unless the parents insist on their improvement, nor even then if, all other schools that are accessible being equally bad, the dissatisfaction can have no practical effect. To make those parents dissatisfied who care but little for good schooling, or are bad judges, and at the same time to make it a necessity for schoolmasters to pay regard to their dissatisfaction, there is but one way; and this is, to give to those who cannot judge of the thing itself, an external criterion to judge by; such as would be afforded by the existence of a certain number of places of education with the *prestige* of public sanction, giving, on a large and comprehensive scale, the best teaching which it is found possible to provide (626).

As a general rule, subject to exceptions, the wishes of parents in regard to the instruction of their children are determined by two considerations. First, what will bring in a direct pecuniary profit. Of this they think themselves judges, though most of them judge even of this very incompetently, being unable to see how any studies, except the direct practice of a business, can conduce to business success. Of other kinds of instruction they neither are, nor consider themselves, to be, judges; and on these their rule of action is that by which they are guided in most other things of which they are personally ignorant – the custom of their class of society. If we desire, therefore, that the education of those who are above poverty, but who are not, for their own bane and that of others, predestined to idleness, should have any better guide than an extremely narrow conception of the exigencies of a business life, we must apply ourselves to the other of the two levers by which those we seek to act upon can be moved; we must introduce a better custom. It must be made the fashion to receive a really good education. But how can this fashion be set except by offering models of good education in schools and colleges within easy reach of all parts of the country? And who is able to do this but such as can afford to postpone all considerations of pecuniary profit, and consider only the quality of the education; either because, like the English Universities, they are certain of sufficient customers, or because they have the means of waiting many years till the time comes which shall show that the pupils they have trained are more than ordinarily fitted for all the uses of life? (623).

Mill's position in 1869 was no different from that expressed three and a half decades earlier. At one point in his early paper on 'Corporation and Church Property' Mill wrote as if the failure of private provision was inevitable: 'Let us do what we may, it will be the study of the merely trading schoolmaster to teach down to the level of the parents, be that level high or low . . . it is in all times, and in all places indispensable, that enlightened individuals and enlightened governments should, from other motives than that of pecuniary gain, bestir themselves to provide (though by no means forcibly to impose) that good and wholesome food for the wants of the mind, for which the competition of the mere trading market affords in general so indifferent a substitute' (IV, 215). But he himself then raised the possibility that, with the progress of enlightened opinion 'the competition of the market will become more and more adequate to provide good education, and endowed establishments will be less and less necessary'. And this outcome could be the very effect of endowments – usefully applied: 'It is only by a right use of endowments that a people can be raised above the need of them' (216).

VII 'SUPERIOR' EDUCATION

Mill's position on 'superior' education differed in certain respects from that on elementary education. A comparison proves revealing of certain matters of principle.

We have encountered Mill's recommendation that free elementary schooling – compulsory schooling – was to be made available at zero or near zero cost subject to a means test. In the case of higher education, while a means test was to be required for those who sought to continue, the state's *obligation* towards those unable to pay (or to pay full fees) was limited only to the 'élite':

The State does not owe gratuitous education to those who can pay for it. The State owes no more than elementary education to the entire body of those who cannot pay for it. But the superior education which it does not owe to the whole of the poorer population, it owes to the *élite* of them – to those who have earned the preference by labour, and have shown by the results that they have capacities worth securing for the higher departments of intellectual work, never supplied in due proportion to the demand ('Endowments', V, 627).[35]

Mill applauded the enlightened attitude of the Schools Enquiry Commission in this regard; and endorsed its proposal that educational endowments be

35 Blaug (1975), 586, refers to Mill's position as unique in this respect in his time: 'No other economist . . . ever went so far.'

combined into funds applicable at the district level 'to pay for the higher education of those who, in the course of their elementary instruction, have proved themselves to be of the sort on whom a higher education is worth bestowing, but whose parents are not in a condition to pay the price'.[36]

The distinction between the state's financial responsibility (always subject to parental means) to all children in the one case, and to the educational élite reflects the obligatory character of elementary education alone. A prime rationale for compulsion was the protection of the child – an argument partly based on justice – for which the parents are in the first place responsible, and the state *in loco parentis* when absolutely necessary. As we know there are also indiscriminate social benefits deriving from an educated population, which reflect Mill's conception of a good community as one composed of human beings capable of rational calculation.

In the case of 'superior' education the formal argument from justice is somewhat less conspicuous, for the claim of the gifted child to training beyond the elementary level is not so strong as to require compulsion of those parents who can afford but refuse to pay. (It is virtually certain, however, that in such an event Mill would have countenanced state support of the student himself.) The case based on social advantage is much emphasized – a case said to be 'beyond human power to estimate' (627). The benefits include a correction of the market disequilibrium characterizing 'the higher departments of intellectual work' alluded to above. But, 'the gain to society, by making available for its most difficult work, not those alone who can afford to qualify themselves, but all those who would qualify themselves if they could afford it, would be but part of the benefit' (627–8). For there was also the fundamentally important consequence of improved equality of opportunity which, for Mill, characterized a 'just' society even within a capitalistic environment:

I believe there is no single thing which would go so far to heal class differences, and diminish the just dissatisfaction which the best of the poorer classes of the nation feel with their position in it. The real hardship of social inequalities to the poor, as the reasonable among them can be brought to see, is not that men *are* unequal, but that they are born so; . . . that the higher positions in life, including all which confer powers or dignity, can not only be obtained by the rich without taking the trouble to be qualified for them, but that even were this corrected (to which there is an increasing tendency), none, as a rule, except the rich, have it in their power to make themselves qualified. By the proposal of the Commissioners, every child of poor parents (for, of course, girls must soon or later be included), would have

36 The district plan would permit large schools, and assure scale economies (good teaching at moderate cost). Three grades of school were to be introduced depending on the number of years parents desired their children to remain.

that power opened to him, if he passed with real distinction through the course of instruction provided for all; and the feelings which give rise to Socialism would be in a great measure disarmed, in as much of them as is unreasonable or exaggerated, by this just concession to that in them which is rational and legitimate (628).

Much earlier Mill had written of the training of a kind of élite – 'superior spirits' – which required 'institutions of education placed above dependence on the immediate pleasure of that very multitude whom they are designed to elevate'; and saw much promise in endowed establishments ('Sedgwick's Discourse', 1835, X, 33).[37] In 1869, and perhaps earlier, Mill insisted that the élite must include those of working-class origin.

VIII PROFESSIONAL TRAINING

Mill expressed doubts whether government intervention was called for in the provision of professional training strictly defined. The 'consumer' could here be relied upon to a far greater degree than in the case of general education:

To educate common minds for the common business of life, a public provision may be useful, but is not indispensable: nor are there wanting arguments, not conclusive, yet of considerable strength, to show that it is undesirable. Whatever individual competition does at all, it commonly does best. All things in which the public are adequate judges of excellence are best supplied where the stimulus of individual interest is the most active; and that is where pay is in proportion to exertion . . . ('Sedgwick's Discourse', CW, 1835, X, 33).

The empirical knowledge which the world demands, which is the stock in trade of money-getting-life, we would leave the world to provide for itself; content with infusing into the youth of our country a spirit, a training them to habits, which would ensure their acquiring such knowledge easily, and using it well ('Civilization', 1836, XVIII, 139).

The foregoing passages are extracted from contexts formally dealing with university education. It is not absolutely certain that Mill intended his readers to generalize the argument to the vocational training of working-class youth. It is, however, likely. Certainly elementary education, where a role for

37 Cf. 'Civilization', 1836, XVIII, 138: 'The regeneration of individual character among our lettered and opulent classes, by the adaptation to that purpose of our institutions, and, above all, of our educational institutions, is an object of more urgency, and for which more might be immediately accomplished, if the will and understanding were not alike wanting'.

government was allowed, was (ideally) to make students 'apprehend with their intellects in what consists the difference between the right way of performing industrial operations and the wrong' (above, p. 704). But this clearly was to be a by-product of good elementary training; the training itself did not extend to the inculcation of vocational skills.[38]

This conclusion calls for a word of caution. The classical economists have been charged with a failure to develop the conception of human capital or to emphasize the function of education in the formation of vocational skills. The characteristic emphasis was, so it is said, on schooling as a training in social behaviour (behaviour appropriate to an industrial society) rather than a means to cognitive knowledge (Blaug, 1975, 568, 574, 590); all the classicists without exception approved state assistance to locally provided schools but did so on grounds of social control; there was scarcely any linkage between national economic performance and the quantity and quality of schooling, so that 'one can pass straight from Adam Smith to Marshall without the slightest loss' concerning education viewed as investment in human capital (592–3). The complaint is also directed against Mill:

John Stuart Mill's treatment of education is an even more striking example of the failure to develop the main implications of the human capital concept. In his discussion of 'the degree of productiveness of productive agents', he lays great stress on 'the economical value of the general diffusion of intelligence among the people' and draws an unflattering comparison between Continental and English workers: 'If an English labourer is anything but a hewer of wood and a drawer of water, he is indebted for it to education, which in his case is almost always self-education.' This sounds indeed as if Mill saw a vital connection between education and economic growth, but when he came later in the book to make his case for government intervention in education, he made no reference of any kind to the economic value of education. The emphasis in the famous 1845 essay on 'The Claims of Labour' and in the chapter 'On the Probable Futurity of the Labouring Classes' in the *Principles* is altogether on character-formation and self-improvement (579).

It is difficult to appreciate why Professor Blaug, who is evidently aware of Mill's observation on the connection between education and economic growth, should so play them down. Mill himself, in the very context cited, stated, and with emphasis, that productivity considerations should enter into the politician's calculation of the social value of elementary education:

A thing not yet so well understood and recognised, is the economical value of the general diffusion of intelligence among the people. The number of persons fitted to direct and superintend any industrial enterprise, or even to execute any process

---

38 Cf. Robson (1968), 211. Mill excluded medical knowledge from the generalization.

which cannot be reduced almost to an affair of memory and routine, is always far short of the demand; as is evident from the enormous difference between the salaries paid to such persons, and the wages of ordinary labour. The deficiency of practical good sense, which renders the majority of the labouring class such bad calculators – which makes, for instance, their domestic economy so improvident, lax, and irregular – must disqualify them for any but a low grade of intelligent labour, and render their industry far less productive than with equal energy it otherwise might be. The importance, even in this limited aspect, of popular education, is well worthy of the attention of politicians, especially in England; since competent observers, accustomed to employ labourers of various nations, testify that in the workmen of other countries they often find great intelligence wholly apart from instruction, but that if an English labourer is anything but a hewer of wood and a drawer of water, he is indebted for it to education, which in his case is almost always self-education (*CW*, II, 107–8).

It is not convincing to suggest that Mill's unambiguous recognition of the economic value of education counted for nothing in his general case for government intervention. We must recall too the explicit statement at the outset, of the *Principles* that '[t]o the community at large, the labour and expense of rearing its infant population form a part of the outlay which is a condition of production, and which is to be replaced with increase from the future produce of their labour' (41).[39]

The role of government in elementary education, therefore, was in part justified in terms of purely economical considerations.[40] Vocational training in the narrow sense of the term on the other hand did not require subsidization since, Mill maintained, private motivation sufficed, as is clear from our earlier citations from 'Sedgwick's Discourse' and 'Civilization'. As he observed in the *Principles* (41) industrial or technical training is undertaken with an eye to 'the greater or more valuable produce thereby attained, and in order that a remuneration equivalent or more than equivalent may be reaped by the learner', in contrast to elementary education where from the perspective of the individual (as distinct from the

39 For the context of this statement see Chapter 4, p. 219.
40 Blaug is unconvincing regarding his version of the classics as a whole, for they paid considerable attention to the purely 'economic' consequences of education. See Hollander (1968), Robbins (1952), 89f, Tu (1969), Vaizey (1962), 15f. This is not to deny their great concern (even their predominant concern) for the generation of 'better men'. See too Miller (1966), 294f who, while charging the classics for 'fail[ing] to develop the idea of education as investment' or 'to emphasize openly the capital accumulation aspect of education' or 'to explore fully the idea that education represents investment in human beings' – rather loose charges – none the less conceded that 'though . . . less overtly interested than many modern economists in the question of education as a form of investment in human beings . . . were familiar with the idea and several of them presented some version of it'.

community) this motive is generally absent. And this is the point at stake: it is precisely because private calculations could not be relied upon to take into account productivity gains that the social returns from elementary training fall short of the private returns, justifying corrective intervention.

However, there is yet a further consideration – the fact that elementary training constituted, for Mill, a precondition for vocational training. The effective operation of private initiative in the provision of industrial and technical skills was predicated upon adequate elementary instruction, a fact reinforcing the economic aspects of such instruction, and implying that the case for state intervention in elementary schooling constitutes, indirectly, a case for intervention in the vocational sphere:

In the existing system of industry these things [an allusion to a pay structure] do adjust themselves with some, though but a distant, approach to fairness. If one kind of work is harder or more disagreeable than another, or requires a longer practice, it is better paid, simply because there are fewer competitors for it; and an individual generally finds that he can earn most by doing the thing which he is fittest for. I admit that this self-adjusting machinery does not touch some of the grossest of the existing inequalities of remuneration, and in particular the unjust advantage possessed by almost the commonest mental over almost the hardest and most disagreeable bodily labour. Employments which require any kind of technical education, however simple, have hitherto been the subject of a real monopoly against the mass. But as popular instruction advances, this monopoly is already becoming less complete, and every increase of prudence and foresight among the people encroaches upon it more and more (III, 977).[41]

Mill's famous critique of the Smithian approach to the wage structure is relevant here. Mill observed that the differential between skilled and unskilled pay exceeded an amount explicable in terms of training costs or various artificial monopolies (apprenticeship and corporation rules and the like) such as Smith envisaged, for there was a *natural* monopoly that Smith had neglected deriving from the requirement of literacy, a requirement increasingly satisfied:

If unskilled labourers had it in their power to compete with skilled, by merely taking the trouble of learning the trade, the difference of wages might not exceed what would compensate them for that trouble, at the ordinary rate at which labour is remunerated. But the fact that a course of instruction is required, of even a low degree of costliness, or that the labourer must be maintained for a considerable time from other sources, suffices everywhere to exclude the great body of the

---

41 This formulation appears in the first two editions. But the principle is restated II, 386–7 and in all editions.

labouring people from the possibility of any such competition. Until lately, all employments which required even the humble education of reading and writing, could be recruited only from a select class, the majority having had no opportunity of acquiring those attainments. All such employments, accordingly, were immensely overpaid, as measured by the ordinary remuneration of labour. Since reading and writing have been brought within the reach of a multitude, the monopoly price of the lower grade of educated employments has greatly fallen, the competition for them having increased in an almost incredible degree (II, 386–7).

The full effects on upward mobility of universal elementary education at an adequate standard still remained to be felt, 'the small degree of education required [of a clerk] being not yet so generally diffused as to call forth the natural number of competitors'. Similarly, 'in the present low state of popular education, all the higher grades of mental or educated labour are at a monopoly price; exceeding the wages of common workmen in a degree very far beyond that which is due to the expense, trouble, and loss of time required in qualifying for the employment' (III, 828).[42]

The belief that Mill failed to appreciate the economic value of education is further brought into question, at least by strong implication, by his support of the subsidization of scientific research. University endowments might be 'very suitably applied . . . [in] the maintenance of professors, and in some cases the encouragement of students, in . . . the highest branches of almost all sciences, even physical: for the speculative researches which lead to the grandest results in science are not those by which money can be made in the general market' (V, 628).

IX   MILL AND EDUCATION: AN OVERVIEW

We shall now take an overview of Mill's position regarding education by reference to the charge against him (above, p. 709) of 'paternalism', a sufficiently marked paternalism to distort his evaluation of the contemporary facts regarding the state of private provision. For it has been argued that his negative estimate was quite unjustified. For example, the Royal Commission on Popular Education (the Newcastle Commission), which reported in 1861, presented data showing that almost the entire population of children of elementary school age was in fact provided for; similarly, Mill's assertions regarding low quality were unjustified (West,

42 Mill was concerned that the too rapid breakdown of barriers might not be advisable while there existed severe population pressure: 'The inequality of remuneration between the skilled and the unskilled is, without doubt, very much greater than is justifiable; but it is desirable that this should be corrected by raising the unskilled, not by lowering the skilled' (II, 388).

1964; 1970a, xvii, Chs. 8, 9, 10; also West, 1970b, 1978a).[43] Mill's hostility towards private provision – attributed also to Nassau Senior and contrasting with Adam Smith's view – is explained by mistrust of parental freedom of choice and Benthamite predilections regarding educational methods: 'The fact was that neither Senior nor Mill liked the type of school that the free market was providing by the middle of the nineteenth century. This was undoubtedly due to their opinion that these schools were inferior to the large-scale models which the poor law institutions were dutifully producing to the order of their Benthamite supervisors' (1970a, 123).[44]

West's argument turns in part on the picture of educational provision – both quantity and quality – provided by the Newcastle Commission. But it is far from the case that the Commission presented an unambiguously favourable picture. Even Professor Blaug, who also refers to Mill's 'quasi-paternalistic' view on government (1975, 582), recognizes the ambiguity at least regarding quality: 'The dispute about quality is as old as the Newcastle Commission itself: the reports of the inspectors held that the standard of teaching in most elementary schools was "excellent, well and fair", while the assistant commissioners pronounced an almost wholly unfavourable verdict on the quality of instruction, particularly for the younger children. The debate is unlikely to be ever effectively settled' (598).[45] Similar doubts have also been expressed regarding earlier favourable estimates (cf. Hurt, 1971; Landes, 1969, 340–1; Crouzet, 1982,

43 Cf. West (1970a), xvii: In 1869, immediately prior to the Forster Act, 'most people were literate, most children had some schooling, and – what may come as the biggest surprise of all – most parents (working-class included) were paying fees for it'.
44 Of Senior (*Suggestions on Popular Education*, 1861) West (1970a) asserts that despite disclaimers to the contrary he did not 'very earnestly look forward one century to the time when every individual of whatever belief could be expected to be able to afford and select his child's education'. Rather 'Senior was really saying that ordinary people could not be trusted to select the right (Benthamite and Protestant) quality of schooling' (xxxiii).
45 Yet Blaug (1975) also writes 'that if we are properly to understand the views of the classical economists, we must begin by putting to one side the standard histories of nineteenth-century education, which seem to have been largely written to prove that education is only adequately provided when the state accepts its responsibility to furnish compulsory education *gratis*' (594). And there is, even in his account, a suggestion of bias in Mill sufficient to distort his perspective. Thus the predominance of Church schools in the private sector is said to be 'perhaps the reason that Mill . . . took a poor view of the growth of voluntary schooling. This is, of course, a pure speculation. But consider what it would have meant to have endorsed the voluntary system. That would be to imply that there was nothing wrong with the powerful grip which the Anglican Church had by then secured over the school system. Surely, this must have been too much to swallow for the son of James Mill and the pupil of Bentham' (584). See also the complaint regarding the 'shrill paternalistic tone' adopted by Senior (1861) who, like Mill, 'shared the increasing tendency of Dissenters to despair of ever competing successfully with Church of England schools' (587) – his despair at the common choice by working-class parents of private schools of deplorable quality 'although good and cheap public schools are at their door'.

726 THE ECONOMICS OF JOHN STUART MILL

415; Sutherland, 1971, 11, 118–19, 24, 26). And one authority has summarized the situation on the eve of the Forster Act of 1870 in the following terms:

An absolute shortage of over a million school places; more than a third of all children between the ages of three and twelve not on the books of any school; an average attendance figure of just over two-thirds; a limited and often broken school life for the scholars; a severe shortage of qualified teachers; unavoidably dreary teaching methods and a less than half-efficient examination system. Fundamentally these problems were the heritage of the low-pitched conception of the aims and possibilities of popular education which had persisted under all governments through the century. Equally they were a pointer to the fact that the voluntary system was increasingly unable to cope with the education of working-class children. The introduction of the Education Bill by the Gladstone administration of 1868 was a recognition that action would no longer be delayed (McCann, 1969, 28).

It is true that Mill did account for the inadequacies (not illiteracy, however, it will be recalled) in terms of class bias (above, p. 703); and it is, of course, possible that he was mistaken in some of his evaluations.[46] But there is no justification for suggesting that he either dissembled or was so biased as to fool himself regarding the actual facts; the 'actual facts' did not point unambiguously towards the conclusions West draws. The same applies to Mill's reading of the Schools Inquiry Commission of 1868 largely devoted to secondary schooling, as being 'as damning to the character of the private, as to that of the endowed schools' (above, p. 716).

It may be noted too that other observers, of a variety of philosophic, religious and political persuasions, questioned the success of private provision. Thus, for example, J. R. McCulloch (three years after the Newcastle Commission had reported):

It is now, indeed, very generally acknowledged, that the providing of elementary instruction, for all classes of its subjects is one of the most pressing duties of government; and during the last half-century, and especially since the termination of the late French wars, some of the principal Continental states have taken every means in their power to ensure the efficient discharge of this important duty. But except in Scotland, no plan of national education has been organized in any part of the United Kingdom. And though much has been done to supply this deficiency by benevolent individuals and societies, and more recently by government, a great

46 In 1848 and in all editions of the *Principles* Mill committed himself to the opinion that the unskilled could not afford educational services and would not even if they could (above, p. 708). But even if West's contention that most working-class parents paid fees is accepted this says nothing about quality – it is 'full cost' to which Mill referred after all, and Mill had high standards. As he put it, 'unfortunately it is much easier to improve education in quantity than in quality' (24 Oct. 1869, *CW*, XVII, 1659).

deal remains to be accomplished, both as respects the diffusion of instruction, and the improvement of its quality (1864, 399).

'Statutory provision' was, accordingly, required for the education of the public. Moreover, 'the public are entitled to superintend its own schools, to decide upon the qualification of the masters, and the species of instruction to be afforded to the pupils', matters which in the private sector 'are left to the discretion of irresponsible individuals' while 'the masters and the instruction may be alike deficient' (399). If McCulloch did not call for the immediate establishment of a system of state schools it was only because of numerous administrative and religious obstacles (401).

As a second example, consider Robert Lowe who (unlike J. S. Mill) receives an excellent press from West and is represented as a follower of Adam Smith in the matter of education (1964, 472). The fact is that even Lowe did not take the data offered by the Newcastle Commission seriously: 'It would be paying too great a compliment to those figures to base any calculation on them' (cited in Adams 1972 [1882], 182) – this, be it noted, a reference to data used by some champions of the *status quo* to demonstrate the *adequacy* of the system as it existed in 1860. In any event, Lowe 'was convinced of the need for public provided elementary education' (even before the Reform Act of 1867) 'as were all Liberals of a "progressive" cast of mind . . . ' (Briggs, 1972, xiv).[47]

* * *

As for Mill's substantive position, far from implying paternalism, the very contrary seems to be true. Although as we have seen, Mill asserted that 'any well-intentioned and tolerably civilized government may think, without presumption, that it does or ought to possess a degree of cultivation above the average of the community which it rules, and that it should therefore be capable of offering better education and better instruction to the people, than the greater number of them would spontaneously demand' (above, p. 706; but see the more qualified statement cited p. 690) he hoped – and there is no reason to question the honesty of the hope – that state provision itself would ultimately prove self-destructive: '[T]his is not one of the cases in which the tender of help perpetuates the state of things which renders help necessary' (above, p. 708). Secondly, he was insistent to a fault upon safeguards: 'the government must claim no monopoly for its education', for '[t]hough the government teachers will probably be superior to the

---

47 Mill favoured the application to government grants of the system of 'payment by result' (above, p. 716 re *CW*, V, 624), which was Lowe's brainchild; cf. Gosden (1969), 33 and Woodward (1962), 481–2 on the Revised Code of 1862.

average of private instructors, they will not embody all the knowledge and sagacity to be found in all instructors taken together, and it is desirable to leave open as many roads as possible to the desired end' (above, p. 709). Government might require that the people 'shall possess instruction in certain things', but not prescribe 'how or from whom they shall obtain it'. Thirdly, we have Mill's allowance that state aid be accorded private schools (although probably not to sectarian schools). Fourthly, the general public would have some voice in the selection of teachers even in state schools. Fifthly, Mill championed endowment as a means of assuring against education falling into the hands of 'an absolute majority' when what was required was 'variety, not uniformity' (above, p. 713); indeed he placed greater faith in the right use of endowments than in direct government provision. Finally, there is no question of Mill's recognition of the need for fees to assure the efficiency of school teachers; while education would not be free for those who could afford it, and the market principle would be retained as far as possible.[48] This was Mill's consistently held position.

Interestingly, even the most severe of Mill's critics has conceded that 'despite his doubts about the efficiency of the market mechanism in education, Mill in the end, like Smith, came down in favour of private schools . . . J. S. Mill . . . despite his misgivings about the ability of ordinary people to buy education themselves, eventually confined his proposals to a law rendering only education (not schooling) compulsory . . . Thus the place or source of . . . education was immaterial after all' (West, 1970a, 124–5; see also Blaug, 1975, 589). Support for this is derived from the passage in *On Liberty* where Mill charges that 'a general State education is a mere contrivence for moulding people to be exactly like one another . . .' and which is read to imply that state intervention was merely to entail the requirement that each child receive a 'good education' leaving parents 'to obtain the education where and how they pleased' with provision of subsidies where necessary (see also West, 1975, 159f).

Mill's proposal, as we have already emphasized (p. 709f), is certainly indicative of the ideal as he saw it. But West is misleading when he implies that this perspective was belatedly arrived at. After all, in the *Principles* itself, throughout all editions, he had written that government 'would be justified in requiring from all the people that they shall possess instruction in certain things, but not in prescribing how or from whom they shall obtain it'. And while it is true that in 1869 Mill expressed himself strongly in favour of endowed schools as a means of avoiding direct government provision, this had been his position as early as 1833 (above, p. 714). Throughout, his concern was with the quality and availability of education rather than its

---

48 The contrast with Smith sometimes drawn (West 1964, 466, Blaug 1975, 585) should therefore not be exaggerated.

source.[49] In any event it is in 1869 that some of his strongest statements of the unreliability of private provision are made (above pp. 696, 715, 717).

West, furthermore, retains a rather forced distinction between Mill and Smith: 'It was Mill's adherence to the principle of liberty which was crucial to his final judgment on the subject. Liberty was required not only as an end in itself but because of certain consequences which Mill thought desirable such as spontaneity, variety and experiment' (1970a, 124). Blaug reiterates this view: 'Although Mill did in the end come down in favour of private schooling, he did not do so because of the classic liberal argument that the experience of making choices in education is itself an education in the art of choices, but rather because he was afraid that the state would abuse its monopoly of education' and concludes with the oddest *nonsequitur*: 'In short, Mill' (as well as Senior) 'moved a long way towards educational paternalism' (1975, 589). Now the insistence upon variety and experiment makes little sense if not seen in large part as a matter of providing opportunities to the public to learn to make wise choices. Much more is at stake than the fear of state abuse – after all the hope was repeatedly expressed that the public would 'learn to appreciate' what a good education amounts to so that the private sector would be reinvigorated.

X FOREIGN TRADE POLICY

The foreign trade context reveals vividly the precise use to which characteristically Ricardian theory was put by Mill in application to particular empirical cases. The early papers on the corn laws of 1825 and 1827 are impressive from this perspective; the basic arguments did not change substantially with the passage of time. The emphasis is upon efficiency: '[I]t is for the interest of a nation to purchase its commodities where they are cheap, and not where they are dear' (*CW*, IV, 47). The anti-Mercantilist 'consumption' perspective is striking. '[I]t is the imports

---

49 On a number of occasions in 1869 Mill wrote warmly of the National Educational League whose activities culminated in the Education Act of 1870; cf. letters of 24 Oct. 1869, XVII, 1658 and Dec. 1869, *ibid.*, 1666. His specific concern in these letters was limited to the principle of compulsory elementary education and that of undenominational state education and he did not here commit himself to the detailed provisions of the bill proposed by Forster (on which see Adams, 1882, 211–12). It is known that he was most disappointed with the final enactment: 'Though brought in by a Government which has earned such high distinction as the destroyer of religious inequality in Ireland, a more effectual plan could have scarcely been devised by the strongest champions of ecclesiastical ascendancy, for enabling the clergy of the Church of England to educate the children of the greater part of England and Wales in their own religion at the expense of the public' (speech at St. James's Hall, 25 March 1870, cited by Adams, 1972, 235–6). But apart from this objection there is no reason to believe that he objected to the allowance for provision as such where necessary.

alone, from which the benefit of foreign commerce is derived' (67); or, as in a paper composed shortly afterwards: 'it is only by our being enabled to import goods, at a less cost than we could afford to produce them at home, that our national wealth derives any sort of advantage from the existence of foreign trade' (130; for similar statements in the *Principles* of this perspective see above, p. 688). In consequence of land scarcity, the only beneficiaries of protection are the landowners; for 'the farmer is effectually prevented, by the competition of other capitalists, from obtaining more than the ordinary profits of stock' (48). Mill has here taken an intermediate-run perspective for presumably the immediate impact would be an increase in agricultural profits at the expense of labourers; and indeed shortly thereafter it is clarified that only with a money-wage increase will labourers be compensated for the corn-price rise. It is the money-wage increase that is responsible for reducing the general (economy wide) return to capital (49–50).

Conspicuous in the account is the fact that (as in Ricardo's treatment) agricultural profits are not represented as governing general profits. Secondly, and also fully in tune with Ricardo, the argument runs in terms of value. Thus regarding the manufacturing sector:

While . . . the labourer continues to receive the same quantity of necessaries as before, corn (the most important of those commodities) has risen in value. He must, therefore, receive a greater *value*, in order to command the same quantity: his money wages must rise. The manufacturers and other capitalists are thus compelled to give a greater value to their labourers, without having a greater value for themselves. They are, therefore, obliged to forego a portion of their profits (50).

But the farmer is in precisely the same position, for 'his gains cannot be permanently greater than those of other capitalists . . . because competition will effectually prevent him from deriving more than a very temporary advantage from [the high corn price] . . . [I]t is not possible that profits should be high when a great value is given to the labourers.'

Some attention is indeed paid to the longer-run consequences of agricultural protection: 'It is the rate of profits which constitutes the inducement to accumulation, and . . . it is on the accumulation of capital that the advancement of the national wealth is wholly dependent'. As for wages, 'the ultimate effect is almost infallibly to diminish them, since by reducing the rate of profit, it retards the accumulation of capital, on which the demand for labour wholly depends' (49). The implicit growth model is therefore not the constant-wage but the declining-wage version. There is certainly no concern with imminent or even prospective stationarity; merely an observation that the return on capital, its growth rate and thus the real wage will be lower than need be the case.

It is clarified also, always in the Ricardian manner, that abolition of the corn laws would be at the cost of landowners in the short run only. For with the expansion of manufactured exports the demand for land services rises to provide the requisite raw materials; moreover – by raising profits and, therefore the demand for labour – population growth would be stimulated: 'The free importation of corn in this respect resembles an improvement in agriculture, which, though it may lower rent for a time, is ultimately beneficial even to the landlord himself' (64).

But the secular consequences of the corn laws play second fiddle to the short-run efficiency consequences – the impact effect prior to population expansion (and assuming a constant commodity wage). The full analysis is of a superb quality. Most impressive are Mill's recognition of a *net* community loss – not merely the transfer to landlords noted above – and of what is now referred to as 'the compensation principle'. As for the net loss:

If, however, there were nothing in the whole process but a transfer; if whatever is lost by the consumer and by the capitalist were gained by the landlord; there might be robbery, but there would not be waste; there might be a worse distribution of the national wealth, but there would be no positive diminution of its aggregate amount. The . . . Corn Laws . . . occasion in all cases an absolute loss, greatly exceeding the gain which can be derived from them by the receivers of rent; and for every pound which finds its way into the pockets of the landlords . . . the community is robbed of several (51).

This net loss reflects, of course, inefficient resource use – the diversion of resources into agriculture 'which would otherwise have produced, not only cloth, or hardware, sufficient to purchase the same quantity of corn in the foreign market, but much more' (52). If society, however, insisted on making a transfer to landlords it would be preferable to do so by direct taxation, landlords estimating 'their probable losses from the repeal of the Corn Laws, and [founding] upon it a claim for compensation'. Whether any claim on grounds of justice could be made was not certain, but Mill wanted merely to convey the advantage over the going system: 'Some, indeed, may question how far they who, for their own emolument, imposed one of the worst taxes upon their countrymen, are titled to compensation for renouncing advantages which they never ought to have enjoyed. It would be better, however, to have a repeal of the Corn Laws, even clogged by a compensation, than not to have it at all' – for 'no one' would lose by such a reform.

In addition to the efficiency and welfare consequences of agricultural protection Mill focusses (like Ricardo) on the issue of corn-price instability (53, 60f). This turns on the near zero elasticity of demand in the case of necessaries:

There is nothing in political economy more certain, than that a small variation in the supply of such a commodity as corn, produces a much more than proportional variation in price . . .

In most other commodities an increase in price induces the purchasers in general to restrict their consumption, and the rise of price, therefore, is little more than proportional to the falling-off in the supply. But corn is a commodity of which, whatever may be its price, all are desirous of consuming the same quantity as before; being willing to renounce almost every other comfort, rather than diminish their consumption of so important a necessary of life. They bid, therefore, against one another, until the poorer competitors are driven out of the market from mere necessity (61; cf. Mill (1827), 145–6).

The principle of demand provides the key to this analysis. Appeal to the principles of Ricardian allocation theory is made also in the discussion of a 'countervailing duty'. Such a duty would only be valid to compensate for a *differential* tax burden on agriculture – such as the ruling tithe charge – and avoid the misallocation implied by the artificial encouragement of agricultural imports:

It is now acknowledged that taxation should be so regulated as to disturb as little as possible that distribution of capital, to which the interests of individuals would lead in a state of perfect freedom. A premium should be given neither on importation nor on home production . . . In both cases, the effect is, that we pay dearer than we ought.

But when other commodities are taxed as well as corn, we think [with McCulloch] that the agriculturists are not entitled to a countervailing duty, unless they can show that they are more heavily taxed than other classes of producers; nor ought the duty even then to exceed the difference between the burthens of the agriculturists and those of others. The reason is, that if all commodities of home production are taxed exactly alike, even without countervailing duties, it is the same thing, with respect to trade, as if they were not taxed at all; since prices are not higher than if there were no tax, and there is no motive to import in a state of perfect freedom . . . But if commodities are taxed unequally, those which are most highly taxed, rise in price, and there is an immediate motive to import them from abroad, paying for them in those which are less heavily taxed. To prevent this, therefore, there is need of a countervailing duty, equal to the difference between the two rates of taxation (68–9).

What is now referred to as the 'second-best' argument is, however, rejected in terms of James Mill's proposition that the existence of protection for various classes of manufactured goods is no justification for agricultural protection (66).

Notwithstanding numerous strong, even arrogant, formulations remi-
niscent of James Mill, the analysis as a whole is most impressive for its
well-balanced blend of theoretical and empirical components. As in the case
of the monetary contribution of 1826 (above, p. 495f) there are signs of
growing independence. The non-dogmatic application of theory may be
illustrated by the attempt to reach a fair evaluation of the actual British
and foreign agricultural cost structures (esp. 53–60). Similarly, there is great
concern with the implications for price stability flowing from the precise
machinery of the going protective system, namely the impediments to
stabilizing speculation on the part of merchants; the argument in this context
too does not proceed in an empirical vacuum: '[W]hen importation is
prohibited until corn shall have attained a certain price, and even then
permitted only for a few months, the importers being compelled to hurry
their corn into the country, without having time to form a judgement as
to the causes of the scarcity, its extent, or probable duration, have no means
of ascertaining how much corn is wanted, and much more than is wanted
is frequently brought; the price is proportionally, or more than proportionally
depressed, and at a time when the farmer, having an unusually small
quantity, has the greatest occasion for a high price, he is forced to content
himself with what would not perhaps be an adequate remuneration even
in an average year' (63).

Mill is also interested in the most effective procedure of reform with an
eye to the transitional period. Here we revert to the allowance for a 'countervailing' duty considering the peculiar burden on agriculture of the 'tithe-
tax'. Ricardo too had allowed a fixed duty from this perspective, but
proposed one to be introduced initially at 20s and lowered by 1s per annum
over a ten-year period to give farmers time to adjust. Mill opposed the
procedure having in mind expectational implications:.

On a recent occasion, when, to save the silk manufacturers from loss, the period
of the reduction of the silk duties was postponed for a year, the silk manufacturers
themselves very generally complained, that they would have suffered less from the
immediate operation of the measure, than they did from the stagnation of business
which was the consequence of the delay; and we suspect, that if the gradual reduction
proposed by Mr. Ricardo, were adopted, the anticipated fall in price would occasion
so general an indisposition to lay in any quantity, beyond what was wanted for
immediate consumption, as might involve the producers in all the evils of a glut (69).

The second of the early papers which deals with the probable consequences
of a sliding scale of duties is equally impressive. Here Mill shows by careful
analysis of specific price data that the scheme (then about to be enacted)
would 'still remain liable to the same *fluctuations* as heretofore' – the going
system of prohibition until the domestic price reached 70s per quarter – since

the average long-run or cost price would not be reduced by the reform. '[T]hese fluctuations, the range of which, during the last twelve years, has been from 112s. to 38s., were wholly occasioned by our high *average* price as compared with that of other countries' – having, of course, in mind the almost zero elasticity of demand for food (146). It is further demonstrated that the diminution of duties with any rise in the price of food acted as a bounty to foreigners thereby imposing a 'third tax' on the community supplementing the misallocation of resources, and the transfer to landowners (147).

In an early paper on the Silk Trade (1826), Mill considers the prospective reduction of duties on the importation of 'wrought silks'. He allows that there is 'distress' in the silk trade, but now denies that it can be attributed to 'the anticipation of the effect which the admission of foreign silks may have on the market' (128); the silk trade was suffering from a depression common to a variety of trades in consequence of a preceding period of 'speculation and overtrading'. To rule out any impact of an announced delay in the abolition of restrictions on the grounds that since 'we have . . . one perfectly sufficient cause of the distress, need we go to look for another?' is scarcely convincing, especially considering Mill's own emphasis upon the phenomenon in 1825.

There are two substantive points of theory to note in this paper. First the application of Ricardo's inverse wage-profit relation. Mill clarifies that the higher general level of money wages paid to British labour relative to their French counterparts (due to the corn laws) in no way constituted an advantage to the French in foreign trade meriting domestic protection. For the relatively low money wages implied relatively high profits not low prices. It is only 'if wages are lower in one employment [that] prices would also be lower in that employment. But wages are lower in all employments; and the supposition of *general* low prices, except from some cause affecting the circulating medium, is absurd' (135). From the British perspective, general profits are lower than they would be in consequence of the corn laws but this is 'not more prejudicial to those who are exposed to foreign competition than to those who are not'. It is readily conceded that the high *relative* wage paid certain specialist labourers would impede British manufacturers in those sectors (136).

A second feature is the contrast made between agricultural protection where there occurs a transfer to landlords as well as a net efficiency loss, and silk protection from which the 'monopolists, in no way gain – a distinction turning on the fixity of land supply: 'Manufacturers do not derive the same advantage from restrictions upon trade that landlords do. The landlord really derives an addition to his income . . . from the operation of the corn monopoly. Not so the manufacturer: he, under a restricted trade, receives no more than the ordinary profits of stock: which he would equally have received had he embarked his capital in any other employment. The tax which the consumer pays, nobody receives; it is a dead loss to the country' (130–1). (The same logic applies to farmers as distinct from landowners as we have seen earlier.) The obvious but questionable implication is that, from Mill's perspective, the manufacturers do not accurately perceive their own interest; in all events, the repeated use of the term 'monopoly' seems inappropriate once entry into the protected trade by domestic capitalists is allowed.

* * *

We turn next to some later contributions. In a 'Petition on Free Trade' (1841) the emphasis is on the inequities to the poor as well as efficiency losses flowing from agricultural protection, with no indication whether the immediate or long run is intended. Here Mill calls for the total abandonment of import duties as the ideal with an allowance for a degree of temporary protection as a transitional step: 'as a means of transition, to prevent too sudden a shock to existing interests, your petitioners fully subscribe to the propriety of retaining, for the present, a moderate [fixed] duty on imported corn' (V, 763). In this latter respect Mill reversed his earlier position which recommended the immediate adoption of tariff reform to avoid undesired expectational consequences. As for the ideal, it is true that in correspondence of 1869 he wrote that Robert Lowe (Gladstone's Chancellor of the Exchequer) had 'certainly much exaggerated the strength of the case against the shilling duty on corn' (2 May, XVII, 1595), yet he proceeded to refer to 'the advantage of getting rid of the last remaining shred of Protectionism' (cf. Bonar, 1911, 722). We must now recall the analytical argument – the terms of trade argument of the essay devoted to trade (1844) and the *Principles* – according to which a nation by the judicious use of import duties may throw part of the burden of taxation on to foreigners (above, pp. 333–4). This case, even in principle, applies solely to duties of a 'non-protecting' kind – such that while domestic consumption may, as it 'almost always' will, be reduced the quantity it still requires at the new prices is imported rather than produced domestically: 'The saving of labour – the increase in the general productiveness of the capital of the world – which is the effect of commerce, and which a *non-protecting* duty would enable the country imposing it to engross, would not be engrossed by a protecting duty, because such a duty prevents any such increased production from existing' ('Of the Laws of Interchange Between Nations', 1844, *CW*, IV, 249; emphasis added).[50]

50 Mill seems to suggest that a revenue tariff has no negative impact on trade volume, which cannot be the case considering the consequences for the export industries of the presumed contraction of demand for imports. The sharp distinction between protective and revenue tariffs seems too sharply drawn.

As for policy, Mill remains vehemently opposed on efficiency grounds to duties which encourage home production of goods otherwise imported; such protective duties are 'purely mischievous, both to the country imposing them, and to those with whom it trades' (250; cf. 231; see also *Principles*, III, 855).[51] Non-protecting or 'revenue' duties – either imposed on commodities which technically could not be produced domestically, or alternatively, at too low a rate to outweigh the cost differential between (prospective) home and (actual) foreign production – are also 'ineligible', but because of the danger of retaliation. (In recognizing the case for retaliation to counter a foreign imposition of revenue tariffs Mill warns that the sum of the duties must 'not be so high as to exceed all that remains of the advantage of the trade . . . [251; also in *Principles*, III, 856].) But existing 'revenue' duties should not – unlike existing 'protective' duties – be abandoned unilaterally: 'any relaxation of such duties, beyond what may be required by the interest of the revenue itself, should in general be made contingent upon the adoption of some corresponding degree of freedom of trade with this country, by the country from which the commodity is imported' (231; cf. also 251).

The case to retain revenue tariffs on reciprocity grounds is not, however, extended to the 'necessaries of life, or the materials and instruments of production', doubtless because of the impact on wages and on profits.

* * *

Although Mill's precise formulation in the case of revenue tariffs seems to imply their justification assuming no danger of retaliation, we must also bear in mind the 'cosmopolitan' flavour to the essay as a whole which would point against 'throwing part of the weight of [a country's] taxes upon other people . . . ' (250). Thus the imposition of export charges whereby a nation in some circumstances can gain at another's expense is said to clash with 'international morality', which if 'rightly understood and acted upon' would rule out all such measures as 'contrary to the universal weal' (248; cf. *Principles*, *CW*, III, 853). Similarly, after demonstrating that the free export

51 Mill also objected to tariffs on revenue grounds where protection is an incidental consequence. Corn is distinguished from manufactures on grounds of increasing costs (at home and abroad), the presumption being that in a freely-operating market corn is also produced domestically. A tariff, it is supposed, will merely reduce but not preclude imports. But although revenue is yielded on the (smaller) quantity imported, a 'tax' is paid by consumers on all units consumed including domestic production; and 'to make the public pay much that the treasury may receive a little' is not an 'eligible mode of obtaining a revenue' (918). In the case of manufactures – Mill implicitly presumes constant-cost industries – a duty which prevents importation is illogical since no revenue will be yielded at all.

of machinery might in certain instances be detrimental Mill none the less proceeds to reject restriction 'on the score of international morality' as well as that of 'sound policy': 'It is evidently the common interest of all nations that each of them should abstain from every measure by which the aggregate wealth of the commercial world would be diminished, although of this smaller sum total it might thereby be enabled to attract to itself a larger share' (252). But even here one notes Mill's realism, for the reciprocity argument is reiterated: 'The exportation of machinery may, however, be a proper subject for adjustment with other nations, on the principle of reciprocity. Until, by the common consent of nations, all restrictions upon trade are done away, a nation cannot be required to abolish those from which she derives a real advantage, without stipulating for an equivalent'.

Like Adam Smith, Mill allowed the case 'in principle' for Navigation Acts on grounds of defence, despite 'economical sacrifice', but believed that contemporary Britain operated under no relative disadvantage in shipping (III, 916–17, cf. 755).[52] The argument for restriction of the corn trade to avoid dependency on foreigners is shown to be questionable on the same grounds as in the early paper of 1825 (IV, 65); we raise the issue here for the allusion again to 'international morality': 'in cases of actual or apprehended scarcity, many countries of Europe are accustomed to stop the exportation of food? Is this, or not, sound policy? There can be no doubt that in the present state of international morality, a people cannot, any more than an individual, be blamed for not starving itself to feed others. But if the greatest amount of good to mankind on the whole were the end aimed at in the maxims of international conduct, such collective churlishness would certainly be condemned by them . . . When the interests . . . of all countries are considered, free exportation is desirable' (III, 917–18).

Mill, even in this striking passage, is realistic enough – the 'greatest good' principle is not yet universally applicable. In any event, the ideal case still rests on the promise of mutual benefit; for although the exporting country would be 'inconvenienced' it might itself be the beneficiary at some future time. Lord Robbins is certainly convincing in maintaining that the classics, including Mill, would not have 'recommended in the interest of the world as a whole policies which they thought would be positively damaging to their own nation' (1971b, 188). That Mill had his feet firmly on the ground is apparent also in his legitimization of retaliation and emphasis on reciprocity negotiations. Yet he is on record as perceiving the extension of the advantages of trade beyond static efficiency gains supplemented by the dynamic gains implied by the stimulus of larger markets for economies of scale and technological change (III, 593) to the even more important intellectual and moral effects. There is no question about the ideal:

---

52 Mill also favoured conscription; cf. letter 5 February 1871, XVIII, 1805–6.

It is hardly possible to overrate the value, in the present low state of human improvement, of placing human beings in contact with persons dissimilar to themselves, and with modes of thought and action unlike those with which they are familiar. Commerce is now what war once was, the principal source of this contact . . . [C]ommerce first taught nations to see with good will the wealth and prosperity of one another. Before, the patriot, unless sufficiently advanced in culture to feel the world his country, wished all countries weak, poor, and ill-governed, but his own: he now sees in their wealth and progress a direct source of wealth and progress to his own country. It is commerce which is rapidly rendering wars obsolete, by strengthening and multiplying the personal interests which are in natural opposition to it. And it may be said without exaggeration that the great extent and rapid increase of international trade, in being the principal guarantee of the peace of the world, is the great permanent security for the uninterrupted progress of the ideas, the institutions, and the character of the human race (*CW*, III, 594).

XI GOVERNMENT AND ECONOMIC DEVELOPMENT

The role of government in development is attended to briefly as a sort of *coda* to the chapter on limits of the *laissez-faire* principle (*CW*, III, 970).[53] In consequence of three specific characteristics which define a state of under-development – 'the public being either too poor to command the necessary resources, or too little advanced in intelligence to appreciate the ends, or not sufficiently practised in joint action to be capable of the means' – Mill maintained that government may have to take responsibility for the provision of services albeit 'intrinsically' more suitable for private initiative: roads, docks, harbours, canals, irrigation works, hospitals, schools, colleges, printing presses – services, it will be noted, not necessarily involving indiscriminate benefit. Indeed, '[in] the particular circumstances of a given age or nation, there is scarcely anything really important to the general interest, which it may not be desirable, or even necessary, that the government should take upon itself, not because private individuals cannot effectually perform it, but because they will not'. Mill clearly intended to supplement, not merely repeat, the allowances for legitimate intervention made earlier which applied to an ad-vanced society. The characteristics now referred to constitute additional sources of divergence between social and private benefits, in special circumstances.

There may perhaps be discerned a paternalistic flavour to Mill's presumption regarding the desirability of development, and the need to act on behalf of subjects 'too little advanced in intelligence to appreciate the ends'. Ricardo, it will be recalled, had avoided the presumption (Hollander, 1979, 554). But so too did Mill in *On Liberty*: 'The spirit of

---

53 Schwartz (1972), 141, believes this issue was here treated as an afterthought. But in fact III, 942, contains a similar discussion; see above (p. 689).

improvement is not always a spirit of liberty, for it may aim at forcing improvements on an unwilling people . . . ' (*CW*, XVIII, 272). In any event, the measure of paternalism in our present context is much qualified.

Government intervention, in the first place, must be always with an eye to the establishment of conditions within which 'individual energy and voluntary cooperation could flourish':

In these cases, the mode in which the government can most surely demonstrate the sincerity with which it intends the greatest good of its subjects, is by doing the things which are made incumbent upon it by the helplessness of the public, in such a manner as shall tend not to increase and perpetuate, but to correct, that helplessness. A good government will give all its aid in such a shape, as to encourage and nurture any rudiments it may find of a spirit of individual exertion. It will be assiduous in removing obstacles and discouragements to voluntary enterprise, and in giving whatever facilities and whatever direction and guidance may be necessary: its pecuniary means will be applied, when practicable, in aid of private efforts rather than in supersession of them, and it will call into play its machinery of rewards and honours to elicit such efforts. Government aid, when given merely in default of private enterprise, should be so given as to be as far as possible a course of education for the people in the art of accomplishing great objects by individual energy and voluntary co-operation (III, 970–1).

Mill's concessions regarding protection of 'infant-industries' are relevant from this perspective:

The superiority of one country over another in a branch of production, often arises only from having begun it sooner. There may be no inherent advantage on one part, or disadvantage on the other, but only a present superiority of acquired skill and experience. A country which has this skill and experience yet to acquire, may in other respects be better adapted to the production than those which were earlier in the field: and besides, it is a just remark of Mr. Rae, that nothing has a greater tendency to promote improvements in any branch of production, than its trial under a new set of conditions. But it cannot be expected that individuals should, at their own risk, or rather to their certain loss, introduce a new manufacture, and bear the burthen of carrying it on until the producers have been educated up' to the level of those with whom the processes are traditional. A protecting duty, continued for a reasonable time, might sometimes be the least inconvenient mode in which the nation can tax itself for the support of such an experiment (III, 918–19).

Mill warned that there must be 'good ground of assurance' as to the temporary nature of the protection. (In later correspondence he specified 'a moderate protecting duty for a certain limited number of years, say ten, or at the very most twenty, during the latter part of which the duty should be

on a gradually diminishing scale, & at this end of which it should expire';
2 May 1865, XVI, 1044).

In the last edition of the *Principles* the warning is strengthened, for Mill had
come to regret the misuse of this concession by private interest, especially in
America and to a lesser degree in Australia. In correspondence he proposed
an alternative: 'I am now much shaken in the opinion, which has so often been
quoted for purposes which it did not warrant; & I am disposed to think that
when it is advisable, as it may sometimes be, to subsidize a new industry in
its commencement, this had better be done by a direct annual grant, which
is far less likely to be continued after the conditions which alone justified
it have ceased to exist' (11 December 1868; XVI, 1520–1; also 7 December,
1516). Insistence upon protection (or subsidization) beyond a 'moderate'
time as by the American cotton and iron industries, is 'a complete proof
that they ought not to have it, & that the longer it is continued the greater
the injustice & the waste of national resources will be' (26 February 1866;
ibid., 1150); American resources could 'in the present circumstances of
America be employed with greater return & greater advantage to the national
wealth, in the production of other articles'. (For comments regarding the
Australian case see letter of 5 July 1868; *ibid.*, 1420.)

There is a further issue peculiarly pertinent to the developmental problem.
I have in mind Mill's rejection (introduced in the edition of 1865) on
standard allocation grounds of Carey's case for protection in his *Principles
of Social Science* (1858) turning on a presumed avoidance of transport costs:

If the commodity is bought in a foreign country with domestic produce in spite
of the double cost of carriage, the fact proves that, heavy as that cost may be,
the saving in cost of production outweighs it, and the collective labour of the
country is on the whole better remunerated than if the article were produced at
home . . . unless America gained more by obtaining her manufactures through
the medium of her corn and cotton than she loses in cost of carriage, the capital
employed in producing corn and cotton in annually increased quantities for the
foreign market would turn to manufactures instead (III, 919).

As for Carey's case for the artificial stimulation of a manufacturing sector
on the grounds that an agricultural economy 'sends away [its] soil' – foreign
consumers not giving back to the land the fertilizing elements abstracted
from it in the manner of domestic consumers, Mill conceded that the problem
of soil exhaustion ('which has only lately come to be understood') was
'henceforth destined to be a permanent element in the thoughts of
statesmen', but denied that this justified protectionist conclusions:

[W]hat I have said respecting cost of carriage, is true also of the cost of manuring.
Free trade does not compel America to export corn: she would cease to do so if

it ceased to be to her advantage. As, then, she would not persist in exporting raw produce and importing manufactures, any longer than the labour she saved by doing so exceeded what the carriage cost her, so when it became necessary for her to replace in the soil the elements of fertility which she had sent away, if the saving in cost of production were more than equivalent to the cost of carriage and of manure together, manure would be imported; and, if not, the export of corn would cease.

Mill pointed out, regarding the United States, that the problem of soil exhaustion had been avoided only because a succession of fresh soils was still available. But a choice would ultimately have to be made between the regular importation of manure and the production both of corn and manufactures as Carey desired.[54]

XII POPULATION CONTROL, POOR RELIEF,
AND FULL EMPLOYMENT POLICY

Like the general case for Free Trade the argument for population control was also made on grounds of expediency. Control was not to be ruled out as an infringement of liberty:

[I]n a country either over-peopled, or threatened with being so, to produce children, beyond a very small number, with the effect of reducing the reward for labour by their competition, is a serious offence against all who live by the remuneration of their labour. The laws which, in many countries on the Continent, forbid marriage unless the parties can show that they have the means of supporting a family, do not exceed the legitimate powers of the State: and whether such laws be expedient or not (a question mainly dependent on local circumstances and feelings), they are not objectionable as violations of liberty. Such laws are interferences of the State to prohibit a mischievous act – an act injurious to others, which ought to be a subject of reprobation, and social stigma, even when it is not deemed expedient to superadd legal punishment (*On Liberty*, *CW*, XVIII, 304).

It is not clear how in practice the presumption that the country be 'either over-peopled, or threatened with being so' limited Mill's case for legal control. But there is certainly nothing to suggest that he intended to recommend intervention in contemporary Britain. His consistent appeal through the years was for the inclusion of responsible (prudential) behaviour, and we know that by the 1860s he was optimistic regarding the course of events. His point then clearly constitutes a matter of principle for emergency circumstances where educational programmes have fallen on deaf ears, and

---

54 In the context of colonization Mill makes further allowances for state intervention. These will be considered presently.

general wages are seriously threatened. It must also be remembered (by analogy to the case of education) that a denigration of principle of liberty is never intended by rejection of the 'inviolability' principle; every step would have to be taken to minimize the impact of intervention on citizens even though society has the 'moral' right to intervene (but see Stigler, 1975, 196 for a rather more critical view).

Mill, of course, insisted upon general recognition that for the State to take on direct responsibility for living standards implied a corresponding necessity for direct control over population. This he considered *unendurable* in contemporary circumstances:

There are governments in Europe who look upon it as part of their duty to take care of the physical well-being and comfort of the people. The Austrian government, in its German dominions, does so. Several of the minor German governments do so. But with paternal care is connected paternal authority. In these states we find severe restrictions on marriage. No one is permitted to marry, unless he satisfies the authorities that he has a rational prospect of being able to support a family . . . If, then, it is intended that the law, or the persons of property, should assume a control over the multiplication of the people, tell us so plainly, and inform us how you propose to do it. But it will doubtless be said, that nothing of this sort would be endurable; that such things are not to be dreamt of in the state of English society and opinion; that the spirit of equality, and the love of individual independence, have so pervaded even the poorest class, that they would not take plenty to eat and drink, at the price of having their most personal concerns regulated for them by others. If this be so, all schemes for withdrawing wages from the control of supply and demand, or raising the people by other means than by such changes in their minds and habits as shall make them fit guardians of their own physical condition, are schemes for combining incompatibilities ('The Claims of Labour', 1845, *CW*, IV, 374–5).

The same perspective governed Mill's approach to the special problem of poor relief.

Mill's hostility towards the poor-law system as administered in Britain during the three or four decades prior to the reform of 1834 was as strong as that of either Malthus or Ricardo. Both the system of relief to the able-bodied without restraint on the freedom of the recipients, and the system of allowances in aid of wages were strongly condemned on grounds of the stimulus given thereby to population growth:

During the last century, under a rather rigid administration of the poor-laws, population increased slowly, and agricultural wages were considerably above the starvation point. Under the allowance system the people increased so fast, and wages sank so low, that with wages and allowance together, families were worse off than they had been before with wages alone . . . This deplorable system, worse than any other form of poor-law abuse yet invented, inasmuch as it pauperizes not merely the unemployed part of the population but the whole, has now been abolished, and of this one abuse at least it may be said, that nobody professes to wish for its revival (II, 362).[55]

A public-relief system was warmly recognized on formal grounds of utility: 'Society mainly consists of those who live by bodily labour; and if society, that is, if the labourers lend their physical force to protect individuals in the enjoyment of superfluities, they are entitled to do so, and have always done so, with the reservation of a power to tax those superfluities for purposes of public utility; among which purposes the subsistence of the people is the foremost' (357). Here the general argument against government interference based on the principle that individuals are the best judge of their own interests was inapplicable since acts were at stake – charitable acts – on behalf of others, so that the only question was how most effectively to satisfy the objective (III, 960).[56]

Systematic relief was necessary to avoid the uncertainty of private provision, raising the problem: 'how to give the greatest amount of needful help, with the smallest encouragement to undue reliance on it' (961). The legislation of 1834 based on the lesser eligibility principle satisfied this matter of fundamental principle and yet avoided the defects attributed to the system it replaced. It is, indeed, represented as a humanitarian measure, solving what had been thought to be an unresolvable dilemma:

It is not at all surprising . . . that Mr. Malthus and others should at first have concluded against all poor-laws whatever. It required much experience, and careful examination of different modes of poor-law management, to give assurance that the admission of an absolute right to be supported at the cost of other people, could exist in law and in fact, without fatally relaxing the springs of industry and the restraints of prudence. This, however, was fully substantiated, by the investigations of the original Poor Law Commissioners. Hostile as they are unjustly accused of being to the principle of legal relief, they are the first who fully proved the compatibility of any Poor Law, in which a right to relief was recognised, with the permanent interests of the labouring class and of posterity. By a collection of facts, experimentally ascertained in parishes scattered throughout England, it was shown

55 By 1865 Mill was more concerned about opinion, for in place of the final clauses he wrote: 'This deplorable system . . . received a severe check from the Poor Laws of 1834: I wish it could be said that there are no signs of its revival.' The view, common to the classical writers, that the outdoor relief system tended to depress wages has been challenged by modern historians (cf. Blaug, 1963, McCloskey, 1973, West, 1978b).

56 It is worth noting Mill's aside that poor relief would not be the central issue if 'prudence' reigned broadly and with a satisfactory 'difusion of property'.

that the guarantee of support could be freed from its injurious effects upon the minds and habits of the people, if the relief, though ample in respect to necessaries, was accompanied with conditions, which they disliked, consisting of some restraints on their freedom, and the privation of some indulgences (II, 359–60).[57]

'Humanity', Mill concluded, 'has no worse enemies than those who lend themselves, either knowingly or unintentionally, to bring odium on this law, or on the principles in which it originated' (II, 360). It was the so-called 'philanthropists' who, failing to appreciate the requirement for a lesser-eligibility provision, referred to 'Union Bastilles' and denied 'that even a workhouse should be a place of regulation and discipline; that any extrinsic restraint should be applied even there. Their bitterest quarrel with the present system of relief is, that it enforces the separation of the sexes' (IV, 375).

Unlike McCulloch (see Hollander, 1979, 723–4, Mill neither considered the advantages of a return to the system operating prior to Speenhamland nor objected to the degree of centralization inherent in the new system of 1834. On the contrary, he found that it satisfied the principle of 'the greatest dissemination of power consistent with efficiency; but the greatest possible centralization of information, and diffusion of it from the centre':

[The] central organ should have a right to know all that is done, and its special duty should be that of making the knowledge acquired in one place available for others. Emancipated from the petty prejudices and narrow views of a locality by its elevated position and comprehensive sphere of observation, its advice would naturally carry much authority; but its actual power, as a permanent institution, should, I conceive, be limited to compelling the local officers to obey the laws laid down for their guidance. In all things not provided for by general rules, those officers should be left to their own judgment, under responsibility to their constituents. For the violation of rules, they should be responsible to law, and the rules themselves should be laid down by the legislature; the central administrative authority only watching over their execution, and if they were not properly carried into effect, appealing, according to the nature of the case, to the tribunals to enforce the law,

---

57 Mill's enthusiasm for the Commission of 1833 was immediate: 'The result is altogether appalling to the dilettanti, and the gigmen, and the ignorant and timid in high stations; to me it has been, & will be I think to you [Carlyle], rather consoling because *we* knew the thing [the existing relief system] to be unspeakably bad, but this I think shews that it may be considerably mended with a considerably less amount of intellect, courage, and virtue in the higher classes, than had hitherto appeared to me to be necessary . . . I regard this enquiry with satisfaction under another aspect too; that it has been more honestly and more ably performed than anything which has been done under the authority of Govt. since I remember . . .' (18 May 1833, XII, 156).

or to the constituencies to dismiss the functionaries who had not executed it according to its spirit. Such, in its general conception, is the central superintendence which the Poor Law Board is intended to exercise over the administrators of the Poor Rate throughout the country. Whatever powers the Board exercises beyond this limit, were right and necessary in that peculiar case, for the cure of rooted habits of maladministration in matters deeply affecting not the localities merely, but the whole community; since no locality has a moral right to make itself by mismanagement a nest of pauperism, necessarily overflowing into other localities, and impairing the moral and physical condition of the whole labouring community. The powers of administrative coercion and subordinate legislation possessed by the Poor Law Board (but which, owing to the state of opinion on the subject, are very scantily exercised by them), though perfectly justifiable in a case of first-rate national interest, would be wholly out of place in the superintendence of interests purely local ('On Liberty', XVIII, 309–10).[58]

There was, however, another possible alternative or supplemental programme. The pledge of full employment given by the French Provisional Government of February 1848 was taken up by Mill in his famous 'Vindication of the French Revolution' published in the *Westminster Review* the following year – the 'obligation on society to find work and wages for all persons willing and able to work who cannot procure employment for themselves' (*Dissertations and Discussions*, II, 384). Subject to one qualification, Mill favoured *le droit au travail* as 'the most manifest of moral truths, the most imperative of political obligations' (385). The formulation seems to imply self-evident natural law or intuitive rights: 'It appeared to the Provisional Government, as it must appear to every unselfish and open-minded person, that the earth belongs, first of all to the inhabitants of it; that every person alive ought to have a subsistence, before any one has more; that whosoever works at any useful thing, ought to be properly fed and clothed before any one able to work is allowed to receive the bread of idleness. There are moral axioms' (385–6). We should recall Mill's Benthamite allowance – as expressed in 1852 (see above p. 642f) – that morality has its source in utility; but the formulation is far too strongly

58 Mill's impatience with those hostile to the poor law is apparent early on: 'The anti-poor law doctrine is now almost universally exploded among political economists, though political economy still continues to be most unjustly bothered with the discredit of it' (1834, cited by Schwartz, 1972, 46). Reference should be made to a letter from Mill, 12 Dec. 1864, XV, 979, regarding James Mill's conversion as a consequence of various articles written for the *Morning Chronicle*: 'Black, as I well remember, changed the opinion of some of the leading political economists, particularly my father's respecting poor laws, by the articles he wrote in the *Chronicle* in favour of a Poor Law for Ireland. He met their objections by maintaining that a poor law did not necessarily encourage overpopulation . . . and he convinced them that he was in the right.'

made on Mill's own terms, and we have noted the utility dimension in the *Principles* in the context of poor relief.

From a practical viewpoint the French scheme was an 'incomparably less injurious form of intervention than had been the English parochial system of poor relief. For it acted on the global labour market, the State being obligated only to 'disburse sufficient funds to create the amount of productive employment that was wanting . . . It relieved no individual from the responsibility of finding an employer, and proving his willingness to exert himself.' In the second edition of the *Principles*, Mill reiterated that this feature reduced considerably objections to support schemes: 'The fund raised by taxation might be spread over the labour market generally . . . without giving to any unemployed labourer a right to demand support in a particular place or from a particular functionary. The power of dismissal as regards individual labourers, would then remain; the government only undertaking to create additional employment when there was a deficiency, and reserving, like other employers, the choice of its own workpeople' (*CW*, II, 357–8).

The qualification, needless to say, arises from the principle of population: 'There is enough to spare for all who *are* born; but there is not and cannot be enough for all who *might* be born; and if every person born is to have an indefeasible claim to a subsistence from the common fund, there will presently be no more than a bare subsistence for anybody, and a little later there will not be even that' (*Dissertations and Discussions*, II, 386; cf. *CW*, III, 358 where the assumption of diminishing returns is made explicit). This should not be read as an instance of the *inevitable* failure of all reform programs. Mill himself specified the way out – that 'some new restraint [be] placed upon the capacity of increase, equivalent to that which would be taken away'; for example: 'all persons living should guarantee to each other, through their organ the State, the ability to earn by labour an adequate subsistence, but that should abdicate the right of propagating the species at their own discretion and without limit: that all classes alike, and not the poor alone, should consent to exercise that power in such measure only, and under such regulations, as society might prescribe with a view to the common good' (*Dissertations and Discussions*, II, 386–7). Holding up such reform was the common 'superstition', amongst conservatives and reformers alike, 'that one of the most important and responsible of moral acts, that of giving existence to human beings, is a thing respecting which there scarcely exists any moral obligation, and in which no person's discretion ought on any pretence to be interfered with'. This formulation confirms what is less clearly expressed in the *Principles*, that Mill himself favoured in principle direct state 'interference' in population decisions, although this need not mean that he would have agreed to a government riding rough-shod over public opinion in this regard.

The implication of all this is remarkable – a Beveridge-like position obligating the State to assure 'full-employment', provided any stimulus to population growth is avoided. Mill recognized that public opinion was not ready for the requisite state intervention in population matters of a general order. It is understandable then that he should have emphasized the Poor Law scheme of 1834 as the immediate solution. But it was the second best.

It remains to note that in the paper on the French Revolution Mill applauds the *ateliers nationaux* as essential in the post-revolutionary circumstances considering the industrial stagnation prevailing, notwithstanding the prospective danger from the population perspective (*Dissertations and Discussions*, II, 387). This suggests a certain flexibility on Mill's part regarding emergency situations, confirmed also by his approach to technological displacement of labour (above, p. 673). It is at the same time, likely that he did not believe direct or fiscal intervention to be usually justified in periods of normal cyclical depression considering the corrective mechanisms at play when supplemented by a degree of monetary intervention (above, pp. 582–3). Moreover, Mill's insistence that protection granted on infant-industry grounds is to be temporary comes to mind here; it parallels the requirement (1845; *CW*, IV, 386–7) that direct intervention in the labour market to provide employment must satisfy the test of ultimate independence – 'that there be a reasonable prospect of their being at some future time self-supporting'. In both cases the implicit assumption is that full use of resources is the norm. But that Mill was even early on moderate in his position is suggested by the fact that despite his assumption of highly mobile labour on empirical grounds in the analysis of the silk trade (1826), he none the less argued for the relief of the 'temporary distress' of the journeymen 'consistently with what is due to the rest of the community' (131). There may also have been some hesitancy on Mill's part to publicize in the *Principles* his allowances considering the ever-present long-term dangers. (On this matter see also Link, 1959, 174).

XIII ON LOCAL AND CENTRAL ADMINISTRATION

The paper on 'Centralisation' (1865) contains an important summary statement of Mill's position on the poor-law system within a broader context of the relation between local and central government and merits attention at this point. A French critic (Dupont-White, *L'Individu et l'Etat*, 1857) had put his faith in central rather than local administration in the course of a general case regarding the inevitability of growing state control with progress. While Mill, as we shall see, rejected this latter theme he wrote scathingly of local authority: 'Any despotism is preferable to local despotism. If we are to be ridden over by authority, if our affairs are to be managed for us at the pleasure of other people, heaven forefend that it should be at that of our nearest neighbours . . . defend us from the leading strings of a Board of Guardians or a Common Council . . . To be under the latter, would be in most localities, unless by the rarest accident, to be the slave of the vulgar prejudices, the cramped, distorted and short-sighted views, of the public of a small town or a group of villages' (*CW*, XIX, 606). But this did not imply Dupont-White's centralization ideal; a happy solution had been found as illustrated from poor relief:

[I]t does not follow, because the local authority ought not to be supreme and absolute, that the central ought; or that the latter should be able, by an act of authority, to overrule the resistance, or dispense with the assent, of the former, in matters on which the legislature had not declared itself. Respecting the degree in which the central executive should cooperate with the localities in the control of local affairs, there are great differences of opinion amongst us. Our author is in the right in saying that our recent legislation has associated central with local authority in a far greater degree than before. The reason is, that the characteristic of the present age is the reform of abuses, and their reform could not be trusted to the persons and the institutions that had introduced them. But our author imagines the tendency, which really exists, to be much stronger than it is. He never wearies of repeating that England has found it necessary to centralise the relief of the poor. He is perhaps not aware that the relief of the poor in England is not central, but local, under central supervision; and that the Poor Law of 1834, which established the Central Board, also created the first tolerably-constituted Local Boards of Poor Law Administration which England has ever possessed.

There was also, of course, the question of liberty, a point made directly to Dupont-White in earlier correspondence. Although Mill agreed that it was desirable for British central government to interfere in local institutions, especially since these latter were worse organized and more corrupt even than the State, there were dangers, and limits had to be found, 'et cela surtout par la raison qu'une nation qui se repose sur son gouvernement du soin de penser pour elle dans les affaires pratiques de la vie sociale, n'est pas et ne peut pas être libre. Je ne connais rien de plus fatal à la liberté qu'une bureaucratie très capable et très fortement organisée, à la tête d'un peuple qui ne cultive pas, par une active gérance de ses intérêts collectifs, le sens pratique des affaires sociales' (1 July 1858, XV, 555–6). But the point is also made that more could be expected from local authority at the 'provincial', e.g. the Quarter Sessions, and County Boards (as distinct from the 'municipal') level which 'composed as they would probably be, could be trusted to do whatever business was assigned to them, without subjection to the central executive; whose functions in regard to them might be limited to collecting and diffusing information, and calling the localities to account if they violated the rules laid down by

Parliament for their observance, or usurped powers not confided to them by law' (XIX, 607).[59]

XIV THE LABOUR MARKET: REGULATION OF HOURS AND UNIONS

The purely economic case both against government productive activity itself and more generally government regulation of private initiative, turned largely on the relative effectiveness of such unfettered initiative in production. This presumption against government intervention no longer held good where 'so-called private management is, in point of fact, hardly better entitled to be called management by the persons interested, than administration by a public officer' – cases of delegated management (*CW*, III, 954). And there were also cases, such as the regulation of factory hours and the disposal of colonial land, requiring legal sanction 'not to overrule the judgment of individuals respecting their own interest, but to give effect to that judgment' (956). These qualifications do not conflict with the general presumption itself but, because of their great practical importance, require close attention.

The issue of factory hours had arisen much earlier in the context of the contemporary debate regarding child and female labour. This entailed a case *par excellence* 'in which it would be highly for the advantage of everybody, if everybody were to act in a certain manner, but in which it is not the interest of any *individual* to adopt the rule for the guidance of his own conduct, unless he has some security that others will do so too' (above, pp. 699–700).

In the *Principles* this specific argument is no longer applied to children; the case for the state is based on protection of minors (on a par with the case for compulsory education): 'Labouring for too many hours in the day, or on work beyond their strength, should not be permitted to them, for if permitted it may always be compelled. Freedom of contract, in the case of children, is but another word for freedom of coercion' (III, 952).[60] Mill

---

59 For a discussion of Mill's position on local institutions and centralization see Brady (1977), xxxix f., lxii f. We shall have more to say on the matter of appropriate government machinery in Section XVI.

60 The rationale for legislative compulsion upon parents and factory owners is expressed very clearly in the course of a subsequent defence of half-time schooling for child workers. The argument from liberty for non-intervention failed in this case: 'On étend cette législation de plus en plus, en sorte qu'elle s'applique maintenant à presque toutes les industries qui ne sont pas purement domestiques, sauf l'agriculture qui jusqu'ici fait exception. L'expérience a prouvé que la loi peut seule faire face à l'intérêt combiné des fabricants et des pères des enfants à exploiter le travail de ces infortunés aux dépens de leur éducation et même de leur développement physique, et cette expérience a graduellement prévalu sur les idées de liberté individuelle. En effet, la liberté individuelle,

objected in this context to the classification of female labour with child labour as a candidate for legal protection on these grounds: 'Children below a certain age *cannot* judge or act for themselves; up to a considerably greater age they are inevitably more or less disqualified for doing so; but women are as capable as men of appreciating and managing their own concerns, and the only hindrance to their doing so arises from the injustice of their present social position' (953).

However, an argument for legal control of *adult* hours is made out along the lines of 1832, although now as a purely hypothetical matter. In fact, Mill expressly added in 1862 that he 'certainly should not, in present circumstances, recommend' such legislation; the argument served to illustrate 'the manner in which classes of persons may need the assistance of law, to give effect to their deliberate collective opinion of their own interest, by affording to every individual a guarantee that his competitors will pursue the same course, without which he cannot safely adopt it himself' (958).

Mill's argument has been ridiculed: 'J. S. Mill . . . gravely argued that the competitive market was incapable of providing a reduction in the hours of work even if all the workers wished it – a mistake I am not inclined to excuse simply because so many later economists repeated it' (Stigler, 1975, 42; cf. 1982, 15). But this is not a fair charge. The problem of market failure in fact arises for Mill because not all workers *do* wish the reduction; if they did the market, Mill conceded, might do the job. But the presentation is certainly unclear. The argument initially turns on the proposition (along the lines of the 1832 model) that '[a] workman who refused to work more than nine hours while there were others who worked ten, would either not be employed at all, or if employed, must submit to lose one-tenth of his wages' (*CW*, III, 957). This is extended, however, to allow for a case where 'nearly all' do restrict themselves voluntarily to nine hours; it is conceded that this might indeed be successfully achieved without legislative intervention – although some individuals would doubtless choose to work ten hours obtaining original wage for a nine-hour day plus pay for the tenth hour: 'short hours [become], by spontaneous choice, the general practice, but those who chose to deviate from it having the fullest liberty to do so'.

n'est sacrée que dans ce qui ne regarde, au moins directement, que l'individu, et ne peut être invoqué pour l'exercice illimité d'un pouvoir quelconque sur les autres, dont les abus sont toujours dans le domaine légitime des lois' (21 June 1870, XVII, 1735-6).

Mill was most enthusiastic about prospects for part-time education, drawing on evidence presented in 1861 by Chadwick. The system resulted in 'attainments and intelligence' superior to full-time schooling, an outcome 'so unexpected as to amount to a discovery . . .', and overcame the objections of parents who wished to withdraw their children from school to enter the work force (1 March 1861, XV, 720; see also XV, 733-4, XVI, 1432). Mill may have been overenthusiastic; see McCann (1969), 25-6 for a rather different picture of the half-time system.

That was, in fact, the ideal. Unfortunately, Mill then changed the terms of the case: 'Probably, however, so many would prefer the ten hours' work on the improved terms, that the limitation could not be maintained as a general practice . . . ' (957–8). This may be true, but here the market fails not because not all or even nearly all workers wish a reduction in the hours of work, but because they do not.

More precisely, the nine-hour day can, Mill insisted, be achieved if sufficient numbers demand it – appropriate contraction in labour supply by the group in concert obviously constituting the mechanism. But should large enough numbers then *expand* the labour supply in the expectation of working a ten-hour day *at the higher wage per hour* they will be disappointed. Government intervention 'is required to assure that the reduction in number of hours insisted upon in unison is adhered to by the group. And assuming there is a preference for a nine-hour day on the improved (hourly) terms over a ten-hour day on the original terms this intervention would, as Mill recognized, not be in conflict with individual preferences but rather giving effect to those preferences.

* * *

Mill, like most other classical economists fervently championed the right of workers to combine. 'Laws against combinations of workmen to raise wages . . . exhibit the infernal spirit of the slave master, when to retain the working classes in avowed slavery has ceased to be practicable' (III, 929).[61] The effectiveness of unions is another matter taken up elsewhere (see Chapter 11). It must be recalled too that for Mill freedom of unionization had an educative function – if forbidden, the law might be blamed for low wages even when not the true source: 'Experience of strikes', for example, 'has been the best teacher of the labouring classes on the subject of the relation between wages and the demand and supply of labour: and it is most important that this course of instruction should not be disturbed' (932; cf. V, 427).

Unions had to be voluntary, however, and here arose a role for legislation. Rarely does Mill express himself so strongly as on this issue: 'No severity, necessary to the purpose, is too great to be employed against attempts to compel workmen to join a union, or take part in a strike by threats or violence' (933). On the other hand, '[m]ere moral compulsion, by the expression of opinion, the law ought not to interfere with; it belongs to more enlightened opinion to restrain it, by rectifying the moral sentiments of the people'. Similarly, restrictive practices of various kinds to the

---

61 For a recent discussion of the response by classicists to the combination laws see Grampp (1979); also Robbins (1952), 103f.

end of making work – though very sharply condemned as 'pernicious' and a 'public mischief' by placing 'the energetic and the idle, the skilful and the incompetent', on a level – were also not to be candidates for legislative restriction. Apart from considerations of 'constitutional liberty',[62] the general good required 'that all economical experiments, voluntarily undertaken, should have the fullest licence, and that force and fraud should be the only means of attempting to benefit themselves, which are interdicted to the less fortunate classes of the community' (934).

This theme was consistently maintained.[63] It is restated in 'Thornton on Labour and Its Claims': 'I do not know of anything that ought to be legally interdicted to workmen in combination, except what would be criminal if done by any of them individually, viz. physical violence or molestation, defamation of character, injury to property, or threats of any of these evils' (V, 659).[64] But here Mill himself raises the free-rider issue and uses it to justify unionists' moral pressure on non-members:

As soon as it is acknowledged that there are lawful, and even useful, purposes to be fulfilled by Trades' Unions, it must be admitted that the members of Unions may reasonably feel a genuine moral disapprobation of those who profit by the higher wages or other advantages that the Unions procure for non-Unionists as well as for their own members, but refuse to take their share of the payment, and submit to the restrictions, by which those advantages are obtained . . . All that legislation is concerned with is, that the pressure shall stop at the expression of feeling, and the withholding of such good offices as may properly depend upon feeling, and shall not extend to an infringement, or a threat of infringement, of

---

62 Mill's problem arose from the fact that the restrictive acts in question would not be illegal, however immoral, if practised by *individuals* (934n).

63 'The difference between employers & workpeople which give rise to strikes are, it appears to me, a subject which wholly escapes the control of legislation. I see nothing which law can do in the matter except to protect from violation the equal liberty of all to combine or to refrain from combination' (17 April 1865, XVI, 1034–5). Compulsory arbitration, in the event of non-settlement is also ruled out.

64 Mill's indictment of restrictive practices is strong: 'There must be some better mode of sharing the fruits of human productive power than by diminishing their amount. Yet this is not only the effect, but the intention, of many of the conditions imposed by some Unions on workmen and on employers. All restrictions on the employment of machinery, or on arrangements for economising labour, deserve their censure. Some of the Unionist regulations go even further than to prohibit improvements; they are contrived for the express purpose of making work inefficient; they positively prevent the workmen from working hard and well . . . ' (V, 665). See also the posthumous chapters on Socialism: '[T]he rules of some trade societies actually forbid their members to exceed a certain standard of efficiency, lest they should diminish the number of labourers required for the work; and for the same reason they often violently resist contrivances for economising labour' (V, 742).

any of the rights which the law guarantees to all – security of person and property against violation, and of reputation against calumny (660).

It will be recalled that the same free-rider principle justified for Mill legislative intervention in the matter of hours. To some extent, therefore, union members would be protected by legislation from potentially damaging activity by non-members and rogue members.

We shall see later (p. 897f) that Mill came to condemn the exclusion from unionized trades by skilled workers of new entrants though able to acquire the skill with ease. His change of position reflected a belief that population pressure among the unskilled was easing – an evaluation discernible in the *Principles* as early as 1852. It cannot be ruled out – despite our present discussion – that Mill might have countenanced legal steps against such restrictive practices on the grounds that they constituted (in Adam Smith's words) a 'plain violation of [a] most sacred property' by preventing the free movement of labour. Unfortunately he did not formally address the issue, limiting himself to moral approbation of the practice.

XV COLONIZATION

The same principle as that justifying the regulation of hours explains Mill's support for E. G. Wakefield's scheme relating to the disposal of colonial lands. The scheme, given a prominent place in the discussion of Book I dealing with 'Co-operation, or the Combination of Labour', was designed to secure 'that every colony shall have from the first a town population bearing due proportion to its agricultural, and that the cultivators of the soil shall not be so widely scattered as to be deprived by distance, of the benefit of that town population as a market for their produce' (*CW*, III, 121). The principle is also laid out in our present context with special reference to the social disadvantages of purely private initiative:

This system is grounded on the important principle, that the degree of productiveness of land and labour depends on their being in a due proportion to one another, that if a few persons in a newly-settled country attempt to occupy and appropriate a large district, or if each labourer becomes too soon an occupier and cultivator of land, there is a loss of productive power, and a great retardation of the progress of the colony in wealth and civilization: that nevertheless the instinct (as it may almost be called) of appropriation, and the feelings associated in old countries with landed proprietorship, induce almost every emigrant to take possession of as much land as he has the means of acquiring, and every labourer to become at once a proprietor, cultivating his own land with no other aid than that of his family. If this propensity to the immediate possession of land could be in some degree restrained, and each labourer induced to work a certain number of years on hire before he became a landed proprietor, a perpetual stock of hired labourers could be maintained, available for roads, canals, works of irrigation, &c., and for the establishment and carrying on of the different branches of town industry; whereby the labourer, when he did at last become a landed proprietor, would find his land much more valuable, through access to markets, and facility of obtaining hired labour. Mr. Wakefield therefore proposed to check the premature occupation of land, and dispersion of the people, by putting upon all the unappropriated lands a rather high price, the proceeds of which were to be expended in conveying emigrant labourers from the mother country (III, 958–9; cf. 965).

The *laissez-faire* case against the proposal is firmly refuted. The social, and indeed the (long-term) individual, advantages alluded to above required intervention since 'it can never be the interest of an individual to exercise this forbearance, unless he is assured that others will do so . . . It is the interest of each to do what is good for all, but only if others will do likewise' (959). The argument is, in fact, generalized from the regulation of hours and colonial property to the entire range of penal law: 'Penal laws exist at all, chiefly for this reason – because even an unanimous opinion that a certain line of conduct is for the general interest, does not always make it people's individual interest to adhere to that line of conduct' (960).

It is important to note that Mill championed the Wakefield scheme to the very end, a matter about which there is some confusion in the literature due to a failure to distinguish the proposal to avoid the dispersion of population by putting a price on unoccupied land, from the proposal to use the proceeds to finance further emigration. (Cf. the debate between Kittrell, 1965, 1966, and Winch, 1965, Ch. ix, 1966.) As we shall now show, it was specifically this latter aspect that Mill came to emphasize less as unsupported private emigration became particularly vigorous. But as for the former, Mill's enthusiasm remained throughout unchecked.

Various objections raised by Cairnes to the discussion in the *Principles* of the efficiency gains deriving from 'separation of employments' or the divisions of activity between agriculture and the towns (letter to Mill 29 Nov. 1864, *CW*, III, 1046) were dismissed out of hand by Mill who made no changes to the next (sixth) edition:

On the Wakefield system I scarcely understand your argument. In the supposed case of the settlers, and in every other, I apprehend the separation of employments to be a real cause and indispensable condition of a larger production. It is true that territorial separation of employments, by international trade, often suffices: but the main justification of Wakefield's system is, that this trade does not take effect when families settle, each of them many miles from its neighbour in the wilderness (12 Dec. 1864, XV, 976).

In 1856 he had expressed the opinion that 'the Wakefield system, unpopular as it now is in Australia, & badly as it has been administered in some of the colonies, has been one of the chief causes of their unexplained growth' (29 Sept. 1856, XV, 511). And thirteen years later he reiterated to an Australian correspondent that 'I am, like yourself, in favour of the Wakefield system' (8 May 1869, XVII, 1598).

Colonization was, of course, also approached by Mill from a broader perspective than the disposal of colonial lands. As we know (see above, p. 698) a case is involved (similar to the poor-relief case) where 'acts done by individuals, though intended solely for their own benefit, involve consequences extending indefinitely beyond them, to interests of the nation or of prosperity, for which society in its collective capacity is alone able, and alone bound, to provide' (III, 963). For the permanent interests of the colony was at stake, not merely that of the first settlers, so that the argument could be made for 'placing the enterprise, from its commencement, under regulations constructed with the foresight and enlarged views of philosophical legislators; and the government alone has power either to frame such regulations, or to enforce their observance'. Further still, the implications of colonization extended beyond the colony itself (even from the perspective of its permanent interests) to touch on 'the collective economical interests of the human race'. Here Mill specified that much more was at stake than the relief of population pressure – 'relieving one labour market and supplying another', for efficiency (as well as distribution) had to be considered, namely the 'exportation of labourers and capital from old to new countries; from a place where their productive power is less, to a place where it is greater, [which] increases by so much the aggregate produce of the labour and capital of the world'. Indeed, so productive did he see such ventures to be, relative to the costs entailed, that colonization 'in the present state of the world' was the 'best affair of business, in which the capital of an old and wealthy country can engage'.

These social advantages would not, Mill maintained in the first two editions, be reaped by individual initiative alone: 'It is . . . obvious . . . that Colonization on a great scale can be undertaken, as an affair of business, only by the government, or by some combination of individuals in complete understanding with the government; . . . Emigration on the voluntary principle cannot have any material influence in lightening the pressure of population in the old country, though as far as it goes it is doubtless a benefit to the colony' (964). Even with respect to the relief of population pressure there was, empirically speaking, too little to be hoped for from the initiative of individual emigrants, since those who could afford to leave were drawn not from the mass of very poor but that limited category of small farmers and labourers with savings; '[a]ny considerable emigration of labour', he concluded, 'is only practicable, when its cost is defrayed, or at least advanced, by others than the emigrants themselves'. But to charge prospective employers in the colonies, or to rely on voluntary contributions by individuals or parishes had been tried and found inadequate.[65] A national scheme could, however, assure that emigration would be self-supporting, the costs financed from the very growth in productivity alluded to above:

One of the principle reasons why Colonization should be a national undertaking, is that in this manner alone can emigration be self-supporting. The exportation of capital and labour to a new country being, as before observed, one of the best of all affairs of business, it is absurd that it should not, like other affairs of business, repay its own expenses. Of the great addition which it makes to the produce of the world, there can be no reason why a sufficient portion should not be intercepted, and employed in reimbursing the outlay incurred in effecting it. For reasons already given, no individual, or body of individuals, can reimburse themselves for the expense; the government, however, can. It can take from the annual increase of wealth, caused by the emigration, the fraction which suffices to repay with interest what the emigration has cost. The expenses of emigration to a colony ought to be borne by the colony; and this, in general, is only possible when they are borne by the colonial government (964–5).

Here allusion is again made to Wakefield's plan 'of putting a price on all unoccupied land devoting the proceeds to emigration' (969): 'The self-supporting system of colonization, once established, would increase in efficiency every year; its effect would tend to increase in geometrical progression: for since every able-bodied emigrant, until the country is fully peopled, adds in a very short time to its wealth, over and above his own consumption, as much as would defray the expense of bringing out another emigrant, it follows that the greater the number already sent, the greater number might continue to be sent, each emigrant laying the foundation of a succession of other emigrants at short intervals without fresh expense, until the colony is filled up' (966). A case is also made for the acceleration in the initial stages of the process by loans from the mother country to colonial governments (to be repaid from the proceeds of land sales).[66]

---

65 Prospective employers had no assurance that those whose transport he financed would work for him; and the enforcement of contracts had proved unsatisfactory.

66 Cf. also CW, II, 376 for Mill's support of 'a grant of public money, sufficient to remove at once, and establish in the colonies, a considerable fraction of the youthful agricultural population. By giving the preference, as Mr. Wakefield proposes, to young couples, or when these cannot be obtained, to families with children nearly grown up, the expenditure would be made to go the farthest possible towards accomplishing the end, while the colonies would be supplied with the greatest amount of what is there in deficiency, and here in superfluity, present and prospective labour.'

Mill's position regarding the necessity for state-supported schemes altered over time with his realization that private initiative was proving more effective than he had originally thought. The implication to be drawn from the changes to the chapter on 'grounds and limits of the *Laissez-Faire* principle' itself are, however, restrained. The strong statement that voluntary emigration 'cannot have any material influence' on population pressure is weakened in 1852 to 'rarely has' any material influence with allusion made in 1862 and thereafter to the 'very peculiar circumstances as those which succeeded the Irish famine' (964).[67] A modifying paragraph is also added in 1852 after the general conclusion regarding 'the obligation on government' to adopt a system encouraging emigration 'without cost to the emigrants themselves':

The importance of these considerations, at the present moment, as regards the British islands, is considerably diminished by the unparalleled amount of spontaneous emigration from Ireland; an emigration not solely of small farmers, but of the poorest class of agricultural labourers, and which is at once voluntary and self-supporting, the succession of emigrants being kept up by funds contributed from the earnings of their relatives and connexions who have gone before. While the stream of this emigration continues flowing, as broad and deep as at present, the principal office required from government would be to direct a portion of it to quarters (such as Australia), where, both for local and national interests, it is most of all required, but which it does not sufficiently reach in its spontaneous course (968).

The closing sentence – though not the general reference to the Irish outflow – is replaced in 1857 by reference to 'a large amount of voluntary emigration to the seats of the gold discoveries'. Mill then steps back: 'But the stream of both these emigrations has already considerably slackened, and there are indications that the aid of government in a systematic form, and on the self-supporting principle, is again becoming necessary to keep the communication open between the hands needing work in England, and the work which needs hands elsewhere.' Yet this is still not the end of the story, for in 1865 Mill further modified his formulation, referring to a 'partial revival' of the Irish (voluntary) outflow and implied some doubt regarding the need for state intervention by replacing the reference to the renewed need for government aid by a more qualified expression – 'it is not certain' that government aid 'will not again become necessary . . .'

That by 1865 (though not yet by 1857) a change had indeed occurred in Mill's evaluation in the need for government intervention is confirmed

---

67 In this edition Mill also deleted a passage alluding to the unsuitability of the Irish for 'colonization, as the exclusive remedy' (II, 376).

by the insertion of a paragraph into the discussion of 'remedies for low wages . . .' (II, Ch. xiii) touching on the implications of cheap transport and improved knowledge. These advances had 'opened up a spontaneous emigration from these islands . . . which does not tend to diminish, but to increase; and which, without any national measure of systematic colonization, may prove sufficient to affect a material rise of wages in Great Britain, as it has already done in Ireland, and to maintain that rise unimpaired for one or more generations' (II, 378; see below, pp. 893–4, for the full passage). The correspondence of 1867 and 1868 contains the same message, and there can then be little doubt as to Mill's late position.

XV MONOPOLY AND THE STATE

Considerable attention is given by Mill to government as a source of monopolistic restrictions: 'Governments . . . are oftener chargeable with having attempted, too successfully, to make things dear, than with having aimed by wrong means at making them cheap', the latter an allusion to efforts at price control. Conferring a monpoly 'upon a producer or dealer, or upon a set of producers or dealers not too numerous to combine, is to give them the power of levying any amount of taxation on the public, for their individual benefit, which will not make the public forego the use of the commodity' (*CW*, III, 927–8; cf. II, 233).[68] Mill conceded that the more numerous and widely scattered the producers the less the damage of protective measures since their combination into a formal monopoly is impeded. But even so monopoly losses can exist, since 'the competition is not so active among a limited as among an unlimited number. Those who feel assured of a fair average proportion in the general business, are seldom eager to get a larger share by foregoing a portion of their profits. A limitation of competition, however partial, may have mischievous effects quite disproportioned to the apparent cause' (928). It does not seem accurate

---

68 Formally Mill like other classicists (including Ricardo) used the term 'monopoly' for situations where there is no tendency of the market price to cost price due to constraint on supply irrespective of numbers (e.g. II, 491). But our concern now is with one or a few sellers.

  Stigler (1982) makes the point that like (Adam Smith), Mill 'saw no way for the state to support competition other than by failing to create monopolies' (39). And to 'the scepticism of the English classical school [including Mill's] about the possibility of monopoly', Viner (1960) attributed 'in significant part the absence of any anti-monopoly legislation in nineteenth-century England' (66). More attention should, however, be paid both to the enthusiastic championship by Smith and Mill of an institutional framework which would positively promote competition; and to the fact that the state was active in countering the adverse effects of monopoly (Crouch, 1967, 212). For a recent discussion of Mill on preferable firm structure in a contemporary context apart from the monopoly issue see Amsler *et al.* (1981).

to ascribe to Mill the opinion that a monopoly 'which was not "perfect" in the modern sense could not yield appreciable monopoly revenue' (Viner, 1960, 66). Moreover, the social consequences of constraints on competition include not merely the supernormal profits paid for by consumers – a static transfer; Mill pointed also to net losses in efficiency from a dynamic perspective:

When relieved from the immediate stimulus of competition, producers and dealers grow indifferent to the dictates of their ultimate pecuniary interest; preferring to the most hopeful prospects, the present case of adhering to routine. A person who is already thriving, seldom puts himself out of his way to commence even a lucrative improvement, unless urged by the additional motive of fear lest some rival should supplant him by getting possession of it before him (CW, III, 928).[69]

Government as a source of monopoly is by no means the whole story. There were important cases where, independently of this source, competition among the few or monopoly ruled – usually entailing joint-stock organization. It cannot fairly be said of Mill that he (in common with other members of the English classical school) 'extended . . . to almost the whole range of industry and trade Smith's argument re the corn-trade that the size of the task, the number of persons involved, and their dispersion over space, made the establishment of an enduring monopoly a practical impossibility' (Viner, 1960, 65).

Let us consider first the problem of joint-stock organization. From the perspective of managerial efficiency there was no presumption in favour of private initiative: 'Government management is, indeed, proverbially jobbing, careless, and ineffective, but so likewise has generally been joint-stock management' (CW, III, 954). Indeed, the advantage lay with government since 'against the very ineffectual security afforded by meetings of shareholders, and by their individual inspection and inquiries, may be placed the greater publicity and more active discussion and comment, to be expected in free countries with regard to affairs in which the general government takes part'.

Yet there is great hesitancy to give the green light to actual state management. There remained, on balance, overriding objections:

69 In the edition of 1852 Mill retracted certain negative pronouncements regarding competition in the previous editions – a matter of profound significance for our later discussion of economic organization – and similarly emphasized that in consequence of 'the natural indolence of mankind' or the 'tendency to be passive, to be the slaves of habit', competition, while perhaps not the 'best conceivable stimulus . . . , is at present a necessary one, and no one can forsee the time when it will not be indispensable to progress' (795).

These reasons have been already pointed out: the mischief of overloading the chief functionaries of government with demands on their attention, and diverting them from duties which they alone can discharge, to objects which can be sufficiently well attained without them; the danger of unnecessarily swelling the direct power and indirect influence of government, and multiplying occasions of collision between its agents and private citizens; and the inexpediency of concentrating in a dominant bureaucracy, all the skill and experience in the management of large interests, and all the power of organized action, existing in the community . . . (955).

Mill's hesitancy is patently clear, for the first reason given had, in fact, been earlier played down (940–1, see above, p. 689) as an argument against government provision.

For all that, Mill did insist firmly on a degree of government regulation – here his presumption that joint-stock organization is peculiarly characteristic of non-competitive structure comes to the fore – and this puts a different complexion on the issue:

[A]lthough, for these reasons, most things which are likely to be given tolerably done by voluntary associations, should, generally speaking, be left to them; it does not follow that the manner in which those associations perform their work should be entirely uncontrolled by the government. There are many cases in which the agency, of whatever nature, by which a service is performed, is certain, from the nature of the case, to be virtually single; in which a practical monopoly, with all the power it confers of taxing the community, cannot be prevented from existing.

Even where 'voluntary agency' is in order, 'the community needs some other security for the fit performance of the service than the interest of the managers; and it is the part of government, either to subject the business to reasonable conditions for the general advantage [including the fixing of maximum charges] or to retain such power over it, that the profits of the monopoly may at least be obtained for the public. This applies to the case of a road, a canal, or a railway' (956).

This matter had been discussed earlier in the *Principles* during the analysis of scale economies:

When, in any employment, the régime of independent small producers has either never been possible, or has been superseded, and the system of many work-people under one management has become fully established, from that time any further enlargement in the scale of production is generally an unqualified benefit. It is obvious, for example, how great an economy of labour would be obtained if London were supplied by a single gas or water company instead of the existing plurality. While there are even as many as two, this implies double establishments of all sorts, when one only, with a small increase, could probably perform the whole operation equally well . . . [Moreover] where competitors are so few, they always end by agreeing not to compete. They may run a race of cheapness to ruin a new candidate, but as soon as he has established his footing they come to terms with him. When, therefore, a business of real public importance can only be carried on advantageously upon so large a scale as to render the liberty of competition almost illusory, it is an unthrifty dispensation of the public resources that several costly sets of arrangements should be kept up for the purpose of rendering to the community this one service. It is much better to treat it at once as a public function; and if it be not such as the government itself could beneficially undertake, it should be made over entire to the company or association which will perform it on the best terms for the public (II, 141–2).

Thus there should be one railway line permitted between any two places which would operate under State regulation, while other (existing) lines might be expropriated, with compensation, on grounds of public utility.

Mill failed to specify the full range of applicability of regulation of this order as distinct from actual state operation. The provision of gas and water services – much emphasized as instances where 'though perfect freedom is allowed to competition, none really takes place, and practically they are found to be even more irresponsible, and unapproachable by individual complaints, than the government' (III, 955–6) – and the paving and cleansing of streets were in fact said to be best undertaken by government. This, however, referred to local government (the operation funded from the rates) doubtless because the various disadvantages listed earlier of direct government agency apply to a much lesser degree at this level.[70] But Mill did not positively rule out state *ownership* of 'public works' of a national character: '[T]he state may be the proprietor of canals and railways without itself working them' for 'they will almost always be better worked by means of a company, renting the railway or canal for a limited period from the state'.

Mill's distrust of centralized activity shines through the entire discussion.[71] There were solutions to the problem of 'monopoly' (and the

---

70 This requires qualification. Mill was also suspicious of local authority – unless under central supervision: 'It is only affairs of a simple character and on a humble scale, not exceeding the levying of a local rate, and the application of it to purposes strictly predetermined, that can with impunity be left to the unassisted and unchecked management of the representatives of a narrow locality' ('Centralisation', 1862, XIX, 606).

   Mill's early knowledge of London's water supply derived apparently from the (Poor Law Commission) *Report into the sanitary condition of the labouring population of Great Britain* (1842). See Mill's enthusiastic letter regarding the substance of a version read in draft (to Chadwick, April 1842, XIII, 516).

71 This was not always clear to his readers (cf. letter to Cairnes, 22 April 1872, XVII, 1888: 'One gets accustomed to strange things, but to find myself held up as an apostle of centralization was indeed something unexpected.') For a more recent example of this misunderstanding, see Hutchison (1953), 53.

efficiency of management) falling far short of recourse to central provision.[72] It is true that in his famous letter of 1852 to the Metropolitan Sanitary Association Mill recommended the consolidation of the London water supply under a central board. But this was because there existed no London government: 'were there a General Council, or Board of Administration for all London, invested with power over every branch of its local affairs, a place in that Council or Board would, like a place in the Municipal Commission of Paris, be sought and diligently filled by persons of high character and standing, as men not only of business capacity, but of general instruction and cultivation. The contrast between such persons and those who usually compose parish vestries . . . is too obvious to require comment' (V, 435). Within the ideal situation – and Mill later campaigned in Parliament for the establishment of Municipal Corporations in the Metropolis (XVI, 1502) – there would be need for an accredited representative of central government on any municipal board: 'I conceive it to be one of the duties of the general government to hold the local government to the performance of its duties' (436). This, however, was not enough for Chadwick who championed a greater degree of centralization.[73]

XVI PATENT PROTECTION

As noted earlier 'monopoly' was said to impede the adoption of new technology; evidently by not encouraging monopoly, the state avoided an impediment to innovation. But Mill justified the need for the monopoly advantage accorded by patents to 'an originator of an improved process'. The patent merely 'postpon[es] a part of the increased cheapness which the public owe to the inventor, in order to compensate and reward him for the service' (CW, III, 927). The essence of the allowance lies in the temporary character of the protection, without which only the 'very opulent or the public-spirited' would undertake inventive effort and 'bring [an] idea into a practical shape'.

Direct government grants are said to provide a less desirable alternative in a passage which casts much light upon Mill's general perspective – his reliance, as far as possible, on market signals emanating from the consumer:

72 Mill to Chadwick 28 Oct. 1864, XV, 961. On the details of the London Water episode and the implications for Mill's position regarding the role of the state, see Harris, 1959, and especially Schwartz (1966).

73 Cf. II, 142, III, 956 regarding temporary monopoly concessions to railway companies and the like. For a critical analysis of Mill's general contention regarding the economic role of patents see Plant (1974).

This has been done in some instances, and may be done without inconvenience in cases of very conspicuous public benefit; but in general an exclusive privilege, of temporary duration, is preferable; because it leaves nothing to any one's discretion; because the reward conferred by it depends on the invention's being found useful, and the greater the usefulness the greater the reward; and because it is paid by the very persons to whom the service is rendered, the consumers of the commodity (928–9).

If, however, patents are excluded the next best alternative would be a small temporary tax on users of the product for the inventor's benefit.

In the edition of 1862 Mill added a most strongly worded criticism of contemporary opponents of patents: 'I have seen with real alarm several recent attempts, in quarters carrying some authority, to impugn the principle of patents altogether; attempts which, if practically successful, would enthrone free stealing under the prostituted name of free trade, and make the men of brains, still more than at present, the needy retainers and dependents of the men of money-bags' (929). In 1865 he remarked further, that, while the patent laws required reform, 'in this case, as well as in the closely analogous one of Copyright, it would be a gross immorality . . . to set everybody free to use a person's work without his consent, and without giving him an equivalent'. To the argument deriving from expediency is thus added that of justice.

XVII   SUMMARY: PROGRESS AND THE STATE

British intellectual opinion, Mill wrote in 1862 – and this reflects a belief that there had been a desirable change since mid-century – had happily struck a sensible balance on the matter of state intervention. This is brought out very clearly during the course of his strong condemnation of French centralization extending to literature and science with its inevitable encouragement of place-seekers:

It is from a sense of these evils, fully as much as from the fortunate national habit of distrusting the government, that nearly all English thinkers regarding the presumption as always unfavourable to any extension of governmental functions, and hold as a rooted conviction that not only are there many of the greatest public concerns from which, as soon as the nation has emerged from the swathing bands of infancy, the State should hold its hand, but that even where no general principle forbids its interference, nothing should be done by it except what has been clearly proved to be incapable of being done by other means . . . there is a strong persuasion that what can be tolerably done in any other way, had better be done in that way than by government. State action is regarded as an extreme remedy, to be reserved, in general for great purposes; for difficult and critical moments in the course of affairs, or concerns too vital to be trusted to less responsible hands. Few Englishmen, we believe, would grudge to the government, for a time, or permanently, the powers necessary to save from serious injury any great national interest; and equally few would claim for it the power of meddling with anything, which it could let alone without touching the public welfare in any vital part. And though the line thus indicated neither is, nor can be, very definitely drawn, a practical compromise of this sort between the State and the individual, and between central and local authority, is, we believe, the result which must issue from all prolonged and enlightened speculation and discussion on this great subject ('Centralisation', 1862, XIX, 609–10).

Practice, Mill suggests, was equally well balanced. There was no presumptive case for intervention. National grants for education were introduced after private organizations were shown to be inadequate; the regulation of emigrant ships resulted from scandals under the unregulated system; and intolerable abuses of the poor laws led to the creation of the Poor Law Board (608–9).

The paper on 'Centralisation' also includes a critique of Dupont-White's argument that State intervention in the sense of administrative authority and control, especially from the centre, was 'an unavoidable consequence and indisputable instrument of progress' (601). That the introduction of a railway system or of joint-stock organization or of new banking instruments required new legislation did not necessarily imply increased executive power: 'no discretionary authority, still less control, still less obligation to ask permission of the executive for every new undertaking'. The creation of inspectorates (schools, factories, endowed charities) also did not imply increased administrative control. This extension of government, Mill did not oppose: 'it does not, or at least need not, weaken the stimulus to individual effort', for it did not 'prescribe how individuals shall carry on their own business for their own profit', but rather protected individuals against others 'from whom it would be either difficult or impossible for them to protect themselves' (602).

Economic growth as such, however, did call for new legislation – for example, to prevent water pollution. 'As respects such new laws, and as much new agency as is needed to ensure their observance, the function of the State naturally does widen with the advance of civilisation. But this part of the case, though sometimes undervalued, is seldom, by English thinkers, denied: and to this extent only can English practice be cited in evidence that State intervention is, or ought to be, a growing fact' (602).

Intervention justified specifically by the principle of indiscriminate benefit, on the other hand, did not, as Dupont-White maintained, necessarily expand with progress.[74] For progress, while 'constantly requiring new things to be done, . . . also multiplies the cases in which individuals or associations are able and willing to do them gratuitously (603). Mill referred here to public-spirited individuals who, in Britain (unlike France where they were 'almost entirely stifled' by centralization) had formed animal-protection, lifeboat, expeditionary, philanthropic and educational societies. (As for education, private munificence had long been at work by way of endowment.) There was no reason to believe 'that the province of government in works of public utility receives accessions at one end, greater than what private zeal and benevolence subtracts from it at the other'. On the contrary:

All the functions of government which do not consist in affording legal protection [even Empire building] are in reality greatest when civilisation is at the lowest; when the poverty of individuals, their ignorance, and inaptness for combination, leaves society no resource but State action for anything requiring large means, co-operation of numbers, or elevated views. There was a time when neither roads, nor canals, nor drainage, nor irrigation, nor banks, nor schools, nor encouragement of arts, letters, or science, could possibly exist except as the work of the government. In an advanced stage of civilisation these things are better done by voluntary associations, or by the public indiscriminately; though we do not deny that, when so done, they create a necessity for new laws, inasmuch as all new good which arises in the world must be expected to bring new evil as its accompaniment (603–4).

Individual capacity and efficiency were, in fact, 'blunted' by dependency. Centralized agency had blunted the initiative of Frenchmen who could only respond to authority. That was the consequence of the French pattern. The solution was not more government – as Dupont-White maintained – but less: 'They are in a state of prostration from which they cannot rise without help. Let help be given to them. They require to be urged, not only by the government, but by everyone else to whom they look up. But urged to what? To let the government act for them? No; but to act for themselves. This is, at least, the ultimatum to which it should be endeavoured to bring them' (605).

74 'Our author makes a stand on another doctrine, quite unassailable in principle – that the State may be required to render all such services as, being necessary or important to society, are not of a nature to remunerate any one for their performance. Thus, the State, or some public authority, must build and maintain light-houses and lay down buoys, it being impossible to make those who benefit by these essential requisites of navigation pay any compensation for their use' (602–3).

Mill, it is true, frequently complained of the 'decay of individual energy' as a concomitant of contemporary progress. This in fact was a major theme of his 1836 paper on 'Civilization'. But it was not inevitable. The solution was seen to lie in 'more perfect combination among individuals' and in reformed education:

Are the decay of individual energy, the weakening of the influence of superior minds over the multitude, the growth of charlatanerie, and the diminishing efficacy of public opinion as a restraining power, – are they the price we necessarily pay for the benefits of civilization; and can they only be avoided by checking the diffusion of knowledge, discouraging the spirit of combination, prohibiting improvements in the arts of life, and repressing the further increase of wealth and of production? Assuredly not. Those advantages which civilization cannot give – which in its uncorrected influence it has even a tendency to destroy – may yet coexist with civilization; and it is only when joined to civilization that they can produce their fairest fruit . . . The evils are, that the individual is lost and becomes impotent in the crowd, and that individual character itself becomes relaxed and enervated. For the first evil, the remedy is, greater and more perfect combination among individuals; for the second, national institutions of education, and forms of polity, calculated to invigorate the individual character ('Civilization', XVIII, 135–6).

But what precisely did Mill have in mind by these recommendations?

The matter is elaborated in a discussion of De Tocqueville (1840).

The point is there again made that business activity encouraged mere selfishness: 'The private money-getting occupation of almost every one is more or less a mechanical routine; it brings but few of his faculties into action, while its exclusive pursuit tends to fasten his attention and interest exclusively upon himself, and upon his family as an appendage of himself; making him indifferent to the public, to the more generous objects and the nobler interests, and, in his inordinate regard for his personal comforts, selfish and cowardly' (168–9). Clearly for Mill genuine individuality was a matter of self-fulfilment *which allows for a sense of social responsibility*. One solution would be found in a range of social occupations – provided, for example, by the electoral and jury systems: 'whatever might be the case in some other constitutions of society, the spirit of a commercial people will be, we are persuaded, essentially mean and slavish, wherever public spirit is not cultivated by an extensive participation of the people in the business of government in detail; nor will the desideratum of a general diffusion of intelligence among either the middle or lower classes be realized, but by a corresponding dissemination of public affairs'. As for the role of education:

Let the idea take hold of the more generous and cultivated minds, that the most serious danger to the future prospects of mankind is in the unbalanced influence of the commercial spirit – let the wiser and better-hearted politicians and public teachers look upon it as their most pressing duty, to protect and strengthen whatever, in the heart of man or in his outward life, can form a salutary check to the exclusive tendencies of that spirit – and we should not only have individual testimonies against it, in all the forms of genius, from those who have the privilege of speaking not to their own age merely, but to all time; there would also gradually shape itself forth a national education, which, without overlooking any other of the requisites of human well-being, would be adapted to this purpose in particular (198).

There can also be no doubt that co-operative commercial ventures were encouraged from the same perspective as co-operative political ventures (see below, p. 909).[75]

Thus far there are no problems. Yet we find Mill complaining in On Liberty that there is 'scarcely any outlet for energy in this country except business' 272). 'The greatness of England is now all collective' he proceeded; 'individually small, we only appear capable of anything great by our habit of combining; and with this our moral and religious philanthropists are perfectly contented'. Mill could not here have had in mind 'combinations' of the kind championed in 1836 and elaborated in 1840, for the co-operative ventures he there called for were designed precisely to encourage genuine individuality. The context refers rather to 'tendencies of the time [which] cause the public to be more disposed than at most former periods to prescribe general rules of conduct, and endeavour to make every one conform to the approved standard'; public opinion was becoming intolerant 'of any marked demonstration of individuality' (271). Mill had particularly harsh words for 'the English philanthropists . . . industriously working at . . . making a people alike, all governing their thoughts and conduct by the same maxims and rules . . .' (273).

However, what were the 'tendencies' of the time which encouraged such 'despotism of custom and conformity'? Mill refers (274–5) to political change which promoted egalitarianism in the broadest sense; educational change which brought people 'under common influences and [gave] them access to the general stock of facts and sentiments'; changes in communication

75 Cf. the emphasis on association in Mill's 'mix of the elements of power' in Petrella (1970).

allowing increased personal contact and easier physical relocation; and the extension of commerce and manufacturing which diffused 'the advantages of easy circumstances [opening] all objects of ambition, even the highest, to general competition'. Above all stood the 'ascendency of public opinion', itself a broad consequence of increased equality:

A more powerful agency than even all these, in bringing about a general similarity among mankind, is the complete establishment, in this and other free countries, of the ascendancy of public opinion in the State. As the various social eminences which enabled persons entrenched on them to disregard the opinion of the multitude, gradually become levelled; as the very idea of resisting the will of the public, when it is positively known that they have a will, disappears more and more from the minds of practical politicians; there ceases to be any social support for nonconformity – any substantive power in society, which, itself opposed to the ascendancy of numbers, is interested in taking under its protection opinions and tendencies at variance with those of the public.

Now several of these tendencies, it will be noted, are implicit in progress itself. And Mill gave a strong warning of the immediacy of the problem:

The combination of all these causes forms so great a mass of influences hostile to Individuality, that it is not easy to see how it can stand its ground. It will do so with increasing difficulty, unless the intelligent part of the public can be made to feel its value – to see that it is good there should be differences, even though not for the better, even though, as it may appear to them, some should be for the worse. If the claims of Individuality are ever to be asserted, the time is now, while much is still wanting to complete the enforced assimilation. It is only in the earlier stages that any stand can be successfully made against the encroachment. The demand that all other people shall resemble ourselves, grows by what it feeds on. If resistance waits till life is reduced *nearly* to one uniform type, all deviations from that type will come to be considered impious, immoral, even monstrous and contrary to nature. Mankind speedily become unable to conceive diversity, when they have been for some time unaccustomed to see it.

Indeed, because 'the only unfailing and permanent source of improvement is liberty, since by it there are as many possible independent centres of improvement as there are individuals' (272) progress itself was threatened. Progress carried within itself the seeds of its own destruction.

Much of this scarcely sits well beside Mill's praise (at precisely the same time) of contemporary British opinion and practice, particularly his contention that the general respect for individuality grows with progress. Evidently Mill's vision of the contemporary scene was a mixed one. It can perhaps be said that while there were dangers to progress these were not yet seen to be inevitable: 'we are progressive as well as changeable, we continually make new inventions in mechanical things, and keep them until they are again superseded by better' (273).[76] It was uniformity of taste that most upset him and which, if not resisted, might ultimately prove disastrous.

76 There is a further complexity. Progress ceases, we read, when a people 'ceases to possess individuality'; but regarding Europe (unlike China) Mill also wrote that 'the despotism of custom with which these nations are threatened is not exactly stationariness'. For *change* itself was not necessarily precluded by the force of custom; uniformity in matters of taste was consistent with change.

TEN

Economic policy: social organization

I   INTRODUCTION

We have argued earlier that Mill at no time envisaged Ricardian deductive methodology as in conflict with the principles of institutional and behavioural relativity. There is nothing 'remarkable' about his continued championship of such methodology despite his profound awareness of the 'provisional' nature of the axiomatic framework. Ricardian procedure was, moreover, fully consistent with a progressive attitude towards social reform; indeed, the fundamental theorem on distribution, as we know, provided a splendid reply to opponents of the union movement.

There remains to discuss a feature of the record that further elucidates Mill's continued adherence to the framework relevant to a capitalist-exchange system throughout his major text. His objectives in writing the *Principles* were, without question, broader than those of Ricardo, yet greater attention by far was paid to an analysis of capitalism than to alternative social arrangements – the theoretical core certainly relates to a competitive-capitalist framework. This requires explanation.

Pertinent here is Mill's self-confessed failure to come to grips with the problem of 'ethology' – the 'science' of human character formation, which he had originally hoped would provide the key to a *general* sociological theory. Without this body of knowledge, political economy, however important, was necessarily relegated to a 'secondary' plane because of the constrained axiomatic basis. This perspective is clearly intimated in the letter to Comte of April 1844 describing the projected *Principles* wherein Mill alludes to his intention to bring the problem into conspicuous relief by distinguishing the laws of production 'common to all industrial societies' from those of production and exchange which are specific to particular social arrangements

(3 April 1844, *CW*, XIII, 626).[1] Two years later, when the project was well under way, Mill reiterated that political economy could make but 'secondary progress' while a broader comprehension of the laws of human behaviour was still a matter for the future:

Quoiqu'il en soit, je tends de plus en plus à faire de l'étude des fonctions intellectuelles et morales ma principale occupation philosophique, en la menant toutefois, comme vous le conseillez, de pair avec les spéculations sociales, car je reconnais pleinement qu'on ne peut pas connaître l'homme individuel en fesant définitivement abstraction de la société, dont il est indispensable de savoir apprécier philosophiquement les diverses influences. Toutefois je persiste à croire que la sociologie, comme science, ne peut plus faire aucun progrès capital sans s'appuyer sur une théorie plus approfondie de la nature humaine. La force de circonstances peut amener des améliorations pratiques importantes, mais la théorie sociologique ne me paraît comporter actuellement que des progrès secondaires, tant qu'on ne s'occupe pas en même temps de perfectionner la théorie intellectuelle et morale de l'homme. Je tâche de payer mon tribut à ces progrès secondaires par le traité d'économie politique dont je m'occupe et qui s'avance rapidement. Après cela je destine mes principaux efforts à cette autre grande tentative et je me propose bien de ne négliger aucun genre d'études qui puisse me rendre plus propre à la poursuivre (26 March, 1846, 613).

But all this is very general. More important is Mill's consciousness of the limitations of a practical order upon the scope of profound social reorganization as an immediate prospect. We touch now on the complex matter of Mill's approach to Socialism. Moreover, it emerges that by his famous self-identification as a Socialist Mill did not intend to relegate competition and self-interest to the dust heap. The tools of analysis pertinent for the study of capitalism, not to speak of the methodology of economic theory, would still retain their relevance.

In his *Autobiography* Mill explained that during the 1820s, as a loyal Benthamite, he had insisted merely upon the mitigation of the defects of contemporary institutions – calling, for example, for the abolition of primogeniture and entails: 'The notion that it was possible to go further than this in removing the injustice – for injustice it is, whether admitting of a complete remedy or not – involved in the fact that some are born to riches and the vast majority to poverty, I then reckoned chimerical; and

---

1 Ethology was formally defined as 'la théorie de l'influence des diverses circonstances extérieures, soit individuelles, soit sociales, sur la formation du caractère moral et intellectuel' (30 Oct. 1843, XIII, 604). It will be recalled that Mill took Comte himself to task in 1848 for a total failure to appreciate 'the laws of human character formation' (above, pp. 91, 173).

only hoped that by universal education, leading to voluntary restraint on population, the portion of the poor might be made more tolerable. In short, I was a democrat, but not the least of a Socialist' (I, 239). Even after his rejection of the doctrine outlined in his father's *Essay on Government*, envisaged as a general 'scientific theory', he still supported representative democracy given the contemporary conditions – 'I was as much as ever a Radical and Democrat for Europe, and especially for England'. His enthusiasm for Owenite, St Simonian and other 'anti-property doctrines' did not reflect a belief that those doctrines were 'true'; neither did he desire that 'they should be acted on'. It reflected no more than a wish to see the upper classes frightened into seeing to it that the poorer classes became better educated – that they 'might be made to see that they had more to fear from the poor when uneducated than when educated' (179).[2] Similarly:

The scheme gradually unfolded by the St. Simonians, under which the labour and capital of society would be managed for the general account of the community, every individual being required to take a share of labour, either as thinker, teacher, artist, or producer, all being classed according to their capacity, and remunerated according to their work, appeared to me a far superior description of Socialism to Owen's. Their aim seemed to me desirable and rational, however their means might be inefficacious; and though I neither believed in the practicability, nor in the beneficial operation of their social machinery, I felt that the proclamation of such an ideal of human society could not but tend to give a beneficial direction to the efforts of others to bring society, as at present constituted, nearer to some ideal standard (175).[3]

According to the account in the *Autobiography* there occurred a significant change in attitude during the 1840s attributed to the influence of Harriet Taylor.[4] On the one hand, Mill explained, 'we were much less democrats'

2 Mill's friend John Austin also 'rejoiced in [the progress of Socialism] as the most effectual means of compelling the powerful classes to educate the people, and to impress on them the only real means of permanently improving their material condition, a limitation of their numbers'. But (apparently unlike himself) Austin was not 'at this time fundamentally opposed to Socialism in itself as an ultimate result of improvement' (*ibid.*, 151).

See also the revealing letter to Gustave d'Eichthal, 8 Oct. 1829, where, after paying warm tribute to Comte's *Système de Politique Positive*, Mill warned against 'mistaking the perfect coherence and logical consistency of his system, for truth' (above, p. 90).

3 Robbins (1952), 147, has written of Mill in the early 1830s as being 'decidedly under the influence of this quite definitely socialist school of thought. But on Mill's own account this influence at the time was a highly qualified one. It was only in the 1840s that serious questions regarding Mill's adherence to 'socialism' arose.

4 'In this third period (as it may be called) of my mental progress [late 30s, early 40s], which now went hand in hand with hers, my opinions gained equally in breadth and

than in the past 'because so long as education continues to be so wretchedly imperfect, we dreaded the ignorance and especially the selfishness and brutality of the mass'. But at the same time,

our ideal of ultimate improvement went far beyond Democracy, and would class us decidedly under the general designation of Socialists. While we repudiated with the greatest energy that tyranny of society over the individual which most Socialistic systems are supposed to involve, we yet looked forward to a time when society will no longer be divided into the idle and the industrious; when the rule that they who do not work shall not eat, will be applied not to paupers only, but impartially to all; when the division of the produce of labour, instead of depending, as in so great a degree it now does, on the accident of birth, will be made by concert, on an acknowledged principle of justice; and when it will no longer either be, or be thought to be, impossible for human beings to exert themselves strenuously in procuring benefits which are not to be exclusively their own, but to be shared with the society they belong to (239).

It will be noted that even this declaration represents 'socialism' as 'an ideal of ultimate improvement', not an immediate prospect. Repeatedly in this very context Mill warned against premature enthusiasm: 'The social problem of the future we considered to be, how to unite the greatest individual liberty of action, with a common ownership in the raw material of the globe, and an equal participation of all in the benefits of combined labour.' But 'we had not the presumption to suppose that we could already foresee by what precise form of institutions these objects could most effectually be attained, or at how near or how distant a period they would become practical'. What was required, at the least, was a profound change of attitudes which would be accomplished 'only by slow degrees, and a system of culture prolonged through successive generations', and this because of the weakness of the motive force of 'interest in the common good' and 'the deep-rooted selfishness which forms the general character of the existing state of society'. These considerations, Mill explained,

depth, I understood more things, and those which I understood before, I now understood more thoroughly. I had now completely turned back from what there had been of excess in my reaction against Benthamism' (*ibid.*, 237).

At the height of his reaction against Benthamism, on this account, Mill had been content merely to 'second the superficial improvements which had begun to take place in those common opinions [of "society" and "the world"]', although his actual convictions differed: 'I was much more inclined, than I can now approve', he confessed, 'to put in abeyance the more decidedly heretical part of my opinions, which I now look upon as almost the only ones the assertion of which tends in any way to regenerate society. But in addition to this, our opinions were far *more* heretical than mine had been in the days of my most extreme Benthamism'. (*ibid.*, 237–8).

774 THE ECONOMICS OF JOHN STUART MILL

did not make us overlook the folly of premature attempts to dispense with the inducements of private interest in social affairs, while no substitute for them has been or can be provided: but we regarded all existing institutions and social arrangements as being (in a phrase I once learned from Austin) 'merely provisional,' and we welcomed with the greatest pleasure and interest all socialistic experiments by select individuals (such as the Co-operative Societies), which, whether they succeeded or failed, could not but operate as a most useful education of those who took part in them, by cultivating their capacity of acting upon motives pointing directly to the general good, or making them aware of the defects which render them and others incapable of doing so (241).

Furthermore, in describing Harriet Taylor's specific contribution, Mill emphasized her practical judgment: 'What was abstract and purely scientific was generally mine; the properly human element came from her: in all that concerned the application of philosophy to the exigencies of human society and progress, I was her pupil, alike in boldness of speculation and cautiousness of practical judgement . . . But while she . . . rendered me bolder in speculation on human affairs, her practical turn of mind, and her almost unerring estimate of practical obstacles, repressed in me all tendencies that were really visionary' (257).

It is clear that Mill took pains to qualify his enthusiasm for a profound social transformation on practical grounds. Indeed the correspondence between Mill and Harriet Taylor regarding the chapter 'On Property' – the proposed draft for the second edition – suggests a yet more qualified view on Mill's part than on Harriet's regarding the fundamental changes in attitudes which any successful reorganization of social arrangement along socialistic lines would require: 'I cannot persuade myself', Mill wrote to Harriet Taylor in 1849, 'that you do not greatly overrate the ease of making people unselfish' (21 March 1849, XIV, 19). Mill in the *Autobiography* emphasized Harriet Taylor's particular contribution to long-run principles – 'the region of ultimate aims' – and matters involving 'the immediately useful and practically attainable'; the 'intermediate' range of problems was his forte although even here, he asserts, she provided 'wise scepticism' putting him on his guard (I, 197). But when Mill writes to her that she greatly overrated 'the ease of making people unselfish' he raises doubts about this evaluation of her 'wise scepticism' and practicality, a comment adding to the impressive body of evidence suggesting how careful we must be not to exaggerate her influence.[5]

The premature character of detailed debate regarding institutional change is discernible also in correspondence with Comte. Here Mill wrote of the

---

5 See on this matter Bain (1882), 171–2, Pappé (1960), Robson (1968), 50–68. Packé (1954) takes a different view of Harriet's importance, as does Hayek (1951), 17. On Mill's general 'hard-headedness', see Viner (1958), 330.

'spiritual development' (the demographic dimension is what above all he had in mind) required before major institutional changes of a specific order could be recommended:

J'apprécie convenablement la sage réserve dont vous avez usé en écartant comme prématurée toute discussion immédiate sur la plupart des institutions politiques proprement dites, au moins dans l'ordre temporel. Vous avez très bien fait sentir que la régénération sociale dépend maintenant de l'essor spirituel, ce qui devient au reste de plus en plus évident aux esprits éclairés par l'impuissance aujourd'hui constatée de toutes les tentatives théoriques et pratiques qu'on fait depuis bientôt cent ans pour renouveler l'état de l'humanité par les seules institutions. Je crois même cette heureuse révolution spéculative plus avancées dans ce pays-ci que partout ailleurs, désenchantés comme nous sommes des institutions soi-disant libres à raison d'une plus intime familiarité pratique. Chez nous aujourd'hui les prolétaires croient presque seuls à l'efficacité réformative [sic] des institutions démocratiques, encore les chefs les plus considérés du mouvement politique prolétaire, parmi lesquels il y en a de très recommandables, mènent aujourd'hui habituellement de front avec leurs projects politiques, des idées de moralisation et de culture intellectuelle pour les masses populaires, dirigées à la vérité jusqu'ici, comme il n'en pouvait être autrement, par une philosophie métaphysique et négative (23 Oct. 1842, XIII, 553–4).

One becomes soon accustomed to read Mill's letters to Comte with a jaundiced eye. But precisely the same sentiments were expressed to others at the same time, and they point in the same direction. Regarding the probable consequence of the abolition of the Corn Laws Mill wrote: 'these things, important as they are, do not occupy so much of my thoughts as they once did; it is becoming more and more clearly evident to me that the mental regeneration of Europe must precede its social regeneration & also that none of the ways in which that mental regeneration is sought, Bible Societies, Tract Societies, Puseyism, Socialism, Chartism, Benthamism &c. will do, though doubtless they have all some elements of truth & good in them. I find quite enough to do in trying to make up my own mind as to the course which must be taken by the present great transitional movement of opinion & society. The little which I can dimly see, this country even less than several other European nations is as yet ripe for promulgating' (19 Dec. 1842, ibid., 563–4).

It transpires that Mill's ideal for the future – evidently the rather distant future – entailed transition from the worker-capital relationship, a relationship of 'dependency', to a system of worker co-operatives; his second-best solution was a system of profit-sharing. Socialism in the modern sense of the term is not in question. Moreover, throughout the discussion of these (and various other) institutional proposals there is conspicuous a deep appreciation of the effectiveness of competition from the perspectives both of resource allocation and of incentive particularly in 'the discovery and adoption of new methods', and even (to some extent) from that of equity. The emphasis on competition throughout the theoretical sections of the *Principles* notwithstanding the (temporary) capitalist environment, is not difficult to appreciate even when we have in mind his longer-term ideals.

II ASPECTS OF THE INDICTMENT OF CAPITALISM

Mill prefaced his remarks in 1852 and thereafter in the famous chapter 'On the Probable Futurity of the Labouring Classes' with the qualification that references to 'a labouring class' did not entail a *permanent* class: 'I do not recognize as either just or salutary, a state of society in which there is any "class" which is not labouring, any human being, exempt from bearing their share of the necessary labours of human life, except those unable to labour, or who have fairly earned rest by previous toil' (*CW*, III, 758). If this is taken seriously, and it surely must be for Mill writes of the existence of a non-labouring class as 'the great social evil', it has profound implications for his ideal state – although the reforms he had in mind for the immediate future still allowed receipts from bequests sufficient to permit a 'moderate independence' and certainly countenanced interest earnings, by and large retaining class-structured social arrangements (755; cf., II, 224–6).

The insertion of 1852 does not, however, constitute a change of position. From the first Mill had insisted that the 'parental' or 'patriarchal' relation characterizing a class-organized society – an allusion to the so-called 'theory of dependence and protection' – was archaic, and crumbling:

The working classes have taken their interests into their own hands, and are perpetually showing that they think the interests of their employers not identical to their own, but opposite to them . . . the poor will no longer [not much longer; 1857] accept morals and religion of other people's prescribing. I speak more particularly of this country, especially the town population, and the districts of the most scientific agriculture, or the highest wages, Scotland and the North of England. Among the more inert and less modernized agricultural population of the southern counties, it might be possible for the gentry to retain, for some time longer, something of the ancient deference and submission of the poor, by bribing them with high wages and constant employment; by insuring them support, and never requiring them to do anything which they do not like (762).[6]

6 See also 'On Labour and its Claims' (1845, IV, 379–80). For Adam Smith's objections to class organization, see Hollander (1972), 150–1.

The battle was a losing one, for to guarantee wages and employment required both population constraint and the enforcement of labour.

Indeed, Mill's remarks on capitalistic class relationships as expressed in 1848 are extraordinarily hostile. He could not conceive, he then wrote, how persons 'who habitually reflect on the condition and tendencies of modern society' could believe 'that the majority of the community will for ever, or even for much longer, consent to hew wood and draw water all their lives in the service and for the benefit of others; or can doubt, that they will be less and less willing to co-operate as subordinate agents in any work, when they have no interest in the result . . .' (1013–14). Rising living standards under capitalism did not provide the solution – on the contrary, the social pressures were greatest in relatively prosperous areas; and in general, 'notwithstanding the effect which improved intelligence of the working classes, together with just laws, may have in altering the distribution of the produce to their advantage, I cannot think that they will be permanently contented with the condition of labouring for wages as their ultimate state' (766). For 'to work at the bidding and for the profit of another, without any interest in the work – the price of their labour being adjusted in hostile competition, one side demanding as much and the other paying as little as possible – is not, even when wages are high, a satisfactory state to human beings of educated intelligence, who have ceased to think themselves naturally inferior to those whom they serve'. A working-class status might be tolerable in 'a new country rapidly increasing in wealth and population' (such as Australia and North America) where upward mobility to the employing class was an option; but 'something else is required when wealth increases slowly, or has reached the stationary state, when positions, instead of being more mobile, would tend to be much more permanent than at present, and the condition of any portion of mankind could only be desirable, if made desirable from the first'.

All of this must be seen within a broader conception of a 'tendency of society towards the disuse of the relation of hiring and service' (766), which is closely related to the notion of progress, entailing an increasing degree of that independency or self-reliance so much emphasized later in *On Liberty*. But there was certainly nothing automatic about the tendency, although Mill was hopeful: 'The poor have come out of leading-strings, and cannot any longer be governed or treated like children. To their own qualities must now be commended the care of their destiny . . . The prospect of the future depends on the degree in which they can be made rational beings.' Progress 'must always be slow';[7] but 'spontaneous education' was proceeding 'in the minds of the multitude, which may be greatly accelerated and improved by artificial aids' (763). There is also at least a hint that unless an alternative

7 In 1852: 'has hitherto been and still is slow'.

to the contemporary social organization were found there would be upheaval – 'the value of this "organization of industry," for healing the widening and embittering feud between the class of labourers and the class of capitalists, must, I think, impress itself by degrees on all who habitually reflect on the condition and tendencies of modern society' (1013).[8]

In 1852 the formulation is altered in various details[9] although the basic hostility to capitalistic class relations remains intact and is in some respects strengthened. It is, as always, 'the moral aspect' that is emphasized,[10] but now supplemented by a cataloguing of various disadvantages even from the employer's perspective, particularly the dishonesty, apparently inevitable under given conditions, of the typical employee:

The relation is nearly as unsatisfactory to the payer of wages as to the receiver. If the rich regard the poor as, by a kind of natural law, their servants and dependents, the rich in their turn are regarded as a mere prey and pasture for the poor; the subject of demands and expectations wholly indefinite, increasing in extent with every concession made to them, while the return given in the shape of service is sought to be reduced to the lowest minimum. It will sooner or later become insupportable to the employing class, to live in close and hourly contact with persons whose interests and feelings are in hostility to them. Capitalists are almost as much interested as labourers in placing the operations of industry on such a footing, that those who labour may feel the same interest in the work they perform, which is felt by those who labour for themselves (767; cf. 783).

The precise stimulus for the adoption of this line is apparently contemporary opposition to piece-work about which Mill disclaimed in strong terms: 'One of the most discreditable indications of a low moral condition given of late by part of the English working classes, is the opposition to piece-work . . . But dislike to piece-work in itself, except under mistaken notions, must be dislike to justness and fairness; a desire to cheat, by not giving work in proportion to pay. Piece-work is the perfection of contract; and contract, in all work, and in the most minute detail – the principle of so much pay for so much service, carried out to the utmost extremity – is the system, of all others, in the present state of society and degree of civilization, most favourable to the worker; though most unfavourable to the non-worker

---

8 On at least one occasion (13 April 1847) Mill declared himself in favour of 'a violent revolution' for 'England has never had any general break-up of old associations & hence the extreme difficulty of getting any ideas into its stupid head' (XIII, 713).

9 The substance, though not the precise formulation, of the observation regarding small upward mobility in a slowly growing economy is retained.

10 'The aim of improvement should be not solely to place human beings in a condition in which they will be able to do without one another, but to enable them to work with or for one another in relations not involving dependence' (768).

who wishes to be paid for being idle' (783). Mill's objections are further reinforced in 1857 by rewording: 'The total absence of regard for justice and fairness in the relations between the two, is as marked on the side of the employed as on that of the employers. We look in vain among the working classes in general for the just pride which will choose to give good work for good wages; for the most part, their sole endeavour is to receive as much, and return as little in the shape of service, as possible' (767).[11] Again, it is not low real earnings and poor working conditions as such that alone can account for Mill's criticism of the employee-employer relationship.

It would, however, be totally misleading to play down Mill's strong condemnation of contemporary income distribution in the chapter 'On Property' – the 'miseries and inequities of a state of much inequality of wealth' (II, 202). There is too the charge formulated in a review of 1851 of Newman's *Lectures on Political Economy* summarizing his position, namely that 'the distinction between rich and poor, so slightly connected as it is with merit and demerit, or even with exertion and want of exertion in the individual, is obviously unjust; such a feature could not be put into the rudest imaginings of a perfectly just state of society; the present capricious distribution of the means of life and enjoyment, could only be defended as an admitted imperfection, submitted to as an effect of causes in other respects beneficial' (V, 444).

Yet we must proceed carefully. For in the review of Newman, Mill seems to declaim against competition as such, alluding – with an eye to rivalry between workers in depressing wages – to 'the physical and moral evils which are not only consistent with, but directly grow out of the facts of competition and individual property . . .' (442), and to competition 'as arming one human being against another, making the good of each depend upon the evil to others, making all who have anything to gain or lose live as in the midst of enemies' (444); and denying that the competitive wage can be identified with the just wage:

If 4*s.* are the fit and proper wages for a day's digging, it is an evil that competition should reduce wages below that amount. Mr. Newman may say that there is no mode of deciding what are the fit and proper wages; but he cannot pretend that competition decides it. The question, then, is resolved into the possibility of determining by law, what wages society can afford to give to those who do its work. Now, what there is to be said as to the difficulty of deciding this, or of enforcing the decision, does not apply to socialists; in their communities no such difficulties would exist; there would be no doubt either what could be given, or that it would be given. Socialists do not say that competition can be dispensed with in society

---

11 But in the 1869 'Chapters on Socialism' (V, 742) Mill conceded much of the case against piece-work from the worker's perspective (see below, pp. 796–8).

as it is. But they say it is a great defect in the constitution of society, that it can only work by such an instrument' (447).[12]

It may be that these aspects of the reply to Newman are instances of Mill's propensity to express himself rather too strongly in the cut and thrust of debate. For even in this review he stated that 'the benefits that flow from private property and competition are, like the evils, too obvious to be missed' (442); his purpose to cut Newman down to size governed the weighting of the argument. And that this is indeed so is suggested by closer analysis of the textual variations to the chapter 'On the Probable Futurity of the Labouring Classes' for the 1852 edition of the *Principles*. For the comment regarding 'hostile competition' in the criticism of the labour-capital relation (above, p. 777 regarding III, 766) is deleted; and a strongly worded case against the notion of competition as 'pernicious' in and of itself is introduced:

I agree . . . with the Socialist writers in their conception of the form which industrial operations tend to assume in the advance of improvement; and I entirely share their opinion that the time is ripe for commencing this transformation, and that it should by all just and effectual means be aided and encouraged. But while I agree and sympathize with Socialists in this practical portion of their aims, I utterly dissent from the most conspicuous and vehement part of their teaching, their declaration against competition. With moral conceptions in many respects far ahead of the existing arrangements of society, they have in general very confused and erroneous notions of its actual working; and one of their greatest errors, as I conceive, is to charge upon competition all the economical evils which at present exist. They forget that wherever competition is not, monopoly is; and that monopoly, in all its forms, is the taxation of the industrious for the support of indolence, if not of rapacity. They forget, too, that with the exception of competition among labourers, all other competition is for the benefit of the labourers, by cheapening the articles they consume; that competition even in the labour market is a source not of low but of high wages, wherever the competition *for* labour exceeds the competition *of* labour, as in America, in the colonies, and in the skilled trades; and never could be a cause of low wages, save by the overstocking of the labour market; while, if the supply of labourers is excessive, not even Socialism can prevent its remuneration from being low' (794–5).

Mill reiterates his concession that there was some legitimacy to the Socialist case against competition 'as a source of jealousy and hostility among those

---

12 What is meant by a 'fit and proper wage for a day's digging' is not clarified and this Mill realized; but as, we shall see, an index would be provided by the alternative earnings available to labour in co-operative ventures when such opportunities existed on a large enough scale.

engaged in the same occupation'. But the advantages were not to be despised, considering now competition in its *dynamic* role as a source of progress:

It is the common error of Socialists to overlook the natural indolence of mankind; their tendency to be passive, to be the slaves of habit, to persist indefinitely in a course once chosen. Let them once attain any state of existence which they consider tolerable, and the danger to be apprehended is that they will thenceforth stagnate; will not exert themselves to improve, and by letting their faculties rust, will lose even the energy required to preserve them from deterioration. Competition may not be the best conceivable stimulus, but it is at present a necessary one, and no one can forsee the time when it will not be indispensable to progress (795).

Feugueray (1851) is here cited approvingly first to the effect that contemporary evils flowed not from competition but from 'l'exploitation du travail par le capital, et la part énorme que les possesseurs des instruments prélèvent sur les produits' – an allusion, it appears, not to the payment of interest as such but the return to property unjustly distributed – and secondly regarding the positive role of competition 'en ce qui concerne le développement des facultés individuelles, et le succès des innovations'.

It should be emphasized that the modification to the 'Futurity' chapter are not a reflection of a new position. The same allowances had appeared already in earlier editions in 'On Property' (985–6; see below, p. 802). Mill was merely tidying up to avoid the unintended impression of a perniciousness from labour's perspectives inherent in competition itself.[13]

The position then from the outset was that competition can act to the benefit of labour as well as to its detriment depending upon the state of the labour market; and that competition, given the going patterns of behaviour, was indispensable from a dynamic perspective – as a discovery process. But there is one conspicuous feature of the 1851 review of Newman that Mill held to – that the competitive wage was not the just wage. This vitally important fact emerges in a letter of 1861:

I shd not be sincere with you if I allowed you to suppose . . . that I look upon questions of wages as capable of being settled in the way of arbitration, on grounds of equity. The insuperable difficulty is that there being no *principle* of equity to rest the settlement upon, any decision must be arbitrary, dependent on the direction of the judge's sympathies. That the workmen should not starve may be said to

---

13 Stigler (1949), 1, writes of Mill's having 'conceded every claim of the communists and attributed grotesque deficiencies to capitalism'. Similarly, for von Mises, 'Mill is the great advocate of socialism' (1978), 195. Here we have a grotesque overstatement indeed. For a balanced perspective on this issue, and on the general theme of the present chapter, see Schwartz, (1972), ch. 7.

be equitable, & also that the employers should get some profit. But between these limits I do not see what standard of equity can possibly be laid down. As long as the employers & their families are able to live better, & expend more on themselves than the labourers & their families, it may always be said that wages are not what they ought equitably to be. I can conceive Socialism, in which the division of the produce of labour is made among all, either according to the rule of equality (Communism) or according to any other *general* rule which may be considered more just than absolute equality. But under a system of private property in past accumulations in which no general rule can be laid down, I think that to give any one the power of deciding according to his own views of equity without a general rule would only perpetuate & envenom instead of healing the quarrel between capital & labour. The only thing which people will in these circumstances submit to as final, is the law of necessity, that is, the demand & supply of the market, *tested* (when not otherwise known) by the result of a strike. All that I consider practicable in the present state of society is to strengthen the weaker side in the competition, which can only be done by the prudence, forethought, wise restraint, & habit of cooperation, of the working people themselves (to S. Paull, 23 Nov. 1861, XV, 749).

Clearly Mill was aware that the competitive labour market might generate rising wages – that is frequently insisted upon as we have seen. The point now made is that the equilibrium wage emerging in the market is in no way a just wage, and this largely because the contemporary distribution of property governing the framework of the market was itself not established on equitable principles. The competitive outcome was acceptable *faute de mieux*, and viewed as such by general opinion. This perspective, Mill also makes clear, legitimized steps 'to strengthen the weaker side in the competition' – and here one must keep in mind both his support of unions and property-reform proposals – a general conclusion strongly stated in the 1869 review of 'Thornton on Labour and its Claims' (V, 658). (Mill's position that the competitive outcome in the wage bargain is not necessarily a just outcome is paralleled by the same position in the context of land tenure and the rent bargain under the cottier system; II, 312, 317; also 328 [III, 994] cited below, p. 802.)

It must be clarified that what has been said applies to the general wage. The structure of wages as determined in an effectively operating competitive system is another matter; as we shall often find Mill championed the outcome from the perspective of justice.[14]

In the posthumous 'Chapters on Socialism' (also written in 1869) Mill makes out an extraordinary sharp set of charges against contemporary capitalism but once again the focus is on social relations of

---

14 Cf. Smith's position that there is no trade off between efficiency and equity discussed by Buchanan (1978), Phelps-Brown (1976).

dependency and the lack of distributive justice not on competition as such:

Notwithstanding all that has been done, and all that seems likely to be done, in the extension of franchises, a few are born to great riches, and the many to a penury, made only more grating by contrast. No longer enslaved or made dependent by force of law, the great majority are so by force of poverty; they are still chained to a place, to an occupation, and to conformity with the will of an employer, and debarred by the accident of birth both from the enjoyments, and from the mental and moral advantages, which others inherit without exertion and independently of desert. That this is an evil equal to almost any of those against which mankind have hitherto struggled, the poor are not wrong in believing. Is it a necessary evil? (V, 710).

Mill thus accepted the factual charge 'that the condition of numbers in civilised Europe, and even in England and France, is more wretched than that of most tribes of savages who are known to us' (713); and that poverty in no way reflected 'desert', rewards being divorced from merit or exertion (715), for it was not the case that everyone 'willing to undergo a fair share of . . . labour and abstinence could attain a fair share of the fruits' (714). On the contrary – and as so often brought out in the *Principles* – '[t]he reward, instead of being proportioned to the labour and abstinence of the individual, is almost in an inverse ratio to it; those who receive the least, labour and abstain the most'. Birth, accident and opportunity were the ruling determinants, so that '[e]ven the idle, reckless, and ill-conducted poor, those who are said with most justice to have themselves to blame for their condition, often undergo much more and severer labour, not only than those born to pecuniary independence, but than almost any of the more highly remunerated of those who earn their subsistence; and even the inadequate self-control exercised by the industrious poor costs them more sacrifice and more effort than is almost ever required from the more favoured members of society' (714). The Socialist contention that much 'crime, vice and folly' resulted from poverty in contemporary conditions was also accepted (715).

However, here Mill drew the line. For he rejected the charge against contemporary competition ('individualism') that 'under the present system hardly any one can gain except by the loss or disappointment of one or of many others', a position leading critics such as Louis Blanc to the 'prediction' of secularly falling real wages and others (such as Considérant, the Fourierist) to that of an increasing tendency towards the failure of small firms. These charges, which he found exaggerated and misleading, were traced to 'ignorance of economic facts, and of the causes by which the economic phenomena of society as it is, are actually determined' (727).

Regarding earnings, even population pressure was no longer an 'irrepressable tendency' and an 'increasing evil' considering the acceleration of capital accumulation, easier emigration and increased prudence (728) – an optimistic viewpoint of the facts of great import since, as we shall presently see, he had in the *Principles* conceded that Socialist arrangements might have the advantage in this regard. Similarly, there was no evidence of increasing monopolization. Mill summarized his position in a remarkable passage insisting on the fact of rising living standards, and moreover, on the relatively limited effect which even a full-fledged redistribution of income would have in raising the lower paid:

It seemed desirable to begin the discussion of the Socialist question by these remarks in abatement of Socialist exaggerations, in order that the true issues between Socialism and the existing state of society might be correctly conceived. The present system is not, as many Socialists believe, hurrying us into a state of general indigence and slavery from which only Socialism can save us. The evils and injustices suffered under the present system are great, but they are not increasing; on the contrary, the general tendency is towards their slow diminution. Moreover the inequalities in the distribution of the produce between capital and labour, however they may shock the feeling of natural justice, would not by their mere equalisation afford by any means so large a fund for raising the lower levels of remuneration as Socialists, and many besides Socialists, are apt to suppose (736).

As for errors of theory, Mill presented (consistently with the *Principles*) a most forceful defence of competition pointing to its potential in assuring low prices and high wages to the benefit of labour:

Next, it must be observed that Socialists generally, and even the most enlightened of them, have a very imperfect and one-sided notion of the operation of competition. They see half its effects, and overlook the other half; they regard it as an agency for grinding down every one's remuneration – for obliging every one to accept less wages for his labour, or a less price for his commodities, which would be true only if every one had to dispose of his labour or his commodities to some great monopolist, and the competition were all on one side. They forget that competition is a cause of high prices and values as well as of low; that the buyers of labour and of commodities compete with one another as well as the sellers; and that if it is competition which keeps the prices of labour and commodities as low as they are, it is competition which prevents them from falling still lower . . . But if, disregarding for the time that part of the effects of competition which consists in keeping up prices, we fix our attention on its effect in keeping them down, and contemplate this effect in reference solely to the interest of the labouring classes, it would seem that if competition keeps down wages, and so gives a motive to the labouring classes to withdraw the labour market from the full influence of competition, if they can, it must on the other hand have credit for keeping down the prices of the articles on which wages are expanded, to the great advantage of those who depend on wages (729–30).

The ellipses in the foregoing extract cover a proposition of profound significance (albeit not Mill's primary concern in this particular context) regarding the role of competition, when operating effectively, in assuring a *just* structure of wages and prices: 'In truth, when competition is perfectly free on both sides, its tendency is not specially either to raise or to lower the price of articles, but to equalise it; to level inequalities of remuneration, and to reduce all to a general average, a result which, in so far as realised (no doubt very imperfectly), is, on Socialistic principles, desirable'.[15] In this latter respect, as well as the notion of a general level of wages which though not 'just' was to be accepted subject to intervention, there is little to distinguish the 'Chapters on Socialism' from earlier pronouncements. If there is a difference it lies in the very forceful denial of a falling wage trend but, as we shall see, there are earlier indications of this perspective in the *Principles* and in correspondence.

There remains one important concession to the Socialists emphasized in the posthumous chapters that requires mention: 'Competition is the best security for cheapness, but by no means a security for quality . . . On this point . . . Socialists have really made out the existence not only of a great evil, but of one which grows and tends to grow with the growth of population and wealth' (731–2). As the matter is expressed elsewhere in the same year: 'Even in commerce properly so called – the legitimate province of self-interest – where it is enough if the ruling motive is limited by simple honesty, . . . the vastness of the field, the greatness of the stakes now played for, and the increasing difficulty to the public in judging rightly of transactions or of character, are making the principle of competition bring forth a kind of effects, the cure of which will have to be sought somewhere else than in the corrective influence of competition itself' ('Endowments', V, 625). But, again, Mill's concern with probity and the need for correction were of long standing.

Our task now is to consider Mill's proposals for dealing with the various indictments made against capitalism.

---

15 The general perspective also governs Mill's approach to women's earnings. It was the competitive market mechanism upon which Mill relied for at least part of the solution to relatively low women's earnings. For one of his concerns was with the fact that 'occupations which law and usage make accessible to them are comparatively so few' (II, 395); 'For improving the condition of women, it should . . . be an object to give them the readiest access to independent industrial employment, instead of closing, either entirely or partially, that which is already open to them' (III, 953) – an allusion to restrictions on women factory workers.

III THE COMMUNIST SOLUTION

The *Autobiography* speaks of the so-called new approach to Socialism as reflected 'less clearly and fully in the first edition [1848], rather more so in the second [1849], and quite unequivocally in the third [1852]' (*CW*, I, 241). Thus the tone of the first edition was rather hostile, whereas that of the third edition represented a 'more advanced' opinion, a progression accounted for by a greater receptivity of the public to such novel ideas following the French Revolution of 1848 and to further investigation of Mill's own part, especially of continental literature. Let us then evaluate the accuracy of this *ex post* account to discern the extent to which the doubts expressed even to Harriet in 1849 (not to speak of those in correspondence with Comte in 1842) were in fact dissipated.

A key chapter for us is 'On Property'. Here (II, 202–3, 210) critics of the contemporary system who championed communal arrangements are classified as Communists, favouring 'the entire abolition of private property' and 'absolute equality' both of income distribution and the allocation of labour in the community (the Owenites *inter alia*); and as Socialists, allowing inequality of various kinds (though on the basis of some principle of justice rather than 'accident'), i.e. 'retaining more or less of the incentives to labour derived from private pecuniary interest', rather than relying on 'the point of honour of industry', and even, in some cases, private ownership of capital in the community.

In the original account given in the *Principles* Mill ruled out as quite unpractical the case of a single 'Co-operative Society' incorporating an entire country, as distinct from a number of small (largely self-contained) Communist communities, each satisfying the conditions of 'community of property and equal distribution of the produce', and linked by 'a Congress to manage their joint concerns':

Supposing that the soil and climate were tolerably propitious, and that the several communities, possessing the means of all necessary production within themselves, had not to contend in the general markets of the world against the competition of societies founded on private property, I doubt not that by a very rigid system of repressing population, they might be able to live and hold together, without positive discomfort. This would be a considerable improvement, so far as the great majority are concerned, over those existing states of society in which no restraint at all is placed on population, or in which the restraint is very inadequate (III, 975).

But the prospects were poor. In addition to the matter of efficacious population control and a presumed isolation from competition from capitalistic systems – a most revealing presumption in itself – 'the standard of industrial duty . . . would be fixed extremely low':

The common operations of industry are the reverse of stirring and stimulating, and the only direct result of extra exertion would be a trifling addition to the common stock shared out among the mass. Mankind are capable of a far greater amount of public spirit than the present age is accustomed to suppose possible. But if the question were that of taking a great deal of personal trouble to produce a very small and unconspicuous public benefit, the love of ease would preponderate. Those who made extra exertions would expect and demand that the same thing should be required from others and made a duty; and in the long run, little more work would be performed by any, than could be exacted from all: the limit to all irksome labour would be the amount which the majority would consent to have made compulsory on themselves (976).

Mill was not at all optimistic, having before him the spectacle of contemporary conditions where, although 'the intensity of competition and the exclusive dependence of each on his own energies tend to give a morbid strength to the industrial spirit, [the majority] are almost everywhere indolent and unambitious; content with little, and unwilling to trouble themselves in order to make it more'.

There was more hope for invention than regular industrial operations (because it was *per se* pleasant) but very little for innovation which involved 'dull and toilsome' tasks. Moreover, innovation required

means and appliances which, in a society so constructed, no one would possess of his own. The many and long-continued trials by which the object is at last attained, could only be made by first persuading the majority that the scheme would be advantageous: and might be broken off at the very time when the work approached completion, if the patience of the majority became exhausted. We might expect therefore that there would be many projects conceived, and very few perfected; while the projects being prosecuted; if at all, at the public expense and not at the projector's, if there was any disposition to encourage them, the proportion of bad schemes to good would probably be even greater than at present (977).

There was also the supposed 'equality'. Formal equality of income was achievable easily enough, but not equality of labour. By what criterion were hours of different occupations to be equated, since the pricing mechanism relied upon in the market system would be absent? (However weak the current operation of the mechanism there was yet hope for improvement.) The dilemma might, in principle, be resolved by abandoning specialization entirely, each working in turn on all varieties of work – but with disastrous effects on productivity, not to speak of the gross injustice involved in neglecting differential strengths, intelligences, temperaments and so forth.

Assuming, however, these obstacles overcome, what would be the positive advantages of a communistic society? The manuscript and first editions play down the outcome and in strong words. The passage is a splendid summary of what Mill himself considered to be the key desiderata of a good society either for its own sake or as conditions for 'mental and moral progress' – enjoyment of the fruits of personal effort, freedom of choice and action, independence, and variety of situation and means:

Those who have never known freedom from anxiety as to the means of subsistence, are apt to overrate what is gained for positive enjoyment by the mere absence of that uncertainty. The necessaries of life, when they have always been secure for the whole of life, are scarcely more a subject of consciousness or a source of happiness than the elements. There is little attractive in a monotonous routine, without vicissitudes, but without excitement; a life spent in the enforced observance of an external rule, and performance of a prescribed task: in which labour would be devoid of its chief sweetener, the thought that every effort tells perceptibly on the labourer's own interests or those of some one with whom he identifies himself; in which no one could by his own exertions improve his condition, or that of the objects of his private affections; in which no one's way of life, occupations, or movements, would depend on choice, but each would be the slave of all: a social system in which identity of education and pursuits would impress on all the same unvarying type of character, to the destruction of that multiform developement of human nature, those manifold unlikenesses, that diversity of tastes and talents, and variety of intellectual points of view, which by presenting to each innumerable actions that he could not have conceived of himself, are the great stimulus to intellect and the mainspring of mental and moral progression (978n).

And here the main outcome of the later *On Liberty* is formulated in summary: 'The perfection of social arrangements would be to secure to all persons complete independence and freedom of action, subject to no restriction but that of not doing injury to others. But the scheme which we are considering abrogates this freedom entirely, and places every action of every member of the community under command' (978).

This summary appears also (with some small modification) in the second edition of 1849, as well as the substance of the extract which precedes it. But the reformulation no longer plays down the advantages of a high income, pointing rather to its attainability within the private enterprise system. The case for the latter is effectively strengthened by the weighting of argument:

On the Communistic scheme, supposing it to be successful, there would be an end to all anxiety concerning the means of subsistence; and this would be much gained for human happiness. But it is perfectly possible to realize this same advantage in a society grounded on private property; and to this point the tendencies of political speculation are rapidly converging. Supposing this attained, it is surely a vast advantage on the side of the individual system, that it is compatible with a far greater degree of personal liberty.

In both editions Mill conceded that the majority of factory workers under contemporary capitalism suffered many of the disadvantages attributed to communism – monotony, perhaps greater and longer monotony (and longer hours); small choice of occupation and location; a dependency 'on the will of others', no less than in 'any system short of actual slavery'; and little incentive in the case of day labourers or fixed-salary recipients who because they work 'for the gain of others, not for their own . . . have no interest in doing more than the smallest quantity of work which will pass as a fulfilment of . . . their engagement' (979).

As for the latter objection, a solution could be found in the extension of piece-working where technically practical, and of opportunities for promotion from the ranks even for day labourers who prove themselves meritorious. The other objections Mill conceded, although as we have noted, he had already spoken of hopes for the future within capitalism from extensions of 'popular instruction'. But that is not the end of the matter. Mill states a belief that 'the condition of the operatives in a well-regulated manufactory, with a great reduction of the hours of labour and a considerable variety of the kind of it, is very like what the condition of all would be in a Socialist community' (980). This, he explains in 1848, was the most to be hoped for in such a community since 'the majority would not exert themselves for any thing beyond this, and . . . unless they did, nobody else would', so that life would settle into 'one invariable round'. To assure these standards would, however, require population control – *public regulation* since under Communism prudential restraint would be precluded. But with the same degree of restraint the lowest paid in a competitive system could enjoy these same standards, without, however, precluding the further progress of individuals (in real earnings and in freedom) who exerted themselves differentially. And precisely here lay the advantage of capitalism:

if we suppose an equal degree of regulation to take place under the present system, either compulsorily, or, what would be so much preferable, voluntarily; a condition at least equal to what the Socialist system offers to all, would fall to the lot of the least fortunate, by the mere action of the competitive principle. Whatever of pecuniary means or freedom of action any one obtained beyond this, would be so much to be counted in favour of the competitive system. It is an abuse of the principle of equality to demand that no individual be permitted to be better off than the rest, when his being so makes none of the others worse off than they otherwise would be (980).

This is a striking formulation of Mill's conception of what equality should and should not entail.

* * *

The Preface to the third edition explains the rewriting of the chapter 'On Property' for that edition, as an attempt to assure against the possible impression that he intended to condemn Socialism [Communism] 'regarded as an ultimate result of human progress' (xciii).[16] On that matter, he now clarified, the only important objection was 'the unprepared state of mankind in general, and of the labouring classes in particular; their extreme unfitness at present for any order of things, which would make any considerable demand on either their intellect or their virtue'. The object of reform – the quite practical object – 'should be to fit mankind by cultivation, for a state of society combining the greatest personal freedom with that just distribution of the fruits of labour, which the present laws of property do not profess to aim at'. Beyond those reforms, however, little could yet be said: 'Whether, when this state of mental and moral cultivation shall be attained, individual property in some form (though a form very remote from the present) or community of ownership in the instruments of production and a regulated division of the produce, will afford the circumstances most favourable to happiness, and best calculated to bring human nature to its greatest perfection, is a question which must be left, as it safely may, to the people of that time to decide. Those of the present are not competent to decide it.' Nothing in all this adds to what Mill had concluded in 1848 and 1849.

There is also a remarkably revealing letter where Mill, writing to a German translator and editor of an earlier edition of his *Principles*, again objects to a misunderstanding regarding his original intentions and explains the recasting of the chapters on 'Property' and 'Futurity':

I only regret that your time & pains were not bestowed on the edition which is

16 That Mill feared he had been misunderstood emerges in a letter of Nov. 1848, (XIII, 740–1) regarding a commendatory notice appearing in the *North American Review*: '[The reviewer] gives a totally false idea of the book and of its author when he makes me a participant in the derision with which he speaks of Socialists of all kinds and degrees. I have expressed temperately and argumentatively my objections to the particular plans proposed by Socialists for dispensing with private property; but on many other important points I agree with them, and on none do I feel towards them anything but respect, thinking, on the contrary, that they are the greatest element of improvement in the present state of mankind. If the chapter in which I mention them had been written after instead of before the late revolutions on the Continent I should have entered more fully into my opinions on Socialism and have done it much more justice.' On the import of the letter as an index of Mill's motivation for the third edition see Robbins (1952), 167–8.

now about to go to press & which I have not only revised throughout but have entirely recast several important chapters . . . The progress of discussion & of European events has entirely altered the aspect of the questions treated in those chapters; the present time admits of a much more free & full enunciation of my opinions on those subjects than would have had any chance of an impartial hearing when the book was first written; & some change has also taken place in the opinions themselves. I observe that in your preface you recommend the book to your readers as a refutation of Socialism: I certainly was far from intending that the statement it contained of the objections to the best known Socialist schemes should be understood as a condemnation of Socialism regarded as the ultimate result of human improvement, & further consideration has led me to attach much less weight than I then did even to those objections, with one single exception – the unprepared state of the labouring classes & their extreme moral unfitness at present for the rights which Socialism would confer & the duties it would impose (18 March 1852, XIV, 85).

Are there, however, any *substantive* modifications in the body of the work between 1849 and 1852? It seems not, a conclusion which must be carefully substantiated.

In the third edition, allusion is once again made to the possible objection that in a system 'of community of property and equal distribution of the produce' – the Communist alternative – there would be little motive to effort. And again this argument is countered by the observation that the same objection applied to day wages under the existing arrangements: 'I am not undervaluing the strength of the incitement given to labour when the whole or a large share of the benefit of extra exertion belongs to the labourer. But under the present system of industry this incitement, in the great majority of cases, does not exist' (204). Mill hints that the advantage might be with Communistic labour since '[the] neglect by the uneducated classes of labourers for hire, of the duties which they engage to perform, is in the present state of society most flagrant', so that presuming universal education under Communism, the general standard would rise to that achieved already by salaried officials on fixed salary – admittedly not 'the maximum of zeal' (205). But any weighing of considerations is in favour of Communism in formal rather than substantive terms, since Mill must have realized that his readers could counter by the obvious insistence – his own insistence in so many other contexts – that day labour must be supposed superseded by piece-work, labour mobility improved, and universal education presumed within capitalism for a valid comparison to be made. (He himself made the latter point explicitly only a few pages later.)

The resounding assertion that 'mankind are capable of a far greater amount of public spirit than the present age is accustomed to suppose possible' reappears in the edition of 1852, but with altered implication.

It is now implied more positively that the prospects under Communism of encouraging 'the public interest' in individuals were promising – 'since all the ambition, and the bodily and mental activity, which are now exerted in the pursuit of separate and self-regarding interests, would require another field of employment, and would naturally find it in the pursuit of the general benefit of the community'. Much weight is placed also on the force of public opinion both as a deterrent against negligence and a positive stimulus. But though the weighting now favoured Communism, Mill none the less still left the issue quite open: 'To what extent . . . the energy of labour would be diminished by Communism, or whether in the long run it would be diminished at all, must be considered for the present an undecided question.'

As for population control, the advantage was now said to lie with Communism. Prudential restraint would be irrelevant since employment was assured to all, but public opinion (supplemented if necessary by penalties) would act in its place against 'selfish intemperance' responsible for reduced standards for all – and recognized as such, there being no employers or social injustices to blame (206). But this concession was withdrawn almost immediately, as we shall see, when attention is drawn to a reformed capitalism.

There is also the matter of allocating labour between occupations. While in 1849 the balance was formulated against the experiment this is no longer so: 'these difficulties, though real, are not insuperable. The apportionment of work to the strength and capacities of individuals, the mitigation of a general rule to provide for cases in which it would operate harshly, are not problems to which human intelligence, guided by a sense of justice, would be inadequate'. At all events 'the worst and most unjust arrangement which could be made of these points, under a system aiming at equality, would be so far short of the inequality and injustice with which labour (not to speak of remuneration) is now apportioned, as to be scarcely worth counting in the comparison' (207).[17] The problems of Communism had only recently been defined and approached; and '[the] impossibility of foreseeing

17 The general tone of Mill's *Westminster Review* notice (1851) of Francis Newman's *Lectures on Political Economy* is in line with these sentiments. Mill there denied that Socialism could be opposed or private property defended 'in principle' or on grounds of a priori justice – general utility must provide the key (V, 443–4). Existing arrangements are, none the less, condemned as unjust: 'The distinction between rich and poor, so slightly connected as it is with merit and demerit, or even with exertion and want of exertion in the individual, is obviously unjust . . . Socialism, as long as it attacks the existing individualism, is easily triumphant; its weakness hitherto is in what it proposes to substitute. The reasonable objections to socialism are altogether practical, consisting in of difficulties to be surmounted, and in the insufficiency of any scheme yet promulgated to provide against them; their removal must be a work of thought and discussion, aided by progressive experiments; and by the general moral improvement of mankind, through good government and education.'

and prescribing the exact mode in which its difficulties should be dealt with, does not prove that it may not be the best and the ultimate form of human society'.

This latter statement was withdrawn in the next edition (1857). But it is clear that while Mill, even in 1852, was deliberately giving Communism the benefit of the doubt to a greater extent than in 1849, he none the less insisted on a fair comparison between alternatives. Despite everything, the net balance of advantage – albeit a balancing of *prospective* considerations – still lay with a reformed capitalism. The choice between an ideal Communism and actual capitalism was obvious; even the very real difficulties likely to be encountered in a Communist regime seeking 'equality' in the allocation of labour between tasks and in pay, fall short 'of the inequality and injustice with which labour (not to speak of remuneration) is now apportioned', the distribution of income 'as we now see it [being] almost in an inverse ratio to the labour – the largest portions to those who have never worked at all, the next largest to those whose work is almost nominal, and so on in a descending scale, the remuneration dwindling as the work grows harder and more disagreeable, until the most fatiguing and exhausting bodily labour cannot count with certainty on being able to earn even the necessaries of life'. Yet what counted was a comparison between 'Communism at its best [and] the régime of individual property, not as it is, but as it might be made' (207; cf. 986). And just here we encounter the fundamentally important assertion that the private property system had never had 'a fair trial':

To judge of the final destination of the institution of property, we must suppose everything rectified, which causes the institution to work in a manner opposed to that equitable principle, of proportion between remuneration and exertion, on which in every vindication of it that will bear the light, it is assumed to be grounded. We must also suppose two conditions realized, without which neither Communism nor any other laws or institutions could make the condition of the mass of mankind other than degraded and miserable. One of these conditions, is universal education; the other, a due limitation of the numbers of the community. With these, there could be no poverty, even under the present social institutions: and these being supposed, the question of Socialism, is not, as generally stated by Socialists, a question of flying to the sole refuge against the evils which now bear down humanity; but a mere question of comparative advantage, which futurity must determine. We are too ignorant either of what individual agency in its best form, or Socialism in its best form, can accomplish, to be qualified to decide which of the two will be the ultimate form of human society (208).[18]

18 A passage to the same effect appears also in 1849 although in a summary statement covering all varieties of Socialism, not specifically Communism narrowly defined. But it is unlikely that this relocation has any substantive import.

There remains the fundamental matter of 'liberty': '[W]hich of the two systems is consistent with the greatest amount of human liberty and spontaneity' would, Mill believed, probably be the key issue rather than those other matters raised in the comparison. For 'after the means of subsistence are assured, the next in strength of the personal wants of human beings is liberty; and (unlike the physical wants, which as civilization advances become more moderate and more amenable to control) it increases instead of diminishing in intensity, as the intelligence, and the moral faculties are more developed' (208). As in 1849 we find the belief repeated that '[the] perfection both of social arrangements and of practical morality would be, to secure to all persons complete independence and freedom of action, subject to no restriction but that of not doing injury to others'. And while there is in 1852 a lesser degree of presumption that the balance lay with a (reformed) capitalism, one yet has the impression that the obligation rested on Communists to make out a convincing case.[19] As Lord Robbins (1952, 155) has put it, 'the nuance of phrase here seems to shade into a certain anxious scepticism':

The question is, whether there would be any asylum left for individuality of character; whether public opinion would not be a tyrannical yoke; whether the absolute dependence of each on all, and surveillance of each by all, would not grind all down into a tame uniformity of thoughts, feelings, and actions. This is already one of the glaring evils of the existing state of society, notwithstanding a much greater diversity of education and pursuits, and a much less absolute dependence of the individual on the mass, than would exist in the Communistic régime. No society in which eccentricity is a matter of reproach, can be in a wholesome state. It is yet to be ascertained whether the Communistic scheme would be consistent with that multiform development of human nature, those manifold unlikenesses, that diversity of tastes and talents, and variety of intellectual points of view, which not only form a great part of the interest of human life, but by bringing intellects into stimulating collision, and by presenting to each innumerable notions that he would not have conceived of himself, are the mainspring of mental and moral progression (209).

* * *

The 'anxious sceptism' is much reinforced by the time Mill composed the elements of the proposed work devoted to 'Socialism' (1869) published posthumously in incomplete form. Here *inter alia* Mill compares capitalism with the Communism of Louis Blanc which (unlike Fourier-type Socialism)

19 Cf. above (p. 778), the similar passage summarizing the main message of *On Liberty* in the earlier editions.

ruled out differential rewards according to the type of work undertaken or the merit of the individual. The comparison did not favour Communism as far as concerned management, Mill's doubts turning on the weak motive force in contrast to contemporary capitalism. The passage is absolutely central for its explicit emphasis on the role of 'personal interest' in the forseeable future:

The difference between the motive powers in the economy of society under private property and under Communism would be greatest in the case of the directing minds. Under the present system, the direction being entirely in the hands of the person or persons who own (or are personally responsible for) the capital, the whole benefit of the difference between the best administration and the worst under which the business can continue to be carried on accrues to the person or persons who control the administration: they reap the whole profit of good management except so far as their self-interest or liberality induce them to share it with their subordinates; and they suffer the whole detriment of mismanagement except so far as this may cripple their subsequent power of employing labour. This strong personal motive to do their very best and utmost for the efficiency and economy of the operations, would not exist under Communism; as the managers would only receive out of the produce the same equal dividend as the other members of the association. What would remain would be the interest common to all in so managing affairs as to make the dividend as large as possible; the incentives of public spirit, of conscience, and of the honour and credit of the managers. The force of these motives, especially when combined, is great. But it varies greatly in different persons, and is much greater for some purposes than for others. The verdict of experience, in the imperfect degree of moral cultivation which mankind have yet reached, is that the motive of conscience and that of credit and reputation, even when they are of some strength, are, in the majority of cases, much stronger as restraining than as impelling forces – are more to be depended on for preventing wrong, than for calling forth the fullest energies in the pursuit of ordinary occupations. In the case of most men the only inducement which has been found sufficiently constant and unflagging to overcome the ever-present influence of indolence and love of ease, and induce men to apply themselves unrelaxingly to work for the most part in itself dull and unexciting, is the prospect of bettering their own economic condition and that of their family; and the closer the connection of every increase of exertion with a corresponding increase of its fruits, the more powerful is this motive. To suppose the contrary would be to imply that with men as they now are, duty and honour are more powerful principles of action than personal interest, not solely as to special acts and forbearances respecting which those sentiments have been exceptionally cultivated, but in the regulation of their whole lives; which no one, I suppose, will affirm. It may be said that this inferior efficacy of public and social feelings is not inevitable – is the result of imperfect education. This I am quite ready to admit, and also that there are even now many individual exceptions to the general infirmity.

But before these exceptions can grow into a majority, or even into a very large minority, much time will be required. The education of human beings is one of the most difficult of all arts, and this is one of the points in which it has hitherto been least successful; moreover improvements in general education are necessarily very gradual, because the future generation is educated by the present, and the imperfections of the teachers set an invincible limit to the degree in which they can train their pupils to be better than themselves. We must therefore expect, unless we are operating upon a select portion of the population, that personal interest will for a long time be a more effective stimulus to the most vigorous and careful conduct of the industrial business of society than motives of a higher character (V, 739–40).

A second weakness of the communistic schemes lay in the small motivation towards risk-taking or 'enterprise':

It will be said that at present the greed of personal gain by its very excess counteracts its own end by the stimulus it gives to reckless and often dishonest risks. This it does, and under Communism that source of evil would generally be absent. It is probably, indeed, that enterprise either of a bad or of a good kind would be a deficient element, and that business in general would fall very much under the dominion of routine; the rather, as the performance of duty in such communities has to be enforced by external sanctions, the more nearly each person's duty can be reduced to fixed rules, the easier it is to hold him to its performance. A circumstance which increases the probability of this result is the limited power which the managers would have of independent action. They would of course hold their authority from the choice of community, by whom their function might at any time be withdrawn from them; and this would make it necessary for them, even if not so required by the constitution of the community, to obtain the general consent of the body before making any change in the established mode of carrying on the concern. The difficulty of persuading a numerous body to make a change in their accustomed mode of working, of which change the trouble is often great, and the risk more obvious to their minds than the advantage, would have a great tendency to keep things in their accustomed track (740–1).

There were serious implications for innovation. The character of the managers likely to be selected would 'be, in all probability, less favourable than private management to the striking out of new paths and making immediate sacrifices for distant and uncertain advantages, which, though seldom unattended with risk, is generally indispensable to great improvements in the economic condition of mankind, and even to keeping up the existing state in the face of a continual increase of the number of mouths to be fed' (742).

Similarly the scales were weighed against Communism as far as concerned worker efficiency. That Mill provides no apologia for contemporary arrangements must first be clarified:

These, under Communism, would have no interest, except their share of the general interest, in doing their work honestly and energetically. But in this respect matters would be no worse than they now are in regard to the great majority of the producing classes. These, being paid by fixed wages, are so far from having any direct interest of their own in the efficiency of their work, that they have not even that share in the general interest which every worker would have in the Communistic organization. Accordingly, the inefficiency of hired labour, the imperfect manner in which it calls forth the real capabilities of the labourers, is matter of common remark. It is true that a character for being a good workman is far from being without its value, as it tends to give him a preference in employment, and sometimes obtains for him higher wages. There are also possibilities of rising to the position of foreman, or other subordinate administrative posts, which are not only more highly paid than ordinary labour, but sometimes open the way to ulterior advantages. But on the other side is to be set that under Communism the general sentiment of the community, composed of the comrades under whose eyes each person works, would be sure to be in favour of good and hard working, and unfavourable to laziness, carelessness, and waste. In the present system not only is this not the case, but the public opinion of the workman class often acts in the very opposite direction: the rules of some trade societies actually forbid their members to exceed a certain standard of efficiency, lest they should diminish the number of labourers required for the work; and for the same reason they often violently resist contrivances for economising labour. The change from this to a state in which every person would have an interest in rendering every other person as industrious, skilful, and careful as possible (which would be the case under Communism), would be a change very much for the better (742).

But there were reforms to be considered 'compatible with private property and individual competition' which altered the weighting of advantages; – first, piece-work, whereby 'the workman's personal interest is closely connected with the quantity of work he turns out'. Yet piece-work, Mill conceded, had its disadvantages, for quality was less easily monitored. Moreover, it was unpopular amongst workers who viewed it 'as a means of (as they think) diminishing the market for labourers. And there is really good ground for their dislike of piece-work, if, as is alleged, it is a frequent practice of employers, after using piece-work to ascertain the utmost which a good workman can do, to fix the price of piece-work so low that by doing that utmost he is not able to earn more than they would be obliged to give him as day wages for ordinary work'. Secondly, Mill alludes to profit-sharing (a matter to which we shall return).

His conclusion is now quite unambiguous: 'It thus appears that as far as concerns the motives to exertion in the general body, Communism has no advantage which may not be reached under private property, while as respects the managing heads it is at a considerable disadvantage. It has also some disadvantages which seem to be inherent in it, through the necessity under which it lies of deciding in a more or less arbitrary manner questions which, on the present system, decide themselves, often badly enough, but spontaneously' (743).

The conclusion is reinforced by the problem of pay. Unless the work is equal, equality of pay is unjust; while for each to engage in all types of work entailed inefficiency:

It is a simple rule, and under certain aspects a just one, to give equal payment to all who share in the work. But this is a very imperfect justice unless the work also is apportioned equally. Now the many different kinds of work required in every society are very unequal in hardness and unpleasantness. To measure these against one another, so as to make quality equivalent to quantity, is so difficult that Communists generally propose that all should work by turns at every kind of labour. But this involves an almost complete sacrifice of the economic advantages of the division of employments, advantages which are indeed frequently over-estimated (or rather the counter-considerations are under-estimated) by political economists, but which are nevertheless, in the point of view of the productiveness of labour, very considerable, for the double reason that the co-operation of employment enables the work to distribute itself with some regard to the special capacities and qualifications of the worker, and also that every worker acquires greater skill and rapidity in one kind of work by confining himself to it. The arrangement, therefore, which is deemed indispensable to a just distribution would probably be a very considerable disadvantage in respect of production (743–4).

But even to ask the same work from each would be unjust considering differential capacities so that some discriminating authority would be required, inevitably generating discord, especially considering the state of conduct:

As long as there are any lazy or selfish persons who like better to be worked for by others than to work, there will be frequent attempts to obtain exemptions by favour or fraud, and the frustration of these attempts will be an affair of considerable difficulty, and will by no means be always successful . . . The institution provides that there shall be no quarrelling about material interests; individualism is excluded from that department of affairs. But there are other departments from which no institutions can exclude it: there will still be rivalry for reputation and for personal power. When selfish ambition is excluded from the field in which, with most men, it chiefly exercises itself, that of riches and pecuniary interest, it would betake itself with greater intensity to the domain still open to it, and we may expect that the struggles for pre-eminence and for influence in the management would be of great bitterness when the personal passions, diverted from their ordinary channel, are driven to seek their principal gratification in that other direction (744–5).

Discord would arise also regarding education. And there was too the problem of inter-community relations: 'It is needless to specify a number of other important questions affecting the mode of employing the productive resources of the association, the conditions of social life, the relations of the body with other associations, &c., and which difference of opinion, often irreconcilable, would be likely to arise'.

Finally, the old spectre is raised – the danger to individual freedom:

But even the dissensions which might be expected would be a far less evil to the prospects of humanity than a delusive unanimity produced by the prostration of all individual opinions and wishes before the decree of the majority. The obstacles to human progression are always great, and require a concurrence of favourable circumstances to overcome them; but an indispensable condition of their being overcome is, that human nature should have freedom to expand spontaneously in various directions, both in thought and practice; that people should both think for themselves and try experiments for themselves, and should not resign into the hands of rulers, whether acting in the name of a few or of the majority, the business of thinking for them, and of prescribing how they shall act. But in Communist associations private life would be brought in a most unexampled degree within the dominion of public authority, and there would be less scope for the development of individual character and individual preferences than has hitherto existed among the full citizens of any state belonging to the progressive branches of the human family. Already in all societies the compression of individuality by the majority is a great and growing evil; it would probably be much greater under Communism, except so far as it might be the power of individuals to set bounds to it by selecting to belong to a community of persons like-minded with themselves (745–6).

The conclusion in the final statement is negative although Mill (as always) recognized the need to allow for experimentation:

From these various considerations I do not seek to draw any inference against the possibility that Communistic production is capable of being at some future time the form of society best adapted to the wants and circumstances of mankind. I think that this is, and will long be, an open question, upon which fresh light will continually be obtained, both by trial of the Communistic principle under favourable circumstances, and by the improvements which will be gradually effected in the working of the existing system, that of private ownership. The one certainty is, that Communism, to be successful, requires a high standard of both moral and intellectual education in all the members of the community – moral, to qualify them for doing their part honestly and energetically in the labour of life under no inducement but their share in the general interest of the association, and their feelings of duty and sympathy towards it; intellectual, to make them capable of estimating distant interests and entering into complex considerations, sufficiently at least to be able to discriminate, in these matters, good counsel from bad. Now I reject altogether the notion that it is impossible for education and cultivation such as is implied in these things to be made the inheritance of every person in the nation; but I am convinced that it is very difficult, and that the passage to it from our present condition can only be slow. I admit the plea that in the points of moral education on which the success of Communism depends, the present state of society is demoralising, and that only a Communistic association can effectually train mankind for Communism. It is for Communism, then, to prove, by practical experiment, its power of giving this training. Experiments alone can show whether there is as yet in any portion of the population a sufficiently high level of moral cultivation to make Communism succeed, and to give to the next generation among themselves the education necessary to keep up that high level permanently. If Communist associations show that they can be durable and prosperous, they will multiply, and will probably be adopted by successive portions of the population of the more advanced countries as they become morally fitted for that mode of life. But to force unprepared populations into Communist societies, even if a political revolution gave the power to make such an attempt, would end in disappointment.

IV THE SAINT-SIMONIAN AND FOURIERIST SOLUTIONS

As for the 'Socialist' recommendations Mill was in all editions of the *Principles* throughout less severe in some respects. Thus the St Simonian version is described as

a system of far higher intellectual pretensions than the other . . . grounded on views of human nature much less limited . . . The St Simonian scheme does not contemplate an equal, but an unequal division of the produce; it does not propose that all should be occupied alike, but differently, according to their vocation or capacity; the function of each being assigned like grades in a regiment, by the choice of the directing authority, and the remuneration being by salary, proportioned to the importance, in the eyes of that authority, of the function itself, and the merits of the person who fulfils it (*CW*, III, 980-1).

Yet such a society had its disadvantages. While it 'would hold out even more abundant stimulus to individual exertion', it would also encourage 'even more of rivalries and animosities than at present'. At all events it was totally visionary – more so even than the Communist alternative – considering the proposed machinery for the dispensing of distributive justice and the allocation of tasks:

[T]o suppose that one or a few human beings, howsoever selected, could, by whatever machinery of subordinate agency, be qualified to adapt each person's work to his capacity, and proportion each person's remuneration to his merits – to be, in fact, the dispensers of distributive justice to every member of a community, were it even the smallest that ever had a separate political existence – or that any use which they could make of this power would give general satisfaction, or would be submitted to without the aid of force – is a supposition too chimerical to be reasoned against. A fixed rule, like that of equality, might be acquiesced in, and so might chance, or an external necessity; but that a handful of human beings should weigh everybody in the balance, and give more to one and less to another at their sole pleasure and judgment, would not be borne unless from persons believed to be more than men, and backed by supernatural terrors (982).

In the second edition of 1849 the Fourierist alternative is taken up and given relatively favourable coverage as 'the least open to objection'. But although a communal organization, it is scarcely accurate to classify it amongst systems totally opposed to private property. For, this system

does not contemplate the abolition of private property, nor even of inheritence: on the contrary, it avowedly takes into consideration, as an element in the distribution of the produce, capital as well as labour. It proposes that the operations of industry should be carried on by associations of about two thousand members, combining their labour on a district of about a square league in extent, under the guidance of chiefs selected by themselves. In the distribution, a certain minimum is first assigned for the subsistence of every member of the community, whether capable or not of labour. The remainder of the produce is shared in certain proportions, to be determined beforehand, among the three elements, Labour, Capital, and Talent. The capital of the community may be owned in unequal shares by different members, who would in that case . . . receive proportional dividends. The claim of each person on the share of the produce apportioned to talent is estimated by the grade or rank which the individual occupies in the several groups of labourers to which he or she belongs; these grades being in all cases conferred by the choice of his or her companions (982–3).[20]

There were advantages over the contemporary system of motivation – 'each person would have much more certainty of reaping individually the

---

20 Schumpeter (1954), 456n, has observed that Fourier's '*phalanstère* organization has but a qualified claim to being called socialist, and it is amusing to note that . . . he actually reserved for interest and profits a relatively larger share than goes to them, on the long-run average, in capitalist reality'. Moreover, common *ménages* in the literal sense were not essential to the scheme, though all would live in the same community of buildings. Private spending was also countenanced.

fruits of increased skill or energy, bodily or mental, than under the present social arrangements can be felt by any but those who are in the most advantageous positions, or to whom the chapter of accidents is more than ordinarily favourable'. Similarly, 'this system does no violence to any of the general laws by which human action, even in the present imperfect state of moral and intellectual cultivation, is influenced. All persons would have a prospect of deriving individual advantage from every degree of labour, of abstinence, and of talent, which they individually exercised' (983–4).[21] But for all that the net evaluation is a negative one – again the arrangements for determining relative rates of pay and the return to capital were totally inadequate given the state of human behaviour:

Before large bodies of human beings could be fit to live together in such close union, and still more, before they would be capable of adjusting, by peaceful arrangement among themselves, the relative claims of every class or kind of labour and talent, and of every individual in every class, a vast improvement in human character must be presupposed. When it is considered that each person who would have a voice in this adjustment would be a party interested in it, in every sense of the term – that each would be called on to take part by vote in fixing both the relative remuneration, and the relative estimation, of himself as compared with all other labourers, and of his own class of labour or talent as compared with all others; the degree of disinterestedness and of freedom from vanity and irritability, which would be required in such a community from every individual in it, would be such as is now only found in the élite of humanity: while if these qualities fell much short of the required standard, either the adjustment could not be made at all, or if made by a majority, would engender jealousies and disappointments destructive of the internal harmony on which the whole working of the system avowedly depends (985).

The *coup de grâce* is provided by Mill's observation that everything said in favour of the Fourierists' experiment related to single communities; but in fact 'the communities themselves are to be the constituent units of an organized whole, (otherwise competition would rage as actively between rival communities as it now does between individual merchants or manufacturers,) and that nothing less would be requisite for the complete

---

21 Cf. the following aspect of the proposal: 'It is inferred from the diversity of tastes and talents, that every member of the community would be attached of several groups, employing themselves in various kinds of occupation, some bodily, others mental, and would be capable of occupying a high place in some one or more; so that a real equality, or a something more nearly approaching to it than might at first be supposed, would practically result: not (as in Communism) from the compression, but, on the contrary, from the largest possible development, of the various natural superiorities residing in each individual' (984).

success of the scheme, then the organisation from a single centre of the whole industry of a nation, and even of the world . . .' – an unlikely prospect.

* * *

The general conclusion of the first two editions drawn from the account of Communism supplemented by the further analysis of St Simonism and Fourierism is a strong affirmation of the case for seeking reform in the improvement and not the displacement of the private property system:

we may, without attempting to limit the ultimate capabilities of human nature, affirm, that the political economist, for a considerable time to come, will be chiefly concerned with the conditions of existence and progress belonging to a society founded on private property and individual competition; and that, rude as is the manner in which those two principles apportion reward to exertion and to merit, they must form the basis of the principal improvements which can for the present be looked for in the economical condition of humanity . . . (985).

In the present stage of human improvement at least, it is not (I conceive) the subversion of the system of individual property that should be aimed at, but the improvement of it, and the participation of every member of the community in its benefits (987).[22]

Moreover, many contemporary evils were by no means inevitable. The potential reforms that could be made within the private enterprise system – which, as we shall see, Mill spent much effort to elucidate – would 'be found to be far more considerable than the adherents of the various Socialist systems are willing to allow. Whatever may be the merit or demerit of their own schemes of society, they have hitherto shown themselves extremely ill acquainted with the economical laws of the existing social system; and have, in consequence, habitually assumed as necessary effects of competition, evils which are by no means inevitably attendant on it. It is from the influence of this erroneous interpretation of existing facts, that many Socialists of high principles and attainments are led to regard the competitive system

---

22 This latter formulation is from the 1849 edition. An almost identical formulation in the ms. and first edition appears at the close of a passage highly laudatory of individual property arrangements: 'There has never been imagined any mode of distributing the produce of industry, so well adapted to the requirements of human nature on the whole, as that of letting the share of each individual (not in a state of bodily or mental incapacity) depend in the main on that individual's own energies and exertions, and such furtherance as may be obtained from the voluntary good offices of others. It is not the subversion of the system of individual property that should be aimed at, but the improvement of it, and the participation of every member of the community in its benefits' (982n).

as radically incompatible with the economical well-being of the mass' (985–6).[23] This statement is of prime importance for it withdraws the implicit barbs from the immediately preceding negative allusion to competition under capitalism.[24] Finally, we have that famous passage where Mill asserts that 'the principle of private property [had] never had a fair trial in any country; and less so, perhaps, in this country than in some others . . .' As for the distant future little could be said – 'we are . . . too ignorant either of what individual agency in its best form, or Socialism in its best form can accomplish, to be qualified to decide which of the two will be the ultimate form of human society'.

* * *

The approach to St Simonism is as negative in 1852 as in the earlier editions. By contrast, reference is made to successful Fourierist experiments and some of the critical comments are deleted including the objection that Fourierist communities would have 'to be constituent units of an organized whole' in order to avoid intercommunity competition (210–11). In his 1851 review of Newman, Mill alludes to the pricing problem under socialism – albeit too casually (cf. Robbins, 1976, 143) – in answer to the charge that socialists failed to see 'that there can be no such thing as price, except through the influence of competition', and therefore, that without competition, there can be no intercommunity exchanges (V, 446). 'Socialists would reply', Mill suggested,

that exchanges between community and community should be at cost price. If it were asked how the cost price is to be ascertained, they would answer, that in the operations of communities, every element of cost would be a matter of public record;

23 See also below (p. 815) regarding a more detailed statement, *ibid.*, 795.
24 In the ms. and the first edition Mill allowed that the 'increasing power of co-operation in any common undertaking, is one of the surest fruits, and most accurate tests, of the progress of civilization: and we may expect, as mankind improve, that joint enterprises of many kinds, which would now be impracticable, will be successively numbered among possibilities, thus augmenting, to an indefinite extent, the powers of the species'. But even this prospect is qualified: 'the proper sphere for collective action lies in the things that cannot be done by individual agency, either because no one can have a sufficiently strong personal interest in accomplishing them, or because they require an assemblage of means surpassing what can be commanded by one or a few individuals. In things to which individual agency is at all suitable, it is almost always the most suitable; working, as it does, with so much greater intensity of motive when the object is personal, with so much stronger a sense of responsibility when it is public, and in either case with a feeling of independence and individual power, unknown to the members of a body under joint government' (986–7n). The respect for private agency is retained in 1849 though in altered formulation.

that every dealer, on the private system, is required and able to ascertain what price will remunerate him for his goods, and the agents of the communities would only be required to do the same thing. This would be, no doubt, one of the practical difficulties, and we think it somewhat undervalued by them; but the difficulty cannot be insurmountable.

Mill also amplifies the surrogate competition within each community in the determination of rates of pay:

According to Owen, the able-bodied would share by turns all kind of necessary labour; the community deciding in general assembly, or by its elected members, what labours *are* necessary. According to Fourier, each would select his or her own occupations; but if some employments were chosen by too many persons, and others by too few, the remuneration of the former would be lowered, and of the latter raised, so as to restore the balance.[25]

Yet notwithstanding the more positive perspective of the third edition, the assertion that private property had 'never had a fair trial' is restated; so too is the criticism of Socialist opinion – that 'the principle of individual property would have been found to have no necessary connexion with the physical and social evils which almost all Socialist writers assume to be inseparable from it' (207–8). The whole chapter closes in 1852 with the explicit statement that (while experimentation was to be welcomed) it was 'for experience to determine how far or how soon any one or more of the possible systems of community of property will be fitted to substitute itself for the ''organization of industry'' based on private ownership of land and capital', Mill reproducing the formulation of 1848 and 1849 that 'the object to be principally aimed at in the present stage of human improvement, is not the subversion of the system of individual property, but the improvement of it, and the full participation of every member of the community in its benefits' (214). He could not have been clearer that his position in 1852 had not substantially altered.

* * *

Projects of the Fourier type are also taken up in the posthumously published

---

25 Mill also alludes to the adoption of piece-work by most associations: 'Almost all the associations, at first, excluded piece-work, and gave equal wages whether the work done was more or less. Almost all have abandoned this system, and after allowing to every one a fixed minimum, sufficient for subsistence, they apportion all further remuneration according to the work done: most of them even dividing the profits at the end of the year, in the same proportion as the earnings' (783).

chapters on Socialism (1869). Here their practicability is recognized – in sharp contrast to that of centrally-organized socialism.[26] In the following definitional passage reference is made to the allowance by Fourierists for private property of a consumer variety, a point in favour of the scheme:

What is characteristic of Socialism is the joint ownership by all the members of the community of the instruments and means of production; which carries with it the consequences that the division of the produce among the body of owners must be a public act, performed according to rules laid down by the community. Socialism by no means excludes private ownership of articles of consumption; the exclusive right of each to his or her share of the produce when received, either to enjoy, to give, or to exchange it. The land, for example, might be wholly the property of the community for agricultural and other productive purposes, and might be cultivated on their joint account, and yet the dwelling assigned to each individual or family as part of their remuneration might be as exclusively theirs, while they continued to fulfil their share of the common labours, as any one's house now is; and not the dwelling only, but any ornamental ground which the circumstance of the association allowed to be attached to the house for purposes of enjoyment. The distinctive feature of Socialism is not that all things are in common, but that production is only carried on upon the common account, and that the instruments of production are held as common property. The *practicability* then of Socialism, on the scale of Mr. Owen's or M. Fourier's villages, admits of no dispute. The attempt to manage the whole production of a nation by one central organization is a totally different matter; but a mixed agricultural and manufacturing association of from two thousand to four thousand inhabitants under any tolerable circumstances of soil and climate would be easier to manage than many a joint stock company (V, 738–9).

The issue of ownership is further clarified subsequently; private ownership even of capital goods was allowed – and thus interest payments – although 'not the arbitrary disposal of it'. Of all socialistic schemes Fourierism receives

---

26 Cf. V, 737: 'Among those who call themselves Socialists, two kinds of persons may be distinguished. There are, in the first place, those whose plans for a new order of society, in which private property and individual competition are to be superseded and other motives to action substituted, are on the scale of a village community or township, and would be applied to an entire country by the multiplication of such self-acting units; of this character are the systems of Owen, of Fourier, and the more thoughtful and philosophic Socialists generally. The other class, who are more a product of the Continent than of Great Britain and may be called the revolutionary Socialists, propose to themselves a much bolder stroke. Their scheme is the management of the whole productive resources of the country by one central authority, the general government. And with this view some of them avow as their purpose that the working classes, or somebody in their behalf, should take possession of all the property of the country, and administer it for the general benefit.'

the most enthusiastic reception in light of this latter consideration, the operation of a surrogate competitive mechanism to determine the wage structure, and various other devices to stimulate initiative and efficiency, including the 'dispensing with the vast number of superfluous distributors':

There is scarcely an objection or a difficulty which Fourier did not foresee, and against which he did not make provision beforehand by self-acting contrivances, grounded, however, upon a less high principle of distributive justice than that of Communism, since he admits inequalities of distribution and individual ownership of capital, but not the arbitrary disposal of it. The great problem which he grapples with is how to make labour attractive, since, if this could be done, the principal difficulty of Socialism would be overcome. He maintains that no kind of useful labour is necessarily or universally repugnant, unless either excessive in amount or devoid of the stimulus of companionship and emulation, or regarded by mankind with contempt. The workers in a Fourierist village are to class themselves spontaneously in groups, each group undertaking a different kind of work, and the same person may be a member not only of one group but of any number; a certain minimum having first been set apart for the subsistence of every member of the community, whether capable or not of labour, the society divides the remainder of the produce among the different groups, in such shares as it finds attract to each the amount of labour required, and no more; if there is too great a run upon particular groups it is a sign that those groups are over-remunerated relatively to others; if any are neglected their remuneration must be made higher. The share of produce assigned to each group is divided in fixed proportions among three elements – labour, capital, and talent; the part assigned to talent being awarded by the suffrages of the group itself, and it is hoped that among the variety of human capacities all, or nearly all, will be qualified to excel in some group or other. The remuneration for capital is to be such as is found sufficient to induce savings from individual consumption, in order to increase the common stock to such point as is desired. The number and ingenuity of the contrivances for meeting minor difficulties, and getting rid of minor inconveniences, is very remarkable. By means of these various provisions it is the expectation of Fourierists that the personal inducements to exertion for the public interest, instead of being taken away, would be made much greater than at present, since every increase of the service rendered would be much more certain of leading to increase of reward than it is now, when accidents of position have so much influence. The efficiency of labour, they therefore expect, would be unexampled, while the saving of labour would be prodigious, by diverting to useful occupations that which is now wasted on things useless or hurtful, and by dispensing with the vast number of superfluous distributors, the buying and selling for the whole community being managed by a single agency (747–8).

In addition 'the free choice of individuals as to their manner of life would be no further interfered with than would be necessary for gaining the full advantages of co-operation in the industrial operations. Altogether, the picture of a Fourierist community is both attractive in itself and requires less from common humanity than any other known system of Socialism; and it is much to be desired that the scheme should have that fair trial which alone can test the workableness of any new scheme of social life'.

Yet despite all this Mill's conclusion still smacks of doubt – a rather unexpected outcome in the light of the foregoing overview of Fourierism: 'The result of our review of the various difficulties of Socialism has led us to the conclusion that the various schemes for managing the productive resources of the country by public instead of private agency have a case for a trial, and some of them may eventually establish their claims to preference over the existing order of things, but that they are at present workable only by the *élite* of mankind, and have yet to prove their power of training mankind at large to the state of improvement which they presuppose' (748).[27] On the whole there was little change in Mill's position over time.

V PROFIT-SHARING

Before turning to the co-operative option (Mill's 'ideal' solution to many of the defects of contemporary organization it transpires) attention must be given to a second-best alternative, that of profit-sharing. The problem as phrased in 1848 and 1849 was to obtain 'the efficiency and economy of production on a large scale, without dividing the producers into two parties with hostile interests, employers and employed, the many who do the work being mere servants under the command of the one who supplies the funds, and having no interest of their own in the enterprise except to fulfil their contract and earn their wages' (*CW*, III, 769). The solution was seen to lie in the *profit-sharing* principle which assures to 'every one who contributes to the work, whether by labour or by pecuniary resources, a partner's interest in it, proportionally to the value of his contribution. It is already a common practice to remunerate those in whom special trust is reposed by means of a percentage on the profits; and cases exist in which the principle is, with the most excellent success, carried down to the class of mere manual labourers' (1007). The scheme is illustrated by an experiment under way in a Paris establishment (Leclaire). These schemes are described as partnerships of labourers with their employer, they 'bringing nothing into the common concern but their labour, while he brings not only his labour

---

27 See Robbins (1952), 164n, for an explanation of Mill's ambivalent attitude to Fourier turning on his recognition of 'the truth relating to this most peculiar and eccentric personality'.

of direction and superintendance but his capital also'. Accordingly, the labourers 'have justly a smaller share of the profits' although 'it is, in the fullest sense, the common concern of all' suffering losses as well as enjoying gains (1013).[28] Here Mill focussed on the major advantage of the scheme over Owenite-type co-operatives, namely recognition of the force of self-interested motivation by rejecting uniform shares. Abstinence, in particular, had to be rewarded appropriately: 'It is expedient that those, whose performance of the part assigned to them is the most essential to the common end, should have a greater amount of personal interest in the issue of the enterprise. If those who supply the funds, and incur the whole risk of the undertaking, obtained no greater reward or more influential voice than the rest, few would practise the abstinence through which those funds are acquired and kept in existence' (1013).[29]

In the posthumous chapters too Mill proposed profit-sharing as the most potent conceivable measure (superior even to piece-work) in the reform of capitalism:

But there is a far more complete remedy than piece-work for the disadvantages of hired labour, viz. what is now called industrial partnership – the admission of the whole body of labourers to a participation in the profits, by distributing among all who share in the work, in the form of a percentage on their earnings, the whole or a fixed portion of the gains after a certain remuneration has been allowed to the capitalist. This plan has been found of admirable efficacy, both in this country and abroad. It has enlisted the sentiments of the workmen employed on the side of the most careful regard by all of them to the general interest of the concern; and by its joint effect in promoting zealous exertion and checking waste, it has very materially increased the remuneration of every description of labour in the concerns in which it has been adopted. It is evident that this system of indefinite extension and of an indefinite increase in the share of profits assigned to the

28 It is not clear that Mill recommended that workers share in losses; a reference is added in 1865 to the fact that until passage of the Limited Liability Act (1855) workmen in England 'could not . . . have been associated with the profits, without being liable for losses. One of the many benefits of that great legislative improvement has been to render partnerships of this description [Leclaire's] possible, and we may now expect to see them carried into practice' (774). Profits to be shared are envisaged as a reflection of improved returns, due to increased efficiency. Whenever the annual net yield exceeded a particular percentage, part of that excess would be allocated to the labourers (775).
29 The Leclaire scheme is represented as 'the ordinary case, in which the whole capital belongs to an individual capitalist' (1011). Another version of what Mill countenanced – a theoretical case discussed by Babbage – presumed that labourers also contributed capital, the breakdown between wages and interest not, as Mill put it, amenable to 'abstract reasoning' (1009). But the Babbage scheme scarcely seems accurately described as 'profit-sharing' in the sense of a partnership between capital and labour; Mill himself points out that the worker and capitalist shade into one another (1010).

labourers, short of that which would leave to the managers less then the needful degree of personal interest in the success of the concern. It is even likely that when such arrangements become common, many of these concerns would at some period or another, on the death or retirement of the chiefs, pass, by arrangement, into the state of purely co-operative associations (V, 743).

Co-operation, it will be seen, was envisaged as the possible destiny of at least some productive establishments adopting profit-sharing. To this outcome we turn next.

VI CO-OPERATION: PROSPECTS AND ADVANTAGES

It was Mill's position up to 1849 that to the principle of profit-sharing 'in whatever form embodied . . . futurity has to look for obtaining the benefits of co-operation, without constituting the numerical majority of the co-operators an inferior caste' (*CW*, III, 1013). The edition of 1852 is rather different. While reference is still made to the Leclaire (and Babbage) varieties of profit-sharing, this solution is no longer emphasized as the primary model for the future: 'The form of association . . . which if mankind continue to improve, must be expected in the end to predominate, is not that which can exist between a capitalist as chief, and work people without a voice in the management, but the association of the labourers themselves on terms of equality, collectively owning the capital with which they carry on their operations, and working under managers elected and removable by themselves' (775). The system of hired labour would 'gradually tend to confine itself to the description of work people whose low moral qualities render them unfit for anything more independent: and . . . the relation of masters and workpeople [would] be gradually superseded by partnership, in one of two forms: temporarily and in some cases, associations of labourers with the capitalist: in other cases, and finally in all, associations of labourers among themselves' (769; cf. 793).

Mill, of course, rejected revolutionary confiscations of property, commenting that such confiscations were mistakenly 'imagined by many people . . . to be the meaning and purpose of Socialism'. He wrote warmly of the change in régime in France since 1848 as creating a promising environment for Socialist experimentation with particular reference to the accumulation of capital by workers:

For the first time it seemed to be intelligent and generous of the working classes of a great nation, that they had obtained a government who sincerely desired the freedom and dignity of the many, and who did not look upon it as their natural and legitimate state to be instruments of production, worked for the benefit of the possessors of capital. Under this encouragement, the ideas sown by Socialist writers,

of an emancipation of labour to be effected by means of associations, throve and
fructified; and many working people came to the resolution, not only that they
would work for one another, instead of for a master tradesman or manufacturer,
but that they would also free themselves, at whatever cost of labour or privation,
from the necessity of paying, out of the produce of their industry, a heavy tribute
for the use of capital; that they would extinguish this tax, not by robbing the
capitalists of what they or their predecessors had acquired by labour and preserved
by economy, but by honestly acquiring capital for themselves (775).[30]

This strongly worded negative perspective on capitalism should not be
read as a charge against payment of interest as such. The charge seems
to be against payment of interest to a separate class (and its excessiveness).
Mill after all so often justified interest as a reward for abstinence. More
specifically, in the present context Mill wrote admiringly of the greater
discipline accepted by members of associations – for example, their voluntary
adoption of the usually disliked piece-work system – precisely because the
rules were 'self-imposed, for the manifest good of the community, and not
for the convenience of an employer regarded as having an opposite interest'
(780).

Mill spelled out in 1852 the implications of the Napoleonic take-over for
the French experiment: 'Before this calamity overtook France, the
associations could be spoken of not with the hope merely, but with positive
evidence, of their being able to compete successfully with individual
capitalists' (784n). Yet he believed that they had proven themselves, that
they had 'existed long enough to furnish the type of future improvement'
and had 'exemplified the process for bringing about a change in society,
which would combine the freedom, and independence of the individual,
with the moral, intellectual, and economical advantages of aggregate
production; and which, without violence or spoliation, or even any sudden
disturbance of existing habits and expectations, would realize, at least in
the industrial department, the best aspirations of the democratic spirit, by
putting an end to the division of society into the industrious and the idle,
and effacing all social distinctions but those fairly earned by personal services
and exertions' (785n., 793).

The 1857 edition expresses yet greater optimism despite the check in
France, consideration made of experiments in Piedmont, Scotland and
England – with particular reference in the latter case to Industrial Societies
and to Associations for Co-operative Consumption (retail outlets), their
progress supported by positive legislative measures (785n).[31] While such

30 On the French experiments see also Mill's 'Vindication of the French Revolution of
February 1848', in *Dissertations and Discussions*, II, 388f.
31 Including the Industrial and Provident Societies Act (1852) and the Limited Liability

progress 'in the present moral condition of the bulk of the population, cannot possibly be rapid . . . those which subsist, continue to do as much business as they ever did: and there are in the North of England instances of brilliant and steadily progressive success. Co-operative stores are increasing both in number and prosperity, especially in the North; and they are the best preparation for a wide application of the principle.' In 1862 Mill expressed himself yet more strongly, writing of the 'brilliant future reserved for the principle of co-operation' (785), alluding again to new and helpful legislation, and to the movement's 'permanency . . . which may now be considered as ensured' (791n). 'It is hardly possible', he observed, 'to take any but a hopeful view of the prospects of mankind, when, in two leading countries of the world, the obscure depths of society contain simple working men whose integrity, good sense, self-command, and honourable confidence in one another, have enabled them to carry these noble experiments to the triumphant issue which the facts recorded in the preceding pages attest' (791). And in 1865, having in mind the further extensions of co-operation in wholesale endeavours in London and the North of England, Mill described the type of organization as 'now one of the recognised elements in the progressive movement of the age . . .' (790).

The late correspondence points to the same conclusion. Mill expressed satisfaction with the expansion of unions from trade to national and even to international level – the latter an allusion to the International Association of Working Men (the First International) formally established in 1864 – for the outcome of the experiment would 'fix the limits of what the trade union principle can do' (to J. R. Ware, 13 Sept., 1868, XVI, 1439). But his own preferences are clear enough:

I am quite of opinion that the various forms of Cooperation (among which the one most widely applicable at present to production, as distinguished from distribution, is what you term the system of small percentage partnerships) are the real and only thorough means of healing the feud between capitalists and labourers; and, while tending eventually to supersede trade unions, are meanwhile a natural and gradually increasing corrective of their operation . . . [The] larger view of questions which these considerations open up, and which is already visibly enlightening the minds of the more advanced workpeople, will dispose them more and more to look for the just improvement of their condition rather in becoming their own capitalists, or allying themselves on fair conditions with the owners of capital, than in their present uncomfortable, and often disastrous, relations with them.

It is then primarily the co-operative solution that Mill had in mind when

Act (1855). Mill alludes to the impulse given by the Owenites and commends the help accorded by individual clergymen and barristers (775, 786).

he pronounced himself and his help-mate to be 'Socialists', at least if we consider the 1850s and thereafter. The apparent contrast between the chapters 'On Property' and 'On the Futurity of the Labouring Classes' – in the former the balance of prospects between Socialism and (reformed) capitalism is even, while in the latter prospects for Socialism seem to have the upper hand – can be appreciated in these terms since Mill's co-operative solution was not taken up in 'On Property'.

Here one notes the observation by Lord Robbins that Mill championed not centralization but a form of syndicalism:

The 'Socialism' which Mill had in mind in the *Autobiography* as possibly ultimately desirable, was not a centralized organisation with an all-powerful state owning and running the means of production, distribution and exchange, but rather a congeries of co-operative bodies of workers practising the virtues of association among themselves but independent, in the same sense in which any part of a social organism can be independent *vis-à-vis* other members of society. That is to say, that the desirable future for the labouring classes lay more in a *syndicalist* rather than a *collectivist* direction (1952, 159; cf. 166).[32]

This formulation may be in one respect a little misleading. While, as we shall show, there can be absolutely no doubt of Mill's rejection of collectivism, it is not certain whether it is syndicalism (or syndicalism alone) that he had in mind, if by that term is meant a combination of all workers throughout society engaged in a particular occupation – 'the sewers for the sewage men' as the Webbs had put it. What was apparently envisaged is the organization of individual productive establishments within each industry as co-operative associations – precluding a separate body of workers distinct from a capitalist (or group of capitalists in the joint-stock case) – where each association would be independent of, and in competition with, similar associations in the same industry (or with capitalist firms if the system was not a universal one). The co-operative system, of course, differs also from Fourierism which entailed arrangements extending far beyond the productive functions.

* * *

In any estimation of Mill's position it is helpful to observe that many of the desirable properties of capitalistic organization were envisaged as being

32 On the role of the law in organizational schemes see *ibid.*, 901f Cf. also Robbins (1967), IV, xl: 'In the last analysis . . . Mill's socialism proves to be much more like non-revolutionary syndicalism than anything which would be called socialism at the present day.' See also Schwartz (1972), 192.

more effectively achievable by co-operation – his preference to this extent entailed a weighing of *means* rather than of *ends*. This is true both of individual freedom and efficiency – advantages normally attributed to capitalistic organization by its champions – as we have seen in his statements of 1852.

The beneficial implications of co-operation for productivity are further amplified in the edition of 1862 in the light of recent experience: 'Their admirable history shows how vast an increase might be made even in the aggregate productiveness of labour, if the labourers as a mass were placed in a relation to their work which would make it (what now it is not) their principle and their interest to do the utmost, instead of the least possible, in exchange for their remuneration' (*CW*, III, 791n). In 1865 the argument is extended with special reference to the efficiency of distributive activity, the assertion being that under existing arrangements the inordinate number of those engaged in distribution 'far more than the gains of capitalists, are the cause why so great a portion of the wealth produced does not reach the producers' (791).[33] Co-operation would release 'a vast number of hands' for 'production' and assure 'great economy of the world's resources'. More generally, the effects on productivity due to the bringing into play of the worker's self-interest is again much underscored; it was 'scarcely possible to rate too highly this material benefit . . .' (792). Differentials when 'fairly earned by personal services and exertions' were to be fully recognized (785n., 793).

It is, moreover, specifically with regard to efficiency that in 'Thornton on Labour and its Claims' Mill even pronounced himself in favour of the 'euthanasia' of unionism, should it reflect a stage on the way to co-operation:

It is palpably for the good of society that its means of production, that the efficacy of its industry, should be as great as possible . . . The identification of the interest of the workmen with the efficiency, instead of the inefficiency of the work, is a happy result as yet only attained by co-operative industry in some of its forms. And if it should prove, in the end, not to be attainable otherwise; if the claims of the workmen to share the benefit of whatever was beneficial to the general interest of the business, became an embarrassment to the masters from which no system of arbitration could sufficiently relieve them, and growing inconvenience to them from the opposition of interest between themselves and the workmen should stimulate the conversion of existing businesses into Industrial Partnerships, in which the whole body of workpeople have a direct interest in the profits of the enterprise; such a transformation would be the true euthanasia of Trades' Unionism, while it would

33 This general issue is taken up in Chapter 5, Allocation, Trade and Distribution. The theme is widespread; see above (p. 1186) regarding the posthumous chapters.

train and prepare at least the superior portion of the working classes for a form of co-operation still more equal and complete (V, 666).[34]

In this regard reference must again be made to the alterations in the 'Futurity' chapter for the edition of 1852 – the deletion of the earlier comment regarding 'hostile competition' in his criticism of the labour-capitalist relationship; and the introduction of a strongly-argued case against the conception of competition as 'pernicious' *in and of itself* (above, p. 780). This formulation in support of competition is then applied to the co-operative solution itself: 'if association was universal, there would be no competition between labourer and labourer [but] that between association and association would be for the benefit of the consumers, that is, of the associations; of the industrious classes generally' (III, 795), a perspective in line with Mill's response to Newman of 1851 regarding intercommunity relations (above, p. 804). Indeed, such interassociation rivalry would be indispensable to avoid stagnation, including a failure to introduce new technology, where again we encounter Mill's concern for innovation rather than invention in Socialist organization:

It is the common error of Socialists to overlook the natural indolence of mankind; their tendency to be passive, to be the slaves of habit, to persist indefinitely in a course once chosen. Let them once attain any state of existence which they consider tolerable, and the danger to be apprehended is that they will thenceforth stagnate; will not exert themselves to improve, and by letting their faculties rust, will lose even the energy required to preserve them from deterioration. Competition may not be the best conceivable stimulus, but it is at present a necessary one, and no one can forsee the time when it will not be indispensable to progress. Even confining ourselves to the industrial department, in which, more than in any other, the majority may be supposed to be competent judges of improvements; it would be difficult to induce the general assembly of an association to submit to the trouble and inconvenience of altering their habits by adopting some new and promising invention, unless their knowledge of the existence of rival associations made them apprehend that what they would not consent to do, others would, and that they would be left behind in the race (795).

Thus Mill's co-operative solution was still to recognize the force of competition, and could only succeed to the extent that it did so.

34 The same position is implied in the *Principles*: 'I must repeat my conviction, that the industrial economy which divides society absolutely into two portions, the payers of wages and the receivers of them, the first counted by thousands, and the last by millions, is neither fit for, nor capable of, indefinite duration: and the possibility of changing this system for one of combination without dependence, and unity of interest instead of organized hostility, depends altogether upon the future developments of the Partnership principle' (III, 896).

The proposal would, of course, allow true democracy by effacing class barriers and permanent wealth differentials characterizing contemporary capitalism. Yet it may legitimately be presumed, considering the very detailed program for reform of the private-property system, that Mill still could not decide whether even these ends might not be achieved, not perhaps entirely but at least to an acceptable degree, within a reformed capitalism. It is certainly the case that he continued to attribute a fundamental role to capitalism into the foreseeable future. As he expressed the matter in 1865 – and it is confirmed in the posthumous chapters on Socialism as we have seen – the practical ideal 'perhaps for a considerable length of time' would be the co-existence of capitalism (preferably with profit-sharing) with co-operatives.

Particular reference is made in this context to the problem of innovation – a regular theme, for we have frequently encountered Mill's doubts regarding the ability of co-operation to assure a rate of technological progress equivalent to that under capitalism:

Unity of authority, makes many things possible, which could not or would not be undertaken subject to the chance of divided councils or changes in the management. A private capitalist, exempt from the control of a body, if he is a person of capacity, is considerably more likely than almost any association to run judicious risks, and originate costly improvements. Co-operative societies may be depended on for adopting improvements after they have been tested by success, but individuals are more likely to commence things previously untried. Even in ordinary business, the competition of capable persons who in the event of failure are to have all the loss, and in case of success the greater part of the gain, will be very useful in keeping the managers of co-operative societies up to the due pitch of activity and vigilence (792–3).

Interestingly enough, therefore, the success of co-operatives would to a degree depend upon the stimulus provided by the competition from private ventures.

Account must also be taken of the possibility emphasized in 1865 that co-operatives might, so to speak, 'degenerate' into joint-stock organizations which retain the employer–employee relationship in that some workers hold no shares in the company.[35] In that case – and he refers to instances in France – it was likely that the competitive advantage would lie with capitalism

---

35 In some cases the solution was for new members, rather than 'receive wages . . . as hired labourers', 'to enter at once into the full benefits of the association, without being required to bring anything in, except their labour: the only condition imposed [being] that of receiving during a few years a smaller share in the annual division of profits, as some equivalent for the sacrifices of the founders' (783).

(though not joint-stock capitalism) considering the peculiar efficacy of 'individual management, by the one person principally interested . . .' This was especially true if profit-sharing schemes were introduced by individual employers:

Co-operation has but one thing to oppose to those advantages [of individual v. collective management] – the common interest of all the workers in the work. When individual capitalists, as they will certainly do, add this to their other points of advantage; when, even if only to increase their gains, they take up the practice which these co-operative societies have dropped, and connect the pecuniary interest of every person in their employment with the most efficient and most economical management of the concern; they are likely to gain an easy victory over societies which retain the defects, while they cannot possess the full advantages, of the old system.

Assuming, however, the successful development of (genuine) co-operatives it was 'not probable that any but the least valuable work-people' – those with 'too little understanding, or too little virtue, to be capable of learning to act in any other system than that of narrow selfishness' – 'will any longer consent to work all their lives for wages merely; both private capitalists and associations will gradually find it necessary to make the entire body of labourers participants in profits. Eventually, and in perhaps a less remote future than may be supposed, we may, through the co-operative principle, see our way to a change in society . . .' Here the edition of 1865 reverts to the formulation of 1852, where Mill had stated his belief – always presuming successful competition from co-operatives for the best workers – that capitalists, rather than employ second-rate workers, would prefer to lend their capital to co-operatives 'at a diminishing rate of interest, and at last, perhaps, even to exchange their capital for terminable annuities. In this or some such mode, the existing accumulations of capital might honestly, and by a kind of spontaneous process, become in the end the joint property of all who participate in their productive employment: a transformation which, thus effected, (and assuming of course that both sexes participate equally in the rights and in the government of the association) would be the nearest approach to social justice, and the most beneficial ordering of industrial affairs for the universal good, which it is possible at present to forsee' (793–4).[36] In the 'Chapters on Socialism' (1869), as in the *Principles,* the vision for the future was a gradual transmutation of capitalism into (genuine) co-operation: 'It is even likely that when such arrangements become common' – Mill's allusion is to profit-sharing in industrial

36 Schumpeter (1954), 457 has suggested that Ferdinand Lassalle's scheme of state-subsidized productive associations which would compete private industry out of existence may have been influenced by Mill.

enterprises – 'many of these concerns would at some period or another, on the death or retirement of the chiefs, pass, by arrangement, into the state of purely co-operative associations' (V, 743).

* * *

But even a less than universal system of co-operatives would leave a profoundly beneficial mark on the private sector. This insight is best clarified in a comment on a question proposed by Fawcett to the Political Economy Club in May 1863: 'To what extent is the principle of Co-operative Trade Societies among the Working Classes economically sound?':

Doubtless many will attempt it and fail, but some, and in the end, many, will succeed. It is not necessary that all should. The success of cooperation on any large scale, will establish a practical minimum of wages, and will strike at the root of the opposition of apparent interest between employers and labourers, since whatever profit the capitalist can obtain in the face of cooperation, must be a mere equivalent for the advantage the enterprise derives from his capital, skill, and unity of management (17 May 1863, XV, 859).

Similarly, to Cliffe Leslie:

It does not seem to me that taskwork even if it could be made universal would destroy the partial opposition of interests between employers & employed. There would still remain the question of the rate of payment & the employers & workmen, supposing them both to be entirely selfish, could not have the same wishes as to that point. Nothing that I can imagine except cooperation would entirely take away the antagonism. But in order to do so, it is not necessary that cooperation should be universal. If it was only very frequent, a labourer who remained in the employment of an individual & who received from him as much (for labour of the same efficiency) as he could earn under cooperation, would see that he had no reason to complain. The employer's profit would then be a mere consequence of increased efficiency in the instruments of production, occasioned by private ownership of them. The capitalist would only take from the workmen what he first gave them (4 May 1863, *ibid.*, 857).

These comments are profoundly significant. For they clarify unmistakably Mill's recognition of an 'exploitative' element in contemporary capitalism – not inherent in the payment of interest as such, but rather a deduction from wages exceeding an amount justified by abstinence, skill and management. The wage available in the co-operative sector would provide the index of the 'fit and proper wage for a day's digging' (cf. above, p. 779).

VII   THE COLLECTIVIST OPTION REJECTED

The 'Chapters on Socialism' were written immediately after the Reform
Act of 1867 which had given new impetus to the 'legitimacy and utility'
of the laws of property from the special perspective of the labouring classes.
There was too the new, if not yet widespread, influence from the Continent.
While British workers focussed on 'certain outlying portions of the
proprietory system' – the merits of free contract in wage determination, and
of state ownership of land – the revolutionary Continentals were championing
'the abolition of the institution of private property' denying 'the legitimacy
of deriving an income in any form from property apart from labour' (*CW*,
V, 708-9). Mill's condemnation of the Continental Socialists was very sharp.
He categorized them as engaging in 'reckless extremities' and 'subversion'
having no concern other than the confiscation of 'property of all kinds out
of the hands of the possessors to be used for the general benefit', but with
little idea of the alternative system to be established.[37] It was precisely
Mill's insistence upon gradualism in social experiment – the practical testing
out of recommended changes – that governed his perspective, as he clarified
in a contrast drawn between the 'self-acting units' constituting the village
communities championed by the Owenites and Fourierists, and 'the
revolutionary Socialists' who proposed 'the management of the whole
productive resources of the country by one central authority' administered
'for the general benefit':

Whatever be the difficulties of the first of these two forms of Socialism, the second
must evidently involve the same difficulties and many more. The former, too, has
the great advantage that it can be brought into operation progressively, and can
prove its capabilities by trial. It can be tried first on a select population and extended
to others as their education and cultivation permit. It need not, and in the natural
order of things would not, become an engine of subversion until it had shown itself
capable of being also a means of reconstruction. It is not so with the other: the
aim of that is to substitute the new rule for the old at a single stroke, and to exchange
the amount of good realised under the present system, and its large possibilities
of improvement, for a plunge without any preparation into the most extreme form
of the problem of carrying on the whole round of the operations of social life without
the motive power which has always hitherto worked the social machinery. It must
be acknowledged that those who would play this game on the strength of their own
private opinion, unconfirmed as yet by any experimental verification – who would

37 Mill spells out for special attention the Swiss paper *La Solidarité*. See also for Mill's hostile
    attitude towards the First International letters to G. Brandes, 4 March 1872, XVII,
    1874-5 and to T. Smith, 4 Oct. 1872, *ibid.*, 1910-12.

forcibly deprive all who have now a comfortable physical existence of their only present means of preserving it, and would brave the frightful bloodshed and misery that would ensue if the attempt was resisted – must have a serene confidence in their own wisdom on the one hand and a recklessness of other people's sufferings on the other, which Robespierre and St. Just, hitherto the typical instances of those united attributes, scarcely came up to (737).

Referring to the need for prior experimentation Mill provided a remarkable forecast of the dangerous consequences of full-fledged centralization:

Far more, of course, may this be said of the more ambitious plan which aims at taking possession of the whole land and capital of the country, and beginning at once to administer it on the public account. Apart from all consideration of injustice to the present possessors, the very idea of conducting the whole industry of a country by direction from a single centre is so obviously chimerical, that nobody ventures to propose any mode in which it should be done; and it can hardly be doubted that if the revolutionary Socialists attained their immediate object, and actually had the whole property of the country at their disposal, they would find no other practicable mode of exercising their power over it than that of dividing it into portions, each to be made over to the administration of a small Socialist community. The problem of management, which we have seen to be so difficult even to a select population well prepared beforehand, would be thrown down to be solved as best it could by aggregations united only by locality, or taken indiscriminately from the population, including all the malefactors, all the idlest and most vicious, the most incapable of steady industry, forethought, or self-control, and a majority who, though not equally degraded, are yet, in the opinion of Socialists themselves, as far as regards the qualities essential for the success of Socialism, profoundly demoralised by the existing state of society. It is saying but little to say that the introduction of Socialism under such conditions could have no effect but disastrous failure, and its apostles could have only the consolation that the order of society as it now exists would have perished first, and all who benefit by it would be involved in the common ruin – a consolation which to some of them would probably be real, for if appearances can be trusted the animating principle of too many of the revolutionary Socialists is hate; a very excusable hatred of existing evils, which would vent itself by putting an end to the present system at all costs even to those who suffer by it, in the hope that out of chaos would arise a better Kosmos, and in the impatience of desperation respecting any more gradual improvement (748–9).

VIII ON SOCIALISM: SUMMARY

It is most important to avoid concluding that Mill can be (almost) all things to all men by failing to commit himself. We must not lose sight of his consistently expressed dislike of the class relationship characterizing capital – relations entailing 'dependency'. His ultimate ideal stands out clearly enough – to see those relations replaced by genuine co-operation. But how exactly this would be achieved was still an open question. For the immediate, indeed foreseeable, future a reformed capitalism, preferably with profit-sharing, and co-operation would hopefully coexist and compete – and Mill gave some estimate of the relative strengths of the respective organizations – the final outcome to be determined in part by that competition.

In 'On Futurity' Mill described the retail and wholesale co-operatives as 'the best preparation for a wider application of the principle' (*CW*, III, 785), suggesting that in themselves they did not yet quite provide the acid test of genuine co-operation – producer co-operatives. In the 'Chapters on Socialism' these same distributive co-operatives are referred to as constituting an experiment 'which, though suggested by and partly grounded on socialistic principles' was 'consistent with the existing constitution of property' (V, 732–3). (The discussion occurs within a section countering Socialist argumentation which is in itself indicative of the same perspective.) We have here a fine illustration of a more general theme that Socialist conceptions provided notions as to how reforms might be undertaken *within* capitalism:

What is incumbent on us is a calm comparison between two different systems of society, with a view of determining which of them affords the greatest resources for overcoming the inevitable difficulties of life. And if we find the answer to this question more difficult, and more dependent upon intellectual and moral conditions, than is usually thought, it is satisfactory to reflect that there is time before us for the question to work itself out on an experimental scale, by actual trial. I believe we shall find that no other test is possible of the practicability or beneficial operation of Socialist arrangements; but that the intellectual and moral grounds of Socialism deserve the most attentive study, as affording in many cases the guiding principles of the improvements necessary to give the present economic system of society its best chance (736).

Similarly, while Mill conceded much of the Socialist charge against competition as an invitation to poor quality goods, and saw it as 'a problem which tends to grow with the growth of population and wealth' (above, p. 785) he emphasized solutions within capitalism: First, resort to the law, a step not yet seriously attempted: 'It must be said, however, that society has never yet used the means which are already in its power of grappling with this evil. The laws against commercial frauds are very defective, and their execution still more so. Laws of this description have no chance of being really enforced unless it is the special duty of some one to enforce them. They are specially in need of a public prosecutor. It is still to be discovered how far it is possible to repress by means of the criminal law a class of misdeeds which are now seldom brought before the tribunals, and to which, when brought, the judicial administration of this country is most unduly lenient' (732).[38] Resort to the law was also incumbent to overcome financial fraud:

> With regard to those greater and more conspicuous economical frauds, or malpractices equivalent to frauds, of which so many deplorable cases have become notorious – committed by merchants and bankers between themselves or between them and those who have trusted them with money . . . the only resources which the present constitution of society affords against them are a sterner reprobation by opinion, and a more efficient repression by the law . . . Until a more moral and rational mode of dealing with culpable insolvency has been tried and failed, commercial dishonesty cannot be ranked among evils the prevalence of which is inseparable from commercial competition (733).

And secondly, there was the co-operative option – a reference to retail and wholesale outlets – as assurance against the unnecessary proliferation of distributors and against product adulteration. We have seen too, Mill's observation in correspondence that the widespread adoption of co-operation would help rid the private sector of its 'exploitative' character.

The closing chapter to the posthumously published work provides the clearest indication that the system of private property and competition was very much alive, and that even *radical* transformations would fail to eradicate the institution, a prescient observation indeed from the perspective of 1985:

> The preceding considerations appear sufficient to show that an entire renovation of the social fabric, such as is contemplated by Socialism, establishing the economic constitution of society upon an entirely new basis, other than that of private property and competition, however valuable as an ideal, and even as a prophecy of ultimate possibilities, is not available as a present resource, since it requires from those who are to carry on the new order of things qualities both moral and intellectual, which require to be tested in all, and to be created in most; and this cannot be done by an Act of Parliament, but must be, on the most favourable supposition, a work of considerable time. For a long period to come the principle of individual property will be in possession of the field; and even if in any country a popular movement were to place Socialists at the head of a revolutionary government, in however many ways they might violate private property, the institution itself would survive, and would either be accepted by them or brought back by their explusion, for the plain reason that people will not lose their hold of what is at present their sole reliance for subsistence and security until a substitute for it has been got into working order. Even those, if any, who had shared among themselves what was

---

38 But cf. III, 884 where opinion is said to reinforce the law in checking mercantile fraud.

the property of others would desire to keep what they had acquired, and to give back to property in the new hands the sacredness which they had not recognised in the old (V, 749–50).

Yet the insistence on *reform* – from the perspective of both 'justice' (which we know already to be a component of utility) and 'prudence' in this case to avoid a (premature) Socialist outcome – is reiterated with force; in which context, as always, the old term 'provisional' is conspicuous:

But though, for these reasons, individual property has presumably a long term before it, if only of provisional existence, we are not, therefore, to conclude that it must exist during that whole term unmodified, or that all the rights now regarded as appertaining to property belong to it inherently, and must endure while it endures. On the contrary, it is both the duty and the interest of those who derive the most direct benefit from the laws of property to give impartial consideration to all proposals for rendering those laws in any way less onerous to the majority. This, which would in any case be an obligation of justice, is an injunction of prudence also, in order to place themselves in the right against the attempts which are such to be frequent to bring the Socialist forms of society prematurely into operation.[39]

There can then be no question in 1869 (as in earlier statements) of the ideal – the gradual transmutation of capitalism into genuine co-operation. There can also be no question of his caution. Following Ashley (1917, App. K) Robbins (1952, 165f.) discerns a more sceptical position on the advantages of Socialism in 1869 than in 1852 – a return, as it were, to the first edition of the *Principles*, but warns us, correctly, not to exaggerate the nuance for much of the weighting of the third edition was a matter of tone induced by apologetic misreadings of the original text – an over-reaction so typical of Mill (144,156n). Little indeed had changed over the years. We know that his critical review of Harriet Martineau in 1834 and his criticism of the 'old political economy' entailed an appeal for an open mind regarding the possibilities for, and merits of, alternative institutional arrangements – rather than the championing of the almost immediate demise of the system of private property and free exchange. We have seen too that in the course of that very same account in the *Autobiography* which defines his state of opinion in the 1840s as Socialist, Mill had warned against premature enthusiasm (see also Hayek, 1942, xxx–xxxi). Considering the continued practical relevance of an economic model founded on 'private property and individual competition', it is scarcely surprising that Mill, in the *Principles*, largely subscribed to the orthodox institutional and

39 Schumpeter (1954), 532, has made the extraordinary assertion that Mill believed socialism to be at hand.

behavioural framework involving the three-factor and three-class schemata as the primary frame of reference – a work he insisted, which 'yielded to none of its predecessors in aiming at the scientific appreciation of the action of these causes, under the conditions which they pre-suppose . . .' (I, 257). The difference with other texts, as we know, simply lay in treating those conditions as provisional: 'The economic generalisations which depend, not on necessities of nature but on those combined with the existing arrangements of society, it deals with only as provisional, and as liable to be much altered by the progress of social improvement' (257).

ELEVEN

Economic policy: the reform programme

I INTRODUCTION

The total transformation of society is one thing; more modest reform is another. This chapter will be concerned with Mill's reform proposals with emphasis upon the 'condition-of-the-people' – both absolute living standards and income distribution – within a capitalist environment. Jacob Viner has maintained that Mill's sympathy with socialism was largely platonic 'for in no major concrete instance did [he] actually commit himself to the desirability of a specific drastic change. Mill aspired after the millennium, but he found abundant reason why it was not and should not be wished to be imminent' (1958, 330). There is much as we have found, that is accurate in a view emphasizing Mill's hard-headedness. Yet it would be an error if that allowance were taken to imply a minimization of the need for sweeping reform, albeit within a 'system of private property'.

Mill's predilection for balance in his argumentation does not facilitate the interpretive task. We have it on high authority that Mill denigrated increases in real income as such, following a tradition extending back at least to Adam Smith – what concerned the classical economists was 'better men', not maximum output (Stigler, 1949, 4). Yet if by this generalization is intended also per capita income one must question whether it reflects accurately Mill's intention, any more than Smith's,[1] although there is no

---

1   'Is this improvement in the circumstances of the lower ranks of the people to be regarded as an advantage or as an inconvenience to the society? The answer seems at first sight abundantly plain. Servants, labourers and workmen of different kinds, make up the far

gainsaying a concern with 'better men'. Productivity gain with an eye to per capita income – assuming, that is, a 'fair' distribution – was at the very forefront of Mill's concern in a wide variety of contexts.[2]

Before proceeding to specifics it is worthwhile taking a broad perspective on the issue at hand. A statement in the review of 'Thornton on Labour and its Claims' (1869) is relevant here:

having regard to the greatly superior numbers of the labouring class, and the inevitable scantiness of the remuneration afforded even by the highest rate of wages which, in the present state of the arts of production, could possibly become general; whoever does not wish that the labourers may prevail [in 'the strife for wages between the labourers and the capitalists'], and that the highest limit, whatever it be, may be attained, must have a standard of morals, and a conception of the most desirable state of society, widely different from those of either Mr. Thornton or the present writer (CW, V, 658).

Although this is a late statement it is quite characteristic of Mill throughout and has much in common with Adam Smith's celebrated formulation.[3] Mill's general sympathies are clear and must be read in terms of the 'greatest happiness' principle. Specifically his overriding concern was social justice – which can be interpreted, as Mill came to interpret it, as the highest category of utility – and by which he understood respect for individuality to be satisfied by equality of opportunity. This is the governing rule and much that otherwise seems obscure in Mill is easily understood if one continually reverts to it. But it is a rule that did not dictate a *specific* position on distribution holding good for all time and space.[4] And it certainly did not provide a licence for the wholesale spoliation of the rich even in his own day and age.[5]

greater part of every great political society. But what improves the circumstances of the greater part can never be regarded as an inconveniency to the whole. No society can surely be flourishing and happy, of which the far greater part of the members are poor and miserable. It is but equity, besides, that they who feed, cloath and lodge the whole body of the people should have such a share of the produce of their own labour as to be themselves tolerably well fed, cloathed and lodged' (Smith, [1937], 78–9).

2 That interpretation is not easy is not denied; cf. Robson (1968), 251–2: 'Whether [Mill] held that further increases in production would be impossible or unnecessary is not clear . . .'

3 '[W]hat improves the circumstances of the greater part can never be regarded as an inconveniency to the whole. No society can surely be flourishing and happy, of which the far greater part of the members are poor and miserable' (see note 1).

4 Cf. Robson (1968), 216: 'Mill's sympathy with the labouring poor was not because their immediate desires are more in accord with utility than those of the middle and upper classes, but because their share of the general interest has received less attention' (see also 246–7, 256).

5 A full treatment of Mill's position on redistribution would require close attention to his political proposals, especially those regarding proportional representation as a device to

Equality of opportunity indeed demanded changes in the distribution of property and its control (including far-reaching restrictions on legacies in general and landed property in particular). And while Mill opposed a progressive income tax on grounds of the principle of proportionality of income to effort and abstinence, progression is strongly recommended in the case of unearned income and in the evaluation of rates of indirect taxation.[6] Mill himself expected that these proposals – especially those regarding inheritance – would cause an uproar. In the event they did not, and this may be explained by his willingness to modify his proposals in the light of the state of opinion; and by the fact that his championship of equality of opportunity did not gainsay a basic insistence upon security of property. Indeed, the greatest weight was placed on it in the account of economic development over long periods, as we have seen, an expediential justification which is reinforced by one from equity (a higher utility) – respect for individuality itself. His proposals, moreover, allowed even major (earned) income differentials.

Mill, in short, made no concessions to green eye. He also made no concessions to fraud wherever he found it – high wages and short hours were desirable, but only if honestly achieved; and, similarly, he placed the blame for low standards wherever he found it, in some cases laying responsibility on privileged classes of labourers. Finally, there were 'laws of production' which had to be thoroughly understood – not all social ills could be blamed on governments or employers.

Unfortunately, Mill's eminently fair and balanced position does not facilitate the task of interpretation. It is in fact a currently disputed issue whether Mill was at all preoccupied with distributive justice in the sense of a concern for the present as distinct from the inhabitants of some future society reeducated according to some élitist model. This position has been argued with reference to Mill's general redistribution proposals and his specific attitude to unions, having in mind his treatment of the poorest strata of contemporary society in the light of the population problem (West, 1978b; West and Hofer, 1978, 1981). Bearing in mind the centrality of the population doctrine, we will demonstrate how questionable is this evaluation in both the general and more specific contexts (a view also maintained in Ekelund and Tollison, 1976, 1978, and Ekelund and Kordsmeier, 1981).

II EQUALITY OF OPPORTUNITY AND PROPERTY RIGHTS

Our concern in what follows is the immediate 'improvements' which Mill had in mind for the system of individual property – his program for a

---

protect minorities in a world with widely extended franchise. For this see Robbins (1952), 203–5; and for a more extensive discussion Hutchison (1981), Ch. 2. On some of Mill's concerns regarding the franchise in the *Principles* itself, see III, 763–4.
6 On some of the contrasts between Millian and Hayekian liberalism see Schwartz (1972), 150f.

reformed capitalism as distinct from its 'subversion'. As we already know Mill declaimed against the 'miseries and inequities of a state of such inequality of wealth' (II, 202). The key to reform was equality of opportunity. Schemes to subsidize the higher education of the poor were given great weight from this perspective:

> The real hardship of social inequalities to the poor, as the reasonable among them can be brought to see, is not that men *are* unequal, but that they are born so; . . . that the higher positions in life, including all which confer power or dignity, can not only be obtained by the rich without taking the trouble to be qualified for them, but that even were this corrected (to which there is an increasing tendency), none, as a rule, except the rich, have it in their power to make themselves qualified. By the proposal of the Commissioners, every child of poor parents (for, of course, girls must sooner or later be included) would have that power opened to him, if he passed with real distinction through the course of instruction provided for all; and the feelings which give rise to Socialism would be in a great measure disarmed, in as much of them as is unreasonable or exaggerated, by this just concession to that in them which is rational and legitimate ('Endowments', 1869, V, 628).

More generally, the contemporary system of private property, as Mill put it in the *Principles*, operated to assure an income distribution such that 'the produce of labour' was

> almost in an inverse ratio to the labour – the largest portions to those who have never worked at all, the next largest to those whose work is almost nominal, and so in a descending scale, the remuneration dwindling as the work grows harder and more disagreeable, until the most fatiguing and exhausting bodily labour cannot count with certainty on being able to earn even the necessaries of life . . . [The laws of property] have made property of things which never ought to be property, and absolute property where only a qualified property ought to exist. They have not held the balance fairly between human beings, but have heaped impediments upon some, to give advantage to others; they have purposely fostered inequalities, and prevented all from starting fair in the race (II, 207).

The foregoing extract provides a provisional, though partial, indication of Mill's conception of justice in income distribution. Conspicuous is the principle that wage income should be proportioned to labour, a principle in part reflecting championship of an optimum structure of earnings in the Smithian sense of that term, and which Mill considered to be subverted both by labour immobility and by excess labour supply in the aggregate. In the present context he wrote very strongly that '[the] generality of labourers in this and most other countries, have as little choice of occupation or freedom of locomotion, are practically as dependent on fixed rules and on the will of others, as they could be on any system short of actual slavery' (209). The contemporary system, in brief, failed to satisfy 'the equitable principle, of proportion between remuneration and exertion' (208).

It is, however, conceded that 'the proportioning of remuneration to work done, is really just, only in so far as the more or less of the work is a matter of choice: when it depends on natural difference of strength or capacity, this principle of remuneration is in itself an injustice: it is giving to those who have; assigning most to those who are already favoured by nature' (210). Mill allowed that, in principle, some compensation might be made to 'the less robust members of the community' (201); and at one point he even defined the principle of 'distributive justice' as a 'redressing of the inequalities and wrongs of nature' (III, 808). But provided 'all were done which it would be in the power of good government to do, by instruction and legislation to diminish this inequality of opportunities' – including in this context apparently, disabilities due to poverty itself – 'the differences of fortune arising from people's own earnings could not justly give umbrage' (811).[7] Acceptance of the distributional consequences flowing from the inevitable residual of natural differences – and insistence upon pay proportionate to effort – was a matter of expedience: 'Considered . . . as a compromise with the selfish type of character formed by the present standard of morality, and fostered by the existing social institutions it is highly expedient; and until education shall have been entirely regenerated, is far more likely to prove immediately successful, than any attempt at a higher ideal' (II, 210). It would, in short, be foolhardy to neglect 'the strength of the incitement given to labour when the whole or a large share of the benefit of extra exertion belongs to the labourer' (204). Mill was evidently prepared to allow some compromise of justice on grounds of expediency, although as we know he regarded justice itself as a matter of utility albeit of a peculiarly high order.

7 This in 1852. The version of 1849 reads thus: '[A]nd it is the part of a good government to provide, that, as far as more paramount considerations permit, the inequality of opportunities shall be remedied. When all kinds of useful instruction shall be as accessible as they might be made, and when the cultivated intelligence of the poorer classes, aided so far as necessary by the guidance and co-operation of the state, shall obviate, as it might so well do, the major part of the disabilities attendant on poverty, the inequalities of fortune arising from people's own earnings could not justly give umbrage'.

Cf. a sharp letter to Arthur Helps of 1847 regarding the assumption 'that inequality is a thing which should be cultivated, that people should be educated with a view to a "just progression of nice distinctions of rank." As I look upon inequality as *in itself* always an evil, I do not agree with any one who would use the machinery of society for the purpose of promoting it. As much inequality as necessarily arises from protecting all persons in the free use of their faculties of body & mind & in the enjoyment of what these can obtain for them, must be submitted to for the sake of a greater good: but I certainly see no necessity for artificially adding to it, while I see much for tempering it, impressing both on the laws & on the usages of mankind as far as possible the contrary tendency' (XVII, 2002).

We must now take into account income from property. The legacy of the past dictated a distribution of property (and accordingly of income) which reflected not the 'fruits of personal exertion' (201) – not a 'just partition, or acquisition by industry' – but the accidental outcome of 'conquest and violence' (207); indeed contemporary arrangements, thus governed by historical accident, failed even to satisfy those expediential 'considerations of utility' which might to some degree justify the system (201).[8]

The defects of the contemporary property system accounted for its basic negative characteristic, namely, that people are prevented 'from starting fair in the race' – the absence of equality of opportunity. It should again be made quite clear that Mill did not recommend 'a fair start' in any extreme sense of that term. Indeed, that all should start 'on perfectly equal terms' was said to be 'inconsistent with any law of private property' (207); allowing private property there were inevitable inequalities thereof arising from 'unequal industry, frugality, perseverence, talents, and to a certain extent even opportunities' (225). But what was the argument for private property; and what could be done to minimize its defects?

As for *landed* property there was no case to be made at all from the perspective of justice. Property was 'only a means to an end, not itself an end' (223) – 'to assure to all persons what they have produced by their labour and accumulated by their abstinence' (227).[9] But this 'essential principle of property' could not apply 'to what is not the produce of labour, the raw material of the earth' (227). The contrast with other forms of property is drawn forcefully:

When the 'sacredness of property' is talked of, it should always be remembered, that any such sacredness does not belong in the same degree to landed property. No man made the land. It is the original inheritance of the whole species. Its appropriation is wholly a question of general expediency. When private property in land is not expedient, it is unjust. It is no hardship to any one, to be excluded

8 For very strong statements see 'Thornton on Labour and its Claims' (1869, V, 653): 'Landed property at least, in all the countries of modern Europe, derives its origins from force; the land was taken by military violence from former possessors, by those from whom it has been transmitted to its present owners . . . the sellers could not impart to others a better title than they themselves possessed. Movable property, no doubt, has on the whole a purer origin, its first acquirers having mostly worked for it, at something useful to their fellow citizens. But, looking at the question merely historically, and confining our attention to the larger masses, the doctrine that the rights of capital are those of past labour is liable even here to great abatements'.

9 Cf. a statement of 1861, V, 558: 'I do not recognize any rights or obligations as existing in property itself, in things; I recognize them only as existing in persons. All moral rights reside in persons; and all moral obligations are towards persons and I should consider nothing but persons in any question of justice.'

from what others have produced: they were not bound to produce it for his use, and he loses nothing by not sharing in what otherwise would not have existed at all. But it is some hardship to be born into the world and to find all nature's gifts previously engrossed, and no place left for the new-comer (230).

It followed from this distinction 'that property in land should be interpreted strictly, and that the balance in all cases of doubt should incline against the proprietor'; 'no exclusive right should be permitted in any individual, which cannot be shown to be productive of positive good' – the precise reverse was the case where other forms of property were concerned – for '[the] privilege, or monopoly, is only defensible as a necessary evil' and 'becomes an injustice when carried to any point to which the compensating good does not follow it' (231–2).[10] Thus, depending upon circumstances, a case could be made for private appropriation of land – pre-eminently where such an arrangement was a precondition for land improvement. But '[w]henever, in any country, the proprietor generally speaking, ceases to be the improver, political economy has nothing to say in defence of landed property, as there established. In no sound theory of private property was it ever contemplated that the proprietor of land should be merely a sinecurist quartered on it' (228). In principle, land nationalization or land redistribution could be justified (with compensation):

[T]he state is at liberty to deal with landed property as the general interests of the community may require, even to the extent, if it so happen, of doing with the whole, what is done with a part whenever a bill is passed for a railroad or a new street. The community has too much at stake in the proper cultivation of the land, and in the conditions annexed to the occupancy of it, to leave those things to the discretion of a class of persons called landlords, when they have shown themselves unfit for the trust. The legislature, which if it pleased might convert the whole body of landlords into fundholders or pensioners, might, *a fortiori*, commute the average receipts of Irish landowners into a fixed rent charge, and raise the tenants into proprietors; supposing always that the full market value of the land was tendered to the landlords, in case they preferred that to accepting the conditions proposed (231).

10 Cf. 'Newman's Political Economy' (1851): 'We agree fully . . . in the doctrine that there can be, morally speaking, only a qualified property in things not produced by labour, such as the raw material of the earth . . . The conclusion is, that property in land is essentially subordinate to public convenience; that the rights of the landed proprietor ought to be construed strictly; that the law should not merely, as is the case of moveable property, forbid him from using it to the injury of others, but should compel him to allow to others all such use as is not incompatible with the purposes for which he is permitted to exercise dominion over it; and, finally, that it may at any time, if the public interest requires, be taken by the legislature, on payment of compensation' (V, 450–1).

In the posthumous 'Chapters on Socialism' (1869) the relativity of the notion of 'property' is forcibly insisted upon with an eye to 'the public good' – in full conformity with Mill's own proposals in the *Principles* and elsewhere:

When . . . it is maintained, rightly or wrongly, that some change or modification in the powers exercised over things by the persons legally recognised as their proprietors would be beneficial to the public and conducive to the general improvement, it is no good answer to this merely to say that the proposed changed conflicts with the idea of property . . . A proposed reform in laws or customs is not necessarily objectionable because its adoption would imply, not the adaptation of all human affairs to the existing idea of property, but the adaptation of existing ideas of property to the growth and improvement of human affairs. This is said without prejudice to the equitable claim of proprietors to be compensated by the state for such legal rights of a proprietary nature as they may be dispossessed of for the public advantage . . . Under this condition, however, society is fully entitled to abrogate or alter any particular right of property which on sufficient consideration it judges to stand in the way of the public good. And assuredly the terrible case which . . . Socialists are able to make out against the present economic order of society, demands a full consideration of all means by which the institution may have a chance of being made to work in a manner more beneficial to that large portion of society which at present enjoys the least share of its direct benefits (V, 753).

In contrast to his rights to landed property, the owner's 'property in moveables, and in all things the product of labour' should be, Mill maintained, 'absolute, except where positive evil to others would result from [such exclusion]' (II, 231). A legitimate and conspicuous exception Mill discerned in the imposition of conditions on the use of legacies for generations to come. The 'mischiefs to society of such perpetuities' had indeed to be balanced against the fact that some persons are motivated 'to acquire a fortune from the hope of founding a family in perpetuity', but still Mill envisaged a net social disadvantage justifying, on grounds of expediency, limitation on the right of bequest (223). Similarly, and yet more widespread in its implications, he justified legislative measures to restrict the magnitude of bequests to any single individual in order to reduce the concentration of wealth.[11] These matters will be elaborated below, having in mind here

11 Cf. III, 811: 'With respect to the large fortunes acquired by gift or inheritance, the power of bequeathing is one of those privileges of property which are fit subjects for regulation on grounds of general expediency; and I have already suggested, as a possible ['as the most eligible' until 1862] mode of restraining the accumulation of large fortunes in the hands of those who have not earned them by exertion, a limitation of the amount which any one person should be permitted to acquire by gift, bequest, or inheritance.'

Mill's insistence that 'the principle of property' would not be infringed by such measures since individuals were still assured 'the fruits of their *own* labour and abstinence'; and that

if as much pains as has been taken to aggravate the inequality of chances arising from the natural working of the principle, had been taken to temper that inequality by every means not subversive of the principle itself; if the tendency of legislation had been to favour the diffusion, instead of the concentration of wealth – to encourage that subdivision of the large masses, instead of striving to keep them together; the principle of individual property would have been found to have no necessary connexion with the physical and social evils which almost all Socialist writers assume to be inseparable from it (208).

A letter of 1870 summarizes well Mill's distinctions betwen forms of property and his approach to social policy in terms of the overriding consideration of public utility:

There is . . . this great practical difference between the case of moveable wealth and that of land, that, so long as land is allowed to be private property (and I cannot regard its private appropriation as a permanent institution) society seems to me bound to provide that the proprietor shall only make such uses of it as shall not essentially interfere with its utility to the public: while, in the case of capital, and moveable property generally, though society has the same right, yet the interests of society would in general be better consulted by laws restrictive of the acquisition of too great masses of property, than by attempting to regulate its use. I have, in my Political Economy, proposed limitations of the right of ownership, so far as the power of bequest is part of it, on the express ground of its being injurious to society that enormous fortunes should be possessed by gift or inheritance (26 June 1870, XVII, 1740).[12]

III LAND REFORM: DISTRIBUTIVE ASPECTS

Let us look now at the actual reform program, as distinct from matters of principle, that Mill had in mind as far as concerns landed property, approaching the issue first from the perspective of distribution. The 'inequity' of the institution of private property had to be balanced against

12 Cf. 'Leslie on the Land Question' (1870): 'The question has been raised whether the administration of the land of a country is a subject to which our current maxims of free trade, free contract, the exclusive power of every one over his own property, and so forth, are really applicable, or applicable without very serious limitations; whether private individuals ought to have the same absolute control, the same *jus utendi et abutendi*, over landed property, which it is just and expedient that they should be permitted to exercise over movable wealth' (V, 672).

efficiency considerations, and it would seem that Mill did not envisage the abolition of the system in its entirety.

There is first Mill's hostility towards primogeniture and legal restraints on the sale of property – feudal remnants designed 'to keep up large hereditary fortunes, and a landed aristocracy' (III, 888).[13] A variety of quite extraordinary arguments, including one by McCulloch, in favour of primogeniture are rejected (see below, pp. 839–40), but for our present purposes we need note only Mill's summary remark regarding distributive equity:

As to the deeper consideration, that the diffusion of wealth, and not its concentration, is desirable, and that the more wholesome state of society is not that in which immense fortunes are possessed by a few and coveted by all, but that in which the greatest possible numbers possess and are contented with a moderate competency, which all may hope to acquire: I refer to it in this place, only to show, how widely separated, on social questions, is the entire mode of thought of the defenders of primogeniture, from that which is partially promulgated in the present treatise (891).[14]

We shall return to the matter of inheritance presently.

There is also the celebrated proposal regarding the taxation of land values or rather the unearned increment of land rent reflecting the consequences of economic growth:

[A] kind of income which constantly tends to increase, without any exertion or sacrifice on the part of the owners: those owners constituting a class of the community, whom the natural course of things progressively enriches, consistently with complete passiveness on their own part. In such a case it would be no violation of the principles on which private property is grounded, if the state should appropriate this increase of wealth, or part of it, as it arises. This would not properly be taking anything from anybody; it would merely be applying an accession of wealth, created by circumstances, to the benefit of society, instead of allowing it to become an unearned appendage to the riches of a particular class . . . They grow richer as it were in their sleep, without working, risking, or economizing. What claim have they on the general principle of social justice, to this accession of riches? (819–20).[15]

---

13 It must be noted (cf. III, 888) that in England the law applied primogeniture only in cases of intestacy; otherwise primogeniture was not binding and the owner could allocate land freely including entail of property on one particular line of descendents. But then it could not be sold since each successive owner had a life-interest only in the property.

14 Cf. also *ibid.*, 892: 'Unless a strong case of social utility can be made out for primogeniture, it stands sufficiently condemned by the general principles of justice; being a broad distinction in the treatment of one person and of another, grounded solely on an accident' (892).

15 Cf. Mill to Baer, 8 Jan. 1873, XVII, 1932: 'Quant aux impôts sur la terre il me paraît juste . . . de retenir pour l'état le tout ou une partie de l'acroissement de la rente qui

Similarly, rentals for houses 'of the favourite situations in large towns' are described as 'among the very few kinds of income which are fit subjects for peculiar taxation . . . being the most gigantic example extant of enormous accessions of riches acquired rapidly, and in many cases unexpectedly, by a few families, from the mere accident of their possessing certain tracts of land, without their having themselves aided in the acquisition by the smallest exertion, outlay, or risk' (835).

Despite the force of these statements Mill yet insisted upon the avoidance of injustice to landowners who might legitimately claim a lack of 'faith' – that their lands had been purchased on the presumption that any impositions on rents would be no greater than on any other income.[16] This problem could however, be overcome by subjecting 'all future increment of rent' beyond a specific date 'to special taxation; in doing which all injustice to landlords would be obviated, if the present market-price of their land were secured to them; since that includes the present value of all future expectations'(821).[17] In brief, 'a tax which, sparing existing rents, should content itself with appropriating a portion of any future increase arising from the mere action of natural causes. But even this could not be justly done, without offering as an alternative the market price of the land' (826).

In taking this position Mill left open the question of the extent of taxation of the increment due to economic progress. But he did effectively come to grips with the problem of justice in the special treatment of that class of income which had so troubled Ricardo.[18]

a lieu par des causes naturelles ou sociales indépendantes du travail ou des frais du propriétaire tandis que l'intérêt du capital tend plutôt à baisser.'

16 Cf. V, 485: 'After a tax has existed for a considerable time, so as to be attached to a particular property, and to be considered in all settlements and all bequests of that property, and in all sales of it, though it may be on the ground of policy expedient and desirable to make an alteration in the tax, it has been never contended for on the ground of justice to the possessors of the property.'

17 Practical suggestions are made (III, 820) regarding how to avoid impinging on increases in rent due to the skill and expenditure of the landlord.

18 Mill also justified, and recommended an increase in, the contemporary English land-tax although a discriminatory tax, there being no counterpart in the case of other incomes (III, 821–2). Cf. V, 479f., on the contemporary land tax, interpreted as a reserve by the State of a certain portion of rent which had never belonged to the owner, constituting a feudal obligation.

Robson (1968), 252, has made the point that Mill's 'early training in Ricardian economics and Benthamite politics taught him to regard the landowning class as one of the chief obstacles to social progress, not only because it desired to maintain the injustice of the economic *status quo*, but also because of its essential inutility. While in general Mill's attitude to land is in accordance with his normal treatment of social topics, he tends to press the argument more strongly against his political opponents, the land-owners, than against his frequent allies, the industrial and commercial class'.

The proposal in question is a key feature of the Programme of the Land Tenure Reform Association, an 'explanatory statement' for which was written by Mill in 1871. Here Mill declared that the Land Laws were designed 'to prop up a ruling class' – indeed, in the post-1867 world, 'of all our leading institutions, none are more unsuited than the Land Laws' – for 'the land has been prevented, to a large extent, from passing out of the hands of the idle into those of the industrious, and its ownership has been retained as the privilege of a small and decreasing number of families' (V, 689).[19] He alluded briefly to proposals to abolish entirely private property in land but hoped that all would go along with the milder measures of the Society bearing in mind that its program in no way justified a permanent system of private property.

As in the *Principles* the general emphasis is on land as a 'natural monopoly' in the sense of fixity of aggregate supply, such that a 'rise of the value of land, and of the incomes of landowners' inevitably followed (independently of any effort) 'increased demand for agricultural products, and for building land . . .' (III, 691).[20] The proposal (again as in the *Principles*) would allow landlords the choice of selling their property to the State at the going market price:

In this manner, that increase of wealth which now flows into the coffers of private persons from the mere progress of society, and not from their own merits or sacrifices, will be gradually, and in an increasing proportion, diverted from them to the nation as a whole, from whose collective exertions and sacrifices it really proceeds. The State will receive the entire rent of the lands voluntarily sold to it by their possessors, together with a tax on the future increase of rent on those properties whose owners have sufficient confidence in the justice and moderation of the State to prefer retaining them. These owners should be allowed at any future period to alter their minds, and give up their lands for the price first offered; or more, if they can show that they have made, during the intervening period, substantial improvements at their own cost. The option thus allowed would be a permanent security to the landowners against any unjust or excessive exercise of the right of taxation by the State (691–2).[21]

19 Even investment in improvements when made by tenants ultimately generated 'an unearned addition to the income of the landlord'.
20 Cf. 'Leslie on the Land Question': '[I]t is an acknowledged principle that when the State permits a monopoly, either natural or artificial, to fall into private hands, it retains the right, and cannot divest itself of the duty, to place the exercise of the monopoly under any degree of control which is requisite for the public good' (V, 672).
21 The options satisfied the landlord's just claims yet benefited the State 'since an individual never gives, in present money, for a remote profit, anything like what that profit is worth to the State, which is immortal' (691).

Mill evidently expected that at least some landlords would choose the option of the sale to the State. And the program of the Society regarding State acquisition goes beyond the formal argument of the *Principles*.[22] For it is now firmly insisted that no new transfers from the public domain were to be permitted. Mill here had in mind the practice whereby 'common lands' could, by Act of Parliament, be taken up for cultivation by their nominal owner – an 'iniquity' involving 'gifts' to the wealthiest class (692–3).[23] Similarly, land owned by public bodies and endowed institutions – much of London and the great towns – had to be regarded as public property (694).

* * *

What though of the disposition of the land in State hands? The overriding consideration is the 'general good' with special reference to the working classes, although the precise form that land use would take was a matter of expediency. The options listed are an index of Mill's typical perspective – his concern with amenity, and with experiment. As for the latter the specific list includes peasant ownership as well as capitalist farming (with guarantees to labour), 'small cultivation' by individuals (who provide both capital and labour) and co-operative farming of State lands, although Mill was doubtful whether public opinion would encourage peasant proprietorship:

When the State thinks fit to exercise its right to these waste lands, the lord of the manor should be compensated for his manorial rights, and the commoners for their rights of common, at the existing value, and the land either kept open for the enjoyment of the people or cultivated for their use. The Society attach great importance to keeping open extensive tracts in a state of wild natural beauty and freedom; and a large portion of the waste lands of the country are of too poor a quality to be worth much for any other purpose. When the land is worth cultivation, and the wants of society require that it should be cultivated, the mode of bringing it into cultivation should be principally determined by the interest of the labouring classes. Were it desirable to give any further extension to private property in land, those classes would have a paramount claim to be admitted to a share in it, by the

22 But it should be noted that in the *Principles*, apart from justifying the discriminatory taxation of land rent, Mill had also insisted upon public access to private land unless necessary for protection against damage to crops, denied that landowners had the right to do or abstain from doing anything inconsistent with the 'public good', and rejected any case for private property where land was not intended for cultivation, from which it followed that the public should at the very least suffer no inconveniences compared with their situation if the land was unappropriated (II, 232).

23 By ancient feudal arrangements, the Lord of the Manor or nominal owner could use the property for game only while the wood growing wild was shared with those who had 'rights in common', namely the adjacent landowners. The peasantry had to all intents and purposes been dispossessed entirely – in exchange for the landowners' forfeiture of various usage rights.

grant of the land in small parcels to respectable agricultural labourers at a fixed rent. But if, as is, perhaps, more to be expected, the opinion prevails that any further permanent alienation of the land is undesirable, these lands will remain with the State, or with local authorities, as a means of trying, with the greatest advantage and under every variety of circumstances, the modes in which land can be most successfully managed on the public account – whether by capitalist farmers, with stipulations for the benefit of the labourers, or by long leases on proper conditions to small cultivators, or, finally, by co-operative farming (693).

In the context of State acquisition of lands owned by endowed institutions, Mill observed – in line with his approach to endowment generally (see below, p. 855f) and with an eye to the 'general good': 'It can keep those lands together, and administer them either for the objects to which they are appropriated, or for such other objects as may be considered preferable, and permit them to be leased or occupied on such terms as it thinks fit by individuals or associations . . . It is obvious what facilitates their possession would give for promoting every improvement that tends to raise the condition of the people: sanitary works, improved dwellings, public gardens, co-operative buildings, co-operative agriculture, useful public institutions of every kind' (694). But since the endowed properties involved largely city areas while fairness required that the proposed advantages should be enjoyed throughout the country Mill further proposed that the State 'should purchase from private owners estates which are in the market, when such purchase is necessary for giving a fair trial in any neighbourhood to co-operative agriculture, or to a properly regulated system of small farming (695).[24]

This latter proposal, introduced rather casually in the present context, played in fact a central role in Mill's reform proposals. This is clear from 'Leslie on the Land Problem' (1870). Here *inter alia* Mill addressed the burning issue of rural poverty, which he attributed – following both Leslie (1870) and Thornton (1846) – to the dispossession of (English) labourers 'of their ancient proprietory rights and beneficial interest in the soil' (V, 680). The consequences were a disaster: 'Economically, the emergency is much greater at this moment in this [England] than in the other island [Ireland]; the main land question here relates to a poorer class than even the Irish tenantry, and there is a much greater amount of material misery and actual destitution in England, traceable mainly to its own land system, though aggravated by that of Ireland and the consequent immigration of

---

24 Mill rejected a case in favour of private speculation in land values on the grounds that individual foresight would assure earlier use of city property than otherwise (694n). Apart from allowance for long leases from the State to individuals who observe an opportunity for profitable land use, the 'Land Department' of the State would, Mill countered, 'exercise for its benefit the foresight now exercised by individuals for theirs'.

poverty' (681).[25] Mill accepted the objective of various proposals by Leslie to 'restrict the power of keeping together large masses of land in a particular line of descent' and assure an increased quantity of land on the market (682) – they were after all a reiteration of his own proposals in the *Principles*. But in his view this would do little 'towards making any great part of the land of this country the property of the actual cultivators,' for in England (unlike France where the poor 'give the highest price, the rich being neither numerous, nor, in general, addicted to rural duties or pleasures') it was to be expected that the sale of land would generally be to the rich, and that the new owners, albeit more numerous, would neither cultivate the land themselves nor grant better leasing conditions to tenants than currently existed (683). The solution demanded direct State intervention:

If the greater marketableness of land is to be made a benefit to the labouring class, it must be in another manner entirely; as, for example, by buying from time to time on account of the public, as much of the land that comes into the market as may be sufficient to give a full trial to such modes of leasing it, either to small farmers with due security of tenure, or to co-operative associations of labourers, as without impairing, but probably even increasing, the produce of the soil, would make the direct benefits of its possession descend to those who hold the plough and wield the spade.

IV LAND REFORM: EFFICIENCY ASPECTS

Mill, we have seen, refused to commit himself to private property in land as a permanent institution – on the contrary his allowance was contingent upon assurance that efficiency considerations outweighed the inequity *inherent* in the system. But as long as the system existed it was desirable to maximize productivity. On these grounds – as well as to avoid excessive concentrations of wealth – a strong case is made against promigeniture, entail and restraints on alienation of land.

Various forced defences of primogeniture as stimulus to effort are examined in the *Principles* and rejected, including one by McCulloch whereby the expenses of the great landlords, though 'injurious to themselves', set a pattern for emulation by others; in Mill's paraphrase 'the custom of primogeniture seems to render all classes more industrious, and to augment at the same time, the mass of wealth and the scale of enjoyment'

---

25 Mill agreed with Leslie that '[t]he land question in Ireland is a tenant's question; and what the case principally requires is reform of the conditions of tenure. The land question in England is mainly a labourer's question, though the tenants also suffer deeply from the same causes which have reduced the labourers to their present state' (679). The distinction implies, of course, the existence of a class of capitalist farmers, distinct from their labourers, in England only.

(*CW*, III, 889–90). The argument is firmly rejected. Mill conceded only that 'a state of complete equality of fortunes would not be favourable to active exertion for the increase of wealth. Speaking of the mass, it is as true of wealth as of most other distinctions – of talent, knowledge, virtue – that those who already have, or think they have, as much of it as their neighbours, will seldom exert themselves to acquire more.' But beyond that he refused to go, illustrating his case from the 'industrial energy and ardour of accumulation' in the United States. Differentials in *earned* income sufficed for the task:

[It] is not therefore necessary that society should provide a set of persons with large fortunes, to fulfil the social duty of standing to be looked at, with envy and admiration, by the aspiring poor. The fortunes which people have acquired for themselves, answer the purpose quite as well, indeed much better; since a person is more powerfully stimulated by the example of somebody who has earned a fortune, than by the mere sight of somebody who possesses one; and the former is necessarily an example of prudence and frugality as well as industry, while the latter much oftener sets an example of profuse expense, which spreads, with pernicious effect, to the very class on whom the sight of riches is supposed to have so beneficial an influence, namely, those whose weakness of mind, and taste for ostentation, makes 'the splendour of the richest landlords' attract them with the most potent spell . . . When a country has once fairly entered into the industrial career . . . the desire of acquisition by industry needs no factitious stimulus: the advantages naturally inherent in riches, and the character they assume of a test by which talent and success in life are habitually measured, are an ample security for their being pursued with sufficient intensity and zeal (890–1).

The discussion of constraints on land transfer provides a conspicuous illustration of Mill's recognition of the role of self-interest, within an appropriate institutional framework, in assuring maximum efficiency of resource use. Contemporary land law is criticized for impeding the process:

It fails, first, by the uncertainty, and the maze of technicalities, which make it impossible for any one, at however great an expense, to possess a title to land which he can positively know to be unassailable. It fails, secondly, in omitting to provide due evidence of transactions, by a proper registration of legal documents. It fails, thirdly, by creating a necessity for operose and expensive instruments and formalities (independently of fiscal burthens) on occasion of the purchase and sale, or even the lease or mortgage, of immoveable property. And, fourthly, it fails by the intolerable expense and delay of law proceedings, in almost all cases where real property is concerned (884–5).

These deficiencies had nefarious effects on productivity. Apart from the impediment of uncertainty of title to capital expenditures in improvement,[26] high transfer costs impeded the market from selecting the most appropriate form of land use and magnitude of land unit.[27] The latter theme is repeatedly alluded to and illustrates a thoroughly 'Chicagoan' perspective:

[T]he expense of making transfers, operates to prevent land from coming into the hands of those who would use it to most advantage; often amounting, in the case of small purchases, to more than the price of the land, and tantamount, therefore, to a prohibition of the purchase and sale of land in small portions, unless in exceptional circumstances. Such purchases, however, are almost everywhere extremely desirable, there being hardly any country in which landed property is not either too much or too little subdivided, requiring either that great estates should be broken down, or that small ones should be bought up and consolidated. To make land as easily transferable as stock, would be one of the greatest economical improvements which could be bestowed on a country; and has been shown, again and again, to have no insuperable difficulty attending it (885-6).

All taxes must be condemned which throw obstacles in the way of the sale of land, or other instruments of production. Such sales tend naturally to render the property more productive. The seller, whether moved by necessity or choice, is probably some one who is either without the means, or without the capacity, to make the most advantageous use of the property for productive purposes; while the buyer, on the other hand, is at any rate not needy, and is frequently both inclined and able to improve the property, since, as it is worth more to such a person than to any other, he is likely to offer the highest price for it. All taxes, therefore, and all difficulties and expenses, annexed to such contracts, are decidedly detrimental; especially in the case of land, the source of subsistence, and the original foundation of all wealth, on the improvement of which, therefore, so much depends. Too great facilities cannot be given to enable land to pass into the hands, and assume the modes of aggregation or division, most conducive to its productiveness. If landed properties are too large, alienation should be free, in order that they may be subdivided; if too small, in order that they may be united. All taxes on the transfer of landed property should be abolished; but, as the landlords have no claim to be relieved from any reservation which the state has hitherto made in its own favour

26 In 'Leslie on the Land Question' (1870) Mill praised a new bill for recognizing 'that in Ireland at least, security of tenure is indispensable to enlist the self-interest of the occupier of land on the side of good cultivation, and that this security cannot, in Ireland, be trusted to the operation of contract, but must be provided by law' (V, 674).

27 The deficiency in the English law was compounded by the fact that stamp duties on contracts fell proportionately more heavily on smaller than larger transactions. (Deleted in the edition of 1852, 857.)

from the amount of their rent, an annual impost equivalent to the average produce of these teaxes should be distributed over the land generally, in the form of a land-tax (858–9).

In an economical point of view, the best system of landed property is that in which land is most completely an object of commerce; passing readily from hand to hand when a buyer can be found to whom it is worth while to offer a greater sum for the land, than the value of the income drawn from it by its existing possessor. This of course is not meant of ornamental property, which is a source of expense, not profit; but only of land employed for industrial uses, and held for the sake of the income which it affords. Whatever facilitates the sale of land, tends to make it a more productive instrument of the community at large; whatever prevents or restricts its sale, substracts from its usefulness. Now, not only has entail this effect, but primogeniture also. The desire to keep land together in large masses, from other motives than that of promoting its productiveness, often prevents changes and alienations which would increase its efficiency as an instrument (893–4).[28]

The self-interest axiom thus appears central enough in this context, as it had done in the second book where Mill argued – with empirical support – that 'cultivation spontaneously finds out the organization that suits it best' where freedom of contract ruled (II, 293; above, p. 242). Yet even here the matter of failures of self-interest arises; for the high costs of litigation and legal documentation, obstacles to land transfer and questionable title, by lowering the sales-value of land, acted against the interest of landowners themselves who, 'though they have been masters of the legislation of England, to say the least since 1688, have never made a single move in the direction of law reform, and have been strenuous opponents of some of the improvements of which they would more particularly reap the benefit . . .' (III, 885). This is precisely the same general perspective as that of Adam Smith who had remarked on the adoption by an agrarian parliament of 'mercantilist' legislation.[29]

28 The complaint extends to contracts or leases as well as sale: 'Some of the taxes on contracts are very pernicious, imposing a virtual penalty upon transactions which it ought to be the policy of the legislator to encourage. Of this sort is the stamp-duty on leases, which in a country of large properties are an essential condition of good agriculture; and the taxes on insurances, a direct discouragement to prudence and forethought' (860). See also, for the general principle, Mill on 'Land Tenure Reform' (1871): Assuming retention of private property, 'whatever facilities its passing into new hands tends to increase its productiveness, and thereby its usefulness to the nation at large: since those among the owners who are least provided with skill, enterprise, and capital, are those who are under the strongest enducement to sell their land' (V, 690).
29 Cf. Stigler (1971). Mill had in mind parliamentary rejection of a register of contracts affecting land. But in 1865 he refers to a new Act as a 'material mitigation' of the deficiency.

The explanation Mill himself gives for such 'irrational hostility to improvement, in a case in which their own interest would be the most benefited by it' is two-fold – 'an intense timidity on the subject of their titles, generated by the defects of the very law which they refuse to alter; and . . . a conscious ignorance, and incapacity of judgment, on all legal subjects, which makes them helplessly defer to the opinion of their professional advisers, heedless of the fact that every imperfection of the law, in proportion as it is burthensome to them, brings gain to the lawyer' (885).

By the first rationalization Mill seems to be alluding to a concern with the ultimate validity of their ownership rights (although in that case their behaviour would scarcely be 'irrational'). But Mill's writings elsewhere suggest an alternative explanation. I allude to his adoption in 'Leslie on the Land Question' (1871) of the position that the self-interest axiom – in its narrower connotation of wealth maximization – does not apply universally, that 'though it has a foundation in truth, [it] is by no means absolutely true; and the limits of its truth ought to be the limits of its practical application' (V, 672). In Leslie's rendition 'the fundamental assumption of political economy . . . is, that men desire to get wealth with the least possible trouble, exertion, and sacrifice; that besides wealth, they desire ease, pleasure, social position, and political power; and that they will combine all the gratification they can of their other desires with the acquisition of wealth' (cited 673). But inductive evidence – 'the assumption their own conduct compels us to make' – suggested that:

The interest of the proprietors of land is . . . to get as much, not only of money, but of amusement, social consideration, and political influence as they can, making as little sacrifice as they can in return for any of those advantages, in the shape of leases to their tenants, the improvement of their estates, or even residence upon them when other places are more agreeable. That they are frequently guided solely by their interest in this sense is borne out by notorious facts; by absenteeism, by the frequent absence of all improvement on the part of the landlord and the refusal of any security to the tenant, by the mischievous extent of the preservation of game and the extension of deer-forests over what once was cultivated land. The single circumstance that tenancy from year to year, a tenure incompatible with good agriculture, is the commonest tenure both in England and Ireland, affords positive proof that the interest of the landlord is no security to the public for the good management of the land in the absence of all interference of law (cited, 673–4).

All this Mill accepted, so that it is somewhat odd that he should in the *Principles* refer to the 'irrational' behaviour of the landlords and give rather unconvincing explanations thereof when there is at hand a very obvious candidate – the fact that 'self-interest' cannot be reduced to wealth-maximization.[30]

It must be emphasized that this broad notion of self-interested behaviour – and consequent social disutility – relates to the great landowners alone, for 'though the self-interest of the landlords frequently operates to frustrate, instead of promoting, the interest which the community has in the most effective use of the productive powers of the soil, there is another party concerned whose self-interest does work in that useful direction; and that is, the actual cultivator of the soil, if he be either a small proprietor, or a tenant on conditions which secure to him the full fruits of his labour and outlay' (674). The self-interest axiom – in the sense of wealth maximization – is in fact implicit in what was said earlier of the consequences of high land-transfer costs, and is used too in response to a case favouring primogeniture which asserted that subdivision dictated 'portions too small to admit of being cultivated in an advantageous manner' (III, 891). This argument, Mill pointed out, 'proceeds on a supposition entirely at variance with that on which all the theorems of political economy are grounded. It assumes that mankind in general will habitually act in a manner opposed to their immediate and obvious pecuniary interest'. For there was a great variety of alternative ways that the heirs might use land – including, for example, common use, or use by one with mortgage payments to others, or sale and division of the proceeds – and '[w]hen the division of the land would diminish its productive power, it is the direct interest of the heirs to adopt some one of those arrangements'.

* * *

In all editions of the *Principles* preference is given on grounds of improved prospects for population control, 'security', and 'independence' to the wide diffusion of property in land amongst peasant and small-landed proprietors over the system of hired labour 'in any form in which it exists at present' (III, 767). But this organization was far from the ideal, and this in part because it failed to take advantage of large-scale production.

Mill was in fact rather concerned lest readers of the *Principles* misunderstand him on this point. His extended demonstrations of the productive potential of peasant proprietorship and the metayer system in

---

30 It may, however, be that the unconcern with wealth maximization can legitimately be regarded as 'irrational'. For Mill has much to say of the improvidence and consequent indebtedness of the great landowners, reflecting their social and family obligations – 'their apparent are . . . habitually greater than their real means, and they are under a perpetual temptation to proportion their expenditure to the former rather than the latter' (892). To sacrifice wealth for other *desiderata* is one thing; to do so to an extreme in this manner is another.

various European countries (above, p. 238f) were designed as a counter to those who exaggerated its defects.[31] But the actual introduction of the system into a country enjoying prudence in matters of population and institutional assurances against a skewed income distribution, so that the benefits of high average productivity are broadly enjoyed, was not to be recommended:

The opinion expressed in a former part of this treatise respecting small landed properties and peasant proprietors, may have made the reader anticipate that a wide diffusion of property in land is the resource on which I rely for exempting at least the agricultural labourers from exclusive dependence on labour for hire. Such, however, is not my opinion. I indeed deem that form of agricultural economy to be most groundlessly cried down, and to be greatly preferable, in its aggregate effects on human happiness, to hired labour in any form in which its exists at present; because the prudential check to population acts more directly, and is shown by experience to be more efficacious; and because, in point of security, of independence, of exercise of any other than the animal faculties, the state of a peasant proprietor is far superior to that of an agricultural labourer in this or any other old country. Where the former system already exists, and works on the whole satisfactorily, I should regret, in the present state of human intelligence, to see it abolished in order to make way for the other, under a pedantic notion of agricultural improvement as a thing necessarily the same in every diversity of circumstances. In a backward state of industrial improvement, as in Ireland, I should urge its introduction, in preference to an exclusive system of hired labour; as a more powerful instrument for raising a population from semi-savage listlessness and recklessness, to persevering industry and prudent calculation.

But a people who have once adopted the large system of production, either in manufacturers, or in agriculture, are not likely to recede from it; and when population is kept in due proportion to the means of support, it is not desirable

31   For example, the evidence regarding the metayer system of Italy – which actually has efficiency disadvantages compared with peasant ownership – proved 'that neither "land miserably cultivated" nor a people in "the most abject poverty" have any necessary connexion with it, and that the unmeasured vituperation lavished upon the system by English writers, is grounded on an extremely narrow view of the subject' (II, 310). In sum, Mill wrote: 'I look upon the rural economy of Italy as simply so much additional evidence in favour of small occupations with permanent tenure. It is an example of what can be accomplished by those two elements, even under the disadvantage of the peculiar nature of the metayer contract, in which the motives to exertion on the part of the tenant are only half as strong as if he farmed the land on the same footing of perpetuity at a money-rent, either fixed, or varying according to some rule which would leave to the tenant the whole benefit of his own exertions.' Not surprisingly, Mill in 1870 commended Leslie's demonstration 'in opposition to a still strong, though diminishing prejudice [of] the great success of peasant properties in France' (V, 685). Leslie was in effect reiterating Mill's long-held position.

that they should. Labour is unquestionably more productive on the system of large industrial enterprises; the produce, if not greater absolutely, is greater in proportion to the labour employed: the same number of people can be supported equally well with less toil and greater leisure; which will be wholly an advantage, as soon as civilization and improvement have so far advanced, that what is a benefit to the whole shall be a benefit to each individual composing it (III, 767–8).

It is clear from the context that by the term 'large industrial enterprises' Mill intended agriculture as well as manufactures, although his argument seems to clash with his insistence elsewhere that 'the distribution of property' should not be identified with that of cultivation (II, 293). It is clear too that Mill insisted upon maximum efficiency provided that labour would enjoy its benefits. He had in fact earlier warned of the dangers of hasty replacement even of an unproductive metayer system by that of 'money rents and capitalist farmers':

Even if the metayers are poor, and the sub-division great, it is not to be assumed as of course, that the change would be for the better. The enlargement of farms, and the introduction of what are called agricultural improvements, usually diminish the number of labourers employed on the land; and unless the growth of capital in trade and manufactures affords an opening for the displaced population, or unless there are reclaimable wastes on which they can be located, competition will so reduce wages, that they will probably be worse off as day-labourers than they were as metayers (311).

In some contexts therefore – the Irish context above all – efficiency might better be sacrificed for the sake of aggregate employment and various other objectives including population control. To the Irish case we shall shortly turn. As for England, Mill seems to have placed his hopes in the shorter run upon capitalist farming – the farmer himself owning land or leasing it under conditions of secure tenure; but in the longer run upon co-operative organization. This latter solution emerges in the course of a 'moral' case pointing away from peasant proprietorship 'as the goal of industrial improvement' (768): 'if public spirit, generous sentiments, or true justice and equality are desired, association, not isolation, of interests, is the school in which these excellences are nurtured. The aim of improvement should be not solely to place human beings in a condition in which they will be able to do without one another, but to enable them to work with or for one another in relations not involving dependence'.[32]

32 In some contexts (see II, 262) Mill referred to co-operative ventures undertaken between peasant proprietors.

V LAND REFORM: IRELAND

The issue of Irish land reform is highly instructive of Mill's general theory of economic policy, particularly his concern both for efficiency and distributive justice with an eye to the well-being of the masses. The worst of all land systems conceivable (from the perspective of population control as well as efficiency) was the Irish cottier system – '[a] situation more devoid of motives to either labour or self-command, imagination cannot conceive. The inducements of free human beings are taken away, and those of a slave not substituted. He has nothing to hope, and nothing to fear, except being dispossessed of his holding, and against this he protects himself by the *ultima ratio* of a defensive civil war' (*CW*, II, 319). But it was the cottier system, not small size *per se*, that was to blame.

What precisely did Mill propose as alternative to the cottier system? There are differences between editions – both substantive and apparent – that we must follow through.

Mill's own preference in the first three editions was for peasant ownership:

Those who, knowing neither Ireland nor any foreign country, take as their sole standard of social and economical excellence, English practice, propose as the single remedy for Irish wretchedness, the transformation of cottiers into hired labourers. I contend that the object should be their transformation, as far as circumstances admit, into landed proprietors. Either, indeed, would be a most desirable exchange from the present nuisance; but as a practical object the latter of the two seems to me preferable in an almost incalculable degree to the former, both as the most desirable in itself, and very much the easiest to effect (III, 989).

His objections to the English system of hired labour were twofold. First, '[to] convert the cottiers into hired labourers is rather a scheme for the improvement of Irish agriculture, than of the condition of the Irish people. The status of a day labourer has no charm for infusing forethought, frugality, or self-restraint, on a people devoid of them' (989). Secondly, workers would be displaced by the English practice of 'throwing together the small holdings into large farms, cultivated by combined labour, with the best modern improvements' (991); two-thirds of the peasantry, he calculated, would be dispensed with, without alternative occupation in manufacturing because labourers were personally unfit for that sector, lack of capital, and English competition. Mill states the problem to perfection: 'The question, what system of agriculture is best in itself, is, for Ireland, of purely theoretical interest: the people are there, and the problem is not how to improve the country, but how it can be improved by and for its present inhabitants' (991).

Reform required then perpetuity of tenure – even better than mere long leases as a stimulus to improvement – combined with limited rents. Competition was inappropriate:

Rent paid by a capitalist who farms for profit, and not for bread, may safely be abandoned to competition; rent paid by labourers cannot, unless the labourers were in a state of civilization and improvement which labourers have nowhere yet reached, and cannot easily reach under such a tenure [as cottiers]. Peasant rents ought never to be arbitrary, never at the discretion of the landlord: either by custom or law, it is imperatively necessary that they should be fixed; and where no mutually advantageous custom, such as the metayer custom of Tuscany, has established itself, reason and experience recommend that they should be fixed in perpetuity: thus changing the rent into a quit-rent, and the farmer into a peasant proprietor (994).

Expropriation of all Irish land by Parliamentary Act is considered as a possible means to the proposed objective, that is the transfer of land to the tenantry who would henceforth pay a fixed rent, with landlords offered the option of surrendering their land entirely at its full value (994–5). Justice would warrant such a radical step of destroying 'the higher classes of Ireland' but 'only if it were the sole means of effecting a great public good'. But there existed 'milder' solutions and preferable ones which allowed for the retention of alternative modes of cultivation, including large-scale capitalist farming: 'Large farms, cultivated by large capitals, and owned by persons of the best education which the country can give, persons qualified by instruction to appreciate scientific discoveries, and able to bear the delay and risk of costly experiments, are an important part of a good agricultural system. Many such landlords there are even in Ireland; and it would be a public misfortune to drive them from their post' (995). Moreover, some existing holdings were too small for the likely success of peasant propriety; and the existing tenants were not always the most appropriate, in which case it was better 'to give them hope of acquiring a landed property by industry and frugality, than the property itself in immediate possession'. What Mill proposed, following W. T. Thornton (1846, 18) was the reclaiming of waste land and its settlement by peasant owners, absorbing enough labour to assure against any surplus in the capitalist-farming sector:

There are then strong objections, as well as great difficulties, opposed to the attempt to make peasant properties universal. But, fortunately, that they should be universal is not necessary to their usefulness. There is no need to extend them to all the population, or all the land. It is enough if there be land available, on which to locate so great a portion of the population, that the remaining area of the country shall not be required to maintain greater numbers than are compatible with large farming and hired labour. For this purpose there is an obvious resource in the waste lands; which are happily so extensive, and a large proportion of them so improvable, as to afford a means by which, without making the present tenants proprietors, nearly the whole surplus population might be converted into peasant proprietors elsewhere (996–7).

Here one notes two revealing details which supplement Mill's objections to competition in the fixing of rents in the Irish case. First, the possible profitability of waste-clearing in some cases is said to be irrelevant: 'it is doubtful whether there be any land, in a temperate climate, which cannot be reclaimed and rendered productive by labourers themselves, under the inducement of a permanent property' (998). Secondly, a role is allowed government in the venture – desirable also as a form of public works:

It would be desirable, and in most cases necessary, that the tracts of land should be prepared for the labours of the peasant, by being drained and intersected with roads at the expense of Government; the interest of the sums so expended, and of the compensation paid for existing rights to the waste land, being charged on it when reclaimed as a perpetual quit-rent, redeemable at a moderate number of years' purchase. The state would thus incur no loss, while the advances made would give that immediate employment to the surplus labour of Ireland, which if not given in this manner, will assuredly have to be given in some other, not only less useful, but far less likely to repay its cost (1000).[33]

Mill waxed eloquent regarding the Waste Land Improvement Society which had shown already 'what an Irish peasantry can be stimulated to do, by a sufficient assurance that what they do will be for their own advantage' (1001).

A supplementary proposal is the Chartist suggestion of a private Joint-Stock Company raising funds to purchase land which would be divided into portions and let to labourers with loans of capital. Labourers would repay the Company at a fixed quit-rent rendering them proprietors, not merely tenants.

In the third edition of 1852 numerous alterations are introduced but it transpires, despite surface appearance, that the substance of Mill's position remains unchanged. This must be demonstrated for there were important changes of an empirical order which caught Mill's eye and seemed to suggest the need for a less radical program.

The primary event in question to which Mill alludes in 1852 is the Wakefield system of self-supporting emigration which 'reduced or is reducing

33 On the advocation, by Mill and others, of drainage and land reclamation schemes, see Black, 1960, 178f.

the population down to the number for which the existing agricultural system can find employment and support' (II, 325).[34] The 'emergency' situation which had prevailed when he first published the *Principles* was over. Excess population would no longer be a problem even were the English agricultural system introduced: 'there can be little doubt that however much the employment for agricultural labour may hereafter be diminished by the general introduction throughout Ireland of English farming – or even if, like the county of Sutherland, all Ireland should be turned into a grazing farm – the superseded people would migrate to America with the same rapidity, and as free of cost to the nation, as the million of Irish who went thither during the last three years' (325). Indeed, 'that flourishing continent . . . for generations will be capable of supporting in undiminished comfort the increase of the population of the whole world' – a strong statement indeed.

However, the crux of the matter for us is Mill's vehement condemnation as 'insolent', 'those who think that the land of a country exists for the sake of a few thousand landowners, and that as long as rents are paid, society and government have fulfilled their function'. 'Justice' and 'policy' required Irish land reforms with an eye to the existing poor *in Ireland*. In a beautiful passage he restated his opposition to the English day-labour system:

But this is not a time, nor is the human mind now in a condition, in which such insolent pretensions can be maintained. The land of Ireland, the land of every country, belongs to the people of that country. The individuals called landowners have no right, in morality and justice, to anything but the rent, or compensation for its saleable value. With regard to the land itself, the paramount consideration is, by what mode of appropriation and of cultivation it can be made most useful to the collective body of its inhabitants. To the owners of the rent it may be very convenient that the bulk of the inhabitants, despairing of justice in the country where they and their ancestors have lived and suffered, should seek on another continent that property in land which is denied to them at home. But the legislature of the empire ought to regard with other eyes the forced expatriation of millions of people. When the inhabitants of a country quit the country *en masse* because its Government will not make it a place fit for them to live in, the Government is judged and condemned. There is no necessity for depriving the landlords of one farthing of the pecuniary value of their legal rights; but justice requires that the actual cultivators should be enabled to become in Ireland what they will become in America – proprietors of the soil which they cultivate (326).

So much for 'justice'. 'Good policy' pointed to the same conclusion; and here Mill reiterated the case presented in earlier editions for 'improving

34 In 1857 the text is modified to read 'has, for the present, reduced the population . . .'.

the condition of the Irish people' – rather than 'Irish agriculture' – by peasant proprietorship:

The status of a day-labourer has no charm for infusing forethought, frugality, or self-restraint, into a people devoid of them. If the Irish peasantry could be instantaneously changed into receivers of wages, the old habits and mental characteristics of the people remaining, we should merely see four or five millions of people living as day-labourers in the same wretched manner in which as cottiers they lived before; equally passive in the absence of every comfort, equally reckless in multiplication, and even, perhaps, equally listless at their work; since they could not be dismissed *en masse*, and if they could, dismissal would now be simply remanding them to the poor-rate. Far other would be the effect of making them peasant proprietors. A people who in industry and providence have everything to learn – who are confessedly among the most backward of European populations in the industrial virtues – require for their regeneration the most powerful incitements by which those virtues can be stimulated: and there is no stimulus as yet comparable to property in land. A permanent interest in the soil to those who till it, is almost a guarantee for the most unwearied labouriousness: against over-population, though not infallible, it is the best preservative yet known, and where it failed, any other plan would probably fail much more egregiously; the evil would be beyond the reach of merely economic remedies (326–7).

As for the precise mode by which reform was to be accomplished there are no changes. The possibility of a universal transformation of all Irish property into peasant proprietorships at a fixed rental, and allowing the option of sale by landlords, is taken up but – though 'just' where no alternatives existed – not recommended for the reasons given in 1849 (II, 328–9; cf. III 994–5). Again, waste reclamation and the private co-operative venture of land purchase for redistribution are given preference (330).[35]

35 The first expedient 'would be, to enact that whoever reclaims waste land becomes the owner of it, at a fixed quit-rent equal to a moderate interest on its mere value as waste. It would of course be a necessary part of this measure, to make compulsory on landlords the surrender of waste lands (not of an ornamental character) whenever required for reclamation.
Another expedient, and one in which individuals could co-operate, would be to buy as much as possible of the land offered for sale, [under the orders of the Encumbered Estates Commission], and sell it again in small portions as peasant-properties . . . This is a mode in which private capital may be employed in renovating the social and agricultural economy of Ireland, not only without sacrifice but with considerable profit to its owners . . .'.
In the editions of 1852 and 1857 (but thereafter deleted) the proposals are prefaced by a sharp warning to the powers that be: 'But though the most direct and drastic mode of creating a peasant proprietary is not in all respects the best, it is far better than no mode at all. If the rulers of Ireland do not exert themselves in time to effect this great

It is in the edition of 1862 that we are faced with a change of position. Here the English system is presented as a practical alternative – indeed the English system had already proven itself, with the introduction of a new class of landowners, for population had already fallen sufficiently to permit full employment of day-labour at good wages, and there was little to fear from a renewal of pressure considering changed attitudes and knowledge of the option of emigration. Cottier tenancy had, of course, to be rooted out, but peasant proprietorship was no longer indispensable:

The new state of things created in Ireland by the vast decrease of her population, and by the effects of that greatest of boons ever conferred on her by any Government, the Encumbered Estates Act, has rendered the introduction, on a large scale, of the English agricultural system for the first time possible in that country. The present population of Ireland is now not greater than can be supported on that system in a state of comfort probably equal to the average lot of English farm labourers . . . and the improved scale of subsistence which is now becoming habitual to the people, together with the familiarity they have now acquired with the resource of expatriation, will probably prevent them for a considerable time from relapsing, through improvident multiplication, into their former degraded state. Ireland, therefore, is not now in a condition to require what are called heroic remedies. The benefits to that country of peasant proprietorship would be as great as ever; but they are no longer indispensable, a prospect has opened to her of making a great advance in civilization without that aid. But though she can now do without peasant-properties, she cannot do without the total extinction of cottier tenancy. Unless that is rooted out, the whole fruits of the improvement now in course of being effected, will be and remain precarious. The lapse of another generation will show whether the landlords of Ireland, now weeded of the reckless and bankrupt portion who formerly held so much of the land, and recruited by the substitution of a more moral and intelligent class, will improve the opportunity by the successful accomplishment of this the only real, permanent, and radical reform in the social economy of that long-suffering country (331n).

This change in position was, however, a temporary one and withdrawn in 1865. The process of replacement of cottier tenancy by the English system was continuing, a process which, though facilitated by vast emigration and the law (an allusion to the Encumbered Estates Act – 'the greatest boon

public end by means less subversive of existing social relations, they will probably find it extorted from them by the compulsion of circumstances, when they will no longer have any power of controlling its conditions. But if they were sincerely desirous to confer this benefit upon Ireland, and only solicitous about the means of conferring it with the least disturbance of individual positions and expectations, there are measures within their reach, liable to none of the objections urged against the proposal of the Tenant League, but which, if pushed to the utmost extent of which they are susceptible, would realize in no inconsiderable degree the object sought' (329–30).

ever conferred on Ireland by any Government'), Mill suggests would probably have been brought about by 'the repeal of the corn laws, necessitating a change in the exports of Ireland from the products of tillage to those of pasturage', since a 'grazing farm can only be managed by a capitalist farmer, or by the landlord' (332–3).[36] Agricultural efficiency was accordingly improving: 'The greatest part of the soil of Ireland, there is reason to believe, is now farmed either by the landlords, or by small capitalist farmers. That these farmers are improving in circumstances, and accumulating capital, there is considerable evidence, in particular the great increase of deposits in the banks of which they are the principal customers. So far as that class is concerned, the chief thing still wanted is security of tenure, or assurance of compensation for improvements.[37] But now, in 1865, Mill's old concern with the Irish labourers is restated. Their wages were not improving as he had expected in 1862. Once again the key to Mill's policy proposals comes to the fore – his primary concern with the living standards of the working masses *remaining in Ireland*. To suggest to the unemployed that they emigrate was a 'disgrace'; recourse had, after all, to be made to peasant proprietorships.

First, as to the facts: 'what . . . is the condition of the displaced cottiers, so far as they have not emigrated; and of the whole class who subsist by agricultural labour, without the occupation of any land? As yet, their state is one of great poverty, with but slight prospect of improvement. Money wages, indeed, have risen much above the wretched level of a generation ago: but the cost of subsistence has also risen so much above the old potato standard, that the real improvement is not equal to the nominal; and according to the best information to which I have access, there is little appearance of an improved standard of living among the class. The population, in fact, reduced though it be, is still far beyond what the country can support as a mere grazing district of England' (333–4). His own forecast of 1862 regarding the employment potential of small capitalist farming (even with adequate security of tenure for improvement) was withdrawn: 'no one will pretend that this resource is sufficient to maintain them in any condition in which it is fit that the great body of the peasantry of a country should exist'. Emigration was indeed a boon from the perspective of those who had chosen to leave and their posterity, and even from that of 'the human race', but this would not do as a just solution for Ireland's remaining workers. It is difficult to exaggerate the significance for Mill's overall perspective on reform of his declaration (drawing on evidence provided by Cairnes) to this effect:

36 Yet Mill expressed fears, due to Cairnes, of the behaviour of a new breed of landlords deriving from the towns; and also of a revival of cottier tenancy.
37 Here Mill refers enthusiastically to Longfield's 'sensational' proposals.

The loss, and the disgrace, are England's: and it is the English people and government whom it chiefly concerns to ask themselves, how far it will be to their honour and advantage to retain the mere soil of Ireland, but to lose its inhabitants. With the present feelings of the Irish people, and the direction which their hope of improving their condition seems to be permanently taking, England, it is probable, has only the choice between the depopulation of Ireland, and the conversion of a part of the labouring population into peasant proprietors. The truly insular ignorance of her public men respecting a form of agricultural economy which predominates in nearly every other civilized country, makes it only too probable that she will choose the worse side of the alternative. Yet there are germs of a tendency to the formation of peasant proprietors on Irish soil, which require only the aid of a friendly legislator to foster them . . .

Attention should also be given to Mill's declaration in his pamphlet 'England and Ireland' (1868) which summarizes well his general perspective (in the context of a case for peasant proprietorships) on the effect of property ownership on effort, improvement and population control:

We are told by many . . . that in a generation after such a change, the land of Ireland would be overcrowded by the growth of population, would be sublet and subdivided, and things would be as bad as before the famine. Just in the same manner we were told that after a generation or two of peasant proprietorship, the whole rural territory of France would be a pauper warren, and its inhabitants would be engaged in "dividing, by logarithms, infinitesimal inheritances." How have these predictions been fulfilled? The complaint now is that the population of France scarcely increases at all, and the rural population diminishes. And, in spite of the compulsory division of inheritances by the Code Civil, the reunions of small properties by marriage and inheritance fully balance the subdivisions. The obsolete school of English political economists, whom I may call the Tory school, because they were the friends of entail, primogeniture, high rents, great landed properties, and aristocratic institutions generally, predicted that peasant proprietorships would lead not only to excessive population, but to the wretchedest possible agriculture . . . Those who still believe that small peasant properties are either detrimental to agriculture or conducive to overpopulation, are discreditably behind the state of knowledge on the subject. There is no condition of landed property which excites such intense exertions for its improvement, as that in which all that can be added to the produce belongs to him who produces it. Nor does any condition afford so strong a motive against overpopulation; becuase it is much more obvious how many mouths can be supported by a piece of land, than how many hands can find employment in the general labour market (VI, 528–9).[38]

38 This work of 1868 has been described as 'probably the most influential single contribution to the extended debate on Irish land problems which was carried out in England between 1865 and 1970' (Black, 1960, 53).

It is also scarcely surprising that in 1870 he fully agreed with Leslie that opposition to farm consolidation – 'a panacea for Irish poverty' according to much English opinion – was quite rational: 'Nor are the Irish peasantry, under anything like fair play, incapable of the qualities necessary for doing the fullest justice to small holdings' (V, 678).

The general principle is abundantly clear and applies quite generally. In the edition of 1862, a charge against landowners in the South of England (as well as Ireland) as backward in scientific improvement and an impediment to progress is withdrawn: 'I must beg the reader to bear in mind that this paragraph was written more than fifteen years ago. So wonderful are the changes, both moral and economical, taking place in our age, that, without perpetually re-writing a work like the present, it is impossible to keep up with them' (II, 230n). Even prior to 1862 Mill had not actually recommended for England land expropriation and redistribution (always with compensation). Indeed, in the first two editions he had made it clear that 'so drastic a measure' would rarely be appropriate, and might be considered merely as 'an extreme remedy, which may happen to be the only suitable one for an extreme case' (231). (Even in the Irish case 'so drastic a measure' was not considered appropriate.) But it is also apparent that notwithstanding the new evidence of improvement Mill continued to believe in the need for far-reaching institutional changes. The explanation will be found in his insistence that productivity gains are nugatory unless they reach the lower strata of society.

VI   ON ENDOWMENT AND PROPERTY RIGHTS

As we have seen, Mill denied a right to private property in land based on justice. His case extended (with qualification) also to endowments in general and provides a further indication of legitimate public control over the disposition of property. Thus a question raised in 1833 ('On Corporation and Church Property') was whether a portion of property 'can be touched . . . without spoliation; whether the diversion of the estates of foundations from the present hands, and from the present purposes, would be disposing of what is justly our own, or robbing somebody else of what is his; violating property, endangering all rights, and infringing the first principles of the social union' (CW, IV, 195–6).[39] The sole argument from justice in favour of the inviobility of the assigned purpose recognized by Mill was temporally limited: 'The sacredness of the founder's assignment should continue during his own life, and for such longer period as the foresight of a prudent man may be presumed to reach, and no

---

39   In the Autobiography, Mill wrote that apart from this paper and the 'Currency Juggle' (also 1833) nothing earlier was 'sufficient[ly] permanent' to be worth reprinting (I, 191).

further . . .' (198). As stated in his paper 'Endowments' in 1869 the founder's will was to be respected, similarly, for the period 'which individual foresight can reasonably be supposed to cover, and during which circumstances are not likely to have so totally changed as to make the effect of the gift entirely different from what the giver intended' – a matter of two or three generations (V, 618, 621). During that period, there was 'an obvious propriety in abiding by his dispositions. To set them aside, unless at the command of a still higher principle, is an offence both against liberty and against property'.

This position – an insistence upon 'respect for the free agency of individuals' beyond their lifetime – is, however, maintained subject to the presumption that the right of bequest itself is recognized, and not regarded as a 'nuisance' (618).[40] Evidently Mill *did* recognize that right, although subject to certain restrictions. Some of these we have encountered with respect to grants to individuals, to which must now be added the restriction against the transfer of lands or houses to a corporate body: 'endowment shall not consist of land' (IV, 222).[41] In addition Mill also spoke of restrictions on the application of funds to uses which have anti-social consequences.[42] For

there are also employments of money which have so mischievous an effect, that they would most likely be prohibited, if it could be done without improper interference with individual liberty; and such an application of funds, though the State may be obliged to tolerate, it may be right that it should abstain from enforcing, on the mandate of the owner, after his death (V, 619).

Apart from these latter constraints, the legator's instructions were to be honoured for the period specified. Beyond that time, while it might be inexpedient for the State to alter the original will, it was never a question of spoliation of property: 'no person ought to be exercising rights of property six hundred years after his death . . . and no reasonable man who gave his money when living, for the benefit of the community, would have desired that his mode of benefiting the community should be adhered to when a better could be found' (IV, 201). Endowments, in brief, were 'national property, which the government may and ought to control' (I, 191); and, accordingly,

40 'If it is right that people should be suffered to employ what is lawfully their own in acts of beneficience to individuals taking effect after their death, why not to the public? . . .'.

41 In the original ms. Mill suggested the sale of all estates in the possession of public trusts and their investment in securities and stock.

42 Such as doles to the poor. But the government should divert funds to as similar a purpose as possible, e.g. schools for the poor.

it is no violation of any right which ought to exist in the founder, to set aside his dispositions many years after his decease; but . . . where individuals have been allowed to acquire beneficial interests in the endowment, these ought in general to be respected; being, in most cases, either rights of property for life, or rights for life by virtue of an implied contract. But, with the reservation of these life interests, the Legislature is at liberty to dispose, at its discretion, of the endowment, after that moderate number of years has elapsed from the date of its formation, beyond which the foresight of an individual cannot reasonably be supposed to extend (205).

In taking this position Mill diverged from 'the great and good Turgot' and Adam Smith, both of whom had objected to foundations as such (211).[43] The problem as Mill saw it lay in perpetuities and could be overcome by his proposals which allowed for their continual modification.[44] Yet even so Mill insisted upon respect for the founder's wishes as far as possible; there were principles by which the admittedly discretionary power of the legislator over endowments should be governed.

Thus the founder's wishes should only be set aside for 'paramount reasons of utility'; his design should be adhered to as long 'as circumstances will admit' (218).[45] And 'even in altering the disposition of the founder' the funds should be applied 'to carry into effect as much of his intention as it is possible to realize without too great a sacrifice of substantial utility' (210); in particular, foundations established originally for educational and cultural purposes should be thus applied with an eye always on the new requirements of the age (212f). It is the spirit not the letter of the original will that matters. The rationale for this consideration is threefold: the utility itself of the foundation; the assurance against irresponsible use by government of fortuitously available funds;[46] and – most important for us in our present context – reasons akin to, though not identical with, justice based on property rights:

43 Although at one time Mill (like Smith and Turgot) opposed endowment as such; cf. *Autobiography*, I, 191.
44 In the original version of 1833 Mill condemned the existing system; his charges were withdrawn in 1859 in the light of recent legislation (IV, 214n).
45 Cf. V, 620: 'Nothing ought to be regarded as a warrant for setting the donor's dispositions prematurely aside, but that to permit their execution would be a clear and positive public mischief.'
46 'Almost any fixed rule, consistent with ensuring the employment of the funds for some purpose of real utility, is preferable to allowing financiers to count upon them as a resource applicable to all the exigencies of the State indiscriminantly' (IV, 218). Diversion of funds to pay off the national debt was strongly condemned as squandering 'for the benefit of a single generation, the inheritance of posterity' (221). Borrowing from an endowment – as from 'any other property, public or private' – was legitimate in an emergency.

Nor would it be right to disregard the great importance of the associations which lead mankind to respect the declared will of every person, in the disposal of what is justly his own. That will is surely not least deserving of respect, when it is ordaining an act of beneficence. And any deviation from it, not called for by high considerations of social good, even when not a violation of property, runs counter to a feeling so nearly allied to those on which the respect for property is founded, that there is scarcely a possibility of infringing the one without shaking the security of the other (218–19).

[By] disregarding entirely the intentions of the original owners, we shall do our best to create a habit of paltering with the sacredness of a trust. It matters not that the property has now become *res nullius*, and is therefore, properly speaking, our own. It is not of our earning; others gave it to us, and for purposes which it may be a duty to set aside, but which cannot honestly be sacrificed to a convenience (221).[47]

VII INCOME DISTRIBUTION AND PUBLIC FINANCE

Mill's general recommendations regarding the tax system will now be taken up, from the perspective of income distribution. Mill adopted Adam Smith's celebrated canons, elaborating only upon the first – equality of taxation, or taxation 'as nearly as possible in proportion to [individuals'] respective abilities: that is, in proportion to the revenue which they respectively enjoy under the protection of the state' (*CW*, III, 805). This maxim Mill interpreted to mean equality of sacrifice – that each 'shall feel neither more nor less inconvenience from his share of the payment [towards the expenses of government] than every other person experiences from his' – which in turn would be satisfied, at least in principle (an important qualification it transpires) by a system of proportionate income taxation (807). The notion of equality of benefit Mill firmly rejected partly on grounds of the impossibility of identifying individual benefit derived from government protection and services.[48]

---

47 As for church endowments: Provided it was deemed advisable that the clergy of a sect should be supported by a public provision, there were no objections; otherwise, the funds should be used for other purposes of highest 'spiritual culture'. And in an advanced age this use would constitute 'a faithful fulfilment' of the intention of the original owners (219–20).

48 Cf. 'The Income and Property Tax (1852)', V, 495, regarding the benefit principle. 'I do not think that the proper test by which to determine the proportional amount of taxation to be paid by different persons. It seems to me to have nothing definite in it. It is not possible to say that one person derives more benefit than another from the protection of the Government; it is necessary for all' (see also *ibid.*, 472).

That the income tax system should not be used to alter the distribution of income – the presumption is that *earned* income is under consideration – is maintained on grounds both of expediency, in the sense of avoidance of disincentive, and the fundamental principle of proportionality of income to effort and abstinence granted always a 'fair start' in the race. Mill accordingly rejected a progressive income tax, the so-called 'graduated property tax':

> I am as desirous as any one, that means should be taken to diminish . . . inequalities, but not so as to relieve the prodigal at the expense of the prudent. To tax the larger incomes at a higher percentage than the smaller, is to lay a tax on industry and economy; to impose a penalty on people for having worked harder and saved more than their neighbours. It is not the fortunes which are earned, but those which are unearned, that it is for the public good to place under limitation. A just and wise legislation would abstain from holding out motives for dissipating rather than saving the earnings of honest exertion. Its impartiality between competitors would consist in endeavouring that they should all start fair, and not in hanging a weight upon the swift to diminish the distance between them and the slow (810–11).

In the early editions Mill had warned against 'opposing obstacles to the acquisition of even the largest fortune by honest exertion' (811).[49] Although perhaps this is stated less sharply subsequently there was evidently no change of substance regarding the principle.

There is some question whether Mill conceded that proportionate taxation imposed a greater burden on lower income recipients. He seems clear enough in the *Principles* that it does not: 'It may be said, indeed, that to take 100*l*. from 1000*l*. . . . is a heavier impost than 1000*l*. taken from 10,000*l*. . . . But this doctrine seems to me too disputable altogether, and even if true at all, not true to a sufficient extent, to be made the foundation of any rule of taxation' (810). But in his evidence of 1861 he is more conciliatory to the opposing position, though still refusing to countenance progression, on grounds of 'justice' and incentive with particular reference to accumulation:

> [I]t is a received maxim to tax persons in proportion to their means; but supposing that there is an income tax of 10 per cent., it is a much easier thing, apart from conventions, from social necessities or social follies, for a rich person to bear a deduction of 10 per cent. from his income than for a poor person. I do not see how you can allow for this consideration . . . I do not see how you can, either with justice or policy, tax a person more heavily because he earns more . . . I do not

---

49 The other side of the coin is Mill's unwillingness to use the tax system in treating extreme poverty – the modern negative income tax. Other solutions were preferable (III, 808).

think that you can lay a tax upon energy, or industry, or prudence. It seems to me that even upon the question of justice, apart from policy, there is no stronger or more valid principle than that of not giving any advantage to self-indulgence over industry and economy, even though the effect may be to give some advantage, or rather, not to interfere with the natural advantage of the rich over the poor (V, 567).

I certainly do think it fair and reasonable that the general policy of the State should favour the diffusion rather than the concentration of wealth, but . . . taxing people on a larger proportion of their income, because they are better off, does not hold the balance fairly between saving and spending; it is contrary to the canon of equity, and contrary to it in the worst way, because it makes that mode of employing income which it is public policy to encourage, a subject of discouragement (569–70).

A contemporary objection to proportional income taxation, that it bears more heavily upon middle-income compared with upper-income contributors by reducing them to a lower social status, is rejected with the same force, and on much the same grounds, as in the case made for restrictions on acquisition through bequests (Section IX). Even were the factual contention valid, which Mill did not concede, he yet objected

to its being considered incumbent on government to shape its course by such considerations, or to recognise the notion that social importance is or can be determined by amount of expenditure. Government ought to set an example of rating all things at their true value, and riches, therefore, at the worth, for comfort or pleasure, of the things which they will buy: and ought not to sanction the vulgarity of prizing them for the pitiful vanity of being known to possess them, or the paltry shame of being suspected to be without them, the presiding motives of three-fourths of the expenditure of the middle classes. The sacrifices of real comfort or indulgence which government requires, it is bound to apportion among all persons with as much equality as possible; but their sacrifices of the imaginary dignity dependent on expense, it may spare itself the trouble of estimating (III, 810).

An objection to the principle of income taxation itself, that it compels the revelation of contributors' pecuniary means, is rejected in precisely the same terms: 'One of the social evils of this country is the practice, amounting to a custom, of maintaining, or attempting to maintain, the appearance to the world of a larger income than is possessed; and it would be far better for the interest of those who yield to this weakness, if the extent of their means were universally and exactly known, and the temptation removed to expending more than they can afford, or stinting real wants in order to make a false show externally' (831). This national characteristic reflected a 'debased state of mind' whereby 'respect (if such a word can be applied to it) is proportioned to what they suppose to be each person's pecuniary means'.

We turn next to the exemption limit allowed on grounds of justice, and the qualifications to the rule against a progressive income tax arising from the regressive incidence of various contemporary commodity taxes. As Mill phrased the first matter (following Bentham on the principle) any burden imposed on incomes below a certain minimum level would entail a sacrifice 'entirely incommensurate' (809; cf. 830–31). Nevertheless, the exemption was to apply generally – all incomes 'taxed only in proportion to the surplus by which they exceed the limit' (831).[50] The degree of progression thereby introduced was acceptable.[51] As Mill expressed the matter in 1861:

The rule of equality and of fair proportion seems to me to be that people should be taxed in an equal ratio on their superfluities; necessaries being untaxed, and surplus paying in all cases an equal percentage. This satisfies entirely the small amount of justice that there is in the theory of a graduated income tax, which appears to me to be otherwise an entirely unjust mode of taxation, and in fact, a graduated robbery. What gives it plausibility is the fact, that at present the lowest incomes which are taxed at all are overtaxed. If an income above 100*l.* a year, supposing that to be the minimum, as at present, were only taxed upon the excess above 100*l.* a year, I think everybody would see that the ratio was in that case fair, and that the lower incomes were exempted as much as they had any just right to be (V, 552; cf. 497).[52]

Much has been made by Professor West of Mill's preoccupation with incomes between £50 and £150 as an indication of an unconcern with the very poorest. For, so runs his argument, those earning below £50 'were *also* paying heavily for items of general consumption in view of the numerous

50 Exemptions to cover educational outlays were also acceptable (V, 592).
51

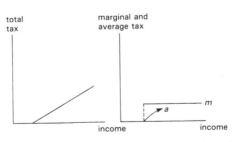

52 The ruling system thus recognized a minimum; but taxed those above it on their *entire* income. Gladstone's 1865 budget only partially accorded with Mill's proposal. For the tax now commenced with incomes exceeding £100 and (over the range £100 to £200) was paid on the excess over £60 (III, 809n). For Mill, if £60 is the minimum limit their taxation should begin at £61.

indirect taxes upon them' (1978b, 572). But this neglects the particular context of Mill's pronouncements which was to emphasize the direct tax burden on the class between £50 and £150 *compared with the rich*. More serious is the failure to note the recommendations for the entire exemption of 'necessaries' from commodity taxation – it was specifically the burden of indirect taxes on 'indulgencies' that Mill said fell most heavily on the middle income (£50–£150) class, without denying the burden on the very poorest of the indirect taxation of necessaries; and for progressive *ad valoram* rates on luxury items. Here again his harsh evaluation of snob appeal by the richer classes is conspicuous.

The specification of the exemption level itself is, however, left vague. In the editions of 1848 and 1849 it is defined as 'an income ordinarily sufficient to provide a moderately numerous labouring family, with the requisites of life and health, and with protection against habitual bodily suffering, but not with any indulgence'. Thereafter, this is altered to an amount 'sufficient to provide the number of persons ordinarily supported from a single income' (809). Later in the text the exemption limit is defined, in the first two editions, as no higher than suffices for 'the necessaries of a labouring family of moderate means', and thereafter for 'the necessaries of the existing population' (830), the latter relating the minimum to the notion of 'subsistence' in the technical sense.[53]

The case for exemption is reinforced in terms of the analysis of the incidence of wage taxation: Even when it might be presumed that the burden falls on profits by way of money-wage adjustments Mill insisted upon exemption, on grounds both of justice and expedience, in this case to avoid a discriminatory burden on capitalists:

We find in the preceding considerations [relating to Taxes on Wages] an additional argument for the opinion already expressed, that direct taxations should stop short of the class of incomes which do not exceed what is necessary for healthful existence. These very small incomes are mostly derived from manual labour; and, as we now see any tax imposed on these, either permanently degrades the habits of the labouring class, or falls on profits, and burthens capitalists with an indirect tax, in addition to their share of the direct taxes; which is doubly objectionable, both as a violation of the fundamental rule of equality, and for the reasons which . . . render a peculiar tax on profits detrimental to the public wealth, and consequently to the means which society possesses of paying any taxes whatever (830).

---

53 Cf. also the 1852 evidence where Mill refers to a sum which 'would provide an individual and an average family, or rather a family just sufficient to keep up the population, with necessaries of life' (V, 473).

A word regarding the specific quantitative limits: In the first three editions of the *Principles* the going exemption level of £150 was said to be too high in itself, but justified because of the existence of indirect taxes on 'necessaries' and because existing taxes on 'indulgencies' fell peculiarly heavily 'on incomes between £50 and £150' (830–1).[54] In the edition of 1857 the exemption limit of £100 then current was also said to be too high in itself, although justified, as was the lower percentage levied between £100 and £150, on similar grounds.[55] But in correspondence of 1868 the limit is reappraised: 'I am very much disposed to think that the limit of £100 is too low, and that it would be an improvement to make the income tax begin at £150 (as it did at first), if not higher.' And, to compensate for the regressiveness of contemporary indirect taxes, a levy on higher incomes is allowed:

If all taxation were direct, it ought to come down to the limit of income just sufficient for the necessaries of life, & everyone ought to pay in proportion to the surplus of the income he possesses beyond those mere necessaries. But so long as the larger part of our revenue is raised by indirect taxation on articles of almost universal consumption, & of which the poor consume more, in proportion to their small means than the rich, so long I think that the incomes between £50 and £150 or £200 pay more than their fair share of indirect taxation, & this requires to be made up to them by levying a tax on the higher incomes, from which they should be exempt (5 Nov. 1868, XVI, 1477).

* * *

Mill's concern with regressiveness extended to the legal system itself. While 'security of property' was accorded a key role in the account of economic development over long periods, in the contemporary British case the state of 'opinion' rather than the law was to be thanked for what security existed since the costs of having recourse to the law ruled it out in many cases:

54 Cf. evidence of 1852: The mass of revenue was derived, Mill asserted, from articles purchased by the middle and lower classes: 'The consequence is, that probably the people in this country who are most heavily taxed in proportion to their incomes, are those receiving incomes of between 50*l*. and 150*l*. a year, because all articles of general consumption are consumed in a greater proportion by that class than by the rich . . . [If] there were no tax but an income tax, it would be fair to commence at as small a sum of 50 *l*., . . . but under present circumstances it is justifiable to begin as high as 150 *l*. The class between 50*l*. and 150*l*. now pay a disproportionate share of our indirect taxes, inasmuch as the articles upon which those taxes principally fall, are articles upon which a larger proportion of small incomes than of large incomes are expended' (V, 473–4). The same burden was also imposed on low as on high quality goods compounding the regression.

55 The lower percentage levied between £100 and £150 was abolished in 1865.

In England the people are tolerably well-protected, both by institutions and manners, against the agents of government; but, for the security they enjoy against other evil-doers, they are very little indebted to their institutions. The laws cannot be said to afford protection to property, when they afford it only at such a cost as renders submission to injury in general the better calculation. The security of property in England is owing (except as regards open violence) to opinion, and the fear of exposure, much more than to the direct operation of the law and the courts of justice (II, 114).[56]

Indeed the law even encouraged dishonesty and crime to the advantage of the wealthy:

The law everywhere ostensibly favours at least pecuniary honesty and the faith of contracts; but if it affords facilities for evading those obligations, by trick and chicanery, or by the unscrupulous use of riches in instituting unjust or resisting just litigation; if there are ways and means by which persons may attain the ends of roguery, under the apparent sanction of the law; to that extent the law is demoralizing, even in regard to pecuniary integrity. And such cases are, unfortunately, frequent under the English system. If, again, the law, by a misplaced indulgence, protects idleness or prodigality against their natural consequences, or dismisses crime with inadequate penalties, the effect, both on the prudential and on the social virtues, is unfavourable. When the law, by its own dispensations and injunctions, establishes injustice between individual and individual; as all laws do which recognise any form of slavery, as the laws of all countries do, though not all in the same degree, in respect to the family relations; and as the laws of many countries do, though in still more unequal degrees, as between rich and poor; the effect on the moral sentiments of the people is still more disastrous (III, 886).

Examples of unfairness include costs of contract, Mill taking McCulloch's position that 'the taxes on contracts are the more objectionable, because, with that tendency to spare the rich which pervades our financial system, they are proportionally much heavier on the smaller transactions' (859n; 1848, 1849 eds). Taxes on auction sales and land purchase provide other instances since in both cases the incidence falls mainly on the more needy party (858).

* * *

56 The injury was compounded. Law taxes, far from being justifiable on the benefit principle as some maintained, constituted 'a tax on redress, and therefore a premium on injury . . . As [Bentham] remarked, those who are under the necessity of going to law, are those who benefit least, not most, by the law and its administration. To them the protection which the law affords has not been complete, since they have been obliged to resort to a court of law to ascertain their rights, or maintain those rights against infringement . . .' (III, 862).

The contentious issue of 'double taxation' is conspicuous in the context of 'equality of sacrifice'. Mill recommended as his ideal the entire exclusion of savings from taxable income:

To tax the sum invested and afterwards tax also the proceeds of the investment, is to tax the same portion of the contributor's means twice over. The principal and the interest cannot both together form part of his resources; they are the same portion twice counted: if he has the interest, it is because he abstains from using the principal; if he spends the principal, he does not receive the interest. Yet because he can do either of the two, he is taxed as if he could do both, and could have the benefit of the saving and that of spending, concurrently with one another (816).[57]

The foregoing argument, which runs in terms of justice, is reinforced by the case from expediency, since what is twice-taxed is 'just the portion employed in a way in which it would rather be public policy to encourage its employment' – that is accumulation (1861, V, 565).[58]

In response to an objection at the 1851 Committee that some savings take the form of investment in non-productive forms, Mill gave a 'Smithian' reply 'that it is more desirable to encourage people to expend money on things which last, and which will be of benefit to future generations, than to expend it on articles which are consumed by the person himself, and from which no other person derives any benefit. Buildings, paintings, sculptures, and other matters of that kind, have an indefinite duration, and money so expended gives pleasure to others as well as to the individual concerned; and it appears to me that such expenditure ought rather to be encouraged than to be subjected to any peculiar tax' (V, 487).

That the scheme would favour the rich over the poor is denied because savings involves a diversion of income from current consumption to a 'productive investment' which is distributed as wages (letter to Cliffe Leslie, 1861, XV, 746–7). The mere fact that it was 'a very much easier thing for the wealthier classes to save than for the poorer ones' – as the examiners at the Committee of 1861 observed – was 'an objection which applies to all the received maxims of taxation' and not to be overcome by unfair and inexpedient double taxation any more than by progressive taxes (on earned income) (V, 567). It was at succession that peculiar burdens on the rich

57 Cf. evidence of 1852, V, 476f.; evidence of 1861, *ibid.*, 553, 565, 597; correspondence with Thornton, 23 Oct. 1863, XV, 892: '. . . I would, if I could, exempt savings from income tax, & make the tax on income virtually a tax on expenditure'; and correspondence with Cliffe Leslie, 1 Dec. 1871, XVII, 1858: 'A tax on total expenditure would be the best tax in principle, because it would exempt savings . . .'.

58 Namely, the same adverse effect as the 'graduated property tax' (i.e. progressive income tax) – that it 'punishes' saving.

might be imposed, as we have seen. It must be added at the same time, that indirect taxation would be abolished in Mill's scheme thus avoiding a regressive feature (evidence of 1851, V, 479).

Gladstone, one of the examiners in 1861, continued to insist that since the poor *must be* a spending class the proposal 'would be, so far as it goes, a change in favour of the richer classes of society as against the poorer' (V, 570); and Mill again conceded that '[i]n one sense it would'. But he was evidently unimpressed; as he saw the matter the proposal 'would be be favourable to the saving classes, whether poor or rich, compared with the spending classes; and that consideration I think is even paramount to the other' (569). Indeed he went so far as to state that to the extent saving is more difficult for the poor the proposed relief 'is a greater advantage to them' (568). But the implications of this position are much reduced by an alternative proposal to which we now turn.

* * *

There was serious danger of fraud in a scheme exempting actual savings by individuals (III, 816–17; V, 478, 565). As an alternative to the expenditure tax Mill proposed an income tax with allowance made for differential classes of savings requirements. This entailed a distinction between 'perpetual' incomes (income from land, stocks, mortgages) and 'life' income (salaries, terminable annuities and professional incomes): 'In principle, I should say that the remission should be on what he does save, neither more nor less; but as this cannot be carried out, I think you must consider, taking people in classes, what difference exists between them as to the necessity or obligation that they are under of saving, with some consideration also of how far you have reason to believe that, practically, as a matter of fact, they do, as a class, save up to the mark of obligation' (V, 586).[59] It was 'a visible injustice' of the contemporary system that it treated both categories alike, despite the fact that those living on life incomes had 'greater necessities' – the obligation to save for retirement and to support dependents after their working years (III, 813–14).[60] The maxim of

59 An important matter is at stake here. For Mill recognized two principles – the avoidance of double taxation and allowance for the savings requirements of different persons, that is a recognition of the differential obligations to make sacrifices (588, 590). To satisfy the former would automatically assure the latter, but not necessarily the reverse. Yet the second-best might be necessary: Avoidance of double-taxation 'is the principle I would apply if I could; but inasmuch as I cannot apply it, I take another standard, to satisfy that which I consider to be the criterion of justice between the tax-payer and another, namely, the difference in their necessities' (594).

60 Cf. III, 831: '[A]ll sums saved from income and invested, should be exempt from the tax: or if this be found impracticable . . . life incomes, and incomes from business and professions, should be less heavily taxed than inheritable incomes, in a degree as nearly

equality of taxation (always in the sense of equality of sacrifice) required that 'people should be taxed, not in proportion to what they have, but to what they can afford to spend' (819).[61] And a rough and ready expedient of what contributors '*ought* to save' – presuming it impossible to evaluate actual savings – was 'a deduction of one-fourth in favour of life-incomes', assuming 'that one-fourth of a life-income is, on the average of all ages and states of health, a suitable proportion to be laid by as a provision for successors and for old age' (817).

Mill further countenanced some discrimination between forms of life income on grounds of relative precariousness. Thus, for example, profits – as distinct from interest – might be preferentially treated:

An income which some not unusual vicissitude may reduce to nothing, or even convert into a loss, is not the same thing to the feelings of the possessor as a permanent income of 1000*l*. a year, even though on an average of years it may yield 1000*l*. a year. If life-incomes were assessed at three-fourths their amount, the profits of business, after deducting interest on capital, should not only be assessed at three-fourths, but should pay, on that assessment a lower rate. Or perhaps the claims of justice in this respect might be sufficiently met by allowing the deduction of a fourth on the entire income, interest included (818–19).

But trading incomes (presumably including interest), he urged in his 1861 evidence, should be taxed more heavily than professional incomes since the

as possible equivalent to the increased need of economy arising from their terminable character'. Cf. also evidence of 1852, V, 466: 'I would therefore tax temporary or precarious incomes at a lower scale than permanent or certain incomes . . . because the possessors of those incomes have one want, which those who possess permanent incomes have not; they are liable to be called upon in most cases to save something out of that income to provide for their own future years, or to provide for others who are dependent upon them; while those who possess permanent incomes can spend the whole, and still leave the property to their descendants or others. It is for this reason that I would tax a temporary income at a lower rate than a permanent income'.

61 Cf. V, 467: 'The true principle of the equality of taxation, I conceive to be, not that it shall be equal in proportion to means, but that it shall, as far as possible, demand an equal sacrifice from all. If two persons have equal incomes, and one of them can afford to spend the whole of that income, while the other is called upon to make a certain reserve to meet future wants, to demand from these two persons the same annual sum, is to require from them not an equal, but an unequal sacrifice'; and V, 551: '[T]he first rule is the general rule of taxation, namely, equality; that is to say, taxation in proportion to means. But this does not, I think, necessarily imply taxation in proportion to the whole of a person's receipts; because the whole of his receipts may greatly exceed what he can, with any propriety, expend upon himself. It seems to me, therefore, that two kinds of allowances are necessary; an allowance for small incomes, and an allowance for incomes that are of temporary duration, or precarious; and I think that the present income tax fails of justice under both those heads, though I do not go nearly so far as many people in my estimate of the amount of that injustice'.

'necessities or obligations for saving . . . are greater in the case of professional men than in the case of traders' (V, 560).[62]

It is not always stated explicitly whether wages – including wages of unskilled labour – were classified as life income; in the *Principles* Mill formally specifies, apart from terminable annuities, only salaries and professional incomes (813). But it would be odd were they excluded, and in the evidence of 1861 Mill in fact spoke of professional income 'and all incomes derived from personal exertion' (V, 559).[63] Indeed much is made of their inclusion. For by treating life incomes more leniently than the perpetual incomes which would pertain typically to upper-income classes the import of his refusal to weight highly the force of Gladstone's argument that the poor cannot save as easily as the rich is reduced:

It is, no doubt, an important question of principle, how far the importance of not taxing twice ought to prevail over other considerations [including any special advantage to the rich]. But this is not the question to be decided practically, since we cannot exempt people on what they actually do save. A tax which was proportioned, not to people's actual savings, but to their necessities and obligations of savings, would not be liable to the objection which you have stated, whatever the force of that objection may be . . . the average that would be taken on the principle of having untaxed what people were bound to save, would of itself exclude the greater portion of the opulent classes from the benefit; it would exclude all but those who were obliged to save in order to fulfil a real necessity (V, 568–9).

Mill had high respect for John Hubbard, chairman of the 1861 Select Committee. Hubbard's proposal, involving a one-third remission for 'industrial' as distinct from 'property' income would be 'a great improvement over the current system' which made no distinctions whatever (570). While his own proposal was designed to assure greater precision within categories – for example some life incomes (of a precarious kind) though derived from property should be treated favourably (570, 579), and trading should be differentiated from professional income – he conceded the need for pragmatism: 'I think it highly desirable in every plan of approximating taxation to justice, that a just principle should be carried out as far as it

---

62 Cf. V, 580, where Mill distinguishes traders' incomes, derived from labour and capital, from professional incomes whose income derived from labour alone (apart from investment in education), and calls for harsher treatment of the former. Earnings of shareholders in joint-stock or public companies would be treated less favourably than the incomes of individual manufacturers or partnerships on the grounds that the latter alone were a reward for industry and talent and thus both precarious and terminable (581). If we read Mill correctly dividends in public companies would be treated as interest.

63 West (1978b, 573) erroneously interprets Mill's suggestion that professional incomes be given special consideration as disconcern with lower (wage) incomes.

can go, that is, to the point at which it is stopped by insurmountable [practical] obstacles; but if other means fail . . . I am forced to give way to them, but not for that reason to relax my support of what I consider justice in cases in which it is practicable' (573). Hubbard's scheme, at least in the broad, captured most of the objectives Mill had in mind.[64] As Gladstone understood his position Mill despaired of 'any mode of adaptation or of reconstruction of the income tax to the principles of justice . . .' (562). And the need for compromise would, Mill believed, be appreciated by the public provided industrial income were given preferential treatment over property income as Hubbard proposed. (For Hubbard's proposal see Appendix pp. 971-6).

As is not surprising for Mill, he found objectionable taxation relief according to family size. The reason offered throws light on the sense of Mill's criterion:

I do not think it would be just to disregard any consideration which is relevant to the real principle, that is, the necessity for saving. You must, I think, make the classification, so as to allow for the greatest number possible of the circumstances that make it necessary for one person to save more than another, with the single exception of those circumstances which depend upon his own will. For instance, I would not admit large families as a ground, because it is not a necessity for anybody to have a large family; it is his choice, and I do not think any allowance should be made for that (576).[65]

* * *

A word is required at this point on the 'house-tax'. Such a tax, as Mill viewed the matter, was 'not intended as a tax on incomes derived from houses, but on expenditure incurred for them. The thing which it is wished to ascertain is what a house costs to a person who lives in it, not what it would bring in if let to some one else' (III, 837). A change in the law of 1851 regrettably retained the feature of rating great residences (Chatsworth and Belvoir are mentioned) 'on an imaginary rent of perhaps 200l. a year, under

64 Thus regarding Hubbard's one-third remission on professional and industrial incomes: 'It is their precariousness, combined with their temporary nature, which constitutes the obligation to make savings from them. It is because the incomes may end sooner, from loss of health and other causes, that professional incomes are under a much stronger necessity of saving, than people who derive their incomes from property' (594); 'There is nothing, generally speaking, to fall back upon in the case of those for whom the saving is made, and, if they are not provided for from that source, they are not so at all' (559).

65 Yet a practical objection to an expenditure tax (apart from easy evasion) given in correspondence is that it falls more heavily on families with many children (1 Dec. 1871, XVII, 1858).

the pretext that owing to the great expense of keeping them up, they could not be let for more'.[66] Indeed, a house tax properly evaluated was 'a nearer approach to a fair income tax, than a direct assessment on income can easily be; having the great advantage, that it makes spontaneously all the allowances which it is so difficult to make, and so impracticable to make exactly, in assessing an income tax: for it what a person pays in house-rent is a test of anything, it is a test not of what he possesses, but of what he thinks he can afford to spend' (835–6).[67]

As we have come to expect there is one objection which did not convince Mill – 'that a person may require a larger and more expensive house, not from having greater means, but from having a larger family' (836). On these grounds 'he is not entitled to complain; since having a large family is at a person's own choice: and, so far as concerns the public interest, is a thing rather to be discouraged than promoted'. But an exemption limit is allowed: 'As incomes below a certain amount ought to be exempt from income tax, so ought houses below a certain value, from house-tax, on the universal principle of sparing from all taxation the absolute necessaries of healthful existence' (837).[68]

* * *

While fairly assessed direct taxation – as we know an expenditure tax or an approximate alternative – would, in principle, be 'the least exceptionable of all taxes', evasion, particularly in the case of professional incomes and profits, would render any such system unjust by discriminating against 'the

---

66 The same point is made in the evidence of 1852 regarding 'some of the largest and most valuable houses in the country' (V, 489); 'the rent which they might be supposed to let for . . . would bear no proportion to what they cost to the proprietor'. And that was the valid index – that 'what a person spends in house rent is generally a fair criterion of what he can afford to spend altogether . . . persons generally expend in house rent something bearing a more equal proportion to the general means of expenditure than almost any other criterion that can be selected'.

67 Cf. V, 496: The house tax was 'much fairer' than the income tax because it 'makes its own allowances, which must be made artificially in the case of the income tax. The house tax, being proportioned to an item of expenditure which approximates to a correct measure of the general scale of a person's expenses, has the advantage that what he saves is spontaneously and naturally excluded, and you are not obliged to exclude it by special regulations'. Yet Mill also urged 'that according to all received opinions, the imposition of a tax on one particular description of property, is only just supposing the general system of taxation to tax other kinds of property in a proportionate degree' (485). Presumably his approval of a house tax must be understood as a special case considering its character as proxy for general expenditure.

68 But see V, 489–90: 'I have not particularly considered whether in the present state of our general taxation, I would make any exemption of low-rented houses.' The going exemption rate (1852) was for houses renting at under £20 annually.

most conscientious' (III, 831–2); and a 'high level of conscientious cooperation, on the part of the contributors [was] not to be hoped for in the present low state of public morality' (867). Mill's general position was well expressed in correspondence: 'I prefer a mixed system of direct & indirect taxation to either alone. If the attempt were made to raise so large a revenue as ours after all due retrenchments [of governmental spending] would still be exclusively by direct taxation, I do not know of any taxes, in themselves just, which, under such strong pecuniary temptation, would not be successfully evaded. The evasions of the income tax are already a disgrace to the national morality (17 April 1865, XVI, 1032).[69]

There was a further consideration weighing against too much reliance on direct taxation – a widespread, though illusory, sentiment that direct taxes impose a greater burden than indirect even when the same aggregate revenue is yielded. A growing appreciation of the real incidence of indirect taxes, Mill believed, characterized contemporary progress; but while the infirmity of mind persisted there was a danger that popular opposition to revenue raising would impede various socially-desirable government expenditures (865–6) – a nice illustration indeed of Mill's high awareness of the cultural constraints on reform.

Some direct taxes were, however, still recommended (868). A tax on land rent, albeit discriminatory, involving (apart from the contemporary land-tax and stamp-duties on the conveyance of land or an equivalent charge) the novel feature of a charge on the 'progressive increase of the incomes of landlords from natural causes'; the taxation of legacies and inheritances at a progressive rate; and also a house-tax.[70] These sources, would constitute 'the prudent limits of direct taxation' to be extended

---

69 Mill in 1852 remarked that the problem of dishonesty was not 'insuperable' (III, 831). Yet a problem it still was; cf. evidence of 1852: 'One thing . . . has always struck me in looking at the estimates, viz., the very small amount of capital which pays income tax under Schedule (D). This seems to me a strong proof of the evasion of the tax. In a country like this, where trade is carried on to so large an extent, it is difficult to believe that there is not a much larger amount of income derived from professions and trades than the amount shown, under that Schedule' (V, 488). 'It seems impossible', he added, 'without a degree of inquisitorialness which no free community will submit to, to dispense with relying mainly upon the returns made by individuals; and those returns, even in the most honourable community which has ever yet existed, could not be implicitly relied upon' (495–6). In 1871 Mill noted that some city men had predicted that Peel's Act of 1842, reinstituting the income tax first introduced by Pitt (1798), would lead to a 'great deterioration of commercial morality' (1 Dec. 1871, XVII, 1858).

70 A moderate tax to avoid any inducement to overcrowding, cf. 1 Dec. 1871, XVII, 1858.

only in times of national emergency when neglect of the 'inequality and unfairness' attached to a general income tax would be justified.[71]

But the proposed direct taxes would require supplementation even in normal times.[72] This should be provided by consumption taxes. Here two general principles are raised: Indirect taxation designed for revenue should be impartial and not act as a discriminatory protective duty; and indirect taxes should not impinge on 'necessaries' – the counterpart to the exemption limit in the case of a general income tax and similarly insisted upon whether or not the incidence is transferred to employers:

An exclusion must . . . be put upon all taxes on the necessaries of life, or on the materials and instruments employed in producing those necessaries. Such taxes are always liable to encroach on what should be left untaxed, the incomes barely sufficient for healthful existence; and on the most favourable supposition, namely that wages rise to compensate the labourers for the tax, it operates as a peculiar tax on profits which is at once unjust, and detrimental to public wealth (868).

'Necessaries', it transpires, include 'ordinary articles of food' for human and animal consumption; timber, metals and tools; soap; tallow and paper (871–2).[73]

Mill's repeatedly encountered hostility towards conspicuous consumption suggested the raising of 'as large a revenue as conveniently may be, from

71 In his evidence of 1852 Mill allowed a broader case for an income tax in normal times: 'Whether [fraud] is such an objection as to render the income tax inadvisable in a country which has to raise by taxation so large a sum as this country has to raise, I should not venture to give an opinion upon. There are many worse taxes than the income tax, but there are many better' (V, 496). In 1861 he stated the matter as in the *Principles*: '[E]xcept in a case of absolute necessity, and as an extraordinary resource, I should be against [the income tax]' (591).

72 It was desirable to have a variety of different modes so that the inevitable inequalities 'may not all fall in the same place' (V, 497).

73 Cf. 12 Dec. 1864, XV, 976, regarding equality of sacrifice: 'I only exclude necessaries. I do not think a distinction can be fairly made between comforts and luxuries, or that I am entitled to call my tea and coffee by the one name, and another person's melons and champagne by the other. I allow for nothing but what is needed to keep an average person alive and free from physical suffering.' Also 17 April 1865, XVI, 1032–33: 'I would in no case tax any of the necessaries of life; but if even a working man expends in luxuries for himself, & especially in stimulants, what is required by the necessities of his family, I think it perfectly just that he should be taxed on such expenditure.' And 28 Dec. 1867, XVI, 1339: 'I would . . . have no direct tax on such incomes as are only sufficient to give mere necessaries of life and health to an average family; nor would I have any indirect taxes on the necessaries of life and health, though I would have on the luxuries, even of the poor; especially luxuries which are apt to be noxious such as intoxicating drinks.' The U.S. cotton tax 'comes within the class of taxes on necessaries . . . I should suspect that it is partly a tax on the laborer . . . by making [money wages] not go so far as they otherwise would, in the purchase of clothing'.

those classes of luxuries which have most connexion with vanity, and least with positive enjoyment; such as the more costly qualities of all kinds of personal equipment and ornament' (870). The theme – which reappears in the case for heavy succession duties – is of the first importance:

I disclaim all asceticism, and by no means wish to see discouraged either by law or opinion, any indulgence (consistent with the means and obligations of the person using it) which is sought from a genuine inclination for, and enjoyment of, the thing itself; but a great portion of the expenses of the higher and middle classes in most countries, and the greatest in this, is not incurred for the sake of the pleasure afforded by the things on which the money is spent, but from regard to opinion, and an idea that certain expenses are expected from them, as an appendage of station; and I cannot but think that expenditure of this sort is a most desirable object of taxation (869).

Accordingly, taxation 'should rise very rapidly with the number of horses and carriages, and with their costliness' (870).[74] But revenue requirements would necessitate also some degree of taxation of the more widely purchased 'real luxuries' or commodities which 'afford pleasure in themselves, and are valued on that account rather than for their cost'; taxes in these cases – Mill's proposal is the counterpart to the principle of proportionate income taxation – should fall 'with the same proportionate weight on small, on moderate, and on large incomes'. But to avoid a regressive burden on the poor – such as characterized the 'flagrantly unjust' contemporary system – Mill proposed that the better qualities of such products, tea, coffee, sugar, tobacco and fermented drinks, be taxed at 'much higher' *ad valorem* rates (870–1).

* * *

Mill maintained that taxation should 'be levied on income, and not on the capital from which the income proceeds; property which does not yield an income being exempt' (e.g. V, 487). A proposal to place the burden entirely on income from 'realized property' or property not under the control of its owner – the public funds, land, mortgages and shares in joint-stock companies – particularly irked him. The proposal, which would effectively free profits of trade, manufactures, and agriculture until retirement from business, he categorized as 'a shameless pretension' by placing the burden on those least able to bear it, since 'realized property' included 'provision made for those who are unable to work' and consisted largely 'of extremely small fractions' (III, 812). 'Why', he asked, 'should those who save pay all the taxes for those who have spent all they got?' (2 March 1859, XV, 597).

---

74 In this context Mill cites Sismondi and Rae (see above, p. 267). Rae himself applies his analysis to taxation (369f). This latter is cited by Mill (III, 869n).

It was 'contrary to both to the rule of equal justice and to economical policy' (28 Dec. 1867, XVI, 1338). The proposal would also free wages from tax obligation, and Mill expressed concern less a powerful but 'unenlightened' working class should one day 'be tempted to throw all taxes on property – or even on realised property, & to make the taxes heavy in order, by their outlay, to benefit as they might think, trade and labour' (25 Sept. 1865, XVI, 1104). The proposal was an inexpedient and unjust as Proudhonism (1 Dec. 1871, XVII, 1858–9). He was incensed by the confiscatory aspects of the proposal for, since purchasers of property would acquire it at a discount, allowance made for the reduced yield expected in the future, the burden – 'exclusively thrown on the owners of the smaller portion of the wealth of the community' – 'would not even be . . . on that *class* of persons in perpetual succession, but would fall exclusively on those who happened to compose it when the tax was laid on' (III, 812). The current owners thus suffer a permanent loss by confiscation: 'That such a proposition should find any favour, is a striking instance of the want of conscience in matters of taxation, resulting from the absence of any fixed principles in the public mind, and of any indication of a sense of justice on the subject in the general conduct of governments' (812–13; cf. 475, 485–6).

However, there is some evidence that late in his life Mill may have been prepared to countenance the *general* taxation of capital although *faute de mieux*. The issue was raised in Baer's *L'Avere e L'Imposta* (1872), which argued that the rule of equity – taxation proportional to means (which Mill we know championed) – would be satisfied by a direct tax on capital value (capital of all kinds both 'realized' and 'unrealized', i.e. whether or not invested in business, and private assets) combined with the indirect taxation of 'unproductive consumption' (30 May 1872, XVII, 1901). To this Mill objected on grounds of double taxation, 'l'egalité dans l'impôt me paraît consister en ce que chacun paie à proportion de ce qu'il peut appliquer à la satisfaction de ses propres besoins. Tant que son capital reste productif il n'en tire pas plus d'advantage personnel que si ce capital lui avait été confié par l'état . . .' (1902). More accurately, 'le capital, tant qu'il reste productif, n'a d'autre valeur pour le capitaliste que celle du revenue qu'il donne et que par conséquent si on le fait payer sur le capital et aussi sur toutes ses dépenses il est en realité imposé deux fois' (22 Sept. 1872, XVII, 1905). In a formal review of Baer for the *Fortnightly* (March 1873) Mill conceded that though the capitalist has no financial advantage from his capital as such while it remains invested 'he has a sense of power and importance connected with it', in consideration of which 'it may be thought equitable to make him pay something additional to the State'. But this would be departing from the principle of taxation in proportion to means, and introducing another principle, that of distributive justice; it was laying a tax on an advantageous social position – a measure which, if defensible, must be so on moral or political grounds, not on economical' (V, 701).

This latter qualification is of some interest, for it does not seem to have been recognized in earlier formulations. What to make of it is another question, since Mill did not investigate further the 'moral or political grounds' in question which might justify Baer's measure. But it is a fact that he did allow a general tax on capital value (in place of the income tax) combined with the indirect taxation of 'luxuries', along Baer's lines, as a practical necessity sooner or later – and this despite the injustice of double taxation – because of the difficulty of assuring that profits bear their share under an income tax and the almost inherent regressiveness of indirect taxation. His position is best stated in the *Fortnightly Review* in the same year:

No tax is in itself absolutely just; the justice or injustice of taxes can only be comparative: if just in the conception, they are never completely so in the application: and it is quite possible that nations may some day be obliged to resort to a moderate tax on all property, as the least unjust mode of raising a part of their revenue. The many injustices of a direct income-tax are generally acknowledged; while perhaps the greatest of all is that which is the least complained of, that it is a tax on conscience, and a premium on deception, and improbity. The increase of commercial dishonesty, so much complained of for many years past, was predicted by good judges as the certain effect of Sir Robert Peel's income-tax; and it will never be known for how much of that evil product the tax may be accountable, or in how many cases a false return of income was the first dereliction of pecuniary integrity. Nevertheless, an income-tax is felt to be indispensable on our present financial system, because without it there are actually no means, recognised by existing opinion, of making the richer classes pay their just share of taxation – a thing which cannot be done by any system of taxes on consumption yet devised. Succession duties are, no doubt, the least objectionable mode of making property, as distinguished from income, contribute directly to the State, and they should be employed as far as practicable; but unless the duty is very light, there is great difficulty in protecting it against evasion. The tax proposed by Mr. Baer, may, therefore, some time or other, have to be taken into serious consideration . . . (V, 701–2).

And similarly, in late correspondence: 'The grand objection which remains unaffected is, that Savings would be taxed doubly and spendings only singly. I have condemned the tax as unjust, but have said that considering the very strong objections to an income tax, a country *may* possibly have at some time or other to make its election for a moderate tax on capital and land as being on the whole the course of least injustice' (to Cairns, 8 Jan. 1873, XVII, 1933).[75]

75 Cf. to Cairns, 9 Dec. 1872, *ibid.*, 1925–6: 'Have you ever turned your attention to

VIII ON INHERITANCE

As a rule government 'ought to make no distinction of persons or classes' (*CW*, III, 806–7), so that a peculiar tax on any class constituted 'a violation of justice' which 'amounts to a partial confiscation' (826). This general rule was taken up in the preceding section. We have encountered already one case of *formal* divergence from the principle of equality of taxation, though 'consistently with that equal justice which is the groundwork of the rule' (819), namely the taxation of the unearned increment of land value. Mill's treatment of succession provides a second key example. The general issue is laid out in 'On Property'.

Private property, in every defence made of it, is supposed to mean, the guarantee to individuals of the fruits of their own labour and abstinence. The guarantee to them of the fruits of the labour and abstinence of others, transmitted to them without any merit or exertion of their own, is not of the essence of the institution, but a mere incidental consequence, which, when it reaches a certain height, does not promote but conflicts with, the ends which render private property legitimate (II, 208).

Accordingly, Mill recommended an absolute upper limit to sums received by legacy or gift:

Each person should have the power to dispose by will of his or her whole property; but not to lavish it in enriching some one individual, beyond a certain maximum, which should be fixed sufficiently high to afford the means of comfortable independence . . . I see nothing objectionable in fixing a limit to what any one may acquire by the mere favour of others, without any exercise of his faculties, and in requiring that if he desires any further accession of fortune, he shall work for it (225; cf. III, 755).[76]

> the merits and demerits of a tax on property, ie: land and capital, realized and unrealized, as a substitute for an income tax? The pros and cons are tolerably obvious, the pros consisting rather in the demerits, of other direct taxes than in the recommendations of this.' Also to Baer himself: 'Or je ne suis pas ennemi de l'impôt sur le capital; je trouve assez probable, qu'à cause de l'incertitude et de l'effet si démoralisateur de l'impôt direct sur les revenus on viendra à imposer le capital comme moyen d'en atteindre les profits' (*ibid.*, 1901).
>
> 76 Mill (223) emphasizes his preference for restrictions on what one may *acquire* not on what one may *bequeath* presumably to avoid interference with an individual's use of his wealth. Expedential qualifications to the recommendation were allowed. Thus in the sixth edition (1865) Mill added that allowances might be made to prevent the break-up of single manufacturing and commercial enterprises or ancestral mansions and parks (225n).

Mill's objections to progressiveness applied solely to *earned* income. This qualification is repeatedly insisted upon and constitutes an essential part of the record. In the *Principles* itself Mill expressed the matter strongly: '[I]nheritances and legacies' – at least beyond a certain amount – were legitimate candidates to be taxed as heavily as was possible 'without giving rise to evasions, by donation *inter vivos* or concealment of property, such as it would be impossible adequately to check. The principle of graduation . . . of levying a larger percentage on a larger sum . . . seems to me, both just and expedient as applied to legacy and inheritance duties' (III, 811–12). Similarly, before the 1852 investigation:

The principle of graduation I do not think is just as applied to incomes derived from personal exertions, or to the savings from incomes derived from personal exertions; but I do not think that the same objection holds good to the principle of graduation when applied to inherited property . . . It is unjust to tax a person because, by his own savings, he acquires a large fortune, and to tax him in a larger proportion than if he had squandered more and saved less; but there is no injustice in taxing persons who have not acquired what they have by their own exertions, but have had it bestowed them in free gift; and there are no reasons of justice or policy against taxing enormously large inheritances more highly than smaller inheritances . . . I would do so to the utmost extent to which the means could be found for imposing it without its being frustrated. The larger the sum demanded by the tax, the more would people try to evade it; but that is the only limitation I would apply to the principle' (V, 491).[77]

And in the evidence of 1861: 'If the rich are to be subject to a greater proportionate amount of taxation than the poor . . . [a] succession duty is the most unobjectionable mode of doing it, because in that way it is confined to hereditary wealth. I think you must allow people to retain the full advantage for their lives of what they have acquired; but the State may deal with it on the occasion of succession' (V, 569).[78]

There emerges in this context a further matter of major principle. Whereas Mill was alert to the problem of double taxation, in the case of succession this was set aside entirely although both the property is taxed at succession and any income yielded thereby subsequently. The entire notion of 'equality of taxation' is said to be inapplicable:

77 See also letter of 28 Dec. 1867, XVI, 1339: '. . . I am quite in favour of some special taxation of all inheritances above a small amount – and graduated taxation too; a percentage rising with the amount of the inheritance.'
78 Mill applied the rule to all forms of property, including personal property such as furniture (cf. V, 491–2). The going system of legacy taxation [apparently] was neither graduated nor extended beyond income-yielding property.

I do not think that the principle of equality of taxation has any application to the case of taxes on succession. It seems to me that taxes on succession stand on a different foundation from all other taxes, and that the State is entitled, in reference to them, to consider public policy and general morality, abstractedly from the special rule of equality of taxation. If a person is allowed by the State to succeed to that which he has not earned, but has obtained without any exertion, that is a privilege which he owes to the existence of law and society, to which the State is entitled to annex conditions, and if these conditions are just, when tried by a higher principle of morality, no general principle of equality of taxation has any application to them (V, 566).

It almost goes without saying, considering Mill's condemnation of primogeniture and other restrictions, that Mill favoured the free disposition by owners of their property subject to the quantitative limits already noted. There is a further constraint – that they may not 'determine the person who should succeed to it after the death of all who were living when the will was made' (III, 895).

* * *

Notwithstanding Mill's proposals for income tax reform and the special treatment of land rent, his own emphasis was always on the reform of succession duties. Here above all, he believed, would be found the key to social justice. This outstandingly important feature of the record is well made in late correspondence with Baer:

J'accorde qu'on peut justement exiger de celui qui vit sans travailler sur le revenu de son capital ou de sa terre une plus grande contribution que de celui qui gagne un revenu équivalent en travaillant, aussi ai-je toujours demandé une réforme de l'income tax dans ce sens. Mais cela est principalement vrai pour ceux qui doivent leur fortune à l'héritage et non à leur propre travail antérieur; aussi c'est surtout par l'impôt sur les successions que je voudrais rétablir, en cette matière, la justice sociale (22 Sept. 1872, XVII, 1905).

[Q]uant aux successions, je ne reconnais aux héritiers même directs aucun droit moral à hériter au delà d'une légitime suffisante pour leur donner de bonnes chances dans la vie. Donc si la société permet d'hériter par delà cette limite, elle a le droit d'y mettre les conditions qu'elle veut; et elle peut user de ce droit dans le but de modérer l'inégalité de richesses ce qui est moins permis lorsqu'il s'agit d'ôter aux travailleurs leurs propres gains. Par là vous verrez qu'au moins je ne suis pas en contradiction avec mes propres principes (8 Jan. 1873, ibid., 1932).

But his proposals had always been the central part of the reform program, as Alexander Bain confirms: '[W]hat I remember most vividly of his talk pending publication of the work [*The Principles*] was his anticipating a tremendous outcry about his doctrines on Property. He frequently spoke of his proposals as to Inheritance and Bequest, which if carried out would pull down all large fortunes in two generations. To his surprise, however, this part of the book made no sensation' (1882, 89).

Now it is not at all clear that surprise was a justified reaction. Consider Mill's own summary of the key clauses:

Freedom of bequest as the general rule, but limited by two things: first, that if there are descendants, who, being unable to provide for themselves, would become burthensome to the state, the equivalent of whatever the state would accord to them should be reserved from the property for their benefit; and secondly, that no one person should be permitted to acquire, by inheritance, more than the amount of a moderate independence. In case of intestacy, the whole property to escheat to the state: which should be bound to make a just and reasonable provision for descendents, that is, such a provision as the parent or ancestor ought to have made, their circumstances, capacities, and mode of bringing up being considered (III, 887).

This summary is, however, immediately followed (in all editions) by an allowance that 'several phases of improvement' would be required 'before ideas so far removed from present modes of thinking will be taken into serious consideration'. The second-best solution then suggested neglects the proposal regarding quantative limits entirely: 'As an intermediate course, therefore, I would recommend the extension to all property, of the present English law of inheritance affecting personal property (freedom of bequest, and in case of intestacy, equal division): except that no rights should be acknowledged in collaterals, and that the property of those who have neither descendants nor ascendants, and make no will, should escheat to the state' (888). The close reader, at least, would not have an impression of the need for great haste in the introduction of the major redistributive measure.

That Mill's position was carried through consistently is confirmed by reference to his 'Leslie on the Land Question' (1870). For Leslie too proposed to limit the amount of land any single person could acquire by inheritance but believed this to be so 'shocking to present proprietory sentiments' that 'only a violent revolution could at present accomplish it' (cited by Mill, V, 681). Accordingly he limited his proposals to the removal of restrictions on land use as a means of increasing the supply of land in the market. We have seen (above, p. 839) that Mill did not think these proposals adequate for their objective of raising rural living standards. Yet in the 1870 review he did not insist on an absolute upper limit on the inheritance of landed property.

IX   LIMITATIONS ON BEQUESTS AND
DISTRIBUTION: DIMINISHING UTILITY

Apart from the desirability of greater equality of opportunity, Mill's argument in favour of the diffusion of wealth derived from a version of the principle of diminishing utility resembling that later adopted by Carl Menger (1871).[79] Limitations on the quantitative right of bequest to any one individual would, Mill maintained, scarcely be regarded 'as a burthensome restraint by any testator who estimated a large fortune at its true value, that of the pleasures and advantages that can be purchased with it: on even the most extravagant estimate of which, it must be apparent to every one, that the difference to the happiness of the possessor between a moderate independence and five times as much, is insignificant when weighed against the enjoyment that might be given, and the permanent benefits diffused, by some other disposal of the four-fifiths'(*CW*, II, 225). What we have here is a condemnation of 'a heap[ing] . . . to satiety' of 'those intrinsically worthless things on which large fortunes are mostly expended' (225). Similarly: 'If the restriction [on bequest] could be made practically effectual, the benefit would be great. Wealth which could no longer be employed in over-enriching a few, would either be devoted to objects of public usefulness, or if bestowed on individuals, would be distributed among a larger number. While those enormous fortunes which no one needs for any personal purpose but ostentation or improper power, would become much less numerous . . .' (226).

Any Mengerian reading has to be understood, however, in peculiarly Millian terms. We must allow for the moral perspective implied by the terms 'intrinsically worthless things', and by the contrast between 'needs for personal purposes' and purchases for 'ostentation or power' – a splendid instance of the role played by value judgement in policy recommendation.[80] There must remain some doubt as to Mill's position in the event that conspicuous consumption did not constitute a characteristic of upper-income expenditures. Yet it is unlikely whether this possibility would have been conceded – whether Mill could conceive how, beyond a certain level, consumption outlays could be other than for 'invalid' objectives, in which case the Menger connection stands.

79   Above, p. 264 Menger does not include a category of status-oriented expenditures but this can be fitted in.
80   Cf. *On Liberty*, XVIII, 260: 'It is desirable . . . that in things which do not primarily concern others, individuality should assert itself. Where, not the person's own character, but the traditions or customs of other people are the rule of conduct, there is wanting one of the principal ingredients of human happiness, and quite the chief ingredient of individual and social progress.'

The perspective, we have already seen, also governed Mill's approach to the selection of appropriate candidates for indirect taxation. But while nothing apparently swayed him from his objections to the progressive taxation of earned income, it is not a far step to apply the allowance made in the case of indirect taxation to that of direct.

X THE DESIRABILITY OF ECONOMIC DEVELOPMENT AND THE STATIONARY STATE

We shall now relate the argument for greater equality to that for a general increase in per capita income. By so doing Mill's preoccupation with the well-being of the masses will become fully apparent.

Some general propositions should be established at the outset, first the belief, expressed in the chapter 'Of the Stationary State', that direct redistribution of income, however desirable, would by itself not provide a permanent solution to low standards: '[W]hat is economically needed is a better distribution, of which one indispensable means is a stricter restraint on population. Levelling institutions, either of a just or of an unjust kind, cannot alone accomplish it; they may lower the heights of society, but they cannot, of themselves, permanently raise the depths' (CW, III, 755). To Austin Mill wrote in 1847: 'What does seem to me essential is that society at large should not be overworked, nor over-anxious about the means of subsistence, for which we must look to the grand source of improvement, repression of population, combined with laws or customs of inheritance which shall favour the diffusion of property instead of its accumulation in masses' (13 April 1847, XIII, 713).[81]

Moreover, while good wages and low hours were desirable they must ideally be earned by freemen with elevated standards:

[I]t seems to me chiefly important to impress on [the working classes] – first, that they are quite right in aiming at a more equal distribution of wealth and social

---

81 By the 1860s, as we shall see, population pressure, Mill believed, had been much assuaged. Accordingly, there seems to be more emphasis on redistribution alone; cf. the emphasis on union activity as a redistributive device in 'Thornton on Labour and its Claims' (1869): '[H]aving regard to the greatly superior numbers of the labouring class, and the inevitable scantiness of the remuneration afforded by even the highest rate of wages which, in the present state of the arts of production, could possibly become general; whoever does not wish that the labourers may prevail, and that the highest limit, whatever it be, may be attained, must have a standard of morals, and a conception of the most desirable state of society, widely different from those of either Mr. Thornton or the present writer' (V, 658). This perspective has in mind the labour force as a whole; the matter is more complex when consideration is given to individual unions especially when non-unionized sectors are allowed for.

advantages; secondly, that this more equal distribution can only be permanently affected (for merely taking from Peter to give to Paul would leave things worse than even at present) by means of their own public spirit and self-devotion as regards others, and prudence and self-restraint in relation to themselves. At present their idea of social reform appears to be simply higher wages, and less work, for the sake of more sensual indulgence. To be independent of master manufacturers, to work for themselves and divide the whole produce of their labour is a worthy object of ambition, but it is only fit for, and can only succeed with people who can labour for the community of which they are a part with the same energy and zeal as if labouring for their own private and separate interest (the opposite is now the case), and who, instead of expecting immediately more pay and less work, are willing to submit to any privation until they have effected their emancipation. The French working men and women contended for a principle, for an idea of justice, and they lived on bread and water till they gained their purpose. It was not more and costlier eating and drinking that was their object, as it seems to be the sole object of most of the well-paid English artisans (7 Jan. 1852, XIV, 81).

And finally, the objective of high wages and low hours must be achieved by honest means, not fraud, a point repeatedly insisted upon (above, pp. 789–9).

Professor Stigler (1949) is certainly right to emphasize Mill's concern with 'better men', but this does not preclude a concern with maximum output (above, pp. 825–6). Indeed the relationship is a mutual one. The savings in resources with increased probity – for criminals, are 'a direct burthen on the national industry' necessitating further costs of police and a legal apparatus – 'would be far outweighed by the immense increase in the produce of all kinds of labour, and saving of time and expenditure, which would be obtained if the labourers honestly performed what they undertake' (CW, II, 110). Similarly, Mill hoped that a 'more liberal and genial mental culture' would reduce the 'intensity of devotion to industrial occupations'; yet by such a transformation 'the labour actually bestowed on those occupations would almost always be rendered more effective' (184) – a case doubtless of less haste, more speed.

Bearing the foregoing qualification in mind higher per capita income was championed. What then of Mill's pronouncements on the stationary state? In the famous chapter of Book IV devoted to the topic, we find a representation of a progressive economy at its best (the United States) as one entailing high earnings and social justice and equality by which, as we would expect, is intended equality of opportunity: '[W]hile riches are power, and to grow as rich as possible the universal object of ambition, the path to its attainment should be open to all, without favour or partially' (III, 754). Impartiality, Mill regarded as universally desirable. But to grow as rich as possible as the universal object of ambition he hoped was 'only one of the phases of industrial progress'. The ideal was a situation in which, 'while no one is poor, no one desires to be richer, nor has any reason to fear being thrust back, by the efforts of others to push themselves forward' (754). More strongly, Mill wrote of the contemporary world that only in 'backward' countries was 'increased production . . . still an important object' (755).

These formulations seem to imply a general unconcern with increased output even as a means to increased average incomes. What is apparently championed is stationarity of aggregate real income as well as of capital and population. This reading, however, would appear not to reflect Mill's general intention. When placed in context it emerges that by these criticisms of 'progressive' society Mill had in mind the ever increasing incomes of the already wealthy. Thus, of 'the kind of economic progress which excites the congratulations of ordinary politicians', namely 'the mere increase of production and accumulation' (III, 755), he maintained that 'in themselves they are of little importance, so long as either the increase of population or anything else prevents the mass of the people from reaping any part of the benefit of them'. And this statement is followed by another expressing equally clearly that it is further increases of income for the already wealthy that cannot be justified: 'I know not why it should be a matter of congratulation that persons who are already richer than any one needs to be, should have doubled their means of consuming things which give little or no pleasure except as representative of wealth; or that numbers of individuals should pass over, every year, from the middle classes into a richer class, or from the class of the occupied rich to that of the unoccupied' (755).[82] It was then Mill's position that diminishing 'utility' attaches, beyond a point, to further increases of real income.

This perspective, it will be recalled, governed Mill's support of limitations on the right of bequest (to which discussion indeed he reverts in the context of the 'Stationary State') and the heavier *ad valorem* taxation of luxuries. But he was very careful not to generalize too far. Thus in *On Liberty* he expressed fears that the democratic tendencies in the United States 'combined with the notion that the public has a right to a veto on the manner in which individuals shall spend their incomes' acted as 'a tolerably effectual sumptuary law', such that in spaces it was 'really difficult for a person possessing a very large income, to find any mode of spending it, which will not incur popular

---

82 It is, it seems, to this feature of contemporary society that Mill alluded in the following often-cited passage: 'I confess I am not charmed with the ideal of life held out by those who think that the normal state of human beings is that of struggling to get on; that the trampling, crushing, elbowing, and treading on each other's heels, which form the existing type of social life, are the most desirable lot of human kind, or anything but the disagreeable symptoms of one of the phases of industrial progress. It may be a necessary stage in the progress of civilization, and those European nations which have hitherto been so fortunate as to be preserved from it, may have it yet to undergo' (754).

disapprobation' (XVIII, 286); but at the same time, '[we] have only further to suppose a considerable diffusion of Socialist opinions', he warned, 'and it may become infamous in the eyes of the majority to possess more property than some very small amount, or any income not earned by manual labour.'[83]

That the principle of 'diminishing utility' was not used to denigrate all further increases in per capita income as such is further confirmed in a summary of the primary purpose of the chapter of the 'Stationary State' placed at the outset of the chapter which follows, 'On the Probable Futurity of the Labouring Classes'. Here Mill explained that his purpose had been the 'negative' one of casting doubt on 'a false ideal', but not actually to recommend stationarity as the immediate objective of economica policy in contemporary circumstances, which remained rising per capita income subject to a 'fair' distribution:

The observations in the preceding chapter had for their principal object to deprecate a false ideal of human society. The applicability to the practical purposes of present times, consists in moderating the inordinate importance attached to the mere increase of production, and *fixing attention upon improved distribution, and a large remuneration of labour, as the two desiderata*. Whether the aggregate produce increases absolutely or not, is a thing in which, after a certain amount has been obtained, neither the legislator nor the philanthropist need feel any strong interest: but, that it should increase *relatively* to the number of those who share in it, is of the utmost possible importance; and this, (whether the wealth of mankind be stationary, or increasing at the most rapid rate ever known in an old country,) must depend on the opinions and habits of the most numerous class, the class of manual labourers (III, 758; italics added).

It is noteworthy that Mill deleted in the 1865 edition the famous reference in the main passage denigrating net accumulation and expansion of wealth in the Northern States where, despite numerous advantages, the net result was a life wherein 'the whole of one sex is devoted to dollar-hunting, and of the other to breeding dollar-hunters' (754). The 'struggle to get on' was now said to be more than 'one of the phases of industrial life': 'It may be a necessary stage in the progress of civilization, and those European nations

---

83 Here again he fulminates against bogus equality and the nefarious devices to assure it: 'It is known that the bad workmen who form the majority of the operatives in many branches of industry, are decidely of opinion that bad workmen ought to receive the same wages as good, and that no one ought to be allowed, through piecework or otherwise, to earn by superior skill or industry more than others can without it. And they employ a moral police, which occasionally becomes a physical one, to deter skilful workmen from receiving, and employers from giving, a larger remuneration for a more useful service.'

which have hitherto been so fortunate as to be preserved from it, may have it yet to undergo. It is an incident of growth, not a mark of decline, for it is not necessarily destructive of the higher aspirations and the heroic virtues; as America, in her great civil war, is proving to the world, both by her conduct as a people and by numerous splendid individual examples, and as England, it is to be hoped, would also prove, on an equally trying and exciting occasion.'

From this perspective we may appreciate Mill's championship of technical progress and rising productivity provided institutional arrangements assured that 'what is a benefit to the whole shall be a benefit to each individual composing it' (768). This reference occurs in a paragraph which argues a case for efficiency in a non-capitalist environment, an allusion to profit-sharing and (better still) to co-operation where productivity gains are yielded 'without dividing the producers into two parties with hostile interests'. Now it is possible that Mill identified what was best in the stationary state with some form of co-operative organization. For it is not clear that capitalist institutions are compatible with a condition of zero net accumulation where productivity increases are entirely to the advantage of labour leaving the return to capital unaffected at its 'minimum'. It has indeed been suggested recently (Levy, 1981, 278–9) that the Stationary State for Mill implied co-operation where incentives exist for the adoption of productivity-increasing technology even in the absence of ordinary profit calculation.[84] We must not forget the role allowed competition within a co-operative environment (Schwartz, 1972, 226).

* * *

It is implied by Mill's account that a time might arise when further increase in aggregate incomes – even permitting increased per capita incomes and assuming an acceptable distribution – would be undesirable; but that was not yet the case in contemporary circumstances, where a higher absolute level (as well as a fairer distribution) of income was called for. Accordingly, the statement that 'it is only in backward countries . . . that increased production is still an important object' is misleading, unless read as a case for increased *aggregate* output as such in backward countries only (notwithstanding a possibly low level of average earnings) without any

---

84 There is some evidence for this, although not conclusive, in Mill's musings regarding the future (above, p. 817) whereby as the return on capital declines secularly capitalists might voluntarily 'lend their capital to co-operatives at [the] diminishing rate of interest and at last, perhaps even . . . exchange their capital for terminable annuities' so that 'the existing accumulations of capital . . . by a kind of spontaneous process, become in the end the joint property of all who participate in their productive employment'.

intention of denigrating increased output in advanced countries as a means to increased *average* income. It should be added, however, that from the perspective of National Defence Mill justified attention to aggregative magnitude even in advanced economies: 'For the safety of national independence it is essential that a country should not fall much behind its neighbours in these things' (*CW*, III, 755) – a reference to 'the mere increase of production and accumulation'.

Mill's interest in the 'Stationary State' can in fact only be fully appreciated in terms of his concern for a high average income with special reference to the masses. In the *Principles*, as in the earlier 'Claims of Labour' (IV, 367–8), he took issue with earlier economists for identifying 'all that is economically desirable with the progressive state, and with that alone' (III, 752) –alluding to Adam Smith and to McCulloch who considered high real wages as necessarily dependent upon rapid accumulation of capital. Mill further objected to those who attributed to Malthus the notion of stationarity as necessarily entailing general misery; it was the argument of the *Essay on Population* in its later editions, Mill pointed out, that population growth is not an exogenous matter beyond human control checked only by ultimate land scarcity – a view 'affirmed by his most distinguished predecessors': 'The publication of Mr. Malthus' Essay is the era from which better views of this subject may be dated; and notwithstanding the acknowledged errors of his first edition, few writers have done more than himself, in the subsequent editions, to promote these juster and more hopeful anticipations' (753).[85] The essence of Mill's perspective, thus based upon a 'Malthusian' foundation, is that whether or not capital is growing, and at whatever rate, living standards of the masses will be high or low depending upon the relative growth of population; low standards were thus compatible with (aggregate) expansion and conversely, high standards were compatible with stationarity:

Even in a progressive state of capital, in old countries, a conscientious or prudential restraint on population is indispensable, to prevent the increase of numbers from outstripping the increase of capital, and the condition of the classes who are at the bottom of society from being deteriorated. Where there is not, in the people, or in some very large proportion of them, a resolute resistance to this deterioration – a determination to preserve an established standard of comfort – the condition of the poorest class sinks, even in a progressive state, to the lowest point which they will consent to endure. The same determination will be equally effectual to keep up their condition in the stationary state, and would be quite as likely to exist. Indeed, even now, the countries in which the greatest prudence is manifested in the regulating of population, are often those in which capital increases least rapidly (753).

85 The reform-oriented perspective of Malthus's position is pointed out very early on; cf. 'McCulloch's Discourse on Political Economy' (1825), V, 758.

Now Mill proceeds to suggest – and this is the main point at issue for us – that the inculcation of appropriate attitudes towards population control might be even more effective in a state of stationarity where there is no 'indefinite prospect of employment for increased numbers' so that it is evident to all that new entrants to the labour market are replacements for those who leave (see also *ibid.*, 753 cited above, p. 449). And precisely because living standards might in consequence of restraint be high he could not 'regard the stationary state of capital and wealth with the unaffected aversion so generally manifested towards it by political economists of the old school' (753–4). From this perspective stationarity becomes the means to the end of high per capita earnings rather than an end itself.

Mill's concern for a high per capita income subject always to equitable distribution must also be evaluated as part of a conception of 'standard of living' of very broad coverage indeed. Consider particularly the emphasis upon 'abridging labour' by means of new technology (alluded to also in the preceding extract):

Even the industrial arts might be as earnestly and as successfully cultivated, with this sole difference, that instead of serving no purpose but the increase of wealth, industrial improvements would produce their legitimate effect, that of abridging labour. Hitherto it is questionable if all the mechanical inventions yet made have lightened the day's toil of any human being. They have enabled a greater population to live the same life of drudgery and imprisonment, and an increased number of manufacturers and others to make fortunes. They have increased the comforts of the middle classes. But they have not yet begun to effect those great changes in human destiny, which it is in their nature and in their futurity to accomplish. Only when, in addition to just institutions, the increase of mankind shall be under the deliberate guidance of judicious foresight, can the conquests made from the powers of nature by the intellect and energy of scientific discoverers, become the common property of the species, and the means of improving and elevating the universal lot (756–7).

But this wide conception of the improvement and elevation of the universal lot by science[86] should not, considering what has been said earlier, be read as a negation of a (quite consistent) championship of rising per capita real income in the narrower sense of that term. In any event, so far as the 'abridging of labour' includes increased leisure – and there is every reason to suppose that it does – there is certainly no conflict.

There were, however, further reasons, apart from improved prospects for per capita earnings and increased leisure, which justified a reconsideration

---

86 Mill, however, early in the *Principles* emphasized the advantages of a *growing* system – in the sense of one undergoing net capital accumulation – for technological change (II, 140).

of the merits of the stationary state – reasons relating to the quality of life in the broad. Mill was careful to reiterate that 'a stationary condition of capital and population implies no stationary state of human improvement. There would be as much scope as ever for all kinds of mental culture, and moral and social progress; as much room for improving the Art of Living, and much more likelihood of its being improved, when minds ceased to be engrossed by the art of getting on' (756). Particularly important in this context is a profound sensitivity towards social amenity – space in particular. Mill did not deny that there was 'room in the world . . . even in old countries, for a great increase of population, supposing the arts of life to go on improving, and capital to increase. But even if innocuous, I confess I see very little reason for desiring it'. Population growth, even assuming an unchanged per capita income, still posed a threat:

The density of population necessary to enable mankind to obtain, in the greatest degree, all the advantages both of co-operation and of social intercourse, has, in all the most populous countries, been attained. A population may be too crowded, though all be amply supplied with food and raiment. It is not good for man to be kept perforce at all times in the presence of his species. A world from which solitude is extirpated, is a very poor ideal. Solitude, in the sense of being often alone, is essential to any depth of meditation or of character; and solitude in the presence of natural beauty and grandeur, is the cradle of thoughts and aspirations which are not only good for the individual, but which society could ill do without. Nor is there much satisfaction in contemplating the world with nothing left to the spontaneous activity of nature; with every rood of land brought into cultivation, which is capable of growing food for human beings; every flowery waste or natural pasture ploughed up, all quadrupeds or birds which are not domesticated for man's use exterminated as his rivals for food, every hedgerow or superfluous tree rooted out, and scarcely a place left where a wild shrub or flower could grow without being eradicated as a weed in the name of improved agriculture. If the earth must lose that great portion of its pleasantness which it owes to things that the unlimited increase of wealth and population would extirpate from it, for the mere purpose of enabling it to support a larger, but not a better or a happier population, I sincerely hope, for the sake of posterity, that they will be content to be stationary, long before necessity compels them to it.

XI THE CONDITION OF THE PEOPLE: THE POVERTY TRAP AND THE SOLUTION

It will be clear that to raise the per capita income of the working masses – to overcome the 'evil of low wages' (CW, II, 367) – was, for Mill, the primary immediate objective of economic policy. A variety of popular expedients to this end were firmly rejected and it is instructive to trace Mill's reasoning, which turns upon the need for population control, and also his conception of the practical difficulties which impeded a solution.

Minimum wage policies were rejected since they would entail unemployment unless the demand for labour were simultaneously increased by 'compulsory saving' – a form of redistribution (356). This Mill does not rule out, provided the problem of poverty entailed the existing generation alone. The passage where this point is elaborated is of the first importance:

If this claim on society could be limited to the existing generation; if nothing more were necessary than a compulsory accumulation, sufficient to provide permanent employment at ample wages for the existing numbers of the people; such a proposition would have no more strenuous supporter than myself. Society mainly consists of those who live by bodily labour; and if society, that is, if the labourers, lend their physical force to protect individuals in the enjoyment of superfluities, they are entitled to do so, and have always done so, with the reservation of a power to tax those superfluities for purposes of public utility; among which purposes the subsistence of the people is the foremost. Since no one is responsible for having been born, no pecuniary sacrifice is too great to be made by those who have more than enough, for the purpose of securing enough to all persons already in existence (357).

The case was, however, entirely different 'when those who have produced and accumulated are called upon to abstain from consuming until they have given food and clothing, not only to all who now exist, but to all whom these or their descendents may think fit to call into existence' (357). If the state 'guarante[es] employment at ample wages to all who are born . . . it is bound in self-protection, and for the sake of every purpose for which government exists, to provide that no person shall be born without its consent. If the ordinary and spontaneous motives to self-restraint are removed, others must be substituted' (358–9; cf. also 'Claims of Labour', IV, 374). The program – particularly in the light of diminishing agricultural returns – would otherwise be an invitation to the destruction of the source of surplus income, and of civilized society. 'No remedies for low wages have the smallest chance of being efficacious, which do not operate on and through the minds and habits of the people. While these are unaffected, any contrivance, even if successful, for temporarily improving the condition of the very poor, would but let slip the reins by which population was previously curbed; and could only, therefore, continue to produce its effect, if, by the whip and spur of taxation, capital were compelled to follow at an equally accelerated pace' (366).

Wage supplements – even supplements divorced from specific family size – were similarly criticized as attempts to regulate wages without regulating labour supply: 'It promises to the labourers that they shall have a certain amount of wages, however numerous they may be: and removes, therefore, alike the positive and prudential obstacles to an unlimited increase' (361). The provision of allotments to supplement wages – which had the advantage of adding to the gross national product – is similarly condemned as far as concerns the effect on wages and population: 'All subsidies in aid of wages enable the labourer to do with less remuneration, and therefore ultimately bring down the price of labour by the full amount, unless a change be wrought in the ideas and requirements of the labouring class; an alteration in the relative value which they set upon the gratification of their instincts, and upon the increase of their comforts and the comforts of those connected with them' (363).

What then was the solution? Only in an environment wherein the standard of living of labourers 'manifestly depends upon their numbers [would] the greatest permanent benefit . . . be derived from any sacrifice made to improve the physical well-being of the present generation, and raise, by that means, the habits of their children' (359). More specifically, the key to the problem of poverty from the 'Malthusian' perspective was to create 'so great a difference in the comforts of the family for a generation to come, as to raise up from childhood a labouring population with a really higher permanent standard of requirements and habits' (365). Half-hearted tinkering would not suffice: 'Unless comfort can be made as habitual to a whole generation as indigence is now, nothing is accomplished; and feeble half-measures do but fritter away resources, far better reserved until the improvement of public opinion and of education shall raise up politicians who will not think that merely because a scheme promises much, the part of statesmanship is to have nothing to do with it' (378). In all this Mill followed W. T. Thornton (1846) although he had less faith than Thornton in the allotment schemes then under discussion.

We find in this context a splendid formulation of the poverty trap. That the masses had been thus far incapable of 'taking any rational view of their own aggregate condition' was explicable, Mill believed, not only in terms of the 'uncultivated state of their intelligence' – encouraged, as we shall see, by a distorted state of public opinion – but also by their very poverty, 'which leaving them neither the fear of worse, nor the smallest hope of better, makes them careless of the consequences of their actions, and without thought for the future' (374). The statement of the problem pointed towards the solution:

For the purpose therefore of altering the habits of the labouring people, there is need of a twofold action, directed simultaneously upon their intelligence and their poverty. An effective national education of the children of the labouring class, is the first thing needful: and, coincidentally with this, a system of measures which shall (as the Revolution did in France) extinguish extreme poverty for one whole generation . . . Education is not compatible with extreme poverty. It is impossible effectually to teach an indigent population. And it is difficult to make those feel the value of comfort who have never enjoyed it, or those appreciate the wretchedness of a precarious subsistence, who have been made reckless by always living from hand to mouth. Individuals often struggle upwards into a condition of ease; but the utmost that can be expected from a whole people is to maintain themselves in it; and improvement in the habits and requirements of the mass of unskilled day-labourers will be difficult and tardy, unless means can be contrived of raising the entire body to a state of tolerable comfort, and maintaining them in it until a new generation grows up (374–5).

And the major increase in living standards required could be achieved – 'without any of the liabilities of mischief attendant on voluntary or legal charity' and at the same time by strengthening incentives to 'industry' and 'forethought' – by state schemes of Foreign and Home Colonization (376f).
   This was the 'system of measures' he had in mind – a two-pronged national program of emigration and education acting on the population variable. Yet it would be an error to suggest that economic growth itself, in the sense of rapid capital accumulation and growth of output – was accorded no role. As we have seen already Mill's discussion of the Stationary State was intended not so much to champion a positive case for stationarity as 'to deprecate a false ideal of human society' in order to moderate 'the inordinate importance attached to the mere increase of production' without reference to per capita wages; it remained of 'the utmost possible importance' that capital and gross output should grow 'relatively to the number of those who share in it'. Growth of capital was essential to provide expanded employment opportunities and allow the maintenance of living standards, assuming a positive growth rate of population.[87]

* * *

What of Mill's vision of prospects for improvement in the condition of the people? Upon the successful inculcation of the principle of population control among the labouring classes turned one aspect of the justification for capitalistic institutions. Unless a successful outcome was assured 'the

87 Mill was imprecise regarding the notion of *excess* population. Sismondi is cited as champion of a stationary population whereas Mill allowed that 'in a country increasing in wealth, some increase of numbers would be admissible' (369); and referred to 'the number of children which the circumstances of society allowed to each . . .' (371). He also (at least in the first edition) extended the imprecisely defined principle 'far beyond' what are commonly called the labouring classes' thereby including it appears the professional classes, but excluding 'the few who being able to give to their offspring the means of independent support during the whole of life, do not leave them to swell the competition for employment' (372n, 419).

industrial system prevailing in this country, and regarded by many writers as the *ne plus ultra* of civilization – the dependence of the whole labouring class of the community on the wages of hired labour, is irrevocably condemned; the system of hired labour would be a positive nuisance' (373). But Mill proceeds to assert that what evidence there was did not justify a pessimistic evaluation of prospects even under capitalism. This is not to say that Mill adopted a naïve attitude towards the magnitude of the task ahead. Far from it. But he did not despair of a successful outcome.[88]

The obstacles which complicated the problem of excess population and which had to be removed are clearly specified. In the first place Mill blamed contemporary opinion for encouraging a totally false perspective: 'Religion, morality, and statemanship have vied with one another in incitements to marriage, and to the multiplication of the species, so it be but in wedlock' (368). The rich, he added, 'provided the consequences do not touch themselves, think it impugns the wisdom of Providence to suppose that misery can result from the operation of a natural propensity . . .'. The clergy and the aristocracy were responsible for keeping the masses in woeful ignorance by encouraging the belief that upon marriage children follow of necessity (369) (see below, pp. 968–70, on Mill's approach to birth control). At one point, indeed, Mill charges the wealthy with a class interest in the encouragement of a large population as an assurance of low wages:

One may be permitted to doubt whether, except among the poor themselves . . . there has ever yet been, in any class of society, a sincere and earnest desire that wages should be high. There has been plenty of desire to keep down the poor-rate; but, that done, people have been very willing that the working classes should be ill off. Nearly all who are not labourers themselves, are employers of labour, and are not sorry to get the commodity cheap (370).

It was scarcely surprising, Mill noted, that in such circumstances the population doctrine had 'not yet penetrated far among those who might be expected to be the least willing recipients of it, the labourers themselves' (371; cf. 352).

However, it is none the less to public opinion – a reformed opinion – that Mill looked to assure prudential behaviour regarding family size in the future: 'Nothing more would probably be necessary to secure that result, than an opinion generally diffused that it was desirable' (370) – a general appreciation inculcated, presumably by education, that the 'principal' or 'special' cause of poverty lay in excess numbers. Regarding what would now be called the problem of the free-rider – in Mill's terms that 'the most thorough perception of the dependence of wages on population will not influence the

88 Contrast Engels (1881), cited below, p. 953n.

conduct of a labouring man' whose individual behaviour regarding numbers could not affect general wages – reliance is placed upon the public 'disgrace' which would attach to such behaviour, a strong inducement indeed since, in Mill's view, so 'large a portion of the motives which induce the generality of men to take care even of their own interest, is derived from regard for opinion – from the expectation of being disliked or despised for not doing it' (371). Some attention is, however, also paid to legal restrictions against 'recalcitrant minorities' – presuming that the vast majority consent voluntarily to the general principle on grounds of its self-evident social utility (372). This matter (which is said to be 'premature') seems to have troubled Mill, who added in 1852 that there would be no need for legal measures in the event that 'women were admitted . . . to the same rights of citizenship with men' for they would exert strong moral pressure in the right direction (372–3).

When we extend our horizon to the agricultural sector, there is the further recommendation of peasant proprietorship much emphasized in the Irish case but not ignored in England, partly on grounds of its potential as a device to encourage population control. As Mill expressed it (above, p. 854): '[I]t is much more obvious how many mouths can be supported by a piece of land, than how many hands can find employment in the general labour market'.

* * *

There are in fact indications in the *Principles* of a growing optimism on Mill's part regarding contemporary population growth and per capita earnings. These indications begin to appear in the third edition of the *Principles* (1852) in the course of a discussion of trade unions and their justification, a matter treated below to which the reader is now referred (Section XII). These indications are further confirmed in the edition of 1865 where Mill inserted a paragraph – one of the most important of the whole work from the perspective of the condition-of-the-people issue – to the effect that technical progress affecting transport and improved knowledge of opportunities abroad promised a rate of 'spontaneous emigration' that (coupled with the consequences of free trade) raised the prospect of a major increase in living standards for British workers, which would be rendered permanent if the splendid opportunity was grasped to inculcate appropriate habits among the rising generation:

I have left the preceding paragraphs as they were written, since they remain true in principle, though it is no longer urgent to apply these specific recommendations to the present state of this country. The extraordinary cheapening of the means of transport, which is one of the great scientific achievements of the age, and the knowledge which nearly all classes of the people have now acquired, or are in the way of acquiring, of the condition of the labour market in remote parts of the world, have opened up a spontaneous emigration from these islands to the new countries beyond the ocean, which does not tend to diminish, but to increase; and which, without any national measure of systematic colonization, may prove sufficient to affect a material rise of wages in Great Britain, as it has already done in Ireland, and to maintain that rise unimpaired for one or more generations. Emigration, instead of an occasional vent, is becoming a steady outlet for superfluous numbers; and this new fact in modern history, together with the flush of prosperity occasioned by free trade, have granted to this overcrowded country a temporary breathing-time, capable of being employed in accomplishing those moral and intellectual improvements in all classes of the people, the very poorest included, which would render improbable any relapse into the overpeopled state (378).

Whether the opportunity of a permanent solution would be used was not absolutely certain but there were grounds for hope, namely 'that there has been no time in our history when mental progress has depended so little on governments, and so much on the general disposition of the people; none in which the spirit of improvement has extended to so many branches of human affairs at once, nor in which all kinds of suggestions tending to the public good in every department, from the humblest physical to the highest moral or intellectual, were heard with so little prejudice, and had so good a chance of becoming known and being fairly considered' (279). It is apparent that with the passage of time the nefarious influence of upper-class opinion with its (class) bias towards a large and growing population was, in Mill's view, declining.

The correspondence is similarly suggestive. In 1850 we find a rather pessimistic evaluation regarding long-term prospects of population control even allowing for subsidized emigration schemes:

At present I expect very little from any plans which aim at improving even the economical state of the people by purely economical or political means. We have come, I think, to a period, when progress, even of a political kind, is coming to a halt, by reason of the low intellectual & moral state of all classes: of the rich as much as of the poorer classes. Great improvements in Education (among the first of which I reckon, dissevering it from bad religion) are the only thing to which I should look for permanent good. For example, the objects of your Association [Poor Law Reform Association], & those of the promoters of Emigration, even if they could be successful in putting an end to indigence, would do no more than push off to another generation the necessity of adopting a sounder morality on the subject of overpopulation – . . . (to Edward Herford, 22 Jan. 1850, XIV, 45).

Indeed at the end of that year Mill expressed doubt whether even a voluntary income redistribution from property to labour would constitute a net social good without a more profound change in behaviour patterns:

[I]f an employer of labour felt bound to divide his profits justly, that is, on some principle of equality among all persons concerned, it is by no means certain that he would in the present state of society & education do a benefit to the individuals equivalent to his sacrifice – & still less certain that he could not in some other manner, make the same amount of sacrifices instrumental to some greater good. These conditions at least seem to be necessary to make such conduct obligatory (27 Nov. 1850, XIV, 53).

But by the mid-1860s Mill's optimism was such that he conceded in correspondence an actual – not merely a perspective – decline in the magnitude of the population issue as an economic (as distinct from a moral) question and this in consequence of rapid economic growth as well as large-scale (spontaneous) emigration:

Le reglement du nombre d'enfants dans les familles me paraît . . . aussi important au point de vue de la moralité qu'au point de vue économique, et même, dans les circonstances actuelles de l'humanité bien davantage; car d'un côté le grand accroissement de la richesse, et de l'autre côté l'habitude croissante de l'émigration, ont fort atténué l'importance de la question de la population économiquement parlant (17 Jan. 1867, XVI, 1229).

I have . . . strongly advocated a national scheme of self-supporting emigration . . . In the present altered state of the labour market in Great Britain and Ireland, occasioned by the great increase of spontaneous emigration, our politicians have grown more afraid of under than of over population . . . (22 Jan. 1867, *ibid.*, 1230).

I have no uneasiness as to the future of England from the two points in its condition which you mention in your letter. Those 'who would work if they could find work to do,' will, I think, find their field of employment greatly widened by the rapid progress of industrial improvement, and such of them as the growth of the national wealth does not provide employment for, will be more and more taken off by emigration . . . 'The ignorance and hopelessness of the mass of the agricultural labourers' are in a fair way to be removed. The movement will soon be irresistable for a national education which will include them; and as soon as they have intelligence to know that better wages are to be had in the manufacturing towns, or in the United States or the Colonies, they will flock thither. Emigration, already so great an element in the social economy of Ireland, is only beginning to reach the agricultural districts of England. It will be the great safety valve, and will, I think, prevent the stir that is sure to take place in the minds of the agricultural labourers from having any other than a wholesome effect (4 Oct. 1868, *ibid.*, 1454–5).

It would doubtless be going too far to say that Mill had se the population problem aside entirely. Early in 1869 he still referred to 'the miserable state of the English agricultural laborers' (7 March 1869, XVII, 1571); and he agreed with Cairnes (9 April 1869, *ibid.*, 1587–8) that Thornton in his *On Labour* (1869) would have done well had he added 'a few pages on the relation of [the population principle] to his doctrine'. In the following year again, he emphasized that in consequence of 'the great addition made annually to the poorer part of our population, the [emigration] scheme would have to be executed on a vast scale indeed if it is to clear out the bad quarters of our towns and leave them a tabula rasa for reconstruction on better principles . . .' (28 March 1870, *ibid.*, 1710). Yet the text of 1865 and the three letters cited from the correspondence of 1867 and 1868 are so very explicitly and strongly worded that one is still left with the impression that at least prospects for a solution were promising, and, perhaps, that even the solution itself was at hand.

There is yet more evidence pointing to the same conclusion. In 1868 he refused, as we know (above, p. 854), to accept the argument that Irish land reform would be nugatory in consequence of population pressure, drawing his argument from French experience. There is too a very explicit passage in the posthumous 'Chapters on Socialism' wherein Mill denied Louis Blanc's notion of a contemporary decline in the general wage. Population pressure was no longer an 'irresistable tendency' and an 'increasing evil' considering the acceleration of capital accumulation, extensive emigration and increased prudence; it was, Mill insisted, patently untrue that only under Communism could excess population growth be prevented although he refused to commit himself to a final judgement of the relative effectiveness of the alternative systems on that score:

It has yet to be proved that there is any country in the civilised world where the ordinary wages of labour, estimated either in money or in articles of consumption, are declining; while in many they are, on the whole, on the increase; and an increase which is becoming, not slower, but more rapid . . . There is much evidence of improvement, and none, that is at all trustworthy, of deterioration, in the mode of living of the labouring population of the countries of Europe; when there is any appearance to the contrary it is local or partial, and can always be traced either to the pressure of some temporary calamity, or to some bad law or unwise act of government which admits of being corrected, while the permanent causes all operate in the direction of improvement.

M. Louis Blanc, therefore, while showing himself much more enlightened than the older school of levellers and democrats, inasmuch as he recognises the connection between low wages and the over-rapid increase of population, appears to have fallen into the same error which was at first committed by Malthus and his followers, that of supposing that because population has a greater power of increase than subsistence, its pressure upon subsistence must be always growing more severe. The difference is that the early Malthusians thought this an irrepressible tendency, while M. Louis Blanc thinks that it can be repressed, but only under a system of Communism. It is a great point gained for truth when it comes to be seen that the tendency to over-population is a fact which Communism, as well as the existing order of society, would have to deal with. And it is much to be rejoiced at that this necessity is admitted by the most considerable chiefs of all existing schools of Socialism. Owen and Fourier, no less than M. Louis Blanc, admitted it, and claimed for their respective systems a pre-eminent power of dealing with this difficulty. However this may be, experience shows that in the existing state of society the pressure of population on subsistence, which is the principal cause of low wages, though a great, is not an increasing evil; on the contrary, the progress of all that is called civilisation has a tendency to diminish it, partly by the more rapid increase of the means of employing and maintaining labour, partly by the increased facilities opened to labour for transporting itself to new countries and unoccupied fields of employment, and partly by a general improvement in the intelligence and prudence of the population. This progress, no doubt, is slow; but it is much that such progress should take place at all, while we are still only in the first stage of that public movement for the education of the whole people, which when more advanced must add greatly to the force of all the two causes of improvement specified above. It is, of course, open to discussion what form of society has the greatest power of dealing successfully with the pressure of population on subsistence, and on this question there is much to be said for Socialism; what was long thought to be its weakest point will, perhaps, prove to be one of its strongest. But it has no just claim to be considered as the sole means of preventing the general and growing degradation of the mass of mankind through the peculiar tendency of poverty to produce over-population. Society as at present constituted is not descending into that abyss, but gradually, though slowly, rising out of it, and this improvement is likely to be progressive if bad laws do not interfere with it (V, 727–9).

XII THE CONDITION OF THE PEOPLE: TRADE UNIONISM

In an analysis of Mill's recantation of 1869 from the wages fund theory Professors West and Hafer consider the statement that '[t]he doctrine hitherto taught by all or most economists (including myself), which denied it to be possible that trade combinations can raise wages, or which limited their operation in that respect to the somewhat earlier attainment of a rise which the competition of the market would have produced without them, – this doctrine is deprived of its scientific foundation, and must be thrown aside' (*CW*, V, 646). In their view, Mill was now accepting the opinion that trade combinations *could* raise wages and on 'Malthusian' grounds – namely on grounds of 'a special theory of survival, under unions, of the most fit and the most prudent workers' whereby 'long-run wages *could* be permanently increased throughout the working population' although 'it was a shrunken population because of the failure of the initially unfit to survive' (1978, 616). Union members were envisaged as 'more foresighted and responsible than other workers', so that 'if unions were allowed, a working population with new tastes for higher standards of living and new control over its numerical size would emerge' (605). In a supplementary article the argument is phrased thus: 'Beyond a certain level of union-negotiated wage increases, Mill believed there would be a ratchet effect after which (surviving) workers would begin to accustom themselves to the higher (irreversible) living standards and smaller families'; unions constituted 'a temporary instrument of social and population control to achieve that precise size and pattern of the future society that he himself preferred' (1981, 547, 549).

The authors' argument is not in all respects clear. On the one hand, Mill's recognition in 1869 that 'union-induced Malthusian effects might occur in the long-run' is represented as a novel contribution to the positive analysis of classical economics, for 'certainly the effects of combinations had not previously been included in Malthus's list of examples of population checks' (1981, 543). Yet it is also an important part of their argument that much the same perspective is to be found in the *Principles*. More specifically, the authors maintain that Mill's case is made out in the *Principles* except in the third and fourth edition (1852 and 1857) where he 'expressed strong criticism of aggressive unions', and this 'because he probably entertained the fleeting belief that in these years of the high tide of the Victorian era, state of the world II had at least been reached' – an allusion to the period after the disappearance from the scene of those unable to adapt, when further upward wage pressure would be unjustified; in later editions and in the recantation, so runs their argument, Mill reverted to his original defence of unions supposing a less advanced state of society (1981, 548; also 1978, 613–14).

These interesting hypotheses deserve serious consideration for, if valid, they cast Mill in a rather poor light. Indeed the main implication of the reading is that, for Mill, social justice is served by a 'plan of social engineering' to design some future society populated with individuals who had been educated out of poverty, and away from their propensity to excessive reproduction (1978a, 585), irrespective of the nefarious implications for some of the existing poor. His concern in short was with a planned future society and this separates him from the 'modern' perspective on social justice. (The West-Hafer perspective points away from the case made out by Ekelund and Tollison, 1976).

The argument is not convincing, however. In the first place, it is not clear from the West-Hafer account wherein precisely lies the recantation. The authors themselves seem doubtful: '[I]f he were recanting anything in the Thornton review, it was the view that unions could not achieve those sustained (disemployment creating) wage increases that would lead to this result. Yet this same "recantation" had been there for all to see at all times through successive editions of his *Principles*' (1981, 549). On our reading of the 1869 article there is no difficulty since we take account of Mill's express statement that '[on] the side of supply, the law as laid down by economists remains intact . . . the population principle and its consequences are in no way touched by anything that Mr. Thornton has advanced . . .' (*CW*, V, 645); Mill's recantation relates solely to the demand side of the labour market – a new allowance for a short-run zero-elastic demand for labour on imputation grounds such that union-induced wage increases can be achieved at no cost to employment. (In Part II of the article the standard allowance is made for the likelihood of ultimate employment loss – that 'there is no keeping up wages without limiting the number of competitors for hire'.)

Secondly, while I certainly do not deny the relevance of the population problem for Mill's approach towards unions, as apparently do Ekelund and Kordsmeier (1981) in their objection to the West-Hafer argument, there is nothing to justify the notion of unions as an instrument to inculcate altered standards. Wherever Mill defends union exclusiveness it is always that of organizations comprising members already practising restraint against the encroachments of the hopelessly irresponsible that he has in mind. Where there were signs of improved prospects for better judgement on the part of the masses his defence is immediately withdrawn. To encourage that judgement, an educational program was required combined with an actual increase in living standards sufficient to alter the expectations of the new generation (*CW*, II, 342); indeed education would be useless unless thus combined: 'Education is not compatible with extreme poverty. It is impossible to teach an indigent population' (375). It could not be further from the truth that Mill turned his back on the existing poor (see also Ekelund and Tollison, 1978, 589).

Finally, in the textual exegesis which follows we shall show that Mill's more optimistic estimate of population pressure and correspondingly stricter attitude to union exclusiveness, first apparent in 1852, remains until the end – scarcely surprising considering the evidence already adduced from the correspondence of the 1860s and the posthumous 'Chapters on Socialism' of 1869. The so-called high tide of the Victorian era lasted rather longer than the half-decade 1852–7 as West maintains.

A case for exclusive unions in the manuscript and first two editions of the *Principles* is strongly formulated on grounds of population pressure in the following terms: While combinations (in particular trades) 'occasionally succeed' in keeping up wages above the competitive level by restrictions to the labour supply, 'I find it impossible to wish, in the present state of the general habits of the people, that no such combinations existed' (II, 397). In the third and fourth editions this latter statement is modified to read that 'their existence, it is probable, has, *in time past*, produced more good than evil' (italics added); while in subsequent editions we have: '[T]he question, whether they are on the whole more useful or mischievous, requires to be decided on an enlarged consideration of consequences . . .'. While the second variation certainly implies the abandonment of the original argument in the supposedly altered circumstances even the final statement does not return all the way to the starting point, but leaves the question open.

That a *permanent* mark was in fact left on Mill's approach by growing optimism regarding the solution to unregulated population growth comes to the fore in the subsequent texts. Thus once again we have a strong defence of restrictive unions in the manuscript and first two editions:

[I]n so far as they do succeed in keeping up the wages of any trade by limiting its numbers, I look upon them as simply intrenching around a particular spot against the inroads of over-population, and making their wages depend upon their own rate of increase, instead of depending on that of a more reckless and improvident class than themselves. And I should rejoice if by trade regulations, or even by trades unions, the employments thus specially protected could be multiplied to a much greater extent than experience has shown to be practicable. What at first sight seems the injustice of excluding the more numerous class from sharing the gains of a comparatively few, disappears when we consider that by being so admitted they would not be made better off, for more than a short time; the only permanent effect which their admission would produce, would be to lower the others to their own level. If indeed the general mass of the people were so improved in their standard of living, as not to press closer against the means of employment than those trades do; if, in other words, there were no greater degree of overcrowding outside the barrier, than within it – there would be no need of a barrier, and if it had any effects at all, they must be bad ones; but in that case the barrier would fall of itself, since there would no longer be any motive for keeping it up. On similar grounds, if there were no other escape from that fatal immigration of the Irish, which has done and is doing so much to degrade the condition of our agricultural, and some classes of our town population, I should see no injustice, and the greatest possible expediency, in checking that destructive inroad by prohibitive laws (397–8).

This stongly-worded formulation is replaced in 1852 and 1857 by a retraction of the defence:

[I]f the present state of the general habits of the people were to remain for ever unimproved, these partial combinations, in so far as they do succeed in keeping up the wages of any trade by limiting its numbers, might be looked upon as simply intrenching round a particular spot against the inroads of over-population, and making their wages depend upon their own rate of increase, instead of depending on that of a more reckless and improvident class than themselves. The time, however, is past when the friends of human improvement can look with complacency on the attempts of small sections of the community, whether belonging to the labouring or any other class, to organize a separate class interest in antagonism to the general body of labourers, and to protect that interest by shutting out, even if only by a moral compulsion, all competitors from their more highly paid department. The mass of the people are no longer to be thrown out of the account, as too hopelessly brutal to be capable of benefiting themselves by any opening made for them, and sure only, if admitted into competition, to lower others to their own level. The aim of all efforts should now be, not to keep up the monopoly of separate knots of labourers against the rest, but to raise the moral state and social condition of the whole body; and of this it is an indispensable part that no one should be excluded from the superior advantages of any skilled employment, who has intelligence enough to learn it, and honesty enough to be entrusted with it.

Now, in the later editions following the first sentence in the preceding extract, we have the criticism of unions ('the time is past . . .') deleted, and a return to the original statement: 'What at first sight seems the injustice of excluding the more numerous body from sharing the gains of a comparatively few, disappears when we consider that by being so admitted they would not be made better off, for more than a short time; the only permanent effect which their admission would produce, would be to lower the others to their own level.' The West-Hafer argument would seem to stand up, were it not for the fact that this is now followed by a statement, not in the early editions, which once again leaves the whole question open: 'To what extent the force of this consideration is annulled when a tendency commences towards diminished over-crowding in the labouring classes generally, and what grounds of a different nature there may be for regarding the existence of trade combinations as rather to be desired than deprecated, will be considered in a subsequent chapter of this work, with the subject of Combination Laws.' The optimism of the early 1850s seems to be carried through, albeit in somewhat more balanced fashion.

Let us then turn, on Mill's instructions, to the formal treatment of Combination Laws. Without question there here emerges a permanent change in Mill's attitude to unions on grounds of a growing optimism regarding population pressure. Thus in the early editions Mill is prepared to accept reduced employment in a unionized trade (or alternatively the loss of employment elsewhere to the extent capital is transferred from other ventures), focussing upon the desirable long-run consequences. A stronger 'hard-line' Malthusian case could not easily be imagined:

Such, indeed, would really be the result of a successful combination in a particular trade or trades, for some time after its formation; but when it is a permanent thing, the principles so often insisted upon in this treatise, show that it can have no such effect. The habitual earnings of the working classes at large can be affected by nothing but the habitual requirements of the labouring people; these indeed may be altered, but while they remain the same, wages never fall permanently below the standard of these requirements, and do not long remain above that standard. If there had been no combinations in particular trades, and the wages of those trades had never been kept above the common level, there is no reason to suppose that the common level would have been at all higher than it now is. There would merely have been a greater number of people altogether, and a smaller number of exceptions to the ordinary low rate of wages. Combinations to keep up wages are therefore not only permissable, but useful, whenever really calculated to have that effect (III, 931).

In 1852 a new paragraph replaces the final sentence in the foregoing passage, clearly reflecting an altered evaluation of the prospects for population control:

If, therefore, no improvement were to be hoped for in the general circumstances of the working classes, the success of a portion of them, however small, in keeping their wages by combination above the market rate, would be wholly a matter of satisfaction. But when the evelation of the character and condition of the entire body has at last become a thing not beyond the reach of rational effort, it is time that the better paid classes of skilled artisans should seek their own advantage in common with, and not by the exclusion of, their fellow-labourers. While they continue to fix their hopes on hedging themselves in against competition, and protecting their own wages by shutting out others from access to their employment, nothing better can be expected from them than that total absence of any large and generous aims, that almost open disregard of all other objects than high wages and little work for their own small body . . . Success, even if attainable, in raising up a protected class of working people, would now be a hindrance, instead of a help, to the emancipation of the working classes at large (931).

Now this paragraph is retained thereafter.[89] So also is a subsequent statement, also introduced in 1852, that combinations designed to raise wages are 'seldom effectual', but 'when effectual, are, for the reasons which I have assigned, seldom desirable . . .' (931–2) – precisely because success

89 West and Hafer (1981), 546–7, recognize this passage but regard it as ambiguous considering the conditional 'would be' in the first sentence. They neglect the 'it is time' in the second, and the 'now' in the last. Moreover, in the first two editions Mill asserts a few paragraphs later (III, 933) that '[h]igh wages and short hours are generally good objects, or, at all events, may be so, and a limitation of the number of persons in employment may be a necessary condition of these'. This latter comment, which justifies refusing to work for an employer 'who employs more than a certain number of apprentices' is removed in 1852.

is at the cost of those excluded who may well have the prospect of becoming responsible members of society.[90]

One other piece of evidence – and it is overwhelming – emerges in the conclusion to the chapter 'On the Probable Futurity of the Labouring Classes', a passage first appearing in 1852 and retained in all later editions with minor variation only:

Instead of looking upon competition as the baneful and anti-social principle which it is held to be by the generality of Socialists, I conceive that, even in the present state of society and industry, every restriction of it is an evil, and every extension of it, even if for the time injuriously affecting some class of labourers, is always an ultimate good. To be protected against competition is to be protected in idleness, in mental dulness; to be saved the necessity of being as active and as intelligent as other people; and if it is also to be protected against being underbid for employment by a less paid class of labourers, this is only where old custom, or local and partial monopoly, has placed some particular class of artizans in a privileged position as compared with all the rest; and the time has come when the interest of universal improvement is no longer promoted by prolonging the privileges of the few. If the slopsellers and others, so unjustly and illiberally railed at – as if they were one iota worse in their motives or practices than other people, in the existing state of society – have lowered the wages of tailors, and some other artizans, by making them an affair of competition instead of custom, so much the better in the end. What is now required is not to bolster up old customs, whereby limited classes of labouring people obtain partial gains which interest them in keeping up the present organization of society, but to introduce new general practices beneficial to all; and there is reason to rejoice at whatever makes the privileged classes of skilled artizans feel they have the same interests, and depend for their remuneration on the same general causes, and must resort for the improvement of their condition to the same remedies, as the less fortunately circumstanced and comparatively helpless multitude (III, 795–6).[91]

Mill's powerful protest on behalf of the slopsellers may be supplemented by the more general protest against the injustices to the very poor of the contemporary wage structure (V, 714; above, p. 783).

A word next regarding the 'recantation' article. Here there will be found the Malthusian case for unions:

90 There is to be found, even in the first two editions, at least one passage where Mill condemns exclusiveness; cf. the panagyric in favour of competition (III, 795–6 cited below).
91 The only change is the replacement in 1857 of the passage regarding shopsellers and others 'so unjustly and illiberally . . . state of society – ' by slopsellers and others 'of their class'.

There is, however, another, and a less elevated, but not fallacious point of view, from which the apparent injustice of Unionism to the non-united classes of labourers may be morally vindicated to the conscience of an intelligent Unionist. This is the Malthusian point of view, so blindly decried as hostile and odious, above all, to the labouring classes. The ignorant and untrained part of the poorer classes (such Unionists may say) will people up to the point which will keep their wages at that miserable rate which the low scale of their ideas and habits makes endurable to them. As long as their minds remain in their present state, our preventing them from competing with us for employment does them no real injury; it only saves ourselves from being brought down to their level. Those whom we exclude are a morally inferior class of labourers to us; their labour is worth less, and their want of prudence and self-restraint makes them much more active in adding to the population. We do them no wrong by intrenching ourselves behind a barrier, to exclude those whose competition would bring down our wages, without more than momentarily raising theirs, but only adding to the total numbers in existence. This is the practical justification as things now are, of some of the exclusive regulations of Trades' Unions (V, 664).

This statement, it has been argued (West and Hafer, 1978, 612–13), indicates Mill's unaltered defence of restrictive unions on Malthusian grounds – the same defence that appears in all editions of the *Principles* bar the third and fourth.[92] It has drawn strong fire:

In all the literature of the effects of policy upon the poor, the statement . . . that 'our preventing them from competing with us for employment does them no real injury,' must be the most astonishing. It is surely difficult, to say the least, to reconcile such words with an outlook that puts social justice and concern for the poor in the highest priority. It is difficult, too, to reconcile these sentiments with those in the author's *Essay on Liberty*. Neither can the argument . . . be dismissed as a temporary aberration at the time of Mill's review of Thornton. The same reasoning appeared in the first and last edition of Mill's *Principles* (West 1978b, 584).

Is this condemnation a justified one? I think not. Allowance must be made for what follows in the review – Mill's insistence that such 'practical justification' held good only if unionists were not indifferent to the fortunes of those excluded (cf. Ekelund and Tollison, 1976, 228). On this matter he expressed himself hopefully with particular reference to educational progress: '[I]t is a strong indication of a better spirit among them, that the operatives and artisans throughout the country form the main strength

92 It has, however, been argued (Ekelund and Kordsmeier, 1981, 532) that this passage does not represent Mill's own position but an attribution to others. But Mill himself tells us it is a 'not fallacious point of view'.

of the demand, rapidly becoming irresistable, for universal and compulsory education. The brutish ignorance of the lowest order of unskilled labourers has no more determined enemies, none more earnest in insisting that it be cured, than the comparatively educated workmen who direct the Unions' (*CW*, V, 665).

Notwithstanding this qualification, West (1978b, 584) reiterates the general charge against Mill: 'Even if unions were pioneers in the quest to obtain compulsory and universal education, and even if their motives were never suspect and self interested (which is doubtful), such political pressure could have been equally applied without recourse to subjecting the poor non-unionist to unemployment and poverty.' The objection is a strong one indeed. And if it holds good it implies a violent inconsistency in Mill with the *Essay on Liberty* and, as West (585) also makes clear, a violent inconsistency with much of what Mill had stood for in his specific economic writings, including the position that it was a central responsibility of government 'to remove every restriction, every artificial hindrance, which legal and fiscal systems oppose' to self-improvement by the poor ('Claims of Labour', 1845, *CW*, IV, 385).

West's case against Mill would be totally unconvincing if the defence of restrictive unions applied solely to those already in existence and presuming no possible alteration in the procreation habits of those excluded. Mill's point would then be that it was necessary to choose between the lesser of two evils: increased freedom of mobility for one group would imply a temporary improvement in their wages but the permanent deterioration of another group.[93] There is nothing patently 'cruel' about this weighting – subject, it must be strongly emphasized, to the proviso that society sets about raising the conception of the 'subsistence' minimum held by the labouring masses. And this responsibility Mill certainly recognized as is patently clear from his case for national education and emigration schemes.[94] But this is not

93 'We do them no wrong by intrenching ourselves behind a barrier, to exclude those whose competition would bring down our wages, without more than momentarily raising theirs, but only adding to the total numbers in existence' is how Mill formulated it in the 1869 article; 'what at first sight seems the injustice of excluding the more numerous class from sharing the gains of a comparatively few, disappears when we consider that by being so admitted they would not be made better off, for more than a short time; the only permanent effect which their admission would produce, would be to lower the others to their own level' is the formulation in the *Principles*.

94 A letter to Henry George of 1869 regarding Chinese immigration into the United States, is tangentially revealing for our issue. The matter relates to the high Chinese population growth rate and the threat to American wages: 'On general principles, this state of things, were it sure to continue, would justify the exclusion of the immigrants, on the ground that with their habits in respect to population, only a temporary good is done to the Chinese people by admitting part of their surplus numbers, while a permanent harm is done to a more civilised and improved portion of mankind' (23 Oct. 1869, XVII, 1654). But there was the other side of the coin to consider: 'Is it justifiable to assume

quite the end of the matter. For in Mill's treatment of Combination Laws in the *Principles* the case for restrictive unions (cited above from III, 931) seems, at first sight at least, to be applied even to newly proposed organizations which would actually *lower* earnings and employment opportunities of those to be excluded from the trade. The damage would last only 'for some time after its foundation' prior to a fall in population, suggesting (as West maintains) that damage to some *present* workers does not count. We know already that in 1852 and thereafter Mill – here and elsewhere in the *Principles* – withdrew his justification of union exclusiveness. But we must face the question whether he originally treated the unskilled labourers as so beyond the pale that even an increased death rate from this group could be justified. The evidence suggests that this cannot be the case. Mill's entire approach to the problem of long-term poverty which was to assure a *major* improvement in the earnings of the current work force sufficient to influence the expectations of the rising generation points diametrically against this perspective. That the phraseology in question must not indeed be taken literally is confirmed at the close of the paragraph where Mill reverts to a situation of an existing union: 'If there had been no combination in particular trades . . . there is no reason to suppose that the common level [of wages] would have been at all higher than it is now'.

A textual matter should be settled here. One of the early formulations justifying restrictive unions discussed above (pp. 899–900) follows immediately upon a discussion of the damage to workers in declining trades who were denied entry into high-paying trades, specifically the displaced hand-loom workers. If the justification of union restriction on entry was intended to apply to this particular case we would be faced by the extraordinary spectacle of the consequences of imprudent behaviour placed on the shoulders of the prudent, an injustice if ever there was one – a blatant restriction on the right to sell labour, a 'plain violation of this most sacred property' as Smith had put it, which scarcely can be justified in terms of someone else's irresponsibility (West, 1978b, 585). But it is clear that Mill accepted the indictment by the Hand-Loom Weavers Commission (Senior) of exclusion of the displaced hand-loom weavers from trades they could easily master: 'It was given in evidence . . . that this is one of the hardships which aggravate the grievous condition of that depressed class. Their own employment is overstocked and almost ruined; but there are many other trades which it

the character and habits of the Chinese are unsusceptible of improvement? The institutions of the United States are the most potent means that have yet existed of spreading the most important elements of civilisation down to the poorest and most ignorant of the labouring masses. If every Chinese child were compulsorily brought under your school system, or under a still more effective one if possible, and kept under it for a sufficient number of years, would not the Chinese population be in time raised to the level of the American?'

would not be difficult for them to learn: to this, however, the combinations of workmen in those other trades are said to interpose an obstacle hitherto insurmountable' (*CW*, II, 396–7).

Mill, in short, conceded 'the cruel manner in which the exclusive principle of these combinations operates in a case of this peculiar nature' and at no time justified union exclusiveness in this kind of case. It would in fact be extraordinary were it otherwise, considering Mill's championship of the structure of wage differentials as 'just' in a competitive system assuming the absence of institutional checks to mobility.

We have based much of our case on evidence drawn from the union issue. If there should be any remaining doubts regarding Mill's attitude towards the *existing* poor, the reader is referred to our earlier discussion of Ireland. The vehemence of Mill's own reaction to the kind of position attributed to him by West is rarely surpassed in his writings (see above, pp. 847, 849–54).

XIII MILL AND 'BOURGEOIS' BIAS

Various commentators have been struck by what they consider to be Mill's élitist paternalism. The charge has been encountered in our earlier discussion of population control, education, unions and various forms of government interference and found wanting. A version of the case appears also in the present context, for Professor West in the course of his analysis of Mill's redistribution policy alludes to Mill's ideal society as one 'populated largely by individuals with "middle-class aspirations" and who had learned, through a new educational system, preferably of Mill's speical design, the secrets of economic independence and population control' (1978b, 571).[95]

That Mill certainly had his own set of value judgements is not in question. But it did not reflect a *bourgeois* ideal. This is absolutely clear from the force

95 As is not uncommon in Mill scholarship the very opposite interpretation can also be found and on high authority: '[T]o Marx, and to many of us, associationism may be nonsense, but it was not nonsense to the Benthamite mind. In fact, a glance at the utilitarian views on the human mind and on the nature of social relations suffices to show that, once these assumptions concerning the quality – the substantive *equality* – of individuals are granted, associationist hopes cease to be absurd. And this accounts for the cautious associationism of J.S. Mill' (Schumpeter, 1954, 457). Yet more specifically, 'the book to which the bourgeoisie accorded such a reception . . . was written by a man palpably out of sympathy with the scheme of values of the industrial bourgeoisie . . . Though repeatedly changing his position in details, he was, from his middle twenties on, an evolutionary socialist of associationist complexion. For a history of analysis this fact is important only in as much as it refutes the absurd indictment that "classic" economists believed in the capitalist order as the last and highest wisdom that was bound to persist in *secular seculorum*' (531). All this is said to be important 'for those who have been taught to look upon the *Principles* as a verbalization of bourgeois ideology'.

of his condemnation of the dependency relationship entailed in the capital-labour nexus. Moreover, Mill repeatedly complained of middle- and upper-class apologetics, and mocked middle-class 'vulgarity' and mania to rise to higher station.

Mill's appeal for independence in fact extended far beyond the 'economic' sphere to opinion and behaviour in the broad sense. And it was not limited to the working class. Thus he wished to apprise consumers – middle- and upper-class consumers especially – of the rationale behind their luxury consumption in the hope that they would alter their behaviour (see above, p. 860). But even the appeal narrowly conceived should not be lightly dismissed since it governed a very broad range of considerations relating to the role of the state: The 'simple test', as he wrote in 1845 regarding intervention in the labour market, was whether 'the assistance [is] of such a kind, and given in such a manner, as to render them [labour] ultimately independent of the continuance of similar assistance' (*CW*, IV, 386–7); and consistently, government was charged 'to remove every restriction, every artificial hindrance, which legal and fiscal systems oppose to the attempts of the labouring classes to forward their own improvement' (385). Similarly, '[t]he aid of Gov^t is often useful, & sometimes necessary, to start improved systems which once started are able to keep themselves going without further help' (4 April 1866, XVI, 1155).

A summary word regarding Mill's educational recommendations. At an early date he referred to the training of 'superior spirits', requiring 'institutions of education placed above dependence on the immediate pleasure of that very multitude whom they are designed to elevate'; and saw much promise in endowed establishments ('Sedgwick's Discourse', 1835, X, 33). But his expectations were obviously disappointed: 'As for education in the best sense of the term, I fear they [the workers] have a long time to wait for it. The higher and middle classes cannot educate the working classes unless they are first educated themselves. The miserable pretence of education, which those classes now receive, does not form minds fit to undertake the guidance of other minds, or to exercise a beneficient influence over them, by personal conduct' (7 Jan. 1852, XIV, 80).[96] Educational reform would have to include all social strata, and the 'élite', as he came to insist would have to be drawn from the working class as we have seen in the previous chapter.

To talk of Mill's bourgeois aspirations as governing his approach to

---

96 Cf. 'Civilization', 1836; XVIII, 138: '[T]he regeneration of individual character among our lettered and opulent classes, by the adaption to that purpose of our institutions, and, above all, of our educational institutions, is an object of more urgency, and for which more might be immediately accomplished, if the will and understanding were not alike wanting'.

working-class education would, therefore, be inappropriate. But in any event there is nothing sinister about his so-called 'special design' to inculcate 'the secrets' of economic independence and population control. The program, even in the narrow sense of school curriculum, we have seen, was remarkably progressive for the age and an honest reflection of Mill's belief that '[w]hat the poor as well as the rich require is not to be indoctrinated, is not to be taught other people's opinions, but to be induced and enabled to think for themselves' (7 Jan. 1852, XIV, 80).

Our perspective is reinforced when we turn from education narrowly conceived as a school program to education in its broader sense, for '[w]hatever acts upon the minds of the labouring classes, is properly their education', and this encompasses the 'whole of their social circumstances' (1845, IV, 376). Now, as Mill saw the matter, '[t]he primary and perennial sources of all social evil, [were] ignorance and want of culture', and their correction depended on the 'unremitting exertions of the more instructed and cultivated, whether in the position of the government or in a private station, to awaken in their minds a consciousness of this want, and to facilitate to them the means of supplying it' (1833, IV, 213–14). True the 'more instructed and cultivated' were to take the initiative, but hopefully it would be a temporary initiative as the cultural lacunae were corrected and the entire community became conscious of what was required.

The range of means to the end of 'education' was broad indeed, extending from schools and colleges to art galleries, theatres, public games. In the *Principles* much weight is placed on the press, lecture institutions, trade unions and political agitation (III, 763–4). And Mill was optimistic: 'The poor have come out of leading-strings, and cannot any longer be governed or treated like children. To their own qualities must now be commended the care of their destiny'. The working classes were 'now part of the public' and at least the town operatives had access to the press: 'With these resources, it cannot be doubted that they will increase in intelligence, even by their own unaided efforts' (764). Interestingly, Mill recognized a danger that workers might demand legislative intervention reflecting an erroneous view of their own interest, but at least it would reflect 'their own will, their own ideas and suggestions . . . and not rules laid down for them by other people'.[97]

97 Mill's general perspective, it may be added, was held in common with the classicals as a whole. As Lionel Robbins (1952) has argued 'although the Classical Economists were less aware than the exponents of avowedly authoritarian systems of the occasional necessity for paternalism, they differed from others in this respect in that they emphasised continually the desirability of getting away from it . . . [It] was only in a society of individuals, free so far as technical conditions permitted to shape their own ends, that positive good was permanently realizable' (184). In Robbins' view Mill argued the position that it was 'more important that choice should be free than that it should be good' in

The same insistence on independence rather than direction as a training ground emerges in the discussion of co-operation:

Combinations such as the associations of workpeople . . . are the most powerful means of effecting the social emancipation of the labourers through their own moral qualities. Nor is the liberty of association important solely for its examples of success, but fully as much so for the sake of attempts which would not succeed; but by their failure would give instruction more impressive than can be afforded by anything short of actual experience . . . From such experiments the active portion of the working classes would derive lessons, which they would be slow to learn from the teaching of persons supposed to have interests and prejudices adverse to their good . . . (903–4; cf. 793).[98]

It should not be necessary to add that this perspective is perfectly compatible with the hope that 'intelligent friends of the working classes . . . work to amend the social condition in which men are born into situations which make social and economic inequality inevitable' (V, 658).

Let us consider the present general issue from the perspective of Mill's 'ideal' future society. Such a society with which the stationary state is said (though without demonstration) to be 'more nearly allied' would entail 'a well-paid and affluent body of labourers; no enormous fortunes, except what were earned and accumulated during a single lifetime; but a much larger body of persons than at present, not only exempt from the coarser toils, but with sufficient leisure, both physical and mental, from mechanical details, to cultivate freely the graces of life, and afford examples of them to the classes less favourably circumstanced for their growth' (III, 755). Now it is perhaps the notion of a leisure class that has encouraged attribution to Mill of bourgeois predilections, an impression reinforced by reference to the discussion of property earlier in the *Principles* where Mill outlines the hoped-for consequences of his proposals regarding bequests:

[T]here would be a great multiplication of persons in easy circumstances, with the advantages of leisure, and all the real enjoyments which wealth can give, except those of vanity; a class by whom the services which a nation having leisured classes is entitled to expect from them, either by their direct exertions or by the tone they give to the feelings and tastes of the public, would be rendered in a much more

part from utility, i.e. opinions should be freely ventilated, for there is no other way of telling in advance what is true or false; but also and independently from liberty: '[I]nsensibly . . . [Mill] had reached a position which, in fact, involved a plurality of ultimate criteria' (186). This matter has been taken up in Chapter 8.

98 Similarly while Mill believe that the too early attainment of political franchises by the least educated class might retard, instead of promoting, their improvement he also maintained 'that it has been greatly stimulated by the attempt to acquire them' (III, 763–4).

beneficial manner than at present. A large portion also of the accumulations of successful industry would probably be devoted to public uses, either by direct bequests to the State, or by the endowment of institutions; as is already done very largely in the United States, where the ideas and practice in the matter of inheritance seem to be unusually rational and beneficial (II, 226).

While Mill's own value judgements once again are in evidence, they do not include championship of a 'leisure class' in the literal sense of that expression. Mill himself insisted on this in a comment conspicuously added in 1852 to the 'Futurity' chapter: 'I do not recognise as either just or salutary, a state of society in which there is any "class" which is not labouring' (III, 758), and the advantage of upward mobility of labour in the United States – albeit not quite the ideal – is not in doubt (766). The underlying point at stake is made explicitly in correspondence:

As far as I see, the influence of democracy on the aristocracy does not operate by giving them any of the strength of the people but by taking away that which was their own; making them bend with a willing submission to the yoke of bourgeois opinion in all private things, and be the slaves, in public matters, of the newspapers which they dislike & fear. I confess I look less & less to that quarter for anything good. Whatever is valuable in the traditions of gentlemanhood is a *fait acquis* to mankind; as it is really grounded on the combination of good feeling with correct intellectual perceptions, it will always be kept alive by really cultivated persons; the most complete *parvenus* now in this country have as much of it as people of family, & for its diffusion must not our real reliance be on the extension & improvement of education? I have even ceased to think that a leisured class, in the ordinary sense of the term, is an essential constituent of the best form of society. What does seem to me essential is that society at large should not be overworked, nor over-anxious about the means of subsistence, for which we must look to the grand source of improvement, repression of population, combined with laws or customs of inheritance which shall favour the diffusion of property instead of its accumulation in masses (13 April 1847, XIII, 713).

There is one concession to be made to West's theme, namely the fact that Mill did raise the spectre of 'paternalism' as the sole solution if 'after all efforts have been exhausted to educate them for freedom and govern them as freemen . . . it has been definitely proved that they can only be governed as children' (XVIII, 299). His full recommendations in such an event can doubtless be garnered from the texts and correspondence; for example in a letter of 1850, already referred to, Mill questioned the desirability even of a voluntary redistribution from profits to wages 'in the present state of society & education' (above, p. 895).[99] But this bleak outlook did not govern his general perspective on reform even prior to 1852, for he recognized the potential of education and believed he had pinpointed the source of 'the deficiency in the power of reasoning and calculation, which makes [the lowest class of the working people] insensible even to their own interests' (1845, IV, 377).[100] After 1852, as we have shown, any fear of irredeemability was finally set aside as promising evidence flowed in to the contrary.[101] That there were transitional problems is scarcely surprising.[102]

99 For analysis of Adam Smith's second-best solution in the event that public opinion could not be appropriately developed see Winch (1983).

100 There is an interesting suggestion in the course of long-term projections that the least responsible and energetic would remain hired workers whereas the large majority would enter co-operative ventures (above, p. 817).

101 There are numerous indications of this as we have seen. Two straws in the wind: before the Select Committee on Taxation of 1862 Mill expressed the opinion that 'generally speaking . . . anything which is just, or which is as near as it is practicable to get to justice, and the grounds of which are laid clearly before the public, does, in time, command their approbation' (V, 593). In 1865 he applauded the sophistication of the Lancashire spinners and weavers who appreciated that the cotton crisis was not imputable to their employers or the government and acted with 'consistent good sense and forbearance' (III, 764).

102 Cf. Mill's reference to the desirability that only 'the élite of the working classes' be represented in Parliament (10 Nov. 1868, XVI, 1485) – an evident temporary limitation. Also relevant is Mill's approach to voting qualification: 'I consider it entirely inadmissable, unless a temporary makeshift, that the superiority of influence should be conferred in consideration of property. I do not deny that property is a kind of test; education in most countries, though anything but proportional to riches, is on the average better in the richer half of society than in the poorer. But the criterion is so imperfect; accident has so much more to do than merit with enabling men to rise in the world; and it is so impossible for any one, by acquiring any amount of instruction, to make sure of the corresponding rise in station, that this foundation of electoral privilege is always, and will continue to be, supremely odious' ('On Representative Government', XIX, 474).

CONCLUSION

Some central themes

I MILL, RICARDIANISM AND THE HISTORICAL SCHOOL

We shall summarize in this section several major features of our position by reference to the relationship between 'Ricardianism' and 'historicism'. Professor T. W. Hutchison (1978) in his account of the record refers to a 'profound, extreme and consequential' break in method in 1817 and then cites with approval the following statement by the economic historian N. B. Harte (1971, xiii) to describe various consequences of this 'methodological revolution' (54) – consequences which include J. S. Mill's 'non-historical manner' in the *Principles*:

Since Adam Smith, economics has made important strides, while the historical aspects of the subject during a period of enormous structural change in the economy were left, by and large, to a handful of non-academic Victorian worthies. Why was the genesis of economic history so long delayed in a country and in a period which presents so much of crucial importance to the economic historian today? The simple answer is that economics as understood by the classical economists of the nineteenth century was an a-historical subject, not to say an anti-historical one, while history was not conceived as being concerned with things economic. The method adopted by what became known as 'the dismal science' was that of logic and deduction from abstract principles rather than that of empirical investigation and historical inquiry. The ample historical digressions employed by Smith in *The Wealth of Nations* (1776) conspicuously did not relieve the pages of David Ricardo's *Principles of Political Economy* (1817), and it was the approach laid down by Ricardo which dominated classical political economy in England. John Stuart Mill's *Principles of Political Economy* (1848), though concerned to some extent with what he called 'applications' as well as with the 'principles' themselves, followed Ricardo in treating economics in a basically non-historical manner. Economic thought in England in the generations dominated by Ricardo, Mill and the Benthamite distaste for the study of the past is to be contrasted with the line of development taking place at the same time in Germany. While Mill's system of economic principles became entrenched in English thought, the approach to economics in Germany was radically altered during the 1840s and after by the so-called 'historical school' of economists (Harte, 1971, xii-xiii).

The only qualification allowed by Hutchison appears in a note to the effect that Harte is 'rather unfair regarding J. S. Mill in about the last five years of his life, when, under the influence of Cliffe Leslie and the Irish Land problem, he was moving towards a historical and inductive approach' (1978, 55n). This supposed re-evaluation on Mill's part – entailing (Hutchison suggests) an abandonment of Ricardianism understood in 'Euclidean' terms and constituting a central feature of the 'decline and fall of English classical theory' – Hutchison finds 'especially intriguing':

It was the emergence of this new cohort of economists [Cliffe Leslie, Fleeming Jenkin, Bagehot, Jevons], with important critical or constructive contributions to make to economic theorising, who all rejected the central theories of value and wages of 'the Ricardo–Mill Economics', which makes a comparatively brief span of years in the late 1860s and early 1870s so important a turning point in the history of economic theory in England. But what is especially intriguing is that Mill himself in these years, his own last years, seems to have come to share the disillusion and impatience with prevailing doctrines, or some of them, which had owed so much to his own prestige and earlier support (62–3).

Evidence for this perspective is found in a letter to Thornton of 1867 where Mill expressed his support for 'the emancipation of pol[itical] economy – its liberation from the kind of doctrines of the old school (now taken up by well-to do people) which treat what they call economical laws, demand & supply for instance, as if they were laws of inanimate matter, not amenable to the will of the human beings from whose feelings, interests, & principles of action they proceed. This is one of the queer mental confusions which will be wondered at by & by . . .' (*CW*, XVI, 1320). Professor Hutchison then asks rhetorically: 'Just what were these doctrines from which "emancipation" and "liberation" were so desirable? And *exactly who were the members and founders of this "old school"* who were responsible for their formulation and influence? Could they *possibly* have included James Mill and Ricardo, with their comparisons with Newton and Euclid?' (63; cf. 1972, 452–3).

Mill's adverse reaction to Robert Lowe's universal *laissez-faire* recommendations in 1868 is also interpreted as a 'concession' to the historical critics – 'a forthright historico-relativism against the rigid, Ricardian, deductive absolutism of Lowe'. (1978, 63–4n). Repeatedly we encounter references to Mill's 'dogmatism' and 'chauvinism' and over-confidence in the *Principles* (e.g. 56, 64, 146, 154, 218, 221), which are contrasted with his 'piquant' change of attitude as reflected in an 1868 speech against Lowe (64). Similarly regarding Mill's 'belated scepticism': '[I]n his very last years Mill certainly became sceptical regarding some of the current *applications* of classical political economy (especially to Irish land policy) and this forced him back to the methodological assumptions of such "orthodox" economists as Robert Lowe. But this belated scepticism on Mill's part did not find much expression outside letters and speeches' (221).

We now come to a feature of the account that is difficult to understand. Notwithstanding his reference to Mill's 'dogmatism' and 'chauvinism', Professor Hutchison at the same time still refers to Mill's 'intellectual sympathies and extensive understanding', finding it remarkable how Mill, originally, 'was prepared to lend his immense influence and prestige' to the 'non-historical and non-historiate economics of Ricardo' (220).

On our reading of the record the foregoing account proves unhelpful. First and foremost, the view of Mill as 'basically' non-historical is a parody. What he opposed throughout his career was vulgar historicism; he was insistent regarding the positive role to be accorded history in the social sciences (above, pp. 162f). His position was consistent with that of members of the historical school who 'did not object to deduction as such – on the contrary – but insisted that deductions should be made from categorical premises obtained from historical material' (Viner, 1962 [1917] 109; cf. Foxwell, 1887, 101; Marshall, 1925, 165–6). We have seen that even Whewell came to realize that the inductivist-deductivist dichotomy was proving a liability in economics and moved towards the view that history and theory were complementary (above, pp. 44–5).[1] Willhelm Roscher's 'historicism' reads like Mill's (Roscher, 1877, I, 110).[2] Any sharp dichotomy involving a British 'distaste for the study of the past', illustrated by Mill, and a contrasting Continental view must be avoided. More specifically (and in line with the above caution) there was no sudden realization of a new problem in 1867 such as Hutchison envisages. Since 1830 Mill had maintained 'a forthright historico-relativistic' position, taking political economists – 'the old school' – to task for a tendency to consider contemporary institutions as immutable and universal (above, p. 85). So much for the historical record – 1830 not 1867 is Mill's personal watershed.

What now of his 'remarkable' willingness to 'lend his immense influence and prestige' to the 'non-historical and non-historiate' economics of Ricardo? Here we may add that even commentators who recognize the essay on method

---

1 For a general review of the 'historist reaction' to orthodox classicism see Coats (1954). On the 'absurd' argument about 'induction vs. deduction', see Schumpeter (1954), 537.
2 But there were extreme cases; for the British literature see Checkland (1951b), 155f.

as an attempt to escape from the trammels of his early education raise similar problems: 'one may have to conclude that the break was not far-reaching enough . . . [W]e can observe a certain rigidity in his unwavering acceptance of the main tenets of Ricardian and Utilitarian doctrine. His new political economy was based on wider premises than his father's was, and reached conclusions more in tune with his times, but basically it consisted of a series of variations (some very original and interesting) on themes present in Bentham, James Mill and Ricardo. John Stuart Mill could not or would not complete his intellectual emancipation' (Schwartz, 1972, 49). Or yet again (regarding the essay) 'perhaps the most interesting fact' is that Mill 'ended up far closer to his father's position than might have been expected' (Winch, 1966a, 370); and, more generally, allusion is made to Mill's 'remarkable ingenuity in admitting evidence adverse to Ricardo's predictions while preserving the essential position embodied in the theory', and to his 'delicate balancing act' of 'reaffirming and expanding the Ricardian framework, while at the same time generously incorporating new ideas and taking account of evidence which others considered to be antagonistic or damaging to the Ricardian system' (Winch, 1970, 28–9).

   To state the problem is to imply that Mill's self-proclaimed adherence to Ricardo was fanciful and superficial – that in some objective sense he ought to have achieved independence. Schumpeter is quite explicit on this matter as far as concerns both pure theory and 'social outlook': 'the economics of the *Principles* are no longer Ricardian. This is obscured by filial respect and also, independently of this, by J. S. Mill's own belief that he was only qualifying Ricardian doctrine. But this belief was erroneous. His qualifications affect essentials of theory, and still more, of course, of social outlook' (Schumpeter, 1954, 529; cf. Bharadwaj, 1978, 269). And it is to the psychiatrist's couch that some have recourse as explanation: 'The key to this continuing servitude no doubt lies in Mill's psyche' – in 'a profound imbalance in the emotional side of his nature' (Schwartz, 49–50).[3]

---

3 Schwartz's (1972) position is, unfortunately, difficult to pin down. For he also defends Mill against the common charge of inconsistency for adhering to Ricardian theory and yet evincing concern with historicist and institutional themes: The charge is 'unimportant' and 'irrelevant' – '[o]f course he was both original and coherent . . .' (4). Yet notwithstanding the 'of course' Schwartz seeks to account for Mill's loyalty to Ricardian analysis. He finds part of the explanation in his philosophical 'inductivism' and 'positivism' according to which progress comes not from refutation of hypotheses and fundamental revisions but the accumulation of factual knowledge (236–7). This is a far more promising approach than the appeal to Mill's psyche' (see below, p. 966).
      The general perspective in the literature now under review has something of a pedigree. Foxwell claimed that Mill, who was 'susceptible to all the newer influences', was yet 'drawn by his over-regard for the authority of a narrow though able clique to adhere to the older forms of expression. Had Mill's education been more scientific and less

Let us consider this perspective step by step. We have shown in this work how much of Mill's substantive economics is in fact the economics of Ricardo. Mill was perfectly objective in his own evaluation that there was scarcely 'a single opinion (on pure political economy) in the book, which may not be exhibited as a corollary from his doctrines' (22 Feb. 1848, *CW*, XIII, 731). And there can be no question here of 'filial piety'. We should have in mind the sharp contrast perceived by Mill – again an 'objective' perception – between Ricardo and his father. Consider, for example, his reference to the 'just appreciation of the great teachers of political economy, particularly Ricardo' (5 April 1852, XIV, 88). This and similar statements of loyalty are not merely lip service or a matter of 'piety'. We need but contrast them with an evaluation of the *Elements* in 1833 which makes it clear that Mill did not consider his father to be one of the 'great masters': '[James] Mill's powers of concatenation and systematic arrangement qualified him to place in their proper logical connexion the elementary principles of the science as established by its great masters, and to furnish a compact and clear exposition of them' (I, 593). There is too the description of the *Elements* in the *Autobiography* as 'a very useful book when first written, but which has now for some time finished its work' (213); in fact, apart from modifications for the third edition to the analysis of international values and profits James Mill had failed to incorporate Ricardo's criticisms. Nothing of the kind was ever said of Ricardo's *Principles*. More specific still is Mill's remark of 1869 regarding his father: 'One of his minor services was, that he was the first to put together in a compact and systematic form, and in a manner adapted to learners, the principles of Political Economy as renovated by the genius of Ricardo . . .' (1869, I, Ch. xiv).

Keeping always to the fore the objectiveness of Mill's representation of his scientific work as 'Ricardian', is there reason for surprise at such willingness to adhere to the doctrine? In my view there is not – and this because of, rather than in spite of, his 'intellectual sympathies and extensive understanding'. The identification with Ricardo can be accounted for without recourse to psychiatry; there is general evidence pointing to Mill's 'eminently sober, balanced and disciplined mind', a view not affected by the episode of his breakdown and subsequent recovery (Hayek, 1951, 15, 35; cf. Wolfe, 1975, 33). And there is certainly nothing 'unbalanced' about a refusal to innovate for the sake of innovation.

In the first place, Ricardian theory provided a powerful weapon in the battle for social reform even within the broad confines of going institutions.[4]

---

literary, he might possibly have shaken off these restraints. As it was he merely put new wine in the old bottles, to the irreparable injury of his logical reputation' (1887), 85.
4 Our argument is much reinforced by the evidence (above, p. 771) of Mill's own doubts regarding immediate prospects for a radical transformation of society. Cf. Ashley (1917), xxiii: 'Until the present social system should be fundamentally changed, Mill clearly

There is no justification whatsoever for the view that Ricardian theory was moribund and irrelevant after corn law repeal in 1846 (Blaug, 1980, 76). The application of the very hallmark of Ricardian theory, the inverse wage–profit relation, to the labour issues of the day – the competitiveness of high-wage economies in international trade and the efficacy of union activity in particular – provides a striking instance.[5] (It will be remembered that in 1867 a Royal Commission on Trade Unions was appointed, the working-class vote was granted by the Reform Act, and the unequal Master and Servant Acts were amended; and that complete legal recognition was accorded trade unions in 1871.)

The effect of a wage-rate change upon the rate of return was not a casual theme. It reappears throughout the *Principles* and correspondence. The analysis was of the first importance in the light of the common opinion which, Mill feared, the concerted efforts of Ricardo and himself had not succeeded in shaking, that wage-rate increases can be passed on to consumers – the 'popular and widely-spread opinion' that high wages make high prices, reflecting 'the amazing folly of the propositions which may and do become, and long remain, accredited doctrines of popular political economy' (*CW* III, 479).[6] This problem was repeatedly raised in the late correspondence: To George Howell in September 1865 (XVI, 1102), to Henry Fawcett in January 1866 (1130–1), to Edwin Chadwick in December 1867 (1335) and to George Adcroft in June 1870 (XVII, 1734–5). The Ricardian theorem was also raised conspicuously in Mill's famous essay 'Thornton on Labour and its Claims' (1869) for the *Fortnightly Review* (V, 660).

A particularly striking indication of the crucial relevance of the matter at hand appears in a letter to Cairnes some six months before Mill's death wherein he expressed the inverse relation between wages and profits, ascribing it explicitly to Ricardo, in terms more forceful than ever before, complaining bitterly of the ignorance of the 'self-selected teachers of political economy':

You must have been struck as I have been, by the thoroughly confused and erroneous ideas respecting the relation of wages to price, which have shown themselves to be almost universal in the discussions about the recent strikes. The

regarded the Ricardian economics as so far applicable to existing conditions as to call for no substantial revision in method or conclusions'.

5 Checkland (1951b, 151, 156) also fails to see that technical 'Ricardianism' contributed for Mill to a 'reformist' approach to the problem of social amelioration.

6 In dealing with the contention that an increase in wages generates higher commodity prices, Mill, for the edition of 1871, replaced the introductory phrase 'it used formerly to be said' by 'it is not infrequently said', implying that the analysis had again become of very immediate relevance (III, 699).

notion that a general rise of wages must produce a general rise of prices, is preached universally not only by the newspapers but by political economists, as a certain and admitted economical truth; and political economy has to bear the responsibility of a self-contradicting absurdity which it is one of the achievements of political economy to have exploded. It provokes one to see such ignorance of political economy in the whole body of its self-selected teachers. The Times joins in the chorus . . . Certainly no one who knows, even imperfectly, what the Ricardo political economy is, whether he agrees with it or not, can suppose this to be it. I hope you will come down upon it with all the weight of your clear scientific intellect, your remarkable power of exposition, and the authority of your name as a political economist (4 Oct. 1872, XVII, 1909–10).[7]

The relevance of the theorem extended to international trade. Mill in the *Principles* refuted the 'absurd' opinion that 'English producers could be undersold by their Continental rivals' because of high wages: 'If wages, in any of the departments of industry which supply exports, are kept, artificially, or by some accidental cause, below the general rate of wages in the country, this is a real advantage in the foreign market. It lessens the *comparative* cost of production of those articles, in relation to others; and has the same effect as if their production required so much less labour' (III, 689–90). By contrast, 'no such advantage is conferred by *low* wages when common to all branches of industry. General low wages never caused any country to undersell its rivals, nor did general high wages ever hinder it from doing so' (691–2; emphasis added). In correspondence Mill expressed his despair at ever getting the principle across to the public: 'I hardly know any point in Pol. Economy which it is more difficult to treat popularly, & so as to carry persuasion to those who have not studied the subject, than that one, of the influence of high & low wages on foreign trade' (15 Dec. 1865, XVI, 1127). The technical argument follows exactly along Ricardian lines.

There is a further reason why Mill's adherence to Ricardianism can easily be appreciated – his repeated insistence upon the universality of its method as distinct from its axioms (above, p. 122). And as in the case of the

7 Robert Lowe, whose use of political economy incensed Mill (below, pp. 923–5), had acted as a leader-writer for the *Times* and retained his influence there, at least until 1866 (XVI, 1184n).

Walter Bagehot, writing for the *Economist* in 1867, stated the inverse profit–wage relation precisely, allowing for cases of uniform and differential factor proportions, and for general and partial wage changes; cf. Bagehot (1974), 26–8. But he did not anywhere indicate that his statement represented Ricardian economic theory. And in a further article for the journal (33) he warned that 'though the result of an introduction of trades unions into a single occupation may be easily stated, and also its introduction into *all* occupations, the mixed cases of its half-and-half introduction require great care in analysing, and if treated hastily may very easily be misconstrued and mistaken'.

substantive theorems so in that of scope and procedure Mill's loyalty may be said to be 'objectively' based. Neil de Marchi has phrased the matter well: 'Mill's methodological position was no different from Ricardo's. Mill only formally enunciated the "rules" which Ricardo implicitly adopted' (1970, 266). As we have shown at the outset of this work, Ricardo was fully aware of the historical relativity of the institutional and behavioural axioms adopted in the treatment of the capitalist-exchange system. And he too had insisted upon the formal distinction between 'science' and applied economics. His 'strong cases' constituted analytical simplifications introduced to clarify the argument for better comprehension, but to be appropriately modified in the treatment of real world problems, the 'principles' of political economy as such providing but limited guidance in applied economics where conflicting causal influences are at play and where allowance is required for time-lags and frictions. Ricardo, furthermore, was keenly conscious of the limitations imposed upon political economy by the very nature of its data; he shared with Smith the view that 'disturbing causes' disqualified the subject as a predictive science. It has been maintained that while 'it may possibly be open to discussion how far James Mill was a trustworthy interpreter of Ricardo . . . what cannot be doubted is the extent and penetrating character of his influence' (Ashley, 1917, vii). But it is precisely this latter aspect of the relationship that is open to serious question. For the conscious use of strong cases as an analytical device only limited to 'scientific', in contrast to applied, work; the distrust of over-simplified models for policy pronouncement; the rejection of universally-valid axioms; and the view of theoretical economics as a set of investigative tools, rather than a body of descriptive truths or a set of moral exhortations characterize Ricardo's position alone. Compare all this with James Mill's articles of 1836, 'Whether Political Economy is Useful' and 'Theory and Practice' (above, pp. 91–2). There is then truth in Ashley's statement that J. S. Mill did not abandon abstract science (a reference to the Ricardian theory) but rather placed it 'in a new setting', that 'he kept it intact, but he sought to surround it . . . with a new environment' (ix). This is also the position of Schwartz (1972): 'From an analytical point of view Mill's treatise followed the pattern of the master, while the doctrinal changes that Mill introduced made it easier to accept the Ricardian heritage' (16–17; cf. 235–6). We would insist only that Ricardo himself – in sharp contrast with James Mill – had opened the door to this wider perspective, and that there is nothing 'remarkable' about J. S. Mill's loyalty to Ricardo.

Nothing that has been said rules out the near certainty that Mill included Ricardo amongst those who did not themselves carry out a concerted examination of alternative institutional arrangements: Ricardo after all had chosen to write a technical monograph dealing with specific aspects of pure theory as it pertained to a strictly defined environment. But there is a further aspect to Mill's complaints against the 'old political economy'. I refer now to his strong charges against extremist *laissez-faire* recommendations and, in general, apologetic class attitudes. It was the apologetic opponents of reform who very often were hostile to orthodox theory; the leading orthodox economists were innocent and Mill came enthusiastically to their defence (above, p. 181f).

Who then were the guilty parties? Amongst economists Harriet Martineau is an early candidate. Mill referred to her in 1833 as '*narrow*, and matter-of-fact I should say, in the bad sense'; and he accepted Carlyle's low opinion: 'she reduces the *laissez-faire* system to absurdity as far as the *principle* goes, by merely carrying it out to all its consequences' (2 Feb. and 11–12 April 1833, *CW*, XII, 140, 152).[8] In his letter to Lalor of July 1852 (above, p. 181) Mill set apart McCulloch as a possible exception to his denial that economists merited the charges brought against them; it may well be that Mill had in mind here McCulloch's *Treatise on the Succession to Property* (1848) which constituted a vindication of aristocratic landed property.[9] In a letter of November 1844 Mill wrote of the need 'to avoid the hard, abstract mode of treating [labour] questions which has brought discredit upon political economists' (XIII, 644); and in correspondence with his wife of 1854, he had harsh words for the *Examiner* newspaper and its approach to those questions which is said to be representative of the 'old political economy': 'Then what can be in a worse spirit than the remarks on the [Socialist] Conference at the Soc^y of Arts. It is the driest & narrowest of the old political economy, utterly unconscious of the existence of a newer & better' (7 Feb. 1854, XIV, 152; see Appendix, pp. 977–8).

Members of the 'Manchester School' have been described as 'the dogmatic exponents of laissez-faire of the time'. Mill 'denied repeatedly, and forcefully almost to the point of blasphemy, that the Cobdenites had either authority or logic to support them when they invoked the "Laws of Political Economy" to stop government from coming to the relief of distress' (Viner, 1958, 330–1; see also Grampp, 1960). The *Economist* also fits the bill. As one close observer has written: '. . . if we wish to find the origin of the mid-nineteenth-century theory of laissez-faire, we can find it nowhere better than in the *Economist* and the people who were connected with the *Economist* during this period [1843–1859]' (Gordon, 1955, 465).[10] It is particularly worth noting that the *Economist* on the one hand championed F. Bastiat (who reciprocated by praising the journal as 'a precious collection of facts, doctrine and

8 Mill was not on speaking terms with Harriet Martineau (XII, 342).
9 I draw here from a paper on 'John Stuart Mill *versus* McCulloch on Landed Property' by Mitsuo Takeshima.
10 Cf. also the suggestions by de Marchi (1974), 136 which include Thomas Hodgskin, from 1844 to 1856 a writer for the *Economist*; and also Edward Baines, Jr., proprietor and editor of the Leeds *Mercury*. On Baines see Fraser (1974).

experience mutually supporting each other'); and on the other, criticized Ricardo for his refusal to condemn unequivocally protective tariffs and his suggestions of a possible divergence of interest between wage-earners and capitalists. Ricardo's high reputation was said to be unjustified and likely to prove ephemeral (28 Nov. 1846, 477–8).[11] As for J. S. Mill's own position one recalls his response to a request from the Metropolitan Sanitary Association for a reply to the *Economist*'s case against public management of the London water supply: 'If they want me as an authority against the nonsense of the Economist &c. they will get what they want' (22 Jan. 1851, *CW* XIV, 55).[12] In all this we have clear evidence that Mill was right to identify various opponents of reform with critics of Ricardo.[13]

Mill's complaints were reiterated throughout the 1860s and beyond, and it becomes very clear that he distinguished between the founders and leaders of the subject and the second-raters. Thus for example, he observed of some reviews of W. T. Thornton's *On Labour* (1869) that '[i]t is very amusing in this and other cases to see how the tyros in Political Economy think themselves bound to give no quarter to heresies, being afraid to make any of the concessions which their masters make' (9 April 1869, XVII, 1588). Particularly significant is a reaction in 1870 against those political economists who misunderstood and distorted the intentions of the 'founders' of the subject – a position similar to that expressed in the letter to Thornton of 19 October 1867 which has been misread as an attack upon Ricardo's so-called 'Euclidean' procedures. I have in mind the following unambiguous statements regarding apologetic second-raters who adopted the catch-phrases of the master economists; these provide an excellent summary of Mill's insistence, going back to the 1830s, upon the universality of the method of economics rather than of its axioms and specific theorems based thereupon:

The founders of Political Economy have left two sorts of disciples: those who have inherited their methods, and those who have stopped short at their phrases; those who have carried on the work of the masters, and those who think their masters have left them no work to do. The former follow the example of their teachers in endeavouring to discern what principles are applicable to a particular case, by analysing its circumstances; the latter believe themselves to be provided with a set of catch-words, which they mistake for principles – free-trade, freedom of contract,

11 On the *Economist*'s hostility to unions, see Clemence (1961), 96.
12 On this matter, particularly Mill's position on the role of local authorities, see Schwartz (1966).
13 See also Gilmour (1967) on the 'Gradgrind School'; Webb (1955) for contemporary pamphlets written to convince the working class of the immutability of economic laws and futility of combination; and Berg (1980), Chs. 5–8) who cites numerous writers who could have upset J. S. Mill.

competition, demand and supply, the wages fund, individual interest, desire of wealth, &c. – which supersede analysis, and are applicable to every variety of cases without the trouble of thought ('Leslie on the Land Question', V, 671).[14]

There is something amusingly *naïf* in the form in which this interference of legislation represents itself to the minds of many who, with considerable reluctance, find themselves forced to support it. According to them, it is deeply to be regretted, but unavoidable, setting aside of what they call the principles of political economy, in consequence of insuperable difficulties. May I venture to suggest that there are no such principles of political economy as those which they imagine themselves to be violating? The principles of political economy, as of every other department of knowledge, are a different thing from its practical precepts. The same principles require different precepts, wherever different means are required for the same ends. If the interest of landlords does not afford sufficient security to tenants, it is not contrary, but in the strictest conformity, to the teachings of political economy, to provide other security instead (674–5).

Mill cited with approval a statement by Cliffe Leslie pointing to the culprits:

A school of economists of no small pretensions, strongly represented in Parliament, supposes itself to be furnished with a complete apparatus of formulas, within which all economic knowledge is comprised; – which clearly and satisfactorily expounds all the phenomena of wealth, and renders all further investigation of the causes and effects of the existing economy of society needless, and even mischievous as tending to introduce doubt and heresy into a scientific world of certainty and truth, and discontent and disturbance into a social world of order and prosperity . . . Political writers and speakers of this school have long enjoyed the double satisfaction of beholding in themselves the masters of a difficult study, and of pleasing the powers that be, by lending the sanction of 'science' to all established institutions and customs, unless, indeed, customs of the poor. Instead of a science of wealth, they give us a science *for* wealth (671).[15]

There can be no doubt that, for Mill, Robert Lowe represented *par excellence* this group of Parliamentary apologists guilty of the misuse of political

14 'Professor Leslie on the Land Question', *Fortnightly Review*, n.s. VII (June 1870). The review is of Cliffe Leslie, *Land Systems* (1870).
15 Mill was hopeful: '[Ireland] cannot and will not bear to have its agricultural economy ruled by the universal maxims which some of our political economists challenge all mankind to disobey at their peril; it has begun to dawn upon an increasing number of understandings, that some of these universal maxims are perhaps not universal at all, but merely English customs; and a few have begun to doubt whether, even as such, they have any claim to the transcendent excellence ascribed to them' (672).

economy.[16] In a speech in the House of Commons on 12 March 1868 opposing Irish land reform Lowe had represented the principles of political economy as 'an oasis in the desert of politics' summed up in the universally applicable rule of laissez-faire – 'a prejudice, derived from Scotland and adopted by Adam Smith, that a man is at liberty to do what he likes with his own . . .' (*Hansard Parliamentary Debates*, 1868, Vol. 190, 1493).[17] Mill's strongly worded response is of the first importance:

In my right hon. Friend's mind political economy appears to stand for a set of practical maxims. To him it is not a science, it is not an exposition, not a theory of the manner in which causes produce effects: it is a set of practical rules, and these practical rules are indefeasible. My right hon. Friend thinks that a maxim of political economy if good in England must be good in Ireland. But that is like saying that because there is but one science of astronomy, and the same law of gravitation holds for the earth and the planets, therefore the earth and the planets do not move in different orbits. So far from being a set of maxims and rules, to be applied without regard to times, places, and circumstances, the function of political economy is to enable us to find the rules which ought to govern any state of circumstances with which we have to deal – circumstances which are never the same in any two cases. I do not know in political economy, more than I know in other art or science, a single practical rule that must be applicable to all cases, and I am sure that no one is at all capable of determining what is the right political economy for any country until he knows its circumstances. My right hon. Friend perhaps thinks that what is good political economy for England must be good for India – or perhaps for the savages in the back woods of America. My right hon. Friend has been very plain spoken, and I will be plain spoken to [sic]. Political economy has a great many enemies; but its worst enemies are some of its friends, and I do not know that it has a more dangerous enemy than my right hon. Friend. It is such modes of argument as he is in the habit of employing that have made political economy so thoroughly unpopular with a large and not the least philanthropic portion of the people of England. In my right hon. Friend's mind political economy seems to exist as a bar even to the consideration of anything that is proposed for the benefit of the economic condition of any people in any but the

16 In this Mill was wholly at one with Leslie who had written: 'The proposal of the Government to give the tenantry of Ireland some legal security for improvements has been encountered by an objection, claiming to possess the authority of an economic maxim, and seeking to stifle *in limine* all legislation in favour of tenants, on the ground that it is a settled principle of political economy that the management of private property should be left to private interest; and that the relation of landlord and tenant being one of contract, the sole duty of the State is to enforce the performance of contracts' (*FR*, 1 June 1866 in *Land Systems*, 117). Lowe is here referred to (123–4) as maintaining that 'the best security the public can obtain for the good management of land is the personal interest of its private holders'.
17 See also Lowe's (1876) address in honour of Adam Smith; (Political Economy Club) 1876.

old ways. As if science was a thing not to guide our judgment, but to stand in its place – a thing which may dispense with the necessity of studying a particular case, and determining how a given cause will operate under its circumstances. Political economy has never in my eyes possessed this character. Political economy in my eyes is a science by means of which we are enabled to form a judgment as to what each particular case requires; but it does not supply us with a ready-made judgment upon any case, and there cannot be a greater enemy to political economy than he who represents it in that light (*ibid.*, 1525–6).[18]

There are too, at the same period, Mill's charges against 'the obsolete school of English political economists, whom I may call the Tory school, because they were friends of entail, primogeniture, high rents, great landed properties, and aristocratic institutions generally [and] predicted that peasant proprietorships would lead not only to excessive population, but to the wretchedest possible agriculture'.[19]

Mill's position in the 1860s and 1870s was, therefore, characteristic of a view of the nature of Ricardian political economy held since the early 1830s. His letter of 1867 is in no way a 'concession' to the historical critics of orthodoxy such as Cliffe Leslie – 'a forthright historico-relativism against the rigid, Ricardian, deductive absolution of Lowe'.[20]

Leslie condemned Ricardo and Ricardian economics envisaged in terms of extreme *a priorism*, it is true, and he considered Lowe to be a follower of

18 On the (negative) reactions in Parliament to Mill's speech see Black, 1960, 61. The general issue at stake has been well formulated by Black: 'Mill and Cairnes in the eighteen-sixties were using the same theoretical apparatus to discuss land problems as Ricardo and Torrens had done in the eighteen-twenties, but drew from it almost a diametrically opposite policy conclusion. This was primarily due to their recognition of the fact stressed by Cairnes himself – "Political Economy stands apart from all particular systems of social or industrial existence" – together with the corollary that the English system of social organization was one form amongst many and not necessarily a norm or ideal in any case' (54–5; see also 158, 245).

19 These charges appear in 'England and Ireland' (1868), issued during the parliamentary debates on Ireland (*CW*, VI, 528). Mill had in mind writers such as J. W. Croker from whose 'Agriculture in France', *Quarterly Review*, Dec. 1846, he quoted.

20 Professor Hutchison recognizes suggestions of Mill's 'thorough-going relativism' in the review of Harriet Martineau (1834) and in the distinction drawn between the laws of production and distribution, but asserts that 'this relativism does not otherwise figure at all strongly or prominently elsewhere in the *Principles* or in his essay on Definition and Method' (1978, 64n). This statement could not be further from the truth, since the essay is a plea for recognition of the temporal and geographical relativity of the axioms of political economy. In any event, why (one might ask) insist upon a 'thorough-going relativism' in 1834 and neglect it in the preparation of the essay on method at about the same time?

Ricardo.[21] It is also the case that Mill much admired Leslie.[22] But this does not necessarily mean that he followed Leslie in every respect such that his condemnation of Lowe implies also condemnation of Ricardo (understood à la Leslie). There is no reason why admiration of an individual's work necessarily implies unqualified approval. Consider a letter to Leslie of 8 May 1869: 'I shall read with great interest your paper on profits . . . I am open to conviction, but at present I cannot see that you are likely to be successful in anything more than in shewing that the doctrine respecting value & cost of production is true within wider limits of error – is true much more roughly & only in the gross, than is often supposed by political economists. This I am quite prepared to admit' (*CW*, XVII, 1600). Evidently Mill downplayed the significance of Leslie's criticisms of Ricardian economics.

Here we arrive at a most revealing aspect of the record. In taking his position in 1870 Leslie was himself making full use of Mill's *Principles*; he was merely reiterating Mill's position in the famous chapters 'Of Property and Government Interference': 'Mr. Mill finds a natural claim on the part of the State for the public to the absolute ownership of land, in the fact that man did not make it: "It is the original inheritance of the whole species" ' (*Land Systems*, 1870, 123, citing *CW*, II, 230; cf. also 125 citing *CW*, III, 928 on self-interest and competition).[23]

This episode is not a minor matter. Leslie envisaged Mill's method as a mixed method of the a priori and the inductive – as indeed it is; he did not classify Mill's *Principles* as 'Ricardian' (as he and Hutchison use this term). This is clear from a discussion of the diverse methodological positions emanating from Smith:

The peculiarity of Adam Smith's phiolosophy is, that it combines these two opposite methods, and hence it is that we have two systems of political economy

---

21 See, e.g., *Fortnightly Review*, 1 Nov. 1870; in *Essays in Political Economy*, ed. 2, 1888, 21f.; also *Fortnightly Review* 1 Jan. 1879, *ibid.*, 192–3. Cf. Coats (1954), 146 on Lowe as 'one of the most outspoken supporters of Ricardianism'.

22 Cf. letter, 18 Dec. 1866 (*CW*, XVI, 1222): Leslie is 'an excellent popular expositor of scientific thought, one of our best political economists, and has thought much and well on several of the proposed subjects, the land laws being one'. See also 8 Feb. 1869, *CW*, XVII, 1557–8: 'I have read your first letter to the Economist with great pleasure & your paper on La Creuse with much interest & instruction. It is very important to put such points as it contains before the conceited Englishmen who fancy they understand all that relates to the land & politics of France when they do not know the first rudiments of it . . .' And there is, of course, the very positive 1870 review of Leslie's *Land Systems*. Mill warmly supported Leslie for the University College Professorship in 1871 and 1872; cf. *CW*, XVII, 1810, 1889, 1895.

23 Marshall related the growing interest in sociological and institutional studies – citing Cliffe Leslie, Bagehot, Cairnes, Toynbee – to Mill's *Principles* (1920, 764–5). On 'Leslie envisaged as Mill's disciple' see Koot (1975), 319–24.

claiming descent from him – one, of which Mr. Ricardo was the founder, reasoning entirely from hypothetical laws or principles of nature, and discarding induction not only for the ascertainment of its premises, but even for the verification of its deductive conclusions; the other – of which Malthus in the generation after Adam Smith, and Mr. Mill in our own, may be taken as the representatives – combining, like Adam Smith himself, the *a priori* and the inductive methods, reasoning sometimes, it is true, from pure hypotheses, but also from experience, and shrinking from no corrections which the test of experience may require in deductions (1888 [1870], 24; cf. 1888 [1879], 174, 193).

We can go further, as the following extract (1868) from the Appendix to *Land Systems* indicates:

'The spirit quickeneth, but the letter killeth.' The followers of a philsopher owe him no literal sequence: they owe, on the contrary, to his fame and example, and to the science or system of investigation which he establishes, to give it all possible correction as well as expansion; but in political economy it has been the fate of both Adam Smith and Mr. Mill that the letter of general propositions found in their pages has been pushed with pitiless logic to the utmost extreme, without even the qualifications in those very pages [regarding wage rate uniformity], as though a *reductio ad absurdam* of the master were the object of the disciple (366).

And although at one juncture in 1879 Leslie talks of the early essay as a defence of the a priori method, it is admitted that even here Mill's case was qualified in a significant way: 'Mr. Mill, though he subsequently much enlarged the scope and method of economic investigation, was in his earlier years an advocate of the *a priori* method; yet in the well known essay in support of it he emphatically insisted that the conclusions deduced from it are "true only in the abstract", and "would be true without qualification only in purely imaginary cases" ' (1888, 199; the context is the 'desire of wealth' assumption).

Let us draw all this together. That Mill in 1870 favoured Leslie's criticism of Lowe is the most natural thing in the world in the light of his own *Principles* and essay. There was nothing new in any of this – he was expressing approval of Leslie's methodological criticisms of economists because, after all, they were his own and he had long made them.

Now Mill had early on come to the defence of orthodox (Ricardian) economics on scope and method and on social reform. And he came to the defence of orthodox economics against Comte's criticisms in 1865 on exactly the same methodological grounds as in the 1834 review of Martineau (above, p. 85). These latter facts pose no problem whatsoever if Mill championed a Ricardianism as we have understood that doctrine. His adherence to Ricardian procedure may be simply understood by the fact that it was envisaged as quite consistent with an appreciation of the 'provisional' nature of institutions and a preoccupation with social reform. He could, on this reading, defend orthodoxy and yet, like Leslie, favour institutional change against the apologists who misunderstood or misused political economy. He could do so in 1870 as he had done throughout his career from the early 1830s. On the other hand, how could he have supported simultaneously the Leslie perspective and 'Ricardianism' understood as an extremist form of a priorism yielding automatically immediately applicable policy prescriptions justifying *laissez-faire*? This is not a problem that arises just for 1870 and thereafter but for Mill's entire career. If we insist on taking that line we must be prepared to pay the psychiatrist's fees.

II MILL AND NEO-CLASSICISM

Unlike Walras, Jevons did not develop an entire theoretical system in the *Theory of Political Economy* (1871); his work, he himself claimed 'was never put forward as containing a systematic view of Economics' (1924, xliii–xliv). The point is made by Léon Walras who in 1879 contrasted Jevons's approach in this regard with his own: 'Jevons a le tort de ne pas dire que le système de Ricardo et Mill est remplacé. Je remplace dans ma *Théorie mathématique de la Richesse Sociale* et dans mes *Eléments d'Economie politique pure* le système de Ricardo et Mill par un système•très beau, très simple dans ses éléments et très vaste dans ses détails . . .' (1965, I, 628). Walras, whose intellectual origins include J. B. Say, objected to the classical pricing and distribution model (as he understood it) – particularly the cost orientation and the natural-wage approach – on the grounds that, by neglecting a final demand dimension and accordingly derived demand, the English had constructed, from a general-equilibrium perspective, an underdetermined system (1954, 424–5). But he recognized the 'ten remarkable pages' of Jevons's Preface to his second edition of 1879, which state 'that the formula of the English school, in any case the school of Ricardo and Mill, must be reversed, for the prices of productive services are determined by the prices of the products and not the other way round' (45). More generally, Jevons here represented distribution (ideally) as a matter of service pricing 'entirely subject to the principles of value and the laws of supply and demand', with input prices 'the effect and not the cause of the value of the produce' – 'I hold labour to be *essentially variable, so that its value must be determined by the value of the produce, not the value of the produce by that of labour*'; and cost of production as a reflection of opportunities foregone (1924, xliiif., 186).[24] He accordingly directed his criticisms at the wage-fund and

---

24 Cf. Stigler (1965), 304: '[J.B.] Say's approach was fundamentally much more modern than that of his English contemporaries.' For an elaboration of this position, see Hutchison (1978), 84f.

subsistence approaches to wage-rate determination and the cost approach to value – as he understood them – paying tribute to the French tradition: 'the only hope of attaining a true system of Economics is to fling aside, once and for ever after, the mazy and preposterous assumptions of the Ricardian school. Our English Economists have been living in a fool's paradise. The truth is with the French School . . .' (xliv–v).[25]

Jevons recognized elements of the 'correct' position in Mill's *Principles* – that rent enters into cost where land has alternative uses, that all inequalities (whether natural or artificial) generate economic rents, and the representation of demand and supply as a law 'anterior' to costs (xlviii, li, 197) but could not resist remarking (in the context of the generalization of the rent concept) that 'those who have studied Mill's philosophic character as long and minutely as I have done, will not for a moment suppose that the occurrence of this section of Mill's book tends to establish its consistency with other positions in the same treatise'.[26]

The notion of a revolutionary breakthrough in the 1870s is also conspicuous in some recent literature. It has been suggested, for example, that once the subsistence theory of wages broke down 'the most natural alternative was to explain wages by the productivity of labor, an explanation only useful if labor was intrinsically scarce. In short labor had to be treated like land'. Moreover, recognition of the phenomenon of non-competing groups implied a multiplicity of primary factors which, so it is argued, 'required a new theory' (Arrow and Starrett, 1973, 132–3). The founders of the neo-classical school 'understood the glaring omission of demand from the classical model'. There is a deeply embedded belief in the profession that the solution to the paradox of value had to await the 1870s (below, note 32). And the theme of a revolutionary break by the general-equilibrium

25 In his introduction to Jevons's *Theory* (1970), 17–20, Professor R. D. C. Black rejects the usual criticism of Jevons that he failed to develop a theory of factor pricing and therefore a full neo-classical perspective. His intention, Black suggests, was Benthamite; he was not concerned with a general pricing system. This interpretation merits careful consideration for it is by no means self-evident, since Jevons's Preface to the Second Edition does imply a preoccupation with the general pricing problem, both by the suggestions made regarding a 'desirable' approach and by the criticisms of orthodoxy. In an alternative formulation Professor Black (1972c, 373–4) suggests that Jevons's adherence to Benthamism may have held him back from developing a full-fledged theory of factor pricing. This interpretation would be fully consistent with Jevons's position in his Preface. But this is only part of the story. Black further maintains that it is in Jevons's emphasis upon 'the importance of the mathematical method' rather than in the development of utility theory as such, that lies 'the essence of his break with the classical tradition' (1972a, 5).

26 But in correspondence Jevons conceded that although 'there is much that is erroneous in [Mill's] 'Principles' and he never had an idea what *capital* was . . . the book is not the maze of self contradictions that his Logic undoubtedly is' (to Foxwell, 7 Feb. 1875, in Black ed., 1977, IV, 101).

economists from classicism is also a feature of modern 'Cambridge' historiography (Robinson, 1961; Roncaglia, 1981).

Marshall took a very different view, insisting against both Jevons and Walras, upon the essential continuity of nineteenth-century doctrine: 'Under the honest belief that Ricardo and his followers had rendered their account of the causes that determine value hopelessly wrong by omitting to lay stress on the law of satiable wants, [Walras] led many to think he was correcting great errors; whereas he was really only adding very important explanations' (Marshall, 1920, 101n). Indeed Marshall found Ricardo's formulation of pricing preferable to that of Jevons who 'substitutes a catena of causes for mutual causation' (818). This view has been reiterated by Gerald Shove who insists on the source of Marshall's economics in the Ricardo–Mill formulations:

[T]he analytical backbone of Marshall's *Principles* is nothing more or less than a completion and generalisation, by means of a mathematical apparatus, of Ricardo's theory of value and distribution as expounded by J. S. Mill. It is not . . . a conflation of Ricardian notions with those of the 'marginal utility' school. Nor is it an attempt to substitute for Ricardian doctrine a new system of ideas arrived at by a different line of approach . . . [So] far as its strictly analytical content is concerned, the *Principles* is in the direct line of descent through Mill from Ricardo . . . (1960 [1942], 712).

Schumpeter, in his account, follows Marshall part of the way, for he emphasizes Marshall's original source in Mill. At the same time he denies the Ricardo linkage; in his estimate, Mill's system had 'absorbed enough of the Say conception – and in addition was sufficiently helped by Senior's notion of abstinence – to be free from any such objection [as Ricardo's inability to deal with simultaneous equations], and it offered all the elements of the complete model that Marshall was to build. But he retained so many Ricardian relics that there is some excuse for Jevons' and the Austrians' not seeing that they were developing his analysis and for believing instead that they had to destroy it' (1954, 569–70). This attempt to split off Mill from Ricardo is conspicuous in other recent accounts:

A silent revolution in the direction of the marginalist supply-and-demand theory was brought about [by Marshall] in the course of adopting, extending and transforming some ideas in Mill. As Mill himself had departed considerably from Ricardo, Marshall was thus moving even further from the Ricardian source (Bharadwaj, 1978, 254).

It was precisely the beginnings in Mill of considerable deviations from Ricardo's theory of value and distribution that called for and received at Marshall's hands . . .

extensions and refinement; so that Marshall's deliberations on value and distribution departed systematically from the questions Ricardo posed and the framework of analysis he employed . . . What Shove regarded as extensions and generalisations of Ricardo in [Marshall's] *Principles* (the introduction of the demand side, the functional relation between costs and output, the supply and demand determination of wages and profits) are radical departures from the Ricardian standpoint (269).

This book offers a contribution to the on-going debate. The evidence suggests how useful in the present context is the notion of altered 'concentrations of attention' (Hicks, 1976, 208–9) which avoids a revolutionary connotation. For what seems to have occurred in the 1870s was a narrowing of focus, specifically a greater concern with exchange and allocation in their own right; a sharpening of theoretical tools, particularly those relating to consumer choice; and the algebraic formulation of general-equilibrium relationships. These are theoretical developments which could have been absorbed by the traditional corpus of analysis whereas the impatience of the marginalists and their apparent wish to wipe the slate clean meant that much of great import in classical theory for their own chosen and relatively narrow sphere of discourse was not recognized, and spurious analytical distinctions were artificially reinforced.[27] My evidence, in short, suggests how justified was Marshall's position, and confirms the validity of Schumpeter's (Marshallian) view that the economists of the 1870s were developing rather than destroying Mill's system. At the same time it also demonstrates the illegitimacy of his belief that Mill had effectively broken away from Ricardo. Finally, that we find both neo-classical and Ricardian features in Mill's *Principles* implies neither inconsistency as I once believed (Hollander, 1973b, 1976), nor a process of attempted escape from his Ricardian heritage.

It has emerged from our investigation that the economics of Ricardo and J. S. Mill in fact comprises in its essentials an exchange system consistent with the neo-classical elaborations. In particular, their cost-price analysis is pre-eminently an analysis of the allocation of scarce resources, proceeding in terms of general equilibrium, with allowance for final demand, and the interdependence of factor and commodity markets. There was a simultaneous (and consistent) attachment to cost theories of value and to the general-equilibrium conception of economic organization as formulated by J. B. Say and much admired by Walras. The demand side, the functional relation between cost and output, the supply and demand determination

27 Cf. the pertinent comments by Hayek (1941, 434) regarding the fourth proposition on capital: 'That . . . the doctrine has suffered a marked eclipse is mainly due to the fact that the modern subjective theory of value was erroneously thought to have provided an effective refutation.' Also Boulding (1966) regarding the partial validity of the wages-fund theory (132).

of wages and profits, far from being 'radical departures' from Ricardianism, are central to that doctrine without which neither the cost theory of price nor the inverse wage–profit relation can be understood. Serious and long-lived misconceptions regarding classicism flow from a failure to recognize that its notions of wages and interest as compensation for effort and abstinence were pertinent only at the macro-economic level where the determinants of aggregate factor supplies are under investigation and not in the micro-economic context where costs refer to foregone opportunities. (In the sense of foregone products alone, and excluding foregone leisure, cf. Robbins, 1970, 18).

To assert that recognition of a multiplicity of primary factors required a new theory based upon the principles of demand or that classical theory could not solve 'the logical problem of explaining relative wages of heterogeneous types of labour' (Arrow, cited in Hutchison, 1978, 69) is historically unjustified.[28] The wage structure had long been analysed in terms of demand–supply with recognition of a productivity dimension on the demand side; and while value productivity is more conspicuous the more specialized to a particular use are individual factors, those same considerations are no less relevant when allowance is made for factor mobility between uses, although now strict limits are placed on the extent returns in different uses can diverge. In any event, although factor specificity is indeed a neo-classical preoccupation, both Ricardo and Mill carried this very matter far in their generalizations of the rent doctrine.

If we take into account the matter of foreign trade and classical analysis in that case – the conspicuous role accorded demand considerations where the mobility axioms are abandoned – it becomes yet clearer that the notion of a paradigmatic transformation in the 1870s is not helpful. And while Mill was largely responsible for the analysis it must be remembered that Ricardo had left the door open by his formulation so that the elaborations, brilliant as they were, were consistent with existing doctrines.

Thus far we have considered the neo-classical 'relaxation' of the general (but far from universal) classical assumptions regarding factor mobility between uses. There is also the reverse of the medal to consider – the Ricardian assumption of single-use land. By adopting this assumption Ricardo had indicated a preoccupation with the macro-dimension; yet the 'class' relationship that concerned him, pre-eminently the inverse wage–profit relationship, could not be understood except in terms of allocation theory. This applies to Mill too. And both economists insisted upon a micro-

28 It may be agreed that the neo-classics 'took as an expository point of departure a model which was the polar opposite of the classical, the model of pure exchange' (Arrow and Starrett, 1973, 133). Clear exposition may require extreme assumptions, as Ricardo repeatedly insisted.

foundation for macro-analysis which seems eminently sensible if capitalist-exchange institutions are taken seriously. To trace through the consequences of a variation in the general wage in the case where (marginal) cost price incorporates land rent in the Smith–Say manner would have been technically impossible given the state of the science. (It is doubtful whether a specific outcome could be generated in the present day and age, for which reason so much analysis proceeds on the basis of two-factors and two-products.)

That there was indeed no paradigmatic displacement is also quite evident from investigation of Walras. For when he set aside his own restrictive assumption of factor immobility between uses he was led to formulations of cost price identical to those of Ricardo and Mill (Hollander, 1982). This theme can be extended. The appropriate axiomatic base depends in part on the context. The early and later nineteenth-century economists were concerned (as was Adam Smith) both with growth and allocation, although the weighting of their preoccupations certainly differed. Depending upon the context it was appropriate to emphasize factor 'scarcity' or factor 'reproducibility' or various combinations. Thus Ricardo frequently dealt with disturbances (demand changes, innovation, taxation) within a static framework, although there is no question of his predominant concern with a broad range of analytical issues relating to the growth process – the aggregate factors (capital and labour) treated as variables. And conversely, Walras extended his own analysis in the *Elements* to the 'Conditions and Consequences of Economic Progress' which deals with the distributional implications of growth in labour and capital supplies (given land): 'What does need to be discussed . . . in view of its extremely weighty consequences, is the fact . . . that the quantity of land cannot possibly increase though it is possible to increase the number of persons and the quantity of capital goods proper in an economy that saves and converts its savings into capital' (1954, 382). Similarly, he recognized the 'excess of income over consumption' in the aggregate – the matter of surplus and accumulation – as the condition of progress (267f). Clearly, the classical growth model was not superannuated by the early neo-classicists.

J. S. Mill's continued preoccupation with growth issues (and with the general profit rate) despite his sharp awareness of the problem of factor immobility, also requires consideration from this perspective. For it is not obviously true that concern with the general wage and profit rates dissipates with recognition of the phenomenon of non-competing groups. There may yet be disturbances affecting all types of labour more or less equally, and for analysis of the growth process the standard classical mobility axiom (subject to qualifications regarding speed of adjustment) may be most appropriate. Jevons and others, including Cliffe Leslie (1870, 360), were critical of Mill's retention of the notion of an 'average' wage rate, but we must recall his justification in the belief that improved educational opportunities were reducing the immobilities that historically had been responsible for the splintering of the labour market.[29]

III MILL AND MARGINAL UTILITY

We proceed to a closer look at the marginal utility issue – the fact that the classical approach to the law of demand (the negative slope to the demand curve) eschewed reference to the principle of satiability of wants. How to explain what, from a neo-classical perspective, is often represented as a 'failing' (cf. de Marchi, 1972, 350)? There is less involved than meets the eye.

It is possible that the marginal utility concept itself was familiar to Mill (de Marchi, 1972, 347; Bowley, 1972; Hollander, 1977b); in fact Mill utilized a version of diminishing utility in his case for income redistribution (above, pp. 880–1). That Mill 'inherited from Ricardo a bias against giving consumption a place equal to that held by production and distribution in the schema of economic science' (de Marchi, 350; cf. 354, 363) is also true, provided that this is not understood as downplaying the law of demand itself which was so central to Ricardian economics or as a blanket denial that the ultimate motive governing production and employment is final purchase. By his statements in the essay regarding consumption Mill merely intended to convey that the 'laws of consumption' – which are identified with the 'laws of human enjoyment' – fall outside the domain of the economist (above, p. 268). The existence of such laws, however, seems to be conceded. Indeed, Mill removes some potential road-blocks along the path. There is his insistence in *Utilitarianism* that 'rules of arithmetic are applicable to the valuation of happiness, as of all other measurable quantities' (*CW*, X, 258). In the *System of Logic* he took strong issue with Comte and others who 'prefer dogmatically to assume that the mental differences which they perceive, or think they perceive, among human beings, are ultimate facts, incapable of being either explained or altered, rather than take the trouble of fitting themselves, by the requisite processes of thought, for referring those mental differences to the outward causes by which they are for the most part produced, and on the removal of which they would cease to exist' (VIII, 859). He maintained that 'the commonest observation shows that different minds are susceptible in very different degrees to the action of the same psychological causes. The idea, for example, of a given desirable object, will excite in different minds very different degrees of intensity of

29 For a very critical view based upon the fundamental significance of the assumption of a stable wage structure see Hutchison (1972), 457.

desire' (856; cf. 857); but he was ready enough to allow the usefulness of 'approximate generalizations' albeit that they constituted the lowest kind of empirical law: '[W]henever it is sufficient to know how the majority of the human race, or of some nation or class of persons, will think, feel, and act, these propositions are equivalent to universal ones. For the purposes of political and social science this *is* sufficient . . . an approximate generalization is, in social inquiries, for most practical purposes equivalent to an exact one: that which is only probable when asserted of individual human beings indiscriminately selected, being certain when affirmed of the character and collective conduct of masses' (847).[30]

There is then no categorical rejection of an investigation of the 'laws of human environment'. And the question would have arisen for Mill whether it might be fruitful to seek a basis in psychology for the law of demand.

As a matter of principle Mill maintained (in a famous letter to Cairnes) that 'the wants of the time' required 'that scientific deductions should be made as simple and as easily intelligible as they can be made without ceasing to be scientific' (5 Dec. 1871, XVII, 1863). Now the law of demand had already been rationalized in terms of the income effect by Ricardo, and more than that may not have been found necessary. We can be rather more specific. Our researches have shown that when pressed to consider the details of consumer reaction to relative price variation, purchasing power held constant, Mill applied brilliantly and effortlessly a 'revealed preference' analysis, thereby confirming a liking for as simple a rationale as possible – eschewing psychologism in favour of the pure logic of choice (above, p. 270f).[31] This illustrates nicely his complaint to Cairnes, in the letter just referred to, regarding Jevons's 'mania for encumbering questions with useless complications' (*ibid.*, 1862). Jevons, for his part, simply asserted that 'it is surely obvious that Economics does rest upon the laws of human enjoyment; and that, if those laws are developed by no other science, they must be developed by economists' (1924, 39). Mill probably did not see the *Theory* (Schabas, 1983b, 284); but he was closer to the truth than Jevons by his realization that recognition of the need for a theory of demand does not necessarily imply need for a psychological theory of consumption.[32]

30 Cf. 603: 'it is generally enough to know that *most* persons act or are acted upon in a particular way; since [the statesman's] speculations and his practical arrangements refer almost exclusively to cases in which the whole community, or some large portion of it, is acted upon at once' (also 879).

31 This predilection for an 'objective' approach is fully in line with his insistence on a conception of demand as far as possible on a par with that of supply ('Notes on Senior', 1945, 134; *CW*, III, 465; cf. de Marchi, 351).

32 It is most regrettable that the profession cannot be shaken from the opinion that Ricardo and Mill were unable to resolve the paradox of value; and that the utility contributions of the 1870s were required to break the deadlock. For the latest example of this error see Cooter and Rappoport (1984), 510.

However, the appeal for simplicity alone might not have led to a refusal to follow through along a route which promised a more profound comprehension of behaviour. There is a further consideration: Mill's appreciation that consumer goods are usually characterized by some degree of durability imposing a 'capital' dimension upon decisions to purchase. For the production process comes to a halt when things are 'in the place where they are required for use' (above, p. 262); to focus on psychology to explain the stage of acquisition would have appeared inappropriate without the further complication of a discount factor, since the 'laws of human enjoyment' come into play only with the *use* of (durable) consumer goods.

There is also the belief that much consumer activity at the retail level is governed by non-maximizing motivation. (From this point of view, it is doubtful whether Mill would have accorded diminishing marginal utility the status even of 'empirical law'.)[33] To the extent that consumer behaviour is not undertaken on terms of 'business principles' economics had nothing much to say. It is not that Mill was 'prevented' from defining optimum consumption patterns because he lacked the principle of marginal utility (de Marchi, 356-7); rather, maximizing behaviour was, empirically speaking, an inappropriate axiom in the first place. But to the extent that the consumer was envisaged as a maximizer – or at least as behaving consistently – an 'objective' approach was preferable. Important matters of principle govern Mill's neglect of diminishing marginal utility; to refer to it as a 'failure' and imply that the contributions of the 1870s were an unambiguous advance is inappropriate.

IV MILL AND MATHEMATICAL ECONOMICS

Schwartz maintains that 'Mill was no mathematician, either by training or, which is more important, by inclination', and accordingly 'resisted the trend towards the formalization of new knowledge' (1972, 238). As an indication of this perspective he cites the letter to Cairnes regarding Jevons's *Theory of Political Economy* (1871) already referred to above (p. 935): 'I have not seen Mr. Jevons' book, but as far as I can judge from such notices of it as

---

33 De Marchi characterizes the law of diminishing marginal utility as an empirical law; and argues that Mill's associationist psychology would not have provided an adequate underpinning for that law 1972, 352-3. That there was no clear-cut promise of any unambiguous results from this perspective is doubtless true, but we do not need to go so far in our speculations regarding Mill's position. In any event, de Marchi himself concludes that an adherence to associationist psychology made it unlikely that [Mill] would enunciate even this 'empirical law' for himself (354).

have reached me, I do not expect that I shall think favourably of it. He is a man of some ability, but he seems to me to have a mania for encumbering questions with useless complications, and with a notation implying the existence of greater precision in the data than the questions admit of. His speculations on logic, like those of Boole and De Morgan, and some of those of Hamilton, are infected in an extraordinary degree with this vice.'[34]

The notion that Mill's mathematics were inadequate can be dismissed (de Marchi, 1972, 347; Schabas, 1983b, 282). A key to Mill's reaction to Jevons will rather be found in an observation by Cairnes regarding *The Theory of Political Economy* in the letter which elicited the foregoing citation – 'I own', Cairnes wrote, that 'I have no faith in the development of economic doctrines by mathematics. What you have said on the subject of nomenclature in the second vol. of your Logic seems to me decisive upon this point' (23 Oct. 1871, cited Schwartz, 295). Cairnes is here referring to Mill's generalization that ' [w]henever the nature of the subject permits our reasoning processes to be, without danger, carried on mechanically, the language should be constructed on as mechanical principles as possible; while in the contrary case, it should be constructed that there shall be the greatest possible obstacles to a merely mechanical use of it' (*CW*, VIII, 707). This is followed by a statement of presumption against the widespread applicability of mathematical language suitable only for the 'mechanical' approach:

[The] admirable properties of the symbolical language of mathematics have made so strong an impression on the minds of many thinkers, as to have led them to consider the symbolic language in question as the ideal type of philosophical language generally; to think that names in general, or (as they are fond of calling them) signs, are fitted for the purposes of thought in proportion as they can be made to approximate to the compactness, the entire unmeaningness, and the capability of being used as counters without a thought of what they represent, which are characteristic of the *a* and *b*, the *x* and *y*, of algebra. This notion has led to sanguine views of the acceleration of the progress of science by means which, I conceive, cannot possibly conduce to that end, and forms part of that exaggerated estimate of the influence of signs, which has contributed in no small degree to prevent the real laws of our intellectual operations from being rightly understood (708).

34 Cf. Mill's letter to Jevons himself dated 15 May 1865, recently discovered by Margaret Schabas, which includes remarks on Boole and De Morgan: 'My impression was, that there is great ingenuity and power of consecutive thought, both in [Boole's] system itself, and in your modification of it. But you are quite right in supposing that I do not see, in the result attained, any value commensurate with the mental effort. I look upon it as I do upon Mr. De Morgan's syllogisms; as a remarkable feat of mental gymnastics, capable of being very useful in the way of a scholastic exercise, but of no considerable utility, for any other purpose' (1983a, 25).

It is likely that this perspective governed at least in part the allusion to Jevons's 'use of a notation implying the existence of greater precision in the data than the question admits of'. The observation extends far beyond the application of mathematics to consumption theory. Quite generally Mill's fear was that the inappropriate use of mathematical language would act as a positive hindrance to scientific progress; Jevons's mathematical program for economics (cf. Schabas, 1983b) must have seemed to Mill an invitation to set out on a false trail.

Of crucial import here is the reaction in the *System of Logic* to the argument that the adoption of a mathematical approach to the deductive sciences 'would reduce all reasonings to the application of a technical form, and enable their conclusiveness to be rationally assented to after a merely mechanical process, as is undoubtedly the case in algebra' (VIII, 709). This case could only be applied 'where the practical validity' of the reasoning derives from the reasoning itself as in geometry and the 'science of number'. But where there arises the problem of 'composition of causes' involving propositions valid only in the absence of countervailing causes and thus having only 'hypothetical certainty' – the key problem in economics (above, p. 122f) – what is called for is an attitude of mind alert to the specifics of the case and the empirical 'meaning' of the axioms; 'A conclusion . . . however correctly deduced, in point of form, from admitted laws of nature, will have no other than an hypothetical certainty. At every step we must assure ourselves that no other law of nature has superseded, or intermingled its operation with, those which are the premises of the reasoning; and how can this be done by merely looking at the words? We must not only be constantly thinking of the phenomena themselves, but we must be constantly studying them; making ourselves acquainted with the peculiarities of every case to which we attempt to apply our general principles' (710).[35]

Mill's fear that a mathematical program would encourage a perspective deflecting attention from 'the meaning of our signs' is very nicely illustrated from the theory of consumption. I refer again to his approach towards the retail sector – consumers, in many cases, were not he believed, maximizers. The science of economics based upon maximizing behaviour had much to offer regarding the determination of outputs and prices up to the wholesale level, but not beyond; the assumption of marginal calculation by final consumers might be totally inappropriate from an empirical perspective.

From this viewpoint the transformation of economics into a mathematical subject would entail an episode in scientific regression. And in point of fact the marginal treatment of consumption did throw overboard Mill's sophisticated empirical approach to demand – the recognition of 'disturbing

---

35 Cf. Cairnes's version of this proposition in his review of Jevons's theory (1872; in Jevons, 1981, VII, 151–2).

causes' which generate failures of the 'law of demand' – in favour of Jevons's excessive simplifications in the interest of mathematization such as the assumptions of independent goods and independent consumers. More generally, Mill's potentially fruitful approach to competitive price formation involving the relation between firm and industry and expectation regarding entry (above, p. 289) fell on unreceptive soil, Jevons and Walras resorting to totally artificial expedients in order to proceed. This loss of 'realism' is particularly conspicuous in the case of Walras who, Jaffé has strenuously argued, was concerned with the workings of an 'ideal' system not a 'real' capitalist economy, and whose *tâtonnement* process was unrelated to price adjustments in actual markets (Jaffé, 1980); but see the counter-argument by Walker, 1984).[36]

Mill's warnings were remarkably prescient considering the fact that he was unfamiliar with the writings of the early 1870s.[37] And equally striking, some of the dangers of over-simplified models had been long before formulated in his letter to d'Eichthal of 1829 (above, p. 90). There he had emphasized that French procedure, by neglecting 'disturbing causes', distorted the operation even of those causes allowed for: 'They deduce politics like mathematics from a set of axioms & definitions, forgetting that in mathematics there is no danger of partial views: a proposition is either true or it is not, & if it is true, we may safely apply it to every case which the proposition comprehends in its terms: but in politics & the social science, this is so far from being the case, that error seldom arises from our assuming premisses which are not true, but generally from our overlooking other truths which limit, & modify the effect of the former'.[38] There is an interesting parallel here with Keynes's celebrated warnings of 1939 regarding econometrics in his paper on 'Professor Tinbergen's Method'.[39]

36 The true danger was of a long-term nature from the perspective of professional trends. See Black (1972a), 7–8, on Jevons's own realization of the limits of mathematics in the 'dynamical' branches of economics. Jevons, of course, himself made brilliant 'inductive' contributions (cf. Black, 1962). Foxwell (1887) pointed out early on in a discussion of historicist reactions, that 'if they only knew it, the mathematical economists are their most effective supporters. There is no greater safeguard against the misapplication of theory than the precise expression of it. No writers have been so truly historical in their use of theory as those who, like Cournot and Jevons, have known its exact limits' (90).

37 There is no proof that Mill knew of Jevons's celebrated 'Notice of a general Mathematical Theory of Political Economy', given at the British Association in 1862 and published with only minor variation in 1866.

38 Cf. *System of Logic*, VIII, 894 for the same perspective.

39 'Am I right in thinking that the method of multiple correlation analysis essentially depends on the economist having furnished, not merely a list of the significant causes, which is correct as far as it goes, but a *complete* list? For example, suppose three factors are taken into account, it is not enough that these should be in fact *verae causae*; there must be no other significant factor. If there is a further factor, not taken account of, then the method is not able to discover the relative quantitative importance of the first three' (1973, XIV, 308).

This is not the end of the matter. There are various pronouncements in the *System of Logic* which together amount in effect to a case against mathematical 'forecasting' in economics – an exercise that requires precise numerical data – and which might also have played a part in Mill's actual (or potential) response to Jevons. First, consider the positive overview in the case of the physical sciences:

The immense part which those laws ['which are the peculiar subject of the sciences of number and extension'] take in giving a deductive character to the other departments of physical science, is well known; and is not surprising, when we consider that all causes operate according to mathematical laws. The effect is always dependent on, or is a function of, the quantity of the agent; and generally of its position also. We cannot, therefore, reason respecting causation, without introducing considerations of quantity and extension at every step; and if the nature of the phenomena admits of our obtaining numerical data of sufficient accuracy, the laws of quantity become the grand instrument for calculating forward to an effect, or backward to a cause (*CW*, VII, 620).[40]

Here the reader is referred to Vols. I and II of Comte's *Cours de Philosophie Positive* for further elaboration, and to Volume III for the 'limits to the applicability of mathematical principles' – limits which cover economics:

Such principles are manifestly inapplicable, where the causes on which any class of phenomena depend are so imperfectly accessible to our observation, that we cannot ascertain, by a proper induction, their numerical laws; or where the causes are so numerous, and intermixed in so complex a manner with one another, that even supposing their laws known, the computation of the aggregate effect transcends the power of the calculus as it is, or is likely to be; or lastly, where the causes themselves are in a state of perpetual fluctuation; as in physiology, and still more, if possible, in the social science. The mathematical solutions of physical questions become progressively more difficult and imperfect in proportion as the questions divest themselves of their abstract and hypothetical character, and approach nearer to the degree of complication actually existing in nature; insomuch that beyond the limits of astronomical phenomena, and of those most nearly analogous to them,

---

40 Cf. also 'Inaugural address to the University of St. Andrews' (1867) regarding the potential of applied mathematics in the appropriate physical sciences: 'We are able, by reasoning from a few fundamental truths, to explain and predict the phenomena of material objects: and what is still more remarkable, the fundamental truths were themselves found out by reasoning, for they are not such as are obvious to the senses, but had to be inferred by a mathematical process from a mass of minute details, which alone came within the direct reach of human observation. When Newton, in this manner, discovered the laws of the solar system, he created, for all posterity, the true idea of science' (*CW*, XXI, 236).

mathematical accuracy is generally obtained 'at the expense of the reality of the inquiry' (620–1; cf. 459).

Mill concludes that the application of mathematical principles would be 'chimerical' in chemistry and physiology and in 'the still more complex inquiries, the subjects of which are phenomena of society and government'.[41]

There are thus two conceptually distinct but complementary cases pointing away from the fruitful applicability of mathematics to economics – one based on the danger of attributing a bogus precision to symbols thereby opening the door for excessively simple 'geometric' procedures; the other turning upon the paucity of numerical data and the complexity of causal relations which rule out precise computation of the combined effect of causes.

In her account of the reaction to Jevons by Cairnes and Mill, Dr. Schabas has remarked upon Mill's own recognition that in so far as scientific knowledge involves the pursuit of causal laws it is 'ultimately quantitative and thus mathematical in principle', so that, she concludes, 'Mill would have to concede, given this claim, that political economy, as the study of the causes which regulate wealth, was in the very same sense as it was for Jevons, inextricably mathematical. Mill, however, did not reach these conclusions . . .' (1983b, 291). Yet as Dr. Schabas proceeds to show Mill went a long way along the Jevonian path. I take issue only with her representation of Mill's position as 'inconsistent' (293). A word of explanation.

Concern with the excessive simplifications characterizing French geometrical procedure, and doubts regarding mathematical forecasting, do not necessarily rule out the use of mathematics in aid of clear logical thought. Mill himself, after all, had dabbled with algebraic formulations (CW, III, 611). A formal statement of his recognition of a legitimate role for mathematics appears in the System of Logic itself where reference is made to 'the value of mathematical instruction as a preparation for those more difficult investigations' (chemistry, physiology, social science and

---

41 J. B. Say had argued along similar lines in his Traité d'économie politique – but for the physical as well as the social sciences – cautioning that it would 'be idle to imagine that greater precision, or a more steady direction could be given to this study, by the application of mathematics to the solution of its problems. The values with which political economy is concerned, admitting of the application to them of the terms plus and minus, are indeed within the range of mathematical inquiry; but being at the same time subject to the influence of the faculties, the wants and the desires of mankind, they are not susceptible of any rigorous appreciation, and cannot, therefore, furnish any data for absolute calculations. In political as well as in physical science, all that is essential is a knowledge of the connexion between causes and their consequences. Neither the phenomena of the moral or material world are subject to strict arithmetical computation' (1880 [1819], xxvi).

government, and aspects of astronomy) 'in the applicability not of its doctrines, but of its method', by providing training in the deductive procedure of employing 'the laws of simpler phenomena for explaining and predicting those of the more complex' (VII, 621). In the *Examination of Sir William Hamilton's Philosophy* (1865), in the chapter containing Mill's reply to a hypo-critic of the study of mathematics, the contrast appears very strikingly. Here (following Comte) Mill defends mathematical instruction as an 'indispensable first stage of all scientific education worthy of the name' on the grounds that it sets high standards of 'proof', encourages precise logical thought based upon given axioms, postulates and definitions, and teaches 'the importance of quantities' (IX, 472f).[42] Thus even though '[i]n the achievements which still remain to be effected in the way of scientific generalization, it is not probable that the direct employment of mathematics will be to any great extent available' (Mill here includes the moral and social sciences) 'the nature of the phenomena [precluding] such an employment for a long time to come – perhaps for ever', yet (applied) mathematics 'affords the only sufficiently perfect type' (481). For

the process itself – the deductive investigation of Nature; the application of elementary laws, generalized from the more simple cases, to disentangle the phaenomena of complex cases – explaining as much of them as can be so explained, and putting in evidence the nature and limits of the irreducible residuum, so as to suggest fresh observations preparatory to recommencing the same process with additional data: *this* is common to all science, moral and metaphysical included; and the greater the difficulty, the more needful is it that the enquirer should come prepared with an exact understanding of the requisites of this mode of investigation, and a mental type of its perfect realization (cf. also XXI, 235–7).

But there was a danger. Once again the perspective of 1829 is reiterated:

And here we come upon the one really grave charge which rests on the mathematical spirit, in respect of the influence it exercises on pursuits other than mathematical. It leads men to place their ideal of Science in deriving all knowledge from a small

42 What Mill says here is pertinent to his observations regarding equations in economics (above, p. 274). See also *ibid.*, 479. Ricardo's famous complaint against Malthus's opinion that Political Economy 'is not a strict science like mathematics' (1951), VIII, 331, has been read as evidence of 'dogmatic, *a priori* deductivism' (Hutchison, 56n). But this is doubtful. Ricardo's statement continues to specify that Malthus, in consequence of his viewpoint, 'thinks he may use words in a vague way, sometimes attaching one meaning to them, sometimes another and quite different'. J. S. Mill pleaded against dogmatic, a priori, deductivism throughout his career yet saw a place for mathematics in deductive theory, basing himself partly on precision of thought; his position, as usual, was fully in line with Ricardo's.

number of axiomatic premises, accepted as self-evident, and taken for immediate intuitions of reason . . . Nearly everything that is objectionable, along with much of what is admirable, in the character of French thought, whether on metaphysics, ethics, or politics, is directly traceable to the fact that French speculation descends from Descartes instead of from Bacon. All reflecting persons in England, and many in France, perceive that the chief infirmities of French thinking arise from its geometrical spirit; its determination to evolve its conclusions, even on the most practical subjects, by mere deduction from some single accepted generalization: the generalization, too, being frequently not even a theorem, but a practical rule, supposed to be obtained directly from the fountains of reason: a mode of thinking which erects one-sidedness into a principle, under the misapplied name of logic, and makes the popular political reasoning in France resemble that of a theologian arguing from a text, or a lawyer from a maxim of law (485).[43]

Thus, unlike Cliffe Leslie – indeed like Cairnes (Checkland, 1951b, 166) – Mill warned only against the abusive use of mathematics not mathematics *per se*. This is further confirmed by his defence of political economy against Comte's low opinion in the course of which he insisted on the applicability to the social sciences of the methods designed for the natural sciences – the 'scientific artifice familiar to students of science, especially of the applications of mathematics to the study of nature': 'When an effect depends on several variable conditions, some of which change less, or more slowly, than others, we are often able to determine either by reasoning or experiment, what would be the law of variation of the effect of its changes depended only on one of the conditions, the remainder being supposed constant. The law so found will be sufficiently near the truth for all times and places in which the latter set of conditions do not vary greatly, and will be a basis to set out from when it becomes necessary to allow for the variations in those conditions also. Most of the conclusions of social science applicable to practical use are of this description' (*CW*, X, 309). Comte's system, Mill complained, 'makes no room for them. We have seen how he deals with the part of them which are the most scientific in character, the generalizations of political economy'.

43 In his critique of Hamilton, Mill pays tribute to Whewell. After a charge against the 'too unqualified predominance of the mental habits and tendencies engendered by elementary mathematics' (486), Mill continued: 'Applied mathematics in its post-Newtonian development does nothing to strengthen, and very much to correct, these errors, provided the applications are studied in such a manner that the intellect is aware of what it is about, and does not go to sleep over algebraical symbols; a didactic improvement which Dr. Whewell, to his honour be it said, was earnestly and successfully labouring to introduce, thus practically correcting the real defects of mathematics as a branch of general education . . .' This concords with Mill's praise of Whewell's sensible approach to mathematics in his discussion of the university program thirty years earlier; 'Civilization' (1836) *London and Westminster Review*, *CW*, XVIII, 142. But it is not clear from this how he classified Whewell's mathematical renditions of Ricardian theory.

By his various allowances Mill is certainly not 'inconsistent'; his balanced perspective defining the role of mathematics in economics bears consideration in our own day. For it is one thing to doubt the usefulness of 'calculating forward' to a precise numerical forecast, or to condemn the application of maximization principles without discrimination however empirically inappropriate the exercise may be. It is quite another to employ mathematics as a check to sound reasoning. Mill's position was in effect taken up by Marshall who certainly allowed for mathematics as an aid to 'clear thought' while at the same time he objected to contrived 'appearance[s] of lucidity' (1920, 357n., 368; cf. also 781f).[44]

Our discussion helps lighten a further grey area in the literature – the notion that the adoption of algebra requires for Mill that the science in question afford precise numerical data (cf. J. N. Keynes, 1891, 249; Schabas, 1983a, 27, 1983b, 288). This view was strongly opposed by Jevons in his Preface: 'Many persons entertain a prejudice against mathematical language, arising out of a confusion between the ideas of a mathematical science and an exact science. They think that we must not pretend to calculate unless we have the precise data which will enable us to obtain a precise answer to our calculations' (1924, 5). But we have shown that Mill recognized the quantitative dimension to economic phenomena notwithstanding the absence of precise data – their basis in 'the psychological law . . . that a greater gain is preferred to a smaller' (above, p. 108) – and more specifically that he was prepared to countenance the (limited) use of algebra in economics notwithstanding the absence of precise data; indeed, he himself supplemented his verbal account of price formation in the trade context by an attempt to generalize in algebraic terms. The pronouncement that 'mathematical solutions to physical questions become progressively more difficult and imperfect in proportion as the questions divest themselves of their abstract and hypothetical character, and approach nearer to the degree of complication actually existing in nature' (above, p. 940) creates no difficulty for us. He intended thereby the ambitious task of mathematical forecasting and the derivation of axioms à la Newton; much easier is the more mundane task of formulating causal relations of the order 'more or less'.[45]

44 Marshall, as is well known, relates his own early mathematical work to a formalization of Mill's verbal statements: '. . . my acquaintance with economics commenced with reading Mill . . . and translating his doctrines into differential equations as far as they would go; and, as a rule, rejecting those which would not go' (1925, 412).

45 The law of demand comes to mind as an instance. But the reader may refer to an alternative view whereby Mill denied that there was a 'uniform relation between price and quantities demanded of different commodities' and accordingly objected to an expression of the demand schedule – let alone a schedule of variations in utility – in symbolic terms (de Marchi, 1972, 349). In our view this cannot be – that there was a wide variety of demand elasticities is true (unlike the demand for money as such which was of unitary elasticity); but this would not preclude a general expression for the law of demand such that $\epsilon \geqslant 0$ (at least in the wholesale sphere).

V MILL AND MALTHUSIANISM

We have encountered in our review of the literature a reference to Mill's 'remarkable ingenuity' in dealing with 'evidence adverse to Ricardo's predictions' (above, p. 916).[46] This charge turns on a failure to recognize that Ricardo like Smith before him did not design his economic models with an eye to specific historical prediction; and that Mill formally adopted this 'classical' position in his own writings on method. Nothing in British economic experience (particularly the movements of wage and profit rates) reflected adversely on Ricardian doctrine and there was nothing 'ingenious' about Mill's response. In particular, Ricardianism provided general tools of analysis, including a fundamentally important theorem of distribution, which proved indispensable to Mill in his social preoccupations quite independently of the actual path of agricultural productivity and real wage rates.

The failure to recognize these features of classical method is partly responsible for the view that Mill was guilty of the so-called 'Ricardian Vice' – the direct application to the real world of results derived from a narrowly constrained growth model based upon a subsistence-wage axiom:

Ricardo and J. S. Mill took a line well towards the 'hard' end of the spectrum, and *their distribution model only had content to the extent that it could derive this from a 'hard', empirical Malthusian proposition.*
Although the hard-line doctrine had been rejected by such classical 'soft-liners' as Senior, McCulloch (in his later years), and Torrens – and by many others – *it was still well entrenched in the orthodox theorising of the 1860s in the dominant, authoritative text of J. S. Mill, and in those of his disciples Cairnes and Fawcett.* Jevons, and the others of the new wave of economists of the late 1860s and early 1870s, were not attacking a defunct Aunt Sally. But after their attacks – apart briefly from Cairnes and Fawcett – *no economist of note attempted to resurrect a hard-line Malthusian doctrine, at any rate in Britain* (Hutchison, 1978, 71–2).[47]

46 For a strongly worded statement of Ricardo as 'predictionist', see Blaug (1980), 75. Blaug proceeds to discuss 'whether Mill, having conceded the increased irrelevance of Ricardian theory as time passed, ought to have admitted that Ricardian theory was not merely irrelevant but invalid' (76). See also Blaug, in Latsis (1976), 165–6, regarding 'unmistakable signs after 1848 of "degeneration" in the Ricardian research programme, marked by proliferation of "ad hoc" assumptions to protect the theory against the evidence that repeal of the Corn Laws of 1846 had failed to bring about the effects predicted by Ricardo'. Even the argument that there was 'nothing "forced"' . . . about Mill's invoking technical change, if these really were occurring' since the twenty-five years from Ricardo's death in 1823 to Mill's *Principles* in 1848 do not 'constitute a conclusive test of Ricardo's predictions' (de Marchi, 1970, 274), is going too far.

47 Bowley (1973) has similarly argued that a great gap existed in the literature when the subsistence wage concept broke down (213), neglecting entirely the Ricardo–Malthus–Mill wage-path analysis.

946 THE ECONOMICS OF JOHN STUART MILL

Similarly: 'John Stuart Mill was as steadfast in his defence of the third pillar of classical orthodoxy – the Malthusian theory – as he was in defending Say's Law or the cost of production theory of value' (Sowell, 1972, 160); 'probably only a man with Mill's massive reputation for an open and forward-looking mind could have so successfully turned the clock back on fundamental developments in economics and perpetuated a population doctrine which had been discredited theoretically and empirically' (163–4).[48]

All this involves serious errors of judgement – regarding Mill's theory, purpose and method. As for the growth model itself, we have seen the wide range of possible outcomes that might be generated even in the absence of new technology, depending on the relative growth rates of capital and population (above, p. 444f). As for the practical object of the theorizing we recall Mill's estimate that the mass of unskilled labour was still largely unreformed from the perspective of 'prudence' although he was hopeful. In manufacturing, rapid population growth over recent decades had been consistent with the maintenance of wages (even their increase) because of an equally rapid rate of accumulation reflecting the impact of new technology. But in the event of a future deceleration in accumulation real wages could fall, and Mill's basic Malthusian message was that the instillation of prudential habits would 'avert [the calamity], by the adaptation of their habits to their circumstances' (CW, II, 351).

More immediately, there is Mill's insistence that an absolute reduction in population would, under the going conditions characterizing an 'old country' raise wages: 'That is the question, and no other: and it is idle to divert attention from it, by attacking any incidental position of Malthus or some other writer, and pretending that to refute that, is to disprove the principle of population' (353).[49] The wages of agricultural labour in particular were atrociously low 'as an existing fact' so that 'whether

48 Cf. Blaug (1956), 48: with Mill 'it became, once again, the key to the Ricardian theory of distribution. In his effort to restore Malthus' arguments Mill indeed affected something of a counter-revolution' Also Hutchison (1972), 462; Stigler, (1965), 172.

49 It is to be noted also that Mill downplayed Malthus's 'arithmetic' rate of food increase and 'geometric' rate of population increase as an illustration not to be taken literally: 'I ask, then, is it true, or not, that if their numbers were fewer they would obtain higher wages? That is the question, and no other: and it is idle to divert attention from it, by attacking any incidental position of Malthus or some other writer, and pretending that to refute that, is to disprove the principle of population. Some, for instance, have achieved an easy victory over a passing remark of Mr. Malthus, hazarded chiefly by way of illustration, that the increase of food may perhaps be assumed to take place in an arithmetical ratio, while population increases in a geometrical: When every candid reader knows that Mr. Malthus laid no stress on this unlucky attempt to give numerical precision to things which do not admit of it, and every person capable of reasoning must see that it is wholly superfluous to his argument' (II, 353). Mill was perfectly correct in making this defence; Malthus had indeed deliberately used the ratios by way of illustration and did not intend to be taken literally (1890, 5–6).

[population] pressed still harder or not quite so hard [against the wages fund] at some former period is practically of no moment . . .' (354). Even regarding higher paid categories who benefited from improving technology, population pressure could be said actually to exist in the sense of a birth rate which precluded yet greater wage improvements – such indeed as would allow North American living standards:

No Malthusian, we believe, thinks that the pressure of population is greater, relatively to the means of subsistence, than it was thirty years ago. No one can think so who believes that there has been any moral or mental improvement in the people. The complaint is, not that there is no improvement, but that there is not improvement enough – that wages which, with greater restraint on population, might be as high as in America, are kept down by too rapid multiplication. Malthusians would deplore that the advancement constantly taking place in the arts of life, and the good which may be expected from improved social institutions, and a better distribution of the fruits of labour, should be nullified for practical purposes, by serving, as such things have always hitherto done, to increase the numbers of the labouring class much more than to improve their condition (1851, V, 449–50).

The perpetual nature of the problem is a major theme of J. S. Mill. 'I do not know', he wrote to W. G. Ward in 1849, 'where you find that on my shewing the evils of over-population are in some distant future. On the contrary, I hold with Malthus that they are, & have been throughout history, almost everywhere present, & often in great intensity' (*CW*, XIV, 26). He complained in 1852 to Lalor for speaking of Malthus's doctrine as 'tottering' (91). But this is a far cry from population pressure understood as *inevitable* downward pressure on the wage. What stands out is the presumption that the observer or policymaker has a conception of what constitutes the desirable wage; if productivity is sufficient to allow its achievement, any wage below that level is inadequate, and population pressure can be said to exist. To Newman's complaint that Malthus and his followers failed to provide a test of excess population Mill replied and with justification: 'They have given the only possible test: they say that population is excessive when, in a country in which labour is tolerably productive, wages are too low' (V, 449).

That the growth model was not designed for positive prediction should have been clear – if only from the obvious fact that Mill was engaged in an exercise in persuasion designed to play upon key behavioural patterns. But the texts are quite explicit. In the *System of Logic* he expressed the matter with the utmost clarity: 'all generalizations which affirm that . . . population increases faster than subsistence, or subsistence than population . . . and the like, propositions of considerable value as empirical laws within certain (but generally rather narrow) limits, are in reality true or false according to times and circumstances' (VIII, 791; cited above, p. 142). In the *Principles* similarly: '[t]here are so many new elements at work in society, even in those deeper strata which are inaccessible to the mere movements on the surface, that it is hazardous to affirm anything positive on the mental or practical impulses of classes and bodies of men, when the same assertion may be true to-day, and may require great modifications in a few years time' (II, 346).

What then was intended by the celebrated 'tendency' of population to increase faster than subsistence? Nothing more than that '[a]fter a degree of density has been attained, sufficient to allow the principal benefits of combination of labour, all further increase tends in itself to mischief, so far as regards the average condition of the people; but the progress of improvement has a counteracting operation, and allows of increased numbers without any deterioration, and even consistently with a higher average of comfort' (188–9). Thus, in the absence of technical change and with no slackening of population growth there must occur a decline in (marginal) product and the wage. Mill, accordingly, refers to the complaint against 'early' Malthusians who were interpreted to be asserting growing poverty by 'the tendency of population to *increase faster* than the means of subsistence' – and were easily refuted – whereas what they in fact intended was such a tendency 'if [population] were not checked either by mortality or by prudence' (353).

It is important to be clear that in arguing thus Mill like Chalmers (above, p. 60) was following directly in Malthus's footsteps (and also in those of Whately whose usage of the term 'tendency' he was throughout implicitly adopting; cf. also de Marchi, 1970, 1974). The Senior–Malthus exchange of 1829 is most instructive in this regard (above, pp. 50–1). Little could Senior have expected that the old saw regarding the inevitability of low standards would be repeatedly resuscitated and this despite Malthus's own efforts to correct the error.

* * *

Despite the extensive common ground between Malthus and Mill there are some significant differences of detail. We attend first to the role of self-interest and the problem of the 'free-rider'.

Allowance was made by Malthus for (state financed) education programs designed to inculcate the principle of prudential control. But educational programs had a limited potential – to assure the maintenance of standards already achieved rather than their actual increase, since the rising generation must know in practice what it is that by imprudence they would be surrendering (1890, 533–4). 'We should always bear in mind', Malthus further warned, 'that no experiment respecting a provision for the poor can be said to be complete till succeeding generations have arisen' (561), appropriately governed by prudential motives. Malthus had hit upon the poverty trap: a taste for comforts requires that they be already experienced (see also 535).

Education, it was hoped, would contribute to assure against the lowering of standards already achieved. Beyond this nothing more was required of the State in Malthus's view, for once the working class was apprised of the facts regarding the role for prudence, it was only necessary for each individual to be made 'responsible for the maintenance of his own children' and 'subjected to the natural inconveniences and difficulties arising from the indulgence of his inclinations [for early marriage], and to no other whatever' (323). Indeed,

[t]he happiness of the whole is the result of the happiness of individuals, and to begin first with them. No co-operation is required. Every step tells. He who performs his duty faithfully will reap the full fruits of it, whatever may be the number of others who fail. This duty is intelligible to the humblest capacity. It is merely, that he is not to bring beings into the world, for whom he cannot find the means of support . . . It is clearly his interest . . . to defer marrying, till by industry and economy he is in a capacity to support the children that he may reasonably expect from his marriage' (457).

Indeed, a major part of the case against Communism was precisely that resort might have to be made to legal control of family size and the age of marriage. The 'greatest objection to a system of equality and the system of the poor-laws (two systems which, however different in their outset, are of a nature calculated to produce the same results) is, that the society in which they are effectively carried into execution, will ultimately be reduced to the miserable alternative of choosing between universal want and the enactment of *direct* laws against marriage' (357).

Malthus may have been rather too optimistic. There is, in the first place, the supposed ability of the individual to make the complex long-run calculations required by the prudential rule, nicely encapsulated thus: 'The lowest prospect, with which a man can be justified in marrying, seems to be the power, when in health, of earning such wages as, at the average price of corn, will maintain the average number of living children to a marriage' (560n).[50] Malthus's optimism had some justification where labour demand is stationary or at least increasing at a constant rate so that a given wage is consistent with a constant growth rate of labour supply and unchanged prudential habits. But prudence is a relative matter – a falling

---

50 In point of fact, Malthus himself recognized a problem and allowed for state aid to cover miscalculation, at least in individual cases presuming that prudential behaviour was the norm (536).

rate of accumulation, such as Malthus generally envisaged, requiring increased prudence generation by generation if wage constancy is to be assured.[51] It is difficult to envisage this degree of complex calculation on the part of individuals – unless the education program extends to the specifics of Malthusian growth theory.

Secondly, there is the so-called 'free-rider' issue. According to Malthus 'he who performs his duty faithfully will reap the full fruits of it, whatever may be the number of others who fail'. This assertion has some validity if the delay before the new generation of workers enters the market is such that current behaviour regarding marriage has no effect on the current labour market. If, however, the lag is brief then calculations of wage prospects must take into account the prudential behaviour of others, and the assertion is patently untrue. Indeed, the greater the prospect for imprudence by the majority, and thus for relatively low wages, the greater the inducement to delay marriage on the part of the individual who exercises forethought, while conversely, the more confidence can be placed on the general exercise of prudence and the maintenance of the wage the less motive for any individual to behave responsibly.

The same problem arises where the new generation of workers enters the labour force after a delay which excludes its competition with current labour, in the event that the adult considers marriage with an eye to the employment and earnings prospects of the children he expects to have. For the greater the prospects of general prudence the less fear he need have of the nefarious consequences of his own imprudence.

Mill was at one with Malthus regarding the need to inculcate by (state-supported) education the principle that population control holds the key to living standards, and emphasized the problem of poverty – that to rise above it required experience of higher standards. He was also conscious of impediments to success, pointing to the peculiar difficulties attached to the system of hired labour compared with peasant proprietorship:

That wages would fall if population were much increased is often a matter of real doubt, and always a thing which requires some exercise of the thinking faculty for its intelligent recognition . . . Few people like to leave to their children a worse lot in life than their own. The parent who has land to leave, is perfectly able to judge whether the children can live upon it or not: but people who are supported

---

51 Similarly, technical progress that raises the potential for improved wages requires the *increased* exercise of prudential restraint to be rendered of permanent benefit to labour. On empirical aspects of the problems of forecasting faced by the individual contemplating marriage see Wrigley and Schofield (1981), 431–2.

by wages, see no reason why their sons should be unable to support themselves in the same way, and trust accordingly to chance (*CW*, II, 284).[52]

Nor does any condition afford so strong a motive against overpopulation [as does peasant proprietorship]; because it is much more obvious how many mouths can be supported by a piece of land, than how many hands can find employment in the general labour market (VI, 529).[53]

However, Mill was rather more concerned than Malthus with the danger of a degradation of standards (cf. Malthus, 1890; Mill, *CW*, II, 341). And unlike Malthus he was exercised by the free-rider dilemma. What was required, he maintained, was behaviour regarding family size motivated by a sense of social responsibility, or at the least socially-oriented behaviour enforced by public opinion.[54] In these terms he answered the practical objection to Malthus raised by Francis Newman in 1851, that 'it is impossible for any poor man to hope that his individual prudence in the delay or renunciation of marriage, will ever be remunerated by a higher rate of wages. He knows that others will swamp his market with *their* children if *he* live childless. If the good alone are Malthusians, the bad families will outbreed them'. 'This is perfectly true', Mill replied, and 'what is wanted is, not that the good should abstain in order that the selfish may indulge, but such a state of opinion as may deter the selfish from this kind of intemperance by stamping it as disgraceful' (V, 449).[55]

The solution, therefore, hinged on a reform of public opinion. Once the Malthusian idea had taken hold amongst workers,

every labourer [would look] (with Sismondi) upon every other who had more than the number of children which the circumstances of society allowed to each, as doing him a wrong – as filling up the place which he was entitled to share. Any one who supposes that this state of opinion would not have a great effect on conduct, must be profoundly ignorant of human nature; can never have considered how large a portion of the motives which induce the generality of men to take care even of

52 Under the Irish cottier arrangement the problem also arises: 'a metayer family' – protected by custom from losing the farm – 'could not be impoverished by any other improvident multiplication than its own, but a cottier family, however prudent and self-restraining, may have the rent raised against it by the consequences of the multiplication of other families' (316).
53 Malthus also emphasized the peculiar advantages under peasant proprietorships from the population perspective; cf. 1830, in Flew (1970), 242–3.
54 For a discussion of Mill's position and its consistency with that of Godwin, see Levy (1980), 2–16.
55 For a good statement of the 'free-rider' issue and its solution in a reformed state of opinion see J. A. Roebuck, 'National education', (1833), 758. This paper was greatly praised by Mill (9 March 1833, XII, 145).

their own interest, is derived from regard to opinion – from the expectation of being disliked or despised for not doing it . . . We are often told that the most thorough perception of the dependence of wages on population will not influence the conduct of a labouring man, because it is not the children he himself can have that will produce any effect in generally depressing the labour market. True . . . [but] it is the disgrace which naturally and inevitably attends on conduct by any one individual, which if pursued by a majority, everybody can see would be fatal (II, 371).[56]

Assuming widespread acceptance of the foregoing opinion except on the part of that minority 'in the habit of making light of social obligations generally' a case might even be made out for legal control: 'there would be then an evident justification for converting the moral obligation against bringing children into the world who are a burthen to the community, into a legal one; just as in many other cases of the progress of opinion, the law ends by enforcing against recalcitrant minorities, obligations which to be useful must be general, and which, from a sense of their utility, a large majority have voluntarily consented to take upon themselves'. (372).

Control of population was one issue considered by Mill in his evaluation of the relative merits of communism and private property. In the posthumous 'Chapters on Socialism' (1869) Mill commended Louis Blanc for recognizing a potential problem under *all* institutional arrangements but, as one would expect, he treated more critically Blanc's notion of an inevitable decline of living standards under capitalism (above, p. 783). Blanc's opinion that the solution could be found *only* under communism Mill also denied. But in taking this position, he objected only to the extreme case which rules out any possibility of control under private enterprise; he recognized that the case for socialism might turn out strongest. It is certain that he here had in mind its potential in stimulating (and enforcing) a sense of social responsibility in individuals:

Mankind are capable of a far greater amount of public spirit than the present age is accustomed to suppose possible. History bears witness to the success with which large bodies of human beings may be trained to feel the public interest their own. And no soil could be more favourable to the growth of such a feeling, than a Communist association, since all the ambition, and the bodily and mental activity, which are now exerted in the pursuit of separate and self-regarding interests, would require another sphere of employment, and would naturally find it in the pursuit of the general benefit of the community . . . And independently of the public motive, every member of the association would be amenable to the most universal, and one of the strongest, of personal motives, that of public opinion (II, 205).

56 For Sismondi's position which relates to a stationary population, see *ibid.*, 369.

The argument that communism (like the pre-1834 poor relief system) would weaken prudential restraint by assuring subsistence to all and to any number of children is recognized – but countered: 'Communism is precisely the state of things in which opinion might be expected to declare itself with the greatest intensity against this kind of selfish intemperance' (206). Since the cause of falling standards would be crystal clear to all (there being no employers or privileged classes to blame) 'opinion could not fail to reprobate, and if reprobation did not suffice, to repress by penalties of some description, this or any other culpable self-indulgence at the expense of the community'.

Here then Malthus and Mill diverged. Mill was caught in the middle ground between Malthus on the one extreme who saw in self-interest the solution to excess population, and objected to communism precisely because it would have to resort to measures of enforcement and punishment; and Blanc (and later Engels)[57] who found the solution in communism and only in communism. Mill, however, did not finally commit himself. We know he had an abiding horror of centralized systems and his more positive comments on other forms of socialism were qualified, for the full potential of private property had not yet been revealed. Moreover, he himself declaimed against paternalism in matters affecting the labour market (IV, 374–5). But we are faced by a problem. It is not at all clear whether he appreciated the full implications of his hopes for 'public opinion' (not to speak of his countenancing of legal measures, involving regulation of population, to confirm that opinion) within a private-property system – a 'society as at present constituted'.[58] For it must be supposed that there exists some generally held conception regarding the key variables, particularly the trend path of labour demand, and a concensus on the desired wage rate in order to fix upon 'acceptable' family size. The implied degree of community prescience and authority is very great, and suggests a high degree of central control – a command economy.

---

57 Cf. Engels to Kautsky (1881); in Meek (1971), 120: 'There is, of course, the abstract possibility that the number of people will become so great that limits will have to be set to their increase. But if at some stage communist society finds itself obliged to regulate the production of human beings, just as it has already come to regulate the production of things, it will be precisely this society, and this society alone, which can carry this out without difficulty. It does not seem to me that it would be at all difficult in such a society to achieve by planning a result which has already been produced spontaneously, without planning, in France and Lower Austria. At any rate, it is for the people in the communist society themselves to decide whether, when, and how this is to be done, and what means they wish to employ for the purpose.'

58 Indeed he seems reluctant to go too far into the issue, noting (until the third edition of the *Principles*) that 'Whether a legal sanction would be ultimately required, or moral sanctions, and the indirect influence of law and policy, would suffice – and if legal measures were necessary, of what nature it would be advantageous that they should be, it would be premature, in the present state of the question, to discuss' (II, 372n).

The problem is reduced (though by no means eradicated) in a stationary state, and Mill indeed argued part of his case for stationarity from precisely this perspective:

Where there is an indefinite prospect of employment for increased numbers, there is apt to appear less necessity for prudential restraint. If it were evident that a new hand could not obtain employment but by displacing, or succeeding to, one already employed, the combined influences of prudence and public opinion might in some measure be relied on for restricting the coming generation within the numbers necessary for replacing the present (III, 753).

* * *

But here there emerges a problem in interpretation of Mill in his later years far more severe than that posed by the recantation from the wages fund in 1869. The prospects for improving standards were good considering the potential for population control. Yet there is a cloud on the horizon. First indications of a complication appear in the sixth edition of the *Principles* (1865) where Mill conceded that despite massive emigration from Ireland, living standards had not increased, as he himself had expected, because of the very heavy displacements of labour by the adoption of English-type capitalist farming (see above, p. 853; Chapter 6, note 26). In effect, Mill was now adopting Marx's view, for Marx in *Capital* used the Irish experience in an attack on the Malthusian perspective:

Here, then, under our own eyes and on a large scale, a process is revealed, than which nothing more excellent could be wished for by the support of its dogma: that misery springs from absolute surplus-population and that equilibrium is re-established by depopulation . . .
What were the consequences for the Irish labourers left behind and freed from the surplus-population? That the relative surplus-population is to-day as great as before 1846; that wages are just as low, that the oppression of the labourers has increased, that misery is forcing the country towards a new crisis. The revolution in agriculture has kept pace with emigration. The production of relative surplus-population has more than kept pace with absolute depopulation (*Capital*, 1965, I, 703–4).

In so far as the disturbance in question reflects exogenous technical progress or reorganization, what is involved is a change in the *ceteris paribus* conditions – a 'disturbing cause'. But more than this was at stake, as is clear from Mill's 'Leslie on the Land Question' (1870). Here he refers to Leslie's denial of any contemporary rise in Irish standards:

He denies the virtue either of emigration, or of the other favourite English prescription – the consolidation of farms – as a cure, or even much of a palliation, for Irish poverty. As a matter of fact, he asserts that the increase of wages which has taken place, considerably as it appears in comparison with the former standard, is not much more than equivalent to the rise in the price of articles of consumption caused by the gold discoveries, and by the railways, which have everywhere so greatly increased the price of agricultural produce in what were once, from the inaccessibility of markets, the cheap regions of the world . . . As far as Ireland is concerned, [Leslie's] opinion is, that the extensive substitution of pasture for tillage which has taken place during the whole period of the emigration, and has been greatly facilitated by it, has curtailed the demand for labour in a proportion fully equal to the diminution of the supply' (*CW*, V, 675–6).

Now Mill was not merely reporting Leslie's position. He accepted it – not surprisingly considering his own discussion in the *Principles*. He reiterated in the review that excess population growth was no longer an issue and that notwithstanding this fact, and the massive emigration, living standards on average had failed to rise – indeed 'production and prosperity are declining through . . . nearly three-fourths of the island' (677, 678–9). But now there is added a rationale in *wage-induced substitution against labour*: 'As a matter of science, [Leslie] justly criticises the sweeping generalization which assumes that whatever reduces the supply of labour must proportionally raise wages, without regard to the effect which, in certain economic conditions, even a small rise in the price of labour may produce on the demand . . .'

It is clear that Mill himself had fully absorbed neither the theoretical implications of this view nor the empirical implications. We are left with an extraordinary spectacle – Mill's apparent abandonment of what had been throughout his life the very key to the poverty problem. Yet we must tread carefully. There is first the mysterious qualification – in certain economic conditions! Secondly, it still remains true that control of the population growth rate to coincide with a deceleration in accumulation is required to prevent falling wages. Substituting against labour is not an issue in this context. (Similarly, population control is still in order to assure that increased wages, when initially due to technological progress, are maintained at the higher level.) More generally, in a growth context the implications of the new view are dampened – what is required to assure a given rise in standards is a relatively higher rate of capital accumulation than otherwise. But in a stationary state – and one of Mill's arguments for such a state was its potential for the encouragement of population control (above, pp. 886–7) – the new view plays havoc.

VI THE CHARGE OF 'SCIENTISM'

The term 'scientism' has been coined to designate the belief that an extension of scientific and engineering techniques can legitimately be made to the study of society with the promise of similarly impressive results. The term is due to Hayek who was particularly incensed by the 'historicism' of the Saint-Simonians – their attribution to the social sciences of the task of discovering the 'natural laws' of the progress of civilization, supposedly as 'necessary' as that of gravitation, from which perspective derived a penchant for collectivist social engineering (Hayek, 1941b, 1942–4; also in Hayek, 1955). For Hayek, the characteristic 'subjectivism' of the social sciences – the role of motive, knowledge, expectation and so forth – ruled out the parallel and precluded, above all, long-term historical prediction. It was Hayek's view that Mill had been early on infected by Saint-Simon and subsequently by Comte and he cites the motto (from Condorcet) to Book VI of the *System of Logic* to that effect: 'The only foundation for the knowledge of the natural sciences is the idea that the general laws, known or unknown, which regulate the phenomena of the universe, are necessary and constant; and why should that principle be less true for the intellectual and moral facilities of man than for the other actions of nature' (1941b, 13; cf. *CW*, VIII, 912). Knight (1956 [1947]) has taken a similar view; and so has Popper (1963, II, 87) who cites Mill's statement that 'the fundamental problem . . . of the social science, is to find the law according to which any state of society produces the state which succeeds it and takes its place' (*CW*, VIII, 912), and (regarding the historical method) that 'by its aid we may hereafter succeed not only in looking far forward into the future history of the human race, but in determining what artificial means may be used, and to what extent, to accelerate the natural progress in so far as it is beneficial . . .' (929).

Yet this perspective on Mill's position does not ring true. It is certainly not suggested by our analysis of Mill's methodology as formulated in the early essay. On the contrary: that specific prediction was ruled out even in the specialist social sciences such as political economy is a key theme of that work and much attention is paid to the complexities of application. But there is also the early letter to Gustave d'Eichthal of October 1829 (above, p. 90) – a beautiful formulation of some of the special problems in social science which, Mill maintained, the Saint-Simonians had failed completely to appreciate, a criticism engendered especially by Comte's *Système de Politique Positive* (1823). Now the criticism proceeds immediately with the fundamentally important observation that Comte's error flowed from his preclusion of the characteristic problem in social science – that of choice between ends. He had transformed the social into a purely technological problem by this procedure:

It appears to me therefore that most French philosophers are chargeable with the fault . . . of insisting upon only seeing *one* thing when there are many, or seeing a thing only on one side, only in one point of view when there are many others equally essential to a just estimate of it . . . [This fault] pervades [Comte's] whole book; & it seems to me, it is this fault which alone enables him to give his ideas that compact & systematic form by which they are rendered in appearance something like a *science positive*. To begin with the very first and fundamental principle of the whole system, that government and the social union exist for the purpose of concentrating and directing all the forces of society to some one end (*CW*, XII, 36).

In the *System of Logic* the major problems of applied social science are further elaborated following the lines established in the essay, leading to Mill's conclusion that social science, precisely because it is 'insufficient for prediction' has to be distinguished from astronomy the data of which are relatively few and stable (see the discussion above, pp. 132–3 regarding *CW*, VIII, 877–8, 898).

Now Mill, of course, devoted attention in the *System of Logic* to the inverse deductive or historical method, and it is these chapters which most preoccupy those who charge him with 'scientism'. The problem defined there is 'to ascertain [the empirical laws of progress], and connect them with the laws of human nature, by deductions showing that such were the derivative laws naturally to be expected as the consequence of those ultimate ones' (916).[59] And the exercise is designed to yield genuine causal laws of progress extending beyond empirical generalization, with which 'we may . . . be prepared to predict the future with reasonable foresight; we may be in possession of the real *law* of the future; and may be able to declare on what circumstances the continuance of the same onward movement will eventually depend' (791).

Yet it is unlikely whether Mill meant, by the foregoing, positive prediction; he probably intended *tendencies* as he certainly did in the simpler specialist branches – secular tendencies extending beyond the limits of individual countries and periods, knowledge of which would permit policy makers to exercise intelligent judgement.[60] Moreover, he had no illusions about the magnitude of the task. For one thing the programme could scarcely proceed

59   The normal sequence appropriate in specialist branches of social science was inapplicable because of the complexity involved – namely, to set out from principles of human nature and 'determine the order in which human development must take place, and to predict, consequently, the general facts of history up to the present time' (915–16).
In his *Autobiography* (*CW*, I, 219), Mill attributes the inverse deductive method to Comte and defines it thus: 'instead of arriving at its conclusions by general reasoning and verifying them by specific experience (as is the natural order in the deductive branches of physical science), it obtains its generalizations by a collation of specific experience, and verifies them by ascertaining whether they are such as would follow from known general principles'.

60   Cf. 930. The passage cited by Popper (above, p. 756) does not necessarily bear an authoritarian connotation any more than similar statements in the context of the specialist social sciences.

without development of the science of human character formation, or ethology, whereby to arrive at the requisite principles of human nature, and he was perfectly aware of the absence of such foundation (906, cf. 914–5). We certainly know how impatient he was with Comte's presumptions (cf. above, pp. 173–4, regarding the *Discours sur l'ensemble du Positivisme* (1848). Most important is Mill's warning that 'the more highly the science of ethology is cultivated, and the better the diversities of individual and national character are understood, the smaller, probably, will the number of propositions become, which it will be considered safe to build on universal principles of human nature' 906). Accordingly, there always existed a danger of claiming too much for empirical generalizations – 'the common wisdom of common life'.[61]

The significance of the chapters on historical progress in fact lies in the caution (864) that in the absence of genuine causal laws of a secular order there was the greatest danger of attributing excessive power to the specialist social sciences (such as political economy) based as they are on locally-relevant and impermanent axioms. Mill's warnings of the limited scope of economics bear repeating to this day.

VII THE EMPIRICAL DIMENSION: ON THE 'REALITY' OF AXIOMS AND MODEL IMPROVEMENT

The role accorded 'induction' in the derivation of individual axioms and in model improvement are central to the early essay, and that essay Mill intended his readers to have at hand in 1848. It will be useful, for purposes of summary, to take a brief overview of Mill's actual practice in the *Principles* from this perspective with particular reference to the self-interest axiom.

We must, first, set aside an unnecessary terminological complexity, turning on the technical usage of 'wealth' to exclude services. This usage has led some commentators to assert that Mill's maximizing individuals concern themselves solely with material goods (e.g. Bowley, 1937, 46–7, 61, 63). In fact Mill had in mind nothing more than the rule that individuals seek to sell goods and services at the highest price attainable and to buy at the lowest price attainable, that 'buying as well as selling is a matter of business; in which buyers take pains to know, and generally do know, the lowest price at which an article of a given quality can be obtained' (*CW*, III, 460). The consequence of such behaviour combined with other

---

61 The passage cited above (p. 113) from *CW*, VIII, 791 is particularly important here. Grossman (1948) refers to William Playfair (1805) as 'the earliest theorist of capitalist development' and argues that Mill 'carefully read' him (80n). But Mill strenuously rejected any approach that made too much of 'empirical laws', and some of the instances given in the *System of Logic* suggest that if he had Playfair in mind, it was as guilty party.

assumptions relating to large numbers and free entry is a single price for the same good (or service) in one market – the 'Jevons rule' which characterizes competition; and, as we know, 'only through the principle of competition has political economy any pretension to the character of science' subject to 'principles of broad generality and scientific precision' (II, 239).

That the maximizing man in the *Principles* refers to the real man in the market place rather than a psychological fiction comes to light with stark clarity in Mill's restriction of the economic analysis of pricing to the wholesale sector. This restriction turns on the observation that buyers at retail outlets do not typically make their purchases 'on business principles' – a reflection of their indolence, carelessness, satisfaction derived from paying high prices, ignorance, defective judgement as well as high search costs and coercion (III, 460; above, p. 266). Equally conspicuous is the discussion of the motives governing employers of domestics (and of clerks) which explain why more is often paid than the 'competitive' wage, in terms of 'obstentation' and a variety of 'more reasonable motives' all of which turn on the personal contact between employee and employer (II, 398–9; above, p. 312). This case-study provides a very clear indication that the assumption of wealth maximization is pertinent to the anonymous market place where personal contacts are reduced to a minimum precluding the range of considerations in question. Quite clearly Mill was fully at one with Smith regarding the supposed empirical accuracy of the maximizing assumption in the capitalist-exchange environment, and more specifically the limitations imposed by that environment on a range of 'self-interested' forms of behaviour (but see Blaug, 1980, 61, for a different perspective).

Marshall maintained of Ricardo and his followers that they 'often spoke as though they regarded man as a constant quantity, and they never gave themselves enough trouble to study his variations' (1920, 762). While little harm was done in the contexts of money and trade they were 'led astray' particularly in that of distribution: Their predilection 'caused them to speak of labour as a commodity without staying to throw themselves into the point of view of the workman; and without dwelling upon the allowances to be made for his human passions, his instincts and habits, his sympathies and antipathies, his class jealousies and class adhesiveness, his want of knowledge and of the opportunities for free and vigorous action. They therefore attributed to the forces of supply and demand a much more mechanical and regular action than is to be found in real life: and they laid down laws with regard to profits and wages that did not really hold even for England in their own time' (762–3). Marshall did not include Mill of the *Principles* in this charge; it was rather Mill of the essay who was supposedly guilty, Marshall supposing that it was written under the influence of James Mill (764–5n.; see also above, p. 163). Now we have argued that this is an unjustified reading of the origins and substance of the essay. As for the *Principles*, Marshall was right in that Mill did not there apply the principles of supply and demand 'mechanically', either in the context of commodity or of service pricing. Yet he took great pains to avoid disparaging competitive pricing, and in so doing *reinforced* the importance of classical theorizing even from an empirical perspective.

His course of action involves the matter of 'disturbing causes' so central to the formal discussion of method. Consider the declaration that while 'there is no proposition which meets us in the field of political economy more often than this – that there cannot be two prices in the same market . . . yet every one knows that there are, almost always two prices, in the same market' (*CW*, II, 242). The solution adopted by Mill in effect is to treat non-maximizing behaviour in the retail sector as involving 'disturbing causes' in pricing – in principle the responsibility of 'some other science'. But this it must be stressed has an empirical justification, in so far as the primary force at work – that governing the determination of the underlying wholesale price – remained pecuniary maximization.

The latter procedure can be further illustrated by reference to the allowance in the essay that the 'perpetually antagonistic principles to the desire of wealth', namely 'aversion to labour, and desire of the present enjoyment of costly indulgences', are in practice taken into account by economics 'to a certain extent' precisely because of their empirical pervasiveness (above, p. 107). This matter is much amplified in the *Principles*, where it is clarified that by desire of wealth is intended pecuniary maximization and by the two antagonistic forces in question a willingness to bypass an opportunity to increase the return per hour or per unit of capital, by movement between sectors, or to forego a bargain in commodity markets. Thus Mill observed regarding continental Europe 'that prices and charges, of some or of all sorts, are much higher in some places than in others not far distant, without its being possible to assign any other cause than that it has always been so: the customers are used to it, and acquiesce in it' (244). Similarly, 'an enterprising competitor, with sufficient capital, might force down the charges, and make his fortune during the process; but there are no enterprising competitors; those who have capital prefer to leave it where it is, or to make less profit by it in a more quiet way'. The same could be said of labour. Now in the British case too, where 'the spirit of competition' is the strongest, custom was still a 'powerful influence'; but in other environments people were 'content with smaller gains, and estimate their pecuniary interest at a lower rate when balanced against their ease or their pleasure'. Clearly Mill intended more than a quantitative difference between Britain and the Continent. In the latter kind of environment the force of the wealth-maximization motive was swamped by the antagonistic motives so that little could be said of the response to a newly created wage or profit differential or a reduction in price; havoc was wrought as far as concerns 'predictions' regarding labour and capital flows or rates of consumption with price change. In the British case there were strong empirical presumptions favouring the process of equalization of returns to labour and to capital, and also the negative slope to the demand curve and thus a tendency to stable equilibrium in competitive markets – at least up to the retail stage.

Thus it is that Mill appeals to the empirical accuracy of the behavioural axiom in his discussion of profit-rate equalization (cost pricing): 'If the value of a commodity is such that it repays the cost of production not only with the customary, but with a higher rate of profit, capital rushes to share in this extra gain, and by increasing the supply of the article reduces its value. This is not a mere supposition or surmise, but a fact familiar to those conversant with commercial operations' (III, 472). We recall too the obvious appeal to the real world of business and the complexity of entrepreneurial decision making in the context of what we have called 'internal adjustment' to cost variation (above, pp. 292–3).

The same perspective emerges in Mill's general analysis of the wage structure with special reference to his allowance for non-competing groups. A variety of features of the real world, conspicuously the impediments to mobility of a financial and social order, underlay his dissatisfaction with Smithian analysis and it was his growing optimism regarding a breakdown of the impediments that ultimately led him to conclude that while 'there are few kinds of [skilled] labour of which the remuneration would not be lower than it is, if the employer took the full advantage of competition' yet competition 'must be regarded, in the present state of society as the principal regulator of wages, and custom or individual character only as a modifying circumstance, and that in a comparatively slight degree' (II, 337).

Moreover, the existence of unusual cases is never denied. The most striking are the instances of excessive entry as in the literary professions (392) or the Canadian timber trade (383–4) generating negative returns even in equilibrium in consequence of the 'principal of human nature' such that a few great prizes stimulates miscalculation. But this principle too was treated as a 'modifying circumstance' in going conditions.'

That the primary behaviour axiom holds good as a first approximation is thus justified on purely empirical grounds as we were led to expect from the essay. But here we must note the fundamentally important caution regarding the allowances that have to be made in practice, a caution that appears following recognition of possible cases of permanent inequalities in the return on capital:

These observations must be received as a general correction to be applied whenever relevant, whether expressly mentioned or not, to the conclusions contained in the subsequent portions of this treatise. Our reasonings must, in general, proceed as if the known and natural effects of competition were actually produced by it, in all cases where it is not restrained by some positive obstacle. Where competition, though free to exist, does not exist, or where it exists, but has its natural consequences overruled by any other agency, the conclusions will fail more or less of being applicable. To escape error, we ought, in applying the conclusions of political economy to the actual affairs of life, to consider not only what will happen supposing the maximum of competition, but how far the result will be affected if competition falls short of the maximum (244).

Again this too reflects what is said in the essay namely that verification of the hypothesis is 'no part of the business of science, but of the application of science'. But it must be understood with all the qualifications outlined in our account of the earlier work (above, p. 126f).

As in the essay, so in the *Principles* we find that Mill allows the absorption into his economic models of market forms that do not fit the purely competitive model. What we have to say on this matter is pertinent to an evaluation of the view that, from Mill's perspective, 'we never test the *validity* of theories, because the conclusions are true as one aspect of human behaviour by virtue of being based on self-evident facts of human experience' (Blaug, 1980, 77). That the notion of 'self-evident' facts is suspect we know already; what emerges, however, is the further circumstance that Mill does attempt model improvement based upon testing against the record; much more is involved than 'a search . . . for sufficient supplementary causes to close the gap between the facts and the causal antecedents laid down in the theory' (75).

Model improvement as defined in the essay is the hoped for consequence of the process of testing against the evidence. Thus, for example, the economist is duty bound to assure himself of the operation of the various tendencies incorporated within his model, and something would be amiss in the event of an unexplained residual. In some instances a new disturbing cause would be discovered which in future use of theory has to be kept in mind – as instanced by the obstacles to wage-rate equalization which Mill's empirical studies brought to light. But model improvement in consequence of verification might be more substantive, taking the form of 'inserting among its hypotheses a fresh and still more complex combination of circumstances, and so adding *pro hâc vice* a supplementary chapter or appendix, or at least a supplementary theorem to the abstract science' (above, p. 124). Thus the exclusion of monopoly from the scientific domain and its treatment as a disturbing cause turns out to be purely a formal matter; in practice Mill admitted that it had 'always been allowed for by political economists' and himself applied the tools of analysis to this case (above, p. 301). Even more striking, he allowed in practice for the absorption of custom – again formally a 'disturbing cause' – where custom establishes prices yet competition acts to reduce profits to the economy-wide rate by reducing market size – the 'monopolistic competition' model (above, pp. 301–2). Here then we have two splendid illustrations of the observation in the essay that 'disturbing causes . . . which operate through the same law of human nature out of which the general principles of the science arise . . . might always be brought within the pale of the abstract science, if it were worthwhile' (above, p. 124).[62]

Equally striking is Mill's recognition of (short-run) excess demand for money to hold (above, p. 498). This too illustrates model improvement, in this case a consequence of the 'anomaly' of contemporaneous excess labour and capital which forced itself on his attention after his escape from his father's influence. And the idea of an endogenous trade cycle is better developed by Mill than any contemporary (above, p. 461f) and clearly related to real-world events.[63]

The inverse wage-profit relation itself provides a fine case study of this theme. A conspicuous application during the 1860s of the theorem on distribution (in terms of Ricardian 'money' wages based upon a stable measure) involves the relative magnitude of the return on capital in Britain and in the United States. This attempt to subject the theory to a process of testing is impressive evidence of continued lively intellectual interest in Ricardian doctrine, and confirms – if further confirmation is still required – the longevity of that doctrine.

The 'anomaly' Mill encountered arose from his insistence that on Ricardian principles the profit rate in the US should have been lower than in Britain, whereas in fact the interest rate was certainly higher and, by implication, the profit rate too. Correspondence on this matter with Cairnes commenced in December 1864:

Have you formed any opinion, or can you refer me to any good authority, respecting the ordinary rate of mercantile and manufacturing profit in the United States? I have hitherto been under the impression that it is much higher than in England, because the rate of interest is so. But I have lately been led to doubt the truth of this impression, because it seems inconsistent with known facts respecting wages

---

62 It is scarcely surprising that Mill excluded 'small numbers' market structures from the domain of political economy. After all, Edgeworth much later did the same, pointing out that '[a]mong those who would suffer by the new regime there would be . . . the abstract economists, who would be deprived of their occupation, the investigation of the conditions which determine value. There would survive only the empirical school, flourishing in a chaos congenial to their mentality' (1925), I, 138–9.

63 Allowance for varying quality is a further interesting illustration; cf. Mill's explanation of the failure of prices to rise as expected in consequence of gold inflows which runs in terms of a deterioration of the quality of commodities (letter of 15 Sept. 1863, XV, 882).

in America. High profits are compatible with a high reward of the labourer through low prices of necessaries, but they are not compatible with a high cost of labour, and it seems to me that the very high *money* wages of labour in America, the precious metals not being of lower value there than in Europe, indicates a high cost as well as a high remuneration of labour (*CW*, XV, 967; also in III, 1055).

The higher US interest rate, Mill himself went on to suggest, might be accounted for by the fact that investment was, by and large, of European (not home) origin and this required an extra inducement (968). Yet he remained uneasy and appealed for more precise statistical data that might throw light on the issue (XVI, 985–6; III, 1088–9).[64] 'I am much obliged to you', he wrote to Cairnes soon after, 'for the trouble you have taken to get information respecting the rate of profit in the U. States, but I fear it is next to impossible to obtain any conclusive evidence on the subject. There is no more difficult point to ascertain in the whole field of statistics. The scientific question remains as great a puzzle to me as ever' (XVI, 993; III, 1092). He expressed appreciation for new data provided by Cairnes from US informants, but remained troubled by the 'scientific puzzle', involving (in effect) the apparent refutation of Ricardian distribution theory: 'From their statements it is clear that the ordinary notion of the extravagantly high rate of profit in the U. States is an exaggeration, and there seems some doubt whether the rate is at all higher than in England. But that does not resolve the puzzles, as even equality of profits, in the face of the higher cost of labour, indicated by higher money wages, is as paradoxical as superiority. This is the scientific difficulty I mentioned, and I cannot yet see my way through it. I have framed a question for the purpose of bringing it before the P. Ec. Club, which will perhaps be discussed at the April meeting and if not, at the July' (XVI, 1002; III, 1093).[65]

Cairnes himself proposed a solution which entailed a denial that the monetary units of the two centres in which wages were expressed, were comparable.[66] But Mill was not satisfied: 'Your solution of the difficulty

---

64 'Respecting the rate of profit in the United States, we must hope to learn something through the kind offices of Mr. Moran. But it is, I imagine, very difficult to ascertain the real average rate of profit, or expectation of profit, in any country. It would, however, be something to have an answer to the more vague question, whether, in the opinion of Mr. Ashworth, or other persons to whom business in both countries is familiar, the profits of capital in the United States are or are not, higher than in England.'

65 Mill's question, discussed at the meeting of 7 July, was: 'Does the high rate of Interest in America and in new Colonies indicate a corresponding high rate of profit? and if so, What are the causes of that high rate?' (*Political Economy Club*, 1921, 84).

66 'I have indeed hitherto taken the supposed high rate of profit in the U.S. for granted.

as to American profits is perfectly scientific, and was the one which had occurred to myself. As far as it goes, I fully admit it; but my difficulty was, and still is, in believing that there can be *so great* a difference between the cost of obtaining the precious metals in America and in England, as to make the enormous difference which seems to exist in money wages, consistent with a difference the contrary way in the cost of labour' (XVI, 1009; III, 1093–4). The formulation in the *Principles* regarding the American profit rate is slightly altered for the edition of 1865 'so as to leave the subject open for further inquiry' (II, 414).

Cairnes was evidently somewhat piqued by Mill's refusal to settle the matter entirely on his terms.[67] But he then suggested that the difference flowed from their different formulations of the theory of profits:

Am I guilty of arrogance in suspecting that the difference between us here – my inability to perceive the difficulty of which you are sensible – is due to the greater simplicity of the theory of profit through which I look at the phenomena? – I refer to that mode of stating the doctrine – differing from yours and Ricardo's only in form – of which a sketch was contained in the papers I sent you [III, 1048–50; see above, p. 000]. Of course if the theory, thus stated, failed to embrace any essential condition, this would be simply its condemnation; but it appears to me to embrace all the conditions included in your doctrine of 'cost of labour', and it renders the phenomena in the case with which we are now concerned unless I deceive myself perfectly intelligible. Might I ask as a favour, when you come to deal with this question at your leisure, that you would consider once again that mode of stating the theory (III, 1094).

Unfortunately Cairnes did not specify precisely what he intended by raising his corn-profit formulation; and Mill was evidently unconvinced. After observing that he preferred his own formulation of the theory of profits

The high rate of *money* wages certainly would make one suspect the correctness of this view, but the fact is not conclusive. The precious metals may not be lower *in value* in America than in Europe, but their *cost* is certainly lower; the only question is whether it is so much lower as to render the high rate of money wages which prevails consistent, with a rate of profit also higher than, or as high as, in this country'. Cairnes also believed that Mill's suggestion that the US interest rate might be a poor reflection of the profit rate had some merit: 'In what you say on the rate of interest in its relation to profit I entirely concur' (III, 1057; cf. 1060n.; O'Brien, 1943, 280).

67 'I see my observations on American wages and profits in their connexion with the theory of profit did not hit the mark; and I fear I must now relinquish the hope – I might say the ambition – of doing this, as on the assumption that the exposition I gave was correct – which you concede to me – I am unable to perceive where the difficulty lies: in short, the scientific problem seems to me to be solved. For the rest, it is (to my apprehension) merely a matter of evidence whether money wages and profits *are*, at one and the same time, so high as is alleged: if they *are* – then the fact on the assumption that my exposition was

he cryptically suggested that he had hit on a satisfactory solution to the apparent anomaly: 'I am inclined to think that the real solution of the difficulty, and the only one it admits of, has been given by myself in a subsequent place' (XVI, 1018–9; III, 1095). This hit home; in his reply Cairnes was far less confident of the significance of his corn-profit formulation: 'Thank you for looking over my note on profits again: I suppose it must be that I overrate the importance of my form of stating the theory . . .' (III, 1095). The proposed solution although not spelled out in detail reverts to the cost of obtaining the precious metals – a line Mill had himself originally abandoned – as elaborated in the chapter 'Of Money, Considered as an Imported Commodity' which takes into account the broad implications of the general theory of international values including transportation costs (619–20).

We have in this episode a patently honest attempt to 'test' Ricardian theory against the evidence, Mill going to considerable lengths to acquire reliable data. The outcome is a strengthening of the under-pinnings of the basic model. It is impossible to tell what steps Mill would have taken had he remained unable to account for the empirical record. But until such time, he treated the Ricardian distribution model as 'robust' – there is in his approach a basic confidence in its validity, reflecting a belief that 1817 opened up a new era in theoretical economics, which would not in all likelihood be reversed. And here Schwartz's suggestion comes into play that Mill's philosophical perspective played down the likelihood of fundamental revisions (above, note 3); it is theory 'improvement' not 'displacement' that is expected to flow from the testing process.[68]

This same perspective might well lie behind Mill's unfortunate pronouncements that the theory of (competitive) value was near perfection. Clearly Mill allowed himself to be carried away for he recognized scope

correct is conclusive, as it seems to me, that the difference between the cost of obtaining the precious metals in America and in England *is* great enough to produce the results which we see' (III, 1094; O'Brien, 1943, 282).

68 Cf. Mill's early comment regarding the physical sciences as 'continually growing, but never changing: in every age they receive indeed mighty improvements, but for them the age of transition is past' (1831; in Hayek, 1942, 20).

It is interesting that Jevons in effect left the door open for a new revolution by his criticism of Mill's philosophical perspective: 'In the writings of some recent philosophers, especially of Auguste Comte, and in some degree John Stuart Mill, there is an enormous and hurtful tendency to represent our knowledge as assuming an approximately complete character. At least these and many other writers fail to impress upon their readers a truth which cannot be too constantly borne in mind, namely, that the utmost successes which our scientific method can accomplish will not enable us to comprehend more than an infinitesimal fraction of what there doubtless is to comprehend' (1907 [1877], ed 2, 752–3); (I am grateful to Margaret Schabas for this reference).

for on-going improvement such as the contributions by Thornton. And he himself, of course, had made major contributions to the theory of equilibration (above, p. 272f). In any event what we have shown here is the flexible character of Ricardian doctrine in Mill's hands and its great relevance to matters of the day.[69]

69 That political economy seemed incapable of further substantial advance was the widely held view after mid-century. But for this Mill himself cannot be held entirely or even mainly responsible. On some pertinent matters touching on the sociology of knowledge in this regard, see Checkland (1951b), Coats (1964). De Marchi (1973b) shows that Jevons's charge that the dominance of the orthodox school must be held responsible for the 'despotic calm' does not stand up to close examination.

Attitudes towards birth control

In his youth Mill championed mechanical contraception by married couples as 'highly moral and virtuous'[1] and personally engaged in the circulation of birth-control literature (the so-called 'diabolical handbills') (Himes, 1928, 628f., Schwartz, 1972, 28–30, 245f).[2] Marriage at an early age would then be economically feasible and 'debauchery' avoided. The argument was presented as a preferable alternative to Malthus's moral restraint (delayed marriage accompanied by abstinence), for Mill had 'no belief in the efficacy of Mr. Malthus's moral check, so long as the great mass of the people are so uneducated as they are at present'.[3] As Schwartz has pointed out, the context entailed solutions to short-term unemployment, but in 1825 Mill took up the issue of solutions to long-term poverty in the face of land scarcity – Malthus's issue.[4]

As for Mill's later position, there is a letter of 1868 to the author of a birth-control manual which indicates that he remained favourably disposed, but also a hesitancy regarding the expediency of public dissemination:

I thank you for your pamphlet. Nothing can be more important than the question to which it relates, nor more laudable than the purpose it has in view. About the

---

1 Letters in the *Black Dwarf*, XI, 22, 27 Nov. 1823, 748–56, XI, 24, 10 Dec. 1823, 791–8, XII, 1, 7 Jan. 1824, 21–3.
2 The handbills are reproduced by Schwartz (1972), 245f.
3 *Black Dwarf*, XII, 1, 21f.
4 Mill addressed himself to the secular problem in a public debate. Doubtless for this reason he did not raise the question of contraception, but alluded implicitly to moral restraint. Schwartz observes 'that the Ricardians understood the Malthusian principle so vaguely that it was emptied of all empirical content; that is to say, they seemed to think that it could be used to explain any conceivable social situation'. There is some justification for this complaint, for Ricardo also had called for greater restraint on the part of labour as a solution to technological displacement (Hollander, 1979, 586).

expediency of putting it into circulation, in however quiet a manner, you are the best judge. My opinion is that the morality of the matter lies wholly between married people themselves, and that such facts as those which the pamphlet communicates ought to be made known to them by their medical advisers. But we are very far from that point at present, and in the meanwhile every one must act according to his own judgement of what is prudent and right (to T. J. Haslam, 19 Feb. 1868, *CW*, XVI, 1363–4).

Bain (1882, 89) has written of a 'veil of ambiguity' surrounding Mill's later position; and the formulations in the *Principles* are indeed vague. Mill pronounced against 'the mystery in which [the subject of population] is shrouded by a spurious delicacy, which prefers that right and wrong should be mismeasured and confounded on one of the subjects most momentous to human welfare, rather than that the subject be freely spoken of and discussed' (*CW*, II, 368). But he himself did not explicitly affirm support for contraception. On the contrary, the reader of the text could easily gain the impression that he put his faith solely in abstinence – by the married as well as the unmarried:

Who meets with the smallest condemnation, or rather, who does not meet with sympathy and benevolence, for any amount of evil which he may have brought upon himself and those dependent on him, by this species of incontinence? While a man who is intemperate in drink, is discountenanced and despised by all who profess to be moral people, it is one of the chief grounds made use of in appeals to be benevolent, that the applicant has a large family and is unable to maintain them.

That it is possible to delay marriage, and to live in abstinence while unmarried, most people are willing to allow; but when persons are once married, the idea, in this country, never seems to enter into any one's mind that having or not having a family, or the number of which it shall consist, is amenable to their own control. One would imagine that children were rained down upon married people, direct from heaven, without their being art or part in the matter; that it was really, as the common phrases have it, God's will, and not their own, which decided the numbers of their offspring (368–9).

This passage, it might be said, is consistent with the practice of contraception as well as abstinence; and so it is. But Mill then cites Sismondi's view (in the context of a stationary state) that '[u]ne fois que cette famille est formée', (and after the birth of the due number of children) 'la justice et l'humanité exigent qu'il s'impose la même contrainte à laquelle se soummettent les célibataires' – which implies abstinence. This is further reinforced by allusions to the hope that a reformed public opinion would encourage a diminution of the 'animal propensity', for in Mill's view 'over-indulgence is as much caused by the stimulus of opinion as by the mere animal propensity' while 'opinion universally, and especially among the most uneducated classes, has [hitherto] connected ideas of spirit and power with the strength of the instinct, and of inferiority with its moderation or absence; a perversion of sentiment caused by its being the means, and the stamp, of a dominion exercised over other human beings' (371).[5]

Mill thus left ambiguous his position regarding mechanical birth control, and gave an impression that he relied on moral restraint by the married and the unmarried. Here we may have a nice instance of the significance of biography, for 'had he been a public advocate of birth control, what extraordinary evidence would have been lent to the accusations already afloat' regarding the nature of his liaison with Mrs. Taylor (Himes, 1929, 481). If this is so then he sacrificed his scientific obligations for personal motives. Mill's procrastinations should be compared with the extraordinary courage of 'the parson Malthus', Marx's derogatory term (Levy, 1978, Hollander, 1985).

5 Cf. also II, 372–3 regarding the probable role of liberated women in assuring a desirable outcome. Levy (1980), 6n; 31, presumes the passage refers to prospects for the practice of contraception. But there is no justification for this presumption. For Mill the issue of population control ranged far beyond the maintenance of standards. Even if there was potential for the unrestricted growth rate of undiminished wages he would have been opposed on grounds of women's rights: '[Y]ou appear to think that no one ought to be blamed for having an inordinately large family if he produces, & brings them up to produce, enough for their support: now this with me is only a part & even a small part of the question . . . limitation of the number of children would be in my opinion absolutely necessary to place human life on its proper footing, even if there were subsistence for any number that could be produced' (to [Henry?] Green, 8 April 1852, XIV, 88–9).

The Hubbard Issue

Mill in 1862 represented Hubbard as 'the first person who, as a practical legislator, has attempted the rectification of the income tax on principles of unimpeachable justice, and whose well-conceived plan wants little of being as near an approximation to a just assessment as it is likely that means could be found of carrying into practical effect . . .' (*CW*, III, 817n). It proves helpful to have at hand Hubbard's memorandum.

J. G. HUBBARD, 'MEMORANDUM SUBMITTED TO THE CHAIRMAN.'
APPENDIX 1 TO THE REPORT OF THE SELECT COMMITTEE ON INCOME
AND PROPERTY TAX, *PARLIAMENTARY PAPERS*, 1861, VII, 315–17.

The Committee being appointed under the same terms as the Committee of 1851, will naturally avail itself of the Evidence and Report communicated to The House of Commons in 1852; but they will be in no degree fettered by the course taken in the former inquiry.

The Property and Income Tax, although in continuous action since 1842, has been and is more than ever now the result of an exigency – a tax accepted because temporary – a tax expiring by virtue of the law which imposed it. In reality, therefore, the inquiry is not 'What change shall be made in an active and permanent law?' but, 'How shall the Income Tax be framed of which the imposition may now or at any future time be requisite?' And it is important to keep in view that, substituted in 1842 for taxes levied on articles of general consumption, the Income Tax has thus far assumed the character of a tax of compensation.

It will assist in limiting discussion to the real purpose of this scheme if I commence by disclaiming objects which I do not entertain. I, therefore, distinctly repudiate any desire to introduce a graduated tax – one, that is, bearing in a heavier ratio on large than on small incomes. All such attempts to favour the less wealthy at the expense of the more wealthy portion of the community are the errors of socialism, and destructive of the rights of property. Neither do I desire to favour the industrial members of the community by encroachments on those who subsist on the fruits of invested property, or to obtain any advantage for one kind of property, or for one class of industry. I know no object but to regulate this mighty engine of taxation upon the principles which, being in harmony with scientific rules, will be just for each, and beneficial for all.

Adam Smith's axiom, 'the subjects of every State ought to contribute towards the support of the Government as nearly as possible in proportion to their respective abilities, that is, in proportion to the revenue which they respectively enjoy under the protection of the State', must be taken as the test of the true policy of taxation; but in its application it is obvious that we must deal with classes and not with individuals, and that arguments founded on contrasts of wealthy individuals of one class with poor individuals in another class, are altogether inadmissible in an inquiry dispassionately pursued in the cause of truth and justice.

In this, as in many other questions, the controversy would be soon concluded if the disputants were agreed in their definitions. The subject of our consideration is an 'Income' Tax. What is 'Income' for the purpose of taxation? not assuredly all that *comes in* to a man's possession in the course of a year.

Compare 10,000 l. *in-coming* as a dividend in Consols, with 10,000 l. *in-coming* as rent of land, of which 1,000 l. *out-goes* for repairs; or with 10,000 l. *in-coming* as rent of houses, of which 1,500 l. *out-goes* for repairs, and it is clear that until deduction is made of the out-goings, you have not a net income – an income available for expenditure – an income proper for taxation. And as, again, the *in-coming* or maturing of an Exchequer bond – of a Railway bond – or of a private loan, does not form part of a taxable income, so neither does the *in-coming* of a loan to Government, in the medium of a terminable annuity, form part of a taxable income. The income for which men may be taxed is, as Adam Smith says, 'the revenue which they enjoy', or, in other words, the net income available for expenditure.

The existing tax is called the 'Property and Income Tax'. Why it is so called is not apparent. It does truly, in many instances, tax both property and the income arising from the property, but it is not probable that to declare the special vice of the tax was the intention of its double name. Obviously, however, the same tax should not be a Property and an Income Tax; and while a tax on the transfer of property may rightly be a Property Tax, occurring as it would at intervals of many years, so an annual tax necessarily payable out of income should be an Income Tax. It would consist with the views of an influential class of financial reformers to make even an Income Tax so far a Property Tax as to confine its incidence to the annual products of property; but the fact that the Income Tax, as a tax of compensation – substituted (that is) for taxes which, attaching to articles of general consumption, affected alike (to the extent of their expenditure) the owners of property incomes and the owners of industrial incomes – is conclusive in establishing the liability of the latter to taxation within the specified limits.

In attempting to re-adjust the Income Tax in harmony with the principles I have enumerated, I am aiming at the removal of defects acknowledged by every living statesman, and deemed by them so serious as to involve, if unredressed, the absolute rejection of the tax itself. Yet I am far from hoping that an Income Tax can ever be free from objections; the necessity of relying upon the co-operation of the tax-payers in the assessment of industrial incomes is a very grievous one, for the temptation to dishonesty must work evil, and the revision is proposed not so much with a view to the perpetuity of the tax as to qualify it for its office when it is indispensable, by a very decided mitigation both of its corrupting influence and of its unjust and unequal incidence. If this object be a desirable one, we must be content, for the sake of the great majority of cases which will obtain substantial justice, to tolerate some unimportant anomalies and apparent inconsistencies.

I have ranked the incomes now divided between Schedules A, B, C, D, and E, under two classes. The first class contains the incomes arising from or ascribed to the possession of real property in this country – from money lent – from pensions – and from investments in public companies of every kind. In the case of incomes subject to out-goings, the net income is to be obtained (for assessment) by such deductions as may be necessary for that purpose. The evidence which may be obtained by the Committee may determine the extent of the allowance which lands and houses may severally require. Tithe rent-charge, with cure of souls, I have treated as an income contingent on a duty performed, and as the remuneration for that duty, I propose a specific allowance of 100l. The net incomes of the first class from l. upwards will be assessed alike; they will be assessed at the source: rents in the hands of the occupier; dividends in the hands of the companies; interest in the hands of the borrower; and pensions in the hands of the agent of the Government. Tithes or commuted tithes, legally assessable in the hands of the payers, may, for convenience sake, be taxed in the possession of the receiver. The characteristic of all these incomes is that, consequent on the possession of the property from which they arise, they accrue spontaneously, and require no exercise of labour on the part of the owners; and I would add that I not only do not desire, but, on the contrary, condemn any proposition for treating incomes of this class differentially, in virtue of any artificial peculiarity in the tenure of the owners.

In the second class, I place incomes derived from the 'profits accruing from trades and professions; and for the purpose of assessment it is necessary to ascertain what proportion of such profits pass into the character of 'income,' available for expenditure, and so far taxable. Whether these profits are the receipts of the professional man whose capital is in his cultivated knowledge – those of the trader whose capital is in his goods – or those of the manufacturer whose capital is in his machinery – the same essential feature characterises them. The labour of these men is an indispensable element in the production of their profits; ability to labour is dependent upon life and health; their profits are, consequently, precarious; and in obedience to the suggestions of prudence, the owners of industrial and precarious profits apply a portion only of those profits as income to the purpose of expenditure. The residue of those profits passes into the character of capital, and, as capital, yields in the following year products for taxation. I have assumed the proper deduction from industrial profits, before rating them on a parity with spontaneous incomes, to be one-third, upon the following computation:-

It is estimated, in a table prepared by Mr. Farr (Appendix to Second Report on Income Tax, folio 463), that the aggregated incomes of persons having 30 l. or upwards, may be 316,380,000 l.; and the late Mr. Porter valued at 80,000,000 l. the annual increase in the real and personal property of the country. If these estimates severally approach the truth, it follows that one-fourth part of the income of the community is saved from expenditure, and becomes capital. It further appears that the income assessed under Schedules A and C, and arising therefore from funded, landed, and other realised property, is equal in amount to that which is assessed under B, D, and E, the aggregate, that is, of industrial incomes.

The amount of income which would be comprised in an area of taxation extended to include incomes of 75 l. a year would be about 240,000,000 l.; and of this, one-fourth, if saved, would be 60,000,000 l. Of realised property incomes, how much is annually saved? I cannot rate the proportion higher than 1-10th, or upon 120,000,000 l. = 12,000,000 l.; and this would leave 48,000,000 l., or 4-10ths of their aggregate amount, to be supplied from the savings of industrial incomes.

I admit that this is an arbitrary estimate of the savings respectively effected out of spontaneous and industrial incomes; but it accords with every one's observation, that the class which makes is essentially the class which saves, and that the habit of accumulating is its especial characteristic. The percentage of abatement which I have assumed is in exact agreement with the average results of the capitalisation plan approved by the actuaries in 1852; and, with that support, I submit it to the consideration of the Committee.

It may be well now to anticipate a question as to the principle and mode of distinguishing trading profits classed as industrial from dividends payable by trading companies, which I have classed with spontaneous incomes.

In one sense *all* incomes are dependent upon labour; neither rents – interest of money – dividends of companies – nor dividends in the funds, can accrue without the labour of those who till the land – employ the money – work for the company, or out of their industry provide the revenue to pay the public dividends; but the sense in which I have called incomes spontaneous is this, – the labour of the owners of those incomes is not requisite for their production, they are to them the perennial growth of their invested capital, and in this quality available in the largest proportion for their enjoyment or expenditure, and, as a consequence, liable to taxation in the same proportion.

In a trading company, the labour of the clerks, managers, and directors, is all paid for; reserves are made for depreciation, casualties, or exhaustion, and the dividends represent the net return for the invested capital.

Compare with such a company a private brewery, the most stable, in general estimation, of manufacturing trades. The management and super-vision is carried on by the partners in the firm: some may provide the capital; some the supervision; but the profits of the brewery compromise the returns for the capital and the remuneration for the management; they are industrial profits, divisible amongst the partners in the firm. But it may be said that of those partners some are sleeping partners, buying possibly their share in the brewery, and contributing no personal labour to the production of the profits which they receive. This is more or less the case in all large establishments – the money of one partner and the skill of another are the titles to their respective shares; but it is the entity of the partnership – the '*firm*' of the brewery which is assessed, and the supposed difficulty does not arise in a practical way. That between a sleeping partner in a large brewery and a share-holder in a brewing company there may be no important differences, so far as their personal fortunes are concerned, might be admitted, without recognising in these individual cases (untouched as they are by the operation of the tax) any impeachment of the reality of the distinction contended for, or any reason why for such or even more serious difficulties the great measure of justice as between class and class should be relinquished. By placing in the first class the dividends of all companies registered under the Joint Stock Companies Acts, I believe that an effective line will be drawn.

I have included farmers amongst those whose industrial profits require an abatement before taxation; but I am not sufficiently familiar with that industry to judge, except on further evidence, whether any improvement on the existing plan of treatment is open to the committee.

Shipping property presents many instances of the sleeping partnerships, the bearing of which I have already considered in a brewery; they may constitute seeming anomalies, but they offer no practical difficulties.

Possessions have been by some authorities on this question treated as requiring a separate category. Professional men, it has been remarked, have no capital contributing to their profits, which are purely the result of their personal exertion, and they should be estimated for assessment upon a more indulgent scale than applies to the combined gains of capital and labour in trading profits. Undoubtedly, the elements of the trading and professional profits are not identical; but I am not prepared to indicate either a separate principle of treatment, or to affirm that it would be practicable always to distinguish *professions* from *trades*, or to obtain from traders the amounts of their capital in trade which would be requisite for the separate assessment of the annual value of their capital, and of the gains created by labour apart from capital. I am disposed, on the contrary, to think that trading profits must be dealt with in their entirety: the capital apart from the labour would be unfruitful; the labour would be unemployed but for the capital. I look upon trading profits as the products of capital fructified by labour, and as entitled to the abatement proposed alike for all industrial incomes.

The incomes thus far enumerated derived from farms, trades, manufactures, shipping, and professions, can only be assessed with the concurrence of the tax-payer – a reason which (apart from the justice of the case) strongly commends the policy of an indulgent treatment; the remaining item salaries may be taxed in the hands of the employers generally, as it is already done partially.

Foreign property, whether securities or possessions, we have lastly to consider. Much of such property may be realised property in its own locality, but in its own locality it is also subject to taxation. Recognising, however, the difference which may exist between incomes arising from foreign property and those which are strictly professional or industrial, it is submitted that their commercial origin, their liability to taxation by the foreign power which protects them, are reasons sufficient to entitle them to a mitigated assessment here; and the powerful practical motive for concession must not be forgotten, that the assessment is mainly in the hands of the interested parties.

Occupying the debateable ground at which skilled labour commences, industrial incomes, varying from 100 l. to 150 l., may in that view be allowed to retain the concession awarded to them by the present Act, of being charged more lightly than incomes exceeding 150 l.

At what amount the assessment of first class incomes should commence, and whether those of small amount should receive any concession, are questions of which the decision of the Committee may be guided by the evidence to be heard, and upon which I therefore forbear an opinion.

I annex a plan of classification, which includes, under two heads, the whole of the present Schedules.

On the Socialist Conference

REPORT IN *EXAMINER* 4 FEBRUARY 1854 (p. 68) ON
THE SOCIALIST CONFERENCE OF THE SOCIETY OF ARTS

We turn out to have been wrong in our anticipations of this conference. There was very little sentiment, but (instead) a good deal of fury in its socialism.

Mr. Ernest Jones, after bullying the chairman, flouted out of the room – banging the door after him, we dare say. Mr. Dickey forced into the chairman's hands a protest abusive of the rich and wealthy, such as could hardly be agreeable or pleasant to a Grosvenor. Mr. Mather justified all the follies of the mechanical engineers' strike. Mr. Cowell defended all the madness of the Preston turn-out. Speeches after speeches insisted on the 'right' of labour to participate in the profits of capital. Mr. C. Hindley first talked some unintelligible nonsense, and then uttered some very intelligible political mischief. Nearly every man present was in favour of combination. And out of all the miserable talkers, there was only Mr. Henderson, Sir Charles Fox's partner, to remind them that, after all, wages *must* be regulated by the law of supply and demand. Of course all ended in disappointment.

Lord Robert Grosvenor had not one supporter of any note in politics, commerce, manufactures, or society – a fact that probably will not be lost upon him; perhaps not even on the Council of the Society of Arts.

In the absence of men of influence, Lord Robert fell back upon, as he thought, a suggestion of importance. This was – to decide all disputes between masters and men by arbitration. The idea is a mere delusion. Masters must be able to conduct their business on their own views and principles. If those views and principles be wrong, experience will either correct what is wrong, or ruin the wrong-doer. But to give other people – third parties – who are under no pecuniary responsibility, power in such matters, is to introduce the element of control, and with it confusion, into private affairs. Lord Robert Grosvenor's tenantry at Rickmansworth are just as much, or as little, entitled to have their rents lowered by means of compulsory arbitration, as the Preston men are to have their wages raised ten per cent by any such device.

Tribunals of commerce and Courts of wages' arbitration are impertinences. Nobody asks for either; and, if offered, nobody would accept either. What commerce and industry require is simply not to be interfered with. And when disputes arise, why – as Mr. Bright remarked at Manchester the other day, in anything however but the spirit of a Quaker – 'they must be *fought* out'. A mode of solving difficulties which Mr. Bright would rather inconsistently deny to nations.

BIBLIOGRAPHY OF WORKS CITED

WORKS BY JOHN STUART MILL

CW = *Collected Works of John Stuart Mill*, ed. J. M. Robson. Toronto.

Books and pamphlets
(1843) *A System of Logic Ratiocinative and Inductive*. In *CW*, VII–VIII, 1973.
Last (8th) ed. by Mill, 1872.
(1844) *Essays on Some Unsettled Questions in Political Economy*, London. Contains:
    I 'Of the Law of Interchange Between Nations.' In *CW*, IV, 1967,
    232–61.
    II 'Of the Influence of Consumption on Production.' *Ibid.*, 262–79.
    III 'Of the Words Productive and Unproductive.' *Ibid.*, 280–89.
    IV 'On Profits and Interest.' *Ibid.*, 290–308.
    V 'On the Definition of Political Economy' (1836) (see Journal Articles).
(1848) *Principles of Political Economy* (ed. W. J. Ashley, 1917), last (7th) ed.
by Mill, 1871.
(1848) *Principles of Political Economy with Some of Their Applications to Social
Philosophy*. In (ed. J. M. Robson) *CW*, II–III, 1965. Last (7th) ed. by
Mill, 1871).
(1859) *Dissertations and Discussions, Political, Philosophical and Historical*, London.
(1859) *Thoughts on Parliamentary Reform*. In *CW*, XIX, 1973, 311–39, London.
(1859) *On Liberty*, Last (4th) ed. by Mill, 1869. In *CW*, XVIII, 1977,
213–310, London.
(1861) *Utilitarianism*, 1st ed. 1863; last (4th) ed. by Mill, 1871, London.
First published in *Fraser's Magazine*, LXIV, Oct. 1861, 391–406, Nov.
1861, 525–34, Dec. 1861, 658–73). In *CW*, X, 1969, 203–59.
(1861) *Considerations on Representative Government*. Last (3rd) ed. by Mill, 1865.
In *CW*, XIX, 1977, 371–577, London.

(1865) *An Examination of Sir William Hamilton's Philosophy*. In *CW*, IX, 1979. Last (4th) ed. by Mill, 1872.

(1865) *Auguste Comte and Positivism*, first published in *Westminster and Foreign Quarterly Review*, LXXXIII, April 1865, 339–405, LXXXIV, July 1865, 1–42. In *CW*, X, 1969, 261–368, London.

(1868) *England and Ireland*, 5th ed. 1869. In *CW*, VI, 1982, 505–32.

(1869) 'Introduction' to James Mill, *Analysis of the Phenomena of the Human Mind*, 2nd ed. London.

(1873) *Autobiography*. In *Autobiography and Literary Essays*. In *CW*, I, 1981, 1–290. (Posthumous 1874) *Three Essays on Religion*. In *CW*, X, 1969, 369–489, London.

Journal articles, other essays and evidence

(1824) 'War Expenditure,' *Westminster Review*, II, July, 27–48. In *CW*, IV, 1967, 1–22.

(1825) 'The Quarterly Review on Political Economy,' *Westminster Review*, III, Jan., 213–32. In *CW*, IV, 1967, 23–43.

(1825) 'The Corn Laws,' *Westminster Review*, III, April, 394–420. In *CW*, IV, 1963, 45–70.

(1825) 'McCulloch's Discourse on Political Economy,' *Westminster Review*, IV, July, 88–92. In *CW*, V, 1967, 757–60.

(1826) 'Paper Currency and Commercial Distress,' *Parliamentary Review, Session of 1826*, 630–62. In *CW*, IV, 1967, 71–123, London.

(1826) 'The Silk Trade,' *Westminster Review*, V, Jan., 136–49. In *CW*, IV, 1967, 125–39.

(1827) 'The New Corn Law,' *Westminster Review*, VII, Jan., 169–86. In *CW*, IV, 1967, 141–59.

(1828) 'Whately's Elements of Logic,' *Westminster Review*, IX, Jan., 137–72. In *CW*, XI, 1978, 1–35.

(1828) 'The Nature, Origin, and Progress of Rent,' 'Note III' to Adam Smith, *'An Inquiry into the Nature and Causes of the Wealth of Nations'*, IV, ed. J. R. McCulloch, Edinburgh, IV, 100–25. In *CW*, IV, 1967, 161–80.

(1832) 'Use and Abuse of Political Terms,' *Tait's Edinburgh Magazine*, I, May, 164–72. In *CW*, XVIII, 1977, 1–13.

(1832) 'Obituary of Bentham,' *Examiner*, 10 June, 370–2. In *CW*, X, 1969, 495–8.

(1833) 'Remarks on Bentham's Philosophy,' 'Appendix B'. In E. L. Bulwer, *England and the English*, II, 321–44. In *CW*, X, 1969, 3–18, London.

(1833) 'A Few Observations on Mr [James] Mill,' 'Appendix D'. In *ibid.*, 345–55. In *CW*, I, 1981, 589–95.

(1833) 'Comment on Bentham.' In *ibid.*, 163–70. In *CW*, X, 1969, 499–502.

(1833) 'The Currency Juggle,' *Tait's Edinburgh Magazine*, II, Jan., 461–7. In *CW*, IV, 1967, 181–92.

(1833) 'Corporation and Church Property,' *The Jurist, or Quarterly Journal of Jurisprudence and Legislation*, IV, Feb., 1–26. In *CW*, IV, 1967, 193–222.

(1834) 'Miss Martineau's Summary of Political Economy,' *Monthly Repository*, VIII, May, 318–22. In *CW*, IV, 1967, 223–8.

(1835) 'Sedgwick's Discourse,' *London Review*, I, April, 94–135. In *CW*, X, 31–74.

(1835) 'Rationale of Representation,' *London Review*, I, July, 341–71. In *CW*, XVIII, 1977, 15–46.

(1836) 'Civilization,' *London and Westminster Review*, III, XXV, April, 1–28. In *CW*, XVIII, 1977, 117–47.

(1836) 'On the Definition of Political Economy; and on the Method of Philosophical Investigation in that Science,' *London and Westminster Review*, IV, XXVI, Oct., 1–29. (Appears as Essay V in *Essays on Some Unsettled Questions of Political Economy*, 1844, with title '. . . and on the Method of Investigation Proper to it'.) In *CW*, IV, 1967, 309–39.

(1837) 'Aphorisms: Thoughts in the Cloister and the Crowd,' *London and Westminster Review*, IV, XXVI, Jan., 348–57. In *CW*, I, 1981, 419–29.

(1838) 'Bentham,' *London and Westminster Review*, VII, XXIX, Aug., 467–506. In *CW*, X, 1969, 75–115.

(1840) 'Coleridge,' *London and Westminster Review*, XXXIII, March, 257–302. In *CW*, X, 1969, 117–63.

(1840) 'De Tocqueville on Democracy in America,' *Edinburgh Review*, LXXII, Oct., 1–47. In *CW*, XVIII, 1977, 153–204.

(1844) 'The Currency Question,' *Westminster Review*, XLI, June, 579–98. In *CW*, IV, 1967, 341–61.

(1845) 'The Claims of Labour,' *Edinburgh Review*, LXXXI, April, 498–525. In *CW*, IV, 1967, 363–89.

(1845) 'De Quincey's Logic of Political Economy,' *Westminster Review*, XLIII, June, 319–31. In *CW*, IV, 1967, 391–404.

(1846) 'Grote's History of Greece,' *Edinburgh Review*, LXXXIV, Oct., 343–77. In *CW*, XI, 1978, 271–305.

(1849) 'Vindication of the French Revolution of February 1848,' *Westminster Review*, LI, April, 1–47. In *Dissertations and Discussions*. 2nd ed. 1867, II, 335–410, London.

(1850) 'The Savings of the Middle and Working Classes,' *Parliamentary Papers*, XIX, 253–66. In *CW*, V, 1967, 405–29.

(1851) 'The Regulation of the London Water Supply,' Metropolitan Sanitary Association, *Public Agency v. Trading Companies*, 19–23. In *CW*, V, 1967, 431–37.

(1851) 'Newman's Political Economy,' *Westminster Review*, LVI, Oct., 83–101. In *CW*, V, 1967, 439–57.

(1852) 'The Income and Property Tax,' *Parliamentary Papers*, IX, 780–91, 794–820. In *CW*, V, 1967, 463–98.

(1852) 'Whewell on Moral Philosophy,' *Westminster and Foreign Quarterly Review*, LVIII, Oct., 349–85. In *CW*, X, 1969, 165–201.

(1857) 'The Bank Acts,' *Parliamentary Papers*, (Session 2), X.i., 189–218. In *CW*, V, 1967, 499–547.

(1861) 'The Income and Property Tax,' *Parliamentary Papers*, VII, 244–64. In *CW*, V, 1967, 549–98.

(1862) 'Centralisation,' *Edinburgh Review*, CXV, April, 323–58. In *CW*, XIX, 1977, 579–613.

(1867) 'Currency and Banking,' *Enquête sur les principes et les faits généraux qui régissent la circulation monétaire et fiduciaire*, V, 589–96. In *CW*, V, 1967, 599–611, Paris.

(1869) 'Endowments,' *Fortnightly Review*, n.s. V, April, 377–90. In *CW*, V, 1967, 613–29.

(1869) 'Thornton on Labour and Its Claims,' *Fortnightly Review*, n.s. V, May, 505–18; June, 680–700. In *CW*, V, 1967, 631–68.

(1870) 'Leslie on the Land Question,' *Fortnightly Review*, n.s., VII, June, 641–54. In *CW*, V, 1967, 669–85.

(1871) 'Land Tenure Reform,' *Programme of the Land Tenure Reform Association*, 6–16. In *CW*, V, 1967, 687–95, London.

(1873) 'Property and Taxation,' *Fortnightly Review*, n.s. XIII, March, 396–8. In *CW*, V, 1967, 697–702.

(1879 Posthumous) 'Chapters on Socialism,' *Fortnightly Review*, n.s. XXV, Feb., 217–37, March, 373–82, April, 513–30. In *CW*, V, 1967, 703–53.

Correspondence
The Earlier Letters 1812 to 1848. In *CW*, XII–XIII, 1963.
The Later Letters 1849 to 1873. In *CW*, XIV–XVII, 1972.
Lettres inédites de John Stuart Mill à Auguste Comte, 1899, ed. L. Lévy-Bruhl, Paris.

Contributions to the press, parliamentary speeches and miscellaneous
(1822) Two Letters on Exchangeable Value, *The Traveller*, 6 Dec. 3, 13 Dec. 2. In ed. J. H. Hollander *John Stuart Mill on the Measure of Value*, Baltimore, 1936.

(1823) On T. Tooke, *Thoughts and Details;* Part I, *The Globe and Traveller*, 4 March, and Parts II–IV, *Morning Chronicle*, 9 August, 3.

(1823–4) Letters in the *Black Dwarf*:
'Question of Population,' XI, 22, 27 Nov., 748–56.
'Question of Population: Arguments of the Anti-populationists,' XI, 24, 10 Dec., 791–8.
'Question of Population,' XII, 1, 7 Jan., 21–3.

(1831–4) Contributions to the *Examiner*:
'Review of J. F. W. Herschel, *A Preliminary Discourse on the Study of Natural Philosophy*,' 20 March 1831, 179.

'Employment of Children in Manufactories,' 29 Jan. 1832, 67–8.

'The New Colony,' 29 June 1834, 403.

'The New Colony,' 6 July 1834, 419–20.

'Review of *The New British Province of South Australia*,' 20 July 1834, 453–4.

(1841) 'Petition on Free Trade,' *Morning Chronicle*, 17 June, 6. In *CW*, V, 1967, 761–3.

(1844) 'Letter to the editor on James Mill,' *Edinburgh Review*, LXXIX, Jan., 269–71; In *CW*, I, 1981, 533–8.

(1845) 'Notes on Senior's *Outline of Political Economy*,' ed. F. A. Hayek. *Economica*, XII, Aug., 134–9.

(1866) 'Tenure and Improvement of Land (Ireland),' *Hansard Parliamentary Debates*, 17 May, 183, cols 1087–97.

(1867) *Inaugural Address Delivered to the University of St. Andrews*. In *CW*, XXI, 1984, 215–57, London.

(1868) 'State of Ireland,' *Hansard Parliamentary Debates*, 3rd series, London, 190, 1515–32.

OTHER PRIMARY WORKS

Attwood, Thomas (1832) 'Evidence taken before the Committee of Secrecy on the Bank of England's Charter,' *Parliamentary Papers*, 1831–2, VI, 452–68.

Babbage, Charles (1832) *On the Economy of Machinery and Manufactures*, 3rd ed. London.

Bagehot, Walter (1895) *Economic Studies*, ed. R. H. Hutton, London.

— (1974) *Collected Works*, ed. N. St. John-Stevas, London.

Bailey, Samuel (1825) *A Critical Dissertation on the Nature, Measures, and Causes of Value*, London.

Bentham, Jeremy (1789) *An Introduction to the Principles of Morals and Legislation*, ed. J. H. Burns and H. L. A. Hart, London.

— (1815) *A Table of the Springs of Human Action*, London.

Blake, William (1823) *Observations on the Effects produced by Expenditure of Government during the Restriction of Cash Payments*, New York, 1969.

Cairnes, J. E. (1872) 'New Theories in Political Economy.' In R. D. C. Black ed. *Papers and Correspondence of William Stanley Jevons*, London, VII, 146–52.

— (1873) *Essays in Political Economy*, London.

— (1874) *Some Leading Principles of Political Economy*, London, 1883.

— (1888) *The Character and Logical Method of Political Economy*, 2nd ed. London.

Chalmers, Thomas (1832) *On Political Economy in Connexion with the Moral State and Moral Prospects of Society*, 2nd ed. Glasgow.

Clark, J. B. (1899) *The Distribution of Wealth: A Theory of Wages, Interest and Profits*, New York, 1965.

Clark, J.M. (1923) *Studies in the Economics of Overhead Costs*, Chicago.

Comte, Auguste (1823) *Système de Politique Positive*, Paris 1824.

— (1848) *Discours sur l'ensemble du Positivisme*, Paris.

— (1864) *Cours de Philosophie Positive*, 2nd ed. (6 vols) Paris.

Edgeworth, F. Y. (1925) *Papers Relating to Political Economy*, London.

Ellis, William (1826) 'Effect of the Employment of Machinery &c. upon the Happiness of the Working Classes,' *Westminster Review*, V, 101–30.

Empson, William (1837) 'Life, Writings, and Character of Mr. Malthus.' *Edinburgh Review*, CXXX, Jan. In B. Semmel ed. *Occasional Papers of T. R. Malthus*, New York, 231–68.

Fawcett, H. (1865) *Economic Position of the British Labourer*, Cambridge and London.

Fullarton, John (1845) *On the Regulation of Currencies &c*, 2nd ed. London.

George, Henry (1879) *Progress and Poverty*, San Francisco.

Gray, John (1848) *Lectures on the Nature and Use of Money*, Edinburgh.

Herschel, J.F.W. (1830) *A Preliminary Discourse on the Study of Natural Philosophy*, London.

— (1841) 'Review of Whewell *History of the Inductive Sciences* (1837), *Philosophy of the Inductive Sciences* (1840),' *Quarterly Review*, LXVIII, June, 177–238.

Hubbard, J.G. (1861) 'Memorandum submitted to the Chairman.' Appendix 1 to the 'Report of the Select Committee on Income and Property Tax.' *Parliamentary Papers*, VII, 315–17.

Jevons, W. S. (1866) 'Notice of a General Mathematical Theory of Political Economy,' (1862), *Journal of the Statistical Society of London*, XXIX, 235–53.

— (1905) *The Principles of Economics*, rev. ed. London.

— (1906) *The Coal Question*, 3rd ed. New York.

— (1907) *The Principles of Science: A Treatise on Logic and Scientific Method*, 2nd ed. 1877. London.

— (1924) *The Theory of Political Economy*, 4th ed. London.

— (1977) *Correspondence 1873–1878*. In R.D.C. Black ed. *Papers and Correspondence*, IV, London.

— (1977) *Lectures on Political Economy, 1875–76*. In R. D. C. Black ed. *Papers and Correspondence*, VI, London.

— (1981) *Papers on Political Economy*. In R. D. C. Black ed. *Papers and Correspondence*, VII. London.

Jones, Richard (1831) *An Essay on the Distribution of Wealth and on the Sources of Taxation: Part I – Rent*, London.

— (1859) *Literary Remains*, ed. William Whewell, New York, 1964.

Keynes, J. M. (1930) *A Treatise on Money*, London, 1965.

— (1973) *The General Theory of Employment, Interest and Money* (1936) ed. D. Moggridge, *Collected Writings*, VII, London.

— (1973) *The General Theory and After Part II. Defence and Development*. In ed. D. Moggridge *Collected Writings*, XIV, London.

Keynes, J. N. (1891) *Scope and Method of Political Economy*, 4th ed. New York, 1955.

Lalor, John (1852) *Money and Morals*, London.

Leslie, T. E. C. (1870) *Land Systems and Industrial Economy*. In *Ireland, England and Continental Countries*, New York, 1968.

— (1879) 'Review of Jevons's *Theory of Political Economy, The Academy*,' no. 377, New Series, 26 July. In R. D. C. Black ed. *Papers and Correspondence of W. S. Jevons*, VII, London, 1981, 157–62.

— (1888) *Essays in Political Economy*, 2nd ed. Dublin and London.

Lloyd, W. F. (1834) *Lecture on the Notion of Value*. Reprinted in *Lectures on Population, Values, Poor Laws and Rent* (1837), New York, 1968.

— (1835) *Four Lectures on Poor-Laws*. Reprinted in *Lectures on Population, Values, Poor Laws and Rent* (1837), New York, 1968.

— (1837) *Two Lectures on the Justice of Poor-Laws, and One Lecture on Rent*. Reprinted in *Lectures on Population, Values, Poor Laws and Rent* (1837), New York, 1968.

Longe, D. F. (1866) *A Refutation of the Wages Fund Theory of Modern Political Economy as Enunciated by Mr. Mill and Mr. Fawcett*, London.

Longfield, Mountifort (1834) *Lectures on Political Economy*. Reprinted in *The Economic Writings of Mountifort Longfield*, New York, 1971.

Lowe, Robert (1868) 'State of Ireland,' *Hansard Parliamentary Debates*, 3rd series, 190, London, 1483–503.

— (1876) Speech at proceedings of Political Economy Club to celebrate the hundredth year of the publication of the *Wealth of Nations*, London, 7–21.

— (1878) 'Recent Attacks on Political Economy,' *The Nineteenth Century*, IV, Nov., 858–68.

Macauley, T.B. (1829) 'Mr. [James] Mill's Essay on Government,' *Edinburgh Review*, March, June, October. Reprinted in J. Lively and J.Rees eds., *Utilitarian Logic and Politics*, Oxford, 1978, 97–129.

McCulloch, J. R. (1824) *A Discourse on the Rise, Progress, Peculiar Objects and Importance of Political Economy*, Edinburgh.

— (1825) *Principles of Political Economy*, 1st ed. Edinburgh.

— (1831) 'Jones on the Theory of rent,' *Edinburgh Review*, LIX, Sept., 84–99.

— (1832) 'Dr. Chalmers on Political Economy,' *Edinburgh Review*, LVI, Oct., 52–72.

— (1845) *The Literature of Political Economy*, London, 1938.

— (1864) *Principles of Political Economy*, 5th ed. Edinburgh, New York, 1965.

Malthus, T. R. (1820) *Principles of Political Economy*, 1st ed. In P. Sraffa ed. *Works and Correspondence of David Ricardo*, II, Cambridge, 1951.

— (1836) *Principles of Political Economy*, 2nd (posthumous) ed. New York, 1964.

— (1890) *An Essay on the Principle of Population*. Reprinted from last ed. revised by author (1826), London.

— (1963) 'Tooke – On High and Low Prices,' *Quarterly Review*, (1823). In B. Semmel ed. *Occasional Papers*, New York, 145–70.
— (1963) 'Political Economy,' *Quarterly Review*, (1824). In B. Semmel ed. *Occasional Papers*. New York, 171–208.
— (1970) *A Summary View of the Principle of Population* (1830). In A. Flew ed. *Malthus, An Essay on the Principle of Population*, Harmondsworth, 219–72.
Marshall, Alfred (1920) *Principles of Economics*, 8th ed. London.
— (1923) *Money, Credit and Commerce*, London.
— (1925) *Memorials*, ed. A. C. Pigou, London.
Martineau, Harriet (1834) *Illustrations of Political Economy*, London.
Marx, Karl (1962) *Capital*, III, Moscow.
— (1965) *Capital*, I, Moscow.
— (1971) *Theories of Surplus Value*, III, Moscow.
Menger, Carl (1950) *Principles of Economics*, (1st German ed. 1871). Glencoe. Translated and edited by B. F. Hoselitz and J. Dingwall.
Merivale, Herman (1837) 'Senior on Political Economy,' *Edinburgh Review*, CXXXIII, Oct., 73–102.
Mill, James (1804) *An Essay on the Impolicy of a Bounty of the Exportation of Corn*, London.
— (1806) 'Sir James Steuart's "Collected Works",' *Literary Journal*, I, 2nd Series, March, 225–35.
— (1808) *Commerce Defended*, London.
— (1813) 'East India Company,' *Monthly Review*, LXX, April, 410–25.
— (1820) *Essay on Government*, Supplement to the *Encyclopaedia Britannica*, 5th ed. (1820). In J. Lively and J. Rees eds. *Utilitarian Logic and Politics*, Oxford, 1978, 53–95.
— (1824) 'Colonies,' *Supplement to the Encyclopaedia Britannica*, III, 4th, 5th and 6th eds, Edinburgh, 257–73.
— (1824) 'Education,' *Supplement to the Encyclopaedia Britannica*, III, 4th, 5th and 6th eds, Edinburgh, 11–33. In F. A. Cavenaugh ed. *James and John Stuart Mill on Education*. Cambridge, 1931, 1–74.
— (1836a) 'Whether Political Economy is Useful? A Dialogue,' *The London Review*, II, No. 4, Jan., 553–71.
— (1836b) 'Theory and Practice,' *The London Review*, III, No. 1, April, 223–34.
— (1844) *Elements of Political Economy*, 1st ed. 1821, 3rd ed. 1826, London.
— (1869) *Analysis of the Phenomena of the Human Mind*, 2nd ed. ed. J. S. Mill, London.
Place, Francis (1822) *Illustrations and Proofs of the Principle of Population*, London.
Playfair, William (1805) *Inquiry into the Permanent Causes of the Decline and Fall of Powerful and Wealthy Nations*, London.

Political Economy Club (1876) Proceedings at the . . . celebration of the hundredth year of the publication of the *Wealth of Nations*, London.

— (1921) *Centenary Volume*, London.

de Quincey, Thomas (1844) *The Logic of Political Economy*. In D. Masson ed. *Political Economy and Politics*, vol. X, *Collected Works of Thomas de Quincey* (1897) New York, 1970.

Rae, John (1834) *Statement of Some New Principles on the Subject of Political Economy*, Toronto, 1965.

Read, Samuel (1829) *Political Economy*, Edinburgh.

Ricardo, David (1951) *Works and Correspondence*, I–XI, P. Sraffa ed. Cambridge.

Roebuck, J. A. (1833) 'National Education,' *Tait's Edinburgh Magazine*, II, March, 755–65.

Roscher, Wilhelm (1878) *Principles of Political Economy*, ed. J. J. Lalor, New York.

Say, J. B. (1814) *Traité d'économie politique*, 2nd ed. Paris.

— (1880) *A Treatise on Political Economy*, tr. C. R. Prinsep, from 4th French ed. 1819, Philadelphia.

Scrope, G. Poullet (1831) 'The Political Economists,' *Quarterly Review*, XLIV, Jan., 1–52.

— (1831) 'Jones on the Doctrine of Rent,' *Quarterly Review*, XLVI, Nov., 81–117.

— (1833) *Principles of Political Economy*, London.

Sedgwick, Adam (1834) *A Discourse on the Studies of the University*, 3rd ed. London.

Senior, Nassau W. (1827) *An Introductory Lecture on Political Economy*, London. In *Selected Writings on Economics*, New York, 1966.

— (1829) *Two Lectures on Population . . . to which is added a Correspondence between the author and the Rev. T. R. Malthus*, London. In *Selected Writings on Economics*, New York, 1966.

— (1848) 'J. S. Mill on Political Economy,' *Edinburgh Review*, CLXXVIII, Oct., 293–339.

— (1852) *Four Introductory Lectures on Political Economy*, London. In *Selected Writings on Economics*, New York, 1966.

— (1938) *An Outline of the Science of Political Economy*, 1st ed. 1836, 6th ed. 1872, London.

Sidgwick, H. (1883) *The Principles of Political Economy*, London.

de Sismondi Simonde, J. C. L. (1951) *Nouveaux principes d'économic politique*, G. Sotiroff ed. 2nd ed. 1827, Geneva.

Smith, Adam (1937) *An Inquiry into the Nature and Causes of the Wealth of Nations* (1776), New York.

— (1966) *The Theory of Moral Sentiments*, 6th ed. (1790), New York.

— (1980) *Of the Nature of that Imitation which takes place in what are called The Imitative Arts* (n.d.). In W. P. D. Wightman and J. C. Bryce eds. *Essays on Philosophical Subjects*, Oxford, 169–213.

Taussig, F. W. (1896) *Wages and Capital: An Examination of the Wages Fund Controversy*, New York, 1968.

Thompson, T. P. (1826) *The True Theory of Rent, in Opposition to Mr. Ricardo and Others*, (9th ed. 1832), London.

Thornton, Henry (1802) *An Enquiry into the Nature and Effects of the Paper Credit of Great Britain*, London, 1962.

Thornton, W. T. (1846) *Over-Population and its Remedy*, London.

— (1867) 'What Determines the Price of Labour or Rate of Wages?' *Fortnightly Review*, May, 551–66.

— (1869) *On Labour*, London.

Todhunter, I. (1876) *William Whewell, D. D.: An Account of His Writings, with Selections from his Literary and Scientific Correspondence*, London.

Tooke, Thomas (1823) *Thoughts and Details on the High and Low Prices of the Thirty Years, 1793–1822*, London (2nd ed. 1824).

— (1826) *Considerations on the State of the Currency*, London.

— (1832) 'Evidence taken before the Committee of Secrecy on the Bank of England Charter,' *Parliamentary Papers*, 1831–2. VI, 269–304, 432–44.

— (1844) *An Inquiry into the Currency Principle: the Connexion of the Currency with Prices and the Expediency of a Separation of Issue from Banking*, 2nd ed. London.

Torrens, Robert (1821) *An Essay on the Production of Wealth*, New York, 1965.

— (1822) *Three Editorial Notes on Value Contributed to the Traveller*, Dec. Reprinted in J. H. Hollander ed. *Two Letters on the Measure of Value by John Stuart Mill*, Baltimore, 1935.

— (1829) *An Essay on the External Corn Trade*, 3rd ed. 1826, 4th ed. 1829, 5th ed. New York, 1972.

— (1834) *On Wages and Combination*, London.

— (1835) *Colonization of South Australia*, London.

— (1844) *An Inquiry into the Practical Workings of the Proposed Arrangements for the Renewal of the Charter of the Bank of England, and the Regulation of the Currency with a Refutation of the Fallacies advanced by Mr. Tooke*, London.

— (1844) *The Budget: On Commercial and Colonial Policy*, London, New York, 1970.

Turgot, A. R. J. (1770) *Reflections on the Formation and Distribution of Riches*, New York, 1963.

Veblen, T. (1919) *The Place of Science in Modern Civilization*, New York.

Wakefield, E. G. (1833) *England and America*, London.

—, ed. (1843) *An Inquiry into the Nature and Causes of the Wealth of Nations by Adam Smith*, London.

Walras, Léon (1954) *Elements of Pure Economics*, ed. W. Jaffé, 4th definitive ed. 1926, London.

— (1965) *Correspondence and Related Papers, I 1857–1883*, ed. W. Jaffé, Amsterdam.

West, Sir Edward (1826) *Price of Corn and Wages of Labour*, London.

Whately, Richard (1826) *System of Logic*, London, 2nd ed. 1827.

— (1832) *Introductory Lectures on Political Economy*, London.

'Whewell Papers,' Trinity College Library, Cambridge. (Designated as WPC).

Whewell, William (1829) *Mathematical Exposition of Some Doctrines of Political Economy* from the *Transactions of the Cambridge Philosophical Society*, New York, 1971.

— (1831) *Mathematical Exposition of Some of the Leading Doctrines in Mr. Ricardo's 'Principles of Political Economy'*. From the *Transactions of the Cambridge Philosophical Society*, New York, 1971.

— (1831) 'Jones – On the Distribution of Wealth,' *British Critic*, X, July, 41–61.

— (1834). *Astronomy and General Physics Considered with Reference to Natural Theology*, III from the *Bridgewater Treatises*, London.

— (1849) *Of Induction, with Especial Reference to Mr. J. S. Mill's System of Logic*. In *On the Philosophy of Discovery*, London, 1860, Ch. xxii.

— (1850) *Mathematical Exposition of some Doctrines of Political Economy: Second Memoir*. From the *Transactions of the Cambridge Philosophical Society*, New York, 1971.

Wicksell, K. (1935) *Lectures on Political Economy I: General Theory*, London.

Wood, S. (1890) 'A Critique of Wages Theories,' *Annals of the American Academy of Political and Social Science*, I, 426–61.

SECONDARY WORKS WITH SPECIAL REFERENCE TO J. S. MILL

Note *CW*: *Collected Works of John Stuart Mill*. ed. J. M. Robson. Toronto.

Anschutz, R.P. (1953) *The Philosophy of J. S. Mill*, Oxford.

Appleyard, D.R. and J.C. Ingram (1979) 'A reconsideration of the additions to Mill's "Great Chapter",' *History of Political Economy*, XI, Winter, 459–76, 500–4.

Ashley, W. J. (1917) 'Introduction' to J. S. Mill, *Principles of Political Economy* ed. W. J. Ashley. London, v–xxvi.

Bain, Alexander (1882) *John Stuart Mill, a Criticism: With Personal Recollections*, London.

Balassa, B. A. (1959) 'John Stuart Mill and the Law of Markets,' *Quarterly Journal of Economics*, LXXIII, May, 263–74.

Bladen, V. W. (1965) 'Introduction' to J. S. Mill, *Principles of Political Economy*, ed. J. M. Robson, *CW*, II, xiii–lxiii.

Bonar, J. (1911) 'The Economics of John Stuart Mill,' *Journal of Political Economy*, XIX, Nov. 717–25.

Bradley, M. E. (1983) 'Mill on Proprietorship, productivity and population,' *History of Political Economy*, XV, 423–50.

Brady, A. (1977) Introduction to J. S. Mill, *Essays on Politics and Society*, *CW*, XVIII–XIX, ix–lxx.

Breit, W. (1967) 'The Wages Fund Controversy Revisited,' *Canadian Journal of Economics and Political Science*, XXXIII, Nov., 509–28.

Buchdahl, G. (1971) 'Inductivist versus Deductivist Approaches in the Philosophy of Science as Illustrated by Some Controversies Between Whewell and Mill,' *The Monist*, LV, July, 343–67.

Burnell, P. (1983) 'On Opinion in *On Liberty*,' *The Mill News Letter*, XVIII, Winter, 2–11.

Bush, W. C. (1975) 'Population and Mill's Peasant Proprietor Economy,' *History of Political Economy*, V, Spring, 110–20.

Chipman, J. S. (1979) 'Mill's "superstructure": how well does it stand up?,' *History of Political Economy*, XI, Winter, 477–500.

Collini, S. (1983) 'The tendencies of things: John Stuart Mill and the philosophic method.' In S. Collini, D. Winch and J. Burrow, *That Noble Science of Politics: A Study in Nineteenth-century Intellectual History*, Cambridge, 127–59.

Dewey, C. J. (1974) 'The Rehabilitation of the Peasant Proprietor in Nineteenth-Century Economic Thought,' *History of Political Economy*, VI, Spring, 17–47.

Dryer, D. P. (1969) 'Essay on Mill's Utilitarianism,' *CW*, X, lxiii–cxiii.

Edgeworth, F. Y. (1910). 'John Stuart Mill,' *Dictionary of Political Economy*, ed. R. H. I. Palgrave, London, II, 756–63.

Ekelund, R. B., Jr. (1976) 'A Short-run Classical Model of Capital and Wages: Mill's Recantation of the Wages Fund,' *Oxford Economic Papers*, XXVIII, March, 66–85.

Ekelund, R. B. Jr. and W. F. Kordsmeier (1981) 'J. S. Mill, Unions, and the Wages Fund Recantation: A Reinterpretation – Comment,' *Quarterly Journal of Economics*, XCV, Aug., 531–41.

Ekelund, R. B. Jr. and E. S. Olsen (1973) 'Comte, Mill and Cairnes: The Positivist-Empiricist Interlude in Late Classical Economics,' *Journal of Economic Issues*, VII, Sept., 383–416.

Ekelund, R. B. Jr. and R. D. Tollison (1976) 'The New Political Economy of J. S. Mill: The Means to Social Justice,' *Canadian Journal of Economics*, IX, May, 213–31.

— (1978) 'J. S. Mill's New Political Economy: Another View,' *Economic Inquiry*, XVI, Oct., 587–92.

Gray, J. (1981) 'John Stuart Mill on Liberty, Utility and Rights.' In J. W. Chapman and J. R. Pennock eds. *Nomos XIII*; XXIII, *Human Rights*, New York and London, 1981, 80–116.

Hamburger, J. (1976) 'Mill and Tocqueville on Liberty.' In J. M. Robson and M. Laine eds. *James and John Stuart Mill: Papers of the Centenary Conference*, Toronto, 111–25.

Harris, A. L. (1959) 'J.S. Mill on Monopoly and Socialism: A Note,' *Journal of Political Economy*, LXVII, 604–11.

Hayek, F. A. (1942) 'John Stuart Mill at the Age of Twenty-Five.' Introduction to J. S. Mill, *The Spirit of the Age*, Chicago, v–xxxiii.

— (1951) *John Stuart Mill and Harriet Taylor: Their Friendship and Subsequent Marriage*, London.

Hicks, J. (1983b) 'From Classical to Post-Classical, The Work of J. S. Mill,' *Collected Essays on Economic Theory*, III, Oxford, 60–70.

Himes, N. E. (1928) 'The Place of John Stuart Mill and of Robert Owen in the History of English Neo-Malthusianism,' *Quarterly Journal of Economics*, XLII, Aug., 627–40.

— (1929) 'John Stuart Mill's Attitude Towards Neo-Malthusianism,' *Economic History* (Supplement to *Economic Journal*), I, Jan. 457–84.

Himmelfarb, G. (1974) *On Liberty and Liberalism: The Case of John Stuart Mill*, New York.

Hollander, S. (1964) 'Technology and Aggregate Demand in J. S. Mill's Economic System,' *Canadian Journal of Economics and Political Science*, XXX, May, 175–84.

— (1968) 'The Role of Fixed Technical Coefficients in the Evolution of the Wages–Fund Controversy,' *Oxford Economic Papers*, XX, Nov., 320–41.

— (1973b) Review of Schwarz, *The New Political Economy of J. S. Mill. Journal of Economic Literature*, XI, June, 1374–6.

— (1976) 'J. S. Mill and the Neo-Classical Challenge.' In M. Laine and J. M. Robson eds. *Essays on James and J. S. Mill*, Toronto, 67–85.

— (1983) 'William Whewell and John Stuart Mill on the Methodology of Political Economy,' *Studies in the History and Philosophy of Science*, IV, No. 2, 127–68.

— (1984b) 'The Wage Path in Classical Growth Models: Ricardo, Malthus and Mill,' *Oxford Economic Papers*, XXXVI, 200–12.

Hunter, L. C. (1959) 'Mill and Cairnes on the Rate of Interest,' *Oxford Economic Papers*, XI, Feb., 63–87.

Kubitz, O. A. (1932) 'Development of John Stuart Mill's *System of Logic*,' *Illinois Studies in Social Science*, XVIII, March–June, 31–6.

Levy, D. (1980) 'Libertarian Communists, Malthusians and J. S. Mill Who is Both,' *Mill News Letter*, XV, Winter, 2–16.

Levy, M. B. (1981) 'Mill's Stationary State and The Transcendance of Liberalism,' *Polity*, XIV, Winter, 273–93.

McRae, R. F. (1973) 'Introduction' to J. S. Mill, *A System of Logic*, CW, VII–VIII, xxi–xlviii.

de Marchi, N. B. (1972) 'Mill and Cairnes and the Emergence of Marginalism in England,' *History of Political Economy*, IV, Autumn, 344–63.

— (1974) 'The Success of Mill's Principles,' *History of Political Economy*, VI, Summer, 119–57.

Marshall, A. (1925) 'Mr. Mill's Theory of Value' (1876). In A. C. Pigou ed. *Memorials*, London, 119–33.

Martin, D. E. (1976) 'The Rehabilitation of the Peasant Proprietor in Nineteenth-Century Economic Thought,' *History of Political Economy*, VIII, Summer, 297–302.

Miller, J. D. Jr. (1940) 'The Wages Fund Theory and the Popular Influence of Economists,' *American Economic Review*, XXX, March, 108–12.

Mueller, I. W. (1956) *John Stuart Mill and French Thought*, Urbana.

Nagel, Ernest (1950) 'Introduction,' *John Stuart Mill's Philosophy of Scientific Method*, New York, xv–xlviii.

Neff, E. (1926) *Carlyle and Mill: An Introduction to Victorian Thought*, New York.

O'Brien, G. (1943) 'J. S. Mill and J. E. Cairnes,' *Economica*, X, Nov., 273–85.

Packe, M. St. John (1954) *The Life of John Stuart Mill*, London.

Pappé, H. O. (1960) *John Stuart Mill and the Harriet Taylor Myth*, Melbourne.

Petrella, F. (1970) 'Individual, Group, or Government? Smith, Mill, and Sidgwick,' *History of Political Economy*, II, Spring, 152–76.

Pigou, A. C. (1949) 'Mill and the Wages Fund,' *Economic Journal*, LIX, June, 171–80.

Priestley, F. E. L. (1969) 'Introduction' to J. S. Mill, *Essays on Ethics, Religion and Society*, *CW*, X, vii–lxii.

Rainelli, M. (1983) 'Entrepreneur et Profits Dans les "Principles" de John Stuart Mill et d'Alfred Marshall,' *Revue économique*, July, 794–810.

Randall, J. H. Jr. (1965) 'John Stuart Mill and the Working-out of Empiricism,' *Journal of the History of Ideas*, XXVI, 59–88.

Robbins, L. C. (1967) 'Introduction' to J. S. Mill, *Essays on Economics and Society*, *CW*, IV–V, vii–xli.

— (1970b) Review of J. M. Robson, *The Improvement of Mankind, Economica*, XXXVII, May, 194–5.

— (1970c) Review of J. S. Mill, *CW*, X, *Economica*, XXXVII, Nov., 422–4.

Robson, J. M. (1964) 'John Stuart Mill and Jeremy Bentham, with Some Observations on James Mill.' In M. Machure and F. F. Watt eds. *Essays in English Literature from the Renaissance to the Victorian Age*, Toronto, 245–68.

— (1968) *The Improvement of Mankind: The Social and Political Thought of John Stuart Mill*, Toronto.

Ryan, A. (1970) *The Philosophy of John Stuart Mill*, London.

— (1979) 'Introduction' to J. S. Mill, *An Examination of Sir William Hamilton's Philosophy*, *CW*, IX, vii–lxvii.

Schabas, M. (1983a) 'John Stuart Mill to William Stanley Jevons: An Unpublished Letter,' *The Mill Newsletter*, XVIII, Summer, 24–8.

Schwartz, P. (1966) 'John Stuart Mill and Laissez Faire: London Water,' *Economica*, XXXIII, Feb., 71–83.

— (1972) *The New Political Economy of J. S. Mill*, London.

Sparshott, F. E. (1978) 'Introduction' to J. S. Mill, *Essays on Philosophy and the Classics*, *CW*, XI, vii–lxxv.

Spengler, J. J. (1960) 'John Stuart Mill on Economic Development.' In B. F. Hoselitz ed. *Theories of Economic Growth*, New York, 113–54.

Stigler, G. J. (1968) 'Mill on Economics and Society,' *University of Toronto Quarterly*, XXXVIII, Oct., 96–101.

— (1976) 'The Scientific Uses of Scientific Biography, with Special Reference to J. S. Mill.' In J. M. Robson and M. Laine eds, *James and John Stuart Mill: Papers of the Centenary Conference*, Toronto, 1976, 55–66.

Strong, E. W. (1955) 'William Whewell and John Stuart Mill: Their Controversy About Scientific Knowledge,' *Journal of the History of Ideas*, XVI, 209–31.

Takashima, M. (n.d.) 'John Stuart Mill versus McCulloch on Landed Property,' unpublished ms.

Ten, C. L. (1980) *Mill on Liberty*, Oxford.

Thompson, J. H. (1975). 'Mill's Fourth Fundamental Proposition: A Paradox Revisited,' *History of Political Economy*, VII, Summer, 174–92.

Viner, J. (1958) 'Bentham and J. S. Mill: The Utilitarian Background,' *The Long View and the Short*, Glencoe.

— (1962) 'Some Problems of Logical Method in Political Economy,' (1917). In E. J. Hamilton *et al.* eds. *Landmarks in Political Economy*, Chicago, 101–24.

de Vivo, G. (1981) 'John Stuart Mill on Value,' *Cambridge Journal of Economics*, V, 67–9.

West, E. G. (1965) 'Liberty and Education: John Stuart Mill's Dilemma.' *Philosophy*, XL, 129–42.

— (1978b) 'J. S. Mill's Redistribution Policy: New Political Economy or Old,' *Economic Inquiry*, XVI, Oct., 570–86.

West, E. G. and R. W. Hafer (1978) 'J. S. Mill, Unions and the Wages Fund Recantation: A Reinterpretation,' *Quarterly Journal of Economics*, XCII, Nov., 603–19.

— (1981) 'J. S. Mill, Unions, and the Wages Fund Recantation: A Reinterpretation – Reply,' *Quarterly Journal of Economics*, XCV, Aug., 543–9.

Whitaker, J. K. (1975) 'John Stuart Mill's Methodology,' *Journal of Political Economy*, LXXXIII, Oct., 1033–49.

Wilson, F. (1982) 'Mill's Proof that Happiness is the Criterion of Morality,' *Journal of Business Ethics*, I, 59–72.

— (1983) 'Mill's "Proof" of Utility and the Composition of Causes,' *Journal of Business Ethics*, II, 135–58.

Winch, D. (1970). 'Introduction to J. S. Mill,' *Principles of Political Economy*. Harmondsworth, 11–48.

SECONDARY WORKS RELATING TO 'CLASSICAL' ECONOMICS

Amsler, C. E., R. L. Bartlett and C. J. Bolton 'Thoughts of some British economists on early limited liability and corporate legislation,' *History of Political Economy*, XIII, Winter, 774–93.

Arnon, A. (1984) 'The transformation of Thomas Tooke's monetary theory reconsidered,' *History of Political Economy*, XVI, Summer, 311–26.

Baumol, W. J. and B. S. Becker (1960) 'The Classical Monetary Theory,' (1952).In J. J. Spengler and W. R. Allen eds, *Essays in Economic Thought*, Chicago, 753–72.

Beach, E. F. (1971) 'Hicks on Ricardo on Machinery,' *Economic Journal*, LXXXI, Dec., 916–22.

Berg, M. (1980) *The Machinery Question and the Making of Political Economy, 1815–1848*, Cambridge.

Bharadwaj, K. (1978) 'The subversion of classical analysis: Alfred Marshall's early writings on Value,' *Cambridge Journal of Economics*, II, 253–71.

Black, R. D. C. (1983) 'The Irish Dissenters and Nineteenth-Century Political Economy,' *Hermathena*, University of Dublin, CXXXV, Winter, 120–37.

Blaug, M. (1956) 'The Empirical Content of Ricardian Economics,' *Journal of Political Economy*, LXIV, Feb., 41–58.

— (1958a) *Ricardian Economics*, New Haven.

— (1958b) 'The Classical Economists and the Factory Acts – a Re-examination,' *Quarterly Journal of Economics*, LXXIII, May, 211–26.

— (1975) 'The Economics of Education in English Classical Political Economy: A Re-examination.' In A. S. Skinner and T. Wilson eds, *Essays on Adam Smith*, Oxford, 568–99.

Boot, H. M. (1983) 'James Wilson and the Commercial crisis of 1847,' *History of Political Economy*, XV, Winter, 567–84.

Bordo, M. D. (1975) 'John E. Cairnes on the Effects of the Australian Gold Discoveries 1851–73: An Early Application of the Methodology of Positive Economics,' *History of Political Economy*, VII, Autumn, 337–59.

Bortkiewicz, L. von (1952) 'Value and Price in the Marxian System' (1907), *International Economic Papers*, No. 2, 5–60.

Bowley, M. (1937) *Nassau Senior and Classical Economics*, London.

— (1972) 'The Predecessors of Jevons – The Revolution that wasn't,' *The Manchester School*, XL, 9–29.

— (1973) *Studies in the History of Economic Theory before 1870*, London.

Buchanan, J. M. (1978) 'The Justice of National Liberty.' In F. R. Glahe ed. *Adam Smith and the Wealth of Nations*, Boulder, 61–81.

Cannan, E. (1917) *A History of the Theories of Production and Distribution from 1776 to 1848*, 3rd ed. New York, 1967.

Caravale, G. (1982) 'Note sulla teoria ricardiana del valore, della distribuzione e dello sviluppo,' *Giornale degli economisti e annali di economia*, March/April, 141–83.

Carr, J. L. and J. Ahiakpor (1982) 'Ricardo on the non-neutrality of money in a world of taxes,' *History of Political Economy*, XIV, Summer, 147–65.

Chipman, J. S. (1965a) 'A Survey of the Theory of International Trade: Part I, The Classical Theory,' *Econometrica*, XXXIII, July, 477–519.

Coats, A. W. (1964) 'The Role of Authority in the Development of British Classicism,' *Journal of Law and Economics*, VII, Oct., 85–106.

Cochrane, J. L. (1970) 'The First Mathematical Ricardian Model,' *History of Political Economy*, II, Autumn, 419–31.

Corry, B. A. (1961) 'Progress and Profits,' *Economica*, XXIII, May, 203–11.

— (1962) *Money, Saving and Investment in English Economics: 1800–1850*, London.

Cramp, A. B. (1962) *Opinion on Bank Rate, 1822–60*, London.

Dobb, M. (1973). *Theories of Value and Distribution since Adam Smith*, Cambridge.

Douglas, J. M. (1881) *The Life and Selections from the Correspondence of William Whewell*, London.

Eltis, W. (1984) *The Classical Theory of Economic Growth*, London.

Fenn, R. A. (1982) 'On Theory and Practice: James Mill's Social Science,' unpublished ms.

Fetter, F. W. (1965) *Development of British Monetary Orthodoxy, 1797–1875*, Cambridge, Massachusetts.

Gordon, B. J. (1966) 'W. F. Lloyd: A Neglected Contributor,' *Oxford Economic Papers*, XVIII, March, 64–70.

Gordon, S. (1971) 'The Ideology of Laissez-Faire.' In A. W. Coats ed. *The Classical Economists and Economic Policy*, London, 180–205.

Grampp, W. D. (1960) *The Manchester School of Economics*, Oxford.

— (1965) *Economic Liberalism, II: The Classical View*, New York.

— (1979) 'The Economist and the Combination Laws,' *Quarterly Journal of Economics*, 93, Nov., 501–22.

Gregory, T. E. (1928) *An Introduction to Tooke and Newmarch, A History of Prices and of the State of the Circulation from 1792 to 1856*, London, 1962.

Groenewegen, P. D. (1974) Review of M. Dobb, *Theories of Value and Distribution, Economic Journal*, LXXXIV, March, 192–3.

— (1982) 'Thomas de Quincey: "Faithful Disciple of Ricardo?",' *Contributions to Political Economy*, I, 51–8.

Grossman, H. (1948) 'W. Playfair, the Earliest Theorist of Capitalist Development,' *Economic History Review*, XVIII, 65-83.

Henderson, J. P. (1973) 'William Whewell's Mathematical Statements of Price Flexibility, Demand Elasticity and the Giffen Paradox,' *The Manchester School*, XLI, Sept., 329-42.

Hicks, J. (1971) 'A Reply to Professor Beach,' *Economic Journal*, LXXXI, Dec., 922-5.

— (1983a) 'Ricardo and the Moderns,' *Collected Essays on Economic Theory*, III, Oxford, 39-59.

— (1985) 'Ricardo and Sraffa – A Critical View.' In G. Caravale ed. *The Legacy of David Ricardo*, Oxford.

Hollander, S. (1968) 'The Role of the State in Vocational Training: The Classical Economists View,' *Southern Economic Journal*, XXXIV, April, 513-25.

— (1973a) *The Economics of Adam Smith*, Toronto.

— (1977a) 'Adam Smith and the Self-Interest Axiom,' *Journal of Law and Economics*, XX, April, 133-52.

— (1977b) 'The Reception of Ricardian Economics,' *Oxford Economic Papers*, XXIX, July, 221-57.

— (1979a) *The Economics of David Ricardo*, Toronto.

— (1979b) 'Historical Dimension of *The Wealth of Nations*.' In G. P. O'Driscoll ed. *Adam Smith and Modern Political Economy*, Ames, Iowa, 71-84.

— (1981) 'Marxian Economics as General-Equilibrium Theory,' *History of Political Economy*, XIII, Spring, 121-54.

— (1982) 'On the Substantive Identity of the Ricardian and Neo-Classical Conceptions of Economic Organization: the French Connection in British Classicism,' *Canadian Journal of Economics*, XV, Nov., 586-612.

— (1984) 'Marx and Malthusianism: Marx's Secular Path of Wages,' *American Economic Review*, 74, March, 139-51.

— (1985) 'The Population Principle and Social Reform,' *History of Political Economy*, forthcoming.

James, R. W. (1965) 'Life and Miscellaneous Writings,' *John Rae: Political Economist*, Toronto.

Kennedy, W. F. (1962) 'Lord Brougham, Charles Knight and the *Rights of Industry*,' *Economica*, XXIX, 57-71.

Kittrell, E. (1965) 'The Development of the Theory of Colonization in English Classical Political Economy,' *Southern Economic Journal*, XXXI, Jan., 189-206.

— (1966) 'The Classical Debate on Colonization: Reply [to Winch],' *Southern Economic Journal*, XXXII, Jan., 346-9.

Laidler, D. (1972) 'Thomas Tooke on Monetary Reform.' In M. Peston and B. Corry eds. *Essays in Honour of Lord Robbins*, London, 168-86.

Lange, O. (1942) 'Say's Law: A Restatement and Criticism.' In O. Lange ed. *Studies in Mathematical Economics and Econometrics*, Chicago, 49–68.

Levy, D. (1976) 'Some Normative Aspects of the Malthusian Controversy,' *History of Political Economy*, X, Summer, 271–85.

— (1982) 'Diamonds, water and Z goods: an account of the paradox of value,' *History of Political Economy*, Autumn, 312–22.

Link, R. G. (1959) *English Theories of Economic Fluctuations*, New York.

Machlup, F. (1972) 'The Universal Bogey.' In M. Peston and B. Corry eds. *Essays in Honour of Lord Robbins*, London, 99–117.

McKinley, E. (1960) 'The Theory of Economic Growth in the English Classical School,' in B. F. Hoselitz ed. *Theories of Economic Growth*, New York, 89–112.

Maital, S. and P. Haswell (1977) 'Why Did Ricardo (Not) Change His Mind? On Money and Machinery,' *Economica*, XLIV, Nov., 359–67.

de Marchi, N. B. (1970). 'The Empirical Content and Longevity of Ricardian Economics,' *Economica*, XXXVII, Aug., 257–76.

— (1983a) 'Scottish Methodology and English Political Economy: the Steuart Connection.' In I. Holt & M. Ignatieff eds. forthcoming.

— (1983b) 'The Case for James Mill.' In R. Coats ed. *Methodological Controversy in Economics: Historical Essays in Honor of T. W. Hutchison*, Connecticut, 155–84.

de Marchi, N. B. and R. P. Sturges (1973) 'Malthus and Ricardo's Inductivist Critics: Four Letters to William Whewell,' *Economica*, XL, Nov., 379–93.

Meek, R. L. (1971) ed. *Marx and Engels on the Population Bomb*, Berkeley.

Miller, W. L. (1966) 'The Economics of Education in English Classical Economics,' *Southern Economic Journal*, XXXII, 294–300.

— (1971) 'Richard Jones: A Case Study in Methodology,' *History of Political Economy*, III, Spring, 198–207.

— (1977) 'Richard Jones' Contribution to the Theory of Rent,' *History of Political Economy*, IX, Autumn, 346–65.

Moss, L. S. (1974) 'Mountifort Longfield's Supply and Demand Theory of Price and its Place in the Development of British Economic Theory,' *History of Political Economy*, VI, Winter, 405–34.

— (1976) *Mountifort Longfield: Ireland's First Professor of Political Economy*, Ottawa, Ill.

— (1979) 'Power and Value Relationships in *The Wealth of Nations*.' In G. P. O'Driscoll ed. *Adam Smith and Modern Political Economy*, Ames, 85–101.

O'Brien, D. P. (1970) *J. R. McCulloch: A Study in Classical Economics*, London.

— (1975) *The Classical Economists*, Oxford.

Petrella, F. (1977) 'Benthamism and the Demise of Classical Economic Ordnungspolitik,' *History of Political Economy*, IX, Summer, 215–36.

Phelps Brown, E. H. (1976) 'The Labour Market.' In A. S. Skinner and T. Wilson eds. *The Market and the State*, Oxford, 243–59.

Pigou, A. C. (1943) 'The Classical Stationary State,' *Economic Journal*, LIII, Dec., 343–51.

Rashid, S. (1979) 'Richard Jones and Baconian Historicism at Cambridge,' *Journal of Economic Issues*, XIII, March, 159–73.

— (1980) 'The Growth of Economic Studies at Cambridge, 1776–1860,' *History of Education Quarterly*, XX, Autumn, 281–94.

Robbins, L. C. (1952) *The Theory of Economic Policy in English Classical Political Economy*, London.

— (1958) *Robert Torrens and the Evolution of Classical Economics*, London.

Romano, R. E. (1977) 'William Forster Lloyd – a non-Ricardian,' *History of Political Economy*, IX, Autumn, 412–41.

— (1982) 'The economic ideas of Charles Babbage,' *History of Political Economy*, XIV, Autumn, 385–405.

Rosenberg, N. (1965) 'Adam Smith on the Division of Labour: Two Views or One?' *Economica*, XXXII, May, 127–39.

— (1984) 'Karl Marx and the Economic Role of Science,' *Journal of Political Economy*, LXXXII, July/August, 713–28.

Samuelson, P. A. (1968) 'What Classical and Neo-Classical Monetary Theory Really Was,' *Canadian Journal of Economics*, I, Feb., 1–15.

— (1978) 'The Canonical Classical Model of Political Economy,' *Journal of Economic Literature*, XVI, Dec., 1415–34.

Sayers, R. S. (1953) 'Ricardo's Views on Monetary Questions.' In T. S. Ashton and R. S. Sayers eds. *Papers in English Economic History*, Oxford, 76–95.

Shove, G. (1960) 'The Place of Marshall's *Principles* in the Development of Economic Theory' (1942). In J. J. Spengler and W. R. Allen eds. *Essays in Economic Thought*, Chicago, 711–40.

Smith, V. E. (1951) 'The Classicists' Use of "Demand",' *Journal of Political Economy*, LIX, June, 242–57.

Sowell, T. (1972) *Say's Law: An Historical Analysis*, Princeton.

— (1974) *Classical Economics Reconsidered*, Princeton.

Spengler, J. J. (1959) 'John Rae on Economic Development: A Note,' *Quarterly Journal of Economics*, LXXIII, Aug., 393–406.

Sraffa, P. (1951) 'Introduction,' *Works and Correspondence of David Ricardo*, I, Cambridge, xiii–lxii.

Stigler, G. J. (1971) 'Smith's Travels on the Ship of State,' *History of Political Economy*, III, Autumn, 265–77.

Tu, P. N. V. (1969) 'The Classical Economists and Education,' *Kyklos*, XXII, 691–717.

Tucker, G. S. L. (1960) *Progress and Profits in British Economic Thought, 1650–1850*, Cambridge.

West, E. G. (1964) 'Private versus Public Education: A Classical Economic Dispute,' *Journal of Political Economy*, 72, 465–75.

West, H. (1982) 'Mill's "Proof" of the Principle of Utility.' In H. B. Miller and Witt Williams eds. *The Limits of Utilitarianism*, Minneapolis, 23–34.

Winch, D. N. (1963) 'Classical Economics and the Case for Colonization,' *Economica*, XXX, Nov., 387–99.

— (1965) *Classical Political Economy and Colonies*, London.

— , ed. (1966a) *James Mill: Selected Economic Writings*, Edinburgh.

— (1966b) 'The Classical Debate on Colonization: Comment,' *Southern Economic Journal*, XXXII, Jan., 341–5.

— (1983) 'Science and the Legislator: Adam Smith and After,' *Economic Journal*, XCIII, Sept., 501–20.

OTHER SECONDARY WORKS IN THE HISTORY OF ECONOMIC THOUGHT

Allet, J. (1981) *New Liberalism: The Political Economy of J.A. Hobson*, Toronto.

Black, R. D. C. (1962) 'W. S. Jevons and the Economists of his Time,' *The Manchester School*, XXX, Sept., 203–21.

— (1970) 'Introduction' to W. S. Jevons, *Theory of Political Economy*, Harmondsworth, 7–40.

— (1972a) 'Jevons, Marginalism and Manchester,' *The Manchester School*, XL, March, 2–8.

— (1972b) 'Jevons, Bentham and De Morgan,' *Economica*, XXXIX, May, 119–34.

— (1972c) 'W. S. Jevons and the Foundation of the Modern Economics,' *History of Political Economy*, IV, Autumn, 364–78.

Bladen, V. W. (1974) *From Adam Smith to Maynard Keynes*, Toronto.

Blaug, M. (1972) 'Was There a Marginal Revolution?' *History of Political Economy*, IV, Autumn, 269–80.

— (1976) 'Kuhn versus Lakatos *or* Paradigms versus research programmes in the history of economics.' In S. Latsis ed. *Method and Appraisal in Economics*. Cambridge, 149–80.

— (1978) *Economic Theory in Retrospect*, 3rd ed. Cambridge.

— (1979) 'The German Hegemony of Location Theory,' *History of Political Economy*, XI, Spring, 21–9.

— (1980) *The Methodology of Economics*, Cambridge.

Cannan, E. (1929) *A Review of Economic Theory*, London.

Checkland, S. G. (1951a) 'The Advent of Academic Economics in England,' *The Manchester School*, XIX, Jan., 43–70.

Checkland, S. G. (1951b) 'Economic Opinion in England as Jevons Found It,' *The Manchester School*, XIX, May, 143–69.

Chipman, J. S. (1965b) 'A Survey of the Theory of International Trade: Part II, The Neo-Classical Theory,' *Econometrica*, XXXIII, Oct., 685–760.

Coats, A. W. (1954) 'The Historist Reaction to English Political Economy,' *Economica*, XXI, May, 143-53.

Foxwell, H. S. (1887) 'The Economic Movement in England,' *Quarterly Journal of Economics*, II, 84-103.

Gordon, S. (1973) 'The Wages-Fund Controversy: The Second Round,' *History of Political Economy*, V, Spring, 14-35.

Hicks, J. (1976) ' "Revolutions" in Economics.' In S. Latsis ed. *Method and Appraisal in Economics*, Cambridge, 207-18.

Hirsch, A. (1980) 'The "Assumptions" Controversy in Historical Perspective,' *Journal of Economic Issues*, XIV, March, 99-119.

Hutchison, T. W. (1953) *A Review of Economic Doctrines, 1870-1929*, Oxford.

— (1972) 'The "Marginal Revolution" and the Decline and Fall of English Classical Political Economy,' *History of Political Economy*, IV, Autumn, 442-68.

— (1978) *On Revolutions and Progress in Economic Knowledge*, Cambridge.

Ingram, J. K. (1888) *A History of Political Economy*, London.

Jaffé, W. (1980) 'Walras's Economics as Others See It,' *Journal of Economic Literature*, XVIII, June, 528-49.

Jonung, L. (1981) 'Ricardo on Machinery and the Present Unemployment: An Unpublished Manuscript by Knut Wicksell,' *Economic Journal*, XCI, March, 195-205.

Kauder, E. (1965) *A History of Marginal Utility Theory*, Princeton.

Knight, F. H. (1956) *On the History and Method of Economics*, Chicago.

Koot, G. M. (1975) 'T. E. Cliffe Leslie, Irish Social Reform, and the Origins of the English Historical School of Economics,' *History of Political Economy*, VII, Autumn, 312-36.

— (1980) 'English Historical Economics and the Emergence of Economic History in England,' *History of Political Economy*, XII, Summer, 174-205.

Machlup, F. (1976) 'Hayek's Contribution to Economics.' In F. Machlup ed. *Essays on Hayek*, Hillsdale, Michigan, 13-59.

de Marchi, N. B. (1973) 'The Noxious Influence of Authority: A Correction of Jevons' Charge,' *Journal of Law and Economics*, XVI, April, 179-89.

Mitchell, W. C. (1967) *Types of Economic Theory*, I, New York.

Robbins, L. C. (1968) *The Theory of Economic Development in the History of Economic Thought*, London.

Roncaglia, A. (1981) 'Hollander's Ricardo,' *Journal of Post-Keynesian Economics*, XV, 373-4.

Schabas, M. L. (1983b) *William Stanley Jevons and the Emergence of Mathematical Economics in Britain*, University of Toronto, PhD thesis.

Schumpeter, J. A. (1954) *History of Economic Analysis*, New York and London.

Stigler, G. J. (1941) *Production and Distribution Theories: The Formative Years*, New York.

— (1965) *Essays in the History of Economics*, Chicago.

Viner, J. (1960) 'The Intellectual History of Laissez Faire,' *Journal of Law and Economics*, III, Oct., 45–69.

Walker, D. A. (1984) 'Is Walras's theory of general equilibrium a normative scheme?' *History of Political Economy*, XVI, Autumn, 445–69.

Winch, D. (1972) 'Marginalism and the Boundaries of Economic Science,' *History of Political Economy*, IV, Autumn, 325–43.

GENERAL ECONOMIC THEORY AND ECONOMIC POLICY

Arrow, K. J. and D. A. Starrett (1973) 'Cost- and Demand-Theoretical Approaches to the Theory of Price Determination.' In J. R. Hicks and W. Weber eds, *Carl Menger and the Austrian School of Economics*, Oxford, 129–48.

Boss, H. H. M. (1981) *Productive Labour, Unproductive Labour, and the Boundary of the Economic Domain, 1662–1980: History, Analysis and Application*, McGill University, PhD thesis.

Boulding, K. E. (1966) 'Wages as a Share in the National Income.' In D. McCord Wright ed. *The Impact of the Labor Union*, New York.

Burns, A. F. (1968) 'Business Cycles,' *International Encyclopaedia of the Social Sciences*, II, 226–44.

Cooter, R. and P. Rappoport (1984) 'Were the Ordinalists Wrong About Welfare Economics?' *Journal of Economic Literature*, XXII, June, 507–30.

Dobb, M. H. (1940) *Political Economy and Capitalism*, rev. ed. London.

Friedman, M. (1968) 'The Role of Monetary Policy,' *American Economic Review*, LVIII, March, 1–17.

— (1969) *The Optimum Quantity of Money and Other Essays*, Chicago.

Harrod, R. (1948) *Towards a Dynamic Economics*, London.

Hawtrey, R. G. (1928) *Trade and Credit*, London.

Hayek, F. A. (1935) *Prices and Production*, 2nd ed. London.

— (1936) 'The Mythology of Capital,' *Quarterly Journal of Economics*, L, Feb., 199–228.

— (1939) *Profits, Interest and Investment*, London.

— (1941a) *The Pure Theory of Capital*, Chicago.

Hébert, R. F. and A. N. Link (1982) *The Entrepreneur*, New York.

Heertje, A. (1977) *Economics and Technical Change*, London.

Hicks, J. (1963) *The Theory of Wages*, 2nd ed. London.

— (1967) *Critical Essays in Monetary Theory*, Oxford.

— (1973) *Capital and Time: A Neo-Austrian Theory*, Oxford.

— (1974) 'Capital Controversies: Ancient and Modern,' *American Economic Review*, LXIV, May, 307–16.

— (1977) *Economic Perspectives: Further Essays on Money and Growth*, Oxford.

— (1982) *Collected Essays on Economic Theory*, II, *Money, Interest and Wages*, Oxford.

Hoselitz, B. F. (1960) 'Theories of Stages of Economic Growth.' In B. F. Hoselitz ed. *Theories of Economic Growth*, New York, 193–238.

Johnson, H. G. (1949) 'Demand for Commodities is *NOT* Demand for Labour,' *Economic Journal*, LIX, Dec., 531–36.

Johnston, J. (1975) 'A Macro-model of Inflation,' *Economic Journal*, LXXXV, June, 288–308.

Knight, F. H. (1921) *Risk, Uncertainty and Profit*, Boston.

Kuznets, S. (1941) *National Income & its Composition, 1919–38*, New York.

— (1948) 'National Income: A New Version,' *Review of Economics and Statistics*, XXX, Aug., 151–97.

Leibenstein, H. (1966) 'Allocative Efficiency vs "X-efficiency",' *American Economic Review*, LVI, June, 392–415.

Lewis, W. A. (1954) 'Economic Development with Unlimited Supplies of Labour.' In A. N. Agarawala and S. P. Singh eds, *The Economics of Development*, Bombay, 1958.

Myint, H. (1948) *Theories of Welfare Economics*, London.

O'Driscoll, G. P. (1977) *Economics as a Coordination Problem*, Kansas City.

Patinkin, D. (1956) *Money, Interest and Prices*, Evanston.

— (1982) *Anticipations of the General Theory? and Other Essays on Keynes*, Chicago.

Pigou, A. C. (1936) *Economics in Practice: Six Lectures on Current Issues*, London.

— (1947) 'Economic Progress in a Stable Environment,' *Economica*, XIV, Aug., 180–8.

— (1960) *The Economics of Welfare*, 4th ed. London.

Plant, A. (1974) 'The economic theory concerning patents for inventions' (1934), *Selected Economic Essays and Addresses*, London and Boston.

Robbins, L. C. (1927) 'The Optimum Theory of Population.' In T. E. Gregory and H. Dalton eds, *London Essays in Honour of Edwin Cannan*, London, 103–34.

— (1930) 'On a Certain Ambiguity in the Conception of Stationary Equilibrium,' *Economic Journal*, XL, June, 194–214.

— (1970a) *The Evolution of Modern Economic Theory*, London.

— (1971a) *Autobiography of an Economist*, London.

— (1971b) *Money, Trade and International Relations*, London.

— (1976) *Political Economy: Past and Present: A Review of Leading Theories of Economic Policy*, London.

— (1981) 'Economics and Political Economy,' *American Economic Review*, 71, May, 1–10.

Robertson, D. (1966) *Essays in Money and Interest*.

Robinson, J. (1942) *An Essay on Marxian Economics*, London.

— (1961) 'Prelude to a Critique of Economic Theory,' *Oxford Economic Papers*, XIII, Feb., 53–8.

— (1980) *Further Contributions to Modern Economics*, Oxford.

Schumpeter, J. A. (1934) *The Theory of Economic Development*, Cambridge.

Stigler, G. J. (1949) *Five Lectures on Economics Problems*, London.

— (1952) *The Theory of Price*, 3rd ed. New York.

— (1975) *The Citizen and the State: Essays on Regulation*, Chicago.

Taylor, C. (1984) 'Design for Living,' *The New York Review of Books*, XXXI, Nov. 22, 51–5.

Viner, J. (1937) *Studies in the Theory of International Trade*, New York.

— (1958) *The Long View and the Short*, Glencoe.

ECONOMIC AND SOCIAL HISTORY, AND PHILOSOPHY

Adams, F. (1882) *History of the Elementary School Contest in England*, Brighton, 1972.

Bacon, R. and W. Eltis (1978) *Britain's Economic Problem: Too Few Producers*, 2nd ed. London.

Blaug, M. (1963) 'The Myth of the Old Poor Law and the Making of the New,' *Journal of Economic History*, XXIII, 151–84.

Briggs, A. (1972) Introduction to Francis Adams, *History of the Elementary School Contest in England*, Brighton, ix–lxi.

Cannon, W. E. (1964) 'Scientists and Broad Churchmen: An Early Victorian Intellectual Network,' *Journal of British Studies*, IV, Nov., 65–88.

Clemence, R. V. (1961) 'British Trade Unions and Popular Political Economy: 1850–1875,' *Economic History Review*, XIV, 93–104.

Crouch, R. L. (1967) 'Laissez-Faire in Nineteenth-Century Britain: Myth or Reality,' *Manchester School of Economic and Social Studies*, XXXV, Sept., 199–215.

Crouzet, F. (1982) *The Victorian Economy*, New York.

Davis, S. (1981) *Scottish Philosophical History: Hume to James Mill*, University of Toronto, PhD thesis.

Edger, E. R. (1907) 'Posthumous Essay on Social Freedom,' *Oxford and Cambridge Review*, Jan.

Finer, S. E. (1982) Review of L. J. Hume, *Bentham and Bureaucracy, Bentham Newsletter*, No. 6, May, 30–4.

Fraser, D. (1974) 'Edward Bains.' In P. Hollis ed. *Pressure from Without in Early Victorian England*, London.

Gilmour, R. (1967) 'The Gradgrind School,' *Victorian Studies*, XI, Dec., 207–24.

Gordon, S. (1955) 'The London *Economist* and the High Tide of *Laissez-Faire*,' *Journal of Political Economy*, LXIII, Dec., 461–88.

— (1980) *Welfare, Justice and Freedom*, New York.

Gosden, P. H. J. H. (1969) *How They Were Taught*, Oxford.

Halévy, E. (1928) *The Growth of Philosophic Radicalism*, Boston.

Harte, N. B. (1971) Introduction to *The Study of Economic History*, ed. N. B. Harte, London, xi–xxxix.

Hayek, F. A. (1942–4) 'Scientism and the Study of Society,' *Economica*, IX, Aug. 1942, 267–91; X, Feb. 1943, 34–63; XI–XII, Feb. 1944, 27–39.

— (1941b) 'The Counter-Revolution of Science,' *Economica*, VIII, Feb., 9–36, May, 119–50, Aug., 281–320.

— *The Counter Revolution of Science: Studies in the Abuse of Reason*, Glencoe, Ill., 1955.

— (1978) *New Studies in Philosophy, Politics, Economics and the History of Ideas*, Chicago.

Hicks, J. (1969) *A Theory of Economic History*, Oxford.

Hurt, J. S. (1971) 'Professor West and Early Nineteenth-Century Education,' *Economic History Review*, XXIV, 624–42.

Hutchison, T. W. (1981) *The Politics and Philosophy of Economics*, New York.

Knight, F. H. (1956) 'Salvation by Science: the Gospel According to Professor Lundberg' (1947). In *On the History and Method of Economics*, Chicago, 227–47.

Landes, D. S. (1969) *The Unbound Prometheus: Technological Change and Industrial Development in Western Europe from 1750 to the Present*, Cambridge.

Lively, J. and J. Rees (1978) *Utilitarian Logic and Politics*, Oxford.

Long, D. G. (1977) *Bentham on Liberty: Jeremy Bentham's idea of liberty in relation to his utilitarianism*, Toronto.

Lyons, D. (1972) 'Was Bentham a Utilitarian?' In *Reason and Reality: Royal Institute of Philosophy Lectures*, V, London, 196–221.

McCann, W. P. (1969) 'Elementary Education in England and Wales on the Eve of the 1870 Education Act,' *Journal of Educational Administration and History*, II, Dec., 20–9.

McCloskey, D. N. (1973) 'New Perspectives on the Old Poor Law,' *Explorations in Economic History*, X, 419–36.

Pappé, H. O. (1979) 'The English Utilitarians and Athenian Democracy.' In R. R. Bolgar ed. *Classical Influences on Western Thought A. D. 1650–1870*, New York, 295–307.

Pollard, S. (1968) *The Idea of Progress*, London.

Popper, K. R. (1963) *The Open Society and its Enemies*, New York.

Rawls, J. (1971) *A Theory of Justice*, Cambridge, Massachusetts.

Steintrager, J. (1977) *Bentham*, Ithaca.

Stephen, L. (1900) *The English Utilitarians*, London.

Stigler, G. J. (1982) *The Economist as Preacher and Other Essays*, Chicago.

Sutherland, G. (1971) *Elementary Education in the Nineteenth Century*, The Historical Association, London.

Thomas, William (1979) *The Philosophic Radicals: Nine Studies in Theory and Practice, 1817–1841*, Oxford.

Vaizey, J. (1962) *The Economics of Education*, London.

Viner, J. (1972) *The Role of Providence in the Social Order*, Philadelphia.

von Mises, L. *Liberalism: A Socio-Economic Exposition*, Kansas City, 1978.

Ward-Perkins, C. N. (1962) 'The Commercial Crisis of 1847,' (1950). In E. M. Carus-Wilson ed. *Essays in Economic History*, III, London, 263–79.

Webb, R. K. (1955) *The British Working Class Reader*, London.

West, E. G. (1970a) *Education and the State: A Study in Political Economy*, 2nd ed. London.

— (1970b) 'Resource Allocation and Growth in Early Nineteenth-Century Education,' *Economic History Review*, XXIII, 68–95.

— (1975) *Education and the Industrial Revolution*, London.

— (1978a) 'Literacy and the Industrial Revolution,' *Economic History Review*, XXXI, Aug., 369–83.

Wolfe, W. (1975) *From Radicalism to Socialism: Men and Ideas in the Formation of Fabian Socialist Doctrines*, New Haven.

Woodward, L. (1962) *The Age of Reform*, 2nd ed. Oxford.

Wrigley, E. A. and R. S. Schofield (1981) *The Population History of England, 1541–1871: A Reconstruction*. Cambridge, Massachusetts.

INDEX

abstinence *see* capital supply
Adams, F.   729n
Adcroft, G.   918
Aftalion, A.   560n
agriculture
  diminishing returns   xiv, 5, 22, 35–6, 42, 46, 52, 63, 183, 185, 188–9, 191, 208–16, 231–2
  limited scope for division of labour 204–5
  constraints on science, experimentation and innovation in   207, 220–1
  small and large scale compared   207–8
  and sectoral interdependence   216, 225, 234–5
  JSM's increasing optimism regarding productivity advance in   225–6
  exhaustible natural resources   451
  soil exhaustion   740–1
  see also landed property; landlord class; land-tenure systems; protection
Ahiakpor, J.   17n
Allett, J.   665n
Amsler, C. E.   758n
Anderson, J.   6
Appleyard, D. R.   329n
Arnon, A.   488n, 599n, 600
Arrow, K. J.   929, 932
Ashley, W. J.   170, 823, 917n, 920
Attwood, M.   42n
Attwood, T.   487, 509, 511, 550–4
Austin, J.   88, 168
autobiography   85, 86–91, 93, 94, 105n, 167, 168, 181, 182, 204, 336, 509n, 617, 620, 627, 631n, 638–9, 698, 771–2, 774, 785, 823, 855n, 857n, 917, 957n

Babbage, C.   38n, 163n, 203, 204, 297, 810
Bacon, F.   40n, 69, 76, 99, 102n, 152, 152n, 155, 165
Bacon, R.   255–6
Baer, C.   283n, 874, 878
Bagehot, W.   2n, 3n, 4, 15, 914, 919n, 926n
Bailey, S.   298, 303, 304n, 346, 347
Bain, A.   100, 774n, 879, 969
Baines, E.   921n
Balassa, B. A.   484n, 523n, 524
Bank Charter Act (1844)   354n, 512, 558, 573–80 *passim*, 584–7, 589–90, 597n
banking *see* money, monetary policy
Banking and Currency School controversy   555n
  see also monetary policy
Bastiat, F.   921
Baumol, W. J.   484n, 504n
Beach, E. F.   376n
Beccaria, C.   603n
Becker, G. S.   484n, 504n
Bentham, J.
  his knowledge of human nature   114n
  his 'interest-philosophy'   117–24
  on science and art   119n
  defended against Comte   175
  and historical basis to his politics   196n
  on 'forced saving'   542n

Bentham, J. *(continued)*
    his utilitarianism
        and selfishness 609, 656; and hierarchy of motives 611; and qualitative differentiation of justice 612, 656, 658; compared with James Mill's 613; a legal and legislative preoccupation 613–14; conventionality of quantification postulates 615, 659–60; principle of utility as value judgement 616, 659;
        on role of government 676, 680–1
    and tax exemption limits 860–1
Berg, M. 376n, 922n
Bharadwaj, K. 300, 916, 930
Birmingham School 487, 509, 511, 550–5
Black, R. D. C. 60, 270n, 745n, 849n, 854n, 925n, 929n, 939n
Bladen, V. W. 219n, 252
Blake, W. 489, 492, 499
Blanc, L. 783, 794, 897, 952
Blaug, M.
    on impact of Jones' *Essay* 44
    on predictive objective of classical theorizing 57, 58, 918, 945n
    on Chalmers 58
    contrasts Mill and Senior on method 69–70
    on von Thünen 99
    on verification as task of applied economics 126, 962
    on distribution and pricing 246
    on natural and market prices 284n
    on measure of value 346–7
    on savings and employment 373n
    on human capital 721
    on economics of education 700n, 701n, 711n, 718n, 725, 729
    on outdoor-relief 743n
    on degeneration of Ricardian research program 945n
    on JSM's Malthusianism 946n
    on 'self-interest' axiom 959
Bonar, J. xi, 735
Boole, G. 937
Boot, H. M. 462n
Bordo, M. D. 148n
Bortkiewicz, L. von 341–2
Bosanquet, C. 20
Boss, H. 259n
Boulding, K. E. 931n

Bowley, M. 64, 144n, 145n, 298, 300n, 303, 391n, 934, 945n, 958
Bradley, M. E. 238n
Brady, A. 749n
Breit, W. 275, 418n
Briggs, A. 727
Brougham, H. 38
Buchanan, J. M. 782n
Buchdahl, G. 154n
Buckle, H. T. 97n, 106n, 138n, 141n
Bulwer, E. L. 93, 94, 637
Burnell, P. 667n
Burns, A. F. 549n
Bush, W. C. 238n

Cairnes, J. E.
    on method 147
    on consumer theory 270–2
    on price formation 277–9
    on nature of costs 285, 357
    on non-competing groups 309, 316n
    on corn-profit model 351–2, 965–6
    his wages-fund model 402–4, 405, 409, 420
    on relation interest and profit rates 439
    on credit and accumulation 528n
    on monetary aspects of interest-rate determination 539–41, 544
    as utilitarian 615
    on Wakefield's land-disposal scheme 754
    and Ireland 853–4
    his review of Jevons 938n
    on mathematics in economics 943
    on US–British interest rate differentials 963–7
Cambridge ('inductive') critics xiii, 38–46, 149–50, 154–5
Cannan, E.
    his evaluation of the *Principles* xi
    on Chalmers 59
    on classical national income accounts 253
    on fourth proposition on capital 372n
    on first proposition on capital 392n
    on wages-fund theory 398n
Cannon, W. E. 157
capital
    human 253–5
    maintenance of 257, 366–71
    fourth proposition on ('demand for commodities is not demand for labour')

capital *(continued)*
  a theorem on aggregate employment 263, 360, 371–6, 398–9, 420–2, 929n; and law of markets 393
  differential structure of, and relative prices 282
  mobility, and cost pricing 284
  Marx on 340, 365
  as accumulated labour 342–4, 359–60, 361–2
  first proposition on ('industry limited by') 360, 364–5, 393, 417, 520
  fixed v. circulating 364–5, 366, 377n, 401
  Fundism v. Materialism 366, 369
  third proposition on ('consumption of capital') 367
  permanent investments of 369–70
  second proposition on ('the result of saving') 371
  investment and labour demand 374–6
  uncertainty and long-lived investment 385n
  investment and risk 437–8
  wastage 464, 465
  exportation 465, 474–5, 561n
  credit-creation v. capital-creation 528
  see also machinery; wages-fund doctrine
capital market
  and restrictions on innovatory investment 214
  and profit-rate equalization 293
capital supply
  its source in surplus 427, 429
  and abstinence 427, 428, 436, 533n, 809, 830, 833, 840
  wages as source of savings 427–8
  and 'effective desire of accumulation' 428, 432, 437
  and interest rate 430–3
  in stationary state 433–8, 450–1
  under socialism 431–2, 806–7
Caravale, G. 449n
Carey, H. C. 213–16, 288, 441n, 740
Carlyle, T. 85, 93, 175n, 182n, 606n, 618–19, 921
Carr, J. L. 17n
Cazenove, J. 38n
centralization 677, 684, 693, 712, 713, 748, 761–2, 763
Chadwick, E. 711, 750n, 762, 918
Chalmers, T. xiii, 55–6, 177, 181, 464n

his population doctrine 58–60, 65
  on stationary state at high wages 60
Chapters on Socialism 302n, 431, 437n, 782–5, 794–800, 806–8, 820–1, 823, 832, 952
Chartism 184, 849
Châteauvieux, J. F. L. de 242
Checkland, S. G. 148n, 155, 156, 181n, 915n, 918n, 943, 967n
Chipman, J. S. 12, 320–1, 328n, 329n
Clark, J. B.
  on capital 366n, 369
  on stationary state 423, 425
  on 'problem of interest' 434
classical economics
  and prediction 57, 58, 917, 945n
  exonerated of apologetic intent 181f, 921
  and utilitarianism 154n, 602–3, 605, 615
  national income accounting 253
  theory of production 261
  entrepreneurship 316n, 319
  international trade theory 321n, 330n
  competition 276n, 379
  monetary policy 552, 572
  human capital 721
  and economic effects of education 722–3
  and non-universalist theory of economic policy 737
  on outdoor poor-relief 743n
  on combination laws 751n
  monopoly 758, 759
  and growth of *per capita* output 875–6, 882
  opposed paternalism 909n
  historicist reaction to 915n
  Jevons and Walras on 928–9
  supposed insolubility of paradox of value 929, 935n
  and one-use land 932
  charged with 'despotic' influence 967n
Clemence, R. V. 922n
Coats, A. W. 915n, 926n, 967n
Cobbett, W. 552n
Cobden, R. 921
Cochrane, J. L. 39n
Coleridge, S. T. 85, 102n, 182n, 197n, 639
Collini, S. 68n, 122n, 124n

colonies
  and Wakefield proposals 475–6
  and market failure 698, 699–700
  and disposal of colonial land 749, 753–5
  and state-supported emigration 755–6, 891
communism, *see* socialism
competition
  and custom 108, 125, 195, 266, 301–2, 303–4
  and science of political economy 120n, 125, 160–1, 265, 301, 959, 962–3
  and land-tenure arrangement 238
  'classical' 276n, 378–9
  and women's earnings 785n
  no guarantee of 'quality' 785, 821
  see also imperfect competition; JSM, his respect for competition
Comte, Auguste xiii, 82n, 87, 90–1, 94, 136, 137n, 159, 196n
  and human character formulation 90–1, 173–4, 771n, 958
  and the *Principles* 168–77, 770
  and progress 170n
  his philosophy of history 171–2
  his view of political economy 173, 174–5, 927
  and specialization in social science 173–4, 195
  and Benthamite utilitarianism 638n
  and mathematics 940–1
Condorcet, M. de 956
Considerant, V. P. 783
consumer behaviour 247
  and wealth-maximization axiom 265–7
  conspicuous consumption 267–8, 672n
  and taxation 664, 860, 872–3; and reform of opinion 907–8
  JSM's denial of 'laws' of consumption 268–9, 324, 934
  and logic of choice 270–2, 935, 936
  see also price theory, utility theory
co-operation (division of labour)
  relation to social progress 188–90, 204–5, 228–9
  limited scope in agriculture 204–5
  and excess capacity 500–1
  see also industry structure
co-operative organization
  and payment of interest 429n, 811

JSM's ideal for future 775, 810–19, 820–1
  French experience of 810–11
  and piecework 811
  and progress 812
  and intra-industry competition 813
  and efficiency 813–14
  and liberty 814
  and euthanasia of unions 814
  and innovation 816
  its impact on capitalist sector
    reduces exploitation 818, 822; reduces product adulteration 827; reduces proliferation of distributors 822
  agricultural 837–8, 846
  as educational training ground 767, 909–10
Cooter, R. 935n
corn laws *see* protection
Corry, B. A. 477n, 478n, 485, 503n, 508n, 511
cost of production
  historical record of 205–6, 232–5
  as compensation for effort and abstinence 285–6, 357, 932
  as alternative opportunities 285, 932
  see also price theory
Cournot, A. 300n
Cramp, A. B. 582n
Croker, J. W. 925n
Crouch, R. L. 680, 758n
Crouzet, F. 725
custom
  and competition 108, 125, 195, 266, 301–3, 303–4
  and wage structure 309, 311–12
  and utilitarianism 624–5, 629
  and liberty 661–2, 663, 664–7

Davis, S. 15n
defence 886
On the Definition and Method of Political Economy (1836)
  and the *Principles of Political Economy* 69, 162–3, 163–4, 189, 209, 212, 266–7, 958, 960
  champions 'mixed method of induction and ratiocination' 71, 925–7
  on science and application ('art') 67, 69, 91, 151, 180–1

On the Definition and Method of Political Economy (1836) *(continued)*

on verification as 'application' of science 67, 69, 126f, 962

accords major role to empirical evidence 68–9, 69–70, 91, 158

on introspection and wealth-maximization axiom 68, 112–15

on political economy as 'science of wealth' 69

compared with Senior's position 69–70, 142–9, 149

on 'disturbing causes' 70, 107, 111, 113, 116f, 960

and *A System of Logic* 71, 90, 174

a response to James Mill's 'geometrical' constructions 91–2, 94, 95, 118, 915–16

opposes universally applicable axioms in political economy 110–11, 116, 120–1, 149

and model improvement 126–8, 962–3

and Cambridge inductivists 149–53, 158

and 'inverse deductive method' 190, 195–6

denies 'laws' of consumption 268–9, 934

see also wealth-maximization axiom

Descartes, R. 82

Dewey, C. J. 238n, 242n

diminishing returns *see* agriculture

distribution

'pseudo' – v. class 28, 248

and organization of *Principles* 177–85, 185–7

and pricing 187, 246–7, 248, 344–5

and surplus 198–9

and derived factor demand ('imputation') 247, 261–4, 412–13

and rental share 248

and joint-demand 262, 413

redistribution and diminishing utility 264–5, 268, 872, 880–1, 883, 934

and configuration of demand 360–2

and accumulation 375, 406, 517, 865

and utilitarianism 653–4

distributive justice 779, 781, 782–3, 828–9, 886

and taxation 826–7, 858–75

see also fundamental theorem on distribution; laws of production and distribution

distributors

role of dealers in price formation 276, 289n

and efficiency loss 302, 814

under Fourierism 807

under co-operation 814–15

Dobb, M. 45n, 360

Dryer, D. P. 646n

Dumont, P. E. L. 618n

Dunoyer, B. C. P. J. 203n, 707n

Dupont-White, C. B. 747–8, 764–5

economic development

desirability of 16, 738, 881–8

'underdevelopment' defined 666, 689, 738

role of government 672n

encouragement of individual energy and voluntary co-operation 739; 'infant industry' case for protection 739–40

education and 721–7

liberty and 738–9

and security of property 827, 863

and unearned increment of land values 834–6

inflationary program rejected 510–11, 515–16, 552, 565–6

see also growth theory; stationary state

The Economist 919n, 921–2

Edger, E. R. 267n

Edgeworth, F. Y.

on scientific character of political economy 159–60

on incremental utility 264, 326

on JSM's international trade theory 325–9 *passim*, 335n, 356, 464–9

as utilitarian 605

on small-numbers market structure 963n

education

and scope of political economy 219–20

and wage structure 308–9, 723

and correction of destabilizing speculative propensities 550, 588

and social control 663

and market failure 696–8, 715, 716

defects of contemporary private provision 700–3, 724–6, 728–9

and productivity 704–5, 722–3

and citizenship 705

government provision of 706–7, 710

education (*continued*)
and means test 707–8, 718–19; avoidance of state monopoly 709, 710, 727; subsidization of private sector 709, 710, 728, 828; voucher system of 711; selection of staff in state-supported schools 711, 728; state intervention to strengthen private system 717–18, 728, 729
and endowed schools 712–15, 728
private fees in 715–16, 728
Schools Inquiry Commission (1868) 718–19, 726
state responsible to 'élite', in superior 718–20
vocational training and the market 720–1, 722–3
and economic development 721–4
Royal (Newcastle) Commission on Popular Education (1861) 724–6
part-time 749–50n
and co-operation 767, 909–10
and population control 890–1, 899, 948–9, 950
and bourgeois bias 908–9
Eichthal, G.d' 88n, 90, 174, 772n, 939, 956
Ekelund, R. B. Jr. 176n, 397n, 414n, 419n, 827, 898, 899, 904
Ellis, W. 386, 435n, 475, 478n
Eltis, W. 256, 376n, 380n
emigration
government funding of 469, 755, 891
private finance of 757, 893–7
employment (aggregate)
and wage structure 307–8
and expectations 375
and aggregate demand 392, 520
and saving 400
and excess capacity as condition of steady growth 499–504, 509–10, 553
full-employment policy a moral imperative 745–7
takes precedence over efficiency 846
see also capital, fourth proposition on; wages-fund doctrine
employment (firm)
see distribution and derived factor demand
Empson, W. 56
Engels, F. 892n, 953
entrepreneurship 319–20

equality
of opportunity 605, 719, 827, 828, 830
and justice 647, 650, 669–70, 719
under communism 798
'false' perspectives on 873–4, 884
equilibrium 272–4, 276, 967
'dynamic' 47, 445
and interest rate 273n, 525n, 533–4
multiple 328–9, 410n
ethology *see* progress
Examination of Sir W. Hamilton's Philosophy 152n
The Examiner 921, 977–8
exchange
as 'machinery' of distribution process 186, 342n, 345
see also price theory
expectations
and short-run price formation 278–9, 488, 513
and cost-price determination 284, 290
and wage-structure analysis 306–7
destabilizing and cycle 495, 503, 513, 513–15, 519n, 530–1n, 550
and interest-rate determination 541–2
and abolition of duties 733, 735
see also trade cycle

Fawcett, H. 410n, 418n, 419, 818, 918
Fenn, R. 14n, 15n, 91n
Ferguson, C. E. 94
Fetter, F. W. 354n, 600, 601
Feugueray, H. 781
Finer, S. E. 119n
firm *see* industry structure
Fisher, I. 428n, 536
Flew, A. 951n
Fonblanque, A. W. 638
Forget, E. 289n
Fourier, C. 431, 800–8
Fourierism *see* socialism
Foxwell, H. S. 915, 916–17n, 939n
France
1789 Revolution 87, 203–4, 226, 233, 454
1848 Revolution 745, 786, 810–11
'le droit au travail' (1848) 745–6
Ateliers Nationaux 747
centralization in 763–4
1852 Napoleonic takeover 811–12
character of land-purchasers in 839

France (*continued*)
  peasant proprietorship and efficiency in 854
Fraser, D. 921n
Friedman, M. 154, 552n, 572n
Fullarton, J.
  on speculation 481
  on monetary theory and policy 530, 566, 574–5, 576
fundamental theorem on distribution
  and allocation economics 65, 245, 248, 344–5, 355–62, 932–3
  as 'law of arithmetic' 187
  and proportionate shares 187, 337, 342–4, 348–9
  and standard measure of value 245, 248, 335, 346–50
  and quantity theory 248, 354–5
  JSM's Marx-like formulation 335
  and 'cost of labour' 339, 342–3, 349–50
  and Torrens 340, 344
  and Longfield 344
  and 'money' wages 349
  and international trade 356–7
  and factor proportions 358–9
  and wages-fund doctrine 417–20
  and foreign trade policy 734, 919
  and trade unions 770, 918
  testing of 963–7

George, H. 398n, 905n
Gilmour, R. 922n
Gladstone, W. E. 861n, 866
Godwin, W. 951n
Goethe, J. W. von. 85
Gold Standard *see* monetary policy
Gomperz, T. 70n, 112n, 175n
Gordon, B. J. 56n
Gordon, S. 91n, 397n, 664n, 921n
Göschen, G. J. 465n
Gosden, P. H. J. H. 727n
government
  Ricardo and theory of, 23–4
  Benthamite theory of 23–4, 88, 91, 117–25, 613–14, 623–5, 640
  Macaulay on James Mill's essay on 89–90, 94
  Comte and theory of 90–1
  and dangers of extended franchise 713n, 826–7n, 909
  in United States 713
  and voting qualifications 912n

government expenditure
  and tendency of profit rate to minimum 468, 487
  support of, not 'Keynesian' 470–4, 478–9, 486–7, 582–3
  and public works 583n
government regulation
  of public utilities 300, 760–2
  and State central banking 584–5, 593
  and 'self-regarding' v. 'other regarding' acts 661–2, 677–80, 681, 686, 700
  and compensation 672–3, 747
  and liberty 677, 684, 685–6, 690, 700
  'authoritative' v. 'unauthoritative' 679, 684, 686, 689, 693
  'self-destructive' 679, 708, 727, 905, 908
  laissez-faire principle
    subordinate to utility 680–1; presumptive case favouring 684
  and case for free trade: efficiency 685, 686, 689; socio-political 690–2; consumer liberty 693–6
  and control of food prices 686
  and emergency shortages 687
  and control of interest rate 687–8
  and market failure
    consumer ignorance 696–7; acts on behalf of second parties 696–7, 755; divergence of social and private return 699, 738; public goods 699; 'free-rider' issue 699, 749, 750, 752–3; monopoly 758–62
  and education 700–20
  and economic development 738–41
  and population control 741–2, 746
  and poor relief 741–4
  and full employment policy 745–6
  administration of 747–9, 761–2
  and delegated management 749
  and labour market 749, 751–3
  and colonization 753–8
  and patent protection 762–3
  and progress 763–9
  State purchase and disposition of land 837–9
Grampp, W. D. 664n, 750n, 921
Grant, R. 6n
Gray, J. 664
Gray, John 518
Gregory, T. E. 488n, 560n, 599n, 600n
Groenewegen, P. D. 281

Grossman, H. 958n
Grote, G. 89, 93, 113n, 638
growth theory
    and land scarcity xiv
    agricultural model 9, 24, 729–30,
        965–6
    and declining wage path 46–9, 52, 54,
        62–3, 444, 730, 945n
    equilibrium status of points on 424–5
    and population 46–50, 426, 444–5,
        946–7
    and subsistence wages 46–50, 445
    and dynamic equilibrium 47, 445
    and steady-state wages 49, 425–6, 443,
        444–5, 445–50
    Longfield and 60–3
    statics and dynamics 136–7, 189,
        422–6
    scope of JSM's analytical formulation
        190–1
    and social progress 223–38
    and size of firm 230, 783
    excess capacity as condition of steady
        growth 499–504, 510
    see also economic development; profit-
        rate trend; stationary state

Hafer, R. W. 414n, 416n, 827, 897–907
Hamburger, J. 667n
Hamilton, Sir William 937
Harris, A. L. 762n
Harrod, R. 434n
Harte, N. B. 165, 913
Haswell, P. 376n
Hawtrey, R. G. 547n, 554n, 560n
Hayek, F. von 168n, 185n, 263n, 368n,
        371n, 376n, 434n, 436, 502n, 509n,
        744n, 827n, 917, 931n, 955–6
Hébert, R. F. 319
Heertje, A. 376n
Helps, A. 179, 183, 700, 829n
Helvetius, C. A. 603n
Henderson, J. P. 39n
Hermann, F. B. W. von xi
Herschel, Sir John 38n, 44, 45, 76, 85,
        149–53
Hicks, Sir John
    on JSM's reputation xi
    on scope of JSM's theory of demand
        247, 320
    on term 'capital' 366, 368–9
    on machinery 376n

on secular wage path 424
on JSM's 'disposal' of growth economics
    426
on *The Influence of Consumption on Production*
    484, 485
on 'Full Performance' 502n
on JSM's theory of cycles 505n
on classical monetary policy 552,
    572–3
Himes, N. E. 968, 970
Himmelfarb, G. 666n
Hirsch, A. 148n
historical school 164, 194n, 196,
    913–15
    and stages of economic growth 197n
    Ricardianism and 913–28
history 165, 193–4, 194–200
Hobson, J. A. 665n
Hodgskin, T. 921n
Hollander, S. 4, 10n, 12, 24–5, 28, 29,
    31, 39n, 49, 62, 63, 65, 70, 80n, 82n,
    149n, 155–6, 191n, 198n, 203, 204n,
    213n, 215n, 221n, 245, 255n, 261,
    266n, 270, 270n, 274, 276n, 280, 283,
    301, 306n, 308n, 313n, 327n, 332,
    344, 348, 359, 360, 373n, 375n, 376n,
    379, 383, 385, 400, 406, 416n, 424,
    428, 488n, 494, 508n, 546n, 613,
    722n, 738, 744, 776n, 968n, 933, 934
Hoselitz, B. F. 197n
Howell, G. 919
Howitt, W. 238
Hubbard, J. G. 868, 971–6
Humboldt, F. H. von 663
Hume, D. 516n, 523n, 551n, 565, 603,
    615, 641n
Hunter, L. C. 366n, 543–4
Hurt, J. S. 725
Hutcheson, F. 603n
Hutchison, T. W. 17n
    on Ricardo and James Mill on method
        1–3, 20, 29
    and methodological revolution (in 1817)
        2, 8f, 913
    on the essay on method 68, 925n
    on the wages-fund doctrine 405
    on the law of markets 470, 478n, 509n
    on JSM as historian of thought 498n
    on JSM and centralization 761n
    on the franchise 827n
    attributes belated 'historicism' to JSM
        913–14

Hutchison, T. W. *(continued)*
  denies 'relativism' characteristic of JSM
    925n
  on J. B. Say 928n
  on demand theory 932
  on JSM and the Ricardian Vice 945
  and wage structure analysis 934n
  on JSM's Malthusianism 946n

imperfect competition
  and increasing returns 300
  monopolistic competition model 301,
    303
  small-numbers case 301, 963n
  custom and non-price competition
    301-3, 304, 963
  efficiency loss 302
  price discrimination 302-3
  professional remuneration 303
  barriers to entry 304
  banking 303
  'dynamic' losses from 758-9
  see also monopoly
income *see* national income; taxation
    (income)
increasing returns 188-9, 204-7, 297
  and innovation 203-4, 221
  and joint-stock organization 207
  and management 207, 208, 221, 229
  test of 297, 378
  machine-intensive processes and size of
    firm 297
  and taxation 297-8, 335n
  compatibility with competition 300
industry structure
  joint-stock organization 207, 218-19,
    228-31, 439
    and efficiency of delegated manage-
      ment 749, 759-60
  concentration and industry size 297
    and impact of low profit rate 462n;
    and secular tendency towards 783
  see also increasing returns; competition;
    imperfect competition
The Influence of Consumption on Production
    (1844) 28, 394-5, 484-5, 498
Ingram, J. K. 68, 162, 329n
innovation 203, 221
  and diminishing returns 191, 209,
    211-12
  and scale 206-7, 230
  constraints on, in agriculture 207, 220-1

  and joint-stock organization 207,
    227n, 230
  financial restrictions on 214
  and sectoral interdependence 216,
    225, 235
  electromagnetic telegraph 219n
  contemporary prospects for 224
  induced by low profit rate 227n,
    466-7
  and role of competition 227n, 758-9,
    762-3, 775-6, 780-1, 815
  and wealth-maximization 230
  and international values 327, 332-3
  agricultural 380
  impact on saving 385-6
  in stationary state 451, 887
  and compensation for displaced
    labour 672, 885
  and patent protection 762
  and communism 787
  and co-operation 816
  facilitated in growing system 887n
  see also machinery
interest rate
  and stable equilibrium 273n, 525n,
    533
  and wages 308n
  and capital supply 430-2, 533n
  and labourers' co-operative associations
    429-30n
  and socialism 431, 806
  secular decline in 438, 462, 535
  and relation to profit rate 438-9,
    533
  and transmutation of capitalism into co-
    operation 817, 885n
  monetary aspects of
    and gold-discoveries 439, 541, 542-3,
    544; interrelation between commodity
    and bond markets 532, 538-9, 541;
    relation of natural and market rates
    532-4; and government borrowing
    533; cyclical movements of 535-6;
    impact of money-supply increase on
    536-9, 543-4; and role of expecta-
    tions 541; and forced savings 542,
    543; and speculation 545
  loanable-fund theory 533-4
  'real' determinants of 544
  short-run monetary impact on 544
  legitimacy of 776, 781, 811
  US-British differential analysed 963-7

international trade
  foreign exchange rate   34, 491n, 546
  comparative advantage   321
  vent-for-surplus   321, 325
  gains from trade
    efficiency 322, 325–6, 737; dynamic
    737; intellectural and moral 737
  terms of trade   322–3, 332
  consumer perspective on   325, 688–9,
    729
  and fundamental theorem on distribu-
    tion   356–7, 919
  see also protection
international values
  and demand analysis   247, 322–4, 328,
    932
  impact of duties on   270–1, 333–5
  Torrens on   321, 325
  Ricardo on   320–1, 321, 322, 325, 329,
    335
  and reciprocal demand   323–4, 326
  and transport costs   324–5, 330–1, 332
  and diminishing marginal utility   326
  and importers' profits   330, 332
  impact of technical change on   326–7,
    332–3
  and multiple equilibria   328–9, 410n
  in money regime   329–31
invention see knowledge
Ireland
  land reclamation and public works
    177n, 583n, 848
  land tenure   177n, 243–4, 847–8
  financial restrictions on agricultural
    innovation   214–15
  and character of Irish   244
  land reform   847–55
  on transformation of agriculture and
    easing of population pressure
    849–50
  on failure of real wage to rise   853,
    954–5
investment see capital

James, R. W.   428n
Jenkin, F.   914
Jevons, W. S.   xi, 914
  his charges against JSM   245, 929
  ascribes to JSM neglect of consumer
    demand   263
  criticizes JSM's first proposition on
    capital   360

his Coal Question   451n
as Utilitarian   605, 929n
his criticisms of British classicism
  928–9
and mathematical method   929n, 939n
JSM's criticisms of   935, 936–7, 939
and psychological basis for demand
  935–6
the 'Jevons rule'   959
his perspective on scientific revolutions
  966n
on despotism of classical orthodoxy
  967n
Johnson, H. G   360
Johnston, J.   255
joint-stock organization see industry structure
Jones, R.   149, 155, 242
  on Ricardo's method   5, 39–42
  criticizes differential rent doctrine   40–2
  on Mill's essay on method   68, 158n
  denounces birth control   156
  on peasant proprietorship as stimulus to
    population   241
  supposed influence on JSM   238n
Jonung, L.   384n
justice
  and protection of individual liberty
    605, 648, 662, 670, 826
  and qualitative ranking of utilities   612,
    647–51, 654–5, 656, 658
  and equality and impartiality   647,
    650, 670, 789–90
  and private property   671, 673–6
  and compensation   672
  and labour   669–71, 673–6, 826
  and equality of opportunity   719, 826,
    827–8, 829
  and patent and copyright protection
    762–3
  and dishonesty of labour   778, 778–9
  on contemporary failure of distributive
    justice   779, 781, 782–3, 792, 828
  and general competitive wage   779–81
  and competitive wage structure   782,
    784–5, 828, 906–7
  and equality under communism   797–8
  and property   830–3, 839

Kames, Lord   94
Kant, I.   647, 657
Kauder, E.   264

Kautsky, K. 953n
Kay, J. 238
Keynes, J. M. 384n, 397n, 434n, 517n, 523-4n, 532, 533n, 939
Keynes, J. N. 68, 143n, 162, 944
Keynesianism 470-4, 478-9, 486-7, 505-6, 513, 515
Kittrell, E. 471n, 478n, 754
Knight, F. H. 246, 284n, 299n, 423, 939n
knowledge
  relation to social progress 188-90, 227
  sources of 190, 193, 220-1, 226-7
  and political economy 191, 218, 219, 220, 226
  as 'disturbing cause' 191, 467
  specialization and invention 204, 220-1
  constraints on science and invention in agriculture 207, 221
  Marx on scientific knowledge 219n
  electromagnetic telegraph, the outcome of pure research 219n
  Smith on inventiveness 221, 230-1
  inventiveness and general level of intelligence 220-1
  and wealth-maximization 229
  prospects for chemical and mechanical invention 235
  inventions within state of knowledge 237n
  inventions induced by low profit rate 466-7
  scientific research and market failure 699
  basic research and market failure 699-700
  and patent protection 762
  invention and competition 776
  invention under communism 787
Koot, G. M. 68, 163, 926n
Kordsmeier, W. F. 827, 899
Kubitz, O. A. 70n
Kuznets, S. 260, 455n

labour
  the condition-of-the-people issue 178-80, 183-5
    and utilitarianism 605, 670, 673-6; higher *per capita* income and redistribution as major policy objectives 426, 825-6, 884, 885; and the poverty trap 888-97, 949, 950; and trade unionism 897-907
  quality of 201-2
  and industrial relations 202
  trustworthiness of 203
  education and health of 219-20
  policy based on wage-fund and population doctrines 390-4
  market for 409-17
    contemporary conditions of 451-7
  short-run supply of 440
  regulation of hours 684, 700, 749-51, 753
  full employment a moral imperative 745
    state intervention to act on global labour market 746
  child and female 749-50
  and piecework 778, 789, 791, 797, 811
  see also capital; distribution; unions; wages-fund doctrine
Laidler, D. 488n, 550, 598, 599-600
Laing, S. 238, 239, 241
Lalor, J. 181, 182n, 438, 921
landed property
  no case for from justice 830
  and utility 830-1, 840
  and taxation of future increment of land values 835, 871-2, 876
  on state purchase and disposition of 837-9
  see also rent
landlord class
  Ricardo's attitude towards 32, 54, 835
  JSM unsympathetic towards 494n
  the sole beneficiaries of agricultural protection 729-30
  justice for 835
  an obstacle to progress 835n
  charge of scientific backwardness withdrawn 855
land-tenure systems
  peasant proprietorship 177n
    not ideal 242n, 844
  and inverse deductive method 194, 238-9
  and productivity 207, 238-40, 243
  competitive analysis of 238
  and custom 238n
  and population control 241-2, 243, 244, 844, 847, 854, 893, 897, 950-1
  'spontaneous' selection of 242, 842

land-tenure systems *(continued)*
    and land reform
        distributive aspects 833–9; efficiency
        aspects 839–47; Irish 847–54
    co-operation   838, 846
Landes, D. S.   725
Lange, O.   484n, 517n
Lardner, D.   38n
Lauderdale, Lord   249n
Lavergne, L. de.   242
law
    and control of mercantile fraud   821–2
    and restraints on land transfer   834,
        838–42 *passim*, 879
    and primogeniture   834, 839
    failure of self-interest by 'agricultural'
        legislature   842–4
    and adoption of British agriculture in
        Ireland   852–3
    regressiveness of contemporary legal
        system   863–4
    and population control   952
law of markets
    James Mill and J. B. Say on   10–12,
        508, 519–20
    Say's Equality v. Say's Identity   27,
        483–4
    Ricardo on   27
    JSM's original subscription to Say's
        Identity   84, 489–94, 508
    and secular trend of profit rate   467–81
    in open economy   472–4, 478–9
    excess demand for money a feature of
        depression   484–5, 486, 497, 499,
        512–13, 513–20
    no concessions to 'general-glut' theorists
        506, 513
    see also *The Influence of Consumption on
        Production* (1844)
laws of production and distribution   xiv,
    86, 167, 191, 216–23, 238, 827, 925n
    and Harriet Taylor   168
    and organization of *Principles*   168–76,
        177–84, 251–2n, 770–1
    and population control   178
    based on given knowledge   191, 193
Leclaire, E.-J.   810
Leibenstein, H.   266n, 467n
Leslie, C.   148, 194, 196, 253n, 279n,
    528–9n
    on JSM's lack of 'doctrine of evolution'
        164

his influence on JSM   254–5n, 914
and inheritance proposals   879
his use of *Principles*   926–7
on JSM's 'mixed' method   927
on mathematics in economics   943
Levy, D.   280, 666n, 951n, 970n
Levy, M. B.   885
Lewis, W. A.   249n, 440n
liberty
    and government intervention   677,
        684, 685–6, 689–90, 693–6, 700
    and education   700
    and desirability of economic develop-
        ment   738
    and population control   741–2, 746
    centralization, a threat to   748
    and unions   751
    and social responsibility   766–7
    public opinion, a threat to   767–8
    and class organization   777–8
    and communism   788, 799
    and Fourierism   807
    and co-operation   813–14
On Liberty
    as individuality   661
    as constituent of 'general good'   662,
        663, 664–7
    and despotism of custom   662, 667
    as key to social-control problem   661–2,
        669–70, 677, 684
    and character formation   662–3, 664,
        671
    and conventionality of utilitarian axioms
        for legislative purposes   662
    justice, as protection of liberty   662,
        669
    legitimate exceptions   666–7
    and suicide   666, 693–4
    social advantage of   667–8
Limited Liability Act (1855)   809n
Link, A. N.   319
Link, R. G.   462n, 464n, 464, 465, 515n,
    581n
Lloyd, W. F.   47n, 56, 270n
Locke, J.   551n, 627
Long, D. G.   609n, 669n
Longe, F. D.   418n
Longfield, M.   xiii, 5, 47
    defends Ricardo's deductive method   39
    defends differential rent doctrine   39,
        423
    and Ricardian growth model   60–1

Longfield, M. (continued)
  and profit-rate determination   60–1
  on population mechanism   65
  his exposition of law of demand   270n
  on non-competing groups   310n
  and fundamental theorem on distribu-
    tion   344
Lowe, R.
  on economics of education   715, 727
  on agricultural protection   735
  his extreme laissez-faire proposals   915,
    923–4
  and The Times   919n
  and Ricardo   925f
Loyd, S. J. (Lord Overstone)   512, 556,
  574, 598
Lubbock, J. W.   38n
Lyons, D.   669n

Macaulay, T. B.   89, 91
McCann, W. P.   726, 750n
McCloskey, D. N.   743n
McCulloch, J. R.   163, 238, 242, 246,
  494, 499
  compares James Mill and Ricardo
    12–13
  on labour theory   26–7
  his review of Jones   44n
  on Malthus and Chalmers as 'pessimists'
    54–6, 60
  and 'disturbing causes'   58, 144n
  on population mechanism   65
  member of 'old school' on stationary
    state   88n, 886
  criticizes Senior on method   148
  as laissez-faire apologist   181, 921
  on productive labour   249–50
  on fourth proposition on capital   361–2
  on capital as antecedent labour   362
  on conspicuous consumption   267–8n
  his monetary policy   512, 556
  on quality of private schooling   727
  and poor relief   744
  and   defence   of   aristocratic
    institutions   834, 839–40, 921
  on regressive legal system   864
Machiavelli, N.   175
machinery ('conversion' of circulating into
    fixed)
  Ricardo on   205, 360, 376–7, 379–80,
    384, 386–7
  output-reducing and output-increasing

  technologies   378–80, 380–1
  economy-wide   implications   of   379,
    381–2
  a problem in capital scarcity   381, 384
  and wages-fund model   383–4
  and net accumulation   384–7
  Marx on JSM's analysis   386–7
  and railway boom 1844–5   462n
  not dangerous considering high saving
    rate   469–70
Machlup, F.   69, 509n
McRae, R. F.   70n, 154n
Maital, S.   376n
Mallet, J. L.   4n, 38, 47, 51, 54, 60n
Malthus, T. R.
  his growth model   2, 47–50
  his differences with Ricardo   17–18,
    83–4, 282
  on political economy and mathematics
    17–18n, 942n
  and wages-fund theory   25
  refrains from endorsing Jones   37–8, 42
  his criticisms of the Ricardo School   37,
    494, 499
  and   dynamic-equilibrium   wage   path
    47–8
  and stationary state at high wages   49
  his Essay on Population   49, 50, 54
  his use of term 'tendency'   50–1, 57,
    948
  his correspondence with Senior   50–1,
    948
  criticized by McCulloch for 'pessimism'
    54–6
  opposes positive prediction regarding
    population growth   58
  and 'disturbing causes'   144n
  JSM's evaluation of   182n
  and four-stages theory   197n
  charges Ricardo with divorce cost and
    demand-supply theory   287
  and agricultural price instability   488n
  and law of markets   508n
  on 'forced saving'   542n
  his differences with JSM on population
    control   948–53
management (superintendence)   203, 205
  and scale   207, 208, 221, 230
  delegated   228–9, 319
  wages of   300–2, 429n
  and 'joint-stock' organization   749, 759
Manchester School   680, 921

Mandeville, B.   267, 630
Marchi, Neil de   18n, 39n, 42n, 57, 231, 948
    on JSM's debt to Dugald Stewart   1, 14
    on James Mill's method   14–15, 93
    on Cambridge inductivists   40, 45
    on attitudes hostile to political economy (1830–48)   42n
    on the Malthus–Whewell correspondence (1829–33)   42n
    on essay on method as basis for *Principles* 164n
    on nature of *Principles* 184
    on JSM's Ricardian method   919–20
    on consumption theory   934, 936n, 944n
    on mathematics   937
    on prediction   945n
    rejects 'despotism' of classical orthodoxy 967n
marginal revolution *see* mathematical economics; post-classical economics
Marshall, A.   4n
    his evaluation of JSM   xii
    contrasts essay on method and *Principles* 68, 163, 959–60
    and scope of economic theory   103n
    on universality of economic method 161n
    on 'custom'   238n
    defends JSM against charges by Jevons 245
    on fourth proposition on capital   263n, 365n, 371n, 373n
    on JSM's long-run price analysis 299–300
    his international trade theory   321n
    on first proposition on capital   392n
    on wages-fund model   405, 416n
    on stationary state   425n
    on steady-state wages   425–6
    on 'waiting'   434n
    on demand for money   525
    on interest-rate determination   532
    on JSM and historicism   915, 926n
    on continuity of 19th-century economics 930–1
    his rendition of JSM into mathematics 944n
Martin, D. E.   238n
Martineau, H.   85, 91n, 149, 160, 823, 921, 925n, 927

Martineau, J.   115n
Marx, K.
    on apparent and actual causation   104, 212, 340–1
    on scientific knowledge   219n
    on alienation   240n
    on impact of wage variation on price structure   282–3
    and heterogeneous labour   304
    his theory of profits   335
    his conception of capital   340
    on JSM and profit theory   341–2, 344n
    predicts declining growth rate of labour demand   385
    on JSM and machinery   385–6
mathematical economics   936–44
    Ricardo and Malthus on   17–18n
    and Whewell   149
    and Jevons   929n, 939n
    mathematical forecasting   940–1, 942
    and Comte   940
    and J. B. Say   941n
    and Leslie and Cairnes   943
    and Marshall   944n
Mazzini, G.   655
Meek, R. L.   197n, 198
Menger, C.   264, 880
mercantilism   325, 543, 688, 729–30
Merivale, H.   56, 146n
Mill, James
    his method   1–2, 5–9, 12–15
        contrasted with Ricardo's 15–36
    his agricultural growth model   9
    and law of markets   10–12, 508–9, 519–20
    his *Elements*   13, 177n, 246–7
    on population and wages   13
    his *British India* criticized by Ricardo   23–4
    his labour theory criticized by Ricardo 26, 304n
    on law of markets   27, 494
    his *Essay on Government*   88–91 *passim*, 118
    his 'geometrical' procedures   89, 91–2, 95, 920
    his *Analysis of the Phenomena of the Human Mind*   94
    compared with Whately on method 148n
    on productive consumption   258n
    and gains from trade   322

Mill, James *(continued)*
  and demand for labour   362n, 400, 401n
  on colonization   469n
  his utilitarianism and Bentham's contrasted   613–14, 658
  his narrowness and danger to minorities in democracy   30, 713
  his conversion in favour of Poor Law Act (1834)   745n
Mill, J. S.
  appeals for fair interpretation   xi
  reacts against James Mill on method   1, 15, 35, 92–4, 916, 920
  his Ricardianism   1, 167, 180–1, 245, 274, 322, 335–6, 354, 400, 471, 472, 475–7, 770, 913–20
  his juvenile defence of labour theory   26–7, 347n
  his mature position on law of markets   27–8, 392–3, 483–7
  at one with Chalmers regarding stationary state at high wages   60
  on Whewell and, proof of hypotheses   83, 153–4
    derivation of axioms 155–6; social apologetics 157–8, 641, 658
  his altered perspective (1830) on political economy   83f, 94
  his emotional crisis   85, 495, 917
  criticizes 'old school' of political economy on permanancy of social organization   85, 87–8, 823–4, 914, 922, 925; on stationary state 88n; for defence of aristocracy 854, 921, 925; for *laissez-faire* apologetics 921–4
  opposes universally applicable axioms in political economy   86, 91, 92–3, 110, 116, 120–2, 149, 958–61
  and 'provisional' social arrangement   88n, 170, 174, 177, 180, 247, 770, 823, 824, 928
  questions 'pliability' of human nature   88n, 774
  discerns error in James Mill's *Essay on Government*   88–91 *passim*, 118, 772n
  his crucial letter to d'Eichthal (Oct. 1829)   90, 772, 939, 956–7
  and Marx on apparent and actual causation   104, 212–13, 341, 342n
  questions Bentham's knowledge of human nature   114n
  protests identification of utilitarianism and selfishness   115n
  his criticisms of Benthamite 'interest-philosophy'   117–25
  absolves Benthamites of confusing science and art   119n
  on universality of method of political economy   122, 159–61, 919–20, 922
  compared with Senior on method   142–9
  hostile to German metaphysics   154n
  seeks to avoid *Methodenstreit*   158
  his essay on method as basis for *Principles*   164, 958, 959–60
  lacks 'doctrine of evolution'   164, 165, 189–90
  puts history in second place   165
  self-description   165–6, 618–19
  his evaluation of *Wealth of Nations*   167, 228–9
    on Smith's tendency to overstatement   229n
  downplays his purely abstract concern   167
  his debt to Harriet Taylor   168, 772–4
  defends political economy against Comte   168–76, 195, 927–8, 943
  his hostility to philanthropic do-gooders   178–9
  defends classical orthodoxy against charge of apologetics   180f, 921
  his Malthusianism   182, 886, 945–55
    denounces opponents of population control 184, 892; Malthus-mongering 237, 481
  warns against 'l'empiricisme systématique'   185
  his limited investigation of sources of knowledge   190
  his supposed late adoption of historicist perspective   194n, 914
  his common ground with historicists   196, 915, 925–6
  opposes Carey on diminishing returns   213–16
    diminishing returns 'the most important proposition in political economy'   212
  aware of untenability of distinction between laws of production and distribution   222–3

Mill, J. S. *(continued)*
  appreciates capitalist dynamics 223–4, 235–8, 474, 480–1, 493
  his increasing optimism regarding agricultural productivity 225–6
  disparages Jones 238n, 241
  peasant proprietorship not his ideal 242n, 844
  rejects racial theory of economic backwardness 244
  innocent of confusing technical and economic problem 251, 956
  his recantation of wages-fund doctrine 362–3, 389–90, 400, 409–17
  condemns conspicuous consumption 267, 860–1, 872–3, 880–1, 883, 908
  his denial of 'laws' of consumption discussed 268–9, 324, 934
  his marginalia to Senior's *Outline* 274n, 338n, 340n, 373n, 396n, 935n
  defends Ricardian demand–supply analysis against W. T. Thornton 275–9
  his rash statement on law of value 279, 966–7
  on theory of value as key to scientific difficulties 281, 345–6
  rejects De Quincey's claims to originality in price theory 281
  rejects labour theory 282, 304
  his criticism of Physiocracy 286
  his novel analysis of cost-price determination 289–95, 320, 939, 961
    Ricardian features of his cost-price analysis 299
  his 1828 defence of differential-rent doctrine 296–7n, 299
  on Smith's wage-structure analysis 304–9, 723–4, 961
  on non-competing groups 308–9
  on contemporary disintegration of barriers 312, 316, 934, 961
  on demand–supply as 'antecedent' to costs 320, 326
  on international trade
    his debt to Ricardo 321, 335; his early essay and *Principles* contrasted 321–2; a consumer perspective 325, 688, 729; on multiple equilibria 328–9, 410n
  his Marxian statement on source of profits 335
  his 1825 defence of McCulloch against Malthus 335, 494, 499

  on rent and population principles as 'great discoveries' 336n
  his ambiguous formulations
    of fundamental theorem on distribution 342–4; of impact of wage variation on price structure 359; of impact of change in demand configuration on distribution 359–62
  objects to Smith on 'competition of capitals' 353
  sceptical of output-reducing capital conversion 379
  optimistic regarding net employment effects of machinery 385
  in Ricardian tradition on economic organization 400
  his misleading account of wages-fund doctrine (in 1869) 409
  his regard for Thornton 420n
  his concern for economic growth and his speculations on the stationary state 426, 450–1, 884–8
  his concern for fair distribution 426, 826, 883–4, 885
  on the profit rate 'within a handsbreadth of the minimum' 426
  on legitimacy of interest 429n, 776, 781, 884, 911
  his respect for William Ellis 435n
  denies secular fall in profit rate 438, 460
  his concern to inculcate 'prudence' among unskilled labour 444, 454, 456
  neglects Ricardo's falling wage-path analysis 449–50
  commends Jevons's *Coal Question* 451n
  on corn-law repeal and population growth 454–5
  recognizes contemporary decline in population growth rate 455, 850, 852–3, 893f
  hesitates to emphasize contemporary real-wage improvement 455–7
  on high contemporary net investment at constant wage and profit rates 460, 473, 478
  on idea of endogenous trade cycle 461, 495, 963
  his altered evaluation of increasing severity of cycles 463n

Mill, J. S. *(continued)*
on increased international capital mobility 465n
his support of government funding of emigration 469, 755–6
his support of government domestic expenditure not 'Keynesian' 470–4, 478–9
on desirability of capital exportation 474–5
understands Wakefield to be Ricardian 475
consistency of his case for government expenditure and defence of law of markets 478–9
proposes discretionary Bank of England policy 487
his juvenile subscription to Treasury View 490–1; Say's Identity 489–94;
unsympathetic to landlord class 494n
his *Paper Currency and Commercial Distress* (1826) a watershed 495f, 733
his early statement of excess demand for money a mental struggle 499
misrepresents own original position on law of markets 508
his objections to Birmingham inflationists 510, 515–16, 550–5, 581
objects to Currency School program as destabilizing and deflationary 512, 531, 548, 573–4
his monetary interest-rate analysis and Marshall's compared 531
his strategic minimization of short-run monetary impact on interest rate 544
no less a monetary interventionist than Tooke 550, 572–3, 599, 600–1
his polemicism on monetary policy 554
his firm commitment to Gold Standard at ruling par 555, 577
opposed to State Central Bank 583–4, 592
undecided on banking control 594
his praise of Tooke 598n
his monetary dilemma 601
his vicissitudes regarding utilitarianism 602, 605, 607, 638–40
dissatisfaction with (1832–33) 620, 628, 639, 640, 656; his analysis of

Sedgwick's *Discourse* (1835) 628–9, 635, 639; his *Bentham* 631–6, 643, 644; his 'return' to Bentham 641–2, 657, 658
and despotism of public opinion 637, 666–7, 883–4
rejects natural rights case for private property 640
and *élitism* in ranking of utilities 650–1
and utilitarian axioms as value judgement 660–1
for legislative purposes 662
on the charge of paternalism 672, 709, 724–5, 727–8, 738–9, 911–12, 953
his debate with Thornton on 'justice' and the 'rights of labour' 673–6
his hostility to centralization 677–8, 684, 693, 712, 713, 748, 761–2, 953
his preference
for 'unauthoritative' government intervention 679, 684, 686, 689–90, 692; for 'self-destructive' intervention 679, 708, 727–8, 740
rejects class-oriented intervention 681, 873, 876, 883–4
his respect for competition 685, 687, 690, 700, 709, 771, 782–3, 784–5, 903
as engine of discovery and innovation 759, 762, 776, 781, 815
criticizes Adam Smith
on prodigals and projectors 688; on education and the state 701
on class bias and contemporary education 703, 726, 892
aims to improve private education sector 717–18, 728, 729
states 'compensation principle' of welfare economics 731
his non-dogmatic analysis of *Corn Laws* (1825) 733
favours conscription 737n
on intellectual and moral effects of international trade 737–8
on the desirability of economic development 738, 881–8
on misuse of 'infant-industry' case 739–40
opposes Carey on protection 740–1
his *Vindication of the French Revolution* (1848) 745

Mill, J. S. (*continued*)

qualified support of Full Employment policy 745

supports 1834 Poor Law Act as second best 747

population control not to be restricted to poor 746, 891n

his evaluation of delegated management 749, 759

government regulation of factory hours unnecessary in practice 749–50

favours freedom of unionization 751–2

supports Wakefield's land-disposal scheme 753–5

on growing adequacy of private finance of emigration 756–8, 894–5

his emphasis on market signals 762

his growing satisfaction with British opinion and practice regarding role of government 763–4

a Benthamite democratic reformer in 1820s 771

on practical limits to profound social reorganization 771, 879, 917–18n and deep-rootedness of self-interest motive 773–4, 795; and necessity for mental rejuvenation 775

his strategic support for anti-property doctrines in 1830s 772

self-description as 'socialist' in 1840s 772–3

his hard-headedness 774, 825, 917

champions profit sharing 775, 797, 808–10

co-operation as ideal for future 775, 810–18, 821

his indictment of labour–capital class organization and 'theory of dependence and protection' 776–7, 782–3, 820; and stationary state 777; rising wages not solution 777, 779; and dishonesty of labour as 'unjust' 778, 827, 882

champions piecework 778–9, 789, 791, 796–7, 811, 884n

on absence of distributive justice in contemporary Britain 778, 781, 783, 792, 828

denies general competitive wage is 'just' wage 779–81

supports unions and property-reform to

counter unequal bargaining power 782

on competitive wage structure as 'just' 781, 785

rejects Considérant on increased concentration 783

on small quantitative benefit from redistribution 784, 881

rejects Louis Blanc on inevitability of secular wage decline 783, 896–7, 952

competition no guarantee of quality 785, 821

liberty and equitable distribution as the objects of reformed property system 790, 793–4, 803–5, 826, 832

his preference for Fourierism amongst social alternatives 806–8

excessive class of distributors rather than profit main defect of capitalist distribution 814

favours euthanasia of unions via co-operation 814

and transmutation of capitalism into co-operation 817, 885n

insists on gradualism in social experiment 819

rejects collectivism 819–20

his position on socialism summarized 820–4

his taxation proposals and income distribution 827, 859–76

favours security of property 827, 874, 884

his case for distributive justice demonstrated 827, 897–907

champions diffusion of wealth 834

critical of McCulloch's defence of aristocratic institutions 834, 839–40, 921

his land proposals 833

proposes taxation of (future) unearned increment of land values 834–6, 871–2, 876

gives precedence to employment over efficiency 846, 847, 855, 885

discerns transformation of agriculture and easing of population pressure in Ireland 849–53

on failure of Irish real wages to rise 853, 954–5

withdraws charge of scientific backwardness against landlords 855

Mill, J. S. *(continued)*
  proposes mixed system of direct and indirect taxation 871
  taxation proposals summarized 871-2
  reform of succession duties as 'key to social progress' 879
  solution to poverty problem summarized 890-7
  on population control and choice between economic systems 892, 896-7, 953
  his new optimism regarding population control 891-7
  his conditional defence of exclusive unions discussed 897-907
  his 'bourgois bias' discussed 907-12
  his aversion to Lowe's *laissez faire* proposals 914-15
  misuse of political economy 919n, 923-4
  his perspective on scientific revolutions 916n, 966-7
  and post-classical economics 928-34
  and marginal utility 934-6
  his criticisms of Jevons 935, 936-7, 938-9
  his differences with Malthus on population control 948-54
  his insistence on the 'reality' of axioms reiterated 958-61
  major instances of his model improvement 962-3
  on birth control 968-70
Miller, J. D. Jr. 418n
Miller, W. L. 40n, 41n, 238n, 772n
mining
  technology 212n, 216
  exhaustibility of 212n, 216, 225n, 451
  and national debt 451n
Mitchell, W. C. 188n
Molesworth, Sir William 93
monetary policy
  Treasury View 479-80, 490, 498
  Currency School
    'gold-certificate' program 487, 556-7; JSM's objections to, as destabilizing and deflationary 512, 531, 548, 558, 564, 573, 574, 576, 580, 598-9; blames cycles on unregulated note issue 512, 556; on notes as superstructure of credit 531
  Birmingham inflationism 511, 515-16, 550-4, 565-6, 581

and small note issue 512n, 545n, 549, 550, 560, 595
commitment to Gold Standard at ruling par 541, 555, 577, 598
  and case for larger reserves 558, 575, 581
counter-cyclical monetary program for Bank of England
  in depression 548-50, 576-83 *passim*; in speculative periods 560-2, 569-74 *passim*, 580
'real bills' doctrine 551n
and country banks 559, 566, 596
and inconvertibility 565
on advantage of paper currency 565n
and credit policies of Bank of England 571n, 580n, 582n, 593
Bank discretion recommended in response to gold drains 574-5, 576, 580, 584
monetary and fiscal policy contrasted 582-3
on Central Bank management
  no formal legislation proposed 583, 587-8; state bank opposed 583-4, 592, 600-1; reliance on social responsibility of directorship 588-9, 589-91, 601
and multiple-banks 895-7
limited control over banking system 597, 600-1
see also Bank Charter Act (1844)
money
  'permanent' (cost) v. 'temporary' (quantity) value of 295, 521, 528-9
  elasticity of demand for 295, 524-5, 526n
  and international values 329-31
  as standard measure 347-8, 353
  bank notes, 'passivity' of and speculation 354n, 510, 546-8, 553, 578-80, 582, 558-71 *passim*, 598-9, 601
  monetary theory and method 489, 509-10, 573n
  'depreciation' and high price of bullion 491n
  inconceivable where coins circulate 545
  and speed of correction of trade imbalance 491n

money *(continued)*
  and growth
    not achievable by inflationary means
    509–11, 515–16, 552, 565–6; secular
    adequacy of money supply 518
  speculative and precautionary demands
    for 513, 521–2, 525–6
  as medium of exchange 520–1, 572–3
  integration of monetary and value
    theory 525
  credit 528, 529
  substitutes for 527, 531
  'cloakroom' banking 527n
  see also employment; interest rate; law of
    markets; quantity theory; trade cycle
monopoly
  and supply inelasticity 298n, 335n
  and revenue maximization 300–1
  and scientific economics 301, 962
  efficiency losses even if not perfect 758–9
  government
    a source of 758–9, 760
    regulation of 760–1
  and joint-stock organization 759–60
  natural 760–1
  public-utility control 761–2
  and patent and copyright protection
    762–3
  see also imperfect competition
monopolistic competition *see* imperfect
  competition
Montesquieu C. de 175
Morgan, A. De 937
Moss, L. S. 198n, 270n
Mueller, I. 176n
Myint, H. 247, 249, 251

Nagel, E. 154n
Napier, M. 180, 183
national debt 451n, 469n, 518n
national income
  accounting 247–61
  and wealth 248–50
  gross and net components of 257–60
  see also productive–unproductive labour
natural rights 640, 673–5
Neff, E. 182n
Newman, F. W. 640, 779, 781, 792n,
  804, 815, 831n, 947, 951
Newton, Sir Isaac 81n, 82
Nightingale, F. 101n
Norman, G. W. 512, 556

O'Brien, D. P. 68, 148n, 163, 346,
  391n, 421n
O'Driscoll, G. P. 377
Olsen, E. S. 176n
Owen, R. 16, 22, 88n, 105n, 182, 786

Packe, M. St. J. 774
Paley, W. 603n, 642
Pappé, H. O. 152n, 774n
Patinkin, D. 504, 517n, 522–6 *passim*,
  532, 534n, 536
peasant proprietorship *see* France, Ireland,
  land-tenure systems
Peel, Sir R. 512
Petrella, F. 470, 643n, 767n
Pennington, J. 321n
Petty, Sir W. xi
Phelps-Brown, E. H. 782n
philosophic radicals 182
Physiocracy 106, 286
Pigou, A. C. 267n, 397n, 434n, 524,
  584n
Place, F. 22, 177n
Plant, A. 762n
Playfair, W. 958n
Pollard, S. 170n
policy
  and theory 193
  and utilitarianism 606–7, 653–4
  and value judgement 663–5, 679, 880
  as constrained by opinion 827, 871,
    879, 951–2
  see also On the Definition and Method of
    Political Economy; government regula-
    tion; labour; monetary policy
political economy
  and prediction 63, 916, 945, 946–8
  on science and application ('art') 67,
    68–9, 91, 116, 118–19, 131, 132–3,
    177, 191, 265–6, 269, 301
  the 'science of wealth' 69
  inapplicability of empirical methods
    74–5, 98–101
  inductive basis for premises 77, 95–6,
    102, 147–8, 958–61
  'old school' of 85, 87, 823, 854, 914,
    921–5
  and ratiocination 96
  and induction from specific experience
    96–7
  and quantitative empirical methods
    101–2

political economy *(continued)*
  fallacies of observation in 104
  scope of 107, 133–4, 194, 770–1
  the case for specialization 108–9, 116–22
  universally applicable axioms opposed 110, 116, 120, 149
  and 'disturbing causes' 111, 116, 120, 122–4, 938
  and 'introspection' 112
  competition and science of 120n, 125, 160, 265, 301
  universality of its method 122, 159–60, 919–20, 923n
  and principle of population 124, 220, 945–55
  Comte's evaluation of 173
  Carlyle's animosity towards 182n
  and knowledge 191, 217–18, 219, 221, 226–7
  diminishing returns its 'most important law' 212–13
  value theory as 'key' 281, 345–6
  and monopoly 301, 962
  its 'secondary' status 770–1
  on Lowe's misuse of 923–4
  on verification and model improvement 962
  see also On the Definition and Method of Political Economy; Principles of Political Economy
Political Economy Club 14, 38, 47, 54, 818, 964
political science *see* government
poor relief 29–30, 54, 178
  and market failure 697–8
  and social utility 743
  1834 Poor Law Act 743, 747
Popper, Sir Karl 956, 957n
population
  in classical growth models 46–50, 426, 442–4, 444, 445–50, 946–8
  prudential control of 49–50, 178, 182–3, 426, 442–4, 455
  and the stationary state 886
  post-Ricardian discussions of Malthusianism 50–8, 64–5, 182–3
  predictions regarding 58, 141–2, 183, 185, 946–8
  and method of political economy 124, 159–60
  birth control 156, 968–70

  optimum 208, 208n, 237n, 947
  contemporary conditions 235–6, 451–7, 849–53, 892–7
  and land tenure arrangement 241–2, 243, 244, 884, 847, 854, 893, 896–7, 950–1
  and wage-rate structure 310–15
  and French Revolution 454–5
  'free rider' problem 699, 892, 950, 951
  control, and liberty 741, 746, 893
  and communism 786, 789, 792, 897, 949, 952–3
  education and population control 890, 899, 948–9, 950
  and women's rights 893
  and exclusive unions 899–906
  see also JSM, his 'Malthusianism'
Porter, G. R. 163
post-classical economics
  JSM and 245, 261, 928–33
  Hicks, on JSM's 'break-through' 320
  and altered 'concentration of attention' 931
  Jevons and Walras on 'revolutionary' break with classicism 928–9
  Marshall and continuity of 19th-century doctrine 930–1
  neo-classical elements in *Principles* 931
  JSM and marginal utility 934–6
  JSM and mathematical economics 930–44
prediction *see* scientific method
price theory
  labour theory of value 26–7, 282
  exchange, the organization of *Principles* 177–84, 185–7, 344, 347–8
  and distribution 186–7, 246–7, 248, 344–5
  derived factor demand 247, 262–3, 412
  joint-demand 262–3, 413
  bilateral exchange 265
  single-price axiom 265, 958–9
  a case of an upward-sloping demand schedule 267–8
  income effect of price change 269, 327, 935
  substitution effect 270–2, 935
  short-run supply schedule 273
  'stable' equilibrium 273
  equation of demand and supply 272–4, 276, 942n, 966–7

price theory *(continued)*
  short-run price formation 272–81
    and expectations 448, 513; stabilizing
    and non-stabilizing price adjustments
    495–6
  and W. T. Thornton 275
  joint-production 280
  solution to paradox of value 280, 929,
    935n
  and value theory as 'master key' 281
  and De Quincey 281
  and relativity of exchange value 281,
    346
  cost price, and impact of wage-rate
    variation 281–2
    and profit-rate equalization 281–6;
    and capital mobility 284; and alterna-
    tive opportunities 284, 315, 931–2; as
    average of market prices 284; and
    expectations 284–5, 290; and quasi-
    rent 285; nature of costs 285–6, 357;
    rent as cost 286–7; and demand and
    supply 287–9, 294–6, 298–9, 320,
    326, 521; and long-run adjustment
    process 289–95, 320, 939; and vari-
    able-cost conditions 296; and stationary
    state 423
  elasticity of demand 295, 322–4,
    327–8, 335
  and non-competing groups 315–16,
    933
  multiple equilibria 328–9
  and labour market 410–16
  pricing and socialism 787–8, 804
  see also consumer behaviour
Priestley, F. E. L. 602n, 605n, 657n
Priestley, Joseph 603n
Principles of Political Economy
  consistency with essay on method 66,
    162–4, 180–1, 189, 209, 211–12, 958
  and history 165, 193–4, 194–200
  JSM's evaluation of 165–7
  Smithian form, Ricardian substance
    165–9, 916–17
  concern with both application and
    abstract theory 167
  and influence of Harriet Taylor 168,
    772–4
  'The Probable Futurity' chapter 168,
    776, 780, 781, 790–1, 813, 815, 821,
    884, 903
  JSM's writing of 177n

its method and organization 177–84,
    191–3, 246, 247, 251–2, 344, 348
factual materials in 188–9, 959–61
restricted scope of 194, 770–1
status of early chapters 200n
variorum modifications regarding
    agricultural productivity 208, 234n,
    237n; on laws of production and
    distribution 222n; international capi-
    tal mobility 465; monetary determi-
    nants of interest rate 539–44;
    socialism, summarized 822–3;
    peasant proprietorship 847–54; popu-
    lation pressure and real-wage deteri-
    oration 852, 893–4; Irish living stan-
    dards 852–4, 954–5; landlords as
    'improvers' 855; privately-financed
    emigration 893–5; exclusive unions
    898–902
labour policy based on population and
    wage-fund analyses 390f
and *The Influence of Consumption on Produc-
    tion* 484–5, 486
and qualifications to the law of markets
    513–20
and *Of Profits and Interest* 542, 543–4
and scope of monetary policy 573
and utilitarianism 605, 623–4
the 'condition of the people' issue and
    justice 670–1
social control and liberty 677–8
program for reform of social attitudes
    679–80
and role of government 681–3
and case for free trade 685–6
its emphasis on capitalist-exchange
    system 770, 823–4
'On Property' chapter 774, 779, 781,
    786, 790, 790–1, 813
'Stationary State' chapter 883–8
historicists' use of 925 7
neo-classical elements in 931
production
  and organization of *Principles* 177–8
  classical and post-classical theories of
    261, 928f
  process ends on final sale to consumer
    263, 936
  and economic organization 383–4,
    387–400
  see also laws of production and distribu-
    tion

productive–unproductive consumption 257–8
productive–unproductive labour 247, 248, 260–1
  and accumulatibility 249, 250, 254, 260
  and utility 249–50, 252–3
  and human capital 253–5
  marketability criterion 256
  and government services 256
  and surplus 260
  differential production functions 261, 407
  and profit-rate trend 261, 459
  and wages-fund model 407
productivity 188, 201–3, 204–15
  and liberty 670–1
  and private property 671, 827, 830–2, 839
  and probity 882
  see also economic development, labour
profit rate
  trend 46, 52, 53–4, 61–3, 261
    contemporary 437n; and productive-unproductive labour 459; and trade cycle 459–60, 461–7, 486–7, 497, 512–13; and law of markets 467–81
  equalization 281–7
  and role of credit 293
  structure 316–20
  and custom 317–18n
  minimum 438
  and interest rate 438–9
  see also growth theory
profits
  source of in surplus labour time 186, 337–8, 340–1, 342, 358
  taxation of and impact on price structure 283
  and entrepreneurship 319–20
  and exchange 344
  corn-profit model rejected 350–1
  and notion of surplus 352
On Profits and Interest (1844) 318–19, 336, 343–4, 350, 390n, 438
progress
  laws of 86–7, 134–42, 194–200
  and specialization in social science 120–1
  'ethology' and 121, 134–6, 194, 198, 227, 770–1
  social dynamics defined 137
  and income inequality 141–2
  and real wages 141–2, 783, 896–8, 952
  JSM's limited analysis of 164, 165, 189–90, 191, 193, 226–8
  Comte's philosophy of history 176n
  security and 188–90, 203–4, 227–8
  knowledge and 188–90, 227
  and inverse deductive method 195
  and four-stages theory 196–8
  and economic growth 223–37
  and ethical standards 644
  threatened by 'despotism' of public opinion 713, 880n
  and role of government 763–9
  and 'dependent' class organization 777–80
  and industry concentration 783–4
  and co-operation 811–13
  land-owing class as obstacle 835n, 855
  and contemporary mental progress 894, 897
  and charge of 'scientism' 955–8
  science and 966n
property rights
  natural rights case for 640
  and utilitarianism 671–2, 673, 831
  and economic development 671–6, 827f, 831–2, 839
  and equality of opportunity 826f, 830
  security of 827, 874, 884
  and justice 830–1, 839
  and endowments 855–7
  see also landed property
protection
  agricultural
    corn laws 179, 191–2, 237, 336, 454, 474, 488n, 497, 512, 582n, 670n, 694n, 729–34, 775, 918, 945n; secular consequences 729–30; efficiency consequences 731; and deadweight welfare loss 731; and 'compensation principle' 731; and countervailing duties 732, 733; and corn-price instability 731, 773–4; and expectational implications of abolition 733, 735; iniquitous to poor 735
  industrial
    and expectational implications of abolition 733–4; net efficiency loss 734; no gain to capitalists 734–5
  revenue duties, and retaliation 735–6
  and reciprocity 736–7

protection *(continued)*
    and international morality 736–7
    'infant industry' case for 739–40
    transport costs and 740
    soil exhaustion and 740–1
Proudhon, P. J. 674, 874
Pusey, E. B. 181–2n

quantity theory of money
    and fundamental theorem on distribu-
      tion 248, 353–5
    and non-transactions demand for money
      513, 526
    and metallic and fiat money 521n
    impact of money supply increase
      in conditions of excess demand for
        money 521–2, 525–6, 548–9, 554,
        561, 578–80; and generation of excess
        demand for commodities ('income
        theory' of price) 522–40, 528n,
        558–61, 569–71
    and velocity 523
    and credit 527, 528–30
Quincey, T. de 63, 263, 265, 281, 413

Rae, J. 37, 204, 267–8n, 428, 873n
Rainelli, M. 318
Randall, J. H. Jr. 154n
Rappoport, P. 935n
Rashid, S. 151, 154n, 158n
Rau, K. 177
Rawls, J. 603, 664n
Read, S. 47n, 52
Reform Act (1867) 819, 918
Reid, T. 620n
rent
    differential 40–2, 42–3, 63, 186, 208f,
      299
    customary under metayage 242–3
    competitive in cottier system 242–3
    share of 248
    quasi- 285
    and land scarcity 286–7, 298–9
    as cost of production 286–7
    as 'great discovery' 336n
Ricardianism
    'Ricardian Vice' 1, 32, 945
    JSM's defence 1, 84, 180–1, 185, 770,
      916–21
    as perspective on economic growth 3
    Longfield and 60–3
    and prediction 64, 916, 945, 946–8

as fundamental theorem of distribution
    based on measure of value 65,
    346–7
Malthus's criticisms of 83–4
Whewell on 153–5
and utilitarianism 154n
and social reform 182n, 770, 917–19,
    920
and neo-classical economics 245,
    928–33
and short-run price formation 273
and long-run price formation 299
and historicism 913–28
Ricardo, D.
    JSM's relation to xii–xviii
    his growth model xiii, 33–4, 35, 46–7
    his method 4–5, 15–36, 147, 167,
      191n
    on the desirability of economic develop-
      ment 16, 738
    on the behavioural postulate 16–17,
      20–1, 23–4
    on political economy and mathematics
      16–17
    his differences with Malthus 17–18,
      21, 28–9, 34–5, 942n
    on wage theory 18–19
    on solutions to poverty 21–2
    on James Mill's theory of government
      23, 613
    his theoretical criticism of James Mill,
      on annual production (corn) growth
      model 24–5, 400
    on capital supply 26, 428; on labour
      theory 26–7, 304n
    on JSM's juvenile defence of labour
      theory 26, 347n
    his embryonic statement of
      JSM's mature position on law of
      markets 28
    his monetary policy 28, 30–1, 554n, 601
    his trade policy 29, 32, 733
    his poor-law policy 29–30, 54
    his attitude to landowners 32–3, 54,
      835–6
    and prediction 33–5, 57, 62, 945n
    on 'disturbing causes' 35–6
    inductivist critics of 36–42
    his growth model 46–7, 730
    his fundamental theorem of distribu-
      tion 62, 65, 245, 337–40, 352, 354,
      734

Ricardo, D. *(continued)*
  on stage of increasing (agricultural) returns 213n
  on net national income 260
  subscribes to Say on derived factor demand 261
  his demand analysis 269, 328, 335
  and demand–supply equation 274
  and cost theory 321
  and impact of wage variation on price structure 282-3, 359
  on rent and land scarcity 286
  and international values 321, 322, 325, 329, 335
  his notion of surplus 352
  on machinery 376, 379, 384, 385-7
  on wages-fund model 383-4, 400
  maintains fourth proposition on capital 399-400
  on natural price and stationary state 424
  on assisted emigration 469n
  on new markets and profit-rate determination 475-6
  on credit 528n
  on money and interest-rate determination 536
  on interrelation commodity and bond markets 541
  on 'depreciation' 545-6n
  on National Bank 583n
  and land reform 836
  The Economist on 921-2
Robbins, L. C.
  on optimum population 208
  on classical notion of 'wealth' 249
  on Torrens
    and capital 344; and union pressure 419n
  on stationary state 423, 451
  on Rae's 'desire of accumulation' 428n
  on 'problem of interest' 433
  on Wakefield and Torrens on savings leakages 477
  on *The Influence of Consumption on Production* 484n, 485, 487n, 508n
  on Banking and Currency School Controversy 555n
  on utilitarianism 602n, 603n, 606n, 615, 658n, 659, 664n

  on value judgement and economic policy 678
  on role of government 677n, 694n, 711n
  on classical economics of education 722n
  on classical theory of policy 737, 909n
  on combination laws 751n
  on JSM and socialism 772n, 790n, 794-5, 804-5, 808n, 813, 822-3
  and the franchise 826-7n
  on foregone opportunities 932
Robinson, J. 434n, 517n, 930
Robson, J. M. 93, 267n, 407n, 603n, 606n, 631n, 657, 664n, 665n, 668n, 679n, 721n, 774n, 826n, 835n
Roebuck, J. A. 638, 711, 951n
Romano, R. E. 56n, 203n
Roncaglia, A. 930
Roscher, W. 915
Rosenberg, N. 219n, 221n
Rousseau, J.-J. 674
Ryan, A. 68n, 93, 154n

Saint-Simonians 86-7, 90, 168, 800, 804, 956
Samuelson, P. A. 398n, 455n, 460n, 572n
saving
  defined 368, 371
  impact on wages 372, 375, 406, 480n, 517
  impact of innovation on 385
  and employment 400-1
  'forced' 439, 542, 544, 566
  see also capital
Say, J. B.
  and law of markets 12
  on economist's function 15-16
  on Ricardian abstraction 37
  his *Treatise* 177n, 246, 268n
  on division of labour 204
  on productive–unproductive categories 249, 258n
  on derived factor demand 261
  on conspicuous consumption 267n
  on mathematical economics 941n
Sayers, R. S. 30
Schabas, M. L. 935, 937, 938, 941, 944, 966n
Schofield, R. S. 950n

Schumpeter, J. A.
  his evaluation of JSM   xii
  on Ricardian Vice   1-2
  on Adam Smith's method   4n
  on JSM's essay on method   68, 163
  on James Mill's *Essay on Government* 120n
  on Whately's method   148n
  on distribution and pricing   246
  on Walrasian and classical theories of
    production   261
  on classical treatment of entrepreneur-
    ship   316n, 319
  on fortunes of fundamental theorem
    based on measure of value   346-7
  on the measure of value   346
  on savings and employment   373n, 400
  on capital and wages-fund   405
  on 'problem of interest'   433
  on the law of markets   484n, 487
  on 'systems' of political economy   602
  on Benthamite utilitarianism   603-5,
    605-6, 907n
  on relation classical economics and utili-
    tarianism   606
  on Fourierism   801n
  on JSM and prospect of socialism   823n
  on inductivism v. deductivism   915n
  on JSM and Ricardianism   900-1, 916
Schwartz, P.
  his evaluation of the *Principles*   xi, 177n
  on JSM and Ricardianism   xii, 916,
    920, 966
  on the Ricardian Vice   1
  on JSM's essay on method   68
  on JSM's appreciation of capitalist
    dynamics   235
  on value and distribution   282n, 283n
  on the recantation of the wages-fund
    doctrine   416n, 418n
  on monetary theory   485-6, 495n,
    581n, 582, 601
  on the role of government in develop-
    ment   738n
  on the role of the State   762n
  contrasts JSM and Hayek on liberalism
    827n
  on socialism   782n
  on co-operation and competition   885
  on birth control   968
  on local government   922n
scientific method
  prediction   5, 15, 35, 50-8, 63, 126,

    131-4, 141-2, 183, 915-16, 945,
    946-8, 956-7
  'disturbing causes'   35, 116, 122-4,
    125-7, 144n, 167, 191, 220, 239, 301,
    460, 465-7, 960
  induction and deduction defined   71,
    72, 76-8, 149
  deduction as 'mixed method of induc-
    tion and ratiocination'   71, 151, 189
  'composition of causes'   72-4, 191,
    231, 938
  use of term 'tendency'   73, 123, 133,
    457, 462, 464-7, 948
  causation defined   74, 105n
  experimental methods of empirical
    inquiry   74-6
  ratiocination   78
  verification   78-80
    and model improvement   125-31, 158
  'hypothetical method of deduction'
    80-1, 110-11
  proof of hypotheses   83, 154
  in astronomy and physiology   95n
  hierarchy of laws   96n
  empirical laws   96-7, 192
  'specific' experience   102, 112f, 192n
  'inverse deductive method'   140, 194,
    195, 239, 957
  and role of history   155
  synthesis of specialisms the ideal   195
science   955-8
  see also knowledge, progress
scientism   955-8
Scrope, G. P.   42n, 52-3, 56, 57
security, 188-90, 203, 227
Sedgwick, A.   115n, 154, 627f
Senior, N.   40n, 44, 143n, 246
  and Ricardo   xiii, 147
  his correspondence with Malthus   50-1,
    948
  and 'disturbing causes'   58
  on population mechanism   64-5
  his 'elementary propositions'   65n, 143n
  on JSM's essay on method   68, 145-6,
    162
  compared with JSM on method   69-70,
    142-9
  Whately as source on method   148n
  and diminishing marginal utility   268,
    270n
  on price formation   298
  on differential rent   299

Senior, N. (*continued*)
  on barriers to entry 304
  on productive–unproductive categories
    249n, 255n, 258n
  JSM's marginalia to his *Outline* 274n,
    338n, 340n, 373n, 396n, 935n
  on increasing returns
    and taxation 298n; and compatibility
    with competition 300n
  opposes fourth proposition on capital
    398–9
  on role of government 680
  on education and the State 707n, 725,
    729
  Hand-loom Weavers' Report 906
Shaftesbury, Earl of 641n
Shove, G. 930
Sidgwick, H. 188n, 189n, 219n, 251n,
  421n, 615
Sismondi, S. de 37, 181n, 238, 241, 243,
  464n, 873n, 891n, 952n, 969
Smith, A. xii, 2, 244
  archetype of abstract theorizing 3, 36,
    167
  on prediction and 'disturbing causes' 4
  on savings process 10
  and 'familiar' axioms 80n
  the 'old school' on stationary state
    88n, 885–6
  and JSM's *Principles* 165–6
  defended against Comte 175
  and four-stages theory 198n
  and wage differentials 203
  and division of labour 204, 221
  on hired management 228–9
  and alienation 240n
  on 'wealth' 249
  his *Theory of Moral Sentiments* 253
  on productive labour 256, 260
  on net national income 260
  and joint-production 280
  on rent as cost 286–7
  his wage-structure analysis 304–9, 723
  his vent-for-surplus theory 325
  and 'competition of capitals' 353
  on conspicuous consumption 267n
  on capital 366
  on natural price and stationary state
    424
  on capital supply 429
  and advantage of paper money 545n
  as utilitarian 603

  on justice and satisfactory *per capita*
    wages 670n, 825–6n
  and role of government 680, 912n
  and control of interest-rate 688
  on education and the state 701–2
  on educational endowments 715
  his objections to class organization
    776n
  his supposed denigration of maximum
    output 825
  opposes foundations 857–8
  his first canon on taxation 858
  and durable consumer goods 865
  Lowe's address on 924n
  and self-interest axiom 958
Smith, V. E. 270n
social control
  and liberty 661, 663–4, 669–70, 677,
    684
  and education 663
  see also government regulation
social science
  and 'composition of causes' 94
  and deductive method 95
  and geometry contrasted 95n
  empirical laws in 96f, 192
  and specialization 104–15, 116–25
  see also political economy; scientific
    method
socialism 167, 169
  and interest 429n, 431–2, 806
  continental and British contrasted 429n,
    819
  in *Principles of Political Economy*,
    variorum changes discussed 786f,
    802–3, 804–6, 808, 813, 823
  communism
    and population control 786–7, 789,
    792, 896; and indolence 787, 789,
    791, 797; and lack of innovation
    786–7, 796; and 'equality' of labour
    and pay 787, 794–5, 798; and liberty
    788, 794, 799; and allocation of
    labour 792; and management 797–8;
    and education 799; and inter-
    communal relations 799
St. Simonianism 800, 804
Fourierism 800–2f
    and interest payments 801n, 806; and
    inter-community relations 802, 804;
    and pricing under socialism 804; and
    surrogate competition 805, 807; allows

socialism *(continued)*
   private property 805; and liberty 807; and efficiency 807
   First International 812
   collectivism 819–20
   The Examiner report on Conference of the Society of Arts (Feb. 1854) 921, 977–8
   see also Chapters on Socialism (1879)
Sowell, T. xii, 513, 516n, 946
Sparshott, F. E. 152n
speculation 687
   see also expectations; money; trade cycles
Spence, W. 9
Spengler, J. J. 194n, 235, 428n
Spring Rice, T. 469n
Sraffa, P. 28, 351
Starrett, D. A. 929, 932n
statics and dynamics 136f, 189, 422–6
stationary state 46, 49, 60, 424
   'old school' on 85, 87, 886
   potential disadvantages compared with growing system regarding innovation 230, 887n; profit-rate equalization process 293; wage determination 313n; capital leakages 438, 473, 474–5, 478; substitution against 'labour' 451, 469–70, 955; class hostility 777
   and natural price 423
   positive interest rate in 433–7, 451
   and easier population control 448–9, 886, 954, 955, 969
   not a positive recommendation 451, 480–1, 882–5
   and exhaustible resources 451
   and co-operative organization 885, 910
   and leisure 887
   and social amenity 888
   see also economic development; growth theory
Steintrager, J. 609n
Stephen, Sir Leslie 421n, 603n, 609n, 615n
Sterling, J. 431n
Steuart, Sir James 5
Stewart, D. 1, 15, 620n
Stigler, G. J.
   his evaluation of JSM xii
   on the law of markets 12
   on diminishing returns 212n
   on the productive–unproductive classification 261n
   on diminishing marginal utility 268n
   on classical 'competition' 276n
   on non-competing groups 310n
   on the wage-fund theory 391n
   on demand for input 414n
   on Wicksell's critique of classical wage analysis 421n
   on JSM and the role of government 678, 684, 685–6, 690, 742, 750
   on JSM and socialism 684, 781n
   on the State, and industry structure 758n
   on JSM and classical 'denigration' of maximum output 825–6, 882
   on failures of self-interest 842n
   on J. B. Say 928n
   on JSM's Malthusianism 946n
Storch, H. F. von 267n
Strong, E. W. 154n
Sturges, R. P. 18n, 39n, 42n, 45
succession proposals 878–9
   on limited acquisition by bequest 264, 860, 880, 883
   and progressive duties on legacies and inheritances 871–3, 872–3
   see also taxation (direct); utility
Sue, E. 182n
supply *see* price theory
surplus
   surplus labour time and profits 186, 337, 340–1, 342, 358
   and mutual relation profits and wages 352
   and savings 427, 429, 808–9
Sutherland, G. 726
System of Logic xiii, 70, 80–1, 90, 94–104, 104–6, 110, 111, 112–15, 117–21, 128–31, 132–4, 134–42, 144, 147, 151, 155, 158, 161, 174, 194, 640, 934, 938, 940, 941–2, 947–8, 957

Takeshima, M. 921n
Taussig, F. W. 371n, 391n, 397n, 414n, 418n, 420n
taxation (commodity)
   of luxuries, and upward sloping demand curves 267–8
   JSM's progression proposal, and diminishing utility 268, 827, 862, 873, 880–1, 884

taxation (commodity) *(continued)*
 and increasing returns 297–8, 335n
 and differential factor proportions
  360–1
 regressiveness of 864–5, 871–2, 875
 illusion 871
 exemptions 872
taxation (income)
 progression, applied to *unearned income*
  264, 480, 827, 859–60, 862, 872–3,
  877
 of profits, and impact on price structure
  283
 of wages 313
 of 'permanent' and 'life' incomes
  434–5, 866–8
 of capital 469n, 873–5
 of legacies and inheritances 469n, 879
  and diminishing utility 872–3, 877
 and tendency of profit rate to a minimum 480
 double 480n, 865
 and price level 489n
 benefit principle on 680
 unearned increment of land values
  834–6, 871–2, 876
 and equality of sacrifice 858
 and exemption limits 861–2
 expenditure tax proposal 865, 870
 Hubbard's memorandum on income
  and property taxation 868, 970–6
 and house tax 869–70
Taylor, C. 605n
Taylor, H. 168, 407n, 638, 684, 772–4,
 970
Thomas, W. 93
Thompson, J. H. 263n, 374n
Thompson, T. P. 38n, 42
Thornton, H. 527, 536, 581, 593n
Thornton, W. T. 354, 420n
 on orthodox price theory 275, 328
 his labour-market analysis 400, 409–10
 on multiple equilibria in international
  exchange 410n
 warns against sudden currency contraction 554
 and 'rights of labour' 673–5
 his Irish land proposals 838, 848f
 and poverty trap 890
Thünen, H. von xi, 99n
The Times 179, 919n
Tinbergen, J. 939

Tocqueville, A. De 766
Tollison, R. D. 827, 898, 899, 904
Tooke, T. 54, 234n
 on speculation and trade cycle 462,
  496n
 his monetary theory and policy 486,
  487–9, 493, 530, 548, 558, 563
 on monetary intervention 550,
  599–602
 JSM's praise of 598n
Torrens, R. 5, 54, 498n
 induced by JSM to defend differential
  rent doctrine 43
 supports JSM on method 147, 160
 and international values 321, 325
 on capital and profit-rate determination
  340, 344
 and fundamental theorem on distribution
  344
 on labour theory 347n
 on capital-mobility axiom 357n
 his wages-fund model 401–2, 407–8,
  409, 420
 and ability of unions to raise wages
  419n
 on minimum rate of profit 437n
 on speculation and cycle 496n
 and law of markets 508n
 on monetary policy 512, 556
 and velocity of circulation 561n
Toynbee, A. 926n
Tractarians 181n
trade cycle
 and cyclical unemployment 392–3,
  520, 549, 581–2
 as 'disturbing cause' 460
 and tendency of profit-rate to decline
  460, 462–7, 486–7, 497, 512–13, 521,
  567
 inventory 461, 464
 periodicity of 463, 503
 and capital wastage 464, 465
 and investment, output and employment 464, 515–16, 520
 and capital exportation 465
 no Keynesian 'unemployment equilibrium' 472, 505–6, 513, 515, 581
 psychological theory of 495, 503, 512,
  513, 513–15, 519n, 530–1n, 550,
  563–4, 573, 582n
 and destabilizing (speculative) price
  adjustments 496

trade cycle *(continued)*
 role of credit in 496–7, 512, 513,
  513–15, 528–9, 531–2, 547–8, 561–3,
  564
 and net demand for money to hold in
  depression 497, 499, 526, 548, 554
 and cyclical implications of over-full
  employment 502, 553
 lower turning-point 505, 515
 upper turning-point 515
 and interest rate 535
 and bank finance 544–72
 and internationalization of speculative
  mood 546–7, 578
 exacerbated by Bank Charter Act (1844)
  584–6, 589–90
 and usury laws 688
Tu, P. N. V. 722n
Tucker, G. S. L. 340, 496n
Tucker, J. 204n
Turgot, A. R. J. 175, 438, 857

United States
 governments not over-centralized 713
 and infant-industry case 739–40
 and upward mobility in 777, 911
 and differentials on earned income in
  840
 a progressive economy 'at its best'
  882, 884f
 democratic tendencies in 883
 and Chinese immigration 905–6n
 and British interest-rate differentials
  analysed 963–7
unions
 and ability to raise wages 400, 410–11,
  416–17, 419n
 and liberty 751
 educational function of 751
 and intimidation 752
 and compulsory arbitration 752n
 conditional defence of exclusive unions
  753, 897–907
 and unequal bargaining power 782
 cooperation and euthanasia of 814
 and fundamental Ricardian theorem on
  distribution 917–18
 legislation (1867), (1871) 918
 Economist hostile to 922n
usury laws 688
utilitarianism
 and selfishness 115n

classical economics and 154n, 602–3,
  605, 614–15
 Carlyle's animosity towards 182n
 and individual liberty 602
 and wealth-maximization axiom 605
 Jevons and 605, 929n
 and justice as protection of individual
  liberty 605
 and custom 625, 629
 and the labour problem 670, 673–6
 and private property 671, 673–6
 and case for *laissez-faire* 680–2
 and public relief 743
 and socialism 792n
 and property 831–2, 839
 and disposition of State land 838
On Utilitarianism 264, 302n, 659, 668
 utility theory not subject to proof 646,
  660, 661
 on justice and qualitative ranking of
  utilities 647–51, 654–5
 on relation of justice and moral sentiments 653
 and income distribution 654, 673–6
 and laws of human enjoyment 934
utility
 and qualitative ranking of pleasures
  264, 266, 650
 diminishing
  and limited acquisition by bequest
   264, 880, 883; not applied to earned
   income taxation 264–5, 880f; and
   progressive succession duties 827,
   872–3, 877; and progressive *ad valoram*
   rates 267, 827, 862, 873, 880f, 883;
   and international trade 326
  and upward sloping demand curves
   267–8
 Senior and implications of relative income
  268, 270n
 and non-uniform functions of 662
 the marginal-utility issue 934–6

Vaizey, J. 722n
value theory *see* price theory
Vansittart, N. 554n
Veblen, T. 369n
verification *see* scientific method
Villari, P. 70
Viner, J.
 on JSM's essay on method 66–7,
  69

Viner, J. *(continued)*
    contrasts essay on method and *Principles* 162
on experimental methods of empirical inquiry 70
on competition and a specialist political economy 120n
on Richard Jones and custom 238n
on the fourth proposition on capital 263n
on classical international trade theory 321n, 330n
on the wages-fund theory 398n
on Thomas Attwood's 'inflationism' 554–5n
on utilitarianism
    JSM's vicissitudes 603n, 631–2; divorces Benthamism and selfishness 609n, 610n; distinguishes Bentham from James Mill 613, 658; Benthamism not a system of private ethics 614n; on conventionality of Bentham's quantification postulates 615n; on lack of incremental concept 650n
on the nature of applied economics 679
on the substantive identity between JSM and Bentham on role of government 680
on classical approach to monopoly 759
on JSM's hard-headedness 774n, 825
on JSM's socialism as 'platonic' 825
on JSM and historicism 915
on the Manchester School 921
Vivo, G. de 300
vocational training *see* education

wage rate
    subsistence 46, 47, 56, 396, 427–8, 659–60
determination of 186
and 'cost-of-labour' 186, 339, 342–3, 350
impact on price structure 282
'money' rate and proportionate shares 348–50
competitive rate and justice 779–82
see also growth theory
wage-rate structure
    and relative prices 282
and heterogeneous labour 305, 932
Smithian analysis 304–9, 723, 828, 961

and expectations 306f
and full-employment axiom 307f, 828
and non-competing groups 308–9
and education 309
and custom 309–10, 311–12
and population principle 310–15
and 'ostentation' 959
and women's wages 314, 785n
competitive structure as 'just' 782, 785, 828f, 907
wages
    and net national income 260
taxation of 313
and accumulation 372, 375, 406, 480n
wages-fund doctrine
    Ricardo and Malthus on 25
recantation 262–3, 389, 400, 409–17
and wage-structure analysis 310
and economic organization 383–4, 387–99
and time-consuming activity 387
and advances 388, 399
and synchronized activity 389
and unitary elastic labour demand 389, 409, 411
accounts of 1869 and *Principles* compared 384–92, 400, 405, 409
and labour policy 390–4
and law of markets 392–3
and elasticity of aggregate wage bill 409, 409–16, 594–9
and rejection of annual production cycle governing labour demand 400
as 'equilibrium' solution 400–9
factor proportions and employment 404, 407, 420–2
and productive v. unproductive labour 407
theoretical scope of 408
and fundamental theorem on distribution 417–18
Wakefield, E. G. 166, 183, 475, 753–5
Walker, D. A. 939
Walras, L. 261, 928, 933
Ward, W. G. 947
wealth 248–9, 958
    concentration of, and equality of opportunity 826–7, 827–8
and restrictions on bequests 832–3
diffusion of, championed 834, 880, 881
see also national income

wealth-maximization axiom ('self interest')
  67, 69–70, 95, 104–15, 161, 192n, 944
verification of, as 'application' of science
  67, 116, 120, 126
not of universal relevance 69–70, 120,
  122, 144–5, 160–1
and introspection 112f, 136
and observation 113–15, 958–61
and egoism 115
and 'disturbing causes' 116, 122–4,
  960
and specialization 119, 120–1, 124
and population 124
Senior on 144–9
and knowledge 191, 229
and consumer behaviour 247, 265–8,
  936, 959
on rational v. non-rational types of non-
  pecuniary interest 266n
and failures of self-interest 735, 843–4
deep-rootedness of 773, 795
and land-use and size of land-
  unit 840–1, 842
and market anonymity 959
Webb, R. K. 922n
West, E. G.
  on wages-fund recantation 414n, 416n,
    646n
  on education 724, 728–9
  on outdoor-relief 743n
  charges JSM with 'social engineering'
    827, 897–907, 907–12
  with 'bourgeois bias' 907, 911
West, Sir Edward 2, 36, 299
Western, C. 487
Whately, R. 5, 44, 45n, 57, 143n, 148n,
  149, 152, 177, 948–9
Whewell, W. xiii, 38n
  on Ricardo's method 42
  doubts regarding inductivist program
    44–5, 915

his mathematical economics 149
on method 153–8
criticizes JSM on land-tenure 238n
and multiple equilibria 328n
and utilitarianism 641–4
on role of government 677
on mathematics 943n
Whitaker, J. K.
  on JSM's ideas on logic 70n
  on JSM's hierarchy of laws 96n
  on competition, custom and political
    economy 124–5
  on prediction 130n
  on 'speculative faculties' 141n
  on inductive establishment of axioms
    189n
  on inverse-deductive method 189n,
    229n
  on JSM's Malthus-mongering 237
Wicksell, K. 376n, 384, 421n
Wieser, F. von 560n
Wilson, F. 646n
Wilson, J. 462n
Winch, D. 16n, 177n, 912n
  on James Mill 6, 13f, 91
  identifies Ricardo and James Mill on
    method 28–9, 35
  on the essay on method 68n
  on the scientific character of political
    economy 159–60
  on colonization policy 477n, 478n,
    754
  on the law of markets 478
  on JSM and Ricardianism 916, 942
Wolfe, W. 172n
Wood, S. 402n
Woodward, L. 727n
Wordsworth, W. 85n
Wrigley, E. A. 950n

Young, A. 50, 242